BAKING

Margaret Fulton
BAKING

THE ULTIMATE SWEET & SAVOURY BAKING COLLECTION

CONTENTS

INTRODUCTION	6
NOTES ON THE RECIPES	8
CONVERSIONS	9
EQUIPMENT	10

CHAPTER 1: BISCUITS	12
HINTS & TIPS	14
DROP BISCUITS	16
SHAPED BISCUITS	32
ROLLED BISCUITS	59

CHAPTER 2: BROWNIES & SLICES	80
HINTS & TIPS	82
BROWNIES	84
SLICES	92

CHAPTER 3: MUFFINS, SCONES, SHORTCAKES & QUICKBREADS	108
HINTS & TIPS	110
PLAIN & SWEET MUFFINS	112
SAVOURY MUFFINS	124
SCONES	128
SHORTCAKES	138
PLAIN & SAVOURY QUICKBREADS	142
SWEET QUICKBREADS	150

CHAPTER 4: CAKES	**158**
HINTS & TIPS	160
BUTTER CAKES	164
TEA CAKES	185
QUICK-MIX CAKES	192
SPONGE CAKES	201
FRUIT CAKES	214
CONTINENTAL CAKES	222
ICINGS, FROSTINGS & FILLINGS	252
CHAPTER 5: SMALL CAKES	**256**
HINTS & TIPS	258
CUPCAKES, FRIANDS & MADELEINES	260
MACARONS & MERINGUES	273
CHAPTER 6: DESSERTS	**284**
HINTS & TIPS	286
FRUIT DESSERTS	288
PUDDINGS	297
CHEESECAKES	304
SOUFFLÉS	312
MERINGUE DESSERTS	316
CHAPTER 7: PASTRY	**324**
HINTS & TIPS	326
BASIC PASTRY DOUGHS	338
FRUIT PIES & TARTS	339
NUT TARTS	369
TREACLE TARTS	375
CREAM & CHEESE TARTS	376
SWEET TARTLETS & PASTRIES	382
SAVOURY PIES & TARTS	404
SAVOURY TARTLETS & PASTRIES	414
CHAPTER 8: YEAST COOKERY	**418**
HINT & TIPS	420
BASIC & SAVOURY BREADS & ROLLS	422
PIZZAS	436
PIROSHKI	440
SWEET BREAD & ROLLS	442
YEASTED CAKES	457
GLOSSARY	466
INDEX	470
ACKNOWLEDGEMENTS	478
BOOKS BY MARGARET FULTON	479

INTRODUCTION

It is 7 o'clock on Sunday morning and my niece is downstairs rustling up some trays of her special date slice, to take to friends. As that reassuring fragrance wafts into my bedroom, I love knowing that someone is in the kitchen and something is baking in the oven. It takes me straight back to my childhood and my mother, for whom home baking played a vital role in everyday life.

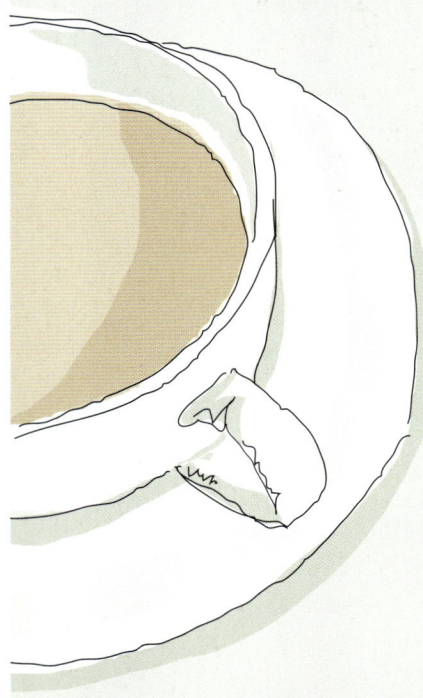

One of my fondest memories growing up was seeing my mother sitting in the kitchen with a mixing bowl on her lap, making her shortbread. The whole thing would be done literally by hand. One hand was kept clean, holding the bowl, and with the other hand she would beat in the butter, sugar and flour until it all got very buttery. She made very good shortbread and I've continued that tradition, as has my daughter Suzanne.

Rich cakes, melt-in-the-mouth biscuits, light-as-air sponges and fluffy scones have held pride of place in the Australian kitchen since pioneering days. And over the years, as we've become more cosmopolitan and sophisticated, the range of recipes has extended to include not only the established fare but also a varied international contribution as well. The inspiration for many of the recipes in this book came from my travels around the world.

My daughter Suzanne (who has been working with me on this book) and I know that many others share our love of baking little specialties for our family and friends. In Holland, spicy speculaas are a favourite biscuit, especially at Christmas. Every self-respecting Scot takes pride in making shortbread. Throughout Scandinavia, Germany and Austria, spiced biscuits are made. In Germany two

INTRODUCTION

stollens are baked, one to keep and one to give away. France has many baked treats, such as madeleines, fruit tarts and pithiviers. From Italy we get sometimes chewy, sometimes crisp specialties like ricotta torte, siena cake and amaretti. We love them, so it is natural that they have been included in this book.

Over the years, I've received letters from all over the world enquiring about my recipes. I once got a letter from a group of men on expedition in Antarctica, wanting a crumpet recipe. I wrote to them for a long time afterwards and they sent photos of the crumpets they made. But the most common thing I get asked about is my Christmas cake. I still get so many letters about this recipe. A lot of people write to me and say 'I love your Christmas cake, and my mother used to make it, and now I make it'. It's wonderful to know these recipes get passed down in families and continue to live on.

Home-baked goods may not always resemble those professional offerings with their perfect edges and level tops, but usually this is a good thing. For me, something that looks handcrafted, a little rustic even, has far more allure than something that comes from a factory. And the bonus is, you've used real ingredients, so you know what you're eating.

Some people avoid baking because they think special skills are needed. The most important thing to remember is to follow the instructions. You've got to learn the rules. If you don't learn the rules you'll get into trouble. There's nothing mysterious about baking. If you're not daunted by something, it's just a matter of going in and doing it. And practise, just keep at it. I love teaching people how to make things like pastry as it's such a wonderful thing to know. It's so easy to do once you've been shown the ways with it. Pastry is the base of all the good things in life!

Baking for me means slowing down enough to roll up your sleeves and bake for the sheer pleasure of it, and for giving and sharing. Suzanne and I invite you to share our joy and love of cooking and baking with these recipes. Enjoy!

Margaret Fulton

NOTES ON THE RECIPES

The metric weights and liquid measures used in this book are those of the Standards Association of Australia. To make these recipes you need a few inexpensive pieces of equipment obtainable at most supermarkets.

These are:
- A standard graduated 250 ml fluid measuring jug for measuring liquids.
- A set of four graduated metric measuring cups comprising 250 ml cup, $1/2$ (125 ml), $1/3$ (approximately 80 ml) and $1/4$ cup (60 ml) – used to measure dry ingredients.
- A set of standard measuring spoons comprising 1 tablespoon (20 ml), 1 teaspoon (5 ml), $1/2$ teaspoon (2.5 ml) and $1/4$ teaspoon (1.25 ml).
- A small set of scales.
- A measuring tape or ruler that gives both metric and imperial measurements.

NOTE North American and British measuring cups and spoons vary from Australian standards. Follow one set of measures; do not mix them.

HOW TO MEASURE CORRECTLY

DRY INGREDIENTS In measuring dry ingredients (flour, sugar, etc.) heap the cup or spoon and level off the excess with a knife or spatula. For flour, pour or spoon the flour into the cup, rather than sweeping the cup into the packet (which can compact the flour, giving you a heavier cup of flour than is standard).

LIQUID INGREDIENTS The metric measuring cup shows 1 cup, $3/4$, $2/3$, $1/2$, $1/4$ and $1/8$ cup measures and their metric equivalents. The litre jug has a similar breakdown from 1 litre to $1/4$ litre and also shows graduations in millilitres (1000 ml = 4 cups = 1 litre).

GENERAL NOTES
- All cup and spoon measures are level.
- The recipes in this book have been made with the 250 ml cup.
- 55–60 g eggs have been used unless otherwise specified.
- Can, pack and bottle sizes are given in metric. Some cans and packs may vary a little from exact sizes given according to the different brands available. It is best to use the nearest size.

ABBREVIATIONS USED

gram	g
kilogram	kg
centimetre	cm
millimetre	mm
millilitre	ml

OVEN TEMPERATURE GUIDE

Oven temperatures are expressed in degrees Celsius (°C). If using a fan-forced oven, as a guide, drop the temperature by 20°C. Oven temperatures vary according to make; therefore, refer to the instruction book that accompanies each oven. All ovens should be preheated to the specified temperature, particularly for cakes, biscuits and pastry recipes. For oven temperature conversions, see opposite.

Know your oven; a new oven may take some getting used to. Most ovens have hotter or cooler spots, and some may run, overall, hotter or cooler than the temperature stated on the thermostat. With practice, you will soon become familiar with any idiosyncracies of your oven and will be able to adjust temperatures and times accordingly.

CONVERSIONS

These conversions are approximate. If using a recipe that gives both cups and weights, stick with one system or the other.

WEIGHT	
METRIC	IMPERIAL
10–15 g	½ oz
20 g	¾ oz
30 g	1 oz
40 g	1½ oz
50–60 g	2 oz
75 g	2½ oz
80 g	3 oz
100 g	3½ oz
125 g	4 oz
150 g	5 oz
175 g	6 oz
200 g	7 oz
225 g	8 oz
250 g	9 oz
275 g	10 oz
300 g	10½ oz
350 g	12 oz
400 g	14 oz
450 g	1 lb
500 g	1 lb 2 oz
600 g	1 lb 5 oz
650 g	1 lb 7 oz
750 g	1 lb 10 oz
900 g	2 lb
1 kg	2 lb 3 oz

VOLUME	
METRIC	IMPERIAL
50–60 ml	2 fl oz
75 ml	2½ fl oz
100 ml	3½ fl oz
120 ml	4 fl oz
150 ml	5 fl oz
170 ml	6 fl oz
200 ml	7 fl oz
225 ml	8 fl oz
250 ml	8½ fl oz
300 ml	10 fl oz
400 ml	13 fl oz
500 ml	17 fl oz
600 ml	20 fl oz
750 ml	25 fl oz
1 litre	34 fl oz

LENGTH	
METRIC	IMPERIAL
5 mm	¼ inch
1 cm	½ inch
2 cm	¾ inch
2.5 cm	1 inch
5 cm	2 inches
7.5 cm	3 inches
10 cm	4 inches
15 cm	6 inches
20 cm	8 inches
30 cm	12 inches

TEMPERATURE		
°C	°F	GAS
140	275	Gas 1
150	300	Gas 2
160	320	Gas 2–3
170	340	Gas 3
180	350	Gas 4
190	375	Gas 5
200	400	Gas 6
210	410	Gas 6–7
220	430	Gas 7

EQUIPMENT

If you're a novice baker and starting from scratch, think first about what you want and like to cook. Cakes need the right tins; biscuits and pastries need good baking trays, pastry tins and a good rolling pin. I am constantly surprised at the difference in baking results because of the type of tin or tray used.

Go for quality and you will usually be rewarded. Generally choose aluminium over tin, particularly a new product called hard-anodised aluminium if you can find it. Silicon is good but doesn't brown as well as metal does.

Start with the basics and gradually build up your equipment as your repertoire and your skills expand. It's irritating to have to struggle to find what you need among a clutter of tins, racks, trays, whisks and electrical appliances.

BISCUITS

ROUND BISCUIT CUTTERS

ALUMINIUM BAKING TRAYS, preferably double-sided. Choose two the same size so you can double them if you want to help protect delicate things from overbrowning on the bases.

SLICES AND BROWNIES

A LAMINGTON TIN, 30 cm x 20 cm

MUFFINS

MUFFIN TINS A 12-hole $1/3$-cup tin should be first on the list, followed by a 24-hole 1–2 tablespoon mini muffin tin, which is wonderful for baking tiny muffins or cakes.

CAKES

A GOOD ELECTRIC STAND MIXER with a paddle beater and a whisk; these are very handy but not cheap, so if you can't afford one, a hand-held electric mixer is an economical and versatile substitute.

SILICON SPATULAS for scraping the sides of the bowl cleanly and for smoothing the tops of mixtures in the tin.

UNCOATED ALUMINIUM CAKE TINS Start with a 20 cm and a 22 cm round cake tin, a deep 19 cm, a 23 cm square cake tin and a 21 cm x 14 cm loaf tin. A 20 cm ring tin is very useful, particularly for cake batters that are likely to sink in the centre, as they allow for more even cooking. It's a bonus to have a 23 cm springform tin. Non-stick coatings are good when the tins are new but are easily scratched, so need careful looking after. Aluminium is light and durable and an excellent conductor of heat, so aids even baking.

SMALL METAL SPATULA for releasing cakes from tins; also useful for spreading icings and fillings

COOLING RACKS are essential for freshly baked cakes and pastries. If the steamy moisture can't escape it will condense inside the cake or dough, making it heavy. Choose one or two made of good quality tinned steel.

EQUIPMENT

ROLLS AND ROULADES
SWISS ROLL TIN, 30 cm x 25 cm

MERINGUES
A COPPER BOWL AND BALLOON WHISK are the very best things for beating egg whites. The copper helps to make a very stable fine-textured foam (most important when making soufflés). Copper bowls are expensive, however, and you'll probably find that a good electric mixer will satisfy your needs. A round-based stainless steel bowl and balloon whisk are a good alternative.

PIPING BAG Choose a large, flexible, tightly woven bag which can be easily washed and dried after use, along with a set of plain nozzles, including a 1 cm diameter one. You might also want one or two rosette nozzles for decorative meringues or cream fillings.

ALUMINIUM BAKING TRAYS (see Biscuits, opposite)

YEAST COOKING
A BABA OR SAVARIN OR KUGELHOPF TIN, if you want to make yeasted cakes

BREAD TINS in various sizes, if you want to make bread

ALUMINIUM BAKING TRAYS if you want to make rolls or round loaves (see Biscuits, opposite)

PASTRIES AND TARTS
A FOOD PROCESSOR is invaluable for making pastry at the drop of a hat.

A HEAVY ROLLING PIN made of a single cylindrical length of close-grained wood with a smooth, silky finish

A MARBLE SLAB – this can be expensive and isn't essential but it will help keep the pastry cool while it is being worked.

A LONG METAL SPATULA for releasing pastry from a floured surface

TWO ALUMINIUM BAKING TRAYS (see Biscuits, opposite)

PASTRY BRUSHES with soft natural or nylon bristles to help dust off excess flour or to spread glazes or melted butter without damaging delicate surfaces.

GENERAL EQUIPMENT
Other equipment that you will already have in the kitchen and that is used for baking includes:

FOR MEASURING Cups and spoons (see page 8) and digital scales

SIFTERS OR SIEVES Buy a large sifter or sieve for sifting flour, and a smaller one for dredging icing sugar or cocoa over finished baked goods

A NEST OF MIXING BOWLS in at least three sizes (small, medium and large); stainless steel, glass or ceramic are better than plastic, which can retain grease, flavours and odours

SPOONS Wooden spoons do not conduct heat or scratch non-stick surfaces; large metal spoons are used for folding in ingredients

BAKING PAPER Essential to line tins; also it's useful to roll out pastry between two sheets of baking paper for ease of handling

CARE OF BAKEWARE
Wash in hot soapy water (do not use abrasive scrubbers on non-stick surfaces) and rinse well. If your oven is still warm after your baking session, put washed and dried bakeware in the oven to dry it completely before putting it away, to prevent rust.

BISCUITS
CHAPTER 1

HINTS & TIPS

The first biscuits were small, flat cakes which were baked twice to make them crisp (the word biscuit means 'twice cooked' in French). The term now describes an infinite variety of crunchy, crisp, chewy or brittle baked goods, from plain water biscuit to sweet confections nibbled with coffee.

TYPES OF BISCUITS

Biscuits can be formed in many ways. The biscuits in this book have been organised according to how they are shaped.

DROP BISCUITS

These are the easiest of all biscuits to shape, as they are simply dropped from a spoon onto a baking tray. They vary in texture. Some fall easily from the spoon and flatten into wafers when baking. Stiffer doughs need a push with the finger or the use of a second spoon to release them. To get drops of uniform size use a standard measuring spoon of the size noted in the recipe – generally a half-teaspoon, teaspoon or tablespoon. If you want the biscuits thinner, press down on top with the tines of a fork dipped in caster sugar. During very hot weather, put the dough in the refrigerator for 20 minutes before using.

Leave a generous amount of space between each mound of mixture on the baking tray; thinner mixtures in particular may spread quite a lot.

SHAPED BISCUITS

These biscuits have very basic shaping. The mixture is generally scooped up in spoonfuls and then rolled into balls by hand. Once placed on the baking trays, the balls can be flattened slightly with the fingers or the tines of a fork dipped in caster sugar or flour.

REFRIGERATOR BISCUITS

The dough is rolled into a log, wrapped in plastic wrap and chilled until firm. Slices are then cut off to form biscuits. Refrigerator biscuit dough is good to keep on hand in the fridge or freezer so you can cut off and bake a few slices when needed at short notice. The dough will keep for two weeks in the fridge or two months in the freezer.

ROLLED BISCUITS

The dough for these biscuits is rolled out then cut into a variety of shapes, either with a knife, a pastry cutter or biscuit cutters. When rolling out biscuit dough, roll each stroke in one direction only (rather than using a back and forth motion), turning the pastry with the help of a metal spatula to ensure evenness. Ensure that the dough is of an even thickness so that the biscuits will all cook in the same amount of time.

Unless the recipe specifies otherwise, the scraps from one rolling can be gathered up, gently pressed together into a pad, then re-rolled and more biscuits cut out.

PIPED BISCUITS

The dough is piped through a piping bag or forced through a metal or plastic biscuit press to form pretty, uniform, formal-looking biscuits of various shapes.

MAKING BISCUITS

HAVE THE RIGHT EQUIPMENT You will need at least one (preferably two) baking trays; a flat-bladed metal spatula for lifting cooked biscuits off the trays; and one or two wire racks.

BISCUITS *hints & tips*

TO PREVENT BISCUITS FROM STICKING to the trays, line trays with baking paper, or grease lightly with butter; too much butter can cause the biscuits to spread. Measure accurately, using level cup and spoon measures unless the recipe states otherwise. See page 10 for more information on measuring.

HAVE BUTTER AT THE RIGHT TEMPERATURE For creamed mixtures, the butter should be at room temperature. This is a slight misnomer, as the temperature of the room depends on the heat of the day. In baking terms, however, 'room temperature' means butter that is soft but still holds its shape. It should not be runny or liquid. Butter straight from the fridge may take an hour to soften adequately, depending on the heat of the room.

FOR MIXTURES WHERE BUTTER IS RUBBED IN, the butter should be chilled so that it is less likely to melt due to the heat of your hands.

ALWAYS PREHEAT THE OVEN so that it is at the right temperature when the biscuits go in.

MAKE SURE THE OVEN RACKS ARE CORRECTLY POSITIONED If baking one tray at a time, place it in the centre of the oven. If baking two trays, place the oven racks as though dividing the oven into thirds. Air needs to circulate around the trays, so it's better to bake a large quantity of biscuits in several batches than to overcrowd the oven.

TURN THE TRAYS OCCASIONALLY Many ovens have hot spots that result in uneven cooking. To compensate for this, turn the baking trays once or twice. If using more than one baking tray, also swap their positions on the oven racks to prevent uneven browning.

KEEP AN EYE ON BISCUITS WHILE THEY BAKE The cooking time in the recipe is a guide only, as all ovens differ. A few minutes before the end of the specified cooking time, check the biscuits, rotating and swapping the trays if needed. Cooked biscuits will be firm and dry on the top. Lift one biscuit off the tray with a spatula and check the underside to see if it is also cooked. If the biscuits need more cooking, return them to the oven for another minute or two. Keep checking them frequently; biscuits can burn quickly.

ONCE THE BISCUITS ARE COOKED, remove them from the oven. They will be very soft and fragile at this stage, so leave them on the tray for a few minutes to cool slightly and set. (The exceptions to this rule are biscuits such as brandy snaps, which are sometimes removed when still hot and then shaped around a rolling pin or similar.) Then use a flat-bladed metal spatula to transfer the biscuits to wire racks to cool completely.

ALLOW BISCUITS TO COOL COMPLETELY before icing, filling or storing them. Once they are cool, store in an airtight container; if left on the racks for too long they can absorb moisture from the air and lose some of their crispness, especially on humid days.

IF ICING OR FILLING BISCUITS, it is best to do so on the day they are to be served, as biscuits may reabsorb moisture from soft icings or fillings if they are stored too long (if the icing is hard, they keep well).

STORE IN AN AIRTIGHT CONTAINER Store each type of biscuit in its own container to prevent flavours from mingling. In particular, keep sweet and savoury biscuits separate.

TO RECRISP BISCUITS that have become a little soft, place on baking trays lined with baking paper and bake in a 180°C oven for about 5 minutes. (This can only be done with biscuits that have not been iced or filled.) Transfer to wire racks to cool.

INGREDIENTS
1½ cups (225 g) plain flour
2 teaspoons baking powder
a pinch of salt
125 g butter, softened
½ cup (55 g) firmly packed brown sugar
2 tablespoons golden syrup
1 egg
1½ teaspoons vanilla essence
3–4 tablespoons milk

BASIC DROP BISCUITS

Although basic and easy enough for a novice biscuit maker, this is a good standby recipe that can be dressed up in different ways (see Variations). Don't make the biscuits too large; they look better when on the dainty side.

MAKES ABOUT 36

METHOD

Preheat the oven to 200°C. Grease baking trays or line them with baking paper.

Sift the flour, baking powder and salt together in a bowl.

Using an electric mixer, cream the butter with the sugar until fluffy. Add the golden syrup, egg and vanilla and beat well. Add the sifted dry ingredients a little at a time alternately with the milk and use a large spoon or silicon spatula to cut and fold the mixture until you have a stiff dough.

Drop teaspoonfuls of the mixture onto the prepared baking trays and bake for 10–12 minutes or until golden. Cool on a wire rack and store in an airtight container.

VARIATIONS

CHOCOLATE DROP BISCUITS Add 60 g cooled, melted chocolate to the creamed butter and sugar, or fold through ⅓ cup chocolate melts. Bake as directed.

CHERRY DROP BISCUITS Add ⅓ cup chopped glacé cherries with the flour and milk. Bake as directed.

NUT DROP BISCUITS Add ½ cup chopped nuts – almonds, walnuts or pecans – with the flour and milk. Bake as directed.

GINGER DROP BISCUITS Add ⅓ cup chopped glacé ginger with the flour and milk. Bake as directed.

INGREDIENTS

1 egg
⅓ cup (75 g) caster sugar
¼ teaspoon vanilla essence
¾ cup (110 g) plain flour
⅓ teaspoon baking powder
½ tablespoon crushed aniseed

ANISE DROP BISCUITS

These tiny biscuits bake to a puffed top on a soft biscuit base. Buy ready-crushed aniseed powder, or for the freshest flavour, crush it yourself using a mortar and pestle or a coffee grinder.

MAKES ABOUT 30

METHOD

Preheat the oven to 160°C. Line baking trays with baking paper.

Using an electric mixer, beat the eggs until fluffy, then beat in the sugar, a little at a time. The mixture should be thick and pale yellow. Add the vanilla, then sift in the flour and baking powder. Add the aniseed and beat for 5 minutes.

Drop half-teaspoonfuls of the mixture, well apart, on the prepared baking trays. Bake for about 12 minutes or until lightly coloured.

Remove from oven, loosen the biscuits on the foil and leave them on it, uncovered and at room temperature, for 18 hours to dry. Store in airtight containers.

FREEZING BISCUITS

Uniced, unfilled biscuits freeze well. Place cooled biscuits in freezer bags, expel as much air as possible, then seal, label and date. Freeze for up to 2 months. To use, remove from the bag and arrange on baking trays lined with baking paper. Allow to thaw at room temperature, then refresh in a 180°C oven for a few minutes. Allow to cool, then fill, ice and decorate if desired.

INGREDIENTS

125 g butter, softened
¾ cup (165 g) firmly packed brown sugar
1 egg
1 tablespoon cocoa powder (see Tip)
1⅓ cups (200 g) self-raising flour
250 g raw unsalted peanuts

CHOCOLATE PEANUT BISCUITS

MAKES ABOUT 30

METHOD

Preheat the oven to 180°C. Grease baking trays or line them with baking paper.

Using an electric mixer, cream the butter with the brown sugar, add the egg and beat well. Sift the cocoa with the flour, stir into the egg mixture, then add the peanuts.

Drop teaspoonfuls of the mixture onto the prepared baking trays and bake for 15 minutes or until firm and golden underneath. Transfer to wire racks to cool.

TIP Try to source Dutch or 'dutched' cocoa powder. It has a richer but less bitter flavour than regular cocoa powder.

NOTE For those with peanut allergies, other nuts may be substituted. Try macadamias or hazelnuts. Chop them if they are large, though not too finely – the crunch of chunky pieces of nut is one of the features of this biscuit.

ANZAC BISCUITS

INGREDIENTS
1 cup rolled oats
¾ cup desiccated coconut
1 cup (150 g) plain flour
1 cup (220 g) caster sugar
125 g butter
1 tablespoon golden syrup
2 tablespoons boiling water
1½ teaspoons bicarbonate of soda

Anzac biscuits came about because there were no eggs during the war. The biscuits were good for the soldiers and they kept well, or so we thought. We made them, packed them in tins and sent them off to our brothers, but when the biscuits arrived at the trenches, the crisp ones were all broken. They were tossed around in the tins so you were lucky to get a whole one. Even today, Anzac biscuits seem to draw people together.

MAKES ABOUT 48

METHOD

Preheat the oven to 150°C. Grease baking trays or line them with baking paper.

Combine the oats, coconut, flour and sugar in a bowl.

Melt the butter and golden syrup over low heat. Mix the boiling water with the bicarbonate of soda and add to the butter and golden syrup mixture. Pour the liquid into the mixed dry ingredients and mix well.

Drop teaspoonfuls of the mixture onto greased baking trays, leaving room for spreading. Bake for 20 minutes or until golden.

Cool on trays for a few minutes, then transfer to wire racks.

NOTE If you prefer your Anzacs slightly chewy rather than crunchy, cook them for about 15 minutes.

INGREDIENTS
1½ cups (225 g) plain flour
2 teaspoons baking powder
a pinch of salt
125 g butter, softened
½ cup (110 g) caster sugar
1½ teaspoons vanilla essence
2 tablespoons honey
1 egg
2 tablespoons milk
2 cups cornflakes, lightly crushed
½ cup glacé cherries, halved (see Note)

CHERRY WINK COOKIES

MAKES ABOUT 36

METHOD

Preheat the oven to 200°C. Grease baking trays or line them with baking paper.

Sift the flour, baking powder and salt. Using an electric mixer, cream the butter with the sugar and vanilla. Add the honey and egg and beat well. Using a large metal spoon or a silicon spatula, fold in dry ingredients, a little at a time, alternating with milk.

Drop heaped teaspoonfuls of mixture into lightly crushed cornflakes and toss gently to coat.

Place on the prepared baking trays and gently press a glacé cherry half in the centre of each. Bake the cookies for 10 minutes or until golden. Transfer to wire racks to cool.

NOTE For a pretty effect, use different colours of glacé cherries. Most glacé cherries are dyed to make them brightly coloured; however, undyed cherries are available. They are a darker, more natural red and are available from larger supermarkets and health food stores.

INGREDIENTS

1 cup rolled oats
1 cup ricotta or cottage cheese
1 cup (150 g) self-raising flour, sifted
½ cup (110 g) caster sugar
¼ cup chopped raisins
¼ cup chopped glacé cherries
125 g butter, melted
⅓ cup milk

CHERRY RAISIN DROPS

These simple biscuits are quick and easy to make. You can also get little ones to help with the mixing as there are no electric beaters involved, just a good old-fashioned wooden spoon.

MAKES ABOUT 36

METHOD

Preheat the oven to 190°C. Grease baking trays or line them with baking paper.

Combine all the ingredients and, using a wooden spoon, mix well to a stiff batter. Place teaspoons of the mixture on the prepared baking trays, allowing space for spreading. Bake for 15–20 minutes or until golden and firm.

Remove from the trays and transfer to wire racks to cool.

VARIATIONS

SULTANA The raisins can easily be replaced with sultanas.

CURRANTS Try using currants instead of raisins.

MIXED PEEL The glacé cherries can be replaced with mixed peel.

BISCUITS *drop biscuits*

INGREDIENTS
125 g butter, softened
1/3 cup (75 g) caster sugar
1 egg
1 teaspoon vanilla essence
3/4 cup (110 g) plain flour, sifted
a pinch of salt

BUTTER WAFERS

This is a very good basic biscuit recipe and useful to have on hand for when unexpected visitors drop by. They are quick to make, the flavourings can be varied and they keep well.

MAKES ABOUT 36

METHOD
Preheat the oven to 190°C. Grease baking trays or line them with baking paper.

Using an electric mixer, cream the butter with the sugar, then beat in the egg and vanilla. Stir in the flour and salt. Drop teaspoonfuls of the mixture onto the prepared baking trays, spacing them well apart.

Bake for 10 minutes or until the biscuits are golden brown around the edges. Transfer to wire racks to cool.

VARIATIONS
CHOCOLATE BUTTER WAFERS Add about 1 tablespoon cocoa powder but reduce the flour in proportion.

COFFEE BUTTER WAFERS Add 1/2–1 teaspoon instant coffee powder (depending on the strength of the coffee) to the dough.

POPPY OR SESAME SEEDS Sprinkle poppy or sesame seeds over the biscuits before baking.

BISCUITS *drop biscuits*

INGREDIENTS
1¼ cups (185 g) plain flour
½ teaspoon bicarbonate of soda
½ teaspoon salt
125 g butter, softened
¼ cup (55 g) firmly packed brown sugar
½ cup (110 g) caster sugar
1 egg, beaten
1 teaspoon vanilla essence
100 g packet choc bits

TOLLHOUSE COOKIES

This is a classic American cookie which remains very popular today. The name comes from the Toll House Inn in Whitman, Massachusetts, which was owned by Ruth Graves Wakefield, who developed the first recipe for chocolate chip cookies in 1930.

MAKES ABOUT 36

METHOD
Preheat the oven to 180°C. Grease baking trays or line them with baking paper.

Sift the flour, bicarbonate of soda and salt together. Using an electric mixer, cream the butter with sugars until light and fluffy. Add the egg and vanilla and beat well. Stir in the sifted dry ingredients and the choc bits.

Drop teaspoonfuls of the mixture onto the prepared baking trays, spacing them about 5 cm apart. Bake for 10 minutes or until golden. Transfer to wire racks to cool.

NOTE Use all the one type of choc bits, or a mixture of milk, dark and white.

BRANDY SNAPS

MAKES ABOUT 12

INGREDIENTS
60 g butter
⅓ cup (60 g) lightly packed brown sugar
⅓ cup golden syrup
½ cup (75 g) plain flour
1 teaspoon ground ginger
grated rind of half a lemon

TO SERVE
1 cup cream
1 tablespoon brandy (optional)

METHOD

Preheat the oven to 180°C. Line two baking trays with baking paper. Grease the round handles of two wooden spoons (the larger the better).

Heat the butter, brown sugar and golden syrup together in a saucepan until the butter melts. Cool, then add the flour sifted with the ginger. Stir in the lemon rind.

Drop teaspoonfuls of the mixture onto a prepared baking tray, spacing them at least 15 cm apart and allowing only two or three biscuits per tray. Bake one tray at a time for about 10 minutes or until golden brown.

Remove from the oven, allow to set for a few seconds, then ease the biscuits off the tray with a palette knife and wrap loosely round the handle of a wooden spoon, lacy side (the upper side) out. When crisp, remove from spoon. As soon as they are completely cold, store in an airtight container unless using immediately.

To serve, whip the cream, fold in the brandy and pipe into both ends of each rolled biscuit. Chill in the refrigerator for at least 30 minutes or until ready to serve.

VARIATION

BRANDY SNAP BASKETS Remove the biscuits from the oven, allow to set for a few seconds, then drape over the upturned bottoms of greased muffin tins or glasses, pressing lightly with a dry cloth. When cool and crisp, remove and store in an airtight container. Fill baskets with ice-cream, sorbet or berries to serve.

NOTE There's a little skill involved in timing the baking, so that the biscuits don't stick to the trays, and in rolling them gently and quickly to shape them. They must be kept in an airtight container once cooled. If filling them, do so close to serving time.

BISCUITS *drop biscuits*

These crisp, lacy rolled wafers are elegant for afternoon tea or to accompany a fruit dessert. They have been made for centuries in Britain, where they were often given as gifts by vendors at medieval fairs. Later they became an afternoon tea treat, filled with whipped cream.

Part of their appeal is the various pretty shapes – tubes, curls or baskets – that they can be formed into, and which can then be filled with cream and fruits, or a mousse mixture.

INGREDIENTS

125 g butter
$2/3$ cup (150 g) caster sugar
2 tablespoons honey
$1/3$ cup cream
a pinch of salt
grated rind of $1/2$ lemon
$1 2/3$ cups (185 g) flaked almonds
2 tablespoons chopped mixed peel
1 tablespoon chopped glacé cherries (optional)
125 g cooking chocolate

FLORENTINES

Florentines are a great European favourite but require some patience to master. This recipe can be a little tricky but the results are worth it once you take the time. The mixture will spread so it needs to be gathered, with the help of a biscuit cutter, into a neat round shape halfway through cooking, and at the end.

MAKES 12

METHOD

Preheated the oven to 190°C. Generously grease baking trays with butter or line them with baking paper.

Put the butter, sugar, honey, cream, salt and lemon rind in a saucepan and lightly boil for about 5 minutes, stirring constantly, until the mixture becomes thick and creamy and leaves the sides of the pan.

Add the almonds, peel and cherries, if using. Mix well and remove from the heat. Spoon tablespoons of the mixture, about four to a tray, and flatten slightly with a wet spoon.

Bake for about 8 minutes. The mixture will spread unevenly, so remove the trays from the oven and gather up the edges of the mixture with a 5 cm biscuit cutter to make the florentines into a round, even shape. Return to the oven for a further 6–8 minutes.

Remove from the oven, allow to cool for a few minutes on the tray then reshape, using a cutter as before. Remove with a metal spatula and transfer to a wire rack to cool.

Melt the chocolate over a bowl of hot water, beat until smooth then spread over the flat side of each cooled biscuit. Using the tines of a fork or a serrated plastic blade made especially for the purpose, mark the chocolate in wavy lines and leave to set. Store in an airtight container.

INGREDIENTS

250 g butter
1 cup (220 g) firmly packed brown sugar
½ cup (110 g) white sugar
1 egg
2 teaspoons vanilla essence
¼ cup water
1⅔ cups (250 g) plain flour
½ teaspoon salt
1½ teaspoons bicarbonate of soda
1 teaspoon ground cinnamon
½ cup chopped nuts
1 cup raisins
2½ cups rolled oats
walnut halves or halved glacé cherries to decorate

HIGHLAND OATMEAL BISCUITS

These hearty oatmeal biscuits have sustained many a hungry Scottish child. Porridge oats, also known as rolled oats, are oats that have been partly cooked. In these biscuits, they give a nice crunch to an otherwise soft mixture.

MAKES ABOUT 60

METHOD

Preheat the oven to 190°C. Grease baking trays or line them with baking paper.

Using an electric mixer, cream the butter with the sugars, egg and vanilla until light and fluffy. Beat in the water. Sift the dry ingredients and stir into the creamed mixture with the nuts, raisins and oats.

Drop heaped teaspoonfuls of the mixture, about 5 cm apart, onto the prepared baking trays. Press a walnut or cherry into the top of each biscuit. Bake for 12–15 minutes or until lightly browned. Transfer to wire racks to cool.

Store in an airtight container or freeze half of the biscuits.

VARIATION

SPICY OAT BISCUITS Add 1 teaspoon each of ground ginger and mixed spice to the dry mixture. Mix well, roll out on a lightly floured surface and cut into fingers. Bake as directed.

INGREDIENTS
2 egg whites
½ cup (110 g) caster sugar
½ cup (75 g) plain flour, sifted
½ teaspoon vanilla essence
¼ cup blanched, slivered almonds
60 g butter, melted and cooled

ALMOND TUILES

Tuiles (French for 'tiles') are thin, crisp, curled wafer biscuits. After baking, the pliable mixture is draped over a rolling pin or similar mould to cool, which gives the characteristic shape. They can be served on their own as petits fours with coffee or with ice cream.

MAKES 10–16 ACCORDING TO SIZE REQUIRED

METHOD
Preheat the oven to 190°C. Grease baking trays or line them with baking paper.

Beat the egg whites until stiff and gradually beat in the sugar. Gently fold in the flour, vanilla, almonds and butter.

Spread 3–4 teaspoons of the mixture to form flat rounds or ovals, well separated from each other, on the prepared baking trays. Bake (in batches of no more than four at a time) for 4–5 minutes or until golden. Remove from the oven and, using a spatula, lift off carefully. Quickly drape over a rolling pin to cool.

When cold, store in an airtight container, as these biscuits are particularly susceptible to softening in humid weather.

VARIATIONS
VANILLA TUILES Follow the recipe for Almond Tuiles, omitting the slivered almonds and increasing the vanilla to ¾ teaspoon.

ORANGE TUILES Follow the recipe for Almond Tuiles, omitting the slivered almonds and vanilla and using 2 teaspoons finely grated orange rind instead (or lemon rind for lemon-flavoured tuiles).

NOTES Once baked, the tuiles need to be handled quickly and lightly, as they cool and crisp quickly. If they crisp too quickly before you've formed them into the right shape, return them briefly to the oven to warm and become pliable again.

For large tuiles, spread 2–3 tablespoons of the mixture on baking trays to form round or oval shapes up to 15 cm across. Bake and finish as for Almond Tuiles.

INGREDIENTS

100 g walnuts, almonds or hazelnuts
125 g butter, softened
¼ cup (55 g) caster sugar
½ teaspoon vanilla essence
1¼ cups (185 g) plain flour
a pinch of salt
vanilla sugar (below) or sifted icing sugar to dust

VANILLA KIPPELS

Vanilla kippels – or kipferls, as they are known in Germany and Austria – are usually made at Christmas. They can be made with different nuts, such as walnuts or almonds, although in Bavaria it is nearly always hazelnuts. Care should be taken to process the nuts to a meal without letting them become a paste. There should be little pieces of nut recognisable in the mixture. The vanilla taste is also important. Store the biscuits in a glass jar together with a piece of vanilla bean – they make a lovely gift when presented in this way and will keep for several weeks.

MAKES ABOUT 40

METHOD

Preheat the oven to 180°C. Grease baking trays or line them with baking paper.

Using the pulse button, process the nuts in a food processor until finely chopped or coarsely ground.

Using an electric mixer, cream the butter with the sugar and vanilla until the mixture is light and fluffy.

Sift the flour with the salt and fold into the creamed mixture along with the ground nuts. Lightly mix to form a dough. If the mixture is too sticky, add a little more flour.

Pinch off small pieces of dough and roll into walnut-sized balls. Roll each ball in the palm of your hand to form a small tube, then curve gently into a crescent. Arrange on the prepared baking trays.

Bake for 20–25 minutes or until lightly coloured. Transfer the biscuits to a wire rack over a sheet of baking paper.

Dredge the kippels lightly with vanilla sugar or sifted icing sugar while they are still warm. Cool on wire racks and store in an airtight container.

NOTE In warmer weather the dough may be a little tricky to handle. In this case, knead lightly until smooth and then form into a ball. Wrap in plastic wrap and chill for 1 hour.

VANILLA SUGAR

Cut 2 vanilla beans into pieces and process in a food processor with 1 cup caster sugar until the beans are incorporated through the sugar, giving it an ashy look. If not using immediately, store in an airtight container; it will keep for many months.

VANILLA BISCUITS

MAKES ABOUT 50

INGREDIENTS
125 g butter
⅓ cup (75 g) caster sugar
1 teaspoon vanilla essence
1 cup (150 g) plain flour
½ teaspoon baking powder
blanched almonds, walnut or pecan halves, hazelnuts or halved glacé cherries to decorate (optional)

METHOD

Preheat the oven to 190°C. Grease baking trays or line them with baking paper.

Melt the butter, then cook over low heat until it browns slightly, without letting it burn. Cool over cold water, then transfer to a mixing bowl, add the sugar and beat until light. Beat in the vanilla.

Gradually fold in the flour sifted with the baking powder. Using floured hands, shape into small balls and flatten them slightly. Top each with a nut or cherry.

Arrange on the prepared trays. Bake for 12–15 minutes or until crisp and golden. Transfer to wire racks to cool.

NOTE Vanilla comes from vanilla beans, actually the pod of a climbing orchid native to central America. The beans are split and the tiny fragrant black seeds added to a recipe, or the chopped pods macerated in alcohol to produce vanilla essence. Good cooks know to store a vanilla bean in a jar of caster sugar, which will gradually absorb the flavour and scent of the vanilla. This vanilla-infused sugar can be used for custards, cakes or biscuits.

BISCUITS *shaped biscuits*

INGREDIENTS

3½ cups (525 g) plain flour
1 teaspoon baking powder
1 teaspoon ground cloves
1 teaspoon ground allspice
a grinding of black pepper
1 teaspoon ground cinnamon
⅔ cup honey
1 cup golden syrup
¾ cup (165 g) caster sugar
45 g butter

PFEFFERNUSSE (SPICE BISCUITS)

These sweet, spicy-flavoured biscuits are an old recipe, made as a special treat in Christmasses past using the exotic spices that came back with spice traders from the east.

MAKES ABOUT 30

METHOD

Preheat the oven to 200°C. Grease baking trays or line them with baking paper.

Sift together the flour, baking powder, cloves, allspice, pepper and cinnamon. Place the honey, golden syrup and sugar in a large, heavy saucepan. Stir over low heat until the sugar dissolves, then bring to the boil, without stirring. Reduce the heat to low and simmer for 5 minutes.

Remove from the heat and stir in the butter. Add the flour mixture, one-quarter at a time, beating well with a wooden spoon until smooth.

Place teaspoonfuls of the mixture on the prepared baking trays, leaving about 2.5 cm space between them.

Bake for 10–15 minutes or until light brown. Transfer to wire racks to cool. Store in an airtight container for up to six weeks.

NOTE Once the biscuits are cold, they can be iced with Glacé Icing (page 252) if you like.

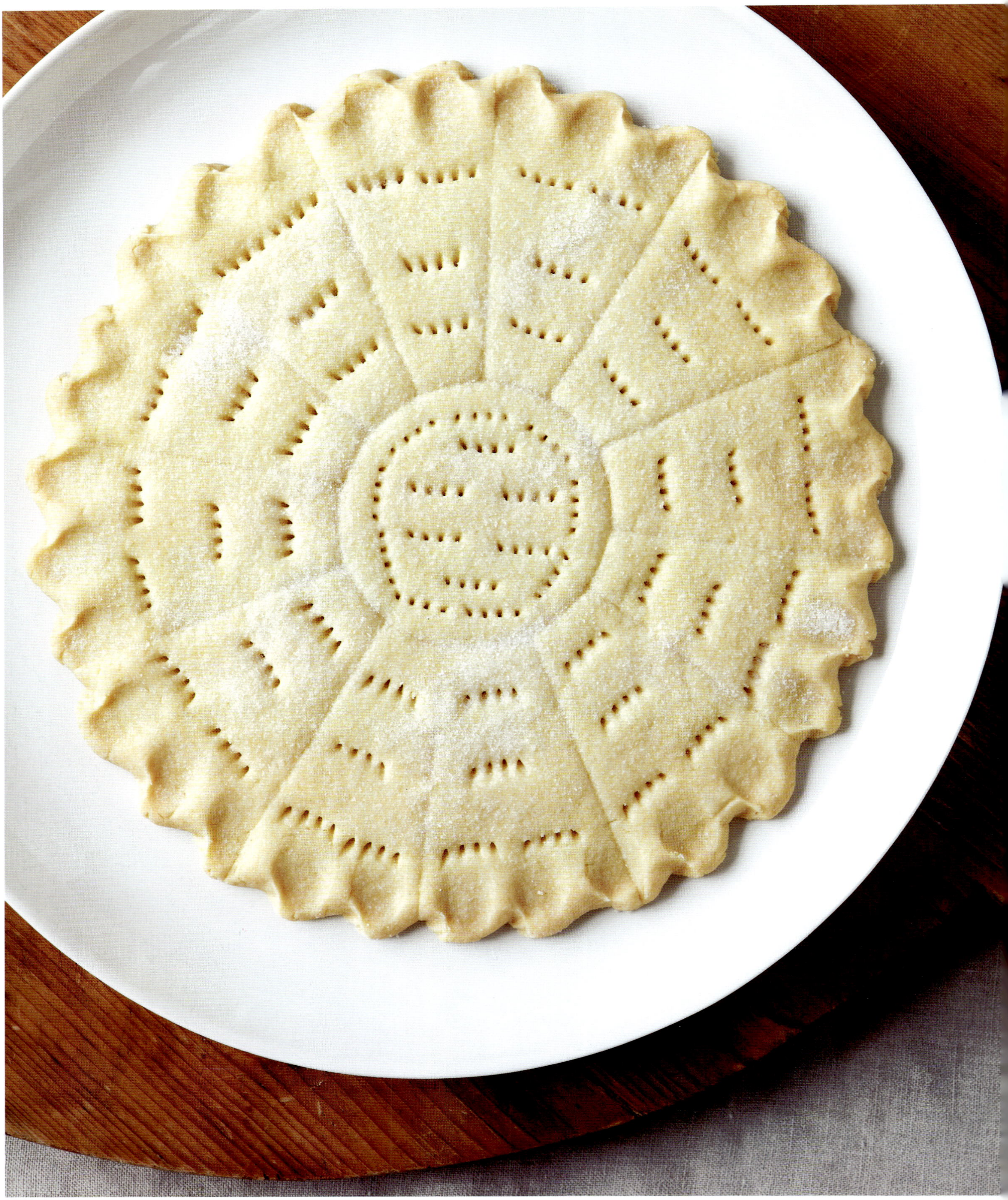

INGREDIENTS
250 g butter, softened
½ cup (110 g) caster sugar, plus extra to dust
3 cups (450 g) plain flour

SHORTBREAD

I love to shape shortbread into petticoat tails. According to legend, the recipe was brought from France by Mary, Queen of Scots. Its French name, 'petits gateaux tailles', means 'little cakes cut off'. The name came to be pronounced as it sounded to the Scots and English – 'petticoat tails'. But the real Highland Scot didn't do any of this. They just put the shortbread on the table and you simply broke it. That was the proper thing to do. Whichever way you make it, if you get it just right, people love it.

MAKES 2 ROUNDS

METHOD
Preheat the oven to 160°C.

Using an electric mixer, cream the butter until light and creamy, then gradually add the sugar, beating it until it is light and fluffy. Work in the flour gradually and then knead the dough with your hands for about 5 minutes until the mixture is very smooth.

Halve the dough and press each piece into a 24 cm circle on baking trays or into flan rings or sandwich tins (there is no need to grease them). You can make them into smaller, thicker circles if you like. With the heel of the hand push the dough out until the mixture is very smooth, then smooth over the surface with a rolling pin, or the heel of your hand over some plastic wrap.

Crimp the edges by pressing the edge of the pastry with your finger and then pinching the edge together. If using a flan ring or sandwich tin, use a fork to decorate the edges. Using a 7 cm round biscuit cutter, cut a circle in the middle. Keeping this smaller circle whole and intact, cut the remaining round into 12 segments. Using a fork, prick the shortbread in a decorative pattern (this is done to release moisture as it cooks, making the shortbread crisp). Dust lightly with extra caster sugar.

Bake for 40 minutes or until very lightly coloured and crisp. Transfer to wire racks to cool and store in an airtight container.

VARIATION
CITRUS SHORTBREAD Add 2 teaspoons each finely grated lemon and orange rind to the butter mixture.

NOTE The dough must be kneaded for about 5 minutes until it becomes smooth and very buttery. This makes a superb shortbread, crisp yet tender. If making ahead, recrisp in a 180°C oven for 15 minutes before serving. For a lighter and crisper shortbread, ¼ cup of the flour could be replaced with the same amount of rice flour.

COCONUT DROPS

INGREDIENTS
1⅓ cups (200 g) self-raising flour
a pinch of salt
1 cup (110 g) caster sugar
1 egg, lightly beaten
1 teaspoon vanilla essence
a few drops of almond essence
125 g butter, melted
1½ cups (135 g) desiccated coconut

MAKES ABOUT 30

METHOD
Preheat the oven to 180°C. Grease baking trays or line them with baking paper.

Sift the flour and salt into a bowl and stir in the sugar. Add the remaining ingredients, except the coconut, and combine. Form the mixture into small balls about the size of a large marble and roll in the coconut.

Arrange on the prepared baking trays, spacing well apart. Bake for 15 minutes or until golden. Transfer to wire racks to cool. Store in an airtight container.

BISCUITS *shaped biscuits*

INGREDIENTS

250 g unsalted butter, softened
1 cup (220 g) firmly packed brown sugar
¼ cup (55 g) caster sugar
1 tablespoon vanilla essence
¼ cup milk
2 large eggs, lightly beaten
2 cups (300 g) plain flour
½ teaspoon ground cinnamon
½ teaspoon salt
1 teaspoon baking powder
1 teaspoon bicarbonate of soda
3 cups rolled oats
1 cup raisins

OATMEAL RAISIN COOKIES

MAKES ABOUT 36

METHOD

Preheat the oven to 180°C. Grease baking trays or line them with baking paper.

Using an electric mixer, cream the butter until soft. Beat in the sugars until light and fluffy. Add the vanilla, milk and eggs and beat thoroughly.

Sift in the flour with the cinnamon, salt, baking powder and soda, and mix until just combined. Stir in the rolled oats and raisins. Place the bowl with the mixture in the refrigerator until firm, for several hours or overnight.

Scoop out large tablespoons of the batter, shape each into a ball and arrange on the prepared baking trays, about 8 cm apart. Press down with a wet fork to flatten slightly.

Bake for 15–20 minutes or until golden. They will still be slightly soft in the centre. Remove from the oven and transfer to wire racks to cool. Store in an airtight container.

INGREDIENTS

125 g butter
½ cup (110 g) firmly packed brown sugar
1 egg, beaten
2 tablespoons honey
1½ cups (225 g) self-raising flour
a pinch of salt
creamed honey, to sandwich

HONEY BUNS

Honey varies greatly in colour, flavour and consistency depending on the flower from which the nectar to make it was gathered. Honey flavours these lovely firm-textured little biscuits, which for good measure are also sandwiched together with creamed honey. If you don't like creamed honey, you can use glacé icing (page 252).

MAKES 10–12 PAIRS

METHOD

Preheat the oven to 180°C. Grease baking trays or line them with baking paper.

Using an electric mixer, cream the butter until soft. Gradually add the brown sugar and beat until light and fluffy. Beat in the egg and honey. Sift the flour with the salt and work into the mixture until it forms a soft dough. Chill until firm.

Shape the dough into small balls each the size of a walnut and place well apart on the prepared baking trays.

Bake for 12 minutes or until risen and golden. Transfer to wire racks to cool then sandwich in pairs with the creamed honey. If making ahead, store unsandwiched biscuits in an airtight container and sandwich just before serving.

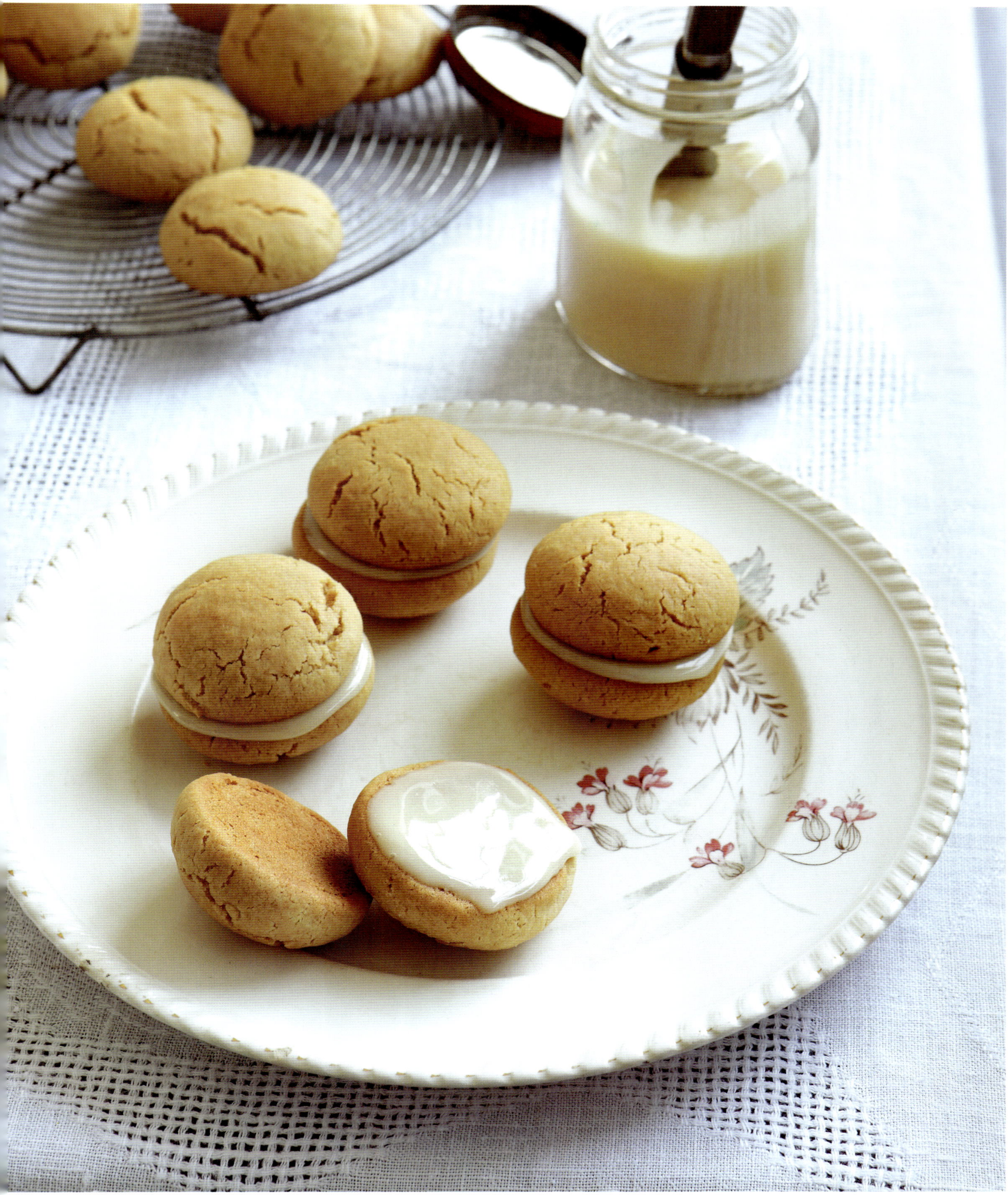

INGREDIENTS

1¼ cups (185 g) plain flour
2 tablespoons caster sugar
125 g butter, diced
½ cup (60 g) very finely chopped hazelnuts
1 egg yolk
extra caster sugar to dust

HAZELNUT CRESCENTS

One of the most beautiful biscuits, especially when the hazelnuts are good and fresh. Walnuts may be used in place of hazelnuts. For long storage, buy whole nuts and store in the freezer. Nuts should be chopped or ground just before using to ensure maximum freshness.

MAKES ABOUT 35

METHOD

Sift the flour into a bowl, stir in the sugar and rub in the butter until the mixture resembles coarse breadcrumbs. Mix in the nuts and stir in the egg yolk. Work with the fingertips to make a dough. Cover and chill for 30 minutes.

Preheat the oven to 180°C and lightly grease two baking trays. Take about 2 teaspoons of dough at a time, roll into 6 cm lengths and shape into crescents. Place on the prepared baking trays and bake for 12 minutes or until lightly coloured.

Remove the crescents and roll them in the extra caster sugar while still warm. Cool on a wire rack and store in an airtight container.

BISCUITS *shaped biscuits*

INGREDIENTS
1 cup (150 g) plain flour
2 tablespoons caster sugar
1 teaspoon bicarbonate of soda
1 teaspoon mixed spice
1 teaspoon ground cinnamon
1 teaspoon ground ginger
60 g butter
2 tablespoons golden syrup
extra ¼ cup (55 g) caster sugar (optional)

GINGERNUTS

These gingernut biscuits have a hard crunchy texture and a wonderful spicy flavour. They are an old favourite.

MAKES ABOUT 20

METHOD

Preheat the oven to 180°C. Grease baking trays or line them with baking paper.

Sift the flour with the remaining dry ingredients. Melt the butter with the golden syrup and pour into the flour mixture. Mix well and roll into balls the size of a walnut. If liked, roll the balls in extra sugar before baking for super crunchiness.

Place on the prepared baking trays and press lightly. Bake for 5 minutes, then reduce the oven temperature to 180°C and bake for a further 7–10 minutes. Cool on the trays.

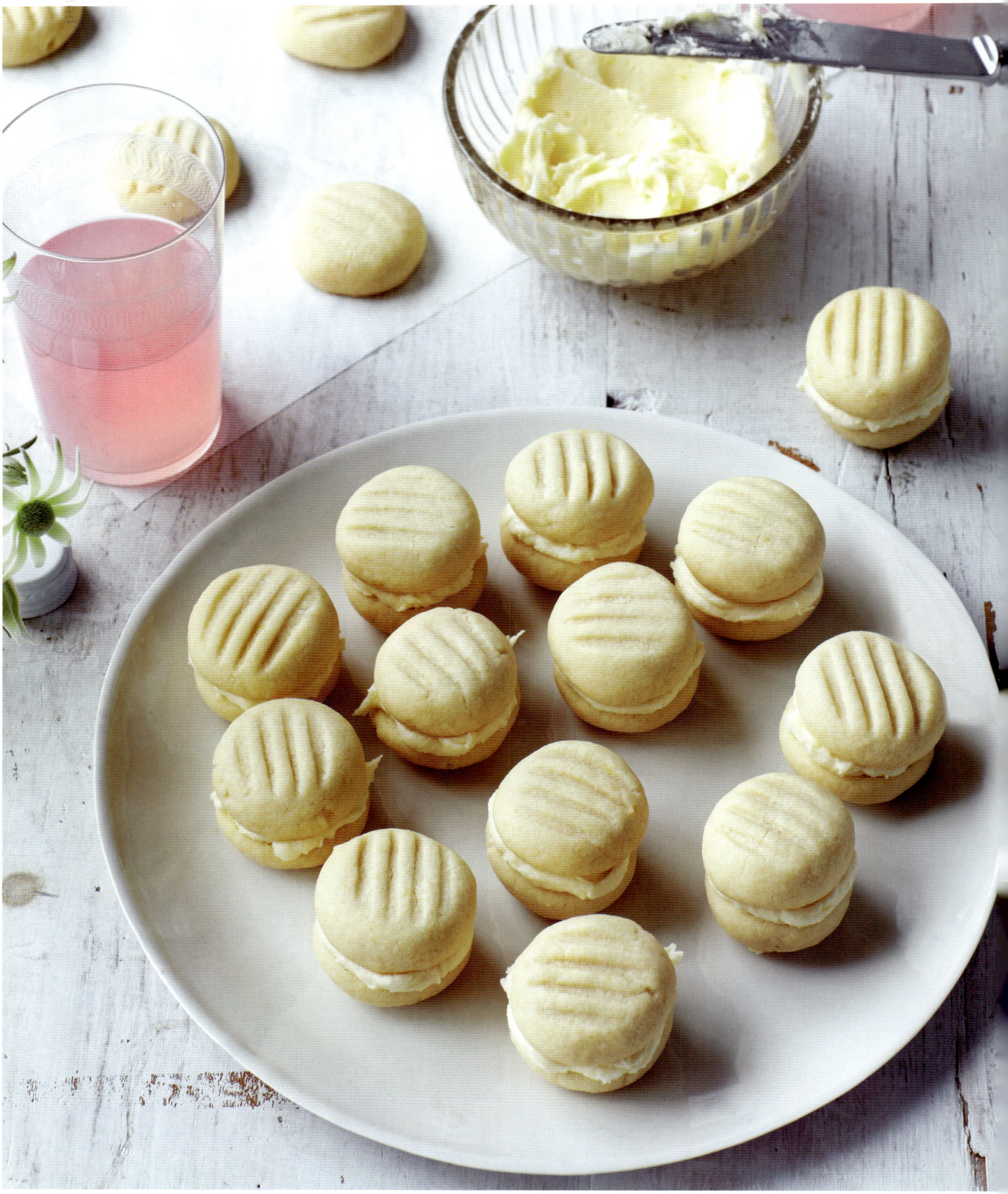

INGREDIENTS
250 g unsalted butter, softened
1/3 cup (50 g) icing sugar, sifted
1 tablespoon grated lemon rind
1 1/2 cups (225 g) plain flour
2 tablespoons cornflour

LEMON FILLING
60 g unsalted butter, softened
1 1/2 teaspoons each lemon juice and rind
3/4 cup (120 g) icing sugar, sifted

LEMON MELTING MOMENTS

These biscuits are truly melt-in-the-mouth and simply irresistible. There are many recipes for melting moments, which are sometimes known as yo-yos. All include cornflour in varying proportions to flour. They can be flavoured with vanilla essence instead of the lemon if you prefer.

MAKES ABOUT 36 PAIRS

METHOD

Preheat the oven to 160°C. Grease baking trays or line them with baking paper.

Using an electric mixer, cream the butter with the icing sugar and lemon rind until light and fluffy.

Sift together the flour and cornflour, add to the butter mixture and mix until a soft dough is formed. Pinch off pieces of dough and roll into small balls each the size of a walnut. Place on the prepared baking trays about 5 cm apart. Press each one down slightly with the heel of your hand, and then, using a fork dipped each time in cold water, mark biscuits lightly to decorate.

Bake for 15 minutes or until lightly golden. Using a metal spatula, carefully remove from trays onto wire racks to cool.

For the lemon filling, beat the butter with the lemon juice and rind until pale and creamy. Add the icing sugar and continue to beat until well combined.

Sandwich the cooled biscuits together with the lemon filling. Store in an airtight container.

INGREDIENTS

250 g butter, softened
1½ cups (240 g) icing sugar, sifted
1 egg
1 teaspoon vanilla essence
2½ cups (275 g) plain flour
½ teaspoon bicarbonate of soda
1 teaspoon baking powder
¼ teaspoon salt
1½ cups finely chopped walnuts
walnut halves to decorate

WALNUT BUTTER BISCUITS

MAKES ABOUT 36

METHOD

Preheat the oven to 180°C. Grease baking trays or line them with baking paper.

Using an electric mixer, cream the butter with the icing sugar until light and fluffy. Add the egg and vanilla and beat well.

Sift the flour with the bicarbonate of soda, baking powder and salt. Stir into the creamed mixture with the chopped nuts. Form the mixture into small balls, place on the prepared baking trays and top each with a walnut half.

Bake for 10–12 minutes or until lightly browned. Transfer to wire racks to cool.

NOTE Walnuts must be fresh, as they are so rich in oils that they can become bitter. To prevent this, store in a cool place, or freeze shelled walnuts. Some cooks buy tinned walnuts, which keep very fresh until opened.

BISCUITS *shaped biscuits*

INGREDIENTS
150 g butter, softened
1 cup (220 g) firmly packed brown sugar
1 egg
1 teaspoon vanilla essence
1 2/3 cups (250 g) plain flour
1/4 teaspoon salt
1/2 teaspoon bicarbonate of soda
375 g pitted dates

DATE SURPRISES

MAKES ABOUT 36

METHOD

Preheat the oven to 180°C. Grease baking trays or line them with baking paper.

Using an electric mixer, cream the butter until soft. Gradually add the brown sugar and beat until light and fluffy. Add the egg and vanilla and beat well.

Sift the flour with the salt and bicarbonate of soda, add to the creamed mixture and mix to make a dough. Chill the dough for about 30 minutes.

Take small pieces of dough and mould them around the dates in cocoon shapes. Alternatively, roll out the dough and cut in 5 cm rounds, and wrap those around the dates. Bake on the prepared trays for 15–20 minutes.

Transfer to wire racks to cool. Any remaining dough may be used to make plain biscuits.

NOTE Dates may be eaten fresh or, more usually, dried. The best dried dates are soft and juicy and are packed whole in small boxes. The harder type of dried date is used in cooking, as here.

INGREDIENTS

125 g butter, softened
¾ cup (165 g) caster sugar plus 2 tablespoons extra
1 egg
1⅓ cups (200 g) self-raising flour
2 tablespoons ground cinnamon

CINNAMON CRINKLES

MAKES ABOUT 36

METHOD

Preheat the oven to 180°C.

Using an electric mixer, cream the butter until soft. Beat in the ¾ cup sugar until light and fluffy. Beat in the egg thoroughly. Sift the flour and add to the creamed mixture. Mix well.

Form about ½ tablespoon of the mixture at a time into a small ball and roll in the combined extra sugar and cinnamon. Place on ungreased baking trays, spacing them about 10 cm apart, flatten slightly and bake for 15 minutes or until golden. Cool on the trays until crisp.

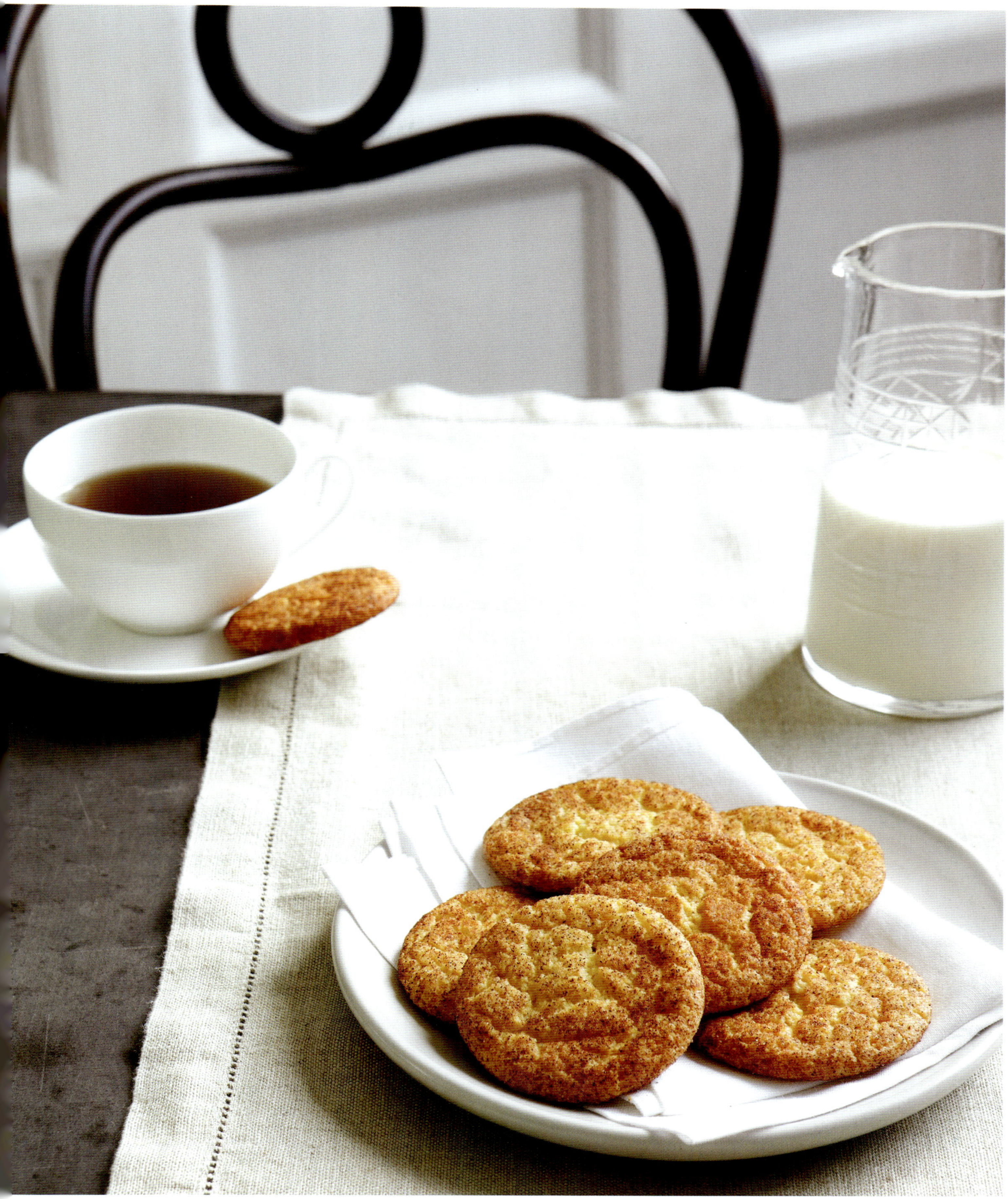

INGREDIENTS

125 g butter
½ cup (110 g) caster sugar
1 egg
1 teaspoon vanilla essence
¾ cup (110 g) self-raising flour
½ cup (75 g) plain flour
a pinch of salt
60 g blanched almonds

BURNT BUTTER BISCUITS

These are one of the best crisp little biscuits, and a personal favourite in my family – simple but very moreish. Don't take the name literally – the butter is cooked until brown and nutty-tasting only.

MAKES ABOUT 24

METHOD

Preheat the oven to 180°C. Grease baking trays or line them with baking paper.

Melt the butter in a saucepan then cook it over a low heat to a light brown, taking care not to let it burn. Cool slightly, add the sugar and beat well. Stir in the egg and vanilla.

Sift the flours with the salt and fold into the creamed mixture. Roll into balls, each about the size of a walnut.

Place on the prepared baking trays, allowing room for spreading. Put a blanched almond on top of each. Bake for 10–12 minutes or until golden and firm. Transfer to wire racks to cool.

BISCUITS *shaped biscuits*

INGREDIENTS

125 g butter, softened
1 teaspoon bicarbonate of soda
1 teaspoon ground cardamom
¼ teaspoon salt
1 cup (220 g) firmly packed light brown sugar
1 egg
1 ²⁄₃ cups (250 g) plain flour, sifted
1 teaspoon cream of tartar

CARDAMOM COOKIES

This is a simple biscuit, with the warm fragrance of cardamon, one of the most exotic spices. For the best flavour, buy whole green cardamom pods, remove the small black seeds and grind them in a spice mill or coffee grinder.

MAKES ABOUT 45

METHOD

Using an electric mixer, cream the butter and add the bicarbonate of soda, cardamom and salt. Mix well and gradually beat in the sugar until the mixture is light and fluffy. Beat in the egg.

Sift together the flour and cream of tartar. Gradually stir into the butter mixture and mix to form a dough. Chill for 3–4 hours or until firm enough to handle.

Preheat the oven to 180°C. Scoop out heaped teaspoonfuls of the chilled dough, shaping them into small balls. Place on ungreased baking trays. Use a wetted fork to press each cookie into a round shape.

Bake for 15–18 minutes or until light golden. Remove from the trays and transfer to wire racks to cool.

TIP When cooking large batches of biscuits, make sure the baking trays are allowed to cool completely between batches, otherwise the mixture will spread too much. Sheets of baking paper used to line the trays may be used for more than one batch.

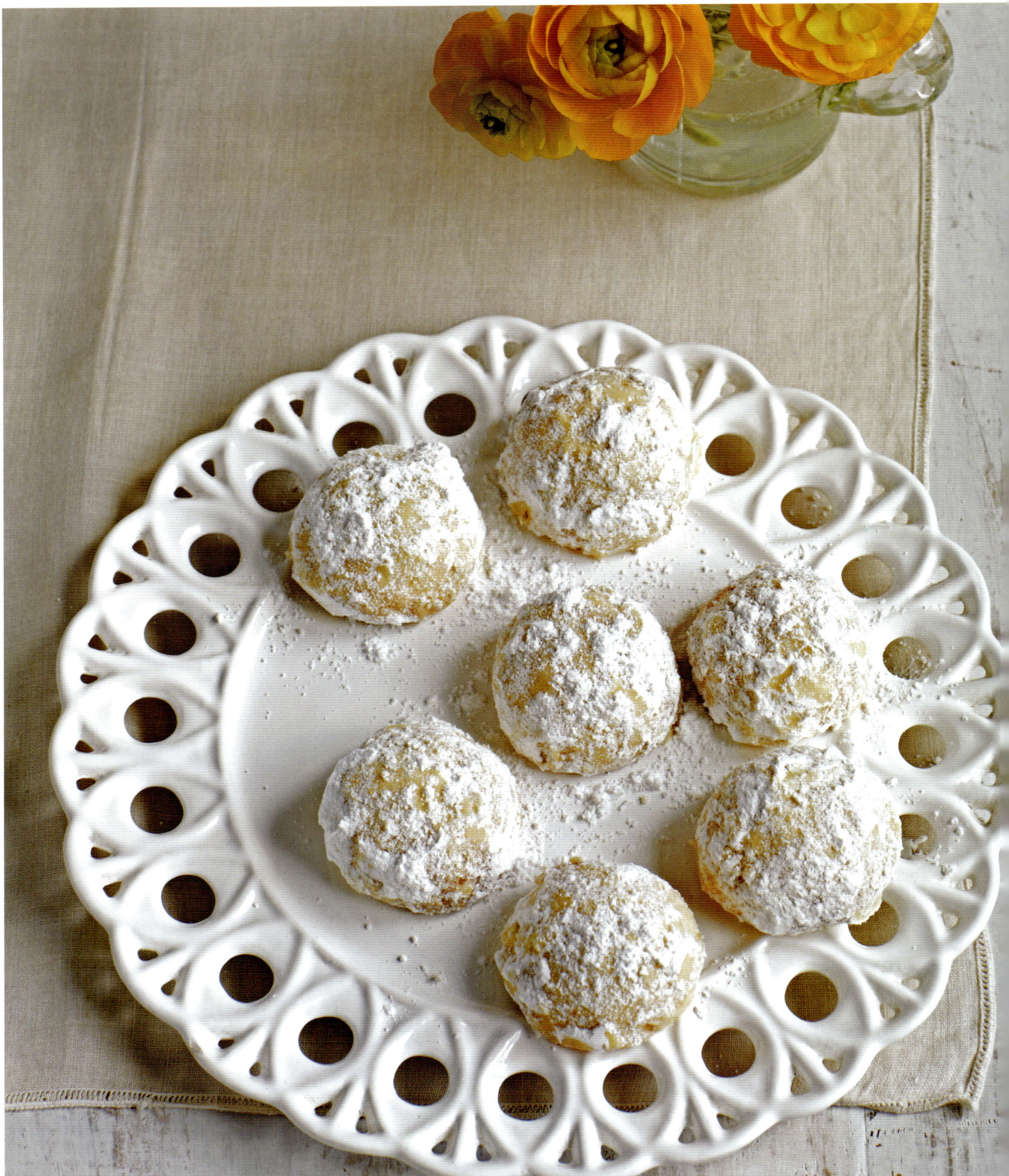

INGREDIENTS
250 g butter, softened
¼ cup (55 g) caster sugar
1 teaspoon vanilla essence
1 ⅔ cups (250 g) plain flour
½ teaspoon salt
¾ cup chopped, blanched almonds
1 cup (160 g) icing sugar

ALMOND BUTTER BALLS

Three favourites – butter, sugar and blanched almonds – are combined to make these delicious butttery balls of flavour. Such simply flavoured biscuits require the best ingredients, so use the freshest almonds and butter.

MAKES ABOUT 24

METHOD

Preheat the oven to 180°C. Lightly grease baking trays.

Using an electric mixer, cream the butter with the sugar and vanilla. Sift the flour and salt and blend into the creamed mixture with the almonds to form a dough.

Shape into balls the size of walnuts, or mould into crescent shapes. Place on the prepared baking trays and bake for about 15 minutes or until firm and lightly coloured.

Remove from the trays and while still warm, roll in the icing sugar. Transfer to wire racks to cool, then roll again in the icing sugar. Store in airtight containers.

INGREDIENTS

185 g butter, softened
1 cup (220 g) firmly packed brown sugar
1 egg
1 teaspoon vanilla essence
2 cups (300 g) plain flour
½ teaspoon salt
½ teaspoon baking powder

REFRIGERATOR BISCUITS

This biscuit dough can be stored, wrapped, in the freezer for months. Take a few slices as you need them and have freshly baked biscuits whenever you want. You can decorate the biscuits with cherries or slivered almonds, or brush them with egg white and sprinkle well with caster sugar, before baking.

MAKES ABOUT 45

METHOD

Using an electric mixer, cream the butter with the brown sugar. Add the egg and vanilla and beat well.

Sift the flour with the salt and baking powder and stir into the creamed mixture. Shape into two rolls about 5 cm in diameter. Wrap in plastic wrap or foil and chill until firm.

Slice thinly, place on a greased baking tray, decorate if desired and bake in a preheated 180°C oven for 7–10 minutes or until golden. Transfer to wire racks to cool.

If wished, store the dough in the refrigerator, wrapped in foil, for up to 2 weeks, or freeze it.

BISCUITS *shaped biscuits*

INGREDIENTS
60 g butter, softened
¼ cup (55 g) caster sugar
2 egg whites
½ cup (75 g) plain flour
¼ teaspoon vanilla essence

LANGUES DES CHATS (CATS' TONGUES)

A flat, crisp biscuit, shaped like a finger or cat's tongue, which originated in 17th-century Europe. These elegant biscuits are perfect for an afternoon tea and can also be served with liqueurs, sparkling wines, ice creams and cream desserts, and also used as an ingredient in some puddings.

MAKES ABOUT 24

METHOD

Preheat the oven to 190°C. Grease two baking trays and dust them with flour.

Using an electric mixer, cream the butter with the sugar until very light and fluffy. Beat the egg whites to a snow and add to the butter mixture alternately with the sifted flour, beating vigorously. Add the vanilla. Spoon into a piping bag fitted with a 1 cm plain tube.

Pipe the mixture onto the prepared tray in the shape of éclairs, about 7.5 cm long. Bang the tray sharply on the work surface once or twice to flatten the biscuits slightly.

Place on the prepared trays and bake for 10–12 minutes, or until the biscuits are pale golden with the edges tinged brown. Leave to cool on the tray.

NOTE The biscuits keep well in an airtight container for up to 2 weeks. You can also recrisp them in a preheated 180°C oven for 3–4 minutes, then cool on a wire rack.

INGREDIENTS

4 large egg whites
500 g ground almonds
1¾ cups (385 g) caster sugar
2 teaspoons baking powder
¼ teaspoon almond essence (optional)
1 cup (160 g) icing sugar mixture
blanched almonds to decorate

AMARETTI

An Italian specialty, known also as mandorlas, amaretti are perfect to have on hand over the festive season. Serve with coffee after dinner, or place in a glass jar for a lovely gift. They can also be decorated with a whole or half glacé cherry rather than an almond.

MAKES ABOUT 40

METHOD

Preheat the oven to 170°C. Line two baking trays with baking paper.

Beat the egg whites in a bowl with a whisk or fork until foamy.

Combine the ground almonds, caster sugar and baking powder in a bowl. Make a well in the centre and add the almond essence, if using. Add the egg whites gradually, mixing all the time. To mix, use a wooden spoon and begin at the centre of the bowl, mixing with a circular motion that gets larger as the ingredients become blended. This method will help to prevent overmixing, which may toughen the dough.

Mix together thoroughly with your hand to form a sticky dough. It should be firm enough to hold together, but not dry. When mixing the dough, use the tips of your fingers as much as you can to keep the dough light.

Roll 1 tablespoon of the dough into a ball. Repeat with the remaining mixture. Roll in the icing sugar mixture to coat and arrange on the prepared baking trays. Press an almond into the centre of each biscuit.

Bake for 15 minutes, until risen, cracked and very lightly coloured. Cool for 5 minutes on the tray before transferring to wire racks to cool completely.

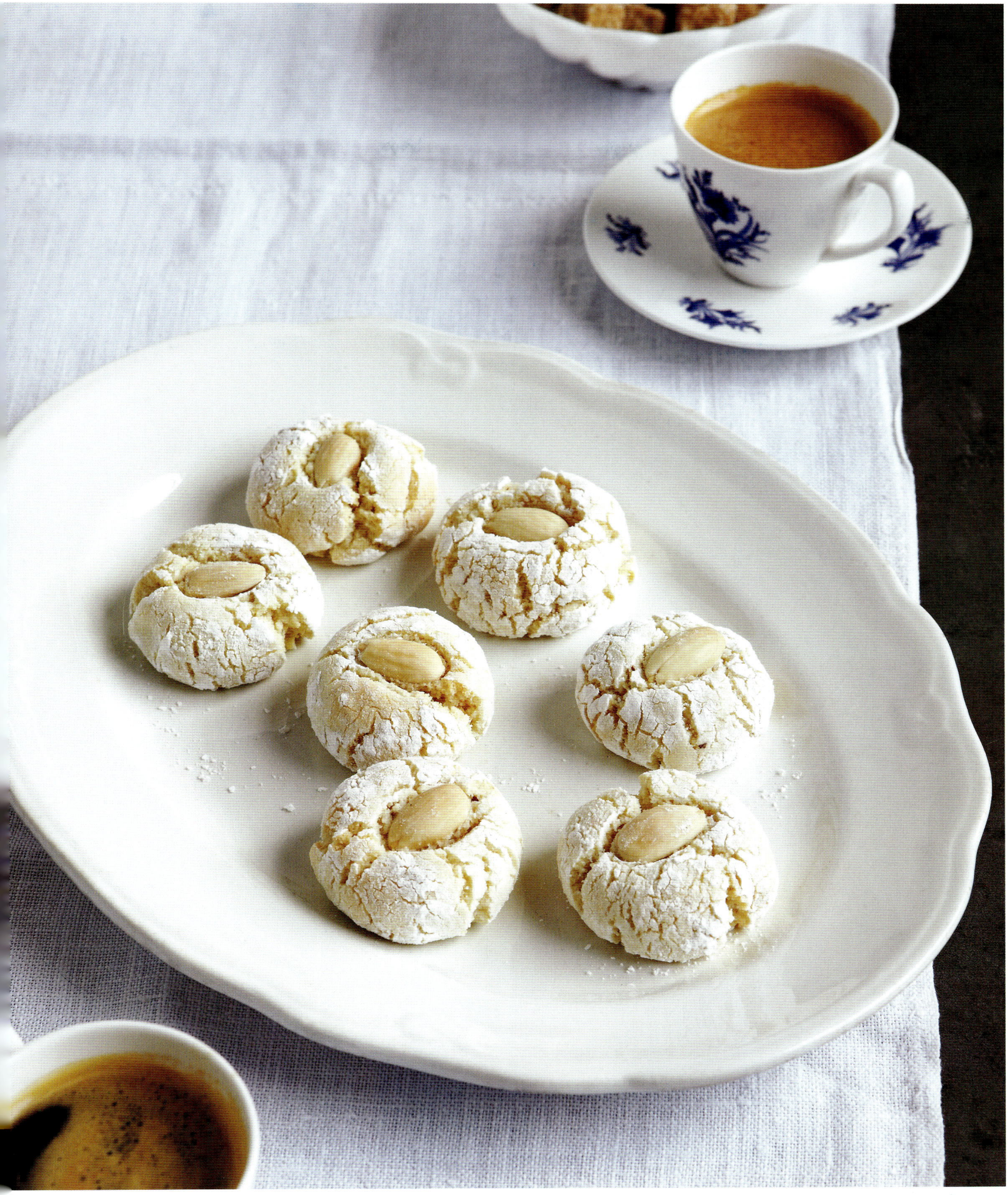

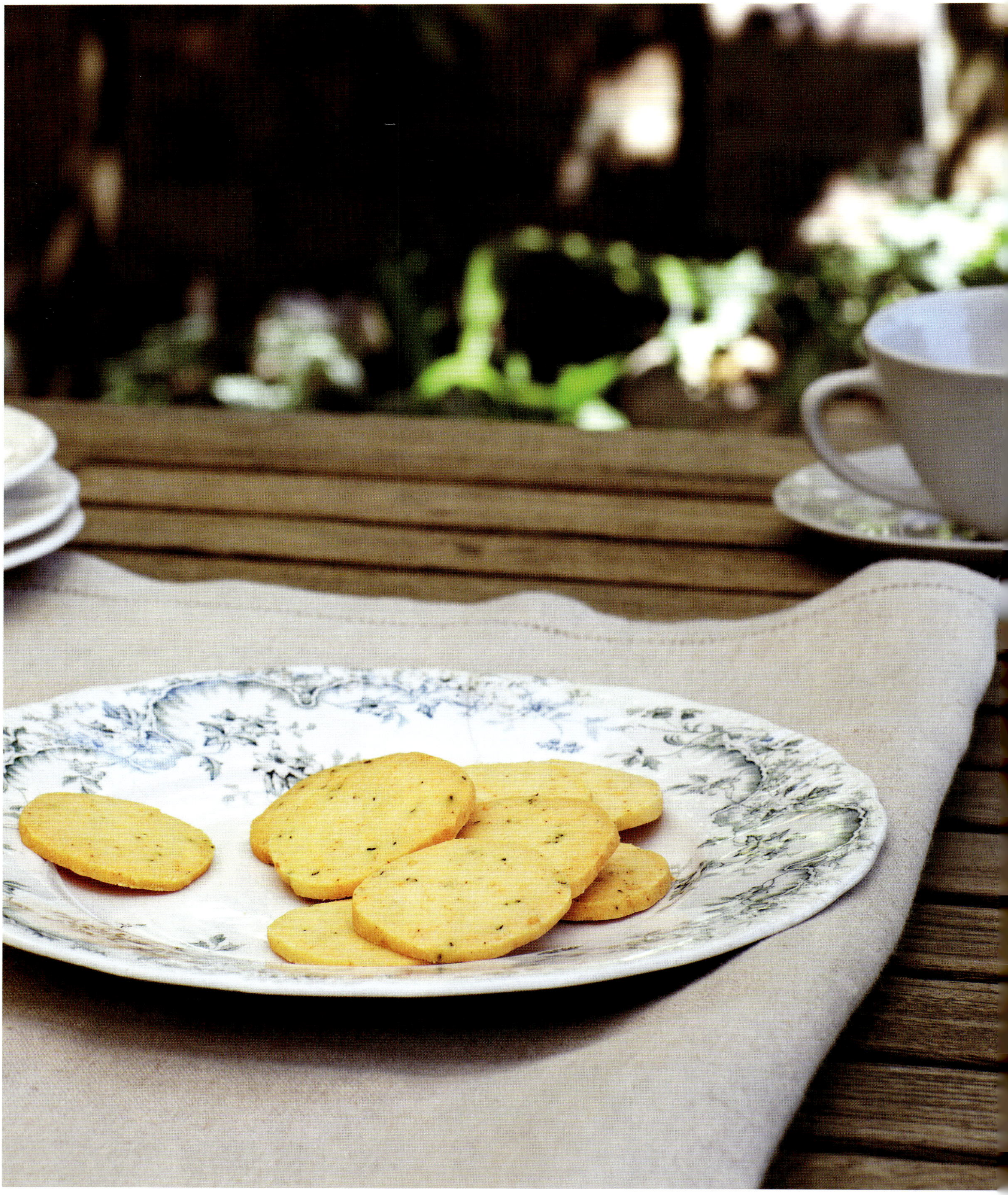

INGREDIENTS

90 g cheddar cheese, finely grated
125 g butter, softened
1½ cups (225 g) plain flour
¼ teaspoon cayenne pepper or ½ teaspoon paprika
¼ teaspoon ground pepper
1 teaspoon salt
1 teaspoon chopped rosemary leaves (see Note)
2 tablespoons grated parmesan cheese

ROSEMARY & CHEESE BISCUITS

Crisp, delicate and savoury, these are perfect to enjoy with drinks. Keep a roll of unbaked dough on hand in the freezer and slice and bake when needed. Vary the herbs, if you like, for different flavours.

MAKES ABOUT 45

METHOD

Using an electric mixer, cream the cheddar cheese and butter until soft.

Sift the flour, cayenne, pepper and salt together. Add to the creamed mixture and knead together with the rosemary and parmesan cheese.

Mix well and form into a roll, 4 cm in diameter. Wrap in plastic wrap and refrigerate for 1 hour.

Preheat the oven to 180°C. Cut into rounds using a sharp knife and place on baking trays. Bake for 15–20 minutes or until golden. Transfer to wire racks to cool.

NOTE Rosemary, the remembrance herb, is lovely in these savoury biscuits. Do not use it freshly picked; leave it for 2–3 days to dry out a little or dry it on a paper towel in a microwave oven set on high for 2 minutes, before crumbling. Store in a small jar.

INGREDIENTS

90 g butter, softened
2 tablespoons crunchy peanut butter
1½ cups (330 g) caster sugar
½ cup (100 g) lightly packed brown sugar
1 teaspoon vanilla essence
1 egg
1⅓ cups (200 g) self-raising flour, sifted
1 teaspoon salt
½ cup rolled oats

PEANUT BUTTER BISCUITS

MAKES ABOUT 36

METHOD

Using an electric mixer, cream the butters with the sugars and vanilla. Add the egg, beat well, then stir in the flour and salt. Mix in the oats.

Form the mixture into two rolls about 2.5 cm in diameter, wrap in plastic wrap and chill for about 30 minutes.

Preheat the oven to 180°C. Grease baking trays or line them with baking paper.

Cut the dough into 6 mm thick slices and arrange on the prepared baking trays. Bake for about 20 minutes.

Cool on the baking trays for 3 minutes, then transfer to wire racks to cool completely.

ALMOND BISCUITS

An interesting little biscuit, with its topping of icing sugar and stiffly beaten egg white, sprinkled with chopped almonds. When baked, the icing hardens to a delectable, shiny, crisp coating.

MAKES ABOUT 60

INGREDIENTS
125 g butter, softened
¼ cup (55 g) caster sugar
1 teaspoon vanilla essence
1 egg yolk
1 ⅔ cups (250 g) self-raising flour, sifted
a pinch of salt
1 egg white
1 cup (160 g) icing sugar, sifted
finely chopped blanched almonds

METHOD
Preheat the oven to 190°C. Grease baking trays or line them with baking paper.

Using an electric mixer, cream the butter with the sugar and vanilla, add the egg yolk and beat well. Mix in the sifted flour and salt to form a firm dough.

Turn the dough out on a floured surface and roll out to a 5 mm thickness.

Beat the egg white until stiff, add the icing sugar gradually and beat until smooth.

Spread the icing over the prepared biscuit mixture. Sprinkle with almonds and cut into diamond or other decorative shapes. Place on greased baking trays and bake for 10–12 minutes. Transfer to wire racks to cool.

INGREDIENTS

1¼ cups (185 g) plain flour
a pinch of salt
¼ cup (55 g) caster sugar
½ cup ground almonds
finely grated rind of 1 lemon
90 g butter
2 egg yolks
sifted icing sugar to dust

SABLÉS

The light, crisp and grainy texture of these lovely shortbreads gives them their French name, sablé – a 'sanded' biscuit. Serve to accompany desserts or as part of a selection for morning or afternoon tea.

MAKES ABOUT 32

METHOD

Grease baking trays or line them with baking paper.

Sift the flour, salt and sugar into a bowl. Mix in the almonds and lemon rind. Rub in the butter until the mixture resembles fine breadcrumbs, then mix in the egg yolks to form a soft dough. Knead lightly until smooth, wrap in plastic wrap and and chill for 15 minutes.

Roll out the dough thinly on a floured surface. Using a biscuit cutter, cut 4 cm rounds from the dough.

Alternatively, cut biscuits by hand with a knife or pastry wheel, cutting the dough into long strips 7.5 cm wide, then cutting across the strips at 4.5 cm intervals to form oblongs. Place them slightly apart on the prepared baking trays. Refrigerate for 30 minutes.

Preheat the oven to 180°C. Bake for 15–20 minutes or until the sablés are very lightly browned. Using a palette knife, carefully transfer them from the baking trays to wire racks to cool. When cold, dust very lightly with icing sugar.

BISCUITS *rolled biscuits*

INGREDIENTS
250 g butter, softened
½ cup (110 g) caster sugar
1⅔ cups (250 g) plain flour
2 teaspoons ground ginger
caster sugar, to sprinkle

GINGER SHORTBREAD BISCUITS

MAKES ABOUT 40

METHOD

Preheat the oven to 160°C. Grease baking trays or line them with baking paper.

Using an electric mixer, cream the butter with the sugar until light and fluffy. Sift together the flour and ginger and gradually work into the butter mixture to form a dough. Chill if necessary.

Knead lightly then roll out on a lightly floured surface until 5 mm thick. Cut into round or star shapes using a biscuit cutter. Transfer to a baking tray and bake for 12–15 minutes or until golden. Sprinkle with caster sugar while still warm. Transfer to wire racks to cool.

VARIATIONS

SPICED BISCUITS Omit the ginger but sift 1 teaspoon ground cinnamon and 1 teaspoon mixed spice with the flour.

BUTTER SHORTBREAD BISCUITS Omit the ginger and add a few drops of vanilla essence to the mixture.

INGREDIENTS

½ cup (110 g) firmly packed brown sugar
½ cup golden syrup
90 g butter
2 teaspoons bicarbonate of soda
3 cups (450 g) plain flour
1 tablespoon ground ginger
a pinch of salt
½ cup very finely chopped hazelnuts
1 egg yolk
2 eggs, lightly beaten
silver cachous and chocolate buttons or drops to decorate

ICING

1 cup (160 g) icing sugar
2–4 tablespoons boiling water
20 g butter

GINGER DAISIES

These pretty little biscuits are good to have on hand and also make a lovely gift. The flavours of ginger and hazelnuts make these daisy biscuits a special treat.

MAKES ABOUT 90

METHOD

Heat the brown sugar, golden syrup and butter in a small saucepan over a low heat, stirring, until the sugar has melted. Remove from the heat, cool for 2 minutes then stir in the bicarbonate of soda.

Sift the flour, ginger and salt into a large bowl. Make a well in the centre and stir in the butter mixture, nuts and eggs to form a soft dough. Wrap the dough in plastic wrap and chill for 1 hour.

Preheat the oven to 200°C. Grease baking trays or line them with baking paper.

Divide the dough into four portions and roll each out to a 3 mm thickness. Cut flower shapes from the dough, using a 5 cm cutter. Arrange on the prepared baking trays and continue with the remaining dough.

Bake for 6 minutes. Leave on the trays until cool enough to handle. Transfer to wire racks to cool completely.

To make the icing, sift the icing sugar into a bowl, make a well in the centre and stir in the combined boiling water and butter until smooth. Spread or pipe lightly on each biscuit and decorate with cachous or chocolate buttons or drops.

TIP These biscuits can be made ahead of time and stored, un-iced, in an airtight container. Simply ice and decorate as required.

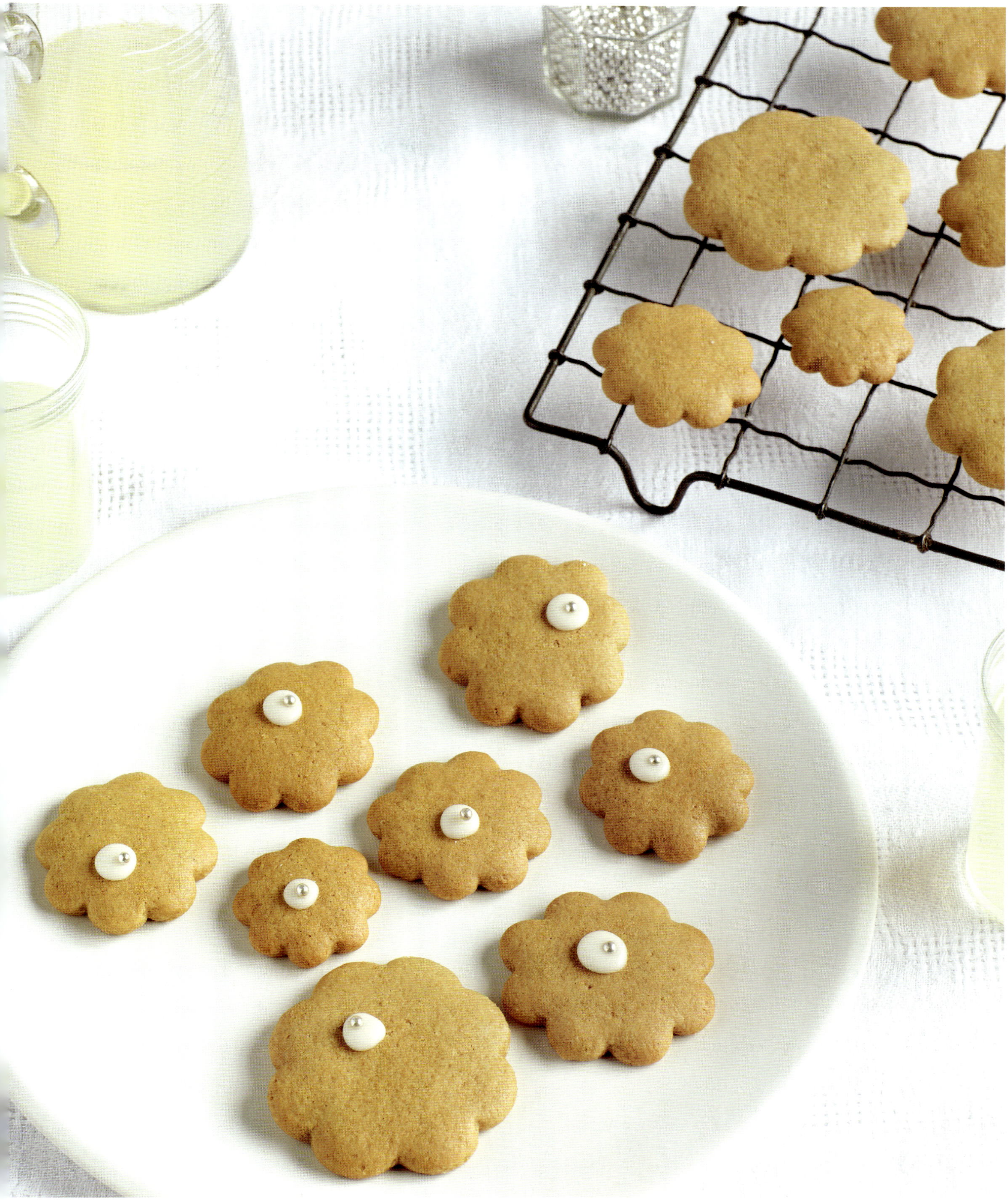

MARGARET FULTON **BAKING**

INGREDIENTS
1½ cups ground toasted hazelnuts
2 cups (300 g) plain flour
a pinch of salt
⅓ cup (75 g) caster sugar
250 g butter, diced
1 cup (160 g) icing sugar, sifted
1 tablespoon hot water
chopped hazelnuts or pistachios to decorate

HAZELNUT COOKIES

MAKES ABOUT 80

METHOD
Put the ground hazelnuts into a bowl. Sift the flour with the salt and add to the bowl with the caster sugar. Rub in the butter and combine well until smooth. Form into a ball, wrap in plastic wrap and chill for 1 hour.

Preheat the oven to 180°C. Grease baking trays or line them with baking paper.

Roll out the dough thinly and cut into rounds with a plain or fluted 4 cm cutter. Place the rounds on the prepared baking trays and bake for about 15 minutes or until firm and lightly coloured.

Allow to cool for 1 minute on the trays, then transfer to a wire rack to cool completely.

Combine the icing sugar with the hot water to make a stiff icing and spread a little on top of each biscuit. Sprinkle over the chopped nuts.

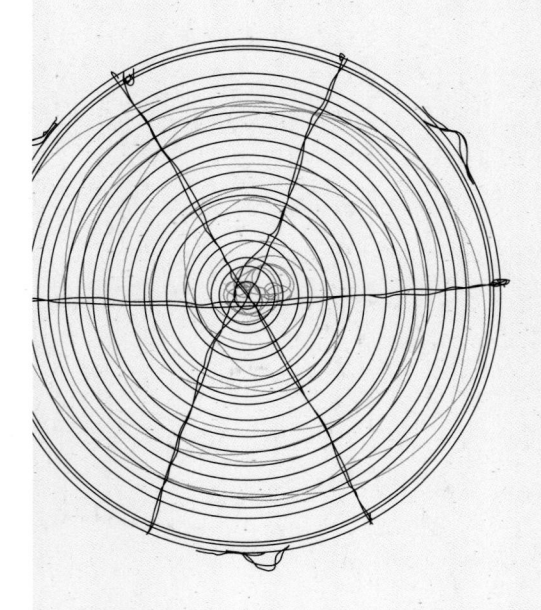

NOTE If liked, half the biscuits may be left un-iced and pairs joined together with a little raspberry jam.

INGREDIENTS
125 g butter
⅓ cup (75 g) caster sugar
⅓ cup golden syrup
3 cups (450 g) plain flour
½ teaspoon ground ginger
1 teaspoon ground cinnamon
3 teaspoons bicarbonate of soda
1 egg
2 teaspoons vanilla essence
currants, glacé cherries, silver cachous and glacé fruits to decorate

ICING
½ cup (80 g) icing sugar, sifted
2 tablespoons hot water

GINGERBREAD MEN

Children love to decorate gingerbread people. Yes, let them do their own thing – eyes, mouths, buttons or bikinis! You can buy traditional gingerbread men cutters as well as girl-shaped cutters. Make the icing, colour small quantities in separate little pots and teach the kids to use the icing to decorate the people as they want. Great fun.

MAKES ABOUT 20 SMALL GINGERBREAD MEN

METHOD

Preheat the oven to 180°C. Grease baking trays or line them with baking paper.

Put the butter, sugar and golden syrup in a saucepan and heat gently, stirring occasionally, until the butter melts. Allow to cool.

Sift the flour, ginger and cinnamon. Add the bicarbonate of soda to the cooled butter mixture and pour onto the flour mixture. Add the egg and vanilla and mix to a soft dough. Roll out to a thickness of 5 mm and chill if necessary.

Cut out shapes with a gingerbread man cutter or a sharp knife. Place on the prepared baking trays. Put currants in place for eyes and buttons, and glacé cherries cut into strips for mouths. Bake for 10 minutes. Transfer to wire racks to cool.

For the icing, combine the icing sugar and water and beat well until smooth. Using an icing pipe (or make baking paper triangles into cones for piping), ice the biscuits and decorate with currants, glacé cherries, silver cachous and glacé fruits.

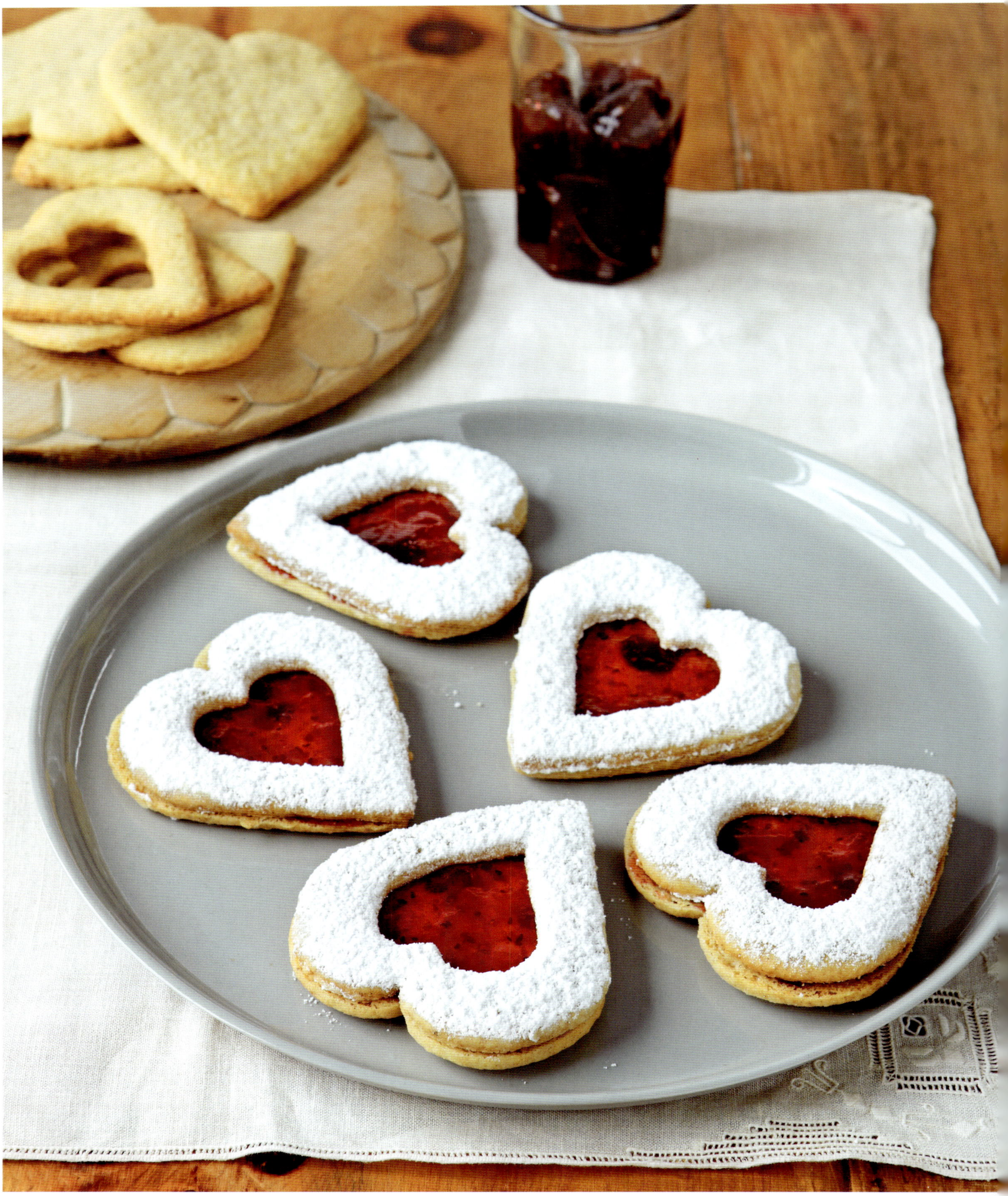

INGREDIENTS

200 g unsalted butter, softened
1 teaspoon vanilla essence
½ cup (110 g) caster sugar
2 cups (300 g) plain flour
1 teaspoon baking powder
¼ teaspoon ground cinnamon
¼ teaspoon ground cloves
1 egg, lightly beaten
1 cup raspberry jam (or ½ cup each raspberry jam and apricot jam)
½ cup (80 g) icing sugar (optional)

LINZER BISCUITS

Linz is a town in Austria famous for its Linzer torte and these pretty biscuits. I had a friend from Linz who gave me this recipe and talked about how important their jam was and how they liked to show it off. It's traditionally always raspberry jam. Also, these were originally made in circles but we've done them as heart shapes, for something different.

MAKES ABOUT 36 PAIRS

METHOD

Preheat the oven to 180°C.

Using an electric mixer, cream the butter and vanilla essnce until light and fluffy. Add the sugar and beat well.

Fold in the flour sifted with the baking powder and spices. Add the beaten egg and mix to combine.

Form the dough into a ball, flatten into a disk and chill, wrapped in plastic wrap, for about 1 hour.

Halve the dough and roll out one half at a time between sheets of baking paper. Chill until firm, then cut into heart shapes with a 5 cm heart-shaped cutter. Re-roll the scraps once and cut out more hearts.

Place on ungreased baking trays, allowing a little room for spreading. Using a smaller cutter, cut out a heart shape from the centres of half of the biscuits.

Bake for 8–10 minutes or until lightly golden. Remove from the oven and transfer to wire racks to cool. Store in an airtight container.

Just before serving, spread slightly warmed jam on the plain hearts. Dust the cut-out shapes with icing sugar, if liked, before placing them over the jam-coated bases.

INGREDIENTS

2⅔ cups (400 g) self-raising flour
a pinch of salt
1½ teaspoons ground cinnamon
1½ teaspoons ground cloves
1½ teaspoons ground nutmeg
1 teaspoon ground white pepper
½ cup (110 g) caster sugar
½ cup (110 g) firmly packed brown sugar
250 g butter, diced
⅓ cup milk
¼ teaspoon bicarbonate of soda
sifted icing sugar to dust

CHRISTMAS SPICE BISCUITS

If you want to hang these biscuits on the Christmas tree, make a hole at a top point of each biscuit before baking then thread a fine ribbon through the hole to tie it to a branch. The baked biscuit may also be decorated with icing to serve. Or, if you prefer, these biscuits can be slipped into small cellophane bags and sealed, to make pretty little gifts for visitors. Let the children help with the decorating; they will add a bit of fun with their often comical ideas.

MAKES 80–100 DEPENDING ON SIZE OF CUTTERS USED

METHOD

Preheat the oven to 180°C. Line two large baking trays with baking paper.

Sift the flour, salt, spices and sugars into a large bowl. Add the butter and rub into the flour mixture until it looks like breadcrumbs.

Combine the milk and bicarbonate of soda in a bowl and stir into the flour mixture. Knead lightly to form a firm but elastic dough. Halve the dough and wrap each piece in plastic wrap. Chill for 30 minutes.

Roll out one half of the dough (leaving the other half in the fridge) to a thickness of 4 mm and cut out biscuits with fancy biscuit cutters, such as hearts, angels, reindeer, stars and trees. Arrange on the trays, allowing room for spreading. Re-knead the dough scraps and chill before rolling out again. Repeat with the remaining dough.

Bake for 15–20 minutes or until golden. Transfer to wire racks to cool and store in airtight containers. Dust with icing sugar if you like before serving.

TIPS Baking trays should always be cold before arranging uncooked biscuits on top, othewise the biscuits will lose their shape.

These biscuits can be decorated with a soft icing (see Ginger Crisp Biscuits, opposite). This is a job children enjoy doing, as they get to use their own imagination.

INGREDIENTS
250 g golden syrup
250 g unsalted butter, at room temperature
¾ cup (165 g) caster sugar
3 cups (450 g) plain flour
3 teaspoons ground ginger
2 teaspoons baking powder
2 teaspoons bicarbonate of soda
1 egg, lightly beaten
silver cachous (optional) to decorate

ICING
½ cup (80 g) icing sugar
2 tablespoons hot water

GINGER CRISP BISCUITS

Spicy, crisp triangular biscuits are decorated in the shape of a Christmas tree – all very festive for the holiday season. Instead of cachous, embellish the biscuits with other small edible decorations, stocked by specialty kitchen stores.

MAKES ABOUT 25

METHOD

Heat the golden syrup, butter and sugar in a small saucepan over a low heat for 3–4 minutes, stirring, until the sugar has dissolved.

Sift the flour with the remaining dry ingredients in a large bowl. Add the butter mixture alternately with the beaten egg and mix until well combined. Divide the dough into a few batches, wrap each in plastic wrap and chill for 1 hour, until firm.

Preheat the oven to 190°C. Line two baking trays with baking paper.

Roll out the dough thinly on a lightly floured board. Using a biscuit cutter or a sharp knife, cut into triangles and place on the prepared baking trays. Re-knead the scraps and chill before rolling out again. Repeat with the remaining dough.

Bake in batches for 8–10 minutes or until very lightly golden. Transfer to wire racks to cool. Store in an airtight container until needed.

To make the icing, beat the icing sugar and hot water together in a bowl until smooth. Using an icing pipe with a fine point (or make baking paper triangles into cones for piping), ice the biscuits and decorate with the cachous to resemble baubles on Christmas trees.

TIP To be sure these biscuits are fully cooked, check underneath – the base should also be pale golden.

INGREDIENTS

3 cups (450 g) plain flour, plus extra for kneading
1 tablespoon baking powder
1 tablespoon ground cinnamon
1 teaspoon ground cloves
1 teaspoon ground nutmeg
½ teaspoon ground aniseed
½ teaspoon salt
½ teaspoon ground ginger or ground white pepper
250 g butter, softened
1½ cups (330 g) firmly packed brown sugar
3 tablespoons rum or brandy
1 egg white, beaten
125 g flaked blanched almonds to decorate

SPECULAAS

Many years ago, I gave a speculaas recipe in a magazine and a reader wrote in saying 'Oh, they're not speculaas!' and then gave me her recipe. Her family turned out to be bakers in Holland. I think this is one of the prize recipes in the book. They are special crisp biscuits, rich in butter and flavoured with brown sugar, spices and rum, made especially for Saint Nicholas' Eve in Holland.

MAKES ABOUT 70

METHOD

Preheat the oven to 190°C. Grease baking trays or line them with baking paper.

Sift the flour, baking powder, cinnamon, cloves, nutmeg, aniseed, salt and ginger or pepper together in a bowl.

Using an electric mixer, cream the butter in a large bowl, then add the brown sugar gradually, beating until the mixture is light and fluffy. Stir in the rum or brandy.

Gradually add the flour and spices to the creamed mixture, stirring until well combined, then form the dough into a ball. Knead the dough on a board sprinkled with about ¼ cup sifted flour.

Roll the dough out between sheets of baking paper into a rectangle about 5 mm thick. With a sharp knife or cutter, cut the dough into 6 cm x 3 cm rectangles. Re-roll scraps and cut more rectangles. Place on the prepared trays, brush with the egg white and decorate with slivered almonds.

Bake for 12 minutes or until they are browned and firm. Transfer to wire racks to cool.

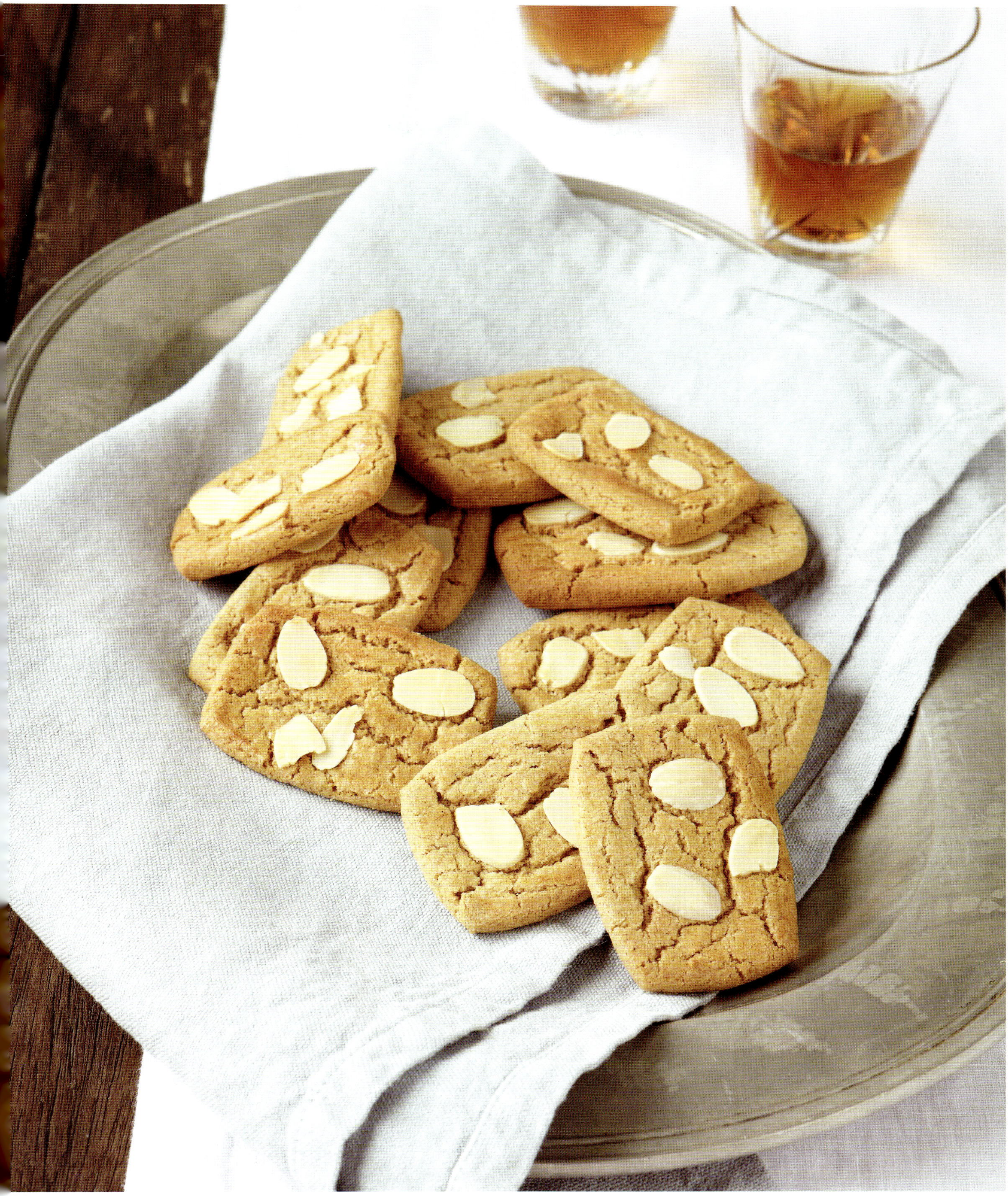

INGREDIENTS
1 cup (150 g) plain flour
1 teaspoon ground cinnamon
¼ teaspoon ground ginger
¼ teaspoon mixed spice
75 g unsalted butter, diced
¼ cup honey

HONEY SPICE COOKIES

Spice and honey always go well together. Cut these cookies into various shapes such as hearts, gingerbread people or stars to dunk into a sweet wine or coffee.

MAKES ABOUT 30

METHOD

Preheat the oven to 180°C. Line two baking trays with baking paper.

Sift the flour and spices into a bowl. Using your fingertips, rub in the butter until the mixture resembles breadcrumbs. Add the honey and mix gently to form a soft dough. Wrap with plastic wrap and chill for 30 minutes.

Roll out the dough between two sheets of baking paper to a thickness of 4–6 mm. Cut out shapes using various cutters of your choice. Arrange the biscuits, slightly apart, on the prepared baking trays. Chill for 10 minutes.

Bake for 10 minutes or until golden. Leave on the trays for 5 minutes before transferring to wire racks to cool completely.

BISCUITS *rolled biscuits*

INGREDIENTS
185 g butter, softened
1½ cups finely grated cheddar cheese
¼ cup grated parmesan cheese
1½ cups (225 g) plain flour, sifted
1 teaspoon paprika
1 teaspoon salt
2 tablespoons finely chopped walnuts

CHEESE & WALNUT SHORTBREADS

Little savoury shortbreads make a welcome nibble with pre-dinner drinks, and are handy to have on hand when people drop in. These would also make a lovely gift, sealed in a cellophane bag tied with a pretty ribbon.

MAKES ABOUT 60

METHOD
Using an electric mixer, cream the butter and grated cheeses. Add the flour, paprika, salt and walnuts. Mix well until the dough comes together to form a ball.

Divide the dough in half, pat each half into a thick round and wrap in plastic wrap. Chill for 1 hour.

Preheat the oven to 180°C. Line two or three baking trays with baking paper.

Roll the dough out thinly and cut into stars using a 5 cm star-shaped or fluted biscuit cutter. Re-roll the trimmings to make more shapes. Arrange on the prepared trays.

Bake in batches for 12–15 minutes or until golden. Transfer to wire racks to cool.

TIP You can also make these shortbreads in the food processor. To do so, first have the butter well chilled and cut into small pieces. Fit the processor with a metal double-bladed knife. Sift the flour, paprika and salt into the bowl. Add the butter to the flour mixture with the cheeses. Process for about 20 seconds or until the pastry clings together and forms a ball. Lightly knead the mixture together to form a smooth dough. Chill until ready to use.

INGREDIENTS
CHEESE PASTRY
2 cups (300 g) plain flour
salt
125 g butter, diced
2 tablespoons grated parmesan cheese
2 eggs
1 teaspoon water

beaten egg to glaze
slivered blanched almonds
sea salt crystals

ALMOND CHEESE ROUNDS

These savoury biscuits keep well if stored correctly, so they may be made days before required. This easily prepared pastry is successful every time, and can also be used to make pastry cases.

MAKES ABOUT 70

METHOD

For the pastry, sift the flour and a pinch of salt into a bowl and rub in the butter until the mixture resembles fine breadcrumbs. Stir in the parmesan.

Beat the eggs and ½ teaspoon salt. Take out 1 tablespoon of the beaten egg, mix with the water and set aside for glazing.

Make a well in centre of the flour mixture and pour in the remaining egg. Lightly mix to a smooth dough. Knead lightly, wrap in plastic wrap and chill for at least 2 hours.

Preheat the oven to 190°C. On a lightly floured board, roll out the dough to about 3 mm thick. Using a fluted round cutter, cut out 4-cm diameter circles, arranging them on an ungreased baking tray. Re-roll the scraps and cut more biscuits. Brush with the egg glaze, then sprinkle with the almonds and a pinch of salt crystals.

Bake for 15 minutes or until golden. Transfer to wire racks to cool.

INGREDIENTS

1⅓ cups (200 g) plain flour
½ teaspoon baking powder
½ teaspoon salt
125 g butter, diced
1½ cups (185 g) medium oatmeal (see Note)
1 egg, lightly beaten
2 tablespoons water

OATCAKES

These are a great Scottish favourite enjoyed throughout the day, either plain or with butter, cheese, honey or jam. They can also be cooked on a griddle or frying pan on the stovetop. Remove when the edges begin to curl and set under a hot grill to cook until crisp.

MAKES ABOUT 50

METHOD

Preheat the oven to 180°C. Grease baking trays or line them with baking paper.

Sift the flour, baking powder and salt into a bowl. Rub in the butter until the mixture resembles breadcrumbs. Stir in the oatmeal, beaten egg and water. Mix and lightly knead to a stiff dough.

Onto a floured surface, roll out the dough to about 3 mm thick. Cut out rounds 4–5 cm in diameter and arrange on the prepared baking trays.

Bake for 15–18 minutes, but remove before any colouring occurs. Transfer to wire racks to cool. Serve with cheese.

NOTE Medium oatmeal is available from good health food stores. A convenient substitute is to grind 2½ cups rolled oats in a food processor for 30–60 seconds.

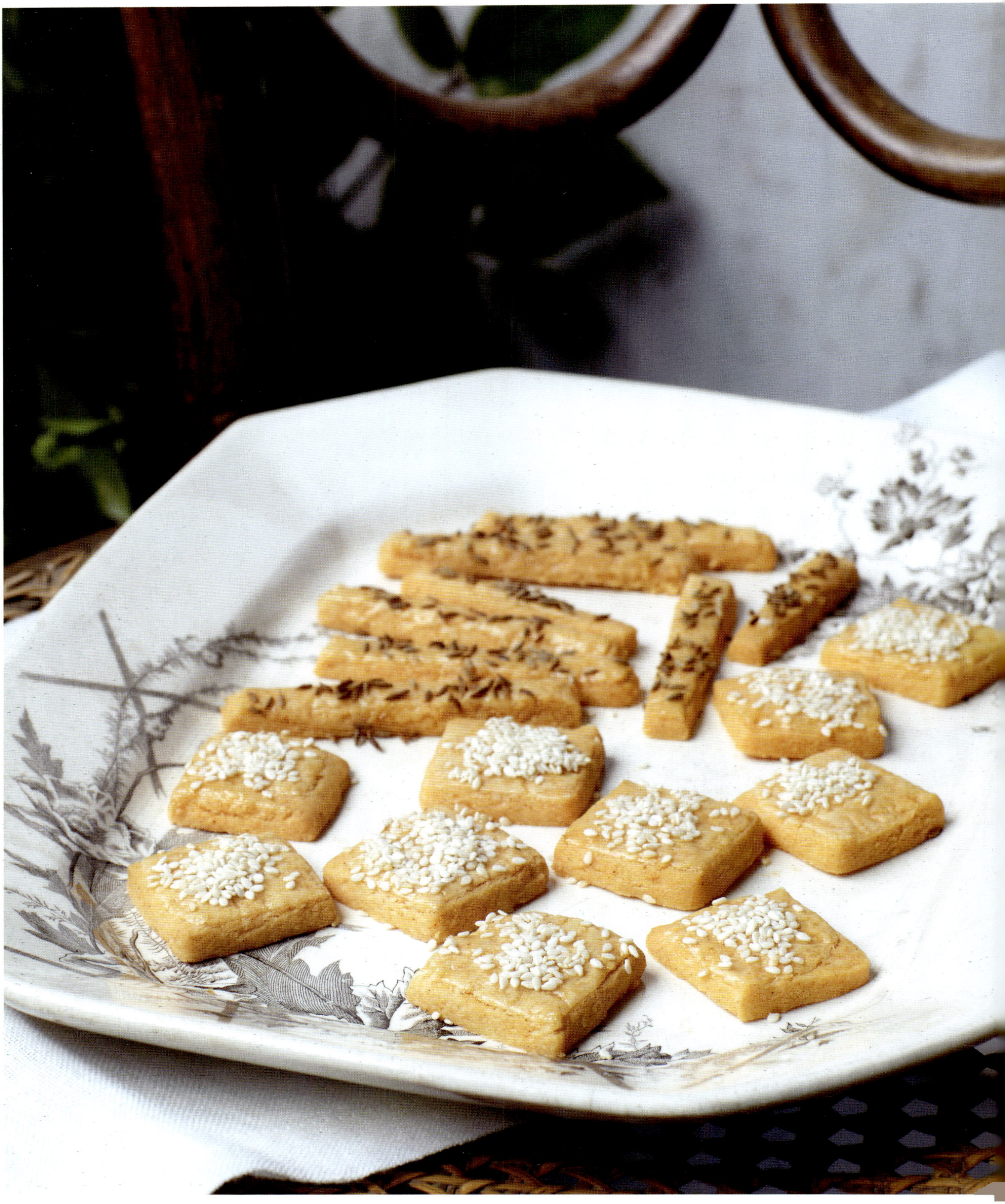

BISCUITS *rolled biscuits*

INGREDIENTS
90 g butter, softened
¾ cup finely grated cheddar cheese
1 tablespoon grated parmesan cheese
¾ cup (110 g) plain flour
½ teaspoon paprika
a pinch of cayenne pepper
½ teaspoon salt
beaten egg for glazing
1 tablespoon sesame or cumin seeds (optional)

CHEESE BISCUITS

MAKES ABOUT 40 FINGERS OR 30 SQUARES

METHOD

Preheat the oven to 180°C. Grease baking trays or line them with baking paper.

Using an electric mixer, cream the butter and cheeses. Sift the flour, paprika, cayenne and salt into the creamed mixture. Mix well to form a dough, wrap in plastic wrap and chill for at least 1 hour.

Roll out on a lightly floured board or between sheets of baking paper until 6 mm thick. Cut into 5 cm squares with a biscuit cutter or into 8 cm x 1 cm fingers.

Put on the prepared baking trays, brush with egg glaze and sprinkle with sesame or cumin seeds if liked. Bake for 8–10 minutes or until lightly browned. Transfer to wire racks to cool.

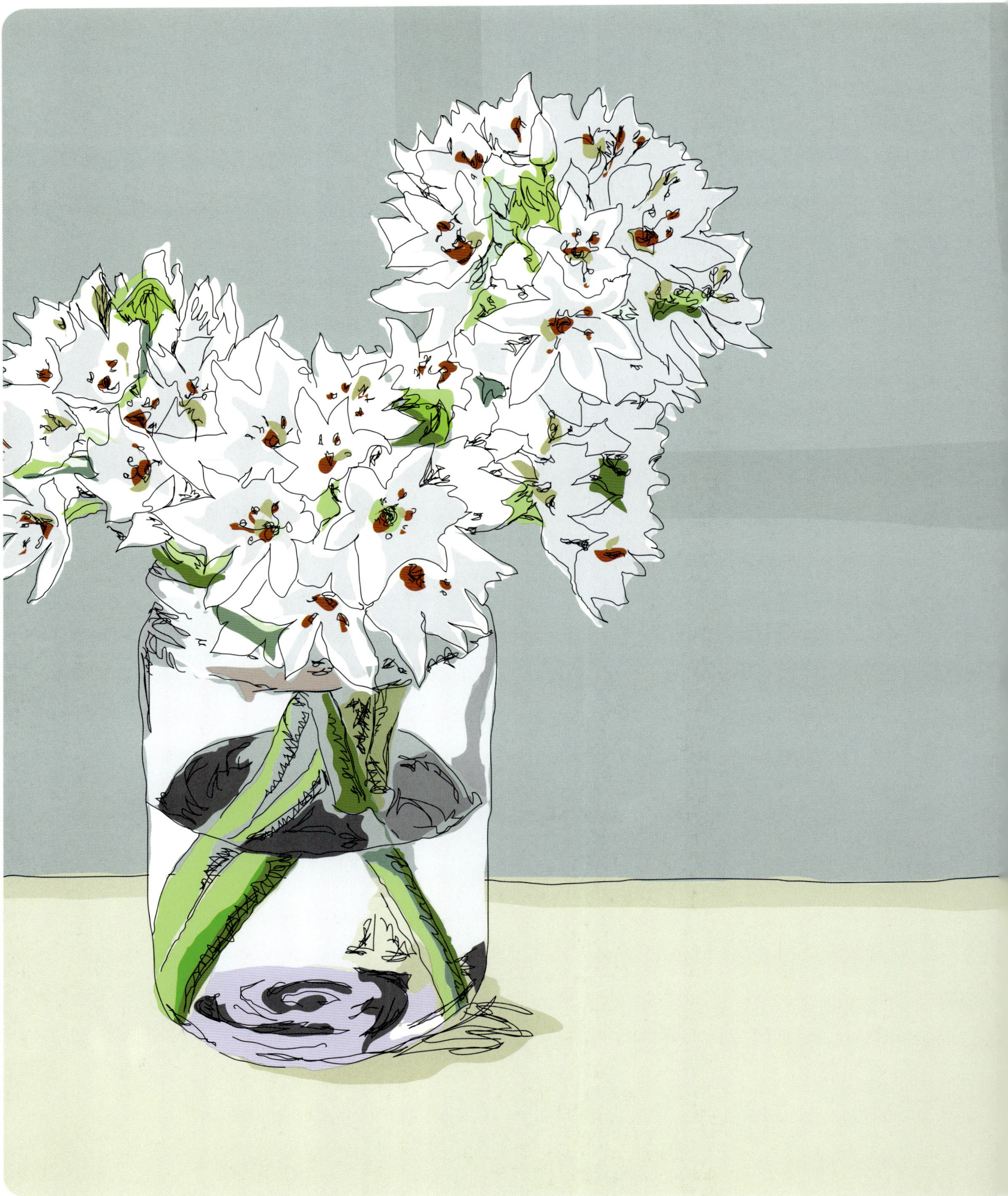

BROWNIES & SLICES
CHAPTER 2

HINTS & TIPS

Brownies are American – an impossibly moreish cross between a cake and a biscuit. They are either fudgy or cakey, depending on their ingredients. The fudgy type is very moist and dense. The cake brownie is light and airy.

Slices (also known as bars or bar cookies) are made as a slab and then cut into squares or fingers. They are quick and easy to make, so are good for nervous or novice bakers. Both brownies and slices keep well in an airtight container, and carry well in lunchboxes.

BROWNIES

The classic brownie has just a few ingredients – butter, sugar, chocolate, eggs and flour. Melting the butter rather than creaming it with sugar gives a denser, fudgy brownie. Dark chocolate is the standard, and either white or brown sugar may be used, or a mixture of both. The darker the sugar, the deeper the molasses flavour. It's a matter of personal taste, so use what you prefer.

Cake-like brownies contain less butter and more flour than fudgy brownies, as well a raising agent to make them softer and lighter. Often the butter is creamed with the sugar rather than melted with the chocolate.

Chewy brownies can get their texture from the addition of extra sugar or an extra egg (or even two) and a combination of different types of chocolate. Sometimes cocoa powder is added to intensify the flavour and thicken the texture, and give a rich, chocolatey, chewy result.

Blondies have a cake-like texture and are a kind of butterscotch bar, made with brown sugar, butter, nuts, eggs, and sometimes white chocolate.

MAKING BROWNIES

ALWAYS USE THE TIN SIZE SPECIFIED in the recipe. Baking in an oversized tin will make thin, dry brownies, while baking in an undersized tin may result in the centre brownies not being quite cooked. If the tin is too large, divide it with a piece of foil folded to the required size, turning up the edge, and fill the empty space with dried beans to keep the folded piece firm.

USE LIGHT-COLOURED, SHINY TINS, which conduct heat evenly. Glass or dark-coloured ones can cause the edges to overbake.

ALWAYS GREASE THE TIN THOROUGHLY or line it with baking paper that has been cut larger than the size of the tin so that the edges hang over two opposite sides, allowing the brownie to be easily lifted out once cooked.

MOST BROWNIE RECIPES START with melting butter and chocolate together. This can be done in a double boiler or a small bowl placed over a saucepan of hot water. Or, if you're using a heavy pan, you can place the butter and chocolate directly over a low heat. Be sure to stir constantly. Butter and chocolate can also be melted together in a microwave oven on medium, stopping the power and stirring the mixture every 20 seconds.

AVOID OVERMIXING THE INGREDIENTS as this can cause brownies to become tough. Mix wet and dry ingredients just long enough to combine them.

FOR FUDGE-STYLE BROWNIES, remove the tin from the oven when the sides have shrunk slightly away from the edges of the tin. The centre will still be slightly soft, but will firm during cooling.

BROWNIES & SLICES *hints & tips*

CAKE-STYLE BROWNIES ARE COOKED when a toothpick inserted into the centre comes out a few moist crumbs attached to it.

BROWNIES WILL BE EASIER TO CUT if they are completely cooled. Have a jug of hot water at hand, dip a sharp knife into it, wipe the knife, then cut across the tin in an up-and-down sawing motion. Re-dip and wipe the knife between cuts.

REDUCING THE FAT CONTENT
Brownies aren't a low-fat treat. Apart from the sometimes large amounts of butter, there's the cocoa butter in the chocolate itself, as well as the fat in the eggs. If you want less fat in your brownie, look for recipes that use cocoa powder instead of chocolate, or that have some chocolate but also use cocoa to top up the chocolate flavour and help reduce kilojoules and fat. 'Dutch-process' cocoa has the smoothest, mildest and richest flavour.

STORING BROWNIES
TO STORE THE BROWNIES, either cover the tin completely with foil or remove the cut pieces from the tin and place in an airtight container. They will keep this way in the refrigerator for about 5 days.

IF YOU WANT TO FREEZE BROWNIES after they've been cut, wrap the pieces individually in plastic wrap, then in foil, and place together in an airtight freezer bag. Or, you can wrap the whole brownie 'block' tightly in plastic wrap, then in foil. Place in a large airtight freezer bag and freeze for up to 4 months. Thaw at room temperature.

SLICES
Slices consist of a pastry or biscuit-like base then a filling and/or topping. If the slice has more than one layer, allow each to cool completely (unless the recipe specifies otherwise) before adding the next layer.

MAKING SLICES
USE LIGHT-COLOURED, SHINY TINS, which conduct heat evenly. Glass or dark-coloured ones can cause the edges to overbake.

ALWAYS GREASE THE TIN THOROUGHLY or line it with baking paper that has been cut larger than the size of the tin so that the edges hang over two opposite sides, allowing the slice to be easily lifted out once cooked.

PRESS THE BASE MIXTURE INTO THE TIN with your hands, smoothing it so that it is flat and level. Alternatively, a pastry base can be rolled out between two pieces of baking paper then transferred to the tin. Any cracks that form can be pushed together with the fingers.

FOR BEST RESULTS, COOK THE SLICE on the middle rack in the centre of the oven. If cooking two slices at the same time, swap their positions on the racks about halfway through the cooking time. If the top begins to overbrown during baking, cover it loosely with a piece of foil.

IF ICING THE SLICE, allow it to cool completely first.

WHEN CUTTING SLICES, first leave the slab to cool. For clean edges, wipe the blade of the knife with a damp cloth between cuts. To cut chocolate-topped slices, dip the blade of the knife in hot water then wipe it; repeat between slices. If cutting a slice while it is still in the tin, remove a corner piece first using a small palette knife, then it will be easier to remove the other pieces cleanly.

STORING SLICES
FOR IMMEDIATE USE, store slices in the tin in which they were baked, cutting the cooked mixture into bars or squares and covering with foil. Most slices can be stored in their tin or in an airtight container, or in the fridge in warmer weather, for up to a week.

FOR LONGER STORAGE, put cut slices in a sealable plastic bag (separating the layers with baking paper) and freeze until required. Thaw at room temperature. If you wrap and freeze slice portions individually, they can be placed frozen in a lunchbox, and will have thawed by lunchtime.

INGREDIENTS

185 g dark chocolate, broken up
125 g butter
2 eggs, lightly beaten
1 cup (220 g) caster sugar
1 teaspoon vanilla essence
1 cup (150 g) plain flour
2/3 cup coarsely chopped walnuts

EASY CHOCOLATE BROWNIES

Nearly everyone loves this classic American treat. Brownies may vary greatly in richness. If you want them chewy and moist, use a 20 cm tin; if you want them cakey, use a smaller tin.

MAKES 9

METHOD

Preheat the oven to 180°C. Grease a deep 20 cm square cake tin and line the base with baking paper.

Place the chocolate and butter in a large heatproof bowl. Place over a saucepan of simmering water on low heat and stir until the chocolate has melted and the mixture is smooth. Remove from the heat. Stir in the eggs, sugar and vanilla essence. Fold through the flour and walnuts.

Spoon into the prepared tin and spread out evenly. Bake for 20–25 minutes until the sides have shrunk slightly from the tin. Cool in the tin before cutting into squares.

MELTING CHOCOLATE

Break up or grate chocolate first so it melts more evenly and quickly. Melt chocolate on a plate or in a bowl (preferably metal, which conducts heat better) over a pan of hot (barely simmering – never boiling) water. Keep it away from all moisture as even a droplet of water may cause it to 'seize' (stiffen and become grainy). Once this has happened you will need to start again with fresh chocolate.

Chocolate can also be successfully melted in the microwave, on low heat in bursts of 1 minute or so. It will keep its shape even when melted, so stir until smooth. If melting butter and chocolate together, do so in the microwave on low heat, or melt the butter first in a small saucepan on the stovetop, then add the chocolate and stir until melted.

INGREDIENTS

250 g butter, softened
2 cups (440 g) caster sugar
3 eggs
1 teaspoon vanilla essence
125 g dark chocolate, broken into pieces
1 cup (150 g) plain flour, sifted
½ teaspoon salt
1 cup chopped walnuts, almonds or pecans

FUDGE BROWNIES

MAKES ABOUT 48

METHOD

Preheat the oven to 180°C. Grease a shallow cake tin about 32 cm x 23 cm and line with baking paper.

Using an electric mixer, cream half the butter with the sugar until light and fluffy. Add the eggs, one at a time, and beat until light. Stir in the vanilla.

Put the remaining butter and the chocolate in a heatproof bowl over a saucepan of hot water on low heat and stir until melted. Cool, then combine well with the creamed butter and sugar mixture. Stir in the flour, salt and nuts.

Pour into the prepared tin and bake for 45 minutes or until a skewer inserted in the centre comes out almost clean.

Allow the brownie mixture to cool in the tin. Cut into small squares to serve.

NOTE Do not overcook or the brownies will not be fudgy – remember that they will set more as they cool. It is always preferable to undercook them.

INGREDIENTS

250 g butter, softened
1 teaspoon vanilla essence
¼ teaspoon almond essence
2 cups (440 g) caster sugar
4 eggs
2 cups (300 g) plain flour, sifted with ½ teaspoon salt
2 cups chopped almonds, pecans, walnuts or Brazil nuts
60 g dark chocolate, broken into pieces

CHOCOLATE ICING (OPTIONAL)

1½ cups (240 g) icing sugar, sifted
1 tablespoon cocoa powder
½ teaspoon vanilla essence
½ teaspoon ground cinnamon
1 teaspoon butter, softened
about 1 tablespoon hot water

TWO-TONE BROWNIES

This recipe is more of a cake-type brownie rather than a fudge-type brownie. It's lighter and fluffier and not as rich or chewy as other brownies.

MAKES 24

METHOD

Preheat the oven to 180°C. Grease a 30 cm x 20 cm cake tin and line it with baking paper.

Using an electric mixer, cream the butter with the essences and sugar until light and fluffy. Add the eggs one at a time, beating well after each addition.

Stir in the flour and half of the nuts, mixing well. Divide the mixture in half. Melt the chocolate in a heatproof bowl placed over hot water. Stir the melted chocolate into one half of the batter.

Drop alternate heaped tablespoons of dark and white batter into the prepared cake tin. Lightly cut through the batter several times, back and forth, to give a marbled effect. Top with the remaining nuts at this stage if you don't intend to ice the brownie.

Bake for 45 minutes or until a skewer inserted in the centre comes out clean. Turn out onto a wire rack to cool. If not icing, cut into bars or squares to serve.

To make the icing, if desired, combine the icing sugar, cocoa, vanilla, cinnamon and butter. Stir in the hot water little by little to give a good spreading consistency. Ice the brownie when cold, if desired, and sprinkle with the reserved nuts.

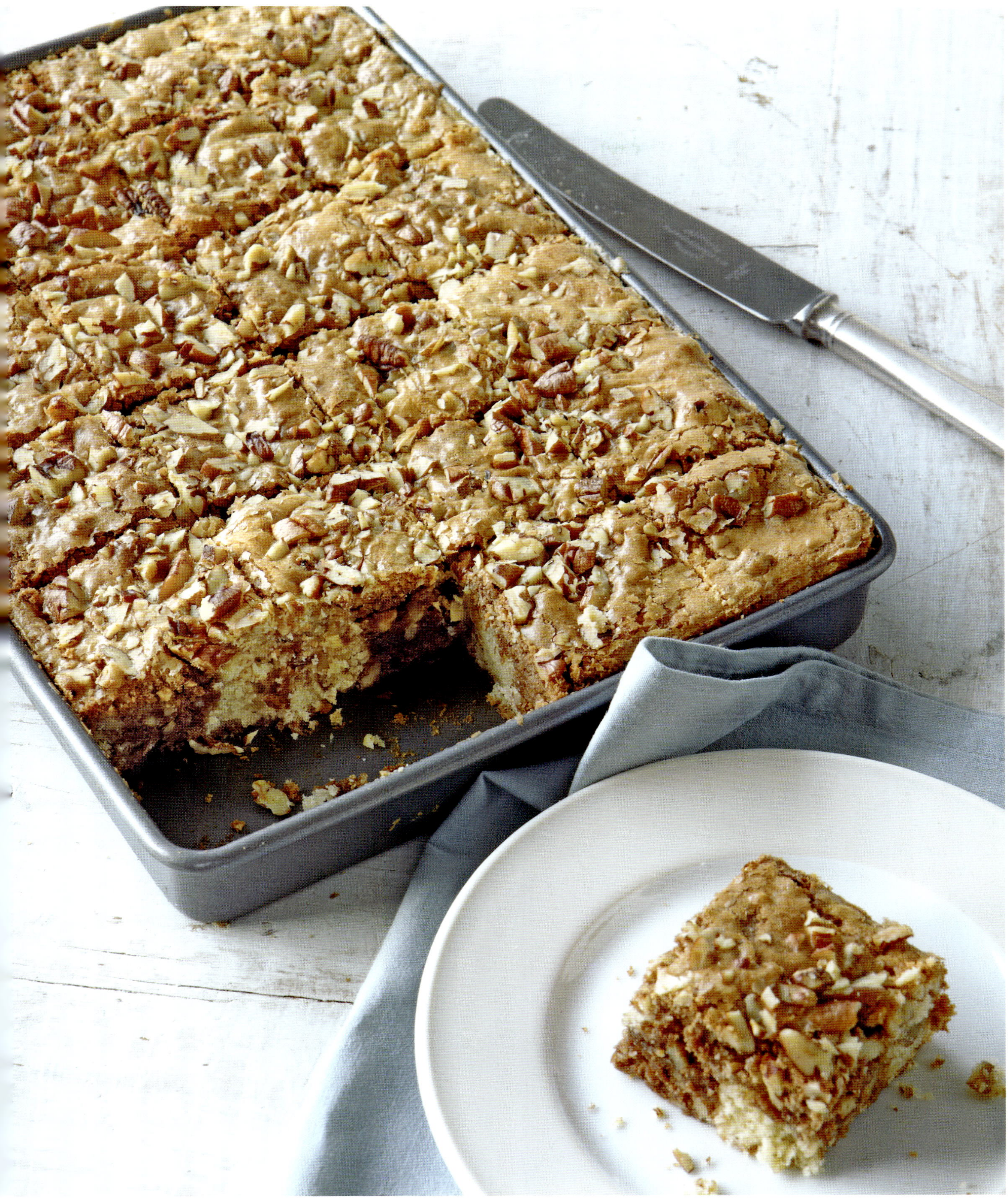

INGREDIENTS

60 g butter, softened
125 g cream cheese, at room temperature
¼ cup (55 g) caster sugar
1 egg
1 tablespoon plain flour
½ teaspoon vanilla essence

CHOCOLATE MIXTURE

125 g dark cooking chocolate, roughly chopped
90 g butter
2 eggs
¾ cup (165 g) caster sugar
½ cup (75 g) plain flour
¼ teaspoon each baking powder and salt
½ cup coarsely chopped pecans or walnuts

MARBLED CHEESECAKE BROWNIES

These brownies have a marvellous fudgy texture – cheesecake with a crisp top, marbled with chocolate and studded with pecans. The mixture is baked in a slab, then cooled and cut into individual squares. Brownies are great for picnics, a casual after-dinner dessert with ice cream, or just served with a glass of ice-cold milk at home.

MAKES 25

METHOD

Preheat the oven to 180°C. Grease a shallow 25 cm cake tin.

Using an electric mixer, cream the butter with the cream cheese. Gradually beat in the sugar until the mixture is light and fluffy. Add the egg and beat in thoroughly. Stir in the flour and vanilla and set aside.

For the chocolate mixture, melt the chocolate and butter in a bowl over hot water, stirring constantly. Allow to cool.

Beat the eggs until well mixed, then gradually beat in the sugar until thick and pale. Sift in the flour, baking powder and salt then fold in with the cooled chocolate mixture and nuts.

Measure 1 cup of chocolate batter and set aside. Spread the remaining chocolate batter in the prepared tin. Top with the reserved cheese mixture, then drop spoonfuls of the reserved chocolate batter on top. Swirl a knife through the batter to make a marbled pattern.

Bake for 30–45 minutes. Remove from the oven and leave to cool in the tin before cutting into 5 cm squares.

INGREDIENTS

185 g dark cooking chocolate, roughly chopped
250 g butter, cubed
3 eggs
1 cup (220 g) caster sugar
2 tablespoons cocoa powder
1 cup (150 g) plain flour
¼ teaspoon salt
1 cup dried cranberries (see Note)

CREAM CHEESE TOPPING

250 g cream cheese, at room temperature
½ cup (110 g) caster sugar
1 egg
2 tablespoons plain flour
1 teaspoon vanilla essence

CRANBERRY CHOCOLATE BROWNIES WITH CREAM CHEESE TOPPING

A rich, soft brownie studded with dried cranberries with a delicious cheesecake topping – a great recipe for a crowd. Take the cream cheese out of the fridge a few hours beforehand so that it is nice and soft for easy beating.

MAKES ABOUT 32 SQUARES

METHOD

Preheat the oven to 180°C and line a 30 cm x 20 cm lamington or slice tin with baking paper.

Melt the chocolate and butter in a small heavy saucepan or a bowl over hot water, stirring constantly. Allow to cool.

Using a hand whisk, beat the eggs until thick and creamy, then gradually beat in the sugar and cocoa.

Sift in the flour and salt then stir through the cooled chocolate mixture and cranberries. Spread the mixture evenly into the prepared cake tin.

To make the topping, using an electric mixer, beat the cream cheese. Gradually beat in the sugar until the mixture is light and fluffy. Add the egg and beat in thoroughly. Stir in the flour and vanilla.

Dollop this mixture over the chocolate mixture then spread evenly with a small metal spatula.

Bake for 40–45 minutes or until a skewer inserted into the centre comes out almost clean. Remove from the oven and leave to cool in the pan before cutting into 4–6 cm squares.

NOTE Dried cranberries are often sold as craisins.

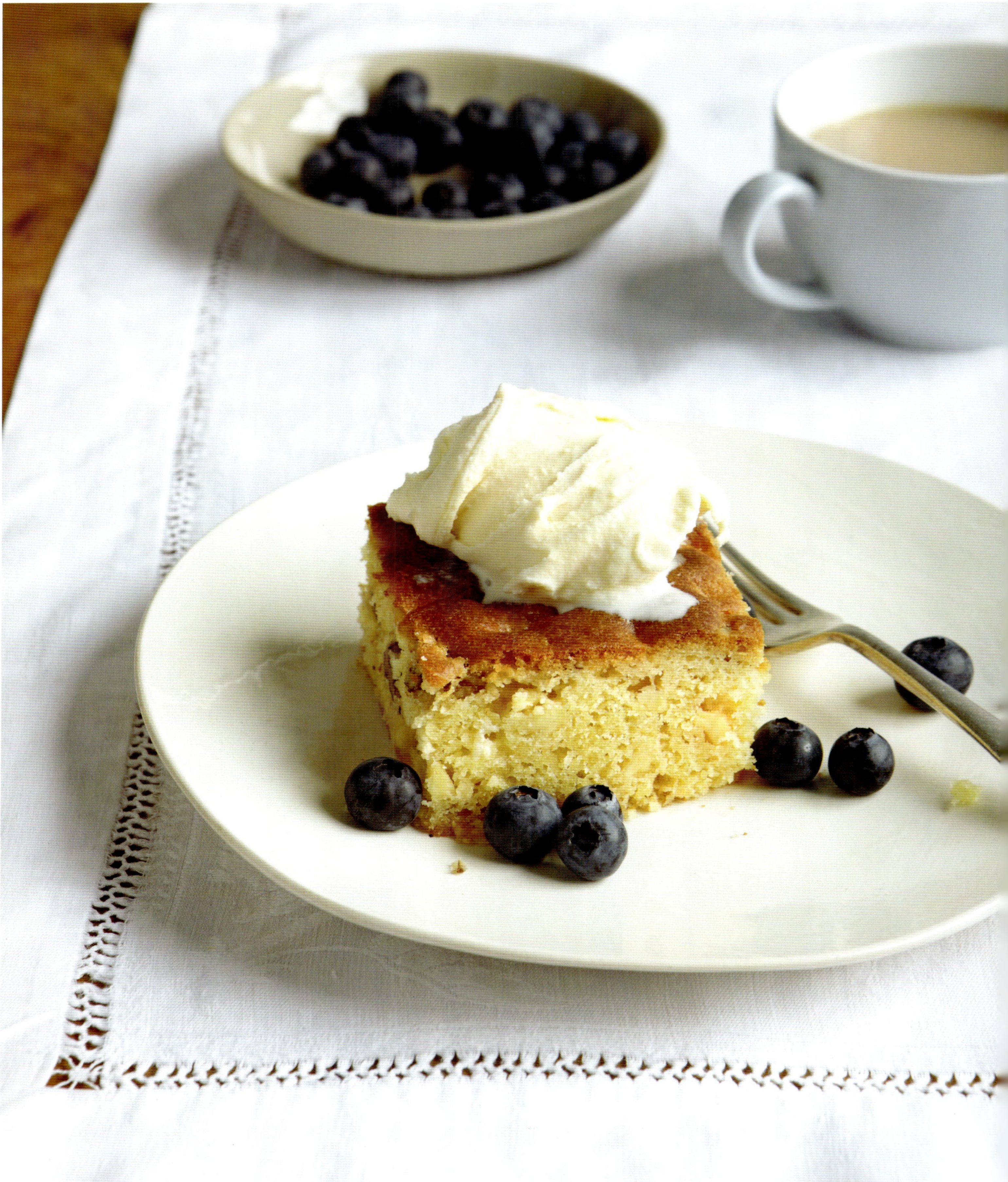

BROWNIES & SLICES *brownies*

INGREDIENTS
185 g white chocolate, chopped
125 g butter
2 eggs, lightly beaten
1 cup (220 g) caster sugar
1 teaspoon vanilla essence
1 cup (150 g) plain flour
²/₃ cup coarsely chopped walnuts or macadamias
½ cup white chocolate bits

EASY BLONDIES

These delicious brownies call for white chocolate and make a lovely dessert when served with ice cream and a small berry fruit such as blueberries or raspberries.

MAKES 9 SQUARES

METHOD
Preheat oven to 180°C. Grease a deep 20 cm square cake tin and line the base with baking paper.

Place the white chocolate and butter in a large heatproof bowl. Place the bowl over a saucepan of simmering water and stir until the chocolate has melted and the mixture is smooth. Remove from the heat. Stir in the eggs, sugar and vanilla. Fold through the flour, nuts and white chocolate bits. Pour into the prepared tin.

Bake for 20–25 minutes until the sides have shrunk slightly from the tin. Cool in the tin before cutting into squares.

APRICOT FINGERS

INGREDIENTS
200 g dried apricots
3 eggs, separated
1 cup (220 g) caster sugar
1 cup (150 g) plain flour, sifted
½ teaspoon baking powder
a pinch of salt
1 cup chopped walnuts
½ teaspoon vanilla essence
extra caster sugar to sprinkle

MAKES ABOUT 24

METHOD

Preheat the oven to 180°C. Grease and line a 29 cm x 19 cm cake tin.

Cook the apricots in water to cover, then drain and chop.

Using an electric mixer, beat the egg whites until stiff, gradually add the sugar and beat well until smooth. Add the egg yolks and beat, then fold in the sifted flour, baking powder and salt. Add the apricots, walnuts and vanilla.

Turn the mixture into the prepared tin and bake for 30 minutes. Sprinkle with a little caster sugar and cut into fingers while still warm.

BROWNIES & SLICES *slices*

INGREDIENTS
125 g butter, softened
2/3 cup (150 g) caster sugar
1 teaspoon vanilla essence
1 egg
1 cup (150 g) self-raising flour, sifted
1 cup sultanas

ICING
1 cup (160 g) icing sugar, sifted
1 teaspoon butter
1 tablespoon strong black coffee
1 tablespoon hot water
2 tablespoons flaked almonds, toasted

COFFEE & ALMOND SLICE

SERVES 12

METHOD

Preheat the oven to 180°C. Grease and line a 20 cm x 30 cm lamington tin.

Using an electric mixer, beat the butter, sugar and vanilla together until pale and creamy. Add the egg and beat well. Fold in the flour and sultanas.

Spread the mixture into the prepared tin. Bake for 25 minutes until golden. Transfer to wire racks to cool.

To make the icing, combine the icing sugar and butter in a small bowl. Add the combined coffee and water, a little at a time, stirring until the mixture is smooth. Spread over the slice and sprinkle with the almonds.

NOTE Make sure the hot water in the icing is very hot, as this sets the icing and ensures it won't be too runny.

INGREDIENTS

BASE
1½ cups (225 g) plain flour
120 g chilled butter, diced
2 tablespoons caster sugar
a pinch each of salt and baking powder
1 egg yolk
1 teaspoon vanilla essence
1–2 tablespoons water
a squeeze of lemon juice

FILLING
½ cup raspberry jam

TOPPING
60 g butter, softened
¼ cup (55 g) caster sugar
1 egg
¼ cup (35 g) self-raising flour, sifted
1½ cups desiccated coconut

COCONUT RASPBERRY SLICE

MAKES ABOUT 20

METHOD

Preheat the oven to 190°C. Line a 28 cm x 18 cm Swiss roll tin with baking paper.

For the base, place the plain flour, chilled butter, sugar, salt and baking powder in a food processor and process, turning the processor rapidly on and off, until the mixture resembles coarse breadcrumbs.

Mix the egg, vanilla, water and lemon juice together and, with the motor running, pour quickly through the feed tube. Process until a ball of dough forms round the blade.

Roll the dough out into a rough rectangle on a floured work surface then transfer to the prepared tin and spread it evenly over the base. If necessary, smooth out with the back of a spoon or hand, having first covered the dough with a sheet of plastic wrap. Spread evenly with jam.

For the topping, using an electric mixer, cream the butter and sugar until light and fluffy. Add the egg and beat well. Fold in the self-raising flour and the coconut. Spread evenly over the jam.

Bake for 10 minutes, reduce heat to 180°C and bake for a further 10–15 minutes or until golden.

Remove from the tin and leave for 10 minutes before cutting into squares and transferring to a wire rack to cool.

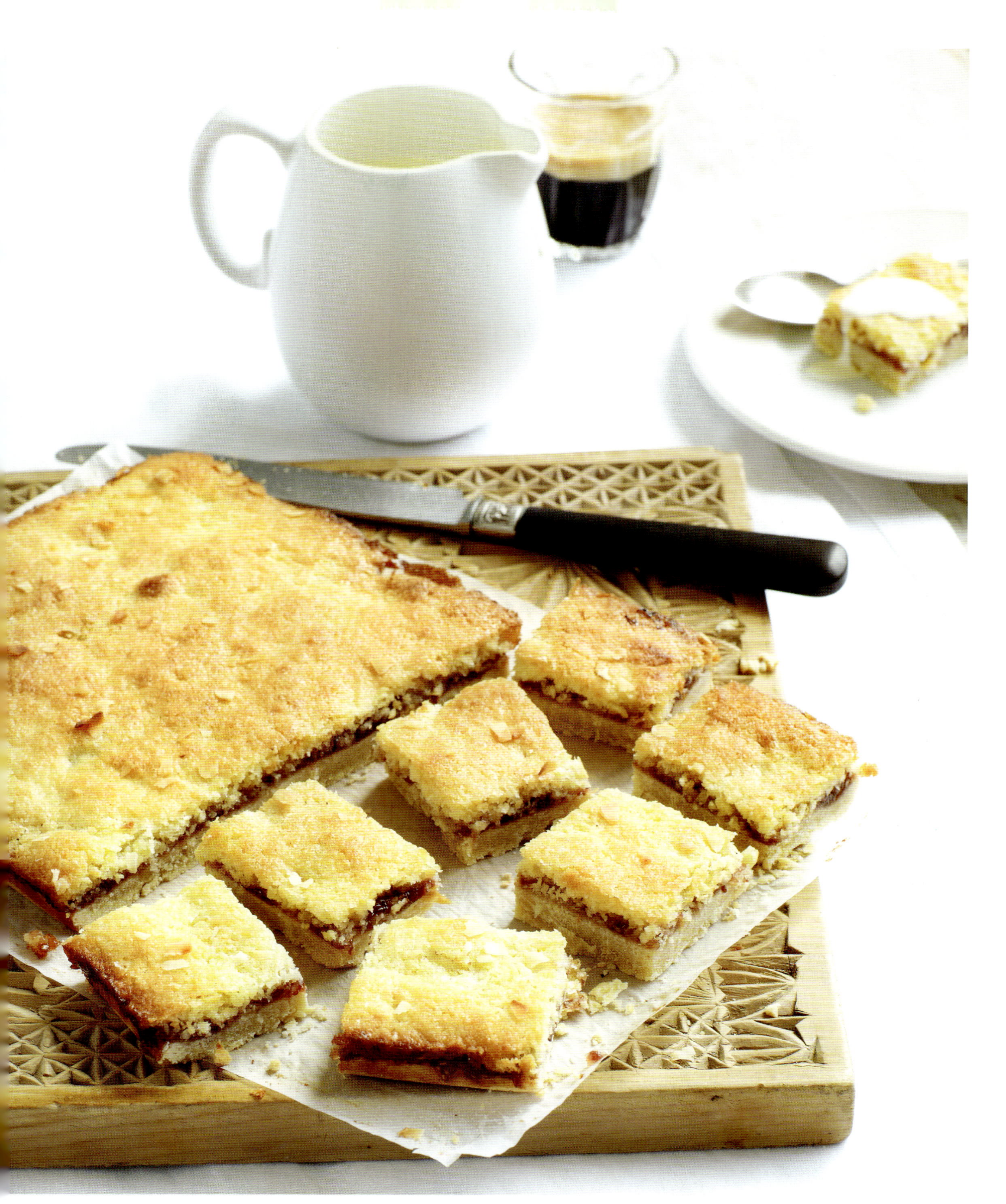

INGREDIENTS

FILLING
1 cup chopped, pitted dates
1 tablespoon lemon juice
2 tablespoons rum or water
2 teaspoons grated lemon rind
¼ cup (55 g) firmly packed brown sugar
1 teaspoon ground cinnamon or allspice

TOPPING
1 cup (150 g) plain flour
1¾ cups rolled oats (plain or quick-cooking)
250 g butter, diced

DATE FINGERS

MAKES 12–14

METHOD

Preheat the oven to 180°C. Grease a 18 cm square cake tin.

To make the filling, place the dates in a saucepan with the remaining filling ingredients and simmer for 20 minutes, stirring often, or until dates are soft. Cool.

Sift the flour into a bowl. Add the oats and rub in the butter until well blended. Divide the mixture in half and press one portion into the prepared tin.

Spoon the date mixture evenly on top, then sprinkle with the remaining rolled oat mixture and press it it into place to cover the filling.

Bake for 25 minutes. Cut into bars while hot and allow to cool in the tin.

NOTE If you want to change the fruit, use chopped dried figs or prunes.

INGREDIENTS
125 g butter
2/3 cup brown sugar
1/2 teaspoon vanilla essence
1 egg, lightly beaten
1 3/4 cups self-raising flour
1 cup sultanas
1/3 cup flaked almonds

SULTANA SLICE

This is a one-bowl or one-pan mix, depending how you want to make it. I melt the butter in a medium bowl in the microwave then mix in the sugar, vanilla, egg, flour and sultanas, or melt the butter in a large-enough saucepan before adding the remaining ingredients.

MAKES 24

METHOD

Preheat the oven to 180ºC. Line a 20 cm x 30 cm lamington tin with baking paper.

Melt the butter, allow to cool, then stir in the sugar, vanilla and egg. Sift in the flour and stir into the butter mixture with the sultanas. When well mixed, spread evenly into the prepared cake tin.

Sprinkle the almonds over evenly and press down lightly with the palm of your hand so they stick against the dough.

Bake for 35 minutes or until lightly browned. Cool in the tin, then cut into bars.

VARIATIONS

GINGER SLICE Sift the flour with 1 tablespoon ground ginger and add 1/2–1 cup chopped glacé ginger in place of the sultanas.

DATE SLICE In place of the sultanas, add 250 g pitted dates which you've chopped using scissors.

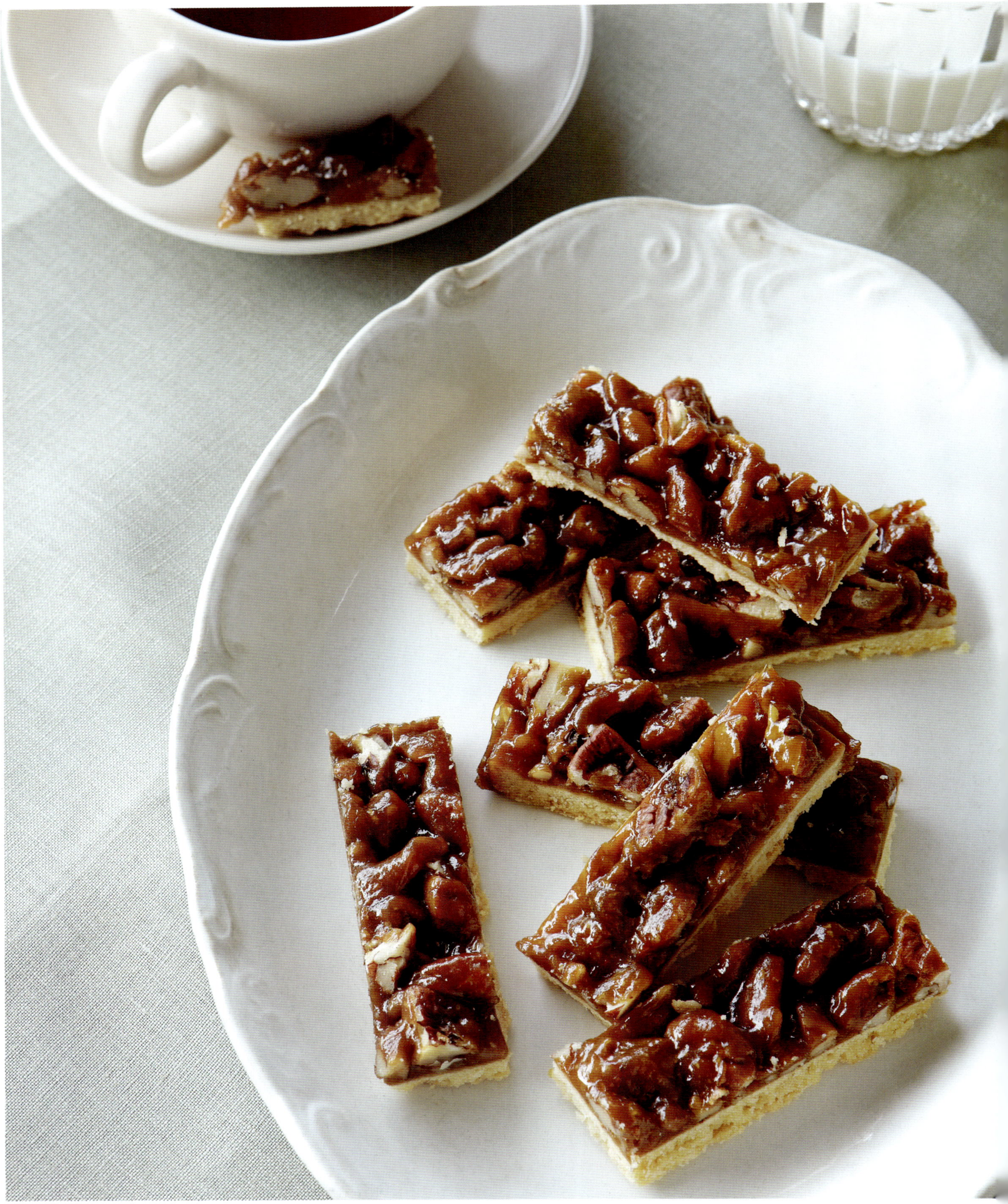

PECAN CARAMEL SLICE

INGREDIENTS
1 cup (150 g) plain flour
½ teaspoon baking powder
90 g butter, diced
1 egg, lightly beaten
1 cup pecans, roughly chopped

CARAMEL TOPPING
60 g butter
⅓ cup golden syrup
⅓ cup (75 g) firmly packed brown sugar
2 tablespoons self-raising flour, sifted

MAKES 14 PIECES

METHOD

Preheat the oven to 180°C. Grease a 25 cm x 19 cm lamington tin and line the base and sides with baking paper.

Sift the flour and baking powder into a bowl. Rub in the butter with your fingertips until the mixture resembles coarse breadcrumbs. Add the egg and mix to form a soft dough. Press over the base of the prepared tin, smoothing with the back of a spoon. Bake for 15 minutes.

Meanwhile, to make the caramel topping, melt the butter in a small saucepan. Remove from the heat and add the golden syrup, sugar and flour. Stir until the mixture is smooth. Sprinkle the slice base with the pecans and pour over the caramel topping. Bake for another 15 minutes. Cool in the tin before cutting into fingers.

TIP You can make the pastry in a food processor. It makes tender, light pastry in moments. Place the flour, baking powder and butter into a food processor fitted with the steel blade. Process until the mixtures looks like coarse breadcrumbs. Add the egg and process until the dough forms a ball. The pastry can be made ahead, wrapped in plastic wrap and stored in the refrigerator until required.

NOTE Pecans have a high oil content so it is advisable to store them in the freezer to prevent any bitter flavour from developing.

INGREDIENTS

2¼ cups rolled oats
½ cup (110 g) raw sugar
125 g butter
2 tablespoons honey
2 tablespoons golden syrup
1 teaspoon molasses (optional)
1 tablespoon sultanas
2 tablespoons chopped dried apricots

ROLLED OAT SQUARES

Honey, golden syrup and a touch of molasses give these squares a distinctive flavour.

MAKES ABOUT 20

METHOD

Preheat the oven to 180°C. Grease a 30 cm x 20 cm lamington tin and line it with baking paper.

In a bowl, combine the rolled oats and sugar. Melt the butter, add the honey, golden syrup and molasses and combine thoroughly. Pour over the oats and sugar. Add the sultanas and apricots and stir well. Spoon into the prepared tin and smooth the top.

Bake for 20–25 minutes. Cut into squares while still warm and leave to cool in the tin.

INGREDIENTS

¾ cup evaporated milk
1 cup chopped dates
1 cup (150 g) self-raising flour
½ teaspoon salt
125 g butter, softened
½ cup (110 g) caster sugar
1 egg, beaten
1 teaspoon vanilla essence
½ cup chopped walnuts
sifted icing sugar

FROSTED DATE BARS

These nutty, economical fruit bars stay moist for a good time. Make them two or three weeks ahead if you like, but don't roll them in the icing sugar until you are about to serve them.

MAKES 24

METHOD

Preheat the oven to 180°C. Grease a 23 cm square cake tin.

Heat the evaporated milk in a small saucepan until small bubbles appear at edge of the pan. Pour over the dates in a bowl and allow to cool.

Sift the flour and salt together. Using an electric mixer, cream the butter with the sugar until light and fluffy. Add the egg and vanilla and beat well. Fold in the sifted flour alternately with the milk and date mixture. Stir in the nuts. Spoon the mixture into the prepared tin.

Bake for 30–35 minutes or until a skewer inserted into the centre comes out almost clean. Turn out and transfer to wire racks to cool. Cut into bars and toss in icing sugar.

DRIED APRICOT & COCONUT SLICE

INGREDIENTS
- 200 g dried apricots, chopped
- ¾ cup water
- 1⅔ cups (250 g) self-raising flour, sifted
- ⅔ cup (150 g) firmly packed brown sugar
- 125 g butter, melted
- 2 eggs
- 1 cup shredded coconut

MAKES 12

METHOD

Preheat the oven to 200°C. Line a 30 cm x 20 cm lamington tin with baking paper.

To make the filling, put the apricots in a small saucepan with the water. Bring to the boil, reduce the heat to low and cook for 5 minutes, stirring frequently, until the fruit is pulpy and the water has been absorbed. Set aside to cool.

To make the pastry, combine 1⅓ cups flour and ⅓ cup of the brown sugar in a large bowl and make a well in the centre. Add the melted butter and mix with a knife until the ingredients have formed a soft dough. Knead lightly.

Press the dough into the prepared tin, spreading firmly with the back of a spoon. Spread the cooled apricots over the pastry.

Beat the eggs lightly in a bowl and whisk in the remaining ⅓ cup brown sugar, remaining ⅓ cup flour and the coconut. Pour the mixture over the apricots, spreading evenly with a spatula.

Bake for 30–40 minutes or until golden brown. Cool in the tin then lift out and cut into squares to serve.

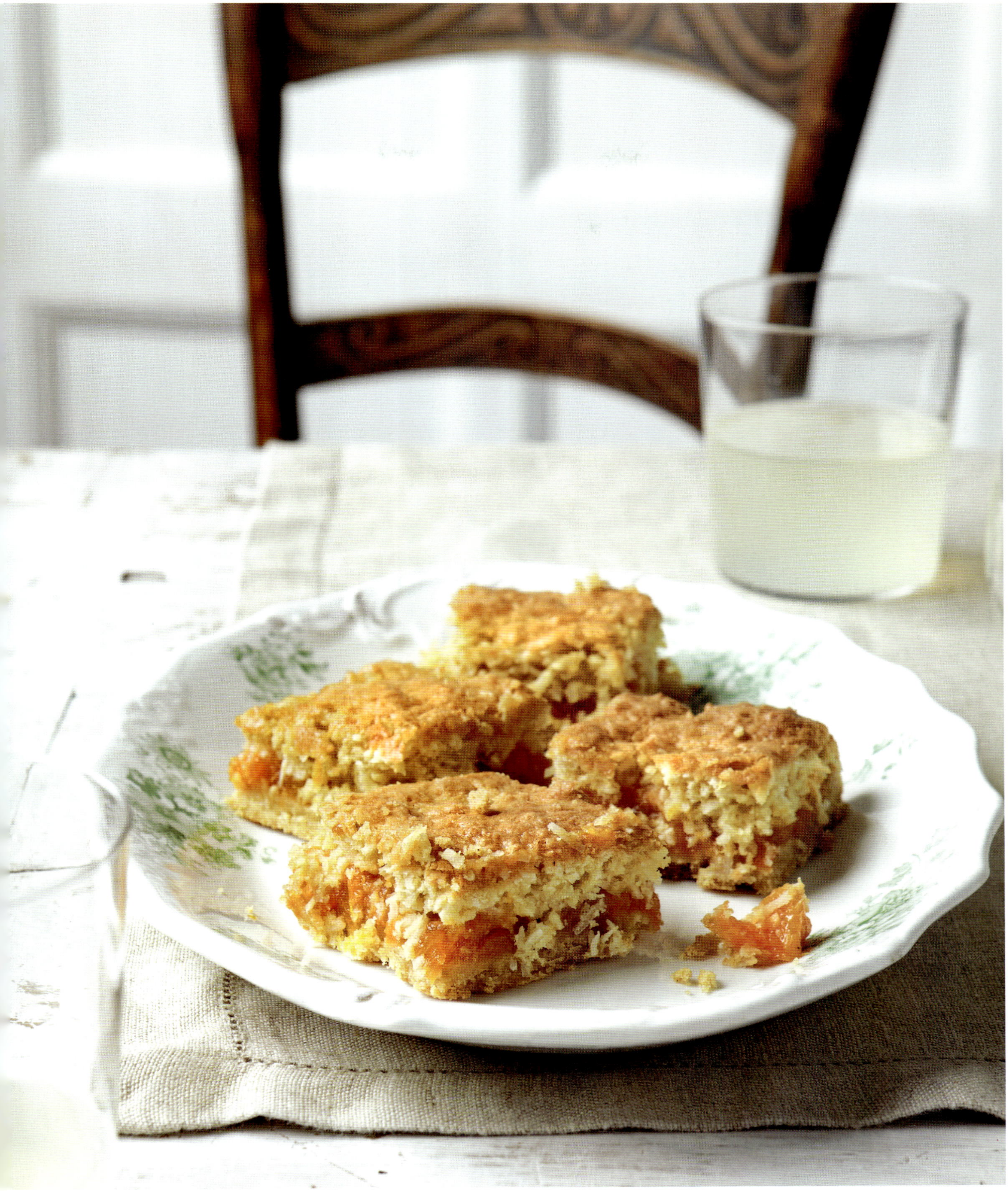

INGREDIENTS
185 g unsalted butter, softened
½ cup (80 g) icing sugar
1½ cups (225 g) plain flour
⅓ cup (50 g) potato flour

LEMON TOPPING
finely grated rind of 3 lemons
1 cup (220 g) caster sugar
3 eggs
½ cup (75 g) plain flour
¾ teaspoon baking powder
¼ cup strained lemon juice
sifted icing sugar to dust

LEMON SPONGE FINGERS

MAKES 30

METHOD

Preheat the oven to 180°C.

Using an electric mixer, cream the butter in a medium bowl until soft. Gradually beat in the icing sugar until the mixture is light and fluffy. Sift the flours into the mixture and mix together, using a spatula or knife, to form a soft dough.

Spread this shortbread dough evenly over the base of a 33 cm x 23 cm Swiss roll tin (there is no need to grease it). If necessary, smooth it out with the back of a spoon, having first covered the dough with a sheet of plastic wrap. Remove the wrap, prick the dough all over with a fork and chill for 30 minutes.

Bake for 15–20 minutes or until pale golden, then remove from the oven. Leave the oven on.

For the lemon topping, place the grated lemon zest, sugar and eggs in a bowl. Whisk together until a pale and thick cream forms. Sift in the flour with the baking powder and fold this into the whisked mixture with the lemon juice.

When the topping is mixed, pour it over the prepared shortbread base and return it to the oven for 25 minutes or until set and very lightly browned. Leave to cool in the tin. When cold, cut the oblong into three even strips lengthwise and ten across. Dust with sifted icing sugar to serve.

INGREDIENTS

250 g cream cheese, softened, or ricotta cheese
2 eggs
½ cup (110 g) caster sugar
1 tablespoon lemon juice
½ cup sultanas
6 sheets filo pastry, cut in half
125 g butter, melted

CREAM CHEESE SLICES

MAKES ABOUT 18

METHOD

Preheat the oven to 180°C.

Place the cheese, eggs, sugar and lemon juice in a large bowl and beat well until smooth. Stir in the sultanas.

Stack filo between two dry tea-towels with a dampened towel on top. Place one sheet of filo in a greased 28 cm x 18 cm baking dish, first brushing the sheet with melted butter. Repeat until you have used half the filo.

Spoon over the cheese filling, and continue adding the remaining filo sheets, brushing each with butter. Using a sharp knife, mark the top filo layers into 6 cm x 4 cm diamond shapes.

Bake for 20–30 minutes or until the pastry is golden and the filling is set. Serve cold.

NOTE Filo pastry is available in the freezer section of supermarkets. It is as thin as paper, so when using it to make layers, make sure the stack of pastry is covered with a tea towel to prevent it from drying out.

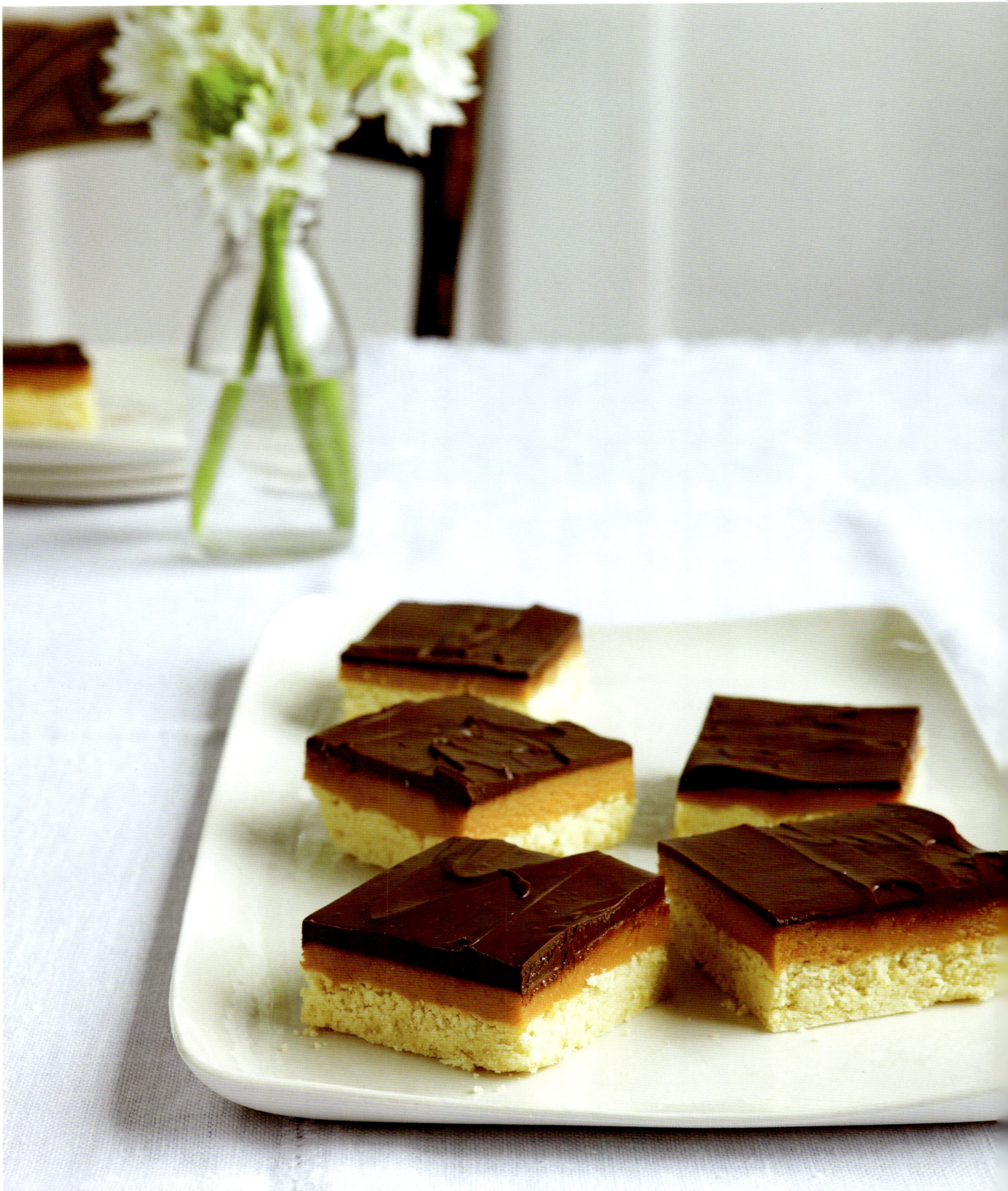

BROWNIES & SLICES *slices*

INGREDIENTS
125 g butter, softened
2 tablespoons caster sugar
1½ cups (225 g) plain flour, sifted

CARAMEL FILLING
80 g butter
2 tablespoons caster sugar
2 tablespoons golden syrup
1 cup condensed milk

CHOCOLATE TOPPING
150 g dark chocolate
20 g butter

CHOCOLATE CARAMEL SLICE

MAKES 14

METHOD

Preheat the oven to 180°C. Line a shallow 20 cm square cake tin with baking paper, letting it hang over two opposite sides to help with taking it out of the tin later.

Using an electric mixer, cream the butter and sugar together in a small bowl until light and fluffy. Add the flour and stir until the mixture is well combined.

Roll out to a square, press evenly into the prepared tin and prick well. Bake for 25–30 minutes. Cool in the tin.

Place the filling ingredients in a saucepan and stir until dissolved. Bring slowly to the boil, then cook, stirring, for 5–7 minutes. Cool slightly, then spread over the biscuit mixture and leave to set and cool completely.

To make the topping, melt the chocolate with the butter over a very low heat without letting the chocolate get at all hot. Spread over the caramel. Leave to set, then lift out using the baking paper and cut into squares or fingers.

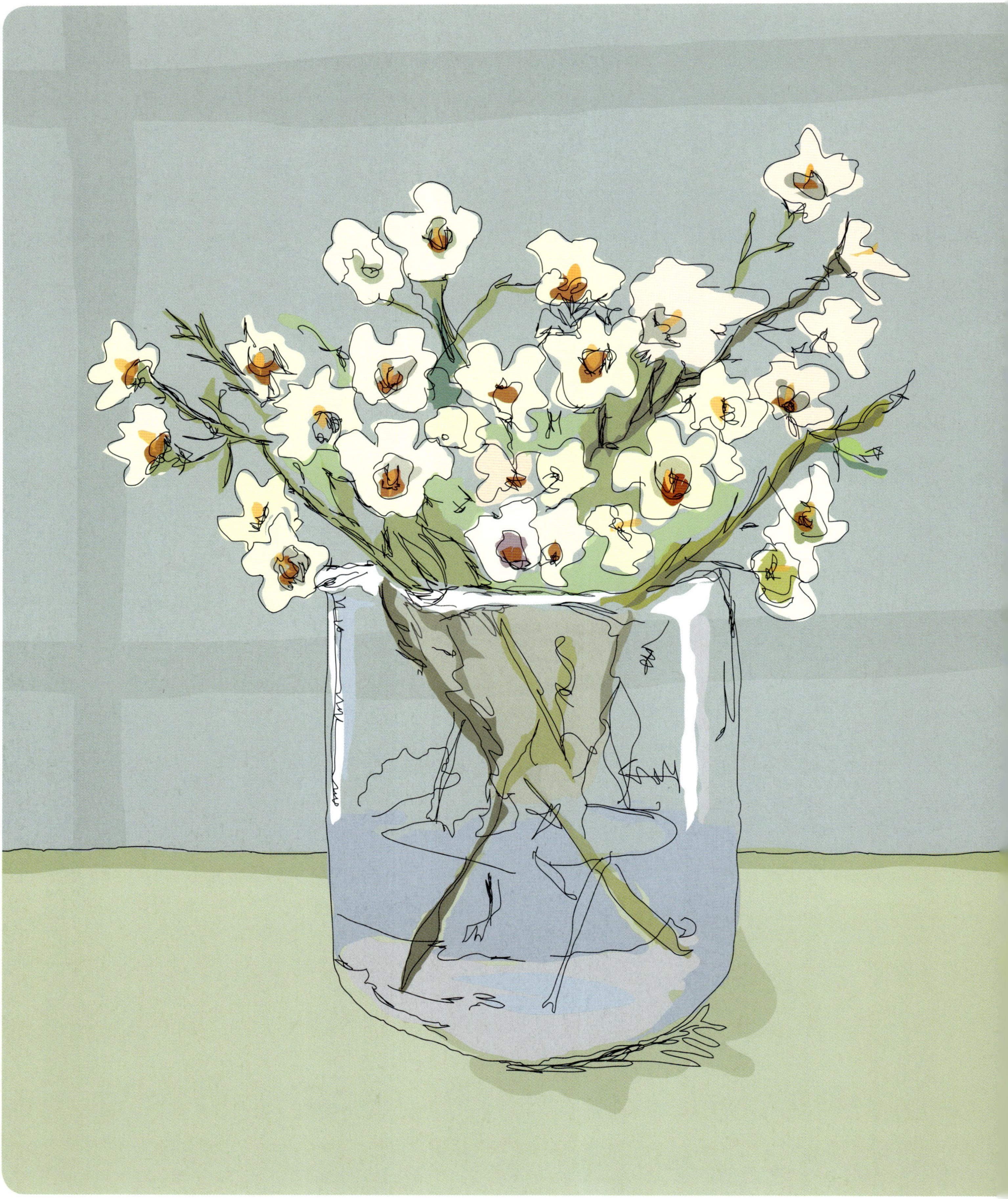

MUFFINS, SCONES, SHORTCAKES & QUICKBREADS

CHAPTER 3

HINTS & TIPS

Muffins, scones and shortcakes are all kinds of quickbreads – mixtures in which all the ingredients are quickly combined, and that rely on fast-acting chemical raising agents such as baking powder and bicarbonate of soda. All require light handling to ensure they do not become tough.

MUFFINS

There are two types of muffins: the flat, bread-like English muffins, which are not dealt with in this book, and the domed American muffins that have a more cake-like texture. These can be sweet or savoury, and are one of America's nicest gifts to the culinary world.

MUFFIN TINS

Half-cup (125 ml) tins are an ideal size, or there are smaller tins for mini muffins. Tin plate is the cheapest material; its only drawback is that it can corrode. Non-stick teflon tins are more expensive but excellent. Alternatively, line muffin tins with paper cases, or use silicone muffin moulds, which are non-stick. All of these materials respond to heat as quickly as possible, helping the muffins to rise well and cook evenly in all directions.

Muffin tins come in three sizes: mini (1 tablespoon), standard (either $1/3$ or $1/2$ cup) and large ($3/4$ cup; also known as Texas). The size of the tins may be changed if you adjust the baking time. A recipe for 12 standard muffins will make about six large muffins and about 24 mini muffins. In general, bake standard muffins for 15 minutes and mini muffins for about 12 minutes.

MAKING MUFFINS

GREASE THE TINS WELL (even non-stick tins should be lightly greased) or line them with paper muffin cases of the right size. It doesn't matter if the case doesn't sit right down in the tin; once it is filled, the mixture will anchor it. Or use silicone moulds, which do not need to be greased.

USE FRESH INGREDIENTS Baking powder and bicarbonate of soda lose their strength over time, so make sure they are fresh by buying them from a high-turnover outlet. Flour, too, needs to be fresh. If you don't have self-raising flour you can make your own by adding 2 teaspoons baking powder to 1 cup of plain flour.

MIX THE WET AND DRY INGREDIENTS with a few swift strokes, just enough to moisten the flour – the mixture should still be a little lumpy. If extra ingredients are added, such as berries or nuts, fold them in gently, being careful not to crush berries or overhandle the mixture. Do not overmix; this will produce tough, coarse-textured muffins.

SPOON THE MIXTURE INTO EACH TIN in one large spoonful, pushing it off with the spoon held low, to avoid stretching the elastic gluten strands in the flour. Fill the tins or paper cases about two-thirds full.

BAKE IMMEDIATELY, or else the raising agents will dissipate and the muffins will not rise. The exceptions are those mixtures, such as Raisin & Bran Muffins (page 116), that can be left in the fridge for days or even weeks and a small quantity baked as needed.

MUFFINS CAN BE PREPARED IN STAGES if time is short or if you want muffins for breakfast in the quickest time possible. Prepare the liquid ingredients and the dry ingredients the night before and store separately. In the morning, combine the two, spoon into the tins and bake.

MUFFINS, SCONES, SHORTCAKES & QUICKBREADS *hints & tips*

They'll be ready by the time you've made your morning coffee. Alternatively, make a prepare-ahead batter such as that for Raisin & Bran Muffins (page 116) and bake only as many muffins as you need at the time.

TEST THE MUFFINS WITH A FINE SKEWER a few minutes before the end of the recommended baking time. If it comes out clean, with no crumbs or batter attached, the muffins are cooked. If not, return them to the oven for another couple of minutes, then test again.

TO REMOVE MUFFINS FROM TINS, run a knife or a small metal spatula around their sides, between muffin and tin. Those cooked in paper cases don't need to be loosened.

MUFFINS ARE BEST EATEN WARM If not eating them straight away, allow to cool completely on a wire rack, then store in an airtight container. Muffins freeze very well; thaw at room temperature (or briefly in the microwave) and then refresh in a preheated 180º oven for about 5 minutes.

SCONES & SHORTCAKES
Scones can be mixed and baked in 20 minutes to enjoy with tea or coffee, or to provide hot savoury snacks or even the basis of a casual meal. They require quick but light handling to achieve the desired flaky result.

Shortcake is a luscious dessert consisting of a tender, scone-like cake which is split, filled and topped with fruit and cream, and served warm. Rounds of rich pastry can also be layered with cream and fruit, Lemon Butter (pages 254–255) or Passionfruit Butter (page 255) to make a Continental-style shortcake.

MAKING SCONES
RUB IN THE FAT with your fingertips or a small palette knife until the mixture resembles breadcrumbs.

ADD THE LIQUID in a slow and steady stream to a well made in the dry ingredients, then mix to a soft dough.

TURN OUT ONTO A FLOURED SURFACE and give the dough a few quick turns with floured hands, then pat gently into a thickness of about 2 cm and cut into rounds with a sharp biscuit or scone cutter.

BRUSH TOPS WITH A LITTLE MILK and bake in a preheated oven for 12–15 minutes or until golden.

MAKING SHORTCAKES
MIX AND HANDLE THE DOUGH LIGHTLY; see Scones. Roll the dough out on a floured surface to about 1 cm thick then cut into rounds the size you want. Bake in a hot oven. When cool sandwich together with a filling of whipped cream and soft fruit.

QUICKBREADS
These loaves and cakes are made with little effort and don't depend on slow-rising yeast. Instead they use quick-acting chemical leaveners such as baking powder and bicarbonate of soda.

MAKING QUICKBREADS
GREASE THE TIN EVENLY BUT SPARINGLY; if you are too generous with greasing the loaf may be sticky.

COMBINE THE DRY INGREDIENTS in a large bowl. Make a well in the centre to pour the liquid into.

IF THE MIXTURE CONTAINS EGGS, beat them with a fork before adding them to the other liquid ingredients.

USE A FORK OR WOODEN SPOON to quickly stir all the ingredients together just until the flour mixture is moistened. Some spots of flour may remain and the butter will be lumpy. It's better to undermix than overmix.

BAKE THE LOAF OR CAKE until it has risen nicely and is golden brown. Test whether it is cooked by inserting a fine skewer or cake tester into the centre; if it comes out with no crumbs or batter attached, the cake is cooked.

ONCE THE LOAF SO COOKED, cool it in the tin for about 5 minutes, then turn it out onto a wire rack. Hot loaves do not slice well, so leave it to cool a little more before slicing with a serrated knife. If icing the loaf or cake, leave it to cool completely before you ice it.

STORE IN AN AIRTIGHT CONTAINER Quickbreads in general do not keep well and are best eaten on the day they are made.

INGREDIENTS

2 cups (300 g) self-raising flour
¼ teaspoon salt
½ cup caster sugar
1 egg, lightly beaten
1 cup milk
90 g butter, melted

BASIC MUFFINS

MAKES 10–12

METHOD

Preheat the oven to 200°C. Grease twelve ⅓-cup muffin tins or line them with paper cases.

Sift the dry ingredients into a large bowl.

Mix the egg, milk and butter together, pour over the dry ingredients and mix just until the flour is moistened; the batter should still be lumpy.

Spoon into the prepared muffin tins, filling each one two-thirds full. Bake for 20–25 minutes or until well risen and golden brown.

VARIATIONS

NUT OR DRIED FRUIT MUFFINS Follow the recipe for Basic Muffins, adding ½ cup chopped nuts or dried fruit to the dry ingredients before mixing in the liquid. Chopped pecans, walnuts, dried apricots, raisins or mixed dried fruit may be used. After filling the muffin tins, sprinkle with sugar.

WHOLEMEAL MUFFINS Follow the recipe for Basic Muffins, using 1 cup (150 g) wholemeal self-raising flour and 1 cup (150 g) white self-raising flour.

WHOLEMEAL ORANGE MUFFINS Follow the method for Basic Muffins, replacing the ingredients with 1 cup (150 g) wholemeal plain flour, 1 cup (150 g) white plain flour, 1 tablespoon baking powder, ¼ teaspoon salt, ½ cup (110 g) firmly packed brown sugar, the juice of 2 oranges, the grated rind of 1 orange, 2 eggs and 60 g butter, melted.

BERRY MUFFINS Follow the recipe for Basic Muffins, and stir in 1 cup frozen blueberries or raspberries to the dry ingredients before mixing in the liquid.

CHOC CHOP MUFFINS Follow the recipe for Basic Muffins, adding ⅔ cup dark or white chocolate bits to the egg, milk and butter mixture along with the flour.

CHRISTMAS MUFFINS Follow the recipe for Basic Muffins, mixing the egg, milk and butter together with 1½ cups Fruit Mincemeat (see page 395), before adding the flour. These muffins are especially nice baked in little Christmassy paper cases placed in mini muffin tins (in which case they should take about 15 minutes to bake).

BACON OR HAM MUFFINS Follow the recipe for Basic Muffins, reducing the sugar to 1 tablespoon and adding 3 rashers bacon, fried crisp and crumbled, or ½ cup finely chopped cooked ham, to the dry ingredients before mixing in the liquid.

MUFFINS, SCONES, SHORTCAKES & QUICKBREADS *plain & sweet muffins*

INGREDIENTS

2 cups (300 g) plain flour
1 teaspoon baking powder
1 teaspoon bicarbonate of soda
¼ teaspoon salt
¼ cup (55 g) sugar
2 tablespoons honey
2 eggs
1¼ cups natural yoghurt
2 tablespoons milk
¼ cup unsalted butter, melted and cooled
1 tablespoon freshly grated lemon rind

LEMON SYRUP

⅓ cup fresh lemon juice
⅓ cup (75 g) caster sugar
3 tablespoons water

LEMON YOGHURT MUFFINS

Muffins first appeared in the late 1950s in America, where they quickly gained popularity. It's important not to make muffins too large … I was rather horrified at the size of them the first time I saw them in America.

MAKES 12

METHOD

Preheat the oven to 190°C. Grease twelve ½ cup muffin tins or line them with paper cases.

In a small bowl, sift together the flour, baking powder, bicarbonate of soda and salt.

In a large bowl, stir together the sugar, honey, eggs, yoghurt, milk, butter and lemon rind until the mixture is combined. Add the flour mixture and stir the batter until just combined.

Divide the batter among the prepared muffin tins and bake for 15–20 minutes, or until they are pale golden.

Make the syrup while the muffins are baking. In a small saucepan, combine the lemon juice, sugar and water, bring the mixture to the boil, and boil for 1 minute.

When the muffins come out of the oven, pierce the top of each muffin gently with a fork two or three times and drizzle the syrup over each of the muffins. Allow to cool in the pan for about 3 minutes, then turn out on a wire rack to cool further.

INGREDIENTS

1¼ cups (185 g) plain flour
½ cup (110 g) sugar
2 teaspoons baking powder
¼ teaspoon bicarbonate of soda
1 teaspoon ground cinnamon
¼ teaspoon ground allspice
¼ teaspoon salt
2 large eggs
1 cup sour cream
60 g butter, melted
1 cup diced unpeeled apples

TOPPING

⅓ cup chopped walnuts
2 tablespoons sugar
2 tablespoons plain flour
2 tablespoons sugar
2 tablespoons butter, diced
½ teaspoon ground cinnamon

APPLE CRUMBLE MUFFINS

MAKES 12–18

METHOD

Preheat the oven to 190°C. Grease eighteen ⅓-cup or twelve ½-cup muffin tins or line them with paper cases.

Into a large bowl, sift the flour, sugar, baking powder, bicarbonate of soda, cinnamon, allspice and salt.

Break the eggs into another bowl, add the sour cream and melted butter and whisk until blended. Stir in the diced apple.

Pour the egg mixture over the flour mixture and fold in just until the dry ingredients are moistened. Divide the mixture among the prepared muffin tins.

For the topping, put all the ingredients into a bowl then rub in the butter until the mixture resembles coarse crumbs. Top each muffin with about 2 teaspoons crumble topping

Bake for 20–25 minutes or until browned. Turn out onto wire racks. Serve warm or cool.

VARIATION

PEAR CRUMBLE MUFFINS Replace the apple with diced ripe but firm pear. Sift ½ teaspoon ground ginger along with the flour mixture if you like.

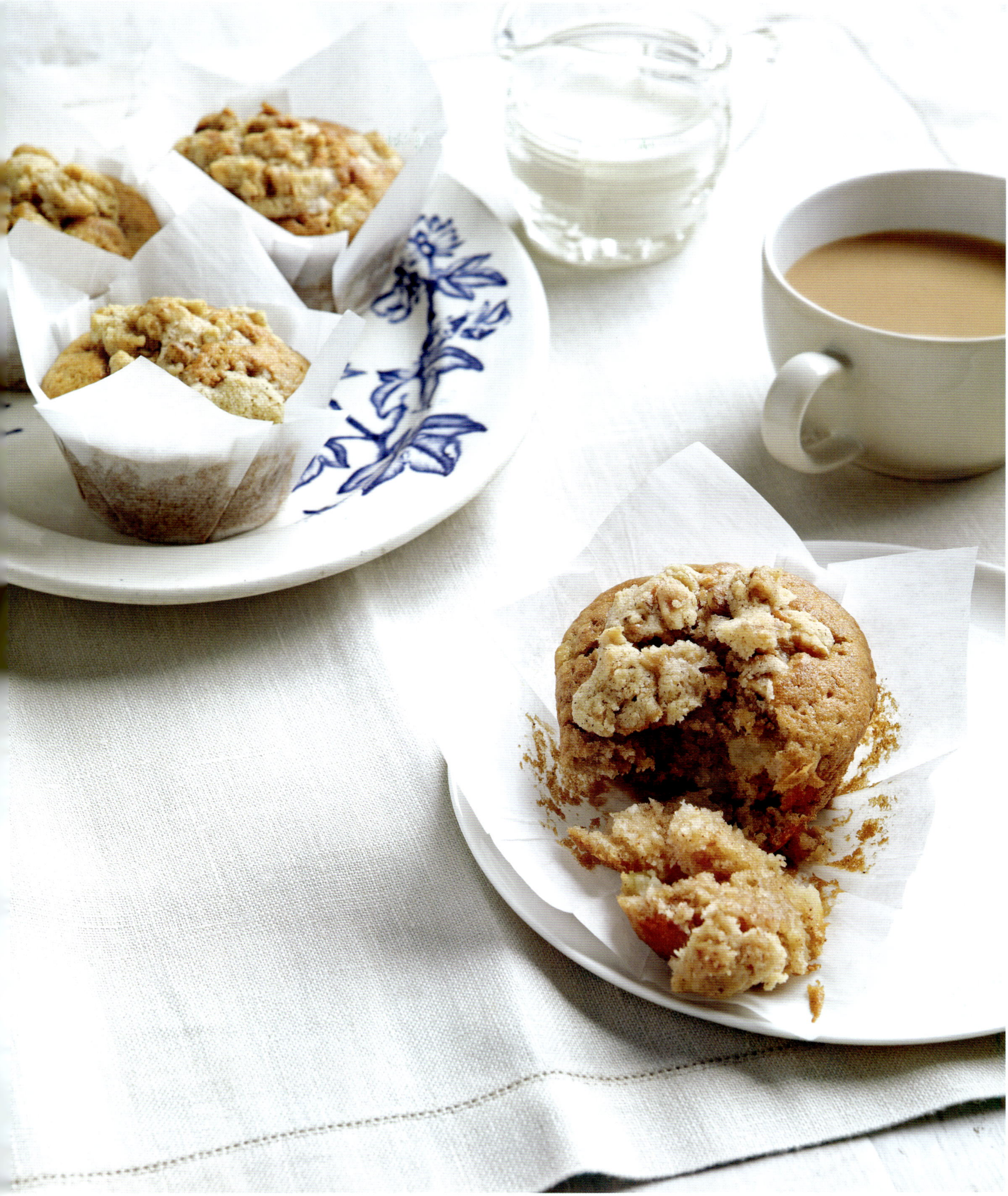

INGREDIENTS

2½ cups (375 g) plain flour
2½ teaspoons bicarbonate of soda
½ teaspoon salt
1 cup (220 g) firmly packed brown sugar
1 cup raisins
1½ cups bran cereal, such as All-Bran
2 eggs
½ cup vegetable oil
1½ tablespoons molasses
2 cups buttermilk, or 2 cups fresh milk soured with 2 tablespoons white vinegar
¾ cup water

RAISIN & BRAN MUFFINS

This is a great recipe for busy households. The batter will keep for up to a fortnight, covered, in the refrigerator. All you have to do to enjoy hot muffins at any time is fill the muffin tins and bake (see Notes). These muffins are delicious served with butter and honey.

MAKES ABOUT 35

METHOD

Sift the flour, bicarbonate of soda and salt into a large bowl. Stir in the brown sugar, raisins and bran cereal.

Beat the eggs with the oil and molasses and mix in the buttermilk and water. Pour into the dry mixture and stir well. Cover with plastic wrap and refrigerate for at least 24 hours.

Stir the mixture lightly, then spoon into greased muffin tins or into paper cases, filling them three-quarters full.

Preheat the oven to 200°C. Bake for 20 minutes or until risen and golden. Serve warm.

NOTES If you are not cooking a whole tray of muffins at once, fill any empty muffin holes with water to encourage even baking.

You can freshen thawed-out frozen or slightly stale muffins by dipping them rapidly in cold milk (or water) and then reheating them in the oven.

MUFFINS, SCONES, SHORTCAKES & QUICKBREADS *plain & sweet muffins*

INGREDIENTS
2 cups (300 g) plain flour
1 tablespoon baking powder
$1/3$ teaspoon salt
$1/2$ cup sultanas
1 cup apple cider
90 g butter, melted
1 egg, lightly beaten

TOPPING
$1/4$ cup (55 g) caster sugar
$1 1/2$ teaspoons ground cinnamon

APPLE CIDER & SULTANA MUFFINS

MAKES 12

METHOD

Preheat the oven to 200°C. Grease twelve $1/3$-cup muffin tins or line them with paper cases.

Sift the flour, baking powder and salt into a bowl. Add the sultanas and toss to coat evenly with flour.

Combine the cider, butter and egg, then pour over the flour mixture, stirring until just mixed. The batter will be lumpy.

Spoon into the prepared muffin tins, filling them two-thirds full. Combine the sugar and cinnamon and sprinkle over the muffins.

Bake for 20–25 minutes or until browned and risen. Turn out onto a wire rack to cool.

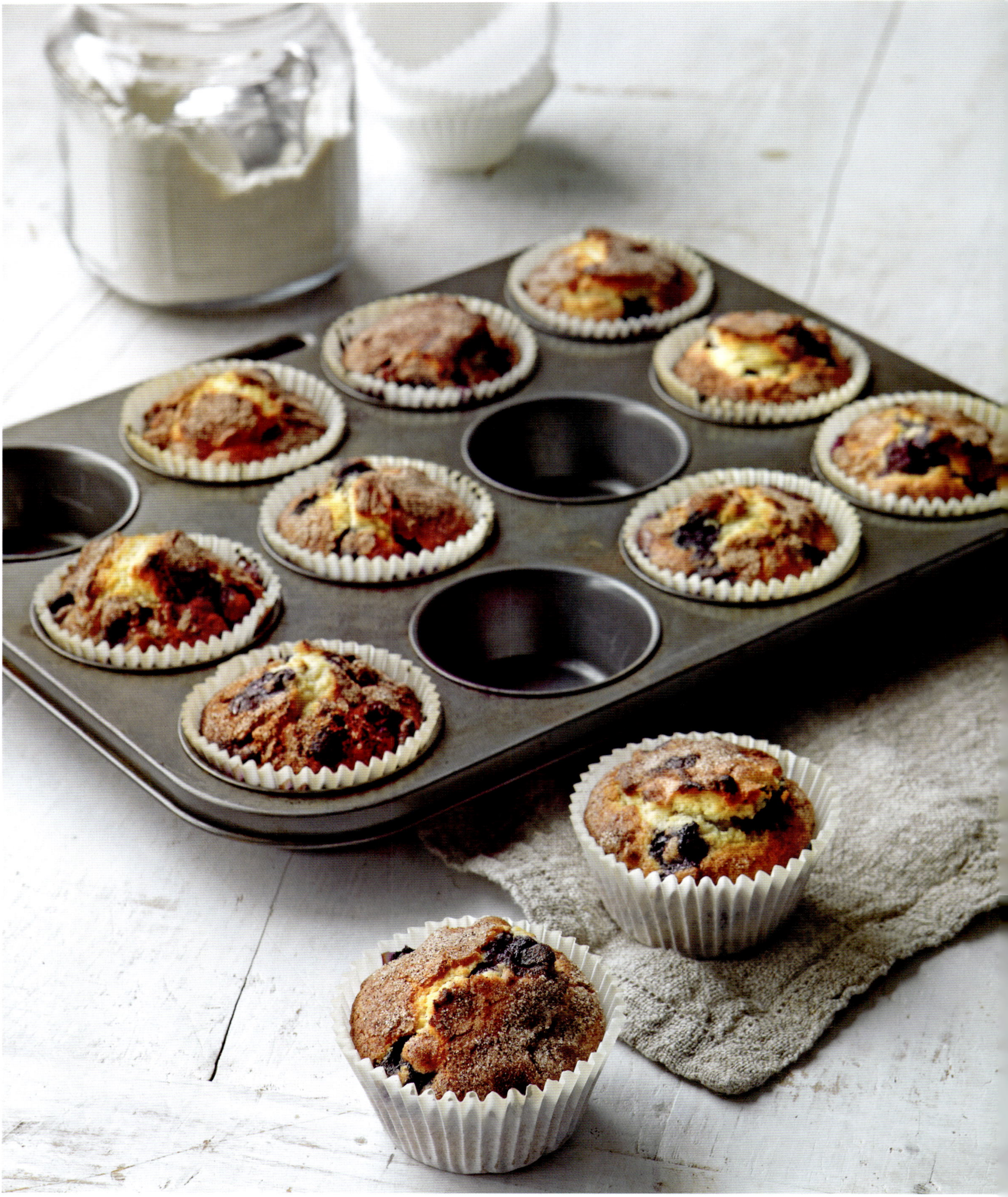

INGREDIENTS

90 g unsalted butter, melted and cooled
½ cup milk
2 eggs
1½ cups (225 g) plain flour
⅔ cup (150 g) caster sugar
2 teaspoons baking powder
a large pinch of salt
½ cup processed bran
1½ cups fresh blueberries
1 tablespoon sugar mixed with 1 teaspoon ground cinnamon

BLUEBERRY BRAN MUFFINS

Muffins also introduced us to the wonderful blueberry. They do seem to work so well together. I think Australians embraced the muffin because it was so quick and portable and there were so many flavour variations.

MAKES 12

METHOD

Preheat the oven to 200°C. Grease twelve ⅓ cup muffin tins or line them with paper cases.

In a bowl, lightly whisk together the melted butter, milk and eggs. Sift the flour, sugar, baking powder and salt over the liquid mixture and add the bran.

Stir the batter until it is just combined; it should still be lumpy. Fold in the blueberries lightly.

Spoon the mixture into the prepared muffin tins. Sprinkle with the cinnamon sugar and bake for 20–25 minutes or until the muffins are risen and golden. Serve warm or at room temperature, with or without butter.

VARIATION

RASPBERRY MUFFINS Replace the blueberries with fresh raspberries.

INGREDIENTS

2 cups (300 g) plain flour
¾ cup (165 g) caster sugar
2 teaspoons baking powder
1½ teaspoons ground cinnamon
¼ teaspoon salt
1 egg
¾ cup light sour cream
¾ cup milk
60 g butter, melted and cooled
sugar and extra cinnamon to dust

SPICED BREAKFAST MUFFINS

MAKES 12

METHOD

Preheat the oven to 200°C. Grease twelve ½-cup muffin tins or line them with paper cases.

Into a large bowl, sift together the flour, sugar, baking powder, cinnamon and salt.

In a small bowl, whisk together the egg, sour cream, milk and butter until the mixture is combined.

Fold the egg mixture into the flour mixture until the batter is just combined. Divide the batter among the prepared muffin tins. Dust well with sugar and ground cinnamon.

Bake for 15–20 minutes or until the muffins are risen and golden. Turn out on to a wire rack to cool.

NOTE The use of light sour cream reduces the fat content of the muffins a little, but it can be replaced with regular sour cream if you prefer.

MUFFINS, SCONES, SHORTCAKES & QUICKBREADS *plain & sweet muffins*

The smell of cinnamon coming from the oven is very enticing. Muffins are a simple option for breakfast, especially on the weekend when you want a special treat. Prepare the wet and dry ingredients separately the night before. In the morning all you need to do is mix the two together and your muffins can be baking while you make the tea and read the paper.

INGREDIENTS

2 cups (300 g) plain flour
¾ cup (165 g) caster sugar
2 teaspoons baking powder
1 teaspoon bicarbonate of soda
¾ teaspoon salt
1 egg
1 egg yolk
1 cup sour cream
⅓ cup milk
30 g unsalted butter, melted and cooled
1 teaspoon vanilla essence
1 cup pitted prunes, roughly chopped
caster sugar to dust

SOUR CREAM & PRUNE MUFFINS

MAKES 12

METHOD

Preheat the oven to 200°C. Grease twelve ½-cup muffin tins or line them with paper cases.

Into a bowl, sift together the flour, sugar, baking powder, bicarbonate of soda and salt.

In another bowl, whisk together the egg, yolk, sour cream, milk, butter and vanilla.

Make a well in the flour mixture, add the egg mixture and lightly stir until just combined. Stir in the prunes.

Divide the batter among the prepared muffin tins and dust the tops thickly with sugar.

Bake for 15–20 minutes or until the muffins are golden. Turn out onto wire racks and allow to cool.

Serve the muffins with butter if you like.

MUFFINS, SCONES, SHORTCAKES & QUICKBREADS *savoury muffins*

INGREDIENTS
2 cups (300 g) plain flour
1 tablespoon baking powder
a pinch of salt
2 eggs
1 cup milk
½ cup (110 g) firmly packed brown sugar
1 teaspoon vanilla essence
⅓ cup vegetable oil or melted butter
about ⅓ cup strawberry jam

TOPPING
60 g butter, melted
¼ cup (55 g) caster sugar
1 teaspoon cinnamon

JAM DOUGHNUT MUFFINS

MAKES 12

METHOD

Preheat the oven to 200°C. Grease twelve ⅓ cup muffin tins or line them with paper cases.

Sift the flour, baking powder and salt into a large bowl.

In another bowl, lightly whisk together the eggs, milk, brown sugar, vanilla and oil or melted butter. Fold into the sifted flour mixture lightly, taking care not to overmix. The batter should not be smooth.

Divide the batter among the prepared muffin tins, filling each two-thirds full. Use a teaspoon to place a dollop of strawberry jam in the centre on the top of each one.

Bake for 12–15 minutes or until they are pale golden and cooked when tested with a skewer.

Remove from the oven, brush quickly with the melted butter and sprinkle with the caster sugar which has been mixed with the ground cinnamon. Serve warm.

INGREDIENTS

2 cups (300 g) plain flour
2 teaspoons baking powder
½ teaspoon bicarbonate of soda
¼ teaspoon cayenne pepper
½ teaspoon salt
½ cup yellow cornmeal (polenta)
2 cups coarsely grated cheddar cheese
½ cup thinly sliced shallots/spring onions (see Note)
1 cup finely diced red capsicum (pepper)
60 g butter, softened
2 tablespoons caster sugar
2 large eggs
1¼ cups buttermilk

CHEESE, CAPSICUM & SHALLOT MUFFINS

These are great lunchtime muffins, with salad. Or try them just on their own with butter as a snack, or even for a workday breakfast on the run. They are also a good addition to children's lunchboxes.

MAKES 18

METHOD

Preheat the oven to 230°C. Grease eighteen ⅓ cup muffin tins or line them with paper cases.

Into a bowl, sift together the flour, baking powder, bicarbonate of soda, cayenne and salt. Add the cornmeal, cheese, shallots and capsicum and stir to combine the mixture well.

In a large bowl, cream together the butter and the sugar, add the eggs and beat the mixture until it is smooth. Gently fold in the flour mixture with the buttermilk until the mixture is just combined.

Divide the batter among the prepared muffin tins and bake the muffins in the middle of the oven for 15 to 18 minutes or until they are golden.

Turn the muffins onto wire racks and leave them to cool.

NOTE The term 'shallot' can be confusing and is used for two different members of the onion family. The type required here, also known as spring onions, are immature onions with very small white bulbs and long green stems; both parts are edible. The small, papery-skinned bulbs that resemble onions are known variously as shallots, French shallots or escallots (these have brown or golden skins) and Asian shallots (purple skins).

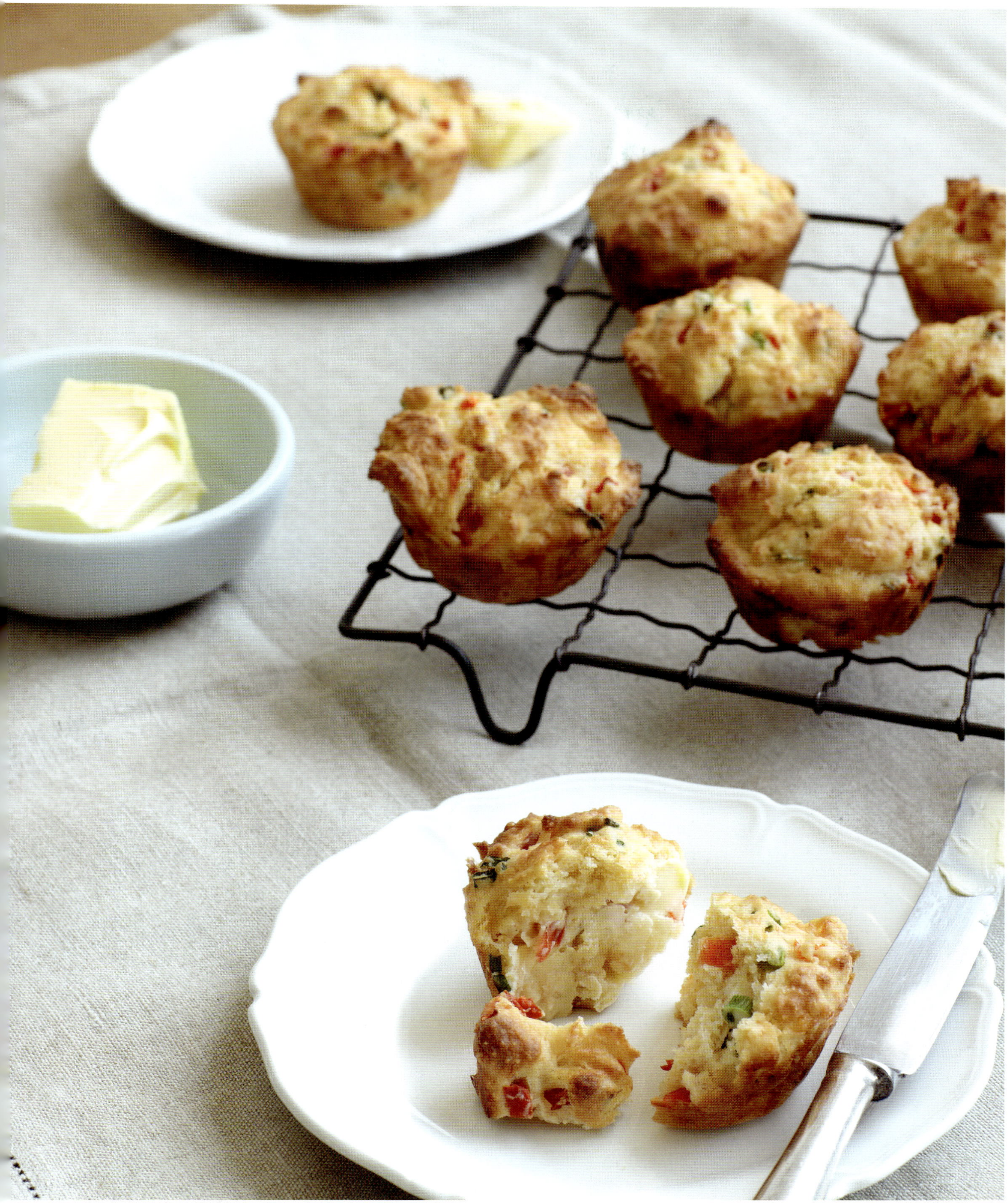

INGREDIENTS

2 cups white cornmeal (polenta)
½ cup (75 g) plain flour
3½ teaspoons baking powder
½ teaspoon bicarbonate of soda
1½ teaspoons salt
1½ cups buttermilk
2 eggs, lightly beaten
2 tablespoons unsalted butter, melted
3 cups fresh corn kernels, cut from the cob

FRESH CORN MUFFINS

When people think of muffins they normally think of the more common sweet or fruity variety, but savoury muffins are just as delicious. Serve these savoury muffins with cheese, a bowl of soup or a salad for a light summer meal.

MAKES 18

METHOD

Preheat the oven to 200°C. Grease eighteen ⅓ cup muffin tins or line them with paper cases.

In a bowl, sift together the cornmeal, flour, baking powder, bicarbonate of soda and salt. Stir in the buttermilk and then the beaten eggs. Do not overmix.

Add the butter and corn, then stir until just mixed.

Divide the mixture among the prepared muffin tins and bake for 25 minutes or until golden and cooked when tested with a skewer.

Turn out onto wire racks to cool. Store in an airtight container for 1–2 days.

INGREDIENTS

1 cup (150 g) plain flour
1 cup yellow cornmeal (polenta)
2 teaspoons baking powder
1 teaspoon bicarbonate of soda
1 teaspoon salt
1½ cups buttermilk
2 eggs, lightly beaten
60 g butter, melted

BUTTERMILK CORNMEAL MUFFINS

Buttermilk makes great muffins that are lighter and fluffier than those made from regular milk. It also combines well with cornmeal and other flours.

MAKES 12

METHOD

Preheat the oven to 200°C. Grease twelve ⅓ cup muffin tins or line them with paper cases. Sift the dry ingredients into a large bowl.

Combine the buttermilk, eggs and melted butter, pour over the dry ingredients and mix until the flour is just moistened; the batter should still be lumpy.

Spoon into the prepared muffin tins, filling each two-thirds full. Bake for 20–25 minutes or until well risen and golden brown. Turn out onto wire racks to cool.

These muffins are good split and served with butter.

INGREDIENTS

3 cups (450 g) self-raising flour
1 teaspoon salt
60 g butter, diced
1¼ cups milk or buttermilk
extra milk for brushing

SCONES

Hot scones with cream and a good berry jam make that delight known as Devonshire tea. The original West England version uses clotted cream, but whipped cream also works well. No afternoon tea is complete without a scone recipe and with so many variations possible, there is something to suit everyone.

MAKES ABOUT 12

METHOD

Preheat the oven to 230°C. Lightly grease a baking tray.

Sift the flour and salt into a bowl. Rub in the butter. Add nearly all the milk at once and mix in quickly with a knife. Add the remaining milk only if necessary to mix to a soft dough.

Turn onto a floured board and knead lightly by turning and pressing with the heel of the hand three or four times.

Pat the dough out to a round 2 cm thick and cut into 4 cm rounds with a floured cutter. Re-roll the dough scraps once and cut more rounds. Place the scones close together on the prepared baking tray. Brush the tops with a little milk and bake in the top of the oven for 10–15 minutes or until well risen and golden.

For soft scones, wrap in a tea towel as soon as they come from the oven. For crusty scones, do not wrap; cool on a wire rack. Serve warm with butter or with jam and cream.

NOTE Scone dough scraps can be gathered up, re-kneaded lightly and re-rolled once, but no more, otherwise the scones made from the scraps will be tough.

VARIATIONS

FRUIT SCONES Follow the recipe for Scones, but stir in 1 tablespoon sugar and ½ cup sultanas or other dried fruit after rubbing in the butter. A little grated orange or lemon rind, or mixed spice, may also be added.

CRUSTED ORANGE SCONES Follow the recipe for Scones, but add 1 tablespoon sugar after rubbing in the butter, and use ¼ cup orange juice and ¾ cup milk for the liquid. Press a sugar cube dipped in orange juice on top of each scone before baking.

SPICED FRUIT PINWHEELS Prepare the dough as for Scones. Roll out to a rectangle 5 mm thick, brush with melted butter and sprinkle with sugar and cinnamon. Sprinkle with mixed dried fruit, roll up and cut into 2 cm thick slices. Place, cut sides up, in a greased, shallow baking tin and bake at 220°C for 10–12 minutes or until browned.

CHEESE SCONES Follow the recipe for Scones, but stir in ⅓ cup grated tasty cheese, ¼ teaspoon dry mustard powder and a good grinding of black pepper or a pinch of cayenne pepper after rubbing in the butter. Bake at 220°C for about 10 minutes.

CHEESE-TOPPED SCONE LOAF Prepare the dough as for Cheese Scones (above), place on a lightly greased baking tray and shape into a round or rectangular loaf 2.5 cm thick. Mix together 45 g softened butter, a pinch of salt, ½ cup grated cheese and a pinch each of cayenne pepper, dry mustard powder and nutmeg. Spread mixture over the loaf. Sprinkle with a little paprika and bake for 12–18 minutes. Transfer to wire racks to cool. Serve cut in slices and buttered.

HERB SCONES Follow the recipe for Scones, but add 1 tablespoon chopped mixed fresh herbs, or 1 teaspoon dried herbs with 1 tablespoon chopped parsley, 2 teaspoons finely chopped green onion and 1 teaspoon sugar after rubbing in the butter. Serve with morning coffee or as a savoury alternative at tea time.

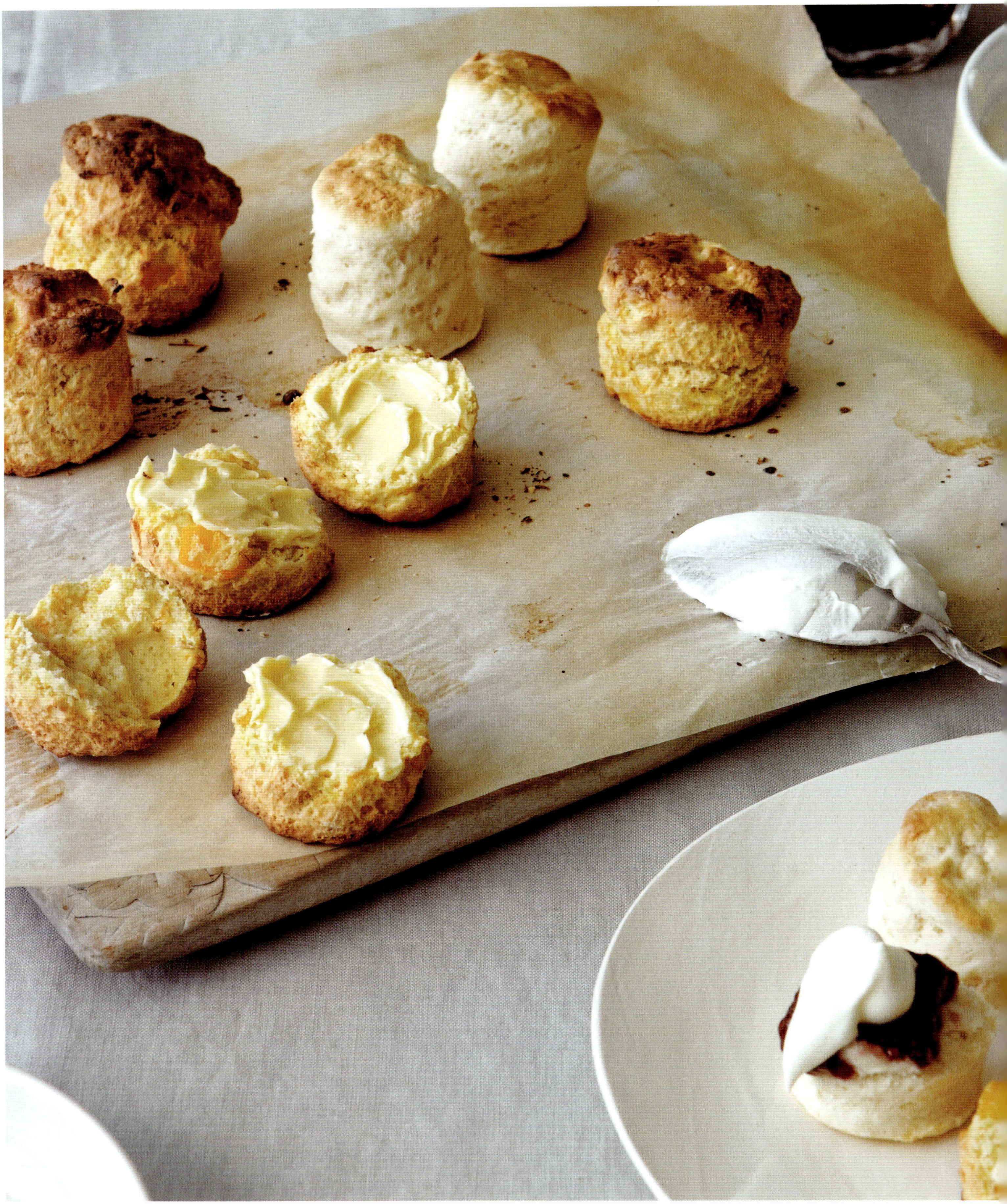

PUMPKIN SCONES

INGREDIENTS
2 cups (300 g) self-raising flour, plus a little extra
½ teaspoon salt
50 g butter, diced
¼ cup (55 g) caster sugar
1 cup drained cooked pumpkin, mashed and cooled
1 egg, beaten lightly
milk for glazing

I learnt to make scones badly at school. And then I learnt how to make them well. I think scones are the one recipe you need to see someone else make. It's so important to rub the butter in properly. Scones to me mean hospitality and warmth, there's just nothing like homemade scones. You can't resist them.

MAKES ABOUT 12

METHOD
Preheat the oven to 225°C. Grease a baking tray with butter.

Sift the flour and salt into a bowl. Rub in the butter, then add the sugar, pumpkin and egg. Mix into a dough, then turn out and knead lightly with a little extra flour. Pat out until 2.5 cm thick and cut into 5 cm rounds with a floured cutter. Lightly knead scraps and re-roll to cut out more scones.

Arrange on the prepared tray and brush the scones with a little milk.

Bake for 20 minutes or until risen and golden. Remove from the oven and wrap in a clean tea towel for a few minutes before splitting and buttering.

NOTE The pumpkin should not be too wet, and it should be mashed without the addition of milk or cream.

INGREDIENTS
2 cups (300 g) self-raising flour
1 teaspoon salt
1 teaspoon sugar
½ teaspoon bicarbonate of soda
60 g butter, diced
⅔–¾ cup buttermilk

BUTTERMILK SCONES

MAKES ABOUT 12

METHOD
Preheat the oven to 230°C.

Sift all the dry ingredients into a mixing bowl. Rub in the butter until the mixture resembles breadcrumbs. Add enough buttermilk to make a fairly soft dough.

Turn out onto a floured surface. Knead lightly, then pat or roll the dough out until about 2 cm thick. Cut into 5 cm rounds with a floured cutter. Place on ungreased baking trays and bake for 10–12 minutes or until golden.

GINGER OATMEAL SCONES

INGREDIENTS

1 cup (150 g) plain flour
1 tablespoon baking powder
2 teaspoons ground ginger
½ teaspoon ground allspice
½ teaspoon salt
1 cup one-minute oats
60 g butter, diced
2 teaspoons honey
¼ cup warm water
⅓ cup milk

MAKES ABOUT 12

METHOD

Preheat the oven to 230°C.

Sift the flour, baking powder, spices and salt into a bowl. Add the oats and rub in the butter. Mix together the honey, water and milk, blending thoroughly. Pour into the dry ingredients and mix to a soft dough.

On a floured surface, lightly pat the dough into a round about 2.5 cm thick. Cut into 5 cm rounds using a floured cutter or sharp knife.

Place on an ungreased baking tray and bake for 10–12 minutes. Serve warm with butter and ginger marmalade or apricot jam.

MARGARET FULTON BAKING

INGREDIENTS

2 cups (300 g) self-raising flour
1 teaspoon baking powder
1 teaspoon mixed spice
a pinch of salt
60 g butter, diced
1½ tablespoons caster sugar
2 tablespoons sultanas (optional)
1 tablespoon treacle
about ⅔ cup milk

TREACLE SCONES

MAKES ABOUT 12

METHOD

Preheat the oven to 230°C. Lightly grease a baking tray.

Sift the flour, baking powder, spice and salt into a bowl. Rub in the butter until the mixture resembles fine breadcrumbs. Stir in the sugar and sultanas, if using.

Gently heat the treacle in a small saucepan and mix thoroughly with half the milk. Add to the dry ingredients with enough of the remaining milk to make a soft dough.

Turn the dough onto a floured work surface and flatten to about 2 cm thick. Cut into 5 cm rounds or squares using a floured cutter or sharp knife. Place on the prepared baking tray and bake for 10–12 minutes or until well risen and golden brown.

Turn out on wire racks to cool.

INGREDIENTS

2 cups (300 g) self-raising flour
½ teaspoon salt
1½ cups (225 g) wholemeal self-raising flour
90 g butter, diced
about 1¼ cups milk

WHOLEMEAL SCONES

MAKES 8–12

METHOD

Preheat the oven to 200°C. Lightly flour a baking tray.

Sift the self-raising flour and salt into a mixing bowl. Stir in the wholemeal flour. Rub in the butter, then make a well in the centre and add sufficient milk to mix to a soft but not sticky dough.

Turn onto a lightly floured board and knead gently. Pat out into a round 2–2.5 cm thick. Place on the prepared baking tray and mark into 8–12 triangles with a sharp, floured knife. Bake for 25–30 minutes or until firm to the touch.

Turn out onto a wire rack to cool. Break into triangles, split in half and spread with butter, or serve with whipped cream and jam.

NOTE Variations given for Scones (see page 129) may also be used for Wholemeal Scones.

SAVOURY SCONE RING

INGREDIENTS

SCONE MIXTURE
2 cups (150 g) self-raising flour
1 teaspoon salt
a pinch of cayenne pepper
60 g butter, diced
½ cup grated cheddar cheese
1 egg, lightly beaten
¾ cup milk

FILLING
125 g (4 oz) salami, ham or corned beef, finely diced
2–3 gherkins, finely diced
2 teaspoons melted butter
2 teaspoons finely chopped parsley
1 small onion, finely chopped
¼ cup grated cheddar cheese
1 tablespoon tomato sauce
1 teaspoon Dijon mustard
salt and freshly ground black pepper

MAKES 10 SLICES

METHOD

Preheat the oven to 190°C. Lightly grease a baking tray.

Sift the flour, salt and cayenne into a bowl. Rub in the butter until the mixture resembles breadcrumbs and stir in the cheese. Mix the egg and milk; reserve about 1 tablespoon of this mixture and stir the remainder into the flour mixture with a knife to form a dough. Pat dough out to a rectangle about 30 cm x 20 cm.

To make the filling, mix the ingredients together and spread over the dough. Roll up from a long side and form into a ring, pressing the ends together to join.

Cut two-thirds of the way through the ring at 3 cm intervals and pull the slices a little way apart. Brush with the reserved egg and milk.

Place on the prepared baking tray and bake for 30–35 minutes. Serve warm.

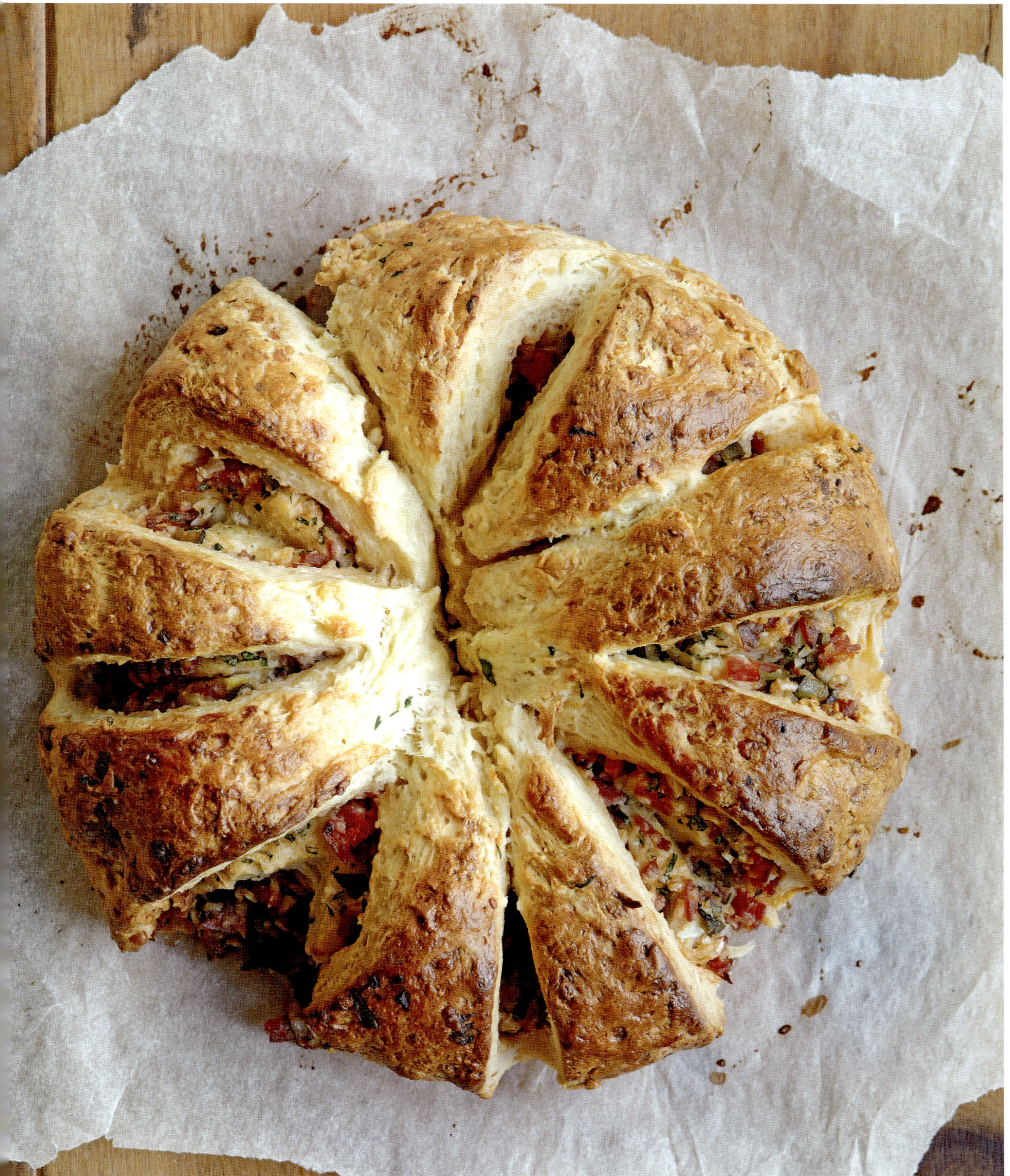

INGREDIENTS

SHORTCAKE PASTRY
2 cups (300 g) plain flour
a pinch of salt
185 g butter, diced
⅓ cup (50 g) icing sugar, sifted
2 egg yolks
a few drops of vanilla essence

FILLING
2 punnets (500 g) strawberries
1 cup cream
2 tablespoons icing sugar, sifted
a few drops of vanilla essence

CONTINENTAL STRAWBERRY SHORTCAKE

SERVES 8

METHOD

Sift the flour and salt onto a work surface and make a well in the centre. Put the remaining pastry ingredients in the well and work everything together with the fingertips of one hand. With the other hand, use a metal spatula to draw the flour quickly into the centre to make a smooth dough. Shape into a ball, wrap in plastic wrap and chill for 30 minutes.

Preheat the oven to 190°C. Lightly grease two baking trays.

Divide the dough in half and roll or pat out into two 23 cm rounds, about 5 mm thick. Place on the prepared baking trays. Prick all over with a fork and crimp the edges with fingers and thumb. Bake for 15–20 minutes or until the pastry is a pale biscuit colour. Do not allow to brown.

Remove from the oven and, while the pastry is warm, cut one round into eight segments. Cool the pastry on a wire rack.

Reserve eight of the best unhulled strawberries for decoration; hull and slice the remainder.

Whip the cream with the icing sugar and vanilla. Reserve one-third of the cream for decoration and mix the remainder with the sliced strawberries.

Place the whole pastry round on a serving plate and cover with the strawberry and cream mixture. Smooth, then arrange the eight pastry segments flat on top. Dust with extra sifted icing sugar and decorate with dollops of cream topped with reserved whole strawberries.

Leave for 1 hour before serving.

NOTE Other prepared fresh fruit (such as sliced peaches, plums, whole raspberries) can replace the strawberries, or use about 1½ cups cooked, puréed dried apricots or 1 quantity Lemon Butter (pages 254–255) or Passionfruit Butter (page 255) folded through the cream.

MUFFINS, SCONES, SHORTCAKES & QUICKBREADS *shortcakes*

INGREDIENTS
2 cups (300 g) plain flour
¼ cup (55 g) caster sugar
2 teaspoons baking powder
½ teaspoon salt
125 g butter, diced
1 egg
about ¾ cup milk
1 tablespoon butter, melted

FILLING
2 punnets (500 g) strawberries
⅓ cup (75 g) caster sugar
1 cup cream
2 tablespoons icing sugar, sifted

AMERICAN STRAWBERRY SHORTCAKE

American shortcake is a luscious dessert consisting of a tender, scone-like cake which is split, filled and topped with fruit and cream, and served warm. Rounds of rich pastry can also be layered with cream and fruit, lemon butter or passionfruit butter to make a Continental-style shortcake.

SERVES 8

METHOD

Make the filling first. Reserve a few of the best strawberries, unhulled to decorate. Hull the remainder and divide in half. Slice one lot in halves, place in a bowl and toss with ¼ cup sugar. Crush the other half of the strawberries with the remaining sugar. Whip the cream with the icing sugar until soft peaks form. Refrigerate the filling.

Preheat the oven to 220°C. Grease a 20 cm sandwich tin.

Sift the flour, sugar, baking powder and salt into a bowl. Rub the butter into the mixture with your fingertips until it forms crumbs the size of small peas. Break the egg into a measuring cup and add enough milk to measure ¾ cup; mix lightly.

Make a well in the centre of the flour mixture, add the milk and egg all at once and mix quickly with a fork until moistened. Turn the mixture into the prepared sandwich tin and smooth the top. Bake for 25–30 minutes or until a skewer inserted in the centre comes out clean.

To serve, immediately turn the shortcake out onto a wire rack and split into two layers. Place the bottom layer, cut side up, on a serving plate and brush with melted butter. Spoon on half of the crushed and sliced strawberries, put the other layer of cake on top, and spoon on the remaining strawberries. Pile the cream in the centre and decorate with the reserved whole strawberries. Serve immediately while still warm.

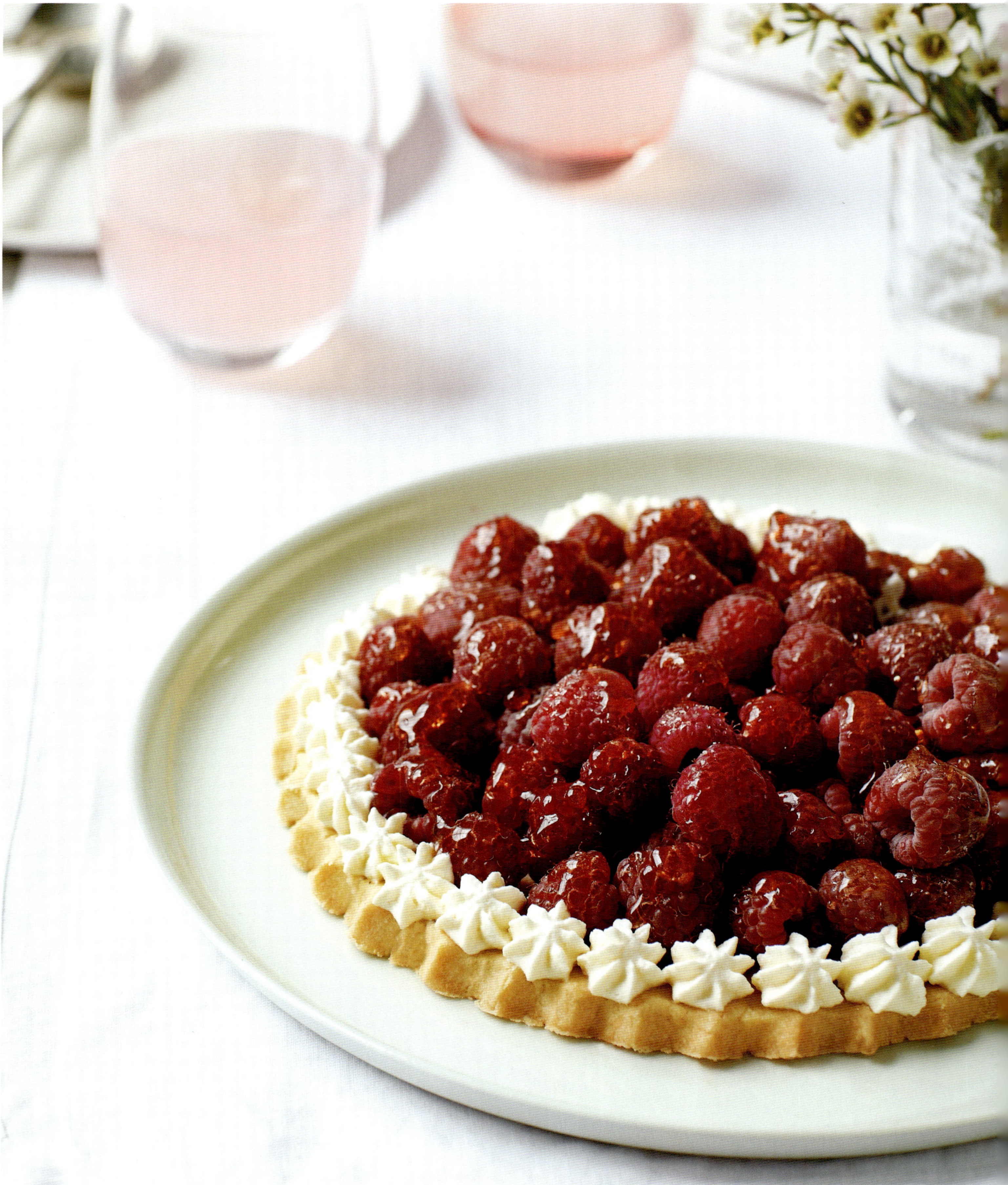

MUFFINS, SCONES, SHORTCAKES & QUICKBREADS *shortcakes*

INGREDIENTS
½ quantity Shortcake Pastry (from Continental Strawberry Shortcake, page 138)

TOPPING
2 punnets (400–500 g) raspberries
⅓ cup redcurrant jelly
1 tablespoon water
½ cup cream

DANISH RASPBERRY SHORTCAKE

I first tried this on a visit to Denmark. I loved Denmark and felt a great affinity with both Denmark and Finland. I think perhaps because there might be some link with the Scots. There is something in our humour and our approach to food that is similar.

SERVES 6

METHOD

Wrap the pastry in plastic wrap and chill for 30 minutes.

Preheat the oven to 190°C. Lightly grease a baking tray.

Roll or pat out the pastry to an 18–20 cm round and crimp the edges. Place on the prepared baking tray and bake for 15–20 minutes or until the pastry is a pale biscuit colour; do not allow to brown. Remove from the oven and cool on a wire rack.

Place the pastry on a serving plate and cover with the raspberries. Rub the redcurrant jelly through a sieve into a small, heavy saucepan. Add the water and heat slowly to boiling point, stirring, then boil until thick enough to coat a spoon thinly and the last drops are sticky as they fall from the spoon. Brush the warm glaze over the raspberries.

When the glaze is quite cold, whip the cream, and, using a piping bag fitted with a 1 cm star tube, pipe a border of tiny rosettes round the edge of the shortcake.

VARIATION

APRICOT SHORTCAKE Follow recipe for Danish Raspberry Shortcake but use well-drained poached or canned apricots instead of the raspberries, and replace the redcurrant glaze with apricot glaze (made by boiling ½ cup apricot jam with 2 tablespoons water, stirring frequently, until mixture is clear and will drop from a spoon). Brush pastry base with 2–3 tablespoons glaze before arranging the fruit on top, to prevent the juices from soaking into the pastry, then use the remaining glaze to brush over the fruit.

WHITE SODA BREAD

INGREDIENTS
5 cups (750 g) plain flour
1 teaspoon bicarbonate of soda
1 teaspoon salt
1 cup buttermilk or soured milk (see Note)

MAKES 1 LARGE LOAF OR 2 SMALL ONES

METHOD

Preheat the oven to 190°C. Lightly grease a baking tray.

Sift the dry ingredients into a bowl and make a well in the centre. Add the buttermilk or soured milk in a steady pouring stream, working in the flour with a large fork. The dough should be slack but not wet and the mixing done lightly and quickly. Add a little more milk if the dough seems too stiff.

With floured hands, turn the dough onto a lightly floured surface and flatten into a round about 4 cm thick. Put onto a greased baking tray and cut a large cross on top with a floured knife. (This is to ensure even distribution of heat.)

Bake for about 40 minutes. To test whether the loaf is cooked, insert a skewer in the centre (it should come out clean) or tap the base of the loaf with your knuckles (it should sound hollow).

Remove from the oven. To keep the bread soft, immediately wrap in a clean tea towel. Allow to cool before cutting.

VARIATIONS

BROWN SODA BREAD Make as for White Soda Bread, using 4 cups (600 g) wholemeal plain flour and 2 cups (300 g) white plain flour. A little more milk will be needed to mix the dough. If a brittle texture is required, add 1 tablespoon melted butter. The bread is best cut when it is quite cold.

TREACLE SODA BREAD Make as for White Soda Bread, but heat 2 tablespoons molasses with the milk, and add $1^{1}/_{2}$ teaspoons sugar and $^{1}/_{2}$ cup sultanas, if liked, to the dough.

NOTE If buttermilk or soured milk is not available, 1 cup fresh milk may be used, in which case add 1 teaspoon cream of tartar to the dry ingredients. Or to sour milk, stir a dash of lemon juice or vinegar into regular milk.

OATMEAL SODA BREAD

INGREDIENTS
1 cup (150 g) wholemeal plain flour
1 cup (150 g) white plain flour
1 teaspoon baking powder
1 teaspoon bicarbonate of soda
1 teaspoon sugar
1 teaspoon salt
1½ cups fine oatmeal
1¼ cups buttermilk or soured milk (see Note, opposite)

MAKES 1 SMALL LOAF

METHOD

Preheat the oven to 190°C. Lightly grease a baking tray.

Sift the flours, baking powder, bicarbonate of soda, sugar and salt into a large bowl and mix in the oatmeal. Stir in the buttermilk or soured milk and mix lightly and quickly to a soft dough.

Turn the dough out on a floured surface, knead once or twice and shape lightly into a round. Place on the prepared baking tray. Using a floured sharp knife, cut a cross in the top of the loaf.

Bake for about 1 hour. To test whether the loaf is cooked, insert a skewer in the centre (it should come out clean) or tap the base of the loaf with your knuckles (it should sound hollow).

Remove from the oven. To keep the bread soft, immediately wrap in a clean tea towel.

Serve while still warm, sliced, with plenty of butter.

INGREDIENTS

4 tablespoons melted butter
½ cup (75 g) plain flour
2½ teaspoons baking powder
1 tablespoon caster sugar
½ teaspoon salt
1½ cups yellow cornmeal (polenta)
1 egg, at room temperature
¾ cup milk, at room temperature

CORNBREAD OR MUFFINS

I had cornbread for the first time when visiting Mexico. You learn to respect the maizes and meals the people use there. I just loved the cornbread. I loved how the Mexicans made a lot of their food, like refried beans and things that were so simple yet delicious. But the cornbread in particular I took a great fancy to.

MAKES 1 LOAF OR 12 MUFFINS

METHOD

Use 1½ tablespoons of the melted butter to grease a shallow 29 cm x 18 cm cake tin or twelve ⅓ cup muffin tins. Place in the top half of a preheated 220°C oven until sizzling hot.

Have all the other ingredients at room temperature. Sift the flour, baking powder, sugar and salt into a bowl and stir in the cornmeal. Beat together the egg, milk and remaining butter, pour into the dry ingredients and combine with a few rapid strokes; the batter will be lumpy.

Spoon the batter into the hot cake tin or muffin tins and bake for about 15 minutes for muffins or 25 minutes for corn bread, or until well risen, browned and cooked when tested with a skewer. Serve immediately.

INGREDIENTS

2 cups (300 g) self-raising flour
⅔ cup (100 g) plain flour
1 teaspoon salt
½ teaspoon bicarbonate of soda
2 small or 1 large zucchini, coarsely grated
¾ cup grated cheddar cheese
1 salad onion, finely chopped
⅓ cup chopped coriander or parsley
2 eggs
1½ cups (375 ml) buttermilk
60 g butter, melted

ZUCCHINI & CHEESE QUICKBREAD

This is the kind of quickbread that makes a meal out of a bowl of soup or salad. I also love it toasted the next day with eggs for breakfast.

MAKES 1 LOAF

METHOD

Preheat the oven to 190°C. Grease a 23 cm x 13 cm loaf tin.

Sift the flours, salt and bicarbonate of soda into a large bowl and add the grated zucchini, cheese, onion and coriander or parsley. Toss together until well mixed.

In another bowl beat the eggs with the buttermilk and butter. Add to the dry ingredients and mix together lightly.

Turn the mixture into the prepared tin and bake for 55 minutes to 1 hour, until a skewer in the centre comes out clean.

Leave in the tin for a few minutes, then turn out onto a wire rack to cool.

INGREDIENTS

4 cups (600 g) self-raising flour
1 teaspoon salt
30 g butter, diced, or dripping
1 cup milk
½ cup water

DAMPER

The traditional Australian bush bread, damper was once made from flour, salt, water and perhaps some dripping. It was baked directly in the ashes of the fire or in a camp oven. Today, milk and butter are used and the damper is baked in a hot oven or, if cooked in the fire, is usually wrapped in several layers of foil so that there is no need to knock the ashes off before eating it.

MAKES ONE 20 CM LOAF

METHOD

Preheat the oven to 200°C. Grease a baking tray and flour it well.

Sift the flour and salt into a large mixing bowl. Rub in the fat. Make a well in the flour and pour in the milk and water. Mix with a knife until the dough leaves the sides of the bowl; add a little more flour if the dough is too slack.

Transfer to the prepared baking tray and pat out to a round about 20 cm across. Cut a cross in the top.

Bake for 25 minutes, then reduce the oven temperature to 180°C and bake for a further 15–20 minutes or until the damper sounds hollow when tapped on the base.

Serve sliced with butter, cheese and chutney, golden syrup or jam.

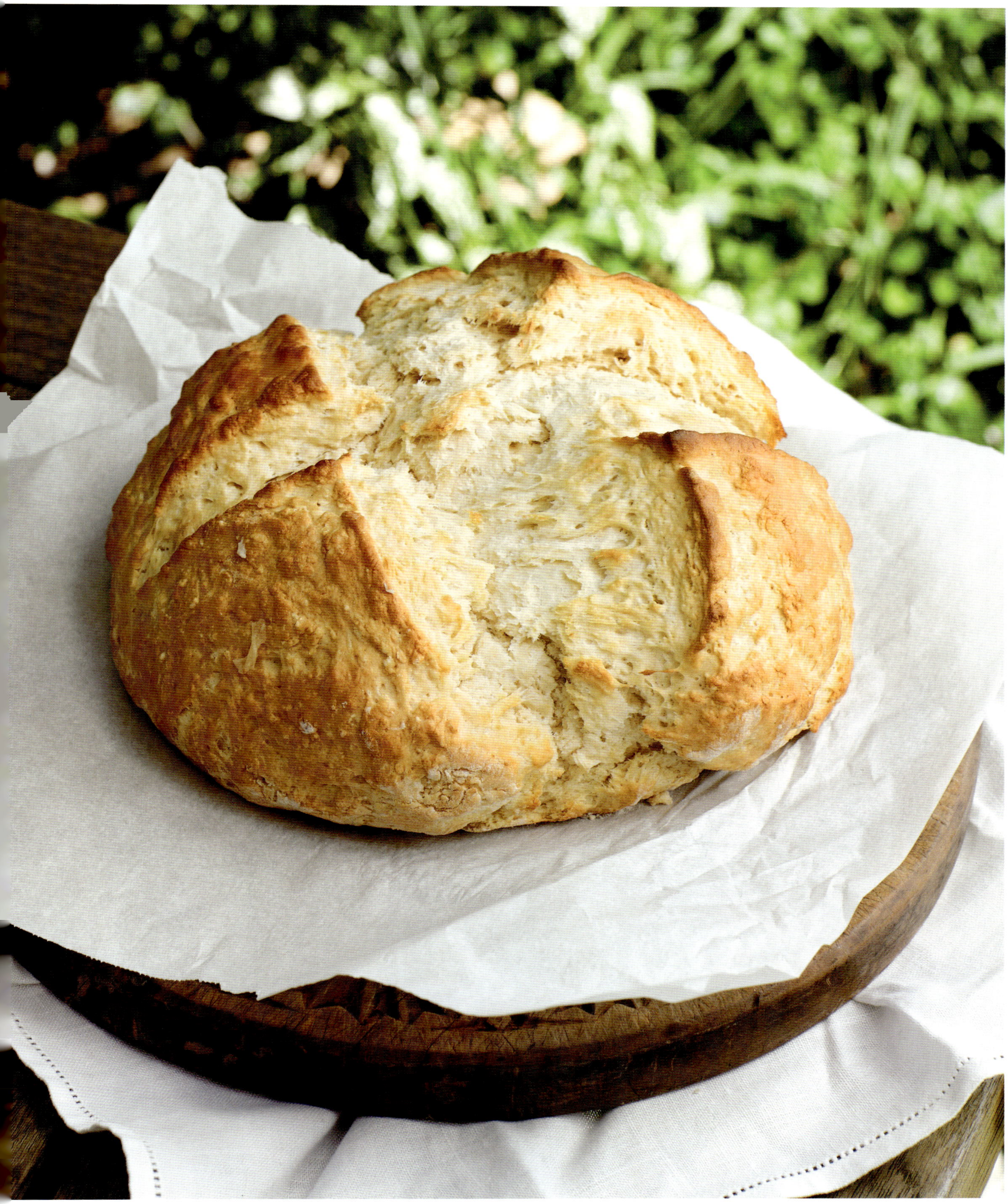

INGREDIENTS

2¼ cups (335 g) plain flour
¼ teaspoon bicarbonate of soda
1 teaspoon salt
¾ cup buttermilk
90 g butter, melted
1 tablespoon molasses or golden syrup

BUTTERMILK BREAD

SERVES 6

METHOD

Preheat the oven to 190°C. Lightly grease a baking tray.

Sift the flour, bicarbonate of soda and salt into a bowl. Stir in the buttermilk, 60 g of the butter and the molasses or golden syrup to form a soft dough.

Transfer the dough to a floured surface and knead until just smooth and elastic. Pat into a round loaf about 15 cm in diameter. With a sharp knife, score the loaf to make six wedges, cutting about 1 cm into the dough. Place on the prepared baking tray.

Bake for 30 minutes or until a skewer inserted in the centre comes out clean. Brush the hot loaf with the remaining melted butter and transfer to a wire rack to cool.

Serve cut into wedges and buttered, with salad or soups.

MUFFINS, SCONES, SHORTCAKES & QUICKBREADS *plain & savoury quickbreads*

INGREDIENTS
2 cups (300 g) plain flour
1½ teaspoons sea salt
1 teaspoon sugar
2 tablespoons poppy seeds
2 tablespoons sesame seeds
1 egg, lightly beaten
1 cup milk
60 g unsalted butter, melted

LAVASH

You can buy lavash (sometimes called lavoche) in delis or gourmet food stores but they are a breeze to make yourself and the result is every bit as good, if not better. Lavash are great for entertaining when arranged in a napkin-lined basket alongside a pâté or a bowl of dip, or as a base for a cheese platter.

MAKES ABOUT 100 5 CM X 3 CM CRACKERS

METHOD

Sift the flour, salt and sugar into a large mixing bowl and stir in the poppy and sesame seeds. Make a well in the centre and add the egg, then the milk and melted butter. Slowly incorporate the flour into the liquids to form a dough.

Knead the dough lightly on a floured board, then wrap in plastic wrap and chill for an hour or so.

Preheat the oven to 180°C. Lightly grease baking trays.

Cut the dough into quarters and roll very thinly, one piece at a time, to 40 cm x 10 cm rectangles – it doesn't matter if you get a few holes. Cut across into serving-sized rectangles or leave in large pieces to break up later, after they are cooked.

Place on the prepared baking trays and bake for 8 minutes or until dry and pale golden. Transfer to wire racks to cool and store in an airtight container.

INGREDIENTS

1½ cups (225 g) plain flour
½ teaspoon salt
2 teaspoons baking powder
½ cup (110 g) caster sugar
½ cup walnut pieces
1 egg, beaten
½ cup milk

SIMPLE WALNUT TEA BREAD

MAKES 2

METHOD

Preheat the oven to 180°C. Grease a 21 cm x 11 cm loaf tin.

Sift the flour, salt and baking powder into a bowl. Add the sugar and walnuts, then stir in the egg and milk. Mix until smooth.

Spoon into the prepared loaf tin and bake for 45 minutes or until a skewer inserted in the centre comes out clean.

Cool on a wire rack. Serve sliced with butter, and cheese if desired.

NOTE If you're not keen on the bitter edge that walnuts sometimes have, they can be replaced with pecans, which are milder.

INGREDIENTS

2 cups (300 g) self-raising flour
a pinch of salt
60 g butter, diced
¼ cup (55 g) caster sugar
⅔ cup raisins, roughly chopped
1 cup chopped walnuts
1 egg, beaten
1 tablespoon golden syrup
1 cup buttermilk

TOPPING

1 tablespoon sugar
2 tablespoons chopped walnuts
a little buttermilk

RAISIN & WALNUT LOAF

A beautiful loaf that keeps fresh for days if stored in an airtight container. Leave to cool completely before cutting and serve sliced, with butter if liked.

MAKES ONE LARGE LOAF

METHOD

Preheat the oven to 180°C. Grease a 23 cm x 13 cm loaf tin.

Sift the flour and salt into a mixing bowl. Rub in the butter until the mixture resembles breadcrumbs, then add the sugar, raisins and walnuts and mix well until combined.

Stir the beaten egg and golden syrup into the buttermilk. Add to the dry ingredients and beat well. Spoon into the prepared loaf tin. Level the top with a spatula.

To make the topping, mix the sugar and walnuts. Brush the loaf with buttermilk, and sprinkle the sugar and nuts over the top. Press gently with a spatula to make sure the topping sticks to the loaf.

Bake for 1 hour 20 minutes or until quite firm to touch. Cool in the tin for 5 minutes, then turn out onto a wire rack to cool completely.

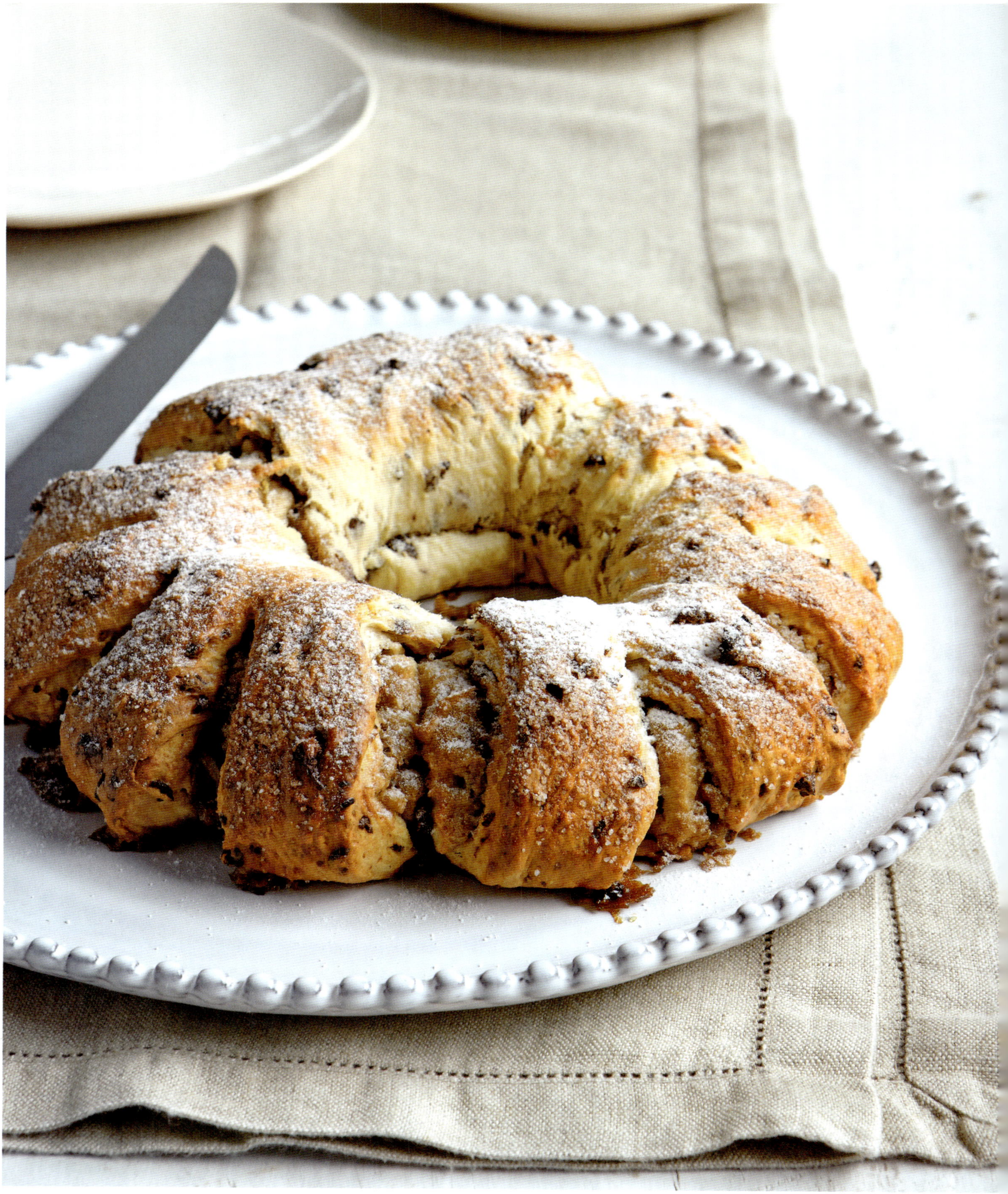

FRUIT & NUT TEA RING

MAKES 10 SLICES

INGREDIENTS

DOUGH
2¼ cups (335 g) self-raising flour
a pinch of salt
60 g butter, diced
¼ cup (55 g) caster sugar
½ cup finely chopped dates or raisins
1 egg yolk
¾ cup milk

FILLING
30 g butter, melted
⅓ cup (75 g) firmly packed brown sugar
¼ cup finely chopped walnuts
1 teaspoon ground cinnamon

GLAZE
egg white, beaten until foamy
white sugar

METHOD

Preheat the oven to 220°C. Grease a baking tray.

Sift the flour and salt into a bowl. Rub in the butter and stir in the sugar and dates or raisins. Mix the egg yolk and milk and stir in quickly with a knife. Pat out the dough to a rectangle 2 cm thick.

To make the filling, mix the ingredients and spread over the dough. Roll up from a long side and form into a ring, pressing the ends together to join. Cut two-thirds of the way through the ring at 3 cm intervals and spread the slices a little way apart. Brush with the beaten egg white and sprinkle with sugar.

Place on the prepared tray and bake for 20–25 minutes or until risen and golden. Serve warm.

INGREDIENTS

1 2/3 cups (250 g) self-raising flour
a pinch of salt
1 teaspoon mixed spice
60 g butter, softened
1/3 cup (75 g) caster sugar
grated rind of 1 lemon
3/4 cup sultanas
1/4 cup treacle
1 egg, beaten
1/2 teaspoon bicarbonate of soda
1/2 cup milk

BARABRITH (WELSH FRUIT BREAD)

MAKES 1 LARGE LOAF

METHOD

Preheat the oven to 180°C. Line a 23 cm x 13 cm loaf tin with baking paper.

Sift the flour, salt and spice into a bowl. Rub in the butter until the mixture resembles breadcrumbs. Stir in the sugar, lemon rind and sultanas. Add the treacle and egg.

Dissolve the bicarbonate of soda in the milk, add to the flour mixture and mix until well blended, adding a little more milk if the mixture is to thick to mix thoroughly. Pour into the prepared loaf tin.

Bake for about 1 hour 25 minutes or until a skewer inserted in the centre comes out clean. Turn out onto a wire rack to cool completely.

Wrap in foil and store for 24 hours before serving, sliced and buttered.

INGREDIENTS

2 ¾ cups (410 g) self-raising flour
¼ teaspoon salt
1 tablespoon grated orange rind
¾ cup (165 g) caster sugar
1 egg
¼ cup orange juice
1¼ cups milk
30 g butter, melted
¾ cup chopped dates

ORANGE & DATE QUICKBREAD

MAKES 1 LOAF

METHOD

Preheat the oven to 180°C. Line a 23 cm x 13 cm loaf tin with baking paper.

Sift the flour and salt into a bowl and stir in the orange rind and sugar. Beat together the egg, orange juice, milk and melted butter and stir in the dates. Pour onto the flour mixture and combine the ingredients with a few swift strokes, stirring lightly until just blended.

Pour into the prepared loaf tin. Bake for 50–55 minutes or until a skewer inserted in the centre comes out clean.

Cool on a wire rack. Serve warm, preferably, with butter.

OAT & RAISIN BREAD

INGREDIENTS
1 egg, beaten
1/3 cup (75 g) firmly packed brown sugar
2 tablespoons golden syrup, warmed
1 1/4 cups buttermilk
60 g butter, melted
2/3 cup rolled oats
1 cup (150 g) wholemeal plain flour
2 teaspoons baking powder
3/4 teaspoon salt
3/4 teaspoon bicarbonate of soda
2/3 cup raisins

MAKES 1 LOAF

METHOD

Preheat the oven to 180°C. Grease a 20 cm x 10 cm loaf tin and line it with baking paper.

Mix the egg with the sugar, syrup, buttermilk, butter and rolled oats. Let stand for 5 minutes.

Sift the flour, baking powder, salt and bicarbonate of soda and fold into the oat mixture. Stir in the raisins lightly.

Turn into the prepared loaf tin and spread the batter evenly with a spatula.

Bake for 1 hour or until a skewer inserted in the centre comes out clean. Cool on a wire rack. Serve sliced and spread with butter.

MUFFINS, SCONES, SHORTCAKES & QUICKBREADS *sweet quickbreads*

INGREDIENTS

3 ripe bananas, well mashed
2 eggs, well beaten
1 2/3 cups (250 g) plain flour
3/4 cup (165 g) caster sugar
1 teaspoon salt
1 teaspoon bicarbonate of soda
1/2 cup coarsely chopped walnuts

BANANA NUT BREAD

This is a simple banana bread, heavy, moist and dark. Recipes such as this and Banana Cake (page 184) are an excellent way to use up overripe bananas.

MAKES 1 LOAF

METHOD

Preheat the oven to 180°C. Grease a 21 cm x 11 cm loaf tin.

Mix the bananas and eggs together in a large bowl. Sift in the flour, sugar, salt and bicarbonate of soda. Mix in the walnuts. Spoon the batter into the prepared loaf tin and bake for 1 hour or until a skewer inserted in the centre comes out clean.

Turn out onto a wire rack. Serve still warm or cooled, as you like, with butter.

NOTE The walnuts can be omitted, or replaced with pecans if you prefer.

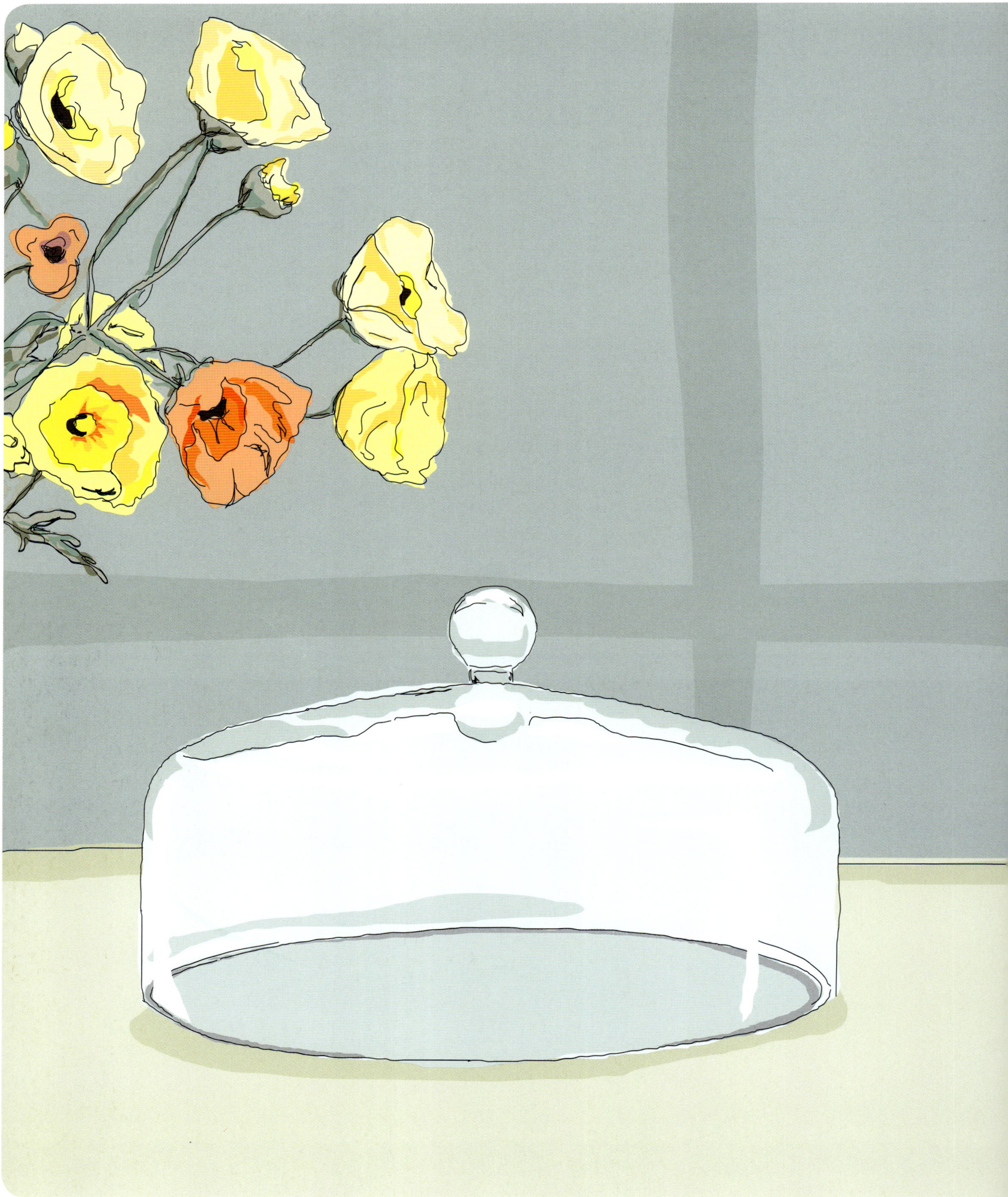

CAKES
CHAPTER 4

HINTS & TIPS

A freshly baked home-made cake has no rival when it comes to flavour. The methods of making cakes may vary, but their popular appeal does not. A good recipe is essential, for this is one branch of cookery where indiscriminate inspiration does not work. The balance of ingredients is critical. Perhaps our grandmothers didn't use a recipe, but they had a sure eye and an experienced hand. Until you have both, don't experiment. Follow a recipe carefully and you'll soon be turning out lovely treats like the best of them.

TYPES OF CAKES
Cakes are categorised according to their ingredients or the method by which they are made.

BUTTER CAKES
Butter cakes are so called because they have a high proportion of butter. There are several methods. Most common is the creaming method, in which butter and sugar are beaten to a creamy consistency first, then the egg is beaten in, and lastly the flour is added. There is also the melting method, which for many cooks is easier; the butter is melted and the remaining ingredients are folded in. Lastly, there is the rubbing-in method, in which the butter is rubbed into the flour then the remaining ingredients are added. The basic butter cake mixture can be varied in many ways; see, for example, page 164.

TEA CAKES
Although certain yeast-based buns are sometimes known as tea cakes, the Australian-style tea cakes in this book are halfway between a sponge and a butter cake. Quickly made from store-cupboard staples, tea cakes are lighter and less rich than butter cakes. With less butter and egg than butter cakes, they do not have the same keeping qualities and are meant to be eaten the day they are made. The butter may be rubbed in or melted depending on the recipe. Tea cakes often have a filling or topping of apple slices or cinnamon, and are so called because they are traditionally served, still warm, as an accompaniment to tea.

QUICK-MIX CAKES
These are also sometimes called 'one-bowl' cakes, because they are made by mixing all the ingredients simultaneously in one bowl. If you are new to baking, or not very confident, quick-mix recipes are good ones to start with. To make mixing easy, the specified fat is often melted butter, but it can be oil or sour cream. There are many delicious cakes made by the quick-mix method. Don't try to adapt ordinary recipes, but use those especially created for quick mixing.

SPONGE CAKES
The lightness of a good sponge depends on beating air into the eggs. There are two basic ways of making a sponge cake. The first method is to beat whole eggs with sugar until thick and light, then fold in the flour – this is called a whisked sponge. The second way is to separate the eggs, make a meringue of the whites and sugar, then add beaten yolks and flour. This is called a sponge sandwich.

The French make a slightly different version called Génoise (page 202), with melted butter added. It is used as the basis for petits fours and other decorated cakes. Swiss rolls are another type of sponge, baked in a shallow tin, rolled while warm, then re-rolled around a filling.

Sponge cakes (except Génoise) contain only a tiny amount of butter, so they don't keep as well as butter cakes, and are at their best when eaten freshly made.

Tins for sponge cakes should have their bases lined with baking paper and the sides should be lightly greased with melted butter, then floured. All sponge cakes should be baked as soon as they are mixed. To test if a sponge is cooked, look for shrinkage around the edge of the tin, and press the centre lightly with your fingers. It will spring back when cooked.

FRUIT CAKES

There are two types: light and dark. They may be made by first creaming the butter and sugar, or by the melt-and-mix method, in which the liquid ingredients (including melted butter) are mixed into the dry ingredients. Many fruit cakes have excellent keeping qualities, and even improve with age. In fact, Christmas cakes are traditionally made a couple of months before Christmas to give them time to mature. The Christmas Cake (page 218) will keep, if stored properly, for 6 months.

CONTINENTAL CAKES

Continental cakes have a richer, closer texture than butter, sponge or quick-mix cakes. When they contain a high proportion of ground nuts instead of flour they are often referred to as tortes, and when they are split into many layers and decorated they may be called gâteaux.

In Continental cakes rich butter-cream fillings are used, and different types of liqueurs, chocolate or coffee are favourite flavourings. Nuts and fruit are used as decorations, and often the cake is chilled before serving. Springform tins make it easy to turn out the richer mixtures, and the interestingly shaped gugelhopf, bundt and ring tins give authentic shapes to Continental cakes.

MAKING CAKES
BEFORE YOU START

READ THE RECIPE THROUGH IN FULL before you start, to ensure you have all the equipment and ingredients.

PREPARE THE TINS before you start making your cake. Make sure they are the correct size and well greased. For some recipes, you will need to line the bases with baking paper cut to fit (see box below). The size of the tin is usually stated but, as a general rule, the mixture should fill the tin by no more than two-thirds. As it bakes, the mixture should rise to the rim or slightly above.

SET THE OVEN SHELF IN POSITION and preheat the oven to the required temperature. Check the oven temperature guide (see page 10) and also check the chart that belongs to your stove for oven positions and temperatures, as these will vary with different types.

HAVE EGGS, BUTTER AND MILK at room temperature for easy mixing and good results.

LINING A TIN WITH BAKING PAPER

Baking paper has a non-stick surface and is very handy to have in the kitchen. Some recipes will tell you to line only the base of the tin, others to line the base and the sides.

When lining a tin with baking paper it is useful to lightly grease the tin first to secure the baking paper in place and prevent it from sliding around. If you are making a meringue mixture on a baking tray, you can secure the baking paper with a few small dabs of the meringue.

Place the cake tin on the baking paper and trace around it. Cut out just inside the line. Cut a strip of paper the circumference and height of the tin. Fit the strip of paper to the sides of the tin and the base piece into the bottom of the tin.

Some recipes (for example, for a soufflé) might tell you to make a paper collar for a tin or dish. In this case, cut a strip of paper the circumference of the tin or dish and the height specified in the recipe (usually a few centimetres taller than the tin or dish). Use to line the tin, or tie on the outside of the dish using kitchen twine, as specified in the recipe.

MIXING & BAKING

IF CREAMING BUTTER AND SUGAR, beat them very thoroughly until very pale and fluffy. Once a light mixture is achieved, add the eggs. Caster sugar is best for cakes, as it dissolves more readily and gives a fine texture. When using an electric mixer, add a little of the cake's liquid when creaming butter and sugar as it helps to dissolve the sugar. When creaming butter or beating in sugar by hand, use a long lifting motion from the bottom of the bowl to trap as much air as possible into the cake mixture.

IF MELTING INGREDIENTS, do not let them boil unless the recipe specifies.

EGGS SHOULD BE BEATEN LIGHTLY and added gradually. If using an electric mixer, it is not necessary to beat the eggs first, simply add them one at a time. Be sure to beat well after each addition. If the creamed mixture looks like it is beginning to curdle or separate, sift in a little flour (about 1 tablespoon) alternately with each egg.

IF THE MIXTURE CONTAINS WHISKED EGG WHITES, ensure your bowl and beaters or whisk are scrupulously clean; the slightest trace of fat will prevent the whites from reaching their full volume. Whisk the whites until stiff but not too dry. Add a spoonful of whisked egg whites to the cake mixture and mix in thoroughly to soften the mixture. Then finally, fold in the remaining egg whites with a large metal spoon, using large cut-and-fold motions to the bottom of the bowl and back to the top.

SIFT POWDERED AND GROUND INGREDIENTS (such as raising agents and spices) together with the flour so they are evenly dispersed.

WHEN FOLDING IN SIFTED DRY INGREDIENTS alternately with the liquid, always begin and end with the flour mixture. Be careful not to beat the mixture, and use a large metal spoon to lift it up gently from the bottom to the top. Give the bowl a small turn between scoops.

TURN THE MIXTURE INTO THE TIN Thinner mixtures can be poured into the prepared tin; thicker mixtures will need to be spooned. Scrape all the batter out of the bowl using a spatula. If necessary, smooth the surface of a thick mixture using the spatula.

LEAVE THE OVEN DOOR CLOSED for the first half of the cooking time, or the cake may collapse (sponge cakes should be left undisturbed for the entire cooking time). When opening and closing the oven door, do so gently.

ABOUT HALFWAY THROUGH THE COOKING TIME, check the cake. If it is cooking unevenly, turn the tin around. Check again 10–15 minutes from the end of the stated cooking time. If the cake is browning too much, loosely cover the top with a sheet of foil or baking paper.

TESTING & COOLING

LEARN TO TEST WHEN A CAKE IS COOKED Lightly press the centre of the cake. If it springs back, it is safe to bring it out of the oven. If your finger leaves an impression, leave the cake in the oven a little longer. A well-cooked cake should also shrink just a little from the sides of the tin. Or buy a fine cake tester, which can be inserted into the centre of the cake and must come out clean.

WHEN REMOVING A CAKE FROM THE OVEN, avoid a draught. Most cakes will need to be left it in the tin for a few minutes after removal from the oven, so they can firm up a little before being turned out. However, this is a general rule only – always check the recipe, as some cakes (such as flourless cakes) need to be cooled completely in the tin before being turned out, or they will break.

TO TURN A CAKE OUT, put a wire rack (or, if you have only one rack, use a large plate) on top of the tin. Using oven gloves, grasp the whole lot and invert it. Ease the tin off the cake. To turn the cake the right way up, put a second wire rack on top of the cake and invert the whole lot again.

IF A CAKE STICKS OR WON'T LEAVE THE TIN, put the tin on a damp cloth for a few minutes to help ease it.

LEAVE THE CAKE TO COOL COMPLETELY before icing or filling it, otherwise the icing or filling will melt. However if you are going to drizzle the cake with hot syrup, do so while the cake is still hot.

CAKES *hints & tips*

STORING

IF YOU'RE GOING TO EAT ALL THE CAKE the day it was made, or even the next day, there is no need to refrigerate it. It should simply be put under a cake dome or in a plastic container and left at room temperature.

IF THE CAKE HAS BEEN CUT, it is worthwhile pressing a piece of plastic wrap against the cut edges to prevent them from drying out. Otherwise place the cake in an airtight plastic container and keep in the refrigerator. Remember to take it out in time to reach room temperature again before eating. Most cakes shouldn't be served chilled.

RICH FRUIT CAKES, such as those made for Christmas and wedding cakes, may be stored (un-iced) in an airtight container. If they are to be stored for a long time, a wrapping of baking paper or foil helps them to age well. Once the cake is cut a wedge of unpeeled apple may be placed beside the cake to enhance freshness – replace with fresh apple as needed.

MOST CAKES CAN BE FROZEN for up to 4 months. The richer the cake, the better it will freeze and retain its flavour and texture on thawing. So rich chocolate cakes, cheesecakes and butter cakes freeze very well. Sponge cakes, on the other hand, have little fat, and will lose their flavour and texture in less than 2 months. Wrap the cake airtight in freezer wrap then in foil before placing in a plastic bag and labelling with the type of cake and the date. Thaw frozen cakes without unwrapping.

TROUBLESHOOTING

A perfect cake should have a light, moist and even texture, with a golden brown crust (unless it is a chocolate cake). If it is a fruit cake, the fruit should be evenly distributed. A skewer inserted in the centre should come out clean, or (for lighter mixtures such as sponges) the cake should spring back when lightly pressed with a fingertip.

However, sometimes a cake will not turn out as you expected or hoped. The following lists some of the common problems and their causes.

BUTTER CAKES, TEA CAKES & CONTINENTAL CAKES

UNDERCOOKED The cake is dense and soggy and has sunk in the centre. A skewer inserted comes out sticky.
CAUSE The cooking time may have been too short or the oven temperature too low. The oven door may have been opened in the early stages of cooking. Too much butter or too little flour may have been used in the mixture.

OVERCOOKED The cake is dry and the crust is very dark.
CAUSE The oven temperature may have been too high or the cooking time too long. The tin may have been the wrong size, or placed too high in the oven.

SPONGE CAKES

UNDERCOOKED The cake is pale and sticky. The cake has not risen properly.
CAUSE The cooking time was too short. The oven door may have been opened during the cooking time.

OVERCOOKED The cake is quite dark on top, has shrunk well away from the side of the tin, and is dry.
CAUSE The egg whites may have been overbeaten. The oven temperature may have been too high or the cooking time too long. The cake may have been placed too high in the oven, or the tin may have been the wrong size.

FRUIT CAKES

UNDERCOOKED The cake is quite pale and has sunk in the centre. The cake is dense and soggy.
CAUSE There might be too little raising agent or too much fruit. The oven temperature may have been too low or the cooking time too short. The tin might not have been placed in the middle of the oven.

OVERCOOKED The crust is very dark and the texture of the cake dry.
CAUSE The cake may have been cooked for too long, or at too high a temperature. The mixture may have too much raising agent or too little butter. The tin may not have been properly lined; due to the long cooking time, the tin should be lined with two layers of brown paper and one layer of baking paper, to protect the cake.

INGREDIENTS

160 g butter, softened
¾ cup (165 g) caster sugar
1 teaspoon vanilla essence
3 eggs, lightly beaten
1⅔ cups (250 g) self-raising flour
a pinch of salt
½ cup milk
whipped cream, jam or Lemon Butter (pages 254–255)

BASIC BUTTER CAKE

Follow this basic butter cake recipe and try a few simple variations such as adding grated orange or lemon rind, sultanas, spices or chopped nuts. Vary the cake tins to make a deeper cake, a loaf or a bar; see Note.

SERVES 8

METHOD

Preheat the oven to 180°C. Grease two 20 cm sandwich tins and line the bases with baking paper.

Using an electric mixer, cream the butter and gradually beat in the sugar with the vanilla, until the mixture is light and fluffy. Gradually beat in the beaten eggs. If using an electric mixer, add the eggs one at a time and beat well after each.

Sift the flour and salt (some cooks do this three times), and then fold into the creamed mixture alternately with the milk, beginning and ending with flour (it is important not to overwork the mixture). Add a little more milk if necessary so that the mixture drops easily from the spoon. Spoon the mixture into the prepared tins and lightly smooth the top.

Bake for 25–30 minutes, or until a skewer inserted in the centre comes out clean. Turn out onto wire racks to cool.

Sandwich with whipped cream, jam or lemon butter and ice as liked.

VARIATIONS

LEMON CAKE Add the grated rind of 1 lemon and 2 teaspoons lemon juice, but omit the vanilla essence.

CHOCOLATE CAKE Sift 3 tablespoons Dutch cocoa with the flour and salt, then add ¼ cup extra milk to the mixture.

SPICE CAKE Sift 2 teaspoons spice (ground ginger, ground cinnamon, ground cardamom or mixed spice) with the flour. Add ⅔ cup chopped dates or chopped walnuts to the mixture.

SULTANA CAKE Fold in ¾ cup sultanas and 1 teaspoon ground cinnamon or mixed spice.

SEED CAKE Add 1 tablespoon caraway seeds to the mixture and sprinkle an extra teaspoon of seeds on top before baking.

NOTE If making one larger cake in a deep 20 cm tin, it will require 45–50 minutes baking time. A 23 cm x 13 cm loaf tin will take 30–40 minutes.

INGREDIENTS

250 g butter, softened
grated rind of half a lemon
1¾ cups (385 g) caster sugar
5 eggs
2¾ cups (410 g) plain flour
2 teaspoons baking powder
a pinch of ground cinnamon
a pinch of salt
½ cup milk
⅓ cup blanched almonds or 3 thin slices candied lemon peel

MADEIRA CAKE

This traditional British cake has the refreshing tang of lemon and orange; it was usually baked with a slice of candied citron peel on top. Citron peel can be difficult to find, so use chopped mixed candied peel or sliced glacé orange. Serve with a glass of Madeira if you like, as was the custom in Victorian England.

SERVES 10

METHOD

Preheat the oven to 180°C. Grease a deep 22 cm cake tin and line the base and sides with baking paper.

Using an electric mixer, cream the butter with the lemon rind and add the sugar gradually. Beat until the mixture is light and fluffy.

Beat in the eggs, one at a time, with a small spoonful of flour added near the end. Sift the remaining flour with the baking powder, cinnamon and salt, and fold into the mixture with the milk.

Spoon into the prepared tin and arrange the almonds or the peel on top. Bake for about 1½ hours, or until a skewer inserted into the centre comes out clean. After 1 hour, reduce the heat to 160°C.

Cool in the tin on a wire rack for 10 minutes, then turn out to cool completely.

ORANGE MARMALADE CAKE

SERVES 8–10

INGREDIENTS
185 g butter, softened
1 cup (220 g) caster sugar
3 eggs
3 tablespoons orange marmalade (see Note)
2½ cups (375 g) self-raising flour, sifted
¼ teaspoon salt
grated rind of 2 oranges
½ cup fresh orange juice, strained

GLAZE
2 oranges
¼ cup orange juice (reserved from the orange used for zesting)
1½ cups caster sugar
¾ cup water

METHOD

Preheat the oven to 180°C. Grease a deep 20 cm round cake tin and line the base and side with baking paper.

Using an electric mixer, cream the butter with the sugar until light and fluffy. Add the eggs, one at a time, beating thoroughly. Stir in the marmalade. Add the flour and salt alternately with the orange rind and juice.

Spoon into the prepared tin and bake for 30–40 minutes or until a skewer inserted in the centre comes out clean. Turn out onto a wire rack set over a baking tray.

To make the glaze, use a zester to remove the skin from one orange and slice the second orange thinly.

Place the sugar, water and orange juice in a saucepan over medium heat and stir until the sugar dissolves. Bring to the boil. Add the zest and orange slices and simmer for 8–10 minutes or until the zest is softened and slightly translucent. Remove from the syrup and set the syrup aside. Allow to cool.

Decorate the cake with the orange zest and slices, then drizzle it with the reserved syrup.

NOTE Although marmalade can be made with any citrus fruits, alone or in combination, the classic marmalade is prepared with Seville oranges. Their characteristic bitterness makes them unpalatable when eaten as is but perfect for marmalade. Use Seville or sweet orange marmalade for this recipe, as you prefer.

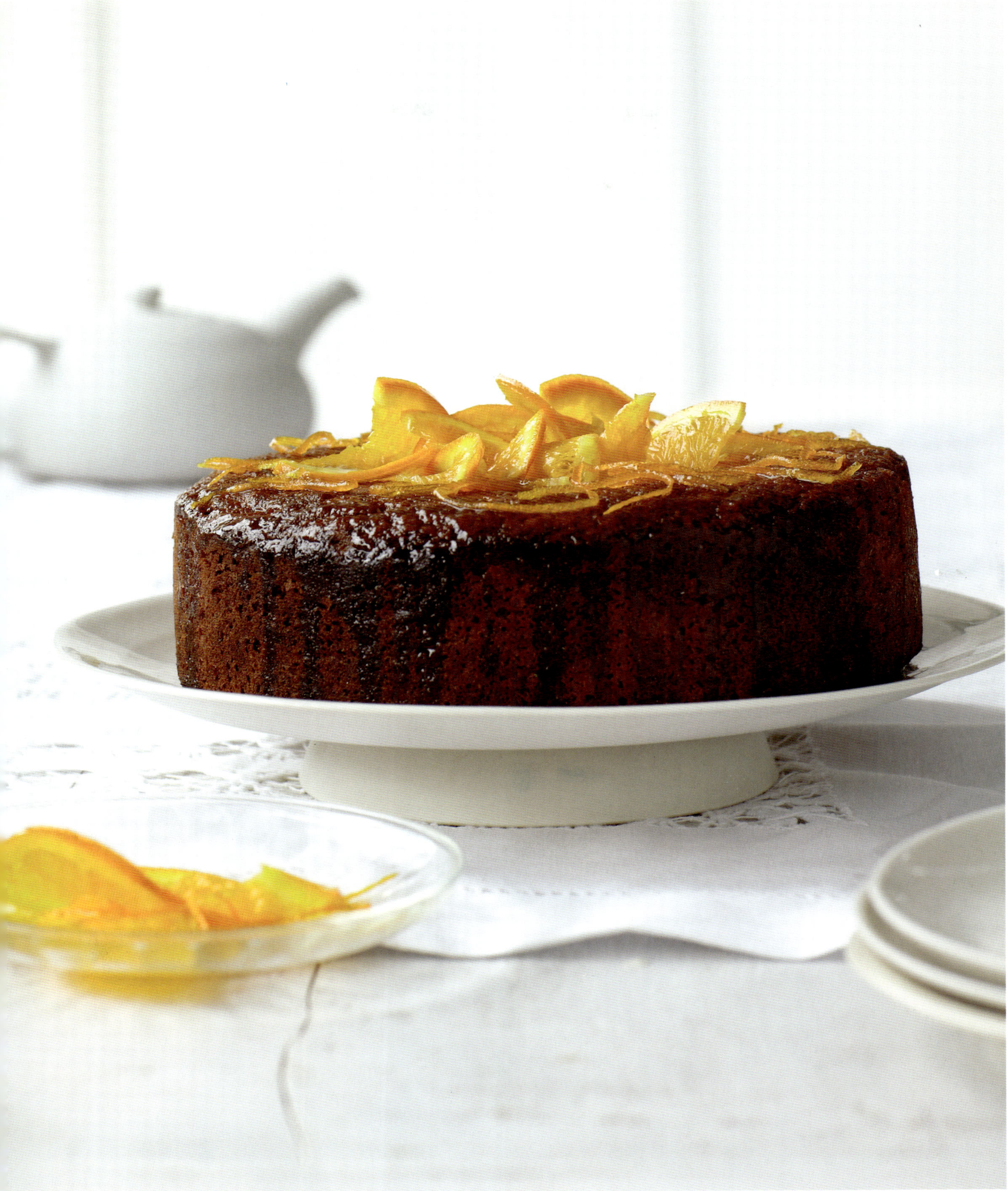

INGREDIENTS

185 g butter, softened
grated rind and juice of 1 orange
¾ cup (165 g) caster sugar
3 eggs, separated
2 cups (300 g) self-raising flour
a pinch of salt
⅓ cup milk
sifted icing sugar to dust

ORANGE CAKE

SERVES 8

METHOD

Preheat the oven to 180°C. Grease a 20 cm round cake tin or a 21 cm x 11 cm loaf tin and line the base with baking paper.

Using an electric mixer, cream the butter with the orange rind and sugar until light and fluffy. Add the egg yolks one at a time and beat well after each.

Sift the flour with the salt into a bowl and fold into the creamed mixture alternately with the strained orange juice and milk, beginning and ending with flour.

Beat the egg whites until stiff peaks form and gently fold in.

Spoon into the prepared tin and bake for 45–50 minutes or until a skewer inserted in the centre comes out clean.

Turn out onto a wire rack, allow to cool, then dust with sifted icing sugar.

CAKES *butter cakes*

INGREDIENTS
250 g butter, softened
1¼ cups (275 g) caster sugar
1 teaspoon vanilla essence
3 eggs
2¼ cups (335 g) self-raising flour
½ teaspoon salt
¾ cup milk
2 tablespoons cocoa powder
2 tablespoons boiling water
red food colouring

MARBLE CAKE

Children love this cake and it's a very popular choice for birthday parties. The white, pink and brown colours form intriguing designs that differ from one slice to the next.

SERVES 8

METHOD
Preheat the oven to 180°C. Grease a deep 20 cm square cake tin and line the base with baking paper.

Using an electric mixer, cream the butter, then gradually beat in the sugar and vanilla until light and creamy. Beat the eggs lightly, and beat gradually into the creamed butter mixture.

Sift the flour and salt intwo a bowl and fold into the creamed mixture alternately with the milk.

Divide the mixture into three portions. Sift the cocoa and blend with the boiling water. Stir this mixture into one portion of the cake mixture. To the second portion, add a few drops of red food colouring to colour it pink. The third portion is left plain.

Drop tablespoons of the mixture into the prepared tin, alternately pink, plain and chocolate. Run a knife gently through the mixture a few times to marble it. Bake for 50–60 minutes.

Turn out onto a wire rack to cool.

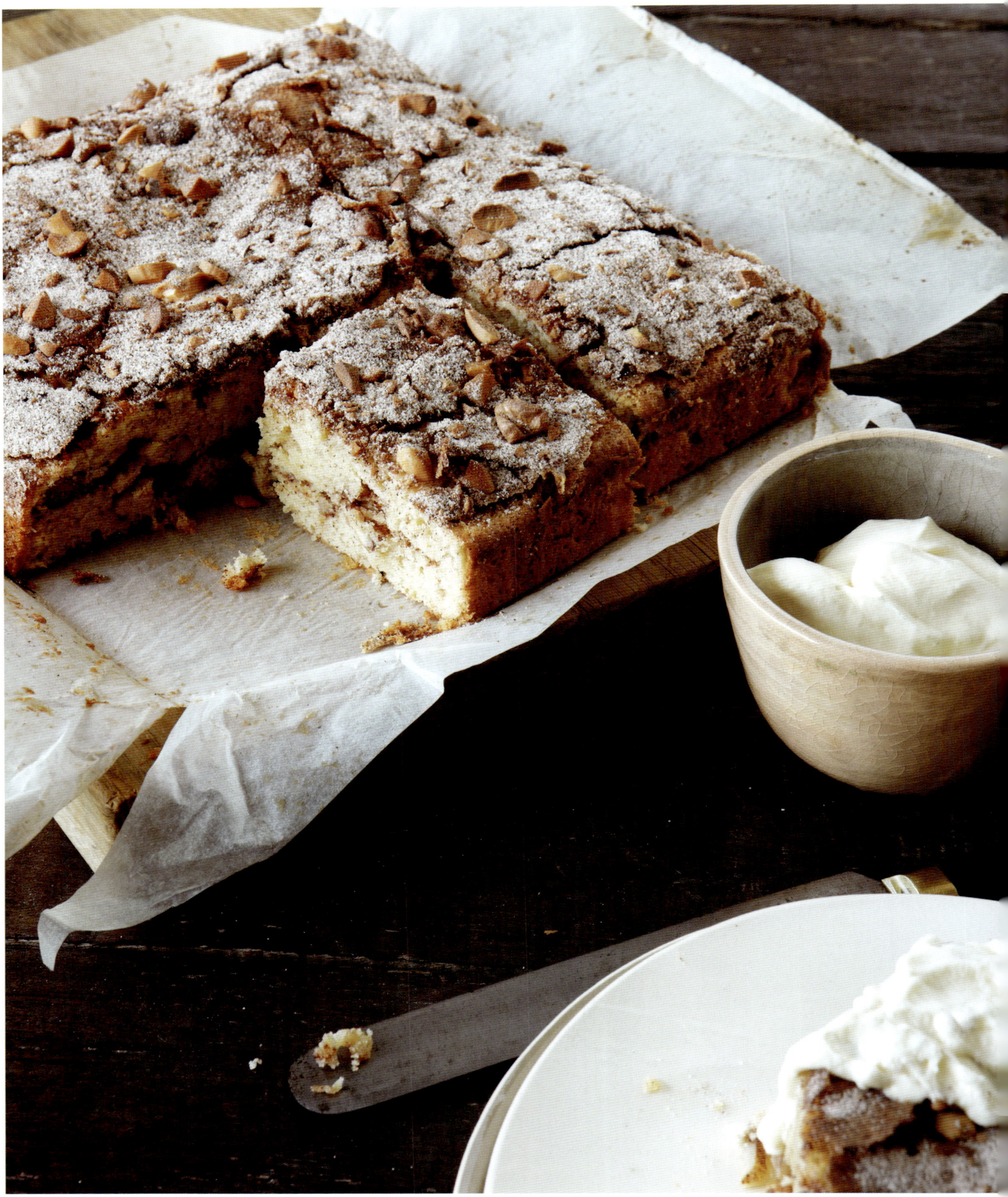

CAKES *butter cakes*

INGREDIENTS

1½ cups (330 g) caster sugar
½ cup mixed chopped nuts
1 tablespoon ground cinnamon
125 g butter, softened
2 eggs, lightly beaten
1 teaspoon vanilla essence
1 tablespoon lemon juice
2 cups (300 g) plain flour
½ teaspoon baking powder
½ teaspoon bicarbonate of soda
¼ teaspoon salt
1 cup sour cream

CINNAMON LAYERED CAKE

SERVES 8

METHOD

Preheat the oven to 180°C. Grease a 23 cm square tin and line the base and sides with baking paper.

Combine ½ cup of the sugar with the nuts and cinnamon and set aside.

Using an electric mixer, cream the butter with the remaining sugar until light and fluffy. Gradually add the eggs with the vanilla and lemon juice, beating well.

Sift the flour with the baking powder, bicarbonate of soda and salt and add alternately to the butter mixture with the sour cream.

Spread half the batter into the prepared tin. Sprinkle with half the cinnamon mixture, then spread the remaining cake batter over the cinnamon. Sprinkle the rest of the cinnamon mixture on top.

Bake for 35–40 minutes or until a skewer inserted in the centre comes out clean.

Remove the cake from the tin and serve warm on its own or with whipped cream flavoured with cinnamon.

INGREDIENTS

½ cup cocoa powder
½ cup boiling water
185 g butter, softened
1½ cups (330 g) caster sugar
1 teaspoon vanilla essence
3 eggs, beaten
2 cups (300 g) self-raising flour
a pinch of salt
¼ teaspoon bicarbonate of soda
¾ cup milk
raspberry jam and whipped cream to serve

CHOCOLATE CAKE

SERVES 8

METHOD

Preheat the oven to 180°C. Blend the cocoa with the boiling water and cool. Line a 28 cm x 19 cm lamington tin with baking paper.

Using an electric mixer, cream the butter with the sugar until light and fluffy. Beat in the vanilla and eggs. Gradually mix in the cooled cocoa mixture.

Sift the flour, salt and bicarbonate of soda and fold into the creamed mixture alternately with the milk. Spoon into the prepared tin and bake for 30–35 minutes or until a fine skewer inserted in the centre comes out clean. Leave to stand in the tin for a few minutes, then transfer to a wire rack to cool.

Cut into squares and serve with raspberry jam and a bowl of whipped cream.

NOTE This recipe is easily doubled to make two cakes if catering for a crowd.

CAKES *butter cakes*

INGREDIENTS
2 tablespoons cocoa powder
2 tablespoons raspberry jam
125 g butter, softened
¾ cup (165 g) caster sugar
1 teaspoon vanilla essence
2 eggs, lightly beaten
2 cups (300 g) self-raising flour, sifted
extra raspberry jam for filling
sifted icing sugar or Chocolate Glaze
   (page 252) to decorate

CHOCOLATE SANDWICH CAKE

A light, fine-textured chocolate cake flavoured and filled with raspberry jam. The raspberry helps cut the sweetness of the chocolate and also adds a bit of a tang. The cake can be simply dusted with icing sugar or given a chocolate glaze for a fancier touch.

SERVES 8

METHOD
Preheat the oven to 180°C. Grease two 18 cm sandwich tins and line the bases with baking paper.

Mix the cocoa to a smooth thin paste with a little boiling water. Add the jam and mix in sufficient boiling water to make ¾ cup. Allow to cool.

Using an electric mixer, cream the butter with the sugar until light and fluffy. Beat in the vanilla, then gradually add the eggs, mixing well after each addition. Fold in the flour alternately with the cocoa and jam mixture.

Spread evenly in the prepared tins. Bake for 25–30 minutes or until the cakes spring back when lightly touched with your finger. Turn out onto wire racks to cool.

Sandwich together with raspberry jam and top with sifted icing sugar or with chocolate glaze.

INGREDIENTS

185 g butter, softened
1 cup (185 g) lightly packed brown sugar
⅓ cup honey
2 eggs, beaten
3 teaspoons rum
½ teaspoon vanilla essence
2 tablespoons cocoa powder
1¾ cups (260 g) self-raising flour
a pinch of salt
½ cup sweet sherry
1 cup cream, ¼ teaspoon almond essence (optional) and icing sugar or Chocolate Glaze (page 252) to decorate

HONEY CHOCOLATE CAKE

SERVES 8–10

METHOD

Preheat the oven to 180°C. Grease a 22 cm round cake tin and line the base and sides with baking paper.

Using an electric mixer, cream the butter with the brown sugar and honey until light and fluffy. Add the eggs gradually, beating well after each addition. Add the rum and vanilla.

Sift the cocoa, flour and salt together. Fold into the creamed mixture alternately with the sherry.

Spoon into the prepared tin and bake for 55–60 minutes or until a skewer inserted in the centre comes out clean. Cool in the tin for 5 minutes, then turn out onto a wire rack.

Whip the cream and, if you like, flavour with the almond essence.

When cold, cut the cake into two layers and fill with the whipped cream. Dust the top with sifted icing sugar or cover with chocolate glaze.

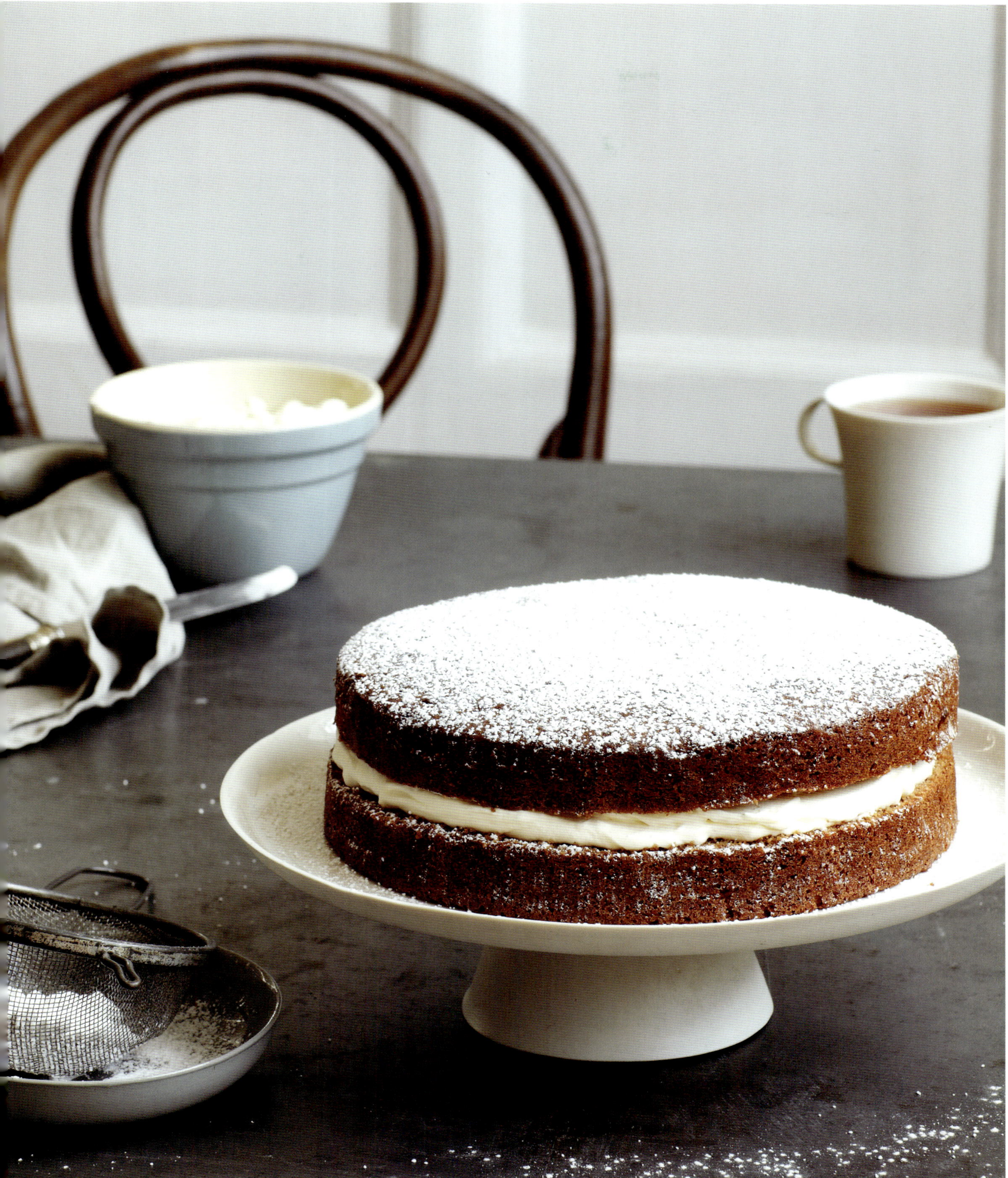

INGREDIENTS

1 2/3 cups (250 g) plain flour
a pinch of salt
2 teaspoons baking powder
125 g butter, diced
3/4 cup (165 g) caster sugar
1/3 cup desiccated coconut
2 eggs, beaten
3/4 cup milk

COCONUT CAKE

SERVES 8

METHOD

Preheat the oven to 180°C. Grease a round 20 cm cake tin and line the base with baking paper.

Sift the flour, salt and baking powder into a large bowl. Add the butter and rub it in until the mixture resembles breadcrumbs. Stir in the sugar and coconut.

Gradually stir the eggs and milk into the flour mixture. Spoon into the prepared tin and smooth the top. Bake in the centre of the oven for 1–1 1/4 hours, or until firm to the touch and golden.

Turn out on a wire rack to cool.

NOTE If you want to ice the cake, try Glacé Icing (page 252) or Liqueur Butter Cream Icing (page 253), omitting the sherry or replacing it with coconut liqueur.

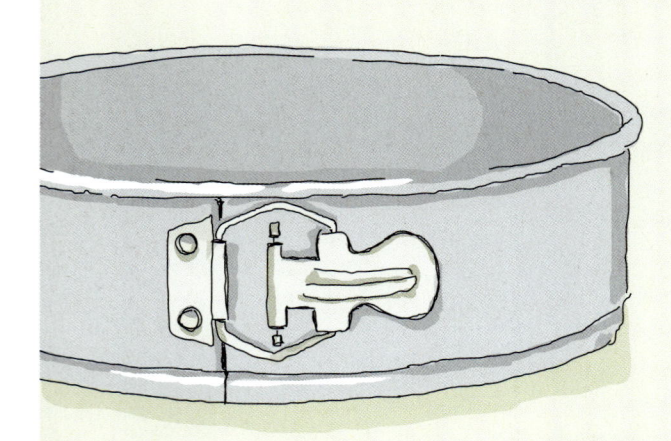

CAKES *butter cakes*

INGREDIENTS
2 cups (440 g) firmly packed brown sugar
2 cups (300 g) self-raising flour, sifted
125 g butter
1 teaspoon bicarbonate of soda
1 cup milk
1 egg, beaten
1 teaspoon grated nutmeg
½ cup chopped walnuts

NUTMEG CAKE

SERVES 10

METHOD

Preheat the oven to 180°C. Generously grease a 20 cm square cake tin and line with baking paper.

Combine the sugar and flour in a large bowl. Rub in the butter until the mixture resembles fine breadcrumbs. Press half the mixture into the prepared tin.

Dissolve the bicarbonate of soda in the milk, add the egg and nutmeg and pour over the remaining sugar and flour mixture. Mix well, then spoon into the tin on top of the pressed-in mixture. Sprinkle walnuts over.

Bake for 1 hour or until a skewer inserted into the centre comes out clean. Cool in the tin for 15 minutes then turn out onto a wire rack to cool completely.

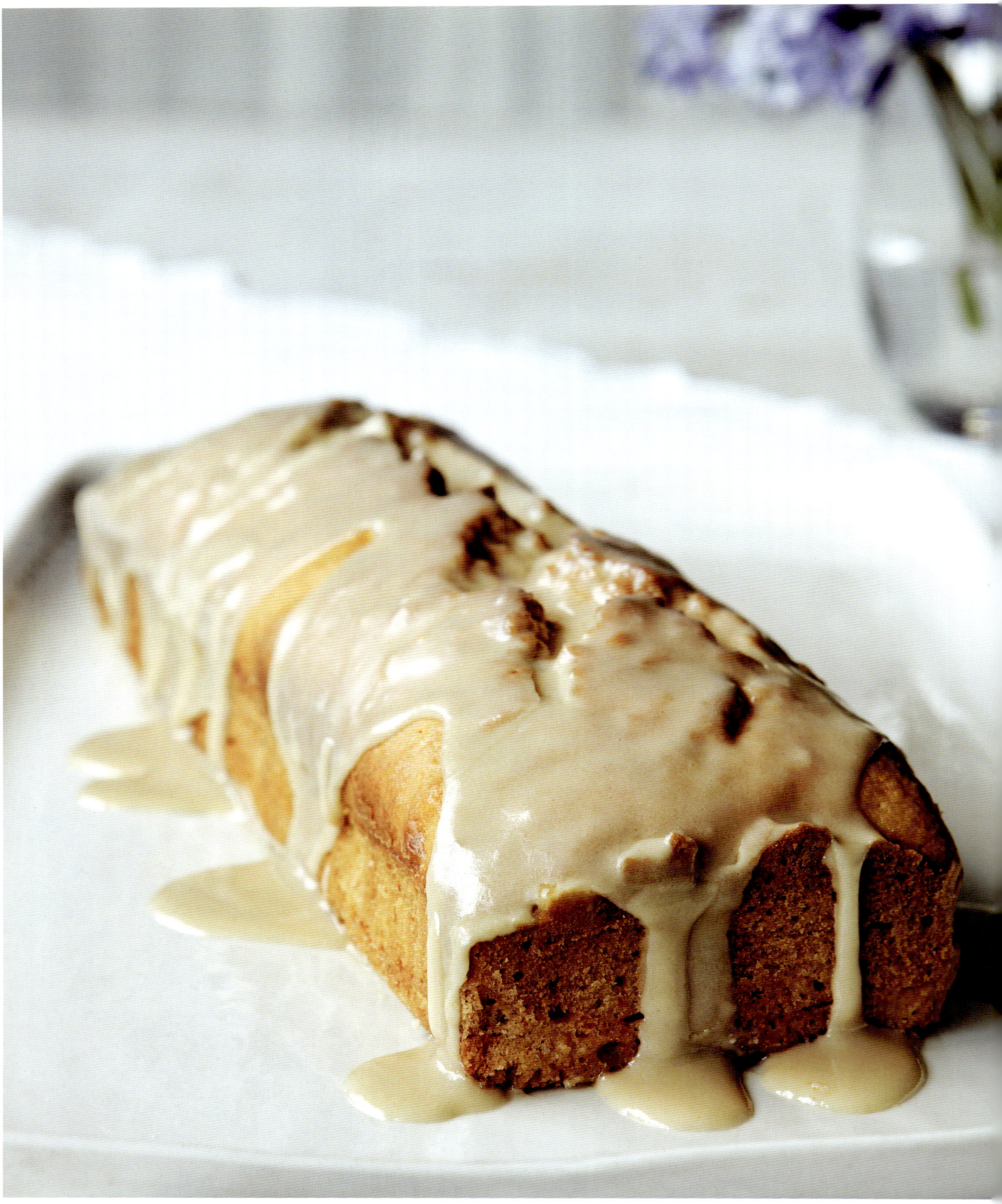

CAKES *butter cakes*

INGREDIENTS
185 g unsalted butter, softened
¾ cup (165 g) caster sugar
2 eggs
2 cups (300 g) plain flour
1 teaspoon baking powder
½ teaspoon bicarbonate of soda
¼ teaspoon salt
1 cup light sour cream
2 tablespoons extra strong espresso coffee

COFFEE GLAZE
1 cup (160 g) icing sugar, sifted
1–2 tablespoons strong espresso coffee

GLAZED COFFEE CAKE

MAKES 2 CAKES; SERVES 16

METHOD
Preheat the oven to 180°C. Grease two 25 cm x 8 cm bar tins and line the base and sides with baking paper.

Using an electric mixer, cream the butter and sugar together until pale and fluffy. Add the eggs, one at a time, beating well after each addition.

Sift the flour with the baking powder, bicarbonate of soda and salt. Fold into the creamed mixture alternately with the sour cream, beginning and ending with flour.

Transfer one-third of the batter to a small bowl. Add the espresso coffee and mix until well combined.

Spoon half the remaining plain batter into the prepared tins, smoothing with a spatula. Top with the coffee batter and the remaining plain batter.

Bake for 45 minutes, until a skewer inserted into the centre comes out clean. Cool in the tin for 10 minutes before turning out onto a wire rack to cool completely.

To make the coffee glaze, put the icing sugar in a small heatproof bowl. Gradually add enough coffee to moisten, stirring until smooth. Place the bowl over a saucepan of simmering water. Stir for 5 minutes or until the icing is glossy and of pouring consistency. Add more coffee if needed.

Pour over the cake and leave to stand for at least 10 minutes before serving to enable the glaze to set.

TIP Do not allow the icing to become too hot as it will lose its glossy appearance.

INGREDIENTS

170 g unsalted butter, softened
1 cup (220 g) caster sugar
2 eggs
1 cup (150 g) self-raising flour
½ cup (75 g) plain flour
⅔ cup buttermilk
2 tablespoons lemon juice
1 tablespoon lemon rind
rind of 2 lemons, finely sliced, for topping

LEMON FROSTING

90 g unsalted butter, softened
½ cup (80 g) icing sugar, sifted
2 teaspoons lemon juice

FROSTED LEMON & BUTTERMILK CAKE

SERVES 8–10

METHOD

Preheat oven to 180°C. Grease a 20 cm square cake tin and line with baking paper.

Using an electric mixer, beat the butter and sugar together until pale and fluffy. Add the eggs, one at a time, beating well after each addition.

Sift the flours together and fold into the creamed mixture alternately with the combined buttermilk, juice and rind, beginning and ending with flour.

Pour into the prepared tin and bake for 45 minutes or until a skewer inserted in the centre comes out clean. Cool in the tin for 10 minutes before turning out onto a wire rack to cool completely.

To make the lemon frosting, using an electric mixer, beat the butter and icing sugar together until pale and fluffy. Gradually beat in the lemon juice and spread over the cake. Top with sliced lemon rind.

CAKES *butter cakes*

INGREDIENTS

250 g butter, softened
1 cup (220 g) caster sugar
3 eggs
$2/3$ cup milk
$1 1/2$ cups sultanas
$1/4$ cup almonds, blanched and chopped
$1/4$ cup chopped mixed candied peel
$2 2/3$ cups (350 g) plain flour
$1 1/2$ teaspoons baking powder

SULTANA CAKE

This cake is beautifully moist and will keep for up to 10 days when stored in an airtight container. It is excellent for lunchboxes, picnics, with tea or coffee, or simply to have on hand to offer guests when they drop in.

SERVES 10

METHOD

Preheat the oven to 160°C. Grease a 20 cm round or square cake tin and line the base with baking paper.

Using an electric mixer, beat the butter and sugar until light and fluffy. Add the eggs one at a time, beating well after each addition. Stir in the milk gradually, then add the sultanas, almonds and peel. Fold in the flour sifted with the baking powder.

Spoon into the prepared tin and bake for about $1 1/2$ hours or until a skewer inserted in the centre comes out clean.

Turn out onto a wire rack to cool.

VARIATION

SULTANA SPICE CAKE Sift 1 teaspoon ground cinnamon, $1/2$ teaspoon ground nutmeg and $1/2$ teaspoon ground allspice along with the flour and baking powder.

INGREDIENTS

250 g butter, softened
1¼ cups (275 g) caster sugar
1 teaspoon vanilla essence
3 eggs
1 cup (150 g) self-raising flour, sifted
⅔ cup (100 g) plain flour, sifted
½ cup ground almonds
a pinch of salt
2 cups frozen raspberries

ALMOND TOPPING

⅓ cup (50 g) plain flour, sifted
2 tablespoons caster sugar
30 g butter, diced
⅓ cup flaked almonds

RASPBERRY & ALMOND SLAB CAKE

When frozen raspberries became readily available, recipes like this were developed, trying to make the most of them. A gorgeous cake, I love the way the raspberries ooze out of the top. And making it as a slab cake is a very Australian thing to do, isn't it? It's something to take to people.

SERVES 16

METHOD

Preheat the oven to 180°C. Grease a deep 22 cm square cake tin and line the base and sides with baking paper. Ensure the paper extends 2 cm above the rim of the tin.

To make the almond topping, combine the flour and sugar in a small bowl. Rub in the butter with your fingertips then fork through the almonds. Set aside.

Using an electric mixer, beat the butter, sugar and vanilla together until pale and fluffy. Add the eggs, one at a time, beating well after each addition. Gently fold in the combined flour, ground almonds and salt. Spread the mixture into the prepared tin and top with raspberries.

Sprinkle the almond topping over the raspberries. Bake for about 1 hour or until a skewer inserted in the centre comes out clean. Cool in the tin for 5 minutes before lifting out carefully onto a wire rack to cool completely.

VARIATION

BLUEBERRY & ALMOND SLAB CAKE Replace the raspberries with blueberries.

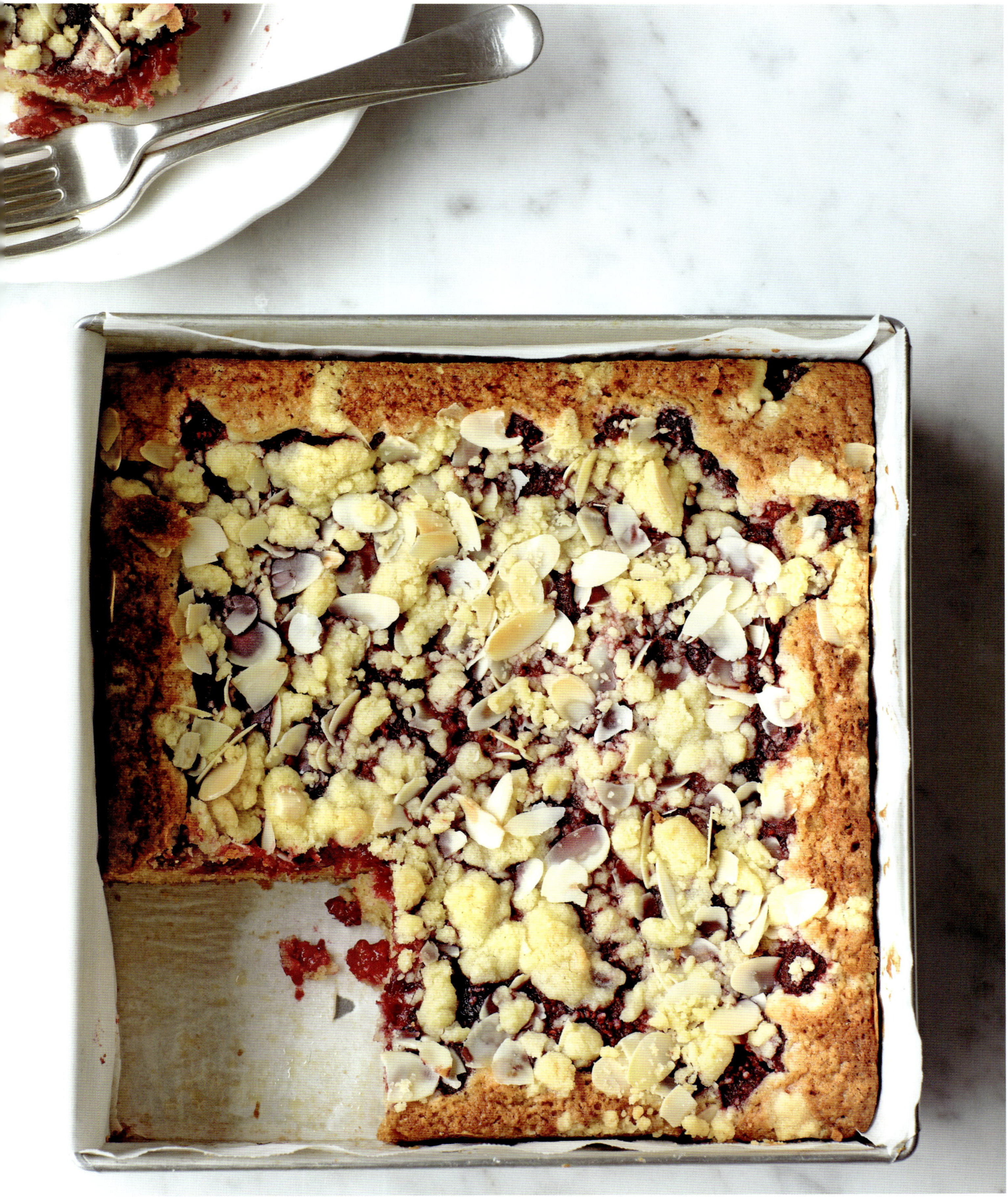

INGREDIENTS
125 g butter, softened
¾ cup (165 g) caster sugar
1 teaspoon vanilla essence
1 egg
2 ripe bananas
1½ cups (225 g) self-raising flour, sifted
¼ teaspoon bicarbonate of soda
¼ cup milk
sifted icing sugar to dust
whipped cream to serve (optional)

BANANA CAKE

My daughter Suzanne's mother-in-law took after her aunts, who were champion pastry cooks. They ran their own successful bakery in New Zealand forty years ago. This is one of her special recipes – a homely banana cake which is always a big hit at family gatherings.

SERVES 8

METHOD

Preheat the oven to 180°C. Grease a 20 cm round cake tin.

Using an electric mixer, cream the butter, and then beat in the sugar and vanilla until light and fluffy. Beat in the egg. Mash the bananas and add to the creamed mixture. Fold in the sifted flour.

Dissolve the bicarbonate of soda in the milk, then stir into the mixture gently but thoroughly.

Spoon the mixture into the prepared tin and bake for 40 minutes or until a skewer inserted in the centre comes out clean. Serve with a light dusting of icing sugar and, if liked, a little whipped cream.

CAKES *tea cakes*

INGREDIENTS
1 egg, separated
½ cup (110 g) caster sugar
½ cup milk
½ teaspoon vanilla essence
1 cup (150 g) self-raising flour, sifted
30 g butter, melted

TOPPING
1 tablespoon butter, melted
1 tablespoon sugar
½ teaspoon ground cinnamon

CINNAMON TEA CAKE

SERVES 6

METHOD

Preheat the oven to 190°C. Line the base of an 18 cm or 20 cm sandwich tin with baking paper.

Beat the egg white until stiff but not dry. Add the egg yolk, then gradually beat in the sugar, beating well between additions.

Mix the milk and vanilla, and add to the mixture a little at a time. Gently stir in the flour and melted butter. Spoon into the prepared tin and bake for 20–25 minutes.

While hot, brush with the butter and sprinkle with the sugar and cinnamon that have been mixed together. Turn out of the tin and place, top side up, on a wire rack. Serve warm or cooled with butter.

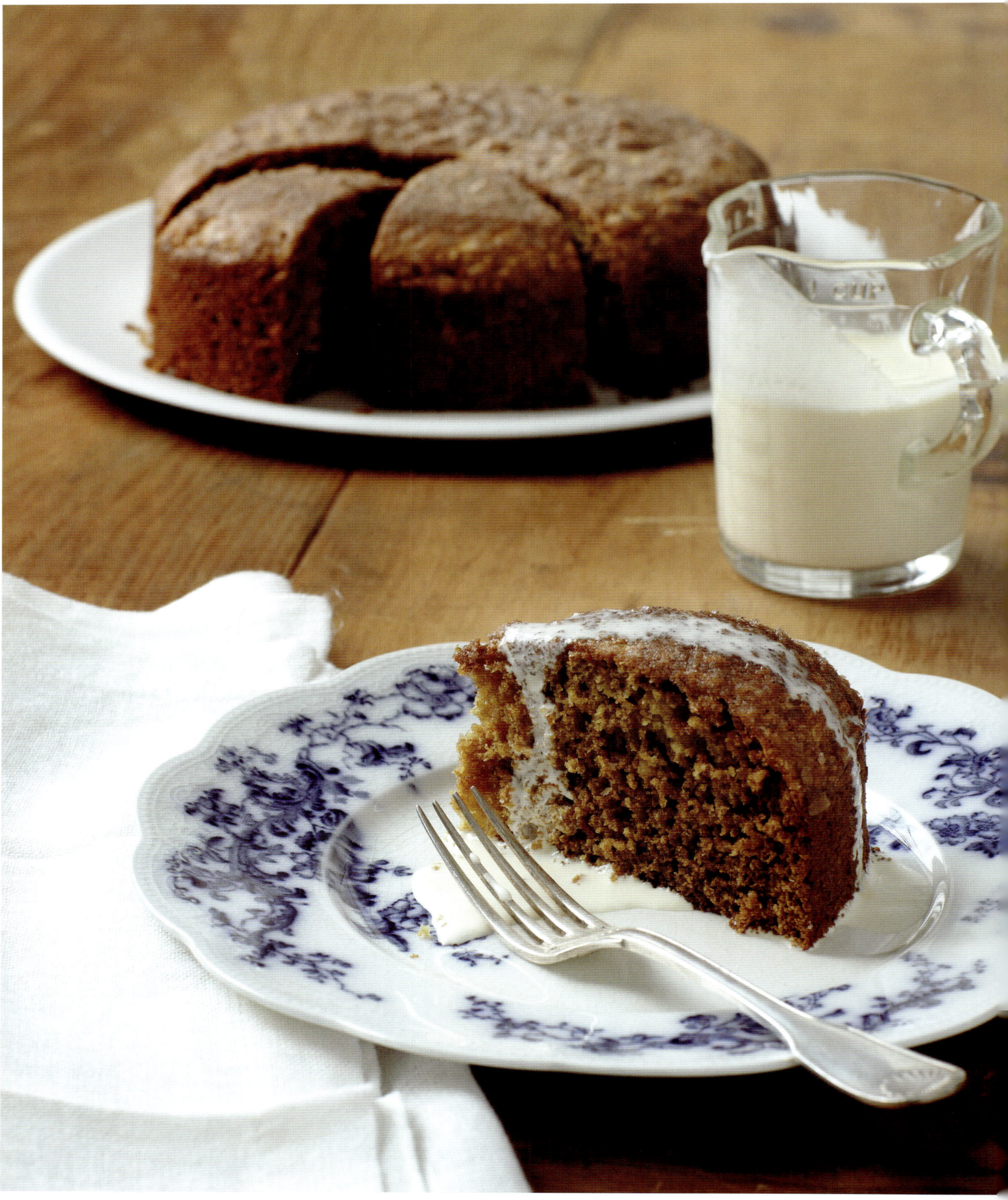

CAKES *tea cakes*

INGREDIENTS
1¼ cups sour cream
¾ cup (165 g) firmly packed brown sugar
1 egg
2¼ cups (335 g) wholemeal plain flour
1 teaspoon bicarbonate of soda
¼ cup warmed honey
½ cup chopped mixed nuts

TOPPING
1 tablespoon caster sugar
¼ teaspoon nutmeg
1 tablespoon butter, softened

HONEY TEA CAKE

SERVES 8-10

METHOD
Preheat the oven to 150°C. Generously grease a 20 cm round cake tin.

Beat together the sour cream, sugar and egg, then sift in the flour and bicarbonate of soda. Mix well. Beat in the warmed honey and chopped nuts.

Spoon the mixture into the prepared tin and bake for about 1½ hours or until a skewer inserted into the centre comes out clean. Turn out onto a wire rack.

Mix together the topping ingredients and brush over the top of the cake. Serve warm or cold, sliced, either buttered or plain.

INGREDIENTS

1 egg, separated
½ cup (110 g) caster sugar
½ cup milk
½ teaspoon vanilla essence
30 g butter, melted
1 cup (150 g) self-raising flour, sifted
1 apple, peeled, cored and thinly sliced

TOPPING

1 tablespoon melted butter
½ teaspoon ground cinnamon mixed with 1 tablespoon caster sugar

APPLE TEA CAKE

This type of tea cake is made from a simple quick-mix batter, sometimes sprinkled with sugar and spices or other toppings, and often served sliced and buttered while still warm. Tea cakes are a comforting treat on a cold afternoon.

SERVES 6

METHOD

Preheat the oven to 190°C. Grease an 18 cm sandwich tin.

Whisk the egg white until stiff and gradually beat in the sugar, then the egg yolk. Stir in the milk, vanilla and melted butter. Fold the flour carefully into the mixture.

Spoon into the prepared tin and arrange the apple slices on top of the batter. Bake for 20–25 minutes.

When cooked, turn out and place, top side up, onto a wire rack. While still hot, brush with melted butter and sprinkle with cinnamon and sugar. Serve warm or cold.

CAKES *tea cakes*

INGREDIENTS

1 2/3 cups (250 g) self-raising flour
125 g butter, diced
1/2 cup (110 g) caster sugar
grated rind of 1 orange
1 egg, beaten
1/2 cup milk
1/2 cup water
1 cup sultanas
1/2 cup chopped candied orange peel

ORANGE & SULTANA LOAF

SERVES 8

METHOD

Preheat the oven to 180°C. Grease an 18 cm x 10 cm loaf tin and line the base with baking paper.

Sift the flour into a bowl and rub in the butter. Stir in the sugar and orange rind. Add the egg, milk and water and beat well.

Stir in the sultanas and candied peel and spoon into the prepared tin. Bake for 1 1/4 hours or until cooked when tested with a skewer. Turn out and place, top side up, onto a wire rack to cool.

Serve sliced and buttered.

INGREDIENTS

1½ cups (225 g) plain flour
1 cup (220 g) caster sugar
1 teaspoon baking powder
¼ teaspoon salt
125 g butter, diced
2 eggs, beaten
½ cup milk
grated rind of 1 lemon
½ cup chopped walnuts

LEMON SYRUP

juice of 1 lemon
¼ cup (55 g) caster sugar

LEMON TEA LOAF

SERVES 6–8

METHOD

Preheat the oven to 180°C. Grease a 21 cm x 11 cm loaf tin and line the base with baking paper.

Sift the flour, sugar, baking powder and salt into a bowl. Rub in the butter using your fingertips. Mix the beaten eggs and milk, stir into the flour mixture, then fold in the lemon rind and walnuts.

Turn into the prepared tin and bake for 1¼ hours or until a skewer inserted in the centre comes out clean.

To make the lemon syrup, mix the lemon juice and sugar together. When the cake is cooked and while it is still hot, pour over the top. Allow the cake to cool in the tin.

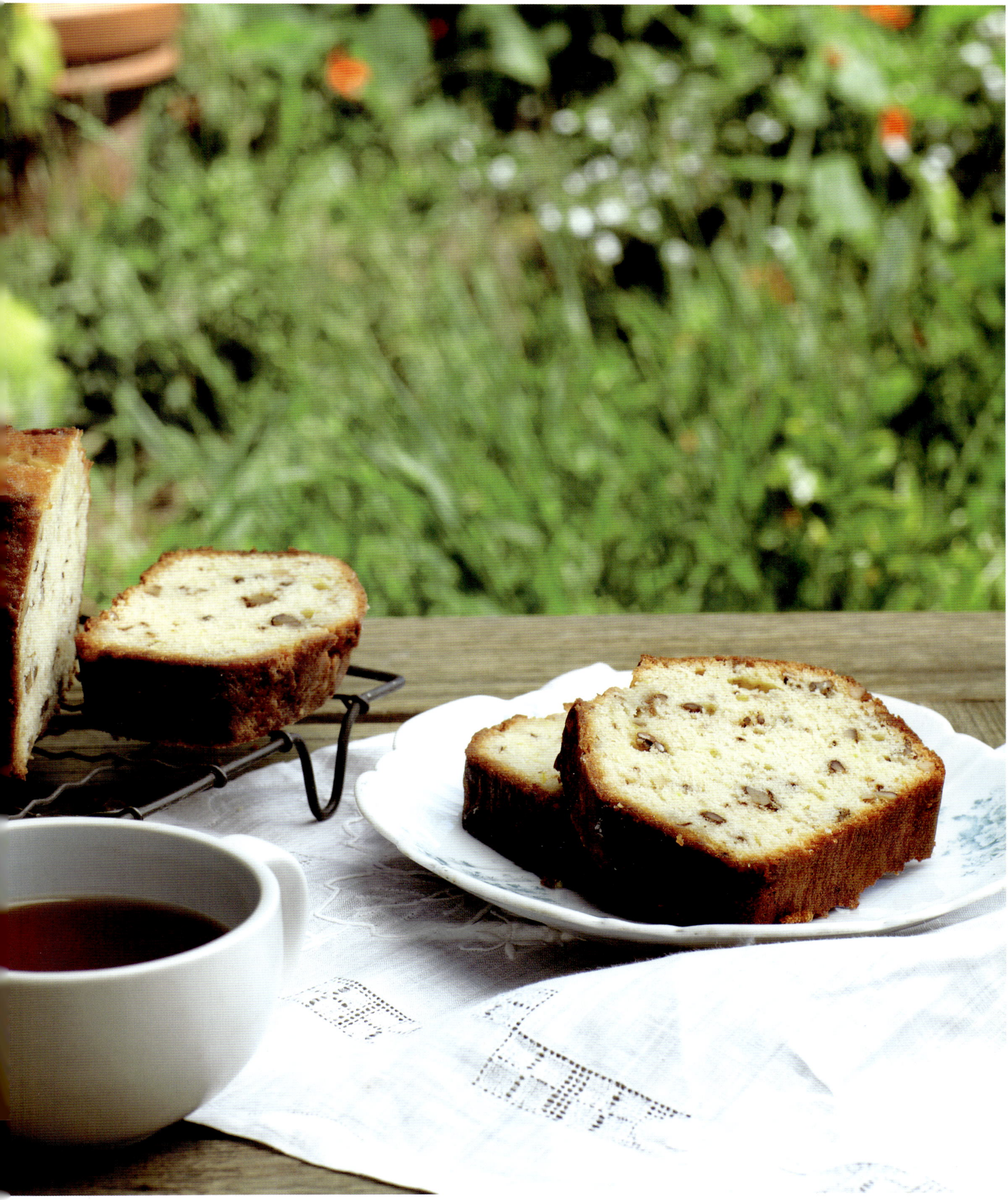

INGREDIENTS

750 g mixed dried fruit
185 g butter
1¼ cups (275 g) firmly packed brown sugar
1 tablespoon grated lemon rind
2 teaspoons mixed spice
1 cup water
2 teaspoons rum or sherry
1 cup (150 g) plain flour
1½ cups (225 g) self-raising flour
¼ teaspoon salt
3 eggs
½ teaspoon bicarbonate of soda

BOILED FRUIT CAKE

An economical and easy cake that keeps well. For Christmas, it may be topped with almonds before baking, or iced and decorated afterwards. The name may sound odd, but it's the fruit mixture that is boiled, not the cake!

SERVES 12

METHOD

Preheat the oven to 180°C. Grease a deep 20 cm cake tin and line it with two layers of baking paper.

Place the fruit, butter, brown sugar, lemon rind, spice, water and rum or sherry in a saucepan and bring to the boil. Reduce the heat and simmer for 5 minutes, then remove from the heat and leave until lukewarm.

Sift the flours and salt together. Beat the eggs with the bicarbonate of soda. Stir the flour and beaten eggs alternately into the fruit mixture.

Spoon into the prepared tin and bake for 45 minutes, then reduce the heat to 160°C and bake for a further 45 minutes or until a skewer inserted in the centre comes out clean.

Turn out of the tin and cool on a wire rack before removing the paper. Store in an airtight container.

This fruit cake will keep in an airtight container for up to 1 month.

CAKES *quick-mix cakes*

INGREDIENTS
1 tablespoon white vinegar
1 cup evaporated milk
1½ cups (225 g) plain flour
a pinch of salt
½ cup cocoa powder
1½ teaspoons bicarbonate of soda
1¼ cups (275 g) caster sugar
155 g butter, melted
1 teaspoon vanilla essence
2 eggs
raspberry jam or whipped cream
Rich Chocolate Icing (page 252) or sifted icing sugar

MELT & MIX CHOCOLATE CAKE

It was such a breakthrough to have ingredients where you could do this — mix them all together in the one bowl. Previously there was a lot of beating things separately. Women loved this melt and mix idea, it was very popular.

SERVES 6-8

METHOD

Preheat the oven to 180°C. Grease two 20 cm sandwich tins and line the bases with baking paper.

Mix the vinegar with the evaporated milk to sour it.

Sift the flour, salt, cocoa, bicarbonate of soda and sugar into a bowl. Add the butter and dry ingredients with the soured milk, vanilla and eggs. Beat vigorously for about 2 minutes or until smooth. Spoon into the prepared tins and bake for 30–35 minutes or until a skewer inserted in the centre comes out clean. Cool on a wire rack.

Sandwich together with raspberry jam or whipped cream and ice with chocolate icing or dust with icing sugar.

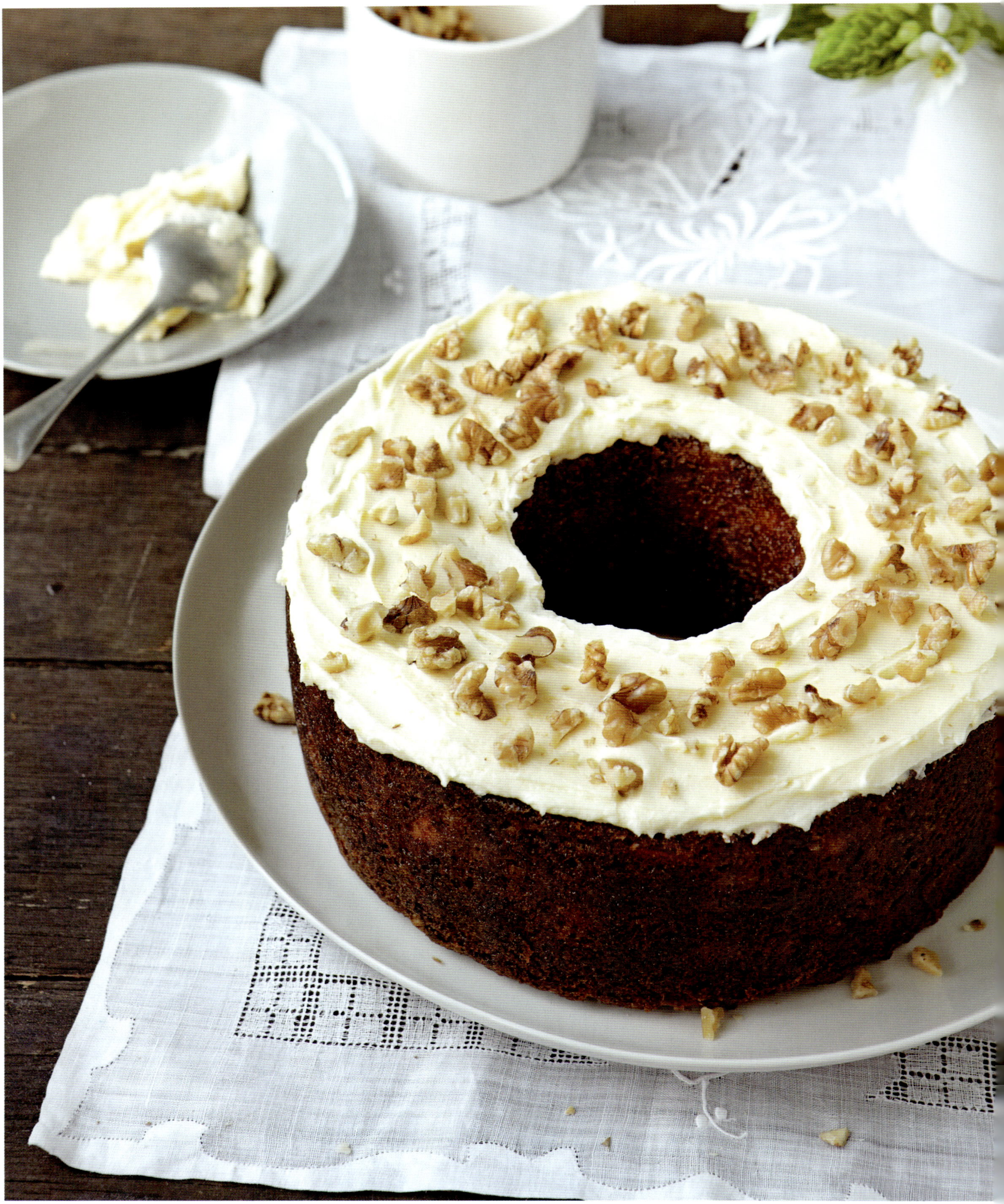

CAKES *quick-mix cakes*

INGREDIENTS
3 cups (450 g) plain flour
2 cups (440 g) caster sugar
1 teaspoon salt
1½ teaspoons bicarbonate of soda
1 cup undrained canned crushed pineapple
2 cups grated carrot
4 eggs
1½ cups vegetable oil
1 teaspoon vanilla essence
1 cup chopped walnuts, pecans or mixed nuts
Lemon Butter Cream Icing (page 253)
chopped walnuts to decorate

CARROT CAKE

This is a very simple recipe and the idea of mixing in a can of pineapple seems extraordinary, but it works. It's what makes the cake so moist. Anything with as much fruit and moisture as this cake would normally sink in the middle, which is why it's best baked in a ring tin. They are very good tins for this sort of cake.

SERVES 12–16

METHOD
Preheat the oven to 180°C. Generously grease a deep 22 cm ring tin.

Sift the flour, sugar, salt and bicarbonate of soda together into a large bowl. Add the pineapple, carrot, eggs, oil and vanilla and beat until combined. Stir in the nuts.

Spoon the batter into the prepared tin and bake for 1 hour or until a skewer inserted in the centre comes out clean. Cool in the tin for 5 minutes, then turn out onto a wire rack to cool completely.

Ice the cooled cake with lemon butter cream icing and scatter with chopped walnuts.

INGREDIENTS

1¾ cups (260 g) plain flour
a pinch of salt
1¾ teaspoons baking powder
1 cup (220 g) firmly packed brown sugar
125 g butter, softened
2 eggs
½ cup milk
1 teaspoon vanilla essence
¾ cup chopped walnuts, almonds or pecans, plus walnut
  or pecan halves to garnish
sifted icing sugar (optional)

CARAMEL NUT CAKE

SERVES 8

METHOD

Preheat the oven to 180°C. Grease a 20 cm round cake tin and line the base with baking paper.

Sift the flour, salt and baking powder into a bowl. Stir in the sugar. Add the butter, eggs, milk and vanilla and beat vigorously until well blended. Fold in the nuts.

Spoon into the prepared tin. Decorate the top of the cake with the nut halves, if using.

Bake for 30–35 minutes or until a skewer inserted in the centre comes out clean.

Cool on a wire rack, then dust with icing sugar if you like. Cut into wedges to serve.

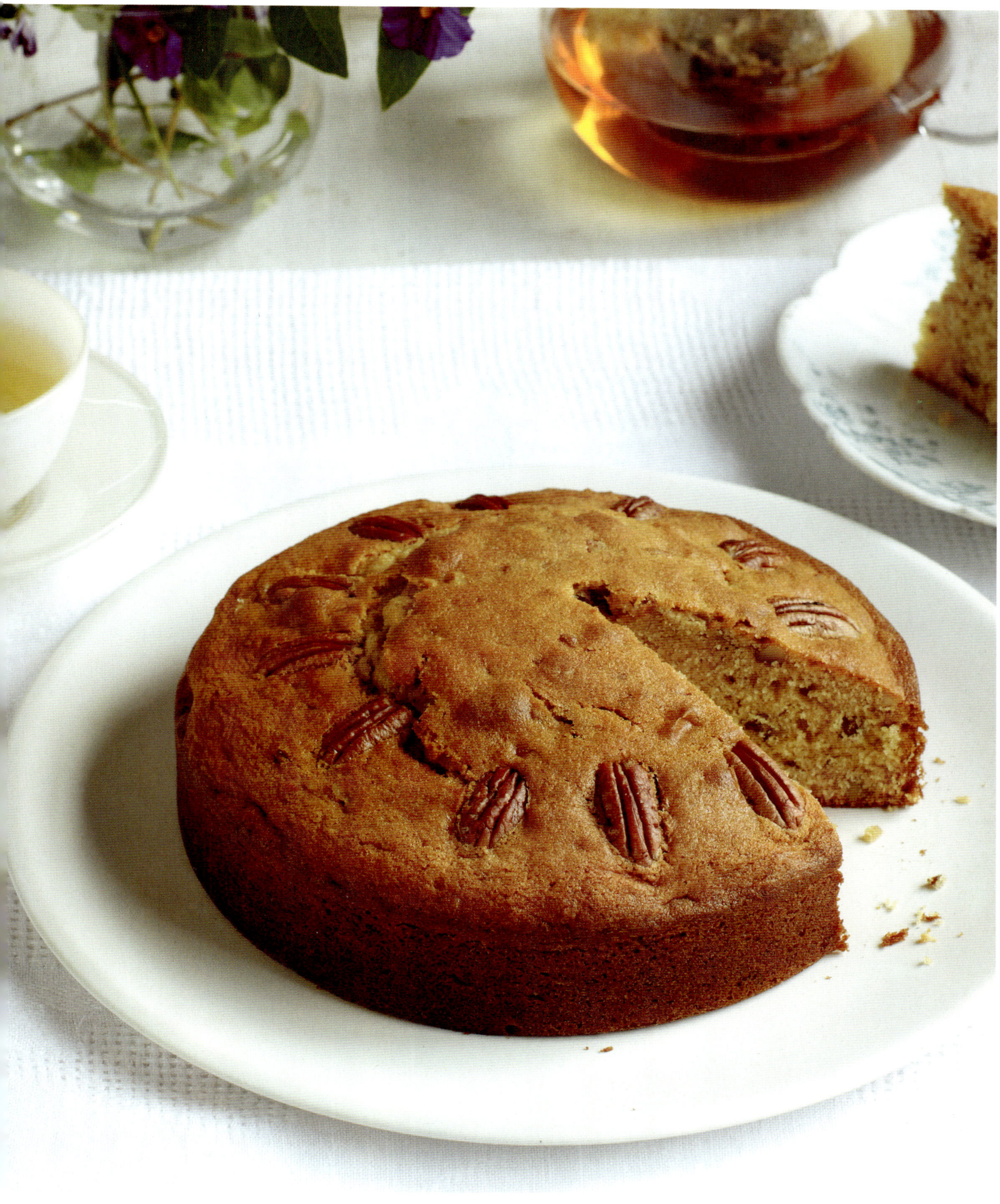

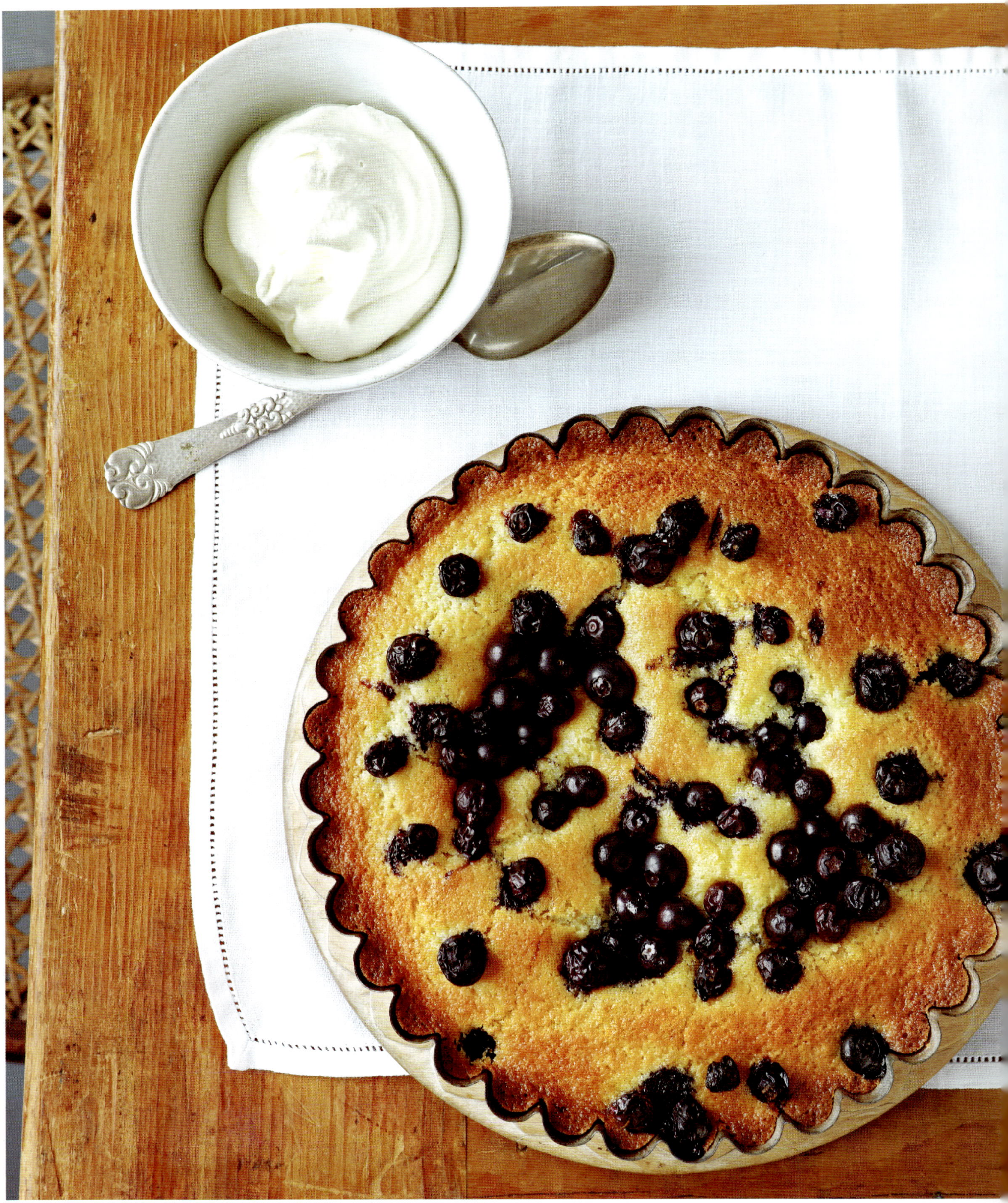

CAKES *quick-mix cakes*

INGREDIENTS
2 cups (300 g) self-raising flour, sifted
1⅓ cups (295 g) caster sugar
2 eggs, lightly beaten
¾ cup milk
grated rind and juice of 1 orange
130 g butter, melted
200 g fresh or frozen blueberries

ORANGE & BLUEBERRY CAKE

SERVES 8–10

METHOD
Preheat the oven to 180°C. Grease a deep 22 cm round loose-based flan tin or cake tin.

Combine the flour and sugar in a large bowl. Add the eggs, milk, rind, juice and butter and mix until combined. Spoon into the prepared tin. Top with half of the blueberries and bake for 20 minutes.

Sprinkle over the remaining blueberries and bake for another 20 minutes.

Cool in the tin for 10 minutes before turning out on a wire rack to cool completely.

TIP If using frozen blueberries there is no need to thaw them first.

INGREDIENTS

2 cups (300 g) plain flour
1 teaspoon mixed spice
2 teaspoons ground ginger
1 teaspoon bicarbonate of soda
125 g butter

1/3 cup (75 g) firmly packed brown sugar
2 tablespoons treacle
1/2 cup golden syrup
2 eggs, beaten
1/2 cup milk

OLD-FASHIONED GINGER CAKE

SERVES 8

METHOD

Preheat the oven to 150°C. Grease an 18 cm square cake tin and line the base and sides with baking paper.

Sift the flour, spice, ginger and bicarbonate of soda into a bowl.

Combine the butter, sugar, treacle and golden syrup in a small heavy saucepan. Heat gently until melted and dissolved, then allow to cool.

Stir the cooled butter mixture into the dry ingredients with the eggs and milk and beat thoroughly until smooth.

Pour into the prepared tin and bake for $1\frac{1}{4}$–$1\frac{1}{2}$ hours or until a skewer inserted in the centre comes out clean.

Cool in the tin for 15 minutes, then turn out. Serve plain or iced with Lemon Glacé Icing (page 252).

CAKES *sponge cakes*

INGREDIENTS
1 cup (150 g) plain flour
1½ cups (330 g) caster sugar
1¼ cups egg whites (10–12 medium eggs)
¼ teaspoon salt
1½ teaspoons cream of tartar
1½ teaspoons vanilla essence
a few drops of almond essence

ANGEL CAKE

A delicate American speciality. Because of its light texture it is not cut, but separated into pieces with two forks. You should be able to find an angel cake tin – a high tube tin, often with a removable base – in a good kitchenware shop.

SERVES 10–12

METHOD
Preheat the oven to 180°C.

Sift the flour and ¾ cup of the sugar together three times. Beat the egg whites with the salt and cream of tartar until soft peaks form. Sprinkle the remaining sugar over the egg whites 2 tablespoons at a time, beating well after each addition. Continue beating until the whites stand in stiff peaks, then fold in the vanilla and almond essences.

Sift about a quarter of the dry ingredients over the egg whites and fold in gently. Repeat until all the mixture is used. Pour the batter into an ungreased 23 cm angel cake tin – if there is a speck of grease on the tin, the cake will not rise. Cut gently through the batter with a spatula to remove any large air bubbles.

Bake for 45–50 minutes or until the crust is golden brown. Remove the cake from the oven and place the tube on a funnel or bottle, so the cake hangs upside down.

When cool, use a thin knife or metal spatula to help remove the cake from the tin.

NOTE Plain angel cakes are nicely complemented with a thin, tangy lemon, orange or passionfruit glacé icing (page 252), or fresh berries and whipped cream. Alternatively you could frost it with a butter cream icing (page 253).

A Génoise is a basic French-style sponge cake used for filled cakes, sponge fingers, petits fours or bombe Alaska. The eggs and sugar are beaten with a balloon whisk over gentle heat until they are warm, thick and a pale lemon colour, and the beating continues at room temperature until the mixture is cool and even thicker.

CAKES *sponge cakes*

INGREDIENTS
4 eggs
½ cup (110 g) caster sugar
½ teaspoon vanilla essence
1 cup (150 g) plain flour, sifted
60 g butter, melted and cooled

GÉNOISE CAKE

To use a Génoise cake when making filled, layered cakes, use whipped cream or Butter Cream Filling (page 255) flavoured with coffee, chocolate, praline or liqueur, and decorate with fruit or nuts. Ice single cakes with Butter Cream Icing (page 253), flavoured to your taste.

MAKES TWO 20 CM ROUND CAKES OR TWO 18 CM SQUARE CAKES

METHOD

Preheat the oven to 180°C. Grease two 20 cm round or 18 cm square tins and line the bases with baking paper.

Put the eggs, sugar and vanilla in a heatproof bowl. Place over warm water over a gentle heat and whisk with a balloon whisk (see Note) until the mixture is a pale lemon colour, thick and doubled in bulk. This will take about 7 minutes.

Remove the bowl from the heat and beat for a further 3–4 minutes or until cool and very thick. Fold in the flour, then add the butter. Mix as lightly and rapidly as possible so as to preserve the mass of air bubbles formed through whisking.

Turn at once into the prepared tins and bake for 20–30 minutes or until cooked. To test, gently press the centre with a finger – if the cake springs back it is cooked. If an impression remains, leave the cake for 5 minutes more and test again.

Turn out onto a wire rack to cool.

NOTE The whisking can be done using a hand-held electric mixer, with or without the use of heat, although the volume of the cake will not be quite as great as it would be if hand-mixed with a balloon whisk.

INGREDIENTS
2 cups (300 g) self-raising flour
a pinch of salt
250 g butter, softened
½ teaspoon vanilla essence
1 cup (220 g) caster sugar
4 eggs, beaten
whipped cream to sandwich

ICING
1 cup (160 g) icing sugar
pulp of 1 passionfruit
1 teaspoon butter

VICTORIA SPONGE

This is the foundation of all sponges. It's an English way of making a sponge. With this sponge in particular, it's all about having the right proportions. The old way of doing it is you put the eggs on one end of the scale and then you measure the flour, sugar and butter on the other end so you get equal quantities. I don't normally add cream to a Victoria sponge, I usually just have it as a plain butter cake and sometimes ice it.

SERVES 8

METHOD

Preheat the oven to 180°C. Grease two 20 cm sandwich tins, line the bases with baking paper and grease the paper.

Sift the flour with the salt.

Using an electric mixer, cream the butter and vanilla thoroughly, then beat in the sugar a little at a time until light and fluffy. Gradually beat in the eggs until thoroughly combined. Be careful to add the eggs slowly or the mixture will curdle and the texture of the cake will be affected. Fold in the flour.

Spoon the mixture into the prepared tins and bake for about 25 minutes or until the cakes have shrunk slightly from the sides of the tins.

Turn out onto a wire rack to cool completely. When cold, sandwich together with whipped cream and ice with passionfruit icing.

For the icing, sift the icing sugar into a bowl and mix smoothly with the passionfruit pulp until the icing will cover the back of a spoon thickly and smoothly. Beat in the butter and warm slightly over a saucepan of hot water, stirring until glossy. Spread over the cooled cake.

NOTE The success of the cake depends on the air beaten into the mixture. Use an electric mixer if you prefer, or beat by hand using a whisking movement from the wrist, lifting the mixture as you whisk.

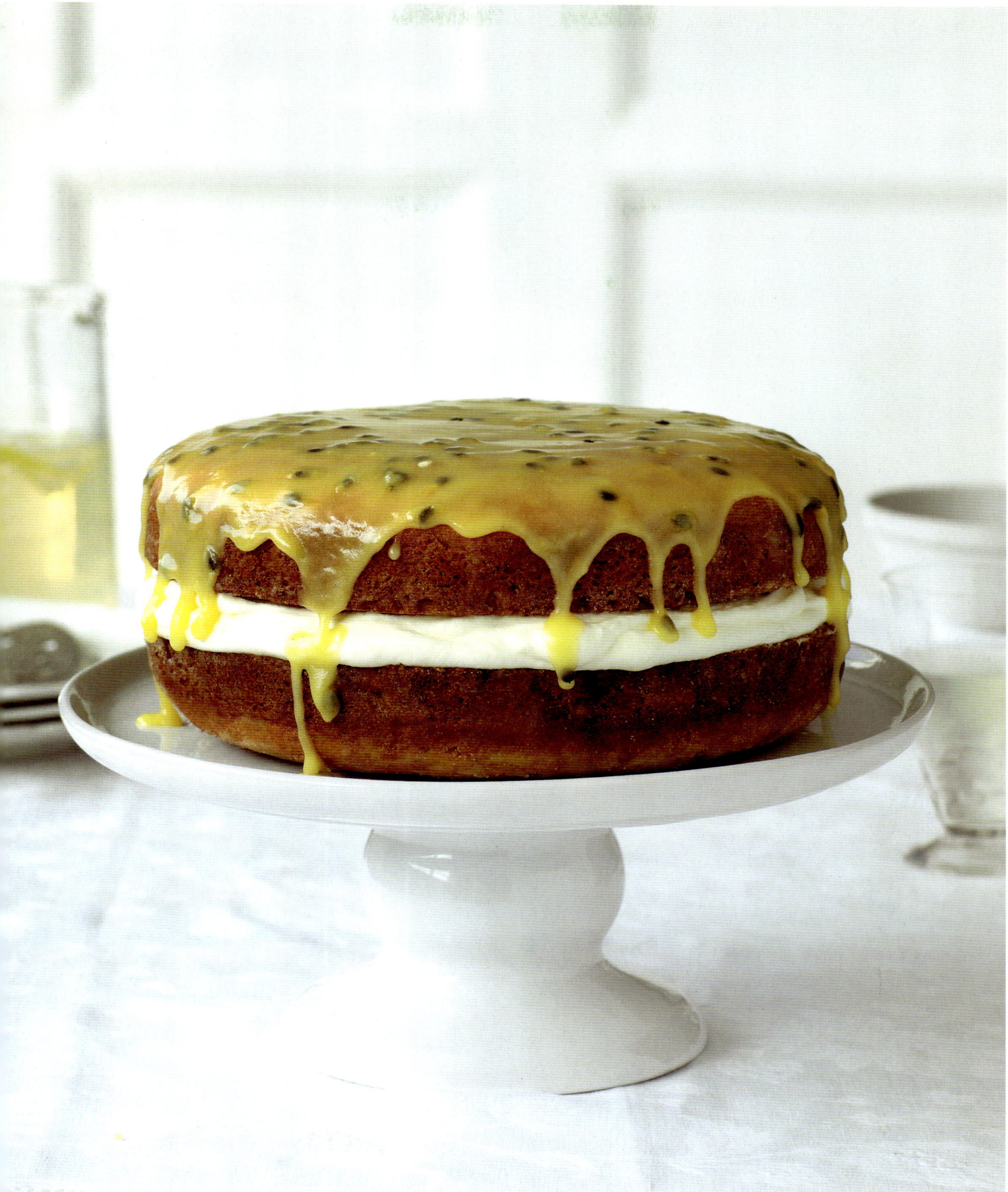

INGREDIENTS

3 eggs
¾ cup (165 g) caster sugar
grated rind of ¼ lemon
1 cup (150 g) self-raising flour
a pinch of salt
1 teaspoon melted butter
2 tablespoons hot water

FILLING & TOPPING

1 cup cream
a few drops of vanilla essence
1–2 teaspoons sugar
pulp of 2 passionfruit, 1 cup sliced strawberries
   or 2 sliced bananas tossed with a little lemon juice
1 tablespoon sifted icing sugar to dust

WHISKED SPONGE CAKE

SERVES 6–8

METHOD

Preheat the oven to 180°C. Grease two 18 cm sandwich tins, line the bases with baking paper, grease the paper and dust with a mixture of 1 teaspoon each of flour and sugar.

Combine the eggs, sugar and lemon rind in a heatproof bowl and place it over a saucepan of simmering water. Whisk for 10 minutes or until a little of the mixture when lifted on the whisk falls in a smooth, steady ribbon onto the mixture in the bowl. Remove from heat and continue whisking for about 5 minutes or until cool.

Sift the flour and salt and, using a metal spoon, gently fold into the egg mixture alternately with the combined butter and hot water.

Spoon into the prepared tins and bake for 20–25 minutes or until the cakes spring back when touched lightly with a finger. Immediately turn out onto a wire rack to cool.

For the filling, whip the cream with the vanilla and sugar until stiff. Combine half the cream with your choice of fruit and use to sandwich the cakes together. Decorate the top with dollops or rosettes of the remaining whipped cream and dust with icing sugar.

TIP When turning out sponges, invert onto a wire rack or a plate and then immediately invert again onto a wire rack so that the top side is uppermost. This prevents rack marks from being pressed into the delicate surface of the cake, and results in a better presentation.

CAKES *sponge cakes*

SPONGE SANDWICH

INGREDIENTS
1 cup (150 g) self-raising flour
a pinch of salt
3 eggs
¾ cup (165 g) caster sugar
1 teaspoon butter, melted
3 tablespoons hot water
jam for filling
sifted icing sugar to dust

SERVES 6-8

METHOD
Preheat the oven to 180°C. Grease two 18 cm sandwich tins and dust lightly with a little flour. Line the bases with baking paper.

Sift the flour and salt together three times.

Separate the eggs. Beat the whites until soft peaks form, then add the sugar gradually, beating until thick. Gently fold in the yolks. Fold in the sifted flour, lightly and evenly. Fold in the melted butter and hot water quickly and lightly.

Spoon into the prepared tins and bake for 20 minutes.

Turn out on a wire rack to cool. When cool, sandwich with slightly warmed jam and dust with icing sugar.

VARIATIONS

FOR A 20 CM SPONGE SANDWICH Preheat the oven to 180°C. Grease two 18 cm sandwich tins and dust lightly with a little flour. Line the bases with baking paper. Follow the method at left, using 1½ cups (225 g) self-raising flour, ¼ teaspoon salt, 4 eggs, 1 cup (220 g) caster sugar, 1 teaspoon melted butter and 4 tablespoons hot water. Bake for 20–25 minutes. Turn out onto a wire rack to cool.

FOR A 23 CM SPONGE SANDWICH Preheat the oven to 180°C. Grease two 23 cm sandwich tins and dust lightly with a little flour. Line the bases with baking paper. Follow the method at left, using 1¾ cups (260 g) self-raising flour, a pinch of salt, 5 eggs, 1¼ cups (275 g) caster sugar, 1½ teaspoons melted butter and 5 tablespoons hot water. Bake for 20–25 minutes. Turn out onto a wire rack to cool.

INGREDIENTS
½ cup (75 g) plain flour
¼ teaspoon salt
½ teaspoon baking powder
60 g cooking chocolate, broken up
4 eggs
¾ cup (165 g) caster sugar
1 teaspoon vanilla essence
2 tablespoons cold water
½ teaspoon bicarbonate of soda
sifted icing sugar
whipped cream flavoured with brandy or vanilla to serve
sliced strawberries to serve (optional)

CHOCOLATE ROLL

A lovely, light-as-air chocolate roll with very little flour. It is delicious with a rich brandy cream filling or, if you want to have it for dessert, a filling of sliced strawberries and cream.

SERVES 6-8

METHOD

Preheat the oven to 200°C. Grease a 30 cm x 25 cm Swiss roll tin and line with baking paper, or make a paper case (see below).

Sift together the flour, salt and baking powder. Melt the chocolate gently in a heatproof bowl over hot water. Cool slightly. Beat the eggs with the caster sugar until very light and thick. Add the flour mixture and vanilla all at once to the egg mixture and fold through gently.

Add the water and bicarbonate of soda to the chocolate, stirring until smooth. Fold quickly and lightly into the egg and flour mixture.

Turn the mixture into the prepared tin or case and bake for about 15 minutes or until the cake springs back when the centre is gently pressed. Loosen the edges and turn the cake out onto a tea towel generously dusted with icing sugar. Peel off the lining paper and trim the edges of the cake with a sharp knife. Roll immediately in the towel, first folding the hem of the towel over the edge of the cake, and rolling the towel in the cake to prevent sticking. After the cake is rolled, cool on a wire rack for at least 1 hour.

Before serving, carefully unroll the cake, remove the towel and quickly spread with whipped cream sweetened with a little sugar and flavoured with vanilla or brandy. Sprinkle with sliced strawberries if you wish. Re-roll the cake, using the tea towel to help, and dust with more icing sugar.

The cake can be decorated with rosettes of whipped cream and the rosettes topped with chocolate shavings or whole strawberries.

TO MAKE A PAPER BAKING CASE Choose a fairly thick greaseproof paper or non-stick paper. Take a piece 30 cm x 35 cm and fold over the ends and sides to form a border about 2.5 cm. Cut a slit at each corner and fold one cut piece over the other to mitre the corner. Fasten each corner with a paper clip so the borders stand up. Slide the case onto a baking tray before filling with the mixture.

CAKES *sponge cakes*

INGREDIENTS
½ cup (75 g) self-raising flour
a pinch of salt
3 eggs
½ cup (110 g) caster sugar
1 tablespoon hot water
caster sugar to sprinkle
3–4 tablespoons warm berry jam or lemon butter

SWISS ROLL

SERVES 6-8

METHOD

Preheat the oven to 220°C. Grease a 30 cm x 25 cm Swiss roll tin and line with baking paper, or make a paper case (see opposite).

Sift the flour with the salt three times. If using a hand-held whisk, place the eggs and sugar in a bowl and stand it over a saucepan of gently steaming (not boiling) water. Whisk together well for about 10 minutes or until the mixture is very thick and creamy. If using an electric mixer, warm the eggs and sugar slightly first, as above (the beating should take less time).

Remove the bowl from the water and continue whisking the mixture until cool.

Fold in the flour with a metal spoon. Lastly, fold in the hot water. Pour the mixture into the prepared tin, shake into the corners and spread evenly using a metal spatula. Bake for 7–10 minutes, until pale golden and springy. Do not overcook as it makes rolling up difficult.

Turn the sponge out onto a tea towel sprinkled with caster sugar. Carefully strip off the lining paper. Trim off the crisp edges with a sharp knife. Starting from the wide end of the sponge, roll in the towel then leave to cool, away from any draughts, before unrolling.

Warm the jam slightly and spread over the unrolled sponge, taking it almost to the edges.

Lifting the edges of the sugared tea towel, re-roll the sponge into a neat, firm roll. Cool the roll on a cake rack with the join underneath.

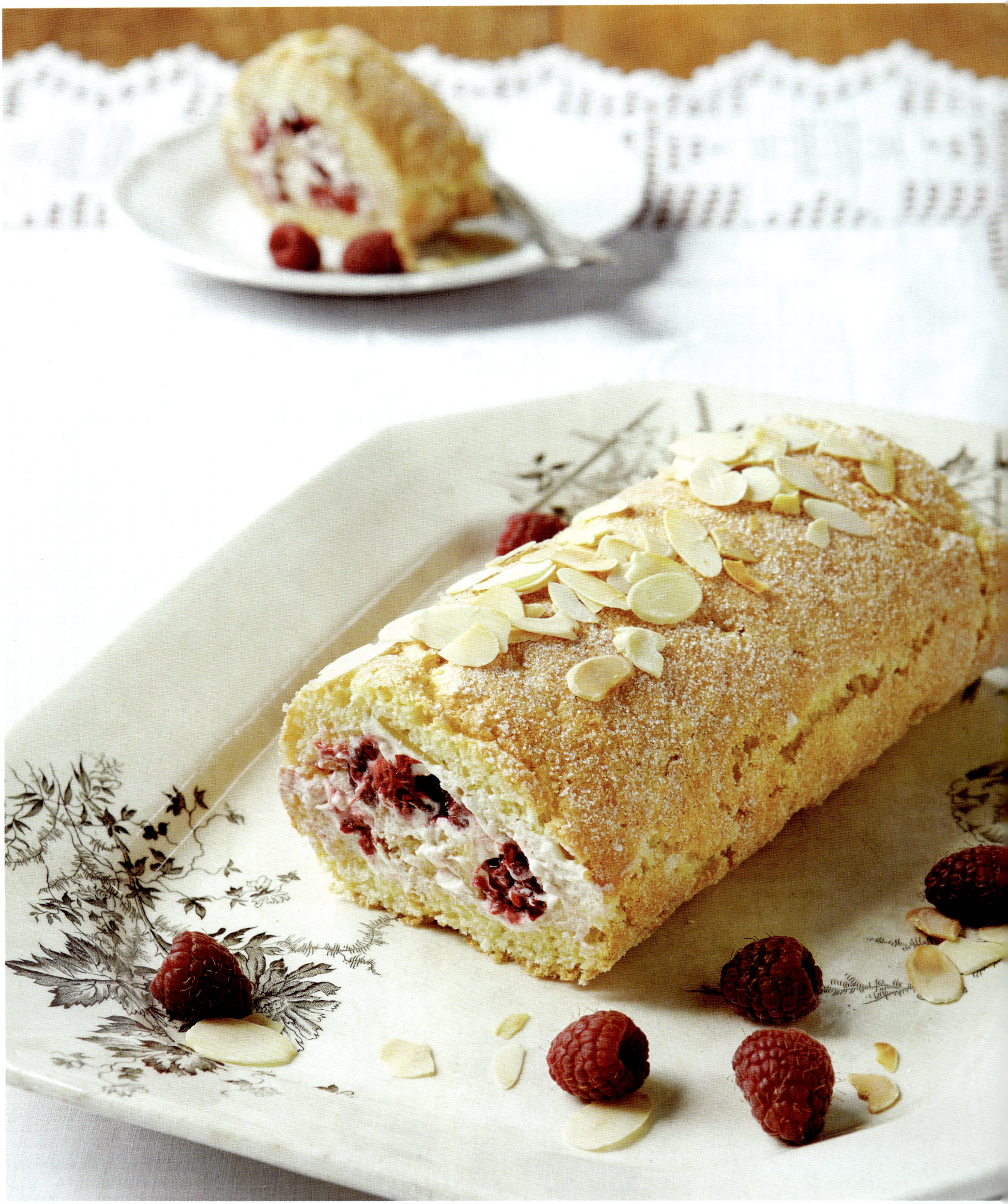

CAKES *sponge cakes*

INGREDIENTS
3 large eggs, separated
½ cup (110 g) caster sugar
½ cup ground almonds
¼ cup (40 g) self-raising flour, sifted
⅓ cup flaked almonds
¾ cup cream, whipped
½ cup fresh raspberries, crushed
sifted icing sugar to dust

ALMOND ROLL

We've been making things like roly-polys for years because sponges and pastries are lovely things to roll. There's nothing mysterious about it, you just have to learn the rules, otherwise you'll get into trouble. With baking I think we should be impressing that following the instructions is very important. With rolls, you've got to have a certain hand. If you're too careful, it won't work. And practise. Just keep at it until you get it right.

SERVES 8

METHOD

Preheat the oven to 180°C. Line a 30 cm x 25 cm Swiss roll tin with baking paper, cutting the corners to fit.

Use a hand-held whisk to beat the egg yolks with the sugar until the mixture is light and creamy. Using an electric mixer, whisk the egg whites until stiff but not dry peaks form and fold into the yolk mixture with the ground almonds and flour.

Gently spread the mixture into the prepared tin. Sprinkle with the flaked almonds (alternatively, the flaked almonds can be toasted and sprinkled on to serve).

Bake for 15 minutes or until cooked (lightly press with a fingertip; the mixture should not remain depressed). Turn out on to a tea towel that has been sprinkled with sugar. Trim away any crisp edges with a sharp knife. Roll up from one long edge and allow to cool.

Stir the crushed berries into the cream. Unroll the cake and spread with the cream mixture. Roll up again and place seam side down on a serving plate. Dust lightly with icing sugar.

INGREDIENTS

3 eggs, separated
2 teaspoons water
¾ cup (165 g) caster sugar, plus extra to sprinkle
1 cup (150 g) plain flour
1 teaspoon baking powder
a pinch of salt
1 cup ground hazelnuts
2 tablespoons icing sugar, sifted

FILLING

1 punnet (250 g) strawberries, hulled
2 tablespoons icing sugar, sifted
185 g dark chocolate
1 tablespoon water
2 egg yolks
90 g unsalted butter, well softened

HAZELNUT & CHOCOLATE ROULADE

SERVES 6-8

METHOD

Preheat the oven to 200°C. Line a 30 cm x 25 cm Swiss roll tin with baking paper.

Whisk the egg whites with the water to a firm snow, then add the sugar a spoonful at a time and continue beating until stiff. Beat in the egg yolks.

Sift the flour with the baking powder and salt, mix with the hazelnuts and fold gently into the egg mixture.

Spoon into the prepared tin and level the top with a palette knife. Bake for 12–15 minutes or until firm to the touch.

Sprinkle a clean tea towel with caster sugar. Turn the roulade out quickly onto the tea towel and carefully peel away the baking paper. Roll up along the long edge. Leave to cool.

To make the filling, purée the strawberries and stir in the icing sugar. Melt the chocolate in a heatproof bowl placed over hot water. Add the 1 tablespoon water. Remove from the heat and add the egg yolks one at a time. Beat well, then gradually mix in the butter. Tip into a bowl and blend in the strawberry purée.

Unroll the sponge roll very carefully. Spread with the filling and re-roll, placing seam side down on a serving plate. Chill for 2–3 hours. Dust with icing sugar before serving.

CAKES *sponge cakes*

INGREDIENTS
½ cup (75 g) arrowroot
1 tablespoon plain flour
½ teaspoon ground cinnamon
1 teaspoon mixed spice
1 teaspoon cream of tartar
½ teaspoon bicarbonate of soda
3 eggs
½ cup (110 g) caster sugar, plus extra to sprinkle
1 tablespoon honey (at room temperature)

HONEY CREAM FILLING
125 g butter, softened
2 tablespoons honey
1 tablespoon boiling water

HONEY SPICED SPONGE ROLL

SERVES 6

METHOD

Preheat the oven to 190°C. Line a 30 cm x 25 cm Swiss roll tin with baking paper, or make a paper case (see page 208).

Sift the dry ingredients three times.

Beat the eggs until thick and add the sugar gradually. Continue beating for about 10 minutes or until the mixture is thick and mousse-like and holds its shape.

Fold the dry ingredients into the egg mixture, then add the honey, mixing until evenly distributed.

Pour into the prepared tin and gently shake to spread the mixture evenly. Bake for 15–20 minutes.

Turn out on a tea towel that has been lightly dusted with caster sugar, quickly peel off the paper and trim the edges. Roll up in the tea towel, starting with the long end.

Allow to cool, then unroll. Fill with the honey cream filling, and roll up again. If serving as a dessert, roll the cake and cut into diagonal slices.

For the honey cream filling, using an electric mixer, cream the butter until light, add the honey a tablespoon at a time, and then add the water. Continue beating until the mixture is smooth and creamy.

INGREDIENTS

1 1/3 cups sultanas
1/3 cup currants
1/3 cup raisins
1/3 cup chopped mixed candied peel
1/3 cup roughly chopped glacé cherries
grated rind of 1/2 lemon or orange
2 1/2 cups (375 g) plain flour
1/2 cup (75 g) self-raising flour
250 g butter, softened
2/3 cup (150 g) caster sugar
2/3 cup (150 g) firmly packed brown sugar
5 eggs
1–2 tablespoons lemon juice

LIGHT FRUIT CAKE

SERVES 12

METHOD

Preheat the oven to 150°C. Grease a deep 20 cm round or square cake tin and line with baking paper.

Combine the dried fruit with the peel, cherries and lemon or orange rind. Sift the flours together.

Using an electric mixer, cream the butter with the sugars until very light and fluffy. Beat the eggs into the creamed mixture one at a time, following each with 1 tablespoon flour. Fold in the remaining flour, then the fruit. Add the lemon juice.

Spoon into the prepared tin and bake for 2 1/2 hours or until a skewer inserted in the centre comes out clean.

Turn out onto a wire rack and leave to cool. When cold, remove the paper lining and store in an airtight tin.

NOTE Spices can be added if liked; sift them in with the flour. Use 1/2 teaspoon ground cinnamon, 1 teaspoon mixed spice and 1/4 teaspoon nutmeg.

CAKES *fruit cakes*

INGREDIENTS

FRUIT
- 250 g raisins, chopped
- 250 g sultanas
- 250 g currants
- 185 g mixed candied peel, finely chopped
- 60 g glacé cherries, diced
- 60 g glacé apricots, diced
- ½ cup brandy or rum
- 3 tablespoons sherry

CAKE MIXTURE
- 250 g butter, softened
- 1⅓ cups (295 g) firmly packed brown sugar
- grated rind of 1 lemon
- 2 tablespoons marmalade
- 5 eggs
- 2½ cups (375 g) plain flour
- 1 teaspoon mixed spice
- 1 teaspoon ground cinnamon
- ¼ teaspoon salt
- 125 g blanched almonds, chopped
- whole blanched almonds (optional)
- extra brandy

RICH FRUIT CAKE

This rich fruit cake is traditionally the base for a wedding cake because it keeps longer (it will keep until the christening, is what they used to say!). It's also good as a Christmas cake or any celebration cake. To use this recipe for an iced Christmas cake, see page 218.

SERVES 16–20

METHOD

Put all the fruit into a bowl and sprinkle with the brandy or rum and the sherry. Leave overnight.

Preheat the oven to 150°C. Grease a deep 20 cm round or square cake tin and line it with one layer of brown paper and two layers of baking paper or greased greaseproof paper.

To make the cake mixture, beat the butter and brown sugar with the lemon rind until light and creamy. Add the marmalade and beat well. Add the eggs one at a time, beating well after each addition. Add 1 tablespoon of the flour with the last egg.

Sift together the remaining flour, the mixed spice, cinnamon and salt, and stir into the creamed mixture alternately with the fruit and chopped almonds.

Spoon the mixture into the prepared tin. If not icing the cake with almond paste and royal icing, decorate with whole almonds arranged in a pattern on top. Bake for 3–3½ hours or until a skewer inserted in the centre comes out clean. Remove from the oven and immediately sprinkle with about 1 tablespoon extra brandy. Remove the cake from the tin, leaving the paper on the cake. Wrap in a tea towel and leave on a wire rack to cool. Remove the towel and wrap the cake in foil, then store in an airtight tin.

INGREDIENTS

250 g butter, softened
1 cup (220 g) caster sugar
grated rind of 2 oranges
5 eggs, lightly beaten
2½ cups (375 g) plain flour
1 teaspoon baking powder
a pinch of salt
¼ cup chopped blanched almonds
1 cup sultanas
1 cup currants
½ cup chopped mixed candied peel
1 tablespoon orange juice
extra blanched almonds, to decorate

DUNDEE CAKE

This is just such a lovely cake, not too rich. It's very reassuring to have in the house. My mother would always make Dundee cake but it wasn't an after-school treat, more of a weekend treat and for when people came to visit. Traditionally it's not cut in wedges, but thin slices.

SERVES 10

METHOD

Preheat the oven to 150°C. Grease a deep 20 cm round cake tin and line first with brown paper then baking paper.

Using an electric mixer, cream the butter with the sugar and orange rind until light and fluffy. Gradually beat in the eggs.

Sift the flour, baking powder and salt into the creamed mixture and fold in gently with the almonds, fruit, peel and orange juice. Mix until smooth then spoon into the prepared tin, level the surface and arrange the extra almonds on top.

Bake for 2–2½ hours, or until a skewer inserted in the centre comes out clean.

Allow to cool in the tin before turning out.

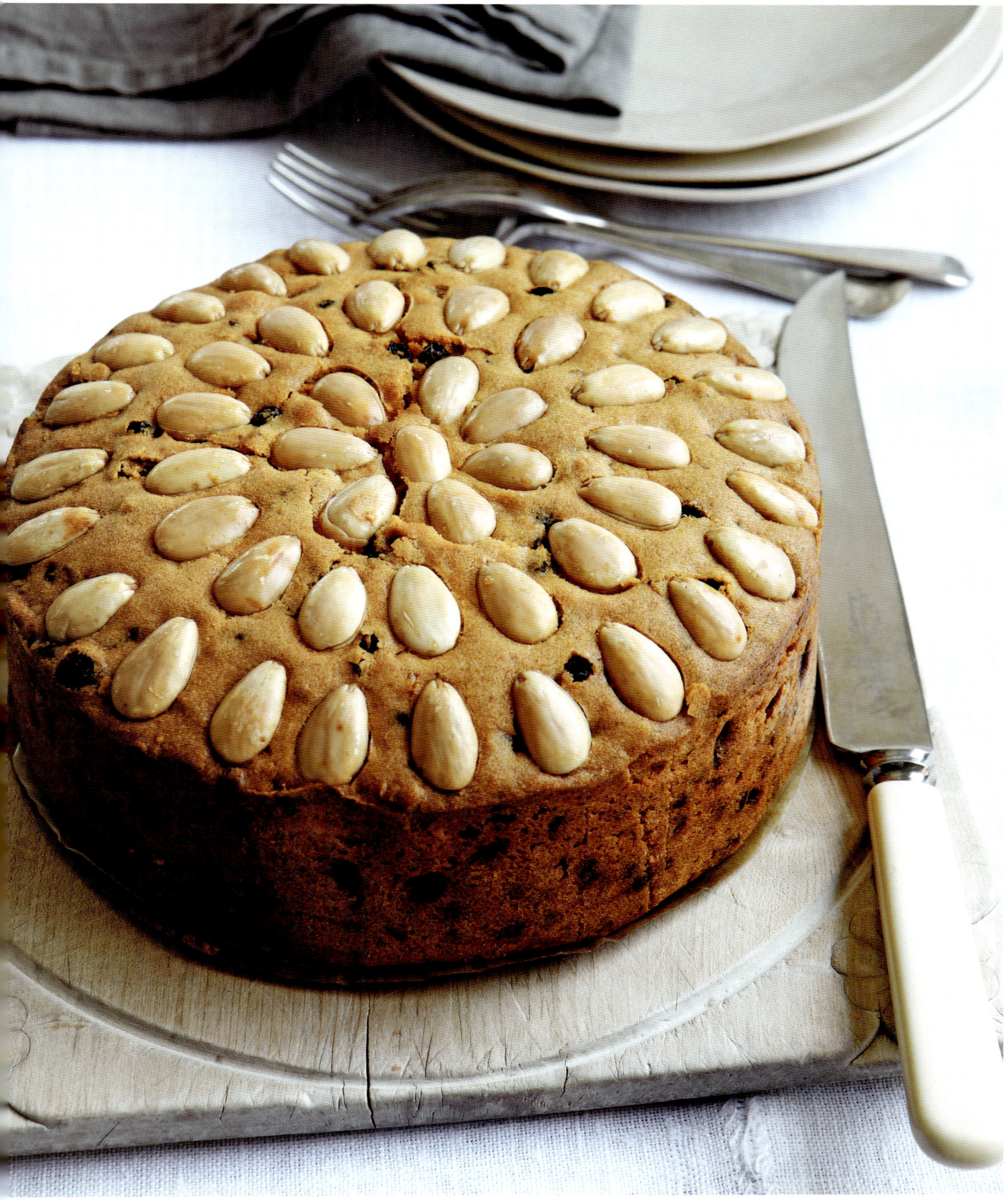

INGREDIENTS

1 Rich Fruit Cake (page 215)

ALMOND PASTE
3 cups (480 g) pure icing sugar, sifted
250 g ground almonds
2 tablespoons lemon juice
2 tablespoons sweet sherry
1 egg yolk
2–3 drops almond essence

GLAZE
3 tablespoons apricot jam
2 tablespoons water
1 teaspoon lemon juice

ICING
2 egg whites
3 ¼ cups (500 g) pure icing sugar, sifted
1–2 teaspoons lemon juice

CHRISTMAS CAKE

I still get a lot of people telling me they make my Christmas cake every year. It's best made a few months ahead of Christmas. It's something to have for when people drop in, and the smell of it in the house is divine. It's very nice to have with a glass of madeira.

SERVES 16–20

METHOD

Make the cake two months before Christmas, and store in an airtight tin until required.

To make the almond paste, combine the icing sugar and ground almonds. Add the lemon juice, sherry, egg yolk and essence and mix to form a firm paste that can be rolled out. If necessary, add a little more sherry.

To make the glaze, bring the jam and water to the boil and boil for 4 minutes. Push through a sieve, return to the pan with the lemon juice and heat through. Brush the hot glaze over the top of the cake.

Roll out the almond paste into a round to fit the top and sides of the cake. Trim off excess paste (see Note). Place on the cake and gently press all over with the edge of a rolling pin until smooth and even. Leave for at least 24 hours before icing.

To make the icing, whisk the egg whites to a light froth and gradually add the icing sugar, beating well. Stir in the lemon juice and continue beating until the icing stands in soft peaks. Spread the icing over the top and sides of the cake. Rough up the icing around the sides and the edge of cake to resemble drifting snow. Decorate as desired. A little of the icing may be set aside, coloured, and used to write 'Merry Christmas' on the cake. Let the icing set overnight.

NOTES Wrap excess almond paste in plastic wrap and store in the fridge for several weeks. It can be used as a sweetmeat to fill pitted dates or to sandwich walnut halves together.

Pure icing sugar, unlike icing sugar mixture, does not have added cornflour to prevent it from caking. Pure icing sugar sets hard, and is the type needed here.

INGREDIENTS

500 g whole, shelled Brazil nuts
12 dates, pitted
1 cup glacé cherries, red and green mixed
¾ cup (110 g) plain flour
½ teaspoon baking powder
½ teaspoon salt
¾ cup (165 g) caster sugar
3 eggs, beaten
1 teaspoon vanilla essence

BISHOP'S CAKE

An old English fruit cake that got its name from the stained-glass window appearance of each slice. It is sometimes known as American Christmas cake, and is more of a fruit-and-nut slab than a cake. This cake should be stored in the refrigerator, wrapped in foil. Being so rich and sweet, only a thin slice is necessary. Bishop's cake may be cut in finger blocks and served with sherry.

SERVES 12–14

METHOD

Preheat the oven to 150°C. Line the base and sides of a 21 cm x 11 cm loaf tin with baking paper.

Put the Brazil nuts, dates and glacé cherries into a large mixing bowl. Sift the dry ingredients over and mix thoroughly. Pour in the eggs and vanilla. Stir well and spoon into the prepared tin.

Bake for about 1½ hours or until a skewer inserted in the centre comes out clean. Remove from the tin, peel away the paper and cool completely on a wire rack.

When cold, wrap in foil and store in the refrigerator. It will keep for up to 3 weeks. Cut into thin slices to serve.

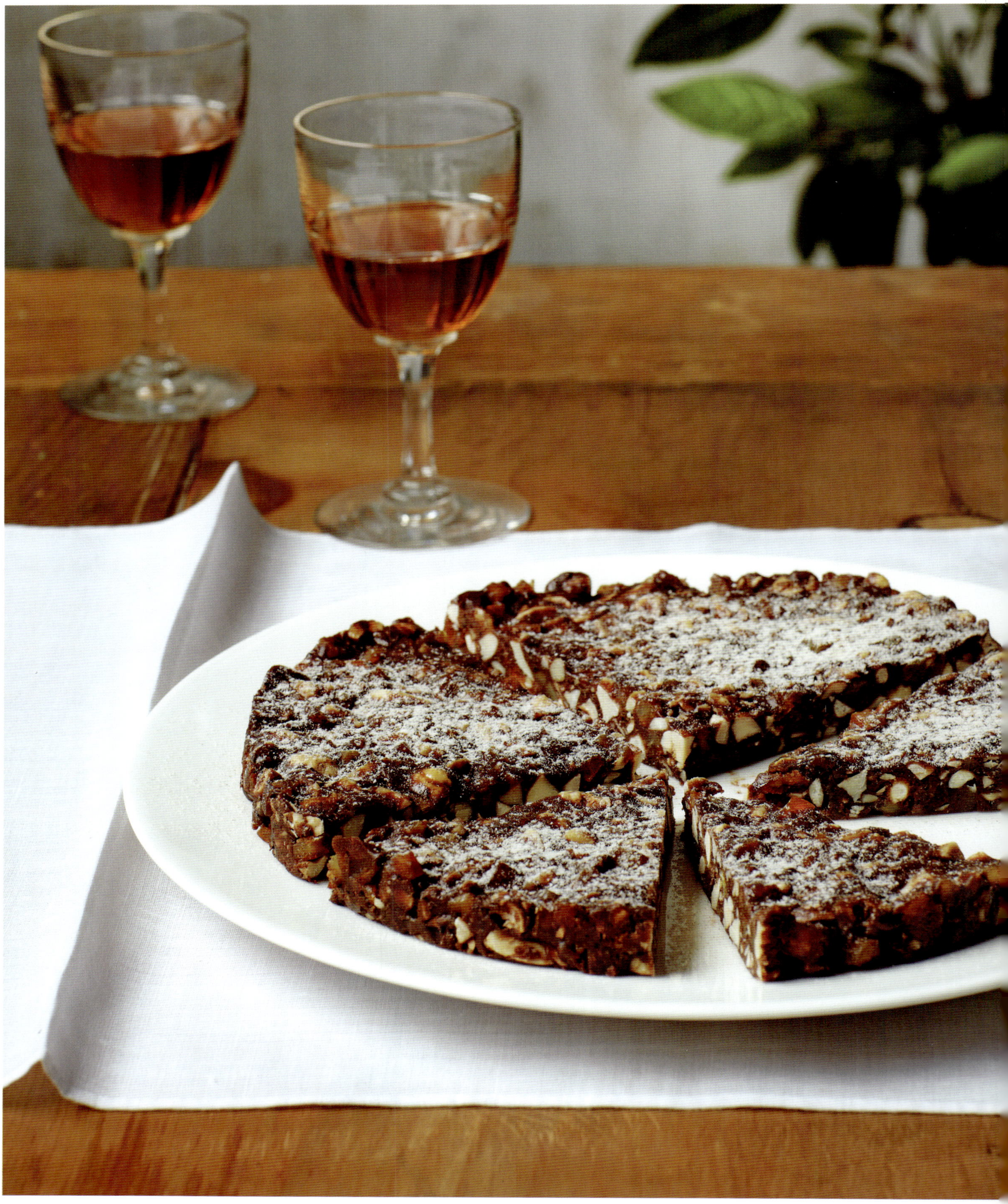

CAKES *fruit cakes*

INGREDIENTS
⅔ cup hazelnuts, toasted, skinned and roughly chopped
¾ cup roughly chopped blanched almonds
1 cup finely chopped mixed candied peel
¼ cup cocoa powder
½ cup (75 g) plain flour, sifted
½ teaspoon ground cinnamon
¼ cup ground nutmeg
½ cup (110 g) caster sugar
⅓ cup clear honey

TOPPING
2 tablespoons icing sugar
1 teaspoon ground cinnamon

SIENA CAKE

I was one of the first people to publish a recipe for Siena cake in Australia. I included it in my encyclopedia after trying it on a trip to Italy. I'd been going to Italy for many years and I was staying in a lovely hotel in the town of Siena. There was a wedding at the hotel and one of the guests gave me some of this cake to try. It is also known as panforte. It is very rich, so serve in small wedges.

SERVES 10–12

METHOD
Preheat the oven to 150°C. Line the base and sides of a 20 cm springform tin with baking paper.

Mix together the hazelnuts, almonds, candied peel, cocoa, flour and spices.

Put the sugar and honey into a small saucepan, heat gently until the sugar dissolves, then boil steadily until a sugar thermometer registers 115°C or until a little of the mixture dropped into a cup of cold water forms a soft ball. Take off the heat immediately and stir in the nut mixture.

Spoon into the prepared tin, spread evenly and press down firmly. If necessary, smooth the surface using dampened hands. Bake for 30–35 minutes. Allow to cool in the tin then turn out and sprinkle the top liberally with the icing sugar sifted with cinnamon.

Cut into small wedges before serving.

NOTE The cake will keep, well wrapped and stored in an airtight container, for 2 months.

INGREDIENTS

185 g butter, softened
1 cup (220 g) caster sugar
3 eggs, lightly beaten
1½ cups (225 g) self-raising flour, sifted
a pinch of salt
2–3 tablespoons milk
1¼ cups cream, whipped
½ cup toasted flaked almonds (see Tip)

COFFEE SYRUP

1 cup strong black coffee
⅓ cup (75 g) sugar
½ cup water
2 tablespoons rum

COFFEE SYRUP CAKE

My daughter Suzanne brought back this recipe from the Cordon Bleu Restaurant in Marylebone Lane, London. Also known as Austrian coffee cake, it's especially moist and has a great flavour, having been soaked in a coffee and rum syrup. It's equally at home for afternoon tea as it is for dessert.

SERVES 8–10

METHOD

Preheat the oven to 180°C. Grease a 5-cup fluted bundt or ring tin (I use a savarin mould).

Using an electric mixer, cream the butter until soft, then add the sugar, a little at a time, and continue beating until light and fluffy. Gradually add the eggs, beating thoroughly after each addition.

Fold in the sifted flour and salt alternately with enough milk to make a dropping consistency. Spoon into the prepared tin, smooth the top and bake for 40–45 minutes or until a skewer inserted in the centre comes out clean. Leave to cool in the tin for a few minutes, then release the sides a little with the help of a metal spatula and turn out onto a wire rack to cool.

To make the coffee syrup, put the coffee in a heatproof jug. (A good instant coffee can be used, but make it strong.)

Heat the sugar and water in a saucepan until the sugar dissolves, then boil for 2 minutes. Add to the coffee and cool. Stir in the rum.

When the cake has cooled, return it to the tin. Slowly pour the coffee syrup evenly over the cake. Cover with plastic wrap and refrigerate until ready to serve. Turn out onto a serving plate and coat with whipped cream and toasted flaked almonds, or serve with a bowl of whipped cream on the side if liked.

TIP To toast the almonds, spread them on a baking tray and cook in a preheated 180°C oven, shaking the tray several times until the almonds turn a pale golden. This can be done in a heavy-based frying pan over a gentle heat but watch that the almonds don't burn. Cool before using.

CAKES *continental cakes*

INGREDIENTS
125 g butter, softened
²⁄₃ cup (150 g) firmly packed brown sugar
2 eggs
½ cup (75 g) self-raising flour, sifted
½ cup ground almonds
75 g dark chocolate, grated
extra grated chocolate (optional)

TOFFEE ICING
60 g butter
²⁄₃ cup (150 g) firmly packed brown sugar
2 tablespoons golden syrup
½ cup cream
sifted icing sugar (optional)

CHOCOLATE TOFFEE CAKE

SERVES 6-8

METHOD

Preheat the oven to 180°C. Grease a 20 cm cake tin and line the base and sides with baking paper.

Using an electric mixer, cream the butter with the sugar until light and fluffy. Beat in the eggs one at a time, then fold in the flour, ground almonds and chocolate.

Spoon into the prepared tin and bake for 1¼ hours or until firm to a light touch. Leave in the tin for 5 minutes, then turn carefully onto a wire rack to cool.

To make the toffee icing, put the butter, brown sugar and syrup into a saucepan. Stir over a gentle heat until the sugar has dissolved. Bring to the boil, reduce the heat immediately and simmer, without stirring, for 5 minutes.

Remove from the heat and slowly pour in the cream in a steady stream, beating well with a wooden spoon. Leave to cool and thicken.

If you prefer a thicker icing, add sufficient icing sugar to give the desired consistency. Spread over the cake and swirl the surface with a spoon. Decorate with extra grated chocolate, if wished.

INGREDIENTS

1¾ cups (260 g) plain flour
2 teaspoons baking powder
a pinch of salt
75 g butter, softened
⅓ cup caster sugar
2 tablespoons milk
1 egg

FILLING

125 g butter
4 tablespoons caster sugar
1 cup thick cold egg custard (custard made from custard powder may be used)
2 teaspoons vanilla essence

TOPPING

75 g butter
3 tablespoons caster sugar
2 tablespoons honey
250 g flaked blanched almonds

BIENENSTICH

This much-loved honey-flavoured 'bee sting' cake of Germany has a creamy custard filling and a delectable topping of sugar-encrusted flaked almonds that add a beautiful golden nuttiness. I've been to Germany a number of times but the first time I tried this cake was in the Barossa Valley in South Australia. I met some Germans who lived there and they made this delicious cake for us.

SERVES 8

METHOD

Preheat the oven to 190°C. Grease a 20 cm springform cake tin.

Sift together the flour, baking powder and salt.

Using an electric mixer, cream the butter with the sugar until light and fluffy.

Combine the milk and egg and gradually add to the creamed mixture. Work in the dry ingredients to make a soft dough. Spread the batter evenly in the prepared tin. Bake for 30–35 minutes.

To make the filling, using an electric mixer, cream the butter and sugar together until light and fluffy, then gradually beat in the cold custard and vanilla.

When the cake is cooked, release the spring and cool the cake on a wire rack. When cold, split the cake into two layers and sandwich together with the filling.

To make the topping, melt the butter in a heavy frying pan over low heat, add the sugar and honey and stir until combined. Remove from the heat, stir in the almonds until the nuts are shiny, then quickly spread the mixture evenly over the cake. Allow to set before cutting.

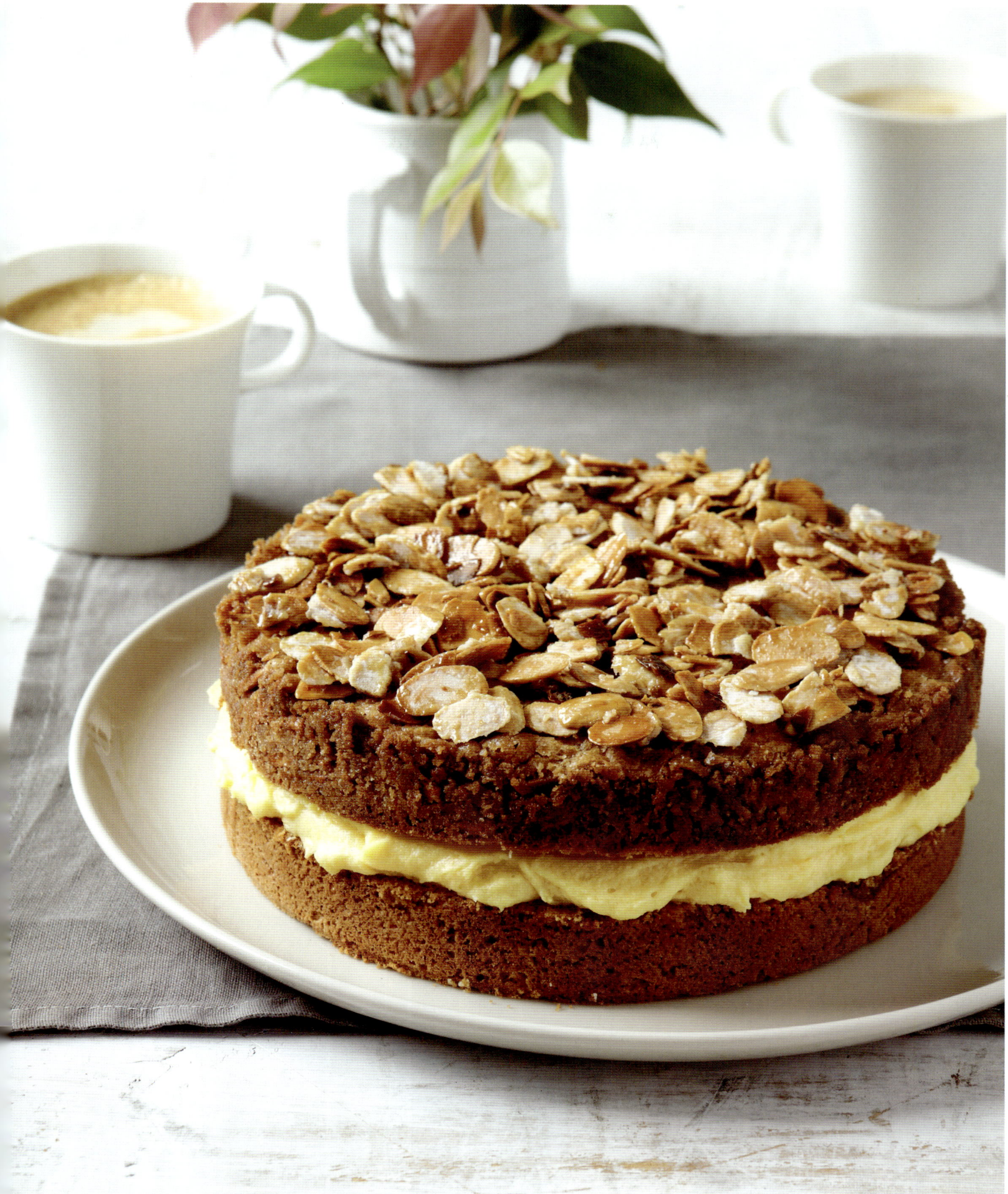

INGREDIENTS

4 eggs
¾ cup (165 g) caster sugar
1¼ cups (185 g) plain flour, sifted

COFFEE BUTTER CREAM
⅓ cup (75 g) caster sugar
½ cup water
3 egg yolks
250 g unsalted butter, creamed
½ cup toasted ground hazelnuts
1 tablespoon coffee essence

CARAMEL
⅔ cup (150 g) caster sugar
⅓ cup water

DECORATION
½ cup toasted ground hazelnuts
8 whole hazelnuts

COFFEE & NUT DOBOZTORTE

SERVES 8

METHOD

Line three baking trays with baking paper. Using a cake tin or plate as a guide, mark five 20 cm circles on the trays: two circles on two of the trays and one on the third tray.

Whisk the eggs with the sugar in a heatproof bowl over a saucepan of very hot water off the heat until the mixture is thick and mousse-like. Remove from the saucepan and continue whisking until the bowl is cold. Using a metal spoon, fold in the sifted flour, lightly and thoroughly. Divide the mixture into five portions and spread inside each circle on the prepared trays. Bake for 5–8 minutes or until pale golden brown. Remove from the oven. Using a sharp knife, trim rounds if necessary. Cool on wire racks.

To make the coffee butter cream, dissolve the sugar in the water in a small saucepan, stirring, over medium heat. Bring to the boil and boil for 5–6 minutes, without stirring, until the syrup reaches thread stage. (To test, drop ½ teaspoon syrup into a cup of ice cold water; it should form threads.) Pour onto the egg yolks and whisk until thick and mousse-like. Gradually beat in the creamed butter, hazelnuts and coffee essence.

Place one round of cake on an oiled baking tray ready to coat with caramel.

To make the caramel, combine the sugar and water in a heavy saucepan over very low heat and stir until the sugar dissolves. Increase the heat, bring to the boil and boil steadily, without stirring, until the mixture is a rich dark brown. Pour at once over the round of cake. Cool for a few minutes until on the point of setting, then mark into eight portions with an oiled knife and trim around edges. To assemble the torte, sandwich the cake rounds together with half the butter cream, placing the caramel-covered round on top. Spread the sides of the cake with half the remaining butter cream, and press ground hazelnuts onto sides. Using the rest of the butter cream, pipe a rosette on each caramel portion and decorate with whole hazelnuts.

NOTE Baking the rounds of cake can be done in rotation using one baking tray.

CAKES *continental cakes*

INGREDIENTS
2 eggs, beaten
2 cups sour cream
2 cups (440 g) caster sugar
3 drops almond essence
2$\frac{2}{3}$ cups (400 g) plain flour
1 teaspoon bicarbonate of soda
½ teaspoon salt
1 teaspoon ground cinnamon
1 teaspoon ground cardamom

FINNISH SOUR CREAM CAKE

I've made quite a few trips to Finland and I had never before seen sour cream used in baking. It's a favourite cake in Finland and I thought it was interesting because it has a little spice in it, that's what appealed to me. Cardamom features a lot in Finland. If I'm serving it as a dessert, I serve it with some cream and raspberries on the side.

SERVES 8–10

METHOD
Preheat the oven to 180°C. Grease a 23 cm gugelhopf, bundt or ring tin and dust with sugar.

Place the eggs, sour cream, sugar and almond essence in a large bowl and mix until combined. Sift the flour with the bicarbonate of soda, salt and spices and add gradually to the egg mixture, beating until the batter is smooth.

Spoon into the prepared tin and bake for 1¼ hours or until a skewer inserted into the centre comes out clean.

Leave in the tin for 10 minutes before turning out to cool on a wire rack.

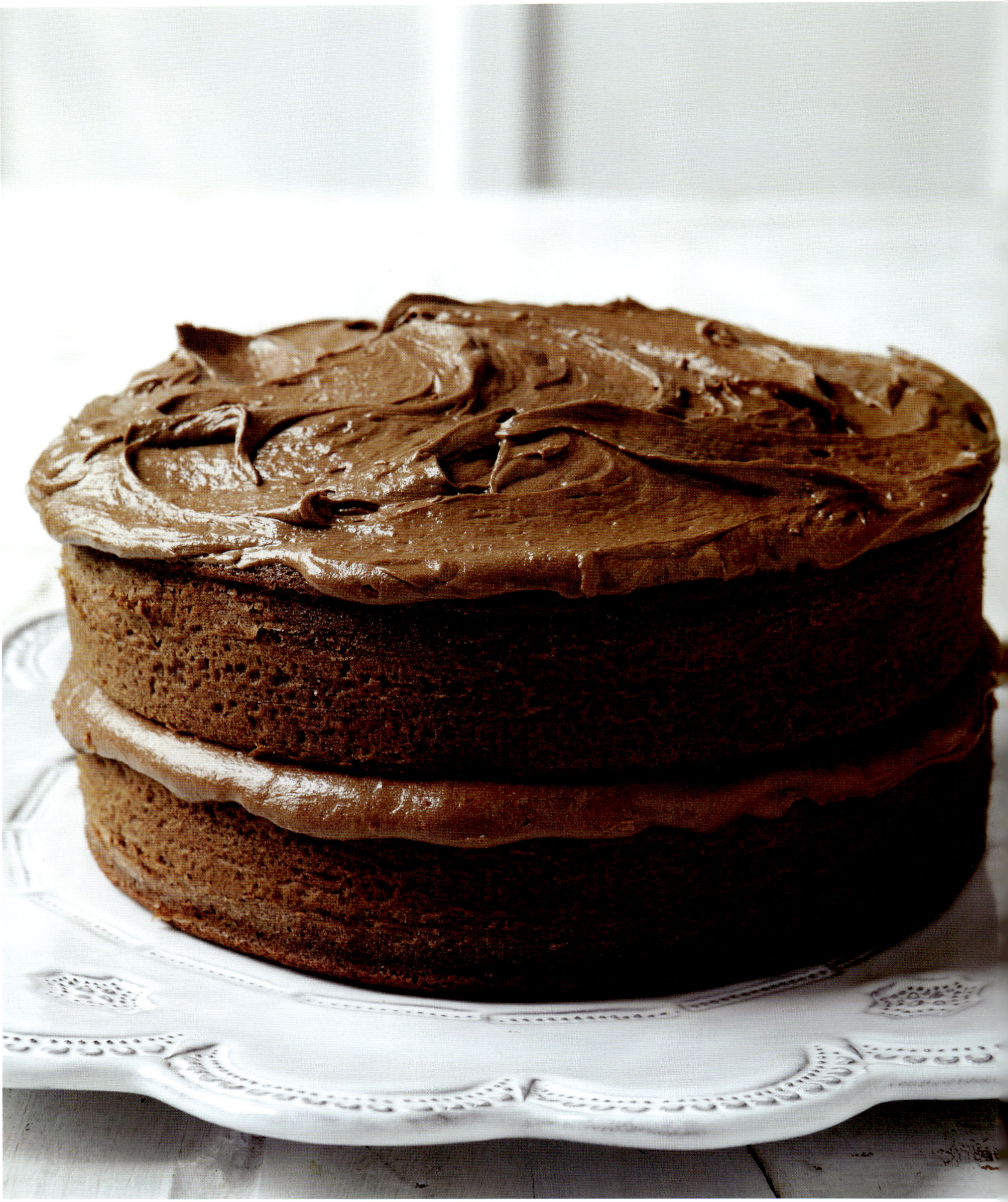

CAKES *continental cakes*

INGREDIENTS
CHOCOLATE FROSTING
185 g cream cheese, softened
125 g butter, softened
½ teaspoon vanilla essence
½ teaspoon peppermint essence
6 cups (960 g) icing sugar, sifted
¼ cup hot water
125 g dark cooking chocolate, melted

CAKE
60 g butter, softened
3 eggs
2 cups (300 g) plain flour
1½ teaspoons bicarbonate of soda
1 teaspoon salt
¾ cup milk

DOUBLE CHOCOLATE CAKE

SERVES 8

METHOD
Preheat the oven to 180°C. Grease two 20 cm round sandwich tins and dust with flour.

To make the chocolate frosting, beat together the cream cheese, butter and essences, blending well. Beat in half the icing sugar, then add the remainder alternately with the hot water. Add the melted chocolate and mix until smooth.

To make the cake, mix the butter with 2 cups of the chocolate frosting. Add the eggs, one at a time, and beat for 1 minute.

Sift the flour, bicarbonate of soda and salt, and stir into the creamed mixture alternately with the milk, beginning and ending with the dry ingredients. Spoon into the prepared tins and bake for 30–40 minutes.

Turn out onto a wire rack to cool.

Sandwich the cooled cakes together with a little of the remaining frosting or jam. Decorate the cake by spreading the rest of the frosting over the top.

INGREDIENTS

1½ cups poppy seeds
6 eggs, separated
1 cup (220 g) caster sugar
½ cup chopped mixed candied peel
1 teaspoon ground allspice
sifted icing sugar to dust
whipped cream to serve (optional)

POPPY SEED CAKE

An unusual but delicious Continental-style cake; it contains no flour and is bound by the poppy seeds and eggs alone. Serve as a dessert or as a tea-time treat, with whipped cream.

SERVES 6–8

METHOD

Preheat the oven to 180°C. Grease a 23 cm springform tin and dust wth flour.

Grind the poppy seeds in a blender. Beat the egg yolks until thick, then gradually add the sugar and continue beating until very thick and pale. Stir in the peel, allspice and poppy seeds.

Beat the egg whites until stiff and fold into the yolk mixture. Pour into the prepared tin and bake for about 50 minutes.

Allow the cake to cool in the tin, then remove the sides. Dust the cake with icing sugar. Serve with whipped cream if liked.

NOTE Allspice is ground pimento (the berry of a tree native to the West Indies). It is not to be confused with mixed spice, which is a combination of cinnamon, nutmeg, allspice, coriander, mace and cloves.

CAKES *continental cakes*

INGREDIENTS

1½ cups (225 g) plain flour
½ teaspoon bicarbonate of soda
1 tablespoon ground ginger
1 teaspoon ground cinnamon
¼ teaspoon ground cloves
¼ teaspoon ground allspice
125 g unsalted butter, softened
½ cup (110 g) firmly packed brown sugar
½ cup treacle
2 eggs
2 teaspoons vanilla essence
½ cup buttermilk

LEMON FROSTING (OPTIONAL)

30 g butter, softened
1 tablespoon lemon juice
1 tablespoon grated orange rind
2 cups (320 g) icing sugar, sifted

GINGERBREAD

SERVES 8

METHOD

Preheat the oven to 180°C. Butter a deep 23 cm round cake tin and line the base with baking paper.

Sift the flour, bicarbonate of soda and spices into a bowl.

Using an electric mixer, cream the butter then beat in the brown sugar, until the mixture is light and fluffy. Beat in the treacle and then the eggs, one at a time. Beat in the vanilla essence. Lastly, fold through the sifted flour mixture thoroughly, and then the buttermilk.

Spoon the mixture into the prepared tin, smoothing the top and making a slight indentation in the centre with a spatula. Bake for 35–40 minutes, or until a skewer inserted in the centre comes out clean.

Cool in the tin on a wire rack. Turn out onto a serving plate and serve plain or spread with lemon frosting.

For the lemon frosting, cream the butter, juice and rind then add the sifted icing sugar, beating until smooth.

INGREDIENTS

6 eggs, separated
1 cup (220 g) caster sugar
grated rind and juice of 1 lemon
$\frac{2}{3}$ cup fine semolina
4 tablespoons ground almonds
$\frac{2}{3}$ cup cream, whipped
1 punnet (250 g) strawberries or raspberries, sprinkled with 1 tablespoon caster sugar

GRIESTORTE

What makes this cake so lovely is the semolina in it, which helps give the cake an interesting texture. This is a German cake. The original griestorte that I used to make was not nearly so high. It's quite a thinnish cake but we've taken to things looking higher. Food is a little bit like fashion. We've used two sponges to make a more dramatic version but you can just make one sponge and halve it. Don't be put off by the idea that it's not so high.

SERVES 8

METHOD

Preheat the oven to 180°C. Grease two 20 cm cake tins, line the bases with baking paper and dust with caster sugar and flour.

Using electric beaters, beat the egg yolks with the sugar over a pan of hot water until thick and mousse-like. Remove from the heat, add the lemon rind and juice and continue beating until very thick and pale. Stir in the semolina and ground almonds.

Whisk the egg whites until stiff peaks form, then fold into the mixture. Pour at once into the prepared tin and bake for 40–45 minutes or until the cakes shrink a little from the sides of the tin.

Turn out onto a wire rack to cool. When cold, spread one cake with whipped cream, cover with the other cake and top with raspberries or strawberries.

VARIATION
GRIESTORTE WITH FRESH PEACHES OR PEARS
Peel, stone or core and slice two fresh peaches or pears, dip in water acidulated with lemon juice to prevent browning, remove, dry well and put in between the cake layers with whipped cream flavoured with a little honey. Dust the top of the cake with sifted icing sugar.

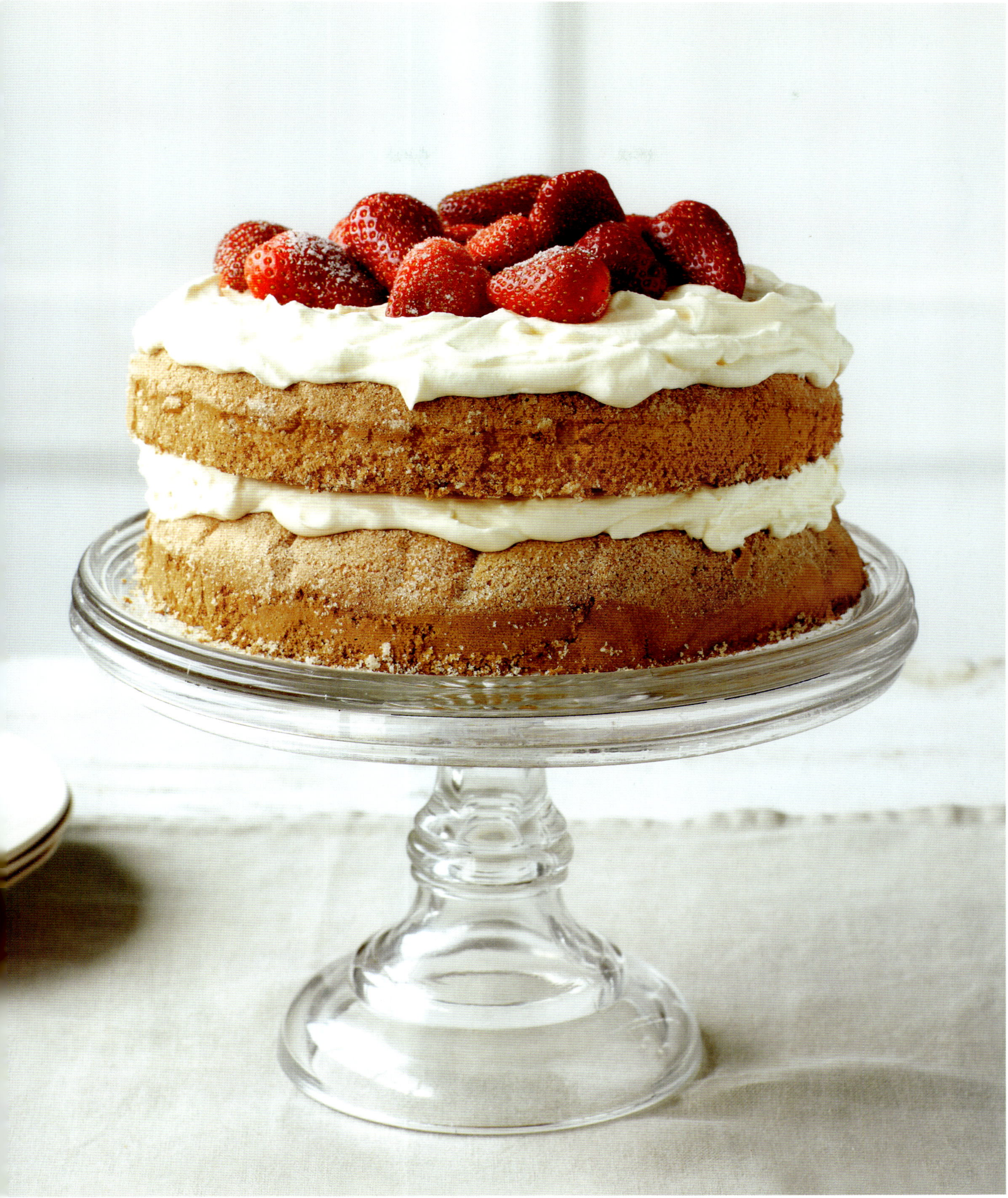

INGREDIENTS
250 g butter, softened
1 cup (220 g) caster sugar
1 teaspoon grated orange rind
4 eggs, separated
1 cup (150 g) plain flour
1 cup fine semolina
4 teaspoons baking powder
1 teaspoon ground cinnamon
½ cup milk
2 cups coarsely ground walnuts

SYRUP
1 cup (220 g) caster sugar
1 cup water
2 whole cloves
5 cm cinnamon stick
1 tablespoon lemon juice
thin strip of lemon rind

GREEK WALNUT CAKE

SERVES 8–10

METHOD

Preheat the oven to 180°C. Generously grease a 33 cm x 23 cm x 5 cm baking dish and line the base with baking paper.

Using an electric mixer, cream the butter with the sugar and orange rind until light and fluffy. Add the egg yolks, beating well after each addition.

Sift the flour, semolina, baking powder and cinnamon. Fold into the creamed mixture alternately with the milk, and add the walnuts, mixing gently.

Beat the egg whites until stiff and fold into the mixture. Spoon into the prepared dish and bake for 45 minutes or until a fine skewer inserted in centre comes out clean.

To make the syrup, combine the ingredients in a heavy saucepan and stir over medium heat until the sugar dissolves. Bring to the boil and boil over moderately high heat for 10 minutes. Strain.

Remove the cake from the oven and pour the hot syrup over the cake while still in the tin. Allow to cool in the tin. When cold, cut into square or diamond shapes to serve.

CAKES *continental cakes*

INGREDIENTS

3 eggs, separated
½ cup (110 g) caster sugar
½ teaspoon vanilla essence
¼ cup Caramel Syrup (below)
⅔ cup (100 g) plain flour
½ teaspoon baking powder
½ teaspoon salt
¼ teaspoon cream of tartar
½ cup chopped toasted almonds

TOPPING

1 cup cream, whipped with 1 tablespoon brown sugar
a few whole toasted almonds

CARAMEL ALMOND TORTE

SERVES 8

METHOD

Preheat the oven to 180°C. Lightly grease a 23 cm springform cake tin.

Beat the egg yolks until thick, pale and creamy, then beat in ¼ cup of the sugar and the vanilla. Gradually add the caramel syrup and beat until well blended.

Sift the flour, baking powder and salt over the mixture and gently fold in.

Whisk the egg whites until foamy, add the cream of tartar and whisk until the whites hold their shape. Gradually whisk in the remaining sugar and continue whisking until the whites are a stiff snow.

Fold the whites into the yolk mixture with the chopped almonds. Pour into the prepared tin and bake for 25 minutes or until golden brown on top and beginning to shrink away slightly from the sides of the tin. Remove the sides of the tin and cool the cake on a wire rack.

Top with whipped cream and almonds to serve.

CARAMEL SYRUP

This syrup, used to flavour cakes and biscuits, keeps indefinitely if stored in a covered container in the refrigerator.

Gently melt 1 cup caster sugar in a heavy-based pan until golden. When bubbles appear over the whole surface, remove from the heat and very slowly pour in 1 cup boiling water. Cool. Makes 1½ cups.

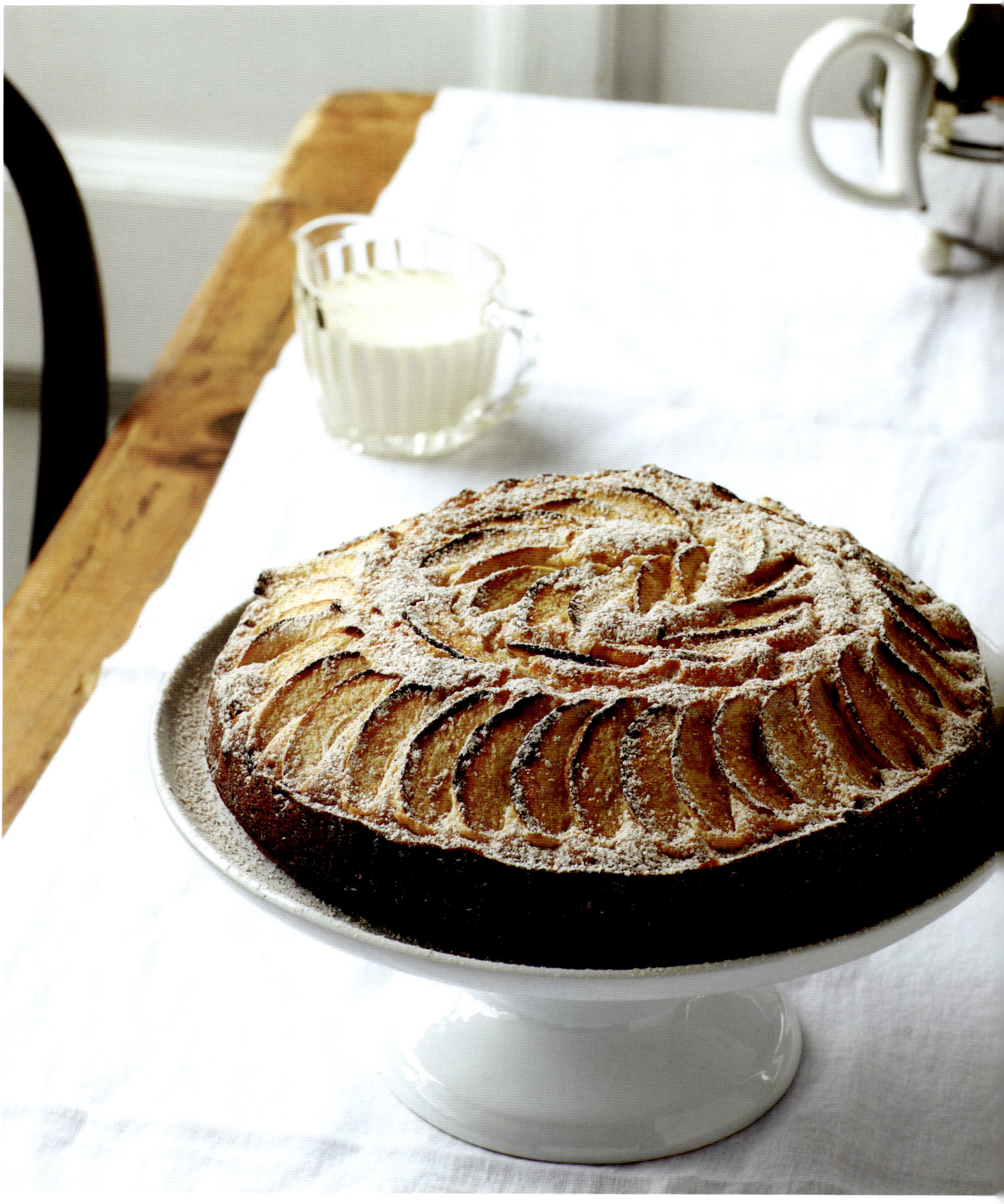

CAKES *continental cakes*

INGREDIENTS
125 g butter, softened
2/3 cup (150 g) caster sugar
2 eggs
1 2/3 cups (250 g) self-raising flour, sifted
1/2 cup milk
4 medium apples
juice of 1 lemon
extra caster sugar and ground cinnamon to sprinkle

GERMAN APPLE CAKE

This is a cake I've always made over the years. It's beautifully presented yet quite simple to make.

SERVES 6-8

METHOD

Preheat the oven to 180°C. Grease a 23 cm springform tin and line the base with baking paper.

Cream the butter with the sugar. Add the eggs and beat well. Add half of the flour and beat to combine. Add the milk and remaining flour alternately (this will make a thick mixture). Spread the mixture in the prepared tin.

Peel, quarter and thinly slice the apples. As you prepare them, put the slices in a bowl and squeeze over the lemon juice to prevent discoloration.

Arrange the drained apples on top of the the cake batter. Bake for 40 minutes or until risen and golden. While still warm, sprinkle with sugar and cinnamon.

INGREDIENTS

1¼ cups fine fresh breadcrumbs
grated rind of 1 orange
juice of 3 large oranges
125 g ground almonds
1 tablespoon orange-flower water
4 eggs, separated
½ cup (110 g) caster sugar
½ teaspoon salt
1 cup cream, whipped

ORANGE & ALMOND CAKE

SERVES 6

METHOD

Preheat the oven to 180°C. Grease a 20 cm square or round tin and sprinkle lightly with ¼ cup of the breadcrumbs.

Mix together the remaining breadcrumbs, the orange rind and juice, ground almonds and orange-flower water. Beat the egg yolks with the sugar and salt until very pale and thick and stir into the orange mixture.

Beat the egg whites until they hold stiff peaks and fold into the orange mixture. Turn into the prepared cake tin.

Bake for about 40 minutes. Allow the cake to cool in the tin. When cold, turn out and spread whipped cream over the top before serving.

NOTE Orange-flower water can be purchased from many health food shops and delicatessens, or in concentrated form from chemists. If using the concentrate, you will need only 2–3 drops.

CAKES *continental cakes*

INGREDIENTS

CARAMEL
75 g butter, softened
⅓ cup (75 g) firmly packed brown sugar

DECORATION
3 rings canned pineapple
6 glacé cherries
6 walnut halves

CAKE
1½ cups (225 g) self-raising flour
½ teaspoon salt
60 g butter
¾ cup (165 g) caster sugar
1 egg, well whisked
½ cup milk

PINEAPPLE UPSIDE-DOWN CAKE

Serve this dessert cake hot with ice cream, egg custard or a sweet sauce.

SERVES 6–8

METHOD

Preheat the oven to 180°C. Grease and line a 20 cm round cake tin.

To make the caramel, cream the butter with the sugar. Spread over the bottom and side of the prepared tin.

To make the decoration, halve the pineapple rings horizontally to make six thin rings; arrange these on the caramel and decorate with cherries and walnuts.

For the cake, sift the flour and salt together three times.

Using an electric mixer, cream the butter with the sugar, then beat in the egg until light and fluffy. Stir in the sifted flour alternately with the milk. Spoon the cake mxture carefully on top of the pineapple arrangement in the tin.

Bake for 50–60 minutes. Invert onto a serving plate as soon as the cake is removed from the oven. Leave for a few minutes then remove the tin.

INGREDIENTS

FRUIT LAYER
1 cup well-drained canned or poached apricots
30 g butter, melted
3 tablespoons brown sugar

CAKE
125 g butter
½ cup (110 g) caster sugar
2 eggs
1 cup (150 g) self-raising flour, sifted

APRICOT UPSIDE-DOWN CAKE

The cake layer in this recipe is light and short, and not very high. This recipe has a number of variations to suit different tastes. It is essential to drain the fruit well.

SERVES 6

METHOD
Preheat the oven to 180°C. Grease an 18 cm round sandwich tin and line the base with baking paper.

For the fruit layer, brush the butter in the base of the prepared tin. Sprinkle evenly with the sugar, and arrange the apricots in a decorative pattern.

To make the cake, using an electric mixer, cream the butter with the sugar until light and fluffy, then add the eggs one at a time and beat well. Fold in the flour.

Spoon the cake mixture over the fruit, being careful not to disturb the fruit. Bake for 30 minutes or until a skewer inserted into the centre comes out clean. Turn out, leaving the cake fruit side up.

Serve warm with cream, ice cream or custard, or cold with tea or coffee.

VARIATIONS

APPLE OR PEAR UPSIDE-DOWN CAKE Replace the apricots with peeled and thinly sliced cooking apple (such as Granny Smith) or ripe but firm pear. Arrange the slices, slightly overlapping them, in concentric circles on the base.

PEACH OR PLUM UPSIDE-DOWN CAKE Replace the apricots with well-drained canned or poached peach slices or plum halves.

CHERRY OR BERRY UPSIDE-DOWN CAKE Replace the apricots with fresh or frozen blueberries or raspberries, or pitted fresh cherries, or well-drained canned pitted cherries. Arrange the fruit in a single layer.

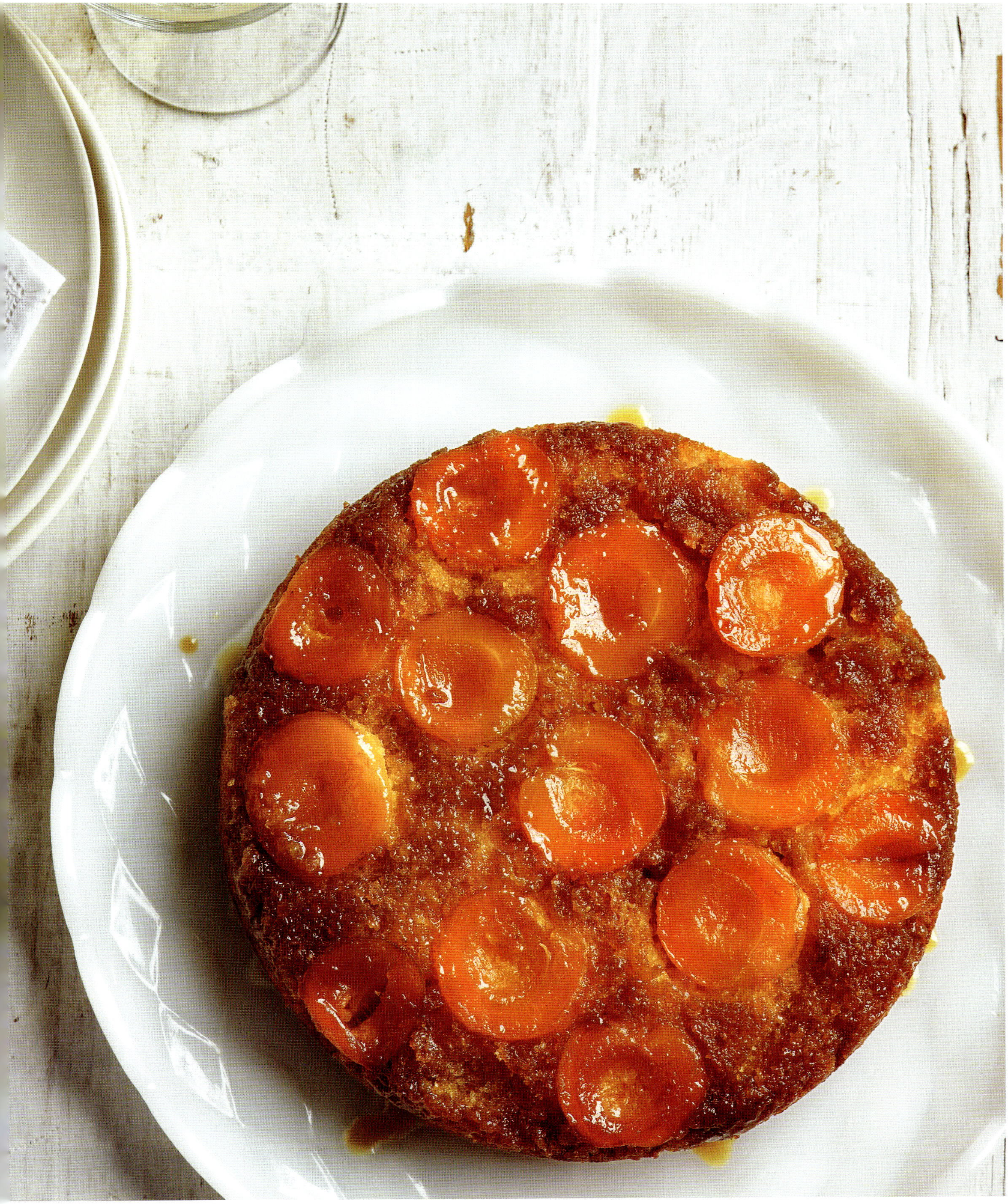

INGREDIENTS

1 2/3 cups (250 g) self-raising flour
2 teaspoons ground ginger
a pinch of salt
125 g butter, softened
3/4 cup (165 g) firmly packed brown sugar
2 eggs
1 cup treacle
1/3 cup sultanas
1/3 cup sliced preserved ginger
1/4 cup milk
1/2 teaspoon bicarbonate of soda

RICH GINGER CAKE

A rich, moist cake with excellent keeping qualities. It is an old family favourite that is good for picnics, lunchboxes and morning and afternoon snacks.

SERVES 6–8

METHOD

Preheat the oven to 180°C. Grease a deep 18 cm round cake tin or a 21 cm x 11 cm x 6 cm loaf tin and line the base with baking paper.

Sift the flour with the ground ginger and salt.

Using an electric mixer, cream the butter with the sugar until light and fluffy. Beat the eggs into the creamed butter mixture one at a time, sprinkling the mixture each time with 2 teaspoons flour. Stir in the treacle, sultanas, preserved ginger and remaining flour.

Warm the milk gently, add the bicarbonate of soda and stir at once into the cake mixture.

Spoon into the prepared tin and bake for 1 hour, then reduce the heat to 160°C and bake for a further 30 minutes. If the cake begins to brown too much on top, cover loosely with a piece of baking paper.

Cool for 5 minutes in the tin before turning out onto a wire rack.

INGREDIENTS

⅓ cup flaked almonds (optional)
1 cup boiling water
125 g dark chocolate, chopped
1 teaspoon bicarbonate of soda
250 g unsalted butter, softened
1½ cups (330 g) caster sugar
3 large eggs, separated
1 teaspoon vanilla essence
2½ cups (375 g) plain flour
a pinch of salt
1 teaspoon baking powder
⅔ cup light sour cream

SOUR CREAM CHOCOLATE CAKE

If I had to choose only one chocolate cake recipe to carry me through life, this would have to be it. It is just as a chocolate cake should be — not the fudgy, flourless kind that everyone loves for dessert, but the perfect cake to slice into wedges for afternoon teas and picnics. The sour cream is the secret to its lightness. The cake cuts easily, yet is rich and beautifully moist. You can keep it plain or add a coating of buttery almonds. The recipe makes one very large cake or two smaller cakes: one to eat and one to freeze for another time or give to a friend.

SERVES 16-20

METHOD

Preheat the oven to 180°C. Generously butter a 3-litre fluted bundt tin or two 20 cm (6-cup) ring tins. Sprinkle with the flaked almonds, if using, pressing them well into the butter to coat the base and sides of the tin(s).

Put the boiling water, chocolate and bicarbonate of soda in a bowl and stir until the chocolate is melted and smooth. Leave to cool.

Using an electric mixer, cream the butter and sugar until light and fluffy, then add the egg yolks one at a time, beating after each addition. Stir in the vanilla, then add the chocolate mixture a little at a time.

Sift the flour, salt and baking powder and fold in alternately with the sour cream, mixing lightly until just combined.

Beat the egg whites until stiff but not dry and fold into the mixture with a large metal spoon. Spoon gently into the prepared tin(s) and bake for 1–1¼ hours for a large cake, 45 minutes for smaller cakes, or until a skewer inserted into the centre comes out clean.

Leave in the tin(s) for a few minutes, then turn out and cool on a wire rack.

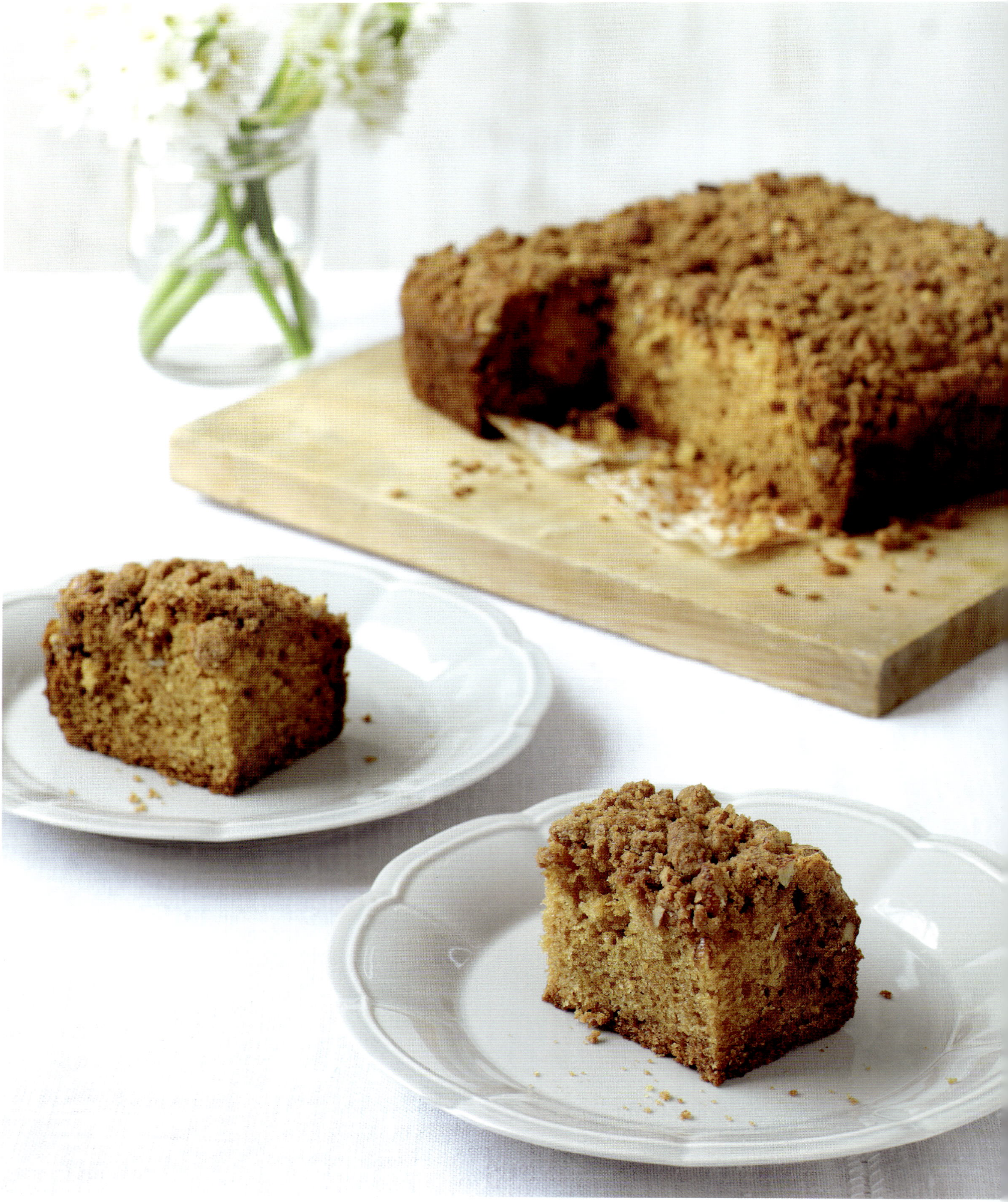

CAKES *continental cakes*

INGREDIENTS
60 g butter, softened
¾ cup (165 g) caster sugar
2 eggs, lightly beaten
300 ml sour cream
1 teaspoon vanilla essence
2 cups (300 g) plain flour, sifted
1 teaspoon baking powder, sifted
1 teaspoon bicarbonate of soda, sifted
½ teaspoon salt, sifted

STREUSEL TOPPING
⅔ cup pecans, roughly chopped
½ cup (75 g) plain flour
½ cup (110 g) brown sugar
75 g butter, melted
1 teaspoon ground cinnamon

SOUR CREAM STREUSEL CAKE

SERVES 10–12

METHOD
Preheat oven to 180°C. Grease a 20 cm square cake tin and line the base and sides with baking paper. Ensure there is an overhang of at least 2 cm above the rim (see Tips).

To make the streusel topping, combine all the ingredients in a bowl, using a fork or fingers, until crumbly. Set aside.

Using an electric mixer, cream the butter and sugar together until pale and fluffy. Gradually add the eggs, beating continuously, until the mixture forms a smooth batter. Add the sour cream and vanilla and beat on low until just combined.

Gently fold the combined flour, baking powder, bicarbonate of soda and salt into the butter mixture. Spoon into the prepared tin and sprinkle with the streusel topping.

Bake for 40–45 minutes. Cool in the pan for 10 minutes before lifting out carefully and transferring to a wire rack to cool completely.

TIPS By extending the baking paper above the rim of the tin it will be much easier to lift the cake out without disturbing the streusel topping. This is a useful technique for many cakes that are too delicate to be turned out or that have a fragile topping.

Almonds or walnuts can be used in place of pecans.

When creaming small amounts of butter and sugar, as here, you may find it more effective to do so in a small bowl, then transfer the creamed mixture to a larger bowl and add the remaining ingredients.

INGREDIENTS

200 g dark chocolate, roughly chopped
150 g unsalted butter
2/3 cup (150 g) caster sugar
1 tablespoon whisky (see Tip)
1 tablespoon espresso coffee
5 eggs, separated
3/4 cup ground hazelnuts
cocoa powder to dust
thick cream to serve

ESPRESSO CHOCOLATE & HAZELNUT CAKE

SERVES 8

METHOD

Preheat the oven to 180°C. Grease a 20 cm springform cake tin and line the base with baking paper.

Put the chocolate, butter, sugar, whisky and coffee in a heatproof bowl. Place over a saucepan of simmering water and stir for 4–5 minutes, until the chocolate has melted and the mixture is smooth. Remove from the heat.

Whisk in the egg yolks, one at a time, until smooth. Fold through the ground hazelnuts. Using an electric mixer or whisk, beat the egg whites until firm peaks form. Stir 2 tablespoons of the whites into the chocolate mixture. Gently fold in the remaining whites.

Pour into prepared the tin and bake for 50 minutes or until firm. Cool in the tin for 5 minutes before transferring to a wire rack to cool completely.

Dust with cocoa and serve with thick cream.

TIP Replace the whisky with brandy or rum, or with milk for a child-friendly option.

CAKES *continental cakes*

INGREDIENTS

CAKE
90 g dark chocolate, broken up
1 tablespoon water or black coffee
4 eggs
¾ cup (165 g) caster sugar
¾ cup (110 g) self-raising flour
1 teaspoon vanilla essence
grated rind of ½ lemon
45 g butter, melted and cooled

TOPPING & FILLING
280 g milk chocolate
700 g jar sour cherries
3 tablespoons Kirsch
2 cups cream

BLACK FOREST CHERRY TORTE

This famous German torte originated in Swabia in the Black Forest region. The basic combination consists of chocolate cake, chocolate, Kirsch and cherries with a wickedly rich amount of whipped cream.

SERVES 10–12

METHOD

Preheat the oven to 180°C. Grease a 23 cm springform cake tin, line the base with baking paper and dust with flour.

To make the cake, melt the chocolate and water or coffee in a heatproof basin over hot water. Beat the eggs with the sugar until thick and mousse-like. Sift in the flour and fold into the egg mixture with the vanilla, lemon rind, melted butter and chocolate mixture. Spoon into the prepared tin and bake for 1 hour, or until a skewer inserted into the centre comes out clean. Release the spring but let the cake cool in the tin.

For the topping, shave thin curls from the side of the block of chocolate with a swivel-bladed vegetable peeler. Chill.

For the filling, drain and reserve the syrup from the cherries. Mix the syrup with the Kirsch. Halve the cherries, leaving a few whole to decorate the cake.

Split the cake into two rounds and prick the base with a fork. Place the bottom layer on a serving plate and soak with half of the Kirsch-flavoured syrup.

Whip the cream until it just holds its shape and pile about one-third over the base. Spoon over half the halved cherries. Place the top cake layer in position, prick with a fork and spoon the remaining syrup over. Arrange the remaining cherry halves on top. Cover the cake with the remaining cream, piling most of it on top. Press chocolate curls around the side of the cake and sprinkle some on top. Decorate with the reserved whole cherries and chill for 1–2 hours before serving.

INGREDIENTS

250 g butter
250 g dark chocolate, broken up
6 eggs, at room temperature
¾ cup (165 g) caster sugar
⅓ cup (75 g) firmly packed brown sugar
3 tablespoons plain flour, sifted
3 tablespoons ground almonds
½ teaspoon cream of tartar
1 tablespoon sifted icing sugar to dust
1 cup cream
a few drops of vanilla essence

RICH CHOCOLATE FUDGE CAKE

Quite the most delicious, melt-in-the-mouth cake, particularly good for desserts or a special occasion. It has a crisp meringue crust and light tender centre with a soft, creamy, almost sauce-like consistency.

SERVES 8

METHOD

Preheat the oven to 180°C. Grease the base and side of a 25 cm springform tin. Line the base with baking paper and flour the tin.

Melt the butter in a large, heavy-based saucepan with the chocolate, stirring constantly over low heat, just until melted and smooth. It should not get much hotter than 50°C. Set aside.

Separate the eggs and beat the sugars into the egg yolks, until just mixed. While the chocolate is still warm, whisk the egg yolk mixture into it, and then stir in the flour and almonds. If the chocolate mixture has cooled, warm it over a low heat, stirring constantly, until it is just barely warm.

Add the cream of tartar to the egg whites and beat until they form soft rounded peaks. Gently fold one third of the whites into the base mixture and mix gently but well, then fold in the rest of the whites, without deflating them.

Pour the mixture into the prepared tin and smooth the top. Bake for 35–45 minutes, or until the cake is completely set around the sides but still has a soft and creamy circle, about 12 cm diameter, in the centre. The cake should tremble in the centre, just slightly, when you shake the tin gently. Cool thoroughly in the tin.

To serve, remove the cooled cake from the tin and dust with the icing sugar. Softly whip the cream and add vanilla and icing sugar to taste. Serve with the cake.

The cake keeps well for 3–4 days. Do not refrigerate or freeze. Store at room temperature, loosely covered with foil, in an airtight container.

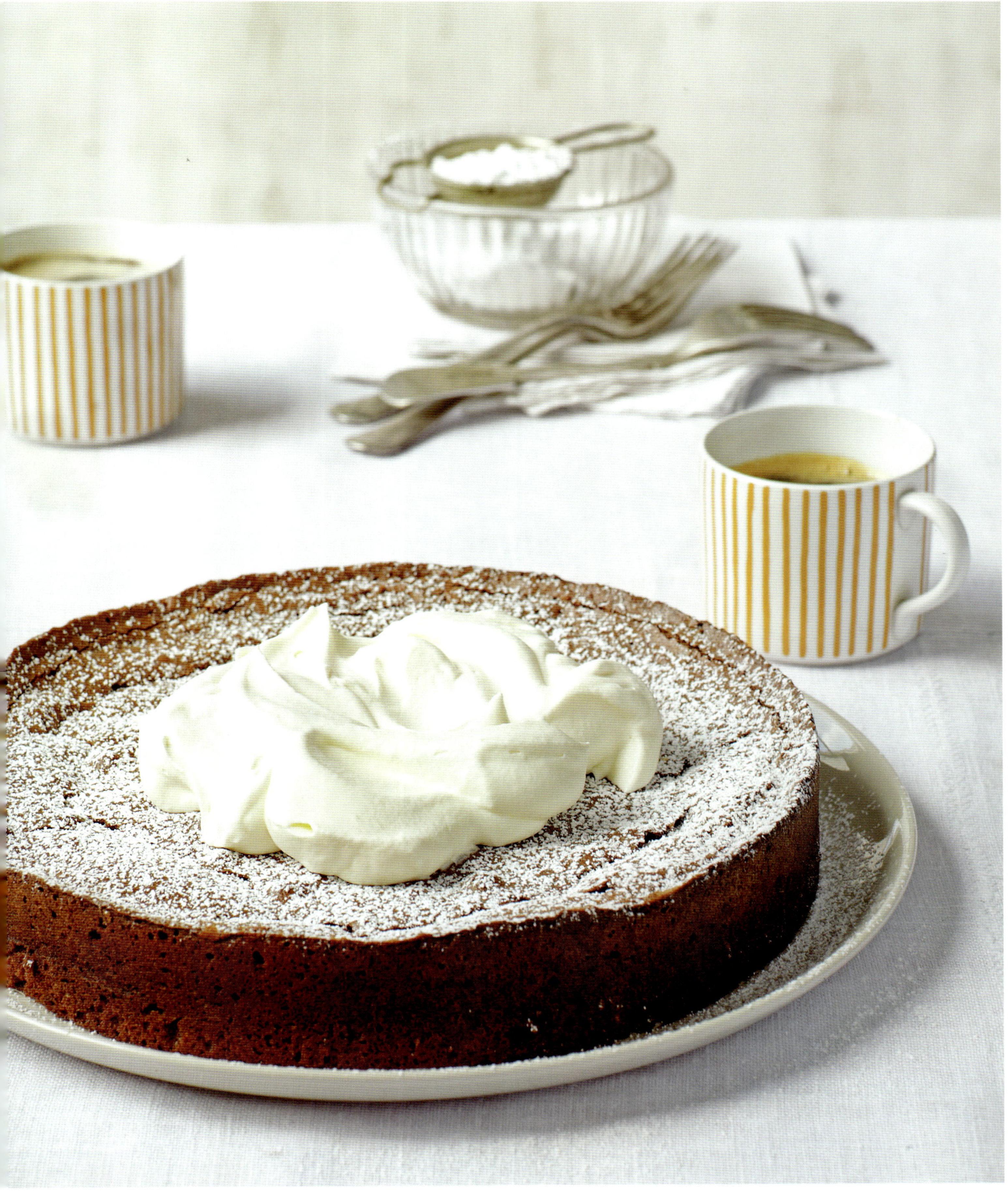

CAKE
125 g unsalted butter
½ cup (110 g) caster sugar
¾ cup (110 g) plain flour
1 teaspoon baking powder
2 teaspoons instant coffee powder
a pinch of salt
2 eggs, lightly beaten
½ cup ground almonds
flaked almonds to decorate

FROSTING
185 g butter
2 cups (320 g) icing sugar, sifted
2 teaspoons instant coffee powder, dissolved in 1 teaspoon hot water

COFFEE ALMOND LAYER CAKE

SERVES 10

METHOD

Preheat the oven to 190°C. Grease two 18 cm sandwich tins and line the bases with baking paper.

To make the cake, using an electric mixer, cream the butter with the sugar until light and fluffy.

Sift together the flour, coffee and salt, and stir into the creamed mixture alternately with the eggs. Stir in the ground almonds. Divide the mixture evenly between the prepared tins.

Bake for about 25 minutes or until a skewer inserted in the centre comes out clean. Turn out and cool on a wire rack.

To make the frosting, cream the butter with the sugar until light and fluffy, then beat in the coffee. Use the frosting to sandwich the cake layers together and to cover the top and sides. Press the flaked almonds lightly into the top and sides to decorate.

CAKES *continental cakes*

INGREDIENTS
5 eggs, separated
1 cup (220 g) caster sugar
1 teaspoon instant coffee powder
½ cup (75 g) flour, sifted
½ cup finely ground hazelnuts or walnuts
sifted icing sugar to dust

FILLING
2 cups cream
2 tablespoons icing sugar, sifted
1 tablespoon instant coffee powder dissolved
   in 1 tablespoon brandy

MOCHA NUT CAKE

SERVES 6

METHOD
Preheat the oven to 160°C. Grease and flour a 23 cm ring tin or springform cake tin.

Beat the egg whites until soft peaks form. Gradually beat in the sugar until the mixture stands in stiff peaks.

Beat the egg yolks separately until thick and light, then fold into the whites.

Mix the coffee, flour and nuts together and fold into the egg mixture gently but thoroughly until no white streaks remain. Spoon into the prepared tin.

Bake for 50–55 minutes or until the cake springs back when lightly pressed with a finger. Cool on a wire rack.

To make the filling, whip the cream until thick, then fold in the sugar and coffee dissolved in brandy. Split the cake into four layers.

Just before serving, sandwich together with the filling and dust icing sugar on top.

ICINGS, FROSTINGS & FILLINGS

Icings, frostings and fillings provide the finishing touches to many cakes, and they need not be elaborate or time-consuming to make. A simple glaze can add an extra level of flavour and visual appeal, and a filling can be as easy as jam or whipped cream.

ICING & FROSTINGS

Icings and frostings add flavour to cakes, give texture contrast, help them stay fresh and moist and, of course, enhance their appearance.

GLACÉ OR WARM ICING
ENOUGH TO COVER TOP OF A 20–23 CM CAKE

A quickly mixed, easily flavoured icing that sets firmly to a decorative glaze. Decorations should be added quickly before the icing sets.

1¼ cups (200 g) pure icing sugar
1 tablespoon boiling water
a few drops of flavouring essence
food colouring as desired

Sift the icing sugar into a small, heatproof bowl. Add the boiling water gradually, mixing to a smooth, thick paste that will coat the back of the spoon. Place the bowl over a small amount of boiling water and stir the icing for 1 minute. Add flavouring and colouring as desired. Pour the icing quickly over the cake and smooth the surface with a spatula or knife dipped in hot water.

VARIATIONS
CHOCOLATE GLACÉ ICING Sift 1 tablespoon cocoa powder with the icing sugar. Melt 1 teaspoon butter in the boiling water before adding to the icing sugar.
COFFEE GLACÉ ICING Add 1 teaspoon instant coffee powder dissolved in 1 tablespoon boiling water to the icing sugar.
LEMON GLACÉ ICING Use 1 tablespoon lemon juice instead of boiling water.
SPICE GLACÉ ICING Add ½ teaspoon each ground cinnamon and nutmeg and ¼ teaspoon ground cloves to the icing sugar.

CHOCOLATE GLAZE
ENOUGH TO COVER TOP OF A 20–23 CM CAKE

60 g butter
60 g dark chocolate
2 tablespoons boiling water
1 cup (160 g) icing sugar, sifted
a pinch of salt
¼ teaspoon vanilla essence

Melt together the butter and dark chocolate in a bowl over a saucepan of hot water. Beat in the boiling water, icing sugar, salt and vanilla. Use as a glaze over chocolate cakes.

RICH CHOCOLATE ICING
ENOUGH TO COVER TOP OF A 23 CM SQUARE CAKE

185 g dark chocolate, roughly chopped
¼ cup dark rum
½ teaspoon vanilla essence
2 cups (320 g) icing sugar, sifted
30 g butter, softened
1 tablespoon hot milk

Melt the chocolate in a heatproof bowl set over simmering water. Stir in the rum and vanilla. Add the icing sugar, butter and milk. Stir vigorously over the hot water until the icing is smooth and glossy. If it is too thick, add a little more milk. Spread at once over the cake.

CAKES *icings, frostings & fillings*

ECONOMICAL CHOCOLATE ICING
ENOUGH TO COVER TOP OF A 20–23 CM CAKE

1½ cups (240 g) icing sugar, sifted
½ teaspoon ground cinnamon
1 tablespoon cocoa powder
30 g butter
1 tablespoon hot water

Mix the icing sugar, cinnamon and cocoa in a bowl, then stir in the softened butter and water. Mix to a smooth paste, adding a little more hot water if necessary.

BUTTER CREAM ICING (VIENNA ICING)
ENOUGH TO FILL A SWISS ROLL OR TOP A 20–23 CM CAKE

This soft and creamy icing can be swirled into decorative shapes and also used for piping.

125 g butter
1½ cups (240 g) pure icing sugar, sifted
1 tablespoon sherry
a few drops of vanilla essence

Beat the butter until light and creamy, then gradually beat in half the icing sugar. Beat in the sherry alternately with the remaining sugar. Stir in the vanilla.

VARIATIONS
CHOCOLATE BUTTER CREAM ICING Sift 1 tablespoon cocoa powder with the icing sugar.
ORANGE BUTTER CREAM ICING Add 1 teaspoon grated orange rind to the icing sugar, and use 1 tablespoon orange juice in place of the sherry.
LEMON BUTTER CREAM ICING Add 1 teaspoon grated lemon rind to the the icing sugar, and use 1 tablespoon lemon juice in place of the sherry.
WALNUT BUTTER CREAM ICING Fold in 2 tablespoons finely chopped walnuts after mixing.
LIQUEUR BUTTER CREAM ICING Replace sherry with Grand Marnier, crème de menthe, crème de cacao, etc.

RUM CHOCOLATE FROSTING
ENOUGH TO FILL AND COVER THE TOP OF A 20 CM CAKE

90 g dark chocolate
½ cup rum, plus extra if needed
4 cups (640 g) icing sugar, sifted
60 g soft butter

Melt the chocolate with the rum over a low heat. Add the icing sugar, 1 cup at a time, beating well after each addition. Beat in the butter. Add a little more rum, if necessary, to make a frosting of spreading consistency. Use to frost and fill chocolate cakes or gâteaux.

MARSHMALLOW FROSTING
ENOUGH TO COVER A 20 CM CAKE

Marshmallow makes a delicious frosting for butter cakes and looks most decorative for special occasions when swirled into rough peaks. For best results use an electric mixer to beat the mixture.

2 teaspoons powdered gelatine
1½ cups boiling water
2 cups (250 g) caster sugar
½ teaspoon vanilla essence

Dissolve the gelatine in half the boiling water in a saucepan, add the remaining water and mix with the sugar. Heat gently, stirring, until boiling, then boil without stirring over medium heat for 15 minutes. Remove from the heat, cool slightly and beat until the mixture doubles in volume and becomes thick. Fold in the vanilla. Spread quickly over the cake with a warm, dry spatula or knife, swirling the top into little peaks for a decorative effect.

CHOCOLATE CREAM CHEESE FROSTING
ENOUGH TO COVER TOPS OF TWO 20–23 CM CAKES

90 g dark chocolate, roughly chopped
90 g cream cheese, softened
¼ cup milk
4 cups (640 g) icing sugar, sifted
½ teaspoon salt

Melt the chocolate in a heatproof bowl over hot water. Remove from heat and gradually beat in the cream cheese and milk. Add icing sugar and salt, beating until smooth and spreadable. Add a little more milk if necessary.

SEVEN-MINUTE FROSTING
ENOUGH TO COVER A BAR CAKE OR 18–20 CM ROUND CAKE

1 cup (160 g) caster sugar
½ teaspoon cream of tartar
1 egg white
2 tablespoons water
¼ teaspoon vanilla essence

Place the sugar, cream of tartar, egg white and water in the top of a double saucepan or in a heatproof bowl placed over simmering water (do not allow bottom of bowl to touch the water). Beat with an electric beater on slow, or with a rotary beater, until the mixture is thick enough to hold its shape. This takes about 7 minutes, which gives the frosting its name. Cool a little, then stir in the vanilla or other desired flavourings and spread roughly over the cake.

NOTE Quantities may be doubled for larger cakes.

VARIATIONS
PEPPERMINT SEVEN-MINUTE FROSTING Add 2–3 drops peppermint essence instead of the vanilla and a little pink or green food colouring.
MARSHMALLOW SEVEN-MINUTE FROSTING When the mixture is thick, after cooking for 7 minutes, stir in 1 cup chopped marshmallows. Stir until melted.
CHOCOLATE SEVEN-MINUTE FROSTING Stir in 90 g melted dark chocolate after cooking for 7 minutes.

FILLINGS
The range of cake fillings seems almost endless, but there are some universal favourites. Sponges are popular with a simple jam filling or whipped cream and fruit. Lemon butter transforms a plain butter cake or sponge sandwich. The smooth butter cream called crème au beurre in France is often sandwiched between many layers of cake to make a Continental gâteau. Cream cheese and ricotta cheese are often the basis of European cake fillings. Dried fruits, nuts, rum, chocolate, ginger and other flavourings are often added to a rich custard cream (crème pâtissière; see page 338) for luscious dessert cakes.

FIRM LEMON BUTTER
MAKES ABOUT 1½ CUPS

Also known as lemon cheese or lemon curd, this is a preserve made from lemons, sugar, butter and eggs. Its tart-sweet flavour makes it a perfect filling for tartlets, sponge cakes, sponge rolls and short biscuits, or use it as a spread. Lemon butter is always a very welcome gift from your kitchen, especially if accompanied by a dozen little baked, unfilled pastry shells.

This recipe makes a fairly firm lemon butter. For a softer version, see opposite.

3 lemons
6 sugar lumps
½ cup (110 g) caster sugar
30 g butter
2 teaspoons cornflour
1 tablespoon water
2 eggs

Wash and dry the lemons. Rub the sugar lumps over the lemons until they are saturated with oil from the skins. Put the sugar lumps into a saucepan with the sugar, butter and the strained juice of the lemons. Place over low heat and stir continuously until the sugar dissolves. Add the cornflour blended with the water and bring to the boil, then remove from the heat. Beat the eggs in a heatproof bowl and slowly add the hot lemon mixture, beating continuously. Place over simmering water and cook for 10 minutes, stirring, or until thick enough to coat the spoon. If not using immediately, pour into hot sterilised

CAKES *icings, frostings & fillings*

jars and seal. Lemon butter keeps for several weeks stored in the refrigerator.

LEMON BUTTER FILLING
MAKES 1 CUP

Delicious as a filling for sponges and cakes, or spread on hot, buttered toast.

60 g butter
grated rind and juice of 2 medium lemons
2 egg yolks (from 60 g eggs)
½ cup (110 g) caster sugar

Melt the butter in the top of double saucepan or heatproof bowl set over hot water. Add the lemon rind and juice, egg yolks and sugar and stir with a wooden spoon over simmering water until the mixture thickens. Allow to cool before using. The quantities may be doubled. The lemon butter will keep well in a covered sterilised jar in the refrigerator.

VARIATION
PASSIONFRUIT BUTTER Replace the lemon juice and rind with the pulp of 4 passionfruit, adding it to the butter along with the egg yolks and sugar.

BUTTER CREAM FILLING (CRÈME AU BEURRE)
MAKES ABOUT 2 CUPS

2 egg yolks
¼ cup (55 g) caster sugar
½ cup milk
250 g unsalted butter
½ teaspoon vanilla essence

Beat the egg yolks with half the sugar until light and creamy. Place the remaining sugar and the milk in a heavy saucepan and bring to the boil, stirring to dissolve the sugar. Pour the milk onto the yolks and blend well. Return to the pan and stir over gentle heat until the custard coats the back of the spoon. Do not allow to boil. Strain and cool. Cream the butter and when soft, add the cooled custard little by little. Flavour with vanilla.

VARIATIONS
COFFEE BUTTER CREAM FILLING Stir 2 teaspoons instant coffee powder into the hot custard. Omit vanilla.
CHOCOLATE BUTTER CREAM FILLING Melt 60 g chopped dark chocolate over hot water. Beat into the creamed butter with the custard.
RUM BUTTER CREAM FILLING Beat 1–2 tablespoons dark rum into the creamed butter with the custard. Omit the vanilla essence.

RICOTTA RUM FILLING
MAKES ABOUT 2 CUPS

250 g ricotta cheese
½ cup (110 g) caster sugar
½ teaspoon vanilla essence
2 tablespoons dark rum
2 tablespoons grated dark chocolate
1 tablespoon chopped glacé fruit (ginger, apricots, pineapple, etc)

Combine the ricotta, sugar, vanilla and rum and beat until light and fluffy. Fold in the chocolate and fruit. Use to fill a sponge or layer cake, wrap cake in foil, and refrigerate for 2–3 hours before serving.

BUTTERSCOTCH FILLING
MAKES ABOUT 2 CUPS

45 g butter
½ cup (110 g) firmly packed brown sugar
1 cup milk
3 tablespoons flour
½ teaspoon salt
2 eggs, lightly beaten
½ teaspoon vanilla essence

Mix the butter and sugar in a heavy saucepan and heat gently, stirring, until melted. Stir in ½ cup of the milk and cook for 2 minutes. Combine the flour, salt and remaining milk, stir into the hot mixture and cook, stirring, until boiling. Stir a little of this mixture into the beaten eggs, pour back into the saucepan and stir over low heat until thickened a little more. Do not allow to boil. Stir in vanilla. Cool and use as a cake or pie filling.

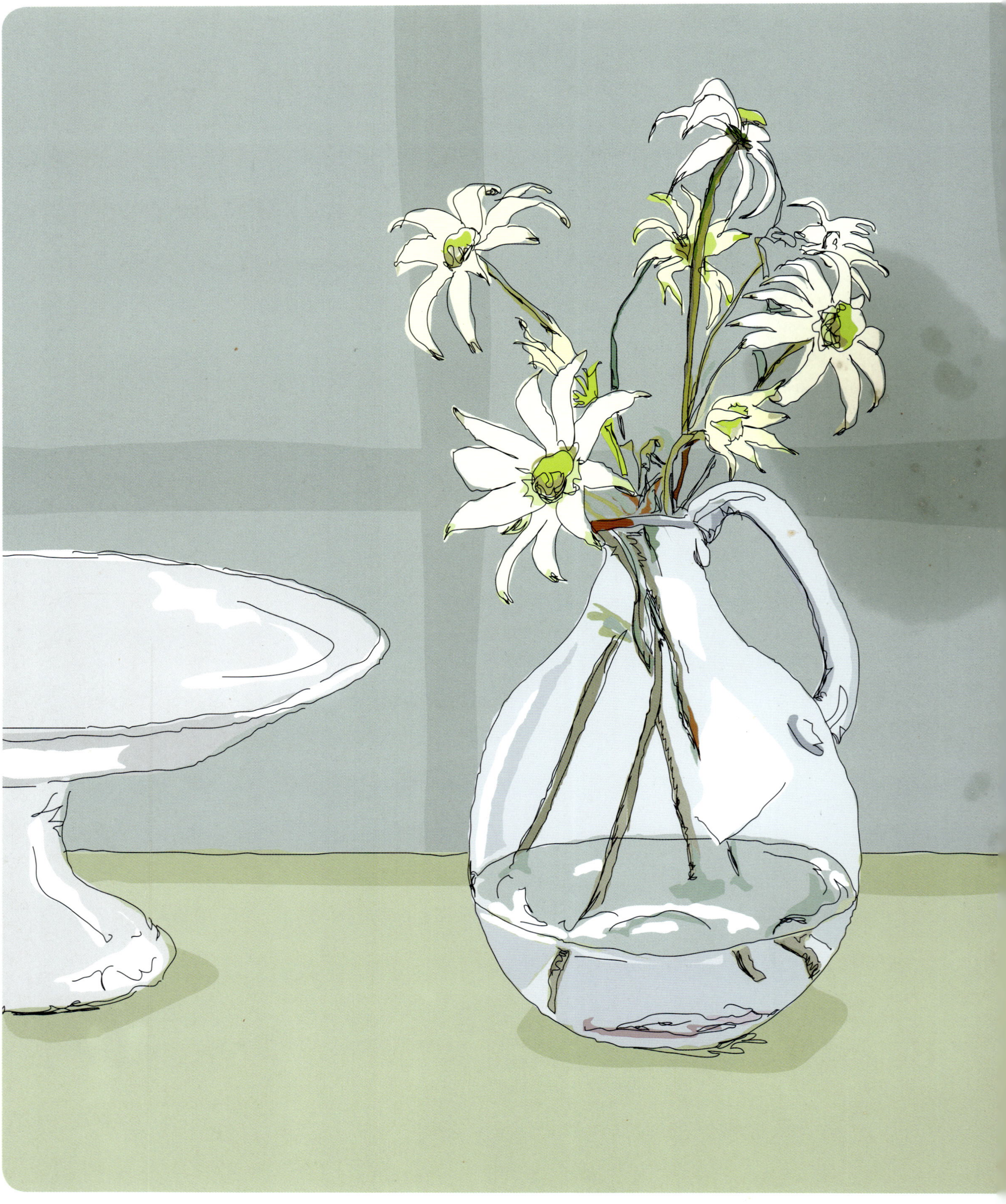

SMALL CAKES
CHAPTER 5

HINTS & TIPS

Nearly all cake mixtures lend themselves to being baked in individual small cakes or portions. There's something very comforting about small cakes, and the indulgence of a cupcake or small sweet treat with a cup of tea or coffee. Meringues, macarons, madeleines, friands and cupcakes are suitable for all sorts of occasions – dress them up for dinner parties, or make them colourful and fun-looking for children's parties, fêtes and fairs.

CUPCAKES & FRIANDS

Bake cupcakes in muffin or patty tins. For children's parties and informal occasions, bake and serve in fluted paper cases, which are available in various colours and patterns. They retain their shape better if the cases are placed in muffin tins for baking. Fill the tins or paper cases about two-thirds full to prevent the mixture from overflowing.

Friands are generally baked in oval-shaped moulds, which may be plain or have a pattern in the base. Alternatively they can be baked in muffin tins.

MACARONS

Macarons are dainty little shiny, domed meringues containing ground nuts, which are sandwiched together with a filling such as butter cream, jam, or ganache (a mixture of chocolate and cream). There are a variety of methods to make macarons. Some start with a base of beaten egg white and sugar syrup, others are made with beaten egg whites and icing sugar before the ground nuts and flavouring are folded through before being piped. A simpler version is made by mixing ground nuts and sugar with egg whites then rolling the mixture into balls.

TIPS FOR SUCCESS

TRY REPLACING SOME OF THE GROUND ALMONDS with other types of nuts such as pistachio, for a different flavour and texture.

SIFT BOTH THE GROUND NUTS AND THE ICING SUGAR separately to make for easy mixing and to minimise imperfections.

FOR BEST RESULTS, use a clean copper bowl and beat the egg whites and sugar with a balloon whisk. Otherwise use a clean dry glass, metal or porcelain bowl and a rotary or hand-held electric beater. Beat the eggs whites until stiff, then add 4 tablespoons of the sugar, one at a time. Continue beating for about 1 minute or until the egg whites are glossy; the meringue should form short peaks when the whisk is lifted. Then, with a spatula, fold in the remaining sugar a few tablespoons at a time. Fold in the vanilla with the last of the sugar and continue folding until the meringue forms long peaks, lastly adding the ground nuts.

TO FLAVOUR AND COLOUR MACARONS, it is preferable to use only dry ingredients and powders; mix them in along with the ground nuts. Liquid flavourings such as fruit purées can spoil the texture and shape of the macarons.

WHEN MIXING THE MACARONS, pour the meringue on top of the dry ingredients and fold together with a spatula until the mixture is combined and is softened. You need to 'slap' the air out of the mixture with a few sharp blows to the mix using the spatula. If you lift the mixture with your spatula and it holds its shape, you need to keep mixing. It should start to run down the bowl.

TO PIPE THE MACARONS, fit a pastry bag with a plain 1.5 cm nozzle, fill it two-thirds full and twist the top. Pipe mounds 3 cm wide on the prepared trays.

ONCE PIPED, LIFT THE TRAY and bang it down hard to spread the macarons to 4 cm and to even the domes and remove ripples. Dust liberally with extra icing sugar. Leave at room temperature for 15 minutes before baking to help them to set and hold their shape.

MERINGUES

There are many variations of meringue – all based on egg white and sugar beaten to a stiff froth, then baked in a very slow oven until light and crisp. Glamorous vacherins, dainty petits fours and fluffy pie toppings are all favourites. Meringues are usually plain but a flavouring may be added such as chopped nuts, chocolate pieces or coconut.

Meringue mixture can be shaped and used in various ways. Small buttons or rosettes baked until dry and crisp may be joined together with whipped cream to make a delicious sweet for afternoon tea or dessert. These tiny meringues may also be used as a topping for desserts or cakes.

Another popular way is to shape meringue with an oval dessertspoon or tablespoon, and these ovals may be joined with whipped cream to form an egg shape. Meringue is often made into a pie shell or basket – individual baskets are very popular, and these may be filled with fruit, whipped cream or any number of creamy desserts.

HINTS FOR SUCCESS

Egg whites for meringue should be at room temperature to ensure maximum volume when beaten. They should be beaten with a pinch of salt, cream of tartar, or a few drops of lemon juice. This may be done in a copper bowl with a wire whisk or in a glass bowl or stainless steel bowl with electric beaters. (Plastic bowls do not give a good result because they can contain residues of oil in their porous walls that will affect your efforts.)

ENSURE THE BOWL IS METICULOUSLY CLEAN. The slightest trace of yolk in the whites will inhibit their rising (as yolks contain fat). The same holds true for bowl and beater: both must be totally free of fat or grease. It is best to wash the bowl and beater with hot water and dry them with a clean, fresh tea towel before beating the whites.

ADD SOME OF THE SUGAR GRADUALLY at first, after the whites become foamy. The meringue has been sufficiently whipped when the whites form soft peaks and cling to the beater in a mass. They are over-beaten if they look dry and stand in sharp, jagged peaks, and the mixture will probably fall when placed in the oven.

THEN FOLD IN THE REMAINING SUGAR. To do this, cut gently down through the mixture and lift some of it up and over onto the top, repeating and turning the bowl until whites and sugar are lightly mixed. Don't worry about mixing thoroughly; it is important not to overwork meringue or the air bubbles will break down. Shaping the meringues will mix the whites and sugar a little more. You must work quickly once the sugar is added or the meringue will wilt.

THE BAKING TRAYS FOR MERINGUES should either be lightly buttered, dusted with flour and the excess flour tapped off, or they may be covered with baking paper. Baking trays coated with non-stick surfaces are also good.

THE OVEN TEMPERATURE should be as low as possible. The point is to dry the meringue by getting all the moisture out of the mixture rather than baking it. A temperature of 120°C is as high as it should go. Higher than this, the meringues brown too quickly, turn leathery and collapse. Properly baked, a meringue is crisp, feather-light, the palest beige in colour, almost white. If liked, meringues may be dusted lightly with caster sugar before baking.

BAKE MERINGUES FOR ABOUT 1 HOUR, although they may be left in the turned-off oven to crisp. Excess moisture in the air makes meringues go soft, so it is best not to bake them on a very damp or rainy day or have anything steaming on the stove while they are cooling on wire racks. Should the meringues absorb any moisture, they can be dried in a very slow oven (100°C) for 15 minutes or so.

TO STORE, transfer cooled meringues to airtight containers, where they will keep for weeks, even months, ready at any time for myriad uses. Fill them with cream, berries or any other soft fruits, finish with a fruit sauce or coulis, or fill or top with a piped rosette of chocolate, coffee or chestnut cream.

CUPCAKES

MAKES ABOUT 12

INGREDIENTS
125 g butter, softened
¾ cup (165 g) caster sugar
1 teaspoon vanilla essence
2 eggs, beaten
2 cups (300 g) self-raising flour
a pinch of salt
⅔ cup milk

GLACÉ ICING
1 cup (160 g) sifted icing sugar
1 tablespoon boiling water
1 teaspoon butter
a few drops of flavoured essence (optional)
food colouring (optional)

METHOD
Preheat the oven to 190°C. Place paper cases in patty or muffin tins.

Using an electric mixer, cream the butter, then gradually add the sugar and beat until light and creamy. Add the vanilla. Add the eggs gradually and beat well after each addition.

Sift the flour and salt and fold lightly into the creamed mixture, alternately with the milk, to make a smooth dropping consistency. Spoon into the paper cases. Bake for about 15 minutes until risen and golden. Remove the paper cases and cool on a wire rack.

To make the glacé icing, sift the icing sugar into a bowl, make a well in the centre and add the boiling water, butter and flavouring if using. Stir until smooth and shiny. Colour as desired and use to ice the cupcakes.

VARIATIONS
BUTTERFLY CAKES Use the same mixture as for cupcakes, but increase the oven temperature to 200°C and bake the cakes in the hottest part of the oven. The tops of the cakes will rise in a peak. When cool, cut a slice from the top of each cake and reserve. Top the cakes with a peak of sweetened whipped cream and a small dollop of jam in the centre. Cut the cake slices in half, arrange on top of the cream to form 'wings' and dust with sifted icing sugar.

NOTE If the cupcakes are to be iced and smooth tops are required, bake in a moderately hot oven, at 190°C. For peaked tops, necessary for butterfly cakes, increase the heat by 10°C and place the cakes in the hottest part of the oven, usually near the top of gas ovens and at the bottom of electric ovens. To make sure, check the guide for your own oven. This recipe is similar to a basic butter cake mixture but calls for extra milk.

SMALL CAKES *cupcakes, friands & madeleines*

There are many possibilities when it comes to decorating cupcakes. For children, try a selection of sweets to decorate, such as fruit jellies and sparkles. A pretty effect is achieved by slicing the fruit jellies first to reveal their shiny centres. Hundreds and thousands, Smarties, chocolate sprinkles, nuts or cherries can be used. Or, top with freshly picked violets and perfect rose petals. Just remember to add the topping while the icing is still not completely set.

INGREDIENTS
30 g butter
4 tablespoons brown sugar
12 canned apricot halves, well drained
310 g packet buttercake or vanilla cake mix

QUICK UPSIDE-DOWN FRUIT CUPCAKES

This is a simple recipe that gives a homemade look to packet cake mix. You can experiment with different fruits and even different flavours of cake mixes. There are good-quality cake mixes available and they come in very handy when you have to make something in a hurry.

MAKES 12

METHOD
Preheat the oven to 190°C.

Melt the butter and spoon evenly into 12 deep patty tins or muffin tins. Sprinkle the bottom of each tin with brown sugar. Place an apricot half, cut side up, in each.

Make up the cake mixture according to the directions on the packet.

Spoon on top of the fruit, filling the tins two-thirds full. Bake for 12–15 minutes or until the cake is cooked. Turn out onto a wire rack, leaving the cakes so that the apricots are facing upwards. Allow to cool before serving.

VARIATIONS
PLUM Try pitted canned plum halves instead of apricots.

BLUEBERRY You can place a few fresh or frozen blueberries into the base of each patty tin.

RASPBERRY Place 3–4 fresh or frozen raspberries in the base of the tin.

STRAWBERRY Try strawberry halves instead of apricots.

SMALL CAKES *cupcakes, friands & madeleines*

INGREDIENTS
1 ½ cups (225 g) self-raising flour
2/3 cup (150 g) caster sugar
125 g butter, softened
3 eggs
¼ cup milk
2 tablespoons currants
icing sugar to dust

QUEEN CAKES

These cakes are little pound cakes with currants mixed through. They are sometimes baked in small fluted pans. Queen cakes originated from Regency recipes to become what we call cupcakes today. They can also be iced with a very thin layer of icing but it's much simpler just to dust them with some icing sugar, creating a very pretty effect.

MAKES 24

METHOD
Preheat the oven to 180°C. Line two 12-hole muffin tins with paper cases.

Sift the flour into a bowl. Add the sugar, butter, eggs and milk. Beat on medium speed for 3 minutes, until the mixture is smooth and pale. Stir through the currants.

Spoon heaped tablespoons of the mixture into the paper cases. Bake for 15 minutes, until golden and firm to touch. Cool in the tins.

Dust with icing sugar before serving.

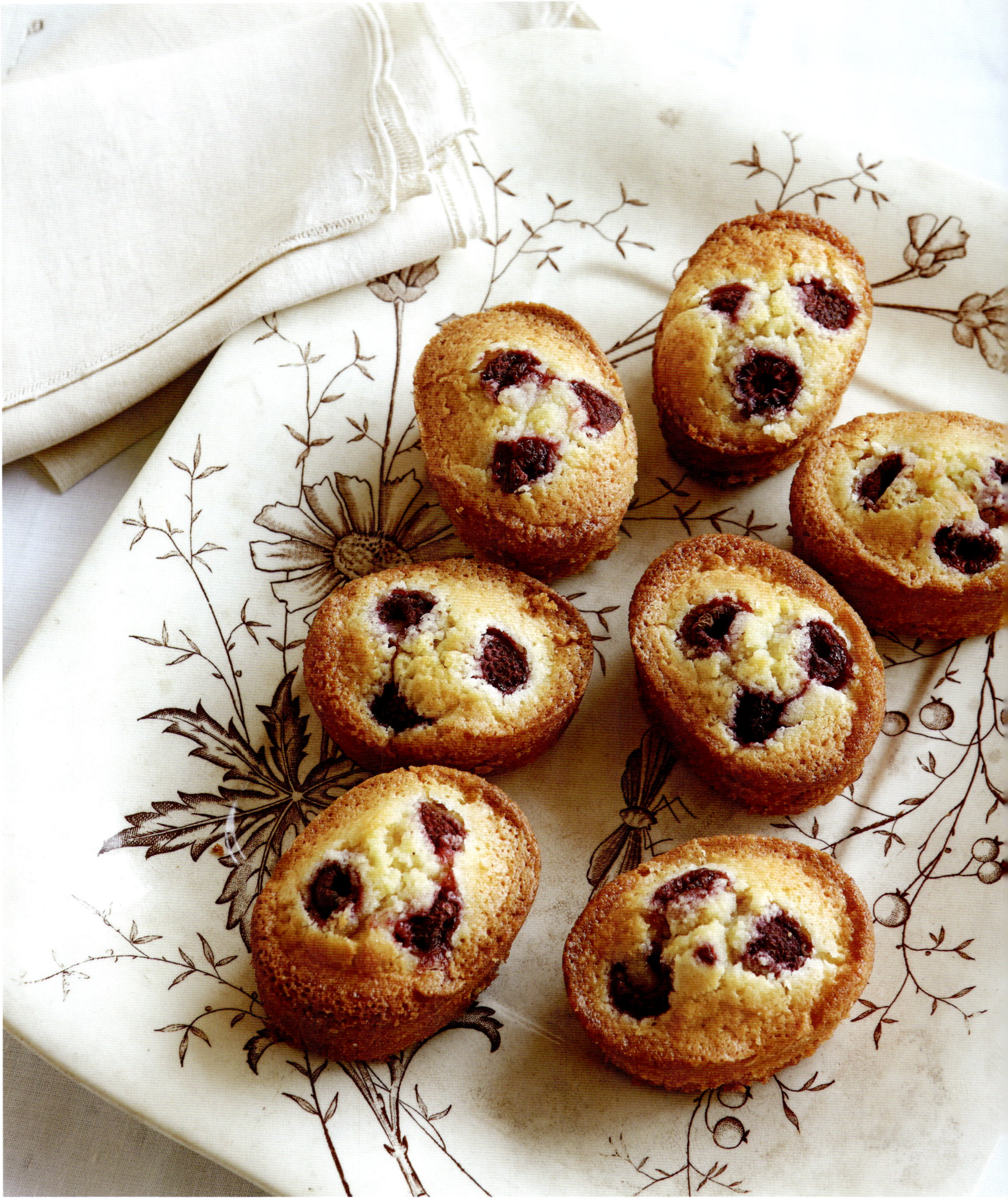

SMALL CAKES *cupcakes, friands & madeleines*

INGREDIENTS
175 g butter
1 cup ground almonds
grated rind of 1 orange
1 2/3 cup (260 g) icing sugar, sifted
1/2 cup (75 g) plain flour, sifted
5 egg whites
200 g fresh or frozen raspberries (optional)

FRIANDS

Originally made in a pastry shop near la Bourse, the financial district of Paris, friands — or financiers, as they are often called — are the same shape as gold bars (the moulds are traditionally rectangular). Perhaps the confusion has come about from the word 'friandise', which is a general French word for 'petits fours'. Whatever you choose to call them, we have all taken to these little almond cakes.

In Australia, friand moulds are oval, 1/2 cup in capacity and deeper than most other small cake tins.

MAKES 10–12

METHOD
Preheat the oven to 230°C. Grease 10–12 individual friand moulds or a 10–12 hole friand tin with butter.

Put the butter in a small saucepan, cook gently until pale golden, then set aside.

Mix the ground almonds in a bowl with the orange rind, icing sugar and flour until combined. Add the egg whites and the warm butter, pouring the butter in carefully and holding back any browned solids that have sunk to the bottom. Mix well together.

Spoon the mixture into the prepared moulds, half-filling each. Top each with 2 or 3 raspberries if using, then place the moulds on a baking tray and bake for 5 minutes.

Reduce the oven temperature to 200°C and bake for a further 12–15 minutes.

Turn the oven off and leave the cakes in the oven for 5 minutes. Remove from the oven and turn out onto a wire rack to cool.

VARIATION
PISTACHIO-HAZELNUT FRIANDS A combination of ground pistachios and ground hazelnuts may replace ground almonds for a different look and taste.

NOTE Friand tins are available at good kitchen shops and department stores. Tiny bite-size oval moulds, miniature patty tins or oblong financier tins are also available for after-dinner friandise. You can also make the friands in mini muffin tins or patty pan cases; this quantity of batter will fill about 20 mini muffin tins or patty pan cases.

INGREDIENTS
1 quantity Basic Butter Cake mixture (page 164)
desiccated coconut

THIN CHOCOLATE ICING
3 cups (480 g) icing sugar
3 tablespoons cocoa powder
4-6 tablespoons boiling water
½ teaspoon butter
a few drops of vanilla essence

LAMINGTONS

This is a popular Australian cake thought to have first been made for a tea party for Lord Lamington, who served as Governor of Queensland from 1896 to 1901. I've judged a lot of lamington competitions over the years and they seem to be getting bigger and bigger. The lamingtons I'm familiar with were always small and dainty. I was on a television show years ago with Barry Humphries and I made some lamingtons for him. When I gave them to him I curtseyed and even he couldn't stop laughing.

MAKES 18-20

METHOD
Preheat the oven to 180°C. Grease a 30 cm x 20 cm lamington tin and line the base with baking paper.

Spread the prepared butter cake mixture evenly in the tin and bake for 30–35 minutes or until cooked. Cool on a wire rack, then cut into small oblong shapes or cubes.

For the chocolate icing, sift the icing sugar and cocoa into a bowl. Add the boiling water, butter and a vanilla then stir until smooth and shiny.

Spread some of the desiccated coconut on a large plate. Dip the cake shapes in the chocolate icing (see Note) then immediately roll in the coconut. Leave on a wire rack to set.

VARIATION
JAM LAMINGTONS Each piece of cake may be cut in half and sandwiched together with a little berry jam before dipping into icing and rolling in coconut. Be careful to use only a small amount of jam so that it does not run out while the cake is being coated.

TIPS Use two forks to hold and turn the lamingtons while they are being dipped in the icing. If the icing thickens too much to dip the cakes into, thin it with a little warm water or stand the bowl in hot water.

Spread only a small amount of coconut on the plate at one time; when it becomes soiled with drips of chocolate icing, replace it with fresh coconut.

NOTE You can bake the basic butter cake for the lamingtons a day before they are required. This helps to prevent the cakes from crumbling when cutting and icing. They keep fresh for several days. You can also freeze the cake but you will need to allow it to thaw for a full 24 hours before using.

SMALL CAKES *cupcakes, friands & madeleines*

INGREDIENTS
185 g butter, softened
½ teaspoon vanilla essence
½ cup (80 g) icing sugar, sifted, plus extra to dust
1¾ cups (200 g) plain flour, sifted
raspberry jam

VIENNA CAKES

Vienna is famous for its cakes and desserts, many of them rich and elaborate. These little cakes, though plainer than many Viennese cakes, are attractive and buttery, and lend themselves to imaginative decoration.

MAKES 12

METHOD

Preheat the oven to 190°C. Grease patty tins or standard muffin tins or line them with paper cases.

Using an electric mixer, cream the butter with the vanilla and sugar until light and fluffy. Fold in the flour.

Pipe or spoon the mixture into the tins or paper cases and make a slight dent in the top of each cake.

Bake for 10–12 minutes. Leave in the tins for a few minutes to firm up a little, then remove from the tins and transfer to wire racks to cool.

Sift extra icing sugar over each cake and drop a little raspberry jam into the centre of each.

VARIATION
ICED VIENNA CAKES Omit the icing sugar and jam and instead ice with a glacé icing of your choice, or with Butter Cream Icing (page 252), plain or flavoured.

INGREDIENTS
1½ cups (225 g) self-raising flour
a pinch of salt
125 g butter, softened
¾ cup (165 g) caster sugar
2 eggs
2 teaspoons coffee essence
2 tablespoons milk

COFFEE GLACÉ ICING
1 cup (160 g) pure icing sugar, sifted
1 tablespoon hot strong coffee
toasted hazelnuts to decorate

ICED COFFEE CAKES

This is a light cupcake topped with coffee icing, perfect for a grown-up afternoon treat. Use pure icing sugar (rather than icing sugar mixture) and strong, very hot coffee; this helps set the icing.

MAKES 12

METHOD

Preheat the oven to 190°C. Line a 12-hole patty or muffin tin with paper cases.

Sift the flour and salt. Using an electric mixer, cream the butter, add the sugar gradually and beat until light and fluffy.

Whisk the eggs and beat, a little at a time, into the creamed mixture. Fold in half the flour with a metal spoon, add the coffee essence and milk and, lastly, the remaining flour.

Spoon into the prepared paper cases and bake for about 15 minutes. Turn out onto a wire rack to cool.

To make the coffee glacé icing, put the icing sugar in a small bowl and mix in enough coffee so that the mixture will cover the back of a spoon smoothly and thickly.

When the cakes are cool, top each with coffee glacé icing and a whole hazelnut.

TIP If the icing seems to be setting before you've topped all the cakes, place the bowl of icing over a small bowl of warm water just until the icing melts again.

SMALL CAKES *cupcakes, friands & madeleines*

INGREDIENTS

45 g butter, softened
2 tablespoons caster sugar
1 egg
1 cup (150 g) self-raising flour, sifted
a pinch of salt
½ cup milk

GEM SCONES

These aren't actually scones, they are a light little cake. They are so simple and easy to make, and everyone loves them. If you haven't inherited a set of gem irons you may be lucky enough to pick some up at a second-hand shop or garage sale. Alternatively you can use shallow patty tins instead, heating them in the oven first.

MAKES ABOUT 12

METHOD

Grease gem irons or patty tins and heat them in a 200°C oven.

Using an electric mixer, cream the butter and sugar until light and fluffy. Add the egg and beat until well incorporated.

Lightly fold in the sifted flour and salt with the milk, and combine until just mixed. Spoon enough mixture to half-fill the gem irons or patty tins. Bake for 10–15 minutes. Turn out onto a wire rack to cool. Serve warm with small squares of good chilled butter.

INGREDIENTS
2 eggs
¾ cup (165 g) caster sugar
½ teaspoon finely grated lemon rind
1 cup (150 g) plain flour, sifted
185 g unsalted butter, clarified (see Tip)
1 tablespoon rum (optional)
sifted icing sugar to dust

MADELEINES

These very light little French tea cakes are usually baked in shallow, scallop-shaped moulds which give them their distinctive shell-like appearance. They are served dusted with icing sugar. English madeleines are a slightly more elaborate version baked in dariole moulds, glazed, coated with coconut and topped with a cherry (see Variations).

MAKES 32 LARGE OR 50 SMALL MADELEINES

METHOD

Preheat the oven to 200°C. Grease the madeleine tins and dust them with flour.

Beat the eggs and sugar until thick and mousse-like using a hand whisk and a bowl set over a pan of gently simmering water, or a very good electric mixer. Remove from the heat (if using that method) and continue to beat until cooled.

Add the lemon rind. Fold in the flour and then the cooled butter, mixing only until everything is blended. A metal spoon or spatula is best for this job. Take care not to overwork the mixture at this point and don't allow the butter to sink to the bottom of the bowl. Lastly fold in the rum, if using.

Spoon the mixture into the prepared madeleine tins. Bake large madeleines for 9 minutes and small madeleines for 6–7 minutes or until pale golden.

Let stand for 1–2 minutes before removing from the tins. Repeat until all the mixture is used. Dust with icing sugar while still warm.

VARIATIONS

CHOCOLATE MADELEINES Sift the flour with 3 tablespoons of cocoa powder.

ORANGE MADELEINES Replace the lemon rind with the grated rind of 1 orange.

ENGLISH MADELEINES Make Madeleines as above but bake in dariole moulds. After baking and when cold, level the tops with a sharp knife to give a flat base when inverted. Turn out upside-down and brush with warm Apricot or Redcurrant Glaze (page 389). Roll immediately in desiccated coconut and top each with ½ glacé cherry.

TIP To clarify the butter, place in a saucepan and melt slowly. When the butter is clear remove from the heat, stand for a few minutes and pour the clear butter into a cup, leaving the sediments in the pan. Cool. This can also be done in the microwave.

NOTE Madeleine tins are available in small and large sizes from kitchen shops and department stores. Dariole moulds, shallow patty tins or muffin tins can be used if madeleine tins are not available.

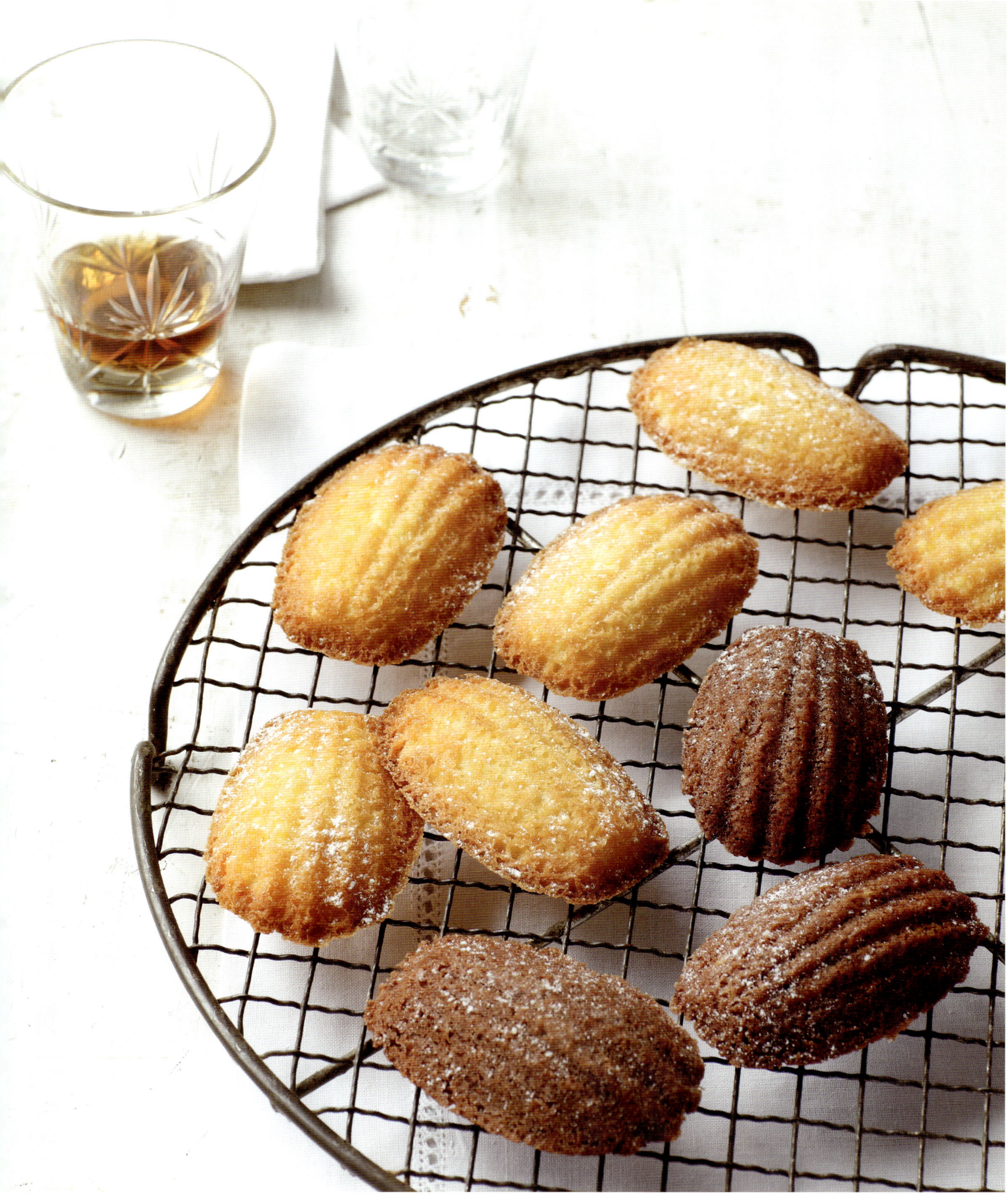

INGREDIENTS

2 cups (300 g) self-raising flour
½ teaspoon mixed spice
a pinch of salt
90 g butter, diced
½ cup (110 g) caster sugar
2 tablespoons each currants, sultanas and chopped mixed peel
1 egg
¼ cup milk

ROCK CAKES

A batch of rock cakes is quickly and easily made and are perfect as a quick snack with morning coffee or afternoon tea. Serve warm or cold, buttered or plain.

MAKES ABOUT 20

METHOD

Preheat the oven to 200°C. Grease baking trays.

Sift the flour with the spice and salt, rub the butter in lightly, and then mix in the sugar. Add the fruits and mix well. Beat the egg, add the milk, then mix into the dry ingredients to form a stiff dough.

Put small tablespoonfuls of the mixture in little rough heaps on the prepared trays.

Bake for 10–15 minutes. Turn out onto a wire rack to cool.

SMALL CAKES *macarons & meringues*

INGREDIENTS

- 1¼ cups (200 g) icing sugar, sifted, plus extra to dust
- 1 cup ground almonds, sifted
- 3 egg whites
- 2 tablespoons caster sugar
- 2–3 drops pink food colouring or a pinch of pink colouring powder

FILLING

- 125 g white chocolate, chopped
- 2 tablespoons thickened cream
- ½ teaspoon strawberry essence

STRAWBERRY MACARONS

Macarons are delightful sweet treats made mainly with eggwhites, ground almonds and sugar. Macarons are usually filled with some type of cream filling sandwiched between the two layers.

MAKES 35

METHOD

Preheat the oven to 130°C (not fan-forced). Lightly grease two baking trays and line with baking paper.

Combine the icing sugar and ground almonds in a bowl.

Using an electric mixer, beat the egg whites until soft peaks form. Add the caster sugar and beat until dissolved. Beat in the food colouring. Fold the egg white mixture thoroughly into the almond mixture.

Using a pastry bag and a plain 1.5 cm nozzle, pipe macarons 3 cm wide on the prepared trays. Lift the tray then bang it down hard to spread the macarons to 4 cm. Dust liberally with extra icing sugar. Leave at room temperature for 15 minutes or for up to 1 hour.

Bake for 20 minutes or until the tops are firm and crisp. Cool on the tray for 5 minutes before sliding the baking paper onto a wire rack to cool completely.

Meanwhile, to make the filling, combine the chocolate and cream in a microwave-safe bowl. Microwave on 50% for 2–3 minutes, stopping and stirring several times until melted and combined. Stir in the strawberry essence. Set aside to cool completely, until of a spreadable consistency.

Scrape the macarons away from the baking paper (they tend to stick a little) and pair according to size. Pipe or spoon a little strawberry filling onto the flat side of one macaron and sandwich together with another. Set aside until the filling sets.

VARIATION

VANILLA MACARONS Omit the pink food colouring and use vanilla essence instead of strawberry.

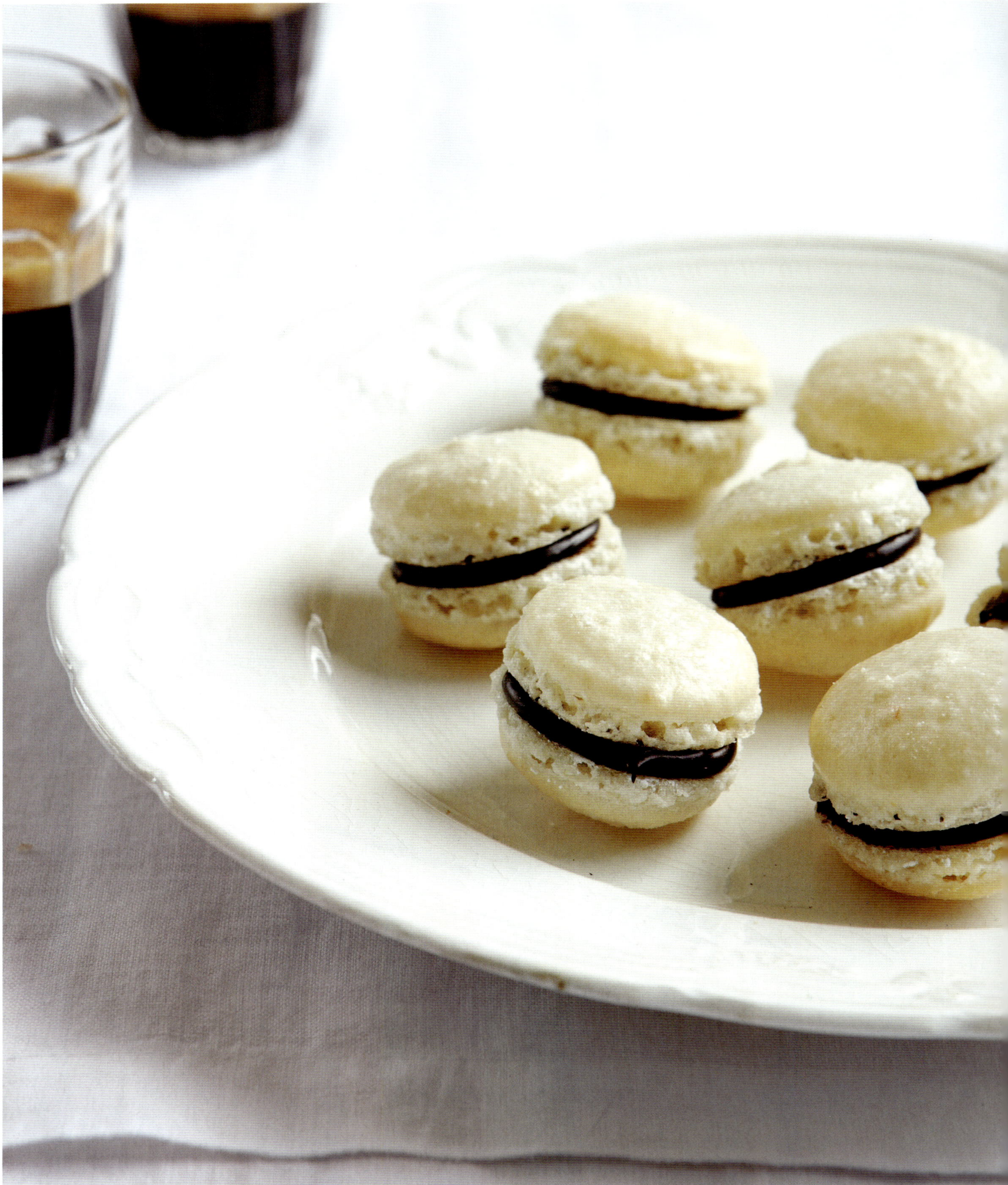

SMALL CAKES *macarons & meringues*

INGREDIENTS
1½ cups (240 g) icing sugar, sifted, plus extra to dust
1 cup ground almonds, sifted
3 egg whites
2 tablespoons caster sugar

GANACHE
135 g dark chocolate, chopped
¼ cup thickened cream

GANACHE-FILLED MACARONS

MAKES ABOUT 24

METHOD

Lightly grease two baking trays and line them with baking paper.

Combine the icing sugar and ground almonds in a bowl. Using an electric mixer, beat the egg whites until soft peaks form. Add the sugar and beat until dissolved. Fold the egg white mixture thoroughly into the almond mixture.

Using a pastry bag and a plain 1.5 cm nozzle, pipe macarons 3 cm wide on the prepared trays. Lift the tray and bang it down hard to spread the macarons to 4 cm. Dust liberally with the extra icing sugar. Leave at room temperature for 15 minutes.

Preheat the oven to 130°C (not fan-forced).

Bake the macarons for 20 minutes or until lightly golden and crisp. Cool on the tray for 5 minutes before sliding the baking paper onto a wire rack to cool completely.

Meanwhile, to make the ganache, combine the chocolate and cream in a small saucepan, then stir until melted and combined. Pour into a bowl and set aside to cool completely, until of a spreadable consistency.

Scrape the macarons away from the baking paper sheet (they tend to stick a little) and pair according to size. Pipe or spoon a little ganache onto the flat side of a macaron and sandwich it together with another.

INGREDIENTS

1½ cups (240 g) icing sugar, sifted, plus extra to dust
1 cup ground almonds or hazelnuts, sifted
3 egg whites
2 tablespoons caster sugar
2 teaspoons coffee flavouring

WHITE COFFEE GANACHE

135 g white chocolate, chopped
¼ cup thickened cream
3 teaspoons coffee flavouring

COFFEE MACARONS

Cooking these treats may seem like a labour of love, but they are well worth the time and effort required.

MAKES ABOUT 35

METHOD

Preheat the oven to 150°C. Lightly grease two baking trays and line them with baking paper.

Combine the icing sugar and ground almonds or hazelnuts in a bowl. Using an electric mixer, beat the egg whites until soft peaks form. Add the caster sugar and coffee flavouring and beat until the sugar dissolves. Fold the egg white mixture into the icing sugar mixture.

Using a 1.5 cm nozzle, pipe macarons 3 cm wide onto the prepared trays. Tap the trays (the macarons will spread to 4 cm) and sprinkle with the extra icing sugar. Leave at room temperature for 15 minutes.

Bake for 20–30 minutes, until lightly golden and crisp. Remove the tray from the oven and stand for 5 minutes. Slide the baking paper sheet onto a wire rack and allow the macarons to cool at room temperature.

Meanwhile, to make the white coffee ganache, put the chocolate and cream in a small saucepan and stir until melted and combined. Stir in the coffee flavouring and refrigerate until nearly set but still spreadable.

Remove the macarons from the baking paper sheet and pair them according to size. Cover the flat side of a macaron with ganache and and stick to its pair. Repeat with the remaining macarons and ganache.

TIP Store macarons in an airtight container in a dry, cool place. Once filled, store macarons in an airtight container in the fridge. You can also freeze the macarons (filled or unfilled) in an airtight container. Allow to stand at room temperature for 30 minutes before serving.

SMALL CAKES *macarons & meringues*

INGREDIENTS
1 cup very strong black coffee
1 cup water
2 cups (440 g) caster sugar
5 egg whites
a pinch of salt
whipped cream to serve

COFFEE KISSES

Use a good coffee to make the syrup for these little meringues; the stronger the coffee the better the flavour. These can be made ahead of serving as they store well in an airtight container for several weeks.

MAKES ABOUT 24

METHOD
Preheat the oven to 150°C. Line baking trays with baking paper or foil.

Heat the coffee, water and sugar together, stirring until the sugar has dissolved, then boil without stirring to make a thick syrup.

Using a balloon whisk or hand-held electric mixer, beat the egg whites in a heatproof bowl until foamy, add the salt and beat the whites to a firm snow. Pour on the syrup in a steady stream, beating all the time. Place the bowl over simmering water and beat for 5 minutes.

Drop the meringue from a teaspoon in small peaked mounds onto the prepared baking tray, spacing the mounds a little way apart.

Bake for 40 minutes or until lightly coloured on the top and firm to the touch. Remove to a wire rack to cool. Store in an airtight container.

To serve, join together in pairs with whipped cream.

INGREDIENTS
3 egg whites
scant ⅛ teaspoon cream of tartar
1 cup (220 g) caster sugar

MINI MERINGUES

This meringue mixture is ideal for miniature meringues, which can be joined together with whipped cream and set in paper cases for a simple yet pretty dessert. You can also use this recipe to make meringue shells, fingers and discs.

MAKES ABOUT 36

METHOD

Preheat the oven to 120°C. Lightly grease baking trays then dust them with flour, or line them with baking paper.

Beat the egg whites with electric beaters on very low speed until frothy. Add the cream of tartar and beat on the highest speed until the peaks hold their shape. Gradually beat in 2 tablespoons of the sugar and continue beating for a further 2–3 minutes.

Add all the remaining sugar at once and fold in quickly and lightly with a metal spoon.

Pipe small amounts onto the prepared baking trays, or shape the meringue mixture into a smooth dollop using two spoons. Bake for 1 hour.

Ease the meringues off the tray with a spatula and leave in the oven for a further 30 minutes or until dry. When cool, store in an airtight container.

VARIATIONS

MERINGUE SHELL Prepare the meringue mixture. Grease a 20–23 cm pie dish and line the base with a round of baking paper. Spread or pipe the meringue mixture over the bottom and side of the dish, building the mixture up on the outside edge. Bake in a preheated 120°C oven for 1–1½ hours or until the surface is set and crusty but only just coloured. Loosen the meringue shell from the pie dish while still warm, and cool before filling. The meringue will crisp as it cools. Use this shell for cream pies. The meringue can also be shaped on a baking tray lined with baking paper. Mark an 18–20 cm circle on the paper and use this as a guide, spreading or piping the meringue inside the circle and building up the outer edge. Bake as above.

INDIVIDUAL MERINGUE SHELLS Prepare the meringue mixture. Line three baking trays with baking paper. Mark 8 cm circles on the paper, leaving at least 5 cm space between the circles. Spread or pipe the meringue mixture inside the circles, building up the outer edges. Bake in a preheated 120°C oven for 45 minutes. Turn the oven off, turn the cases over and allow to cool in the oven. Use as nests for fresh fruit salad with whipped cream, fruit fool or other creamy desserts. Makes 12.

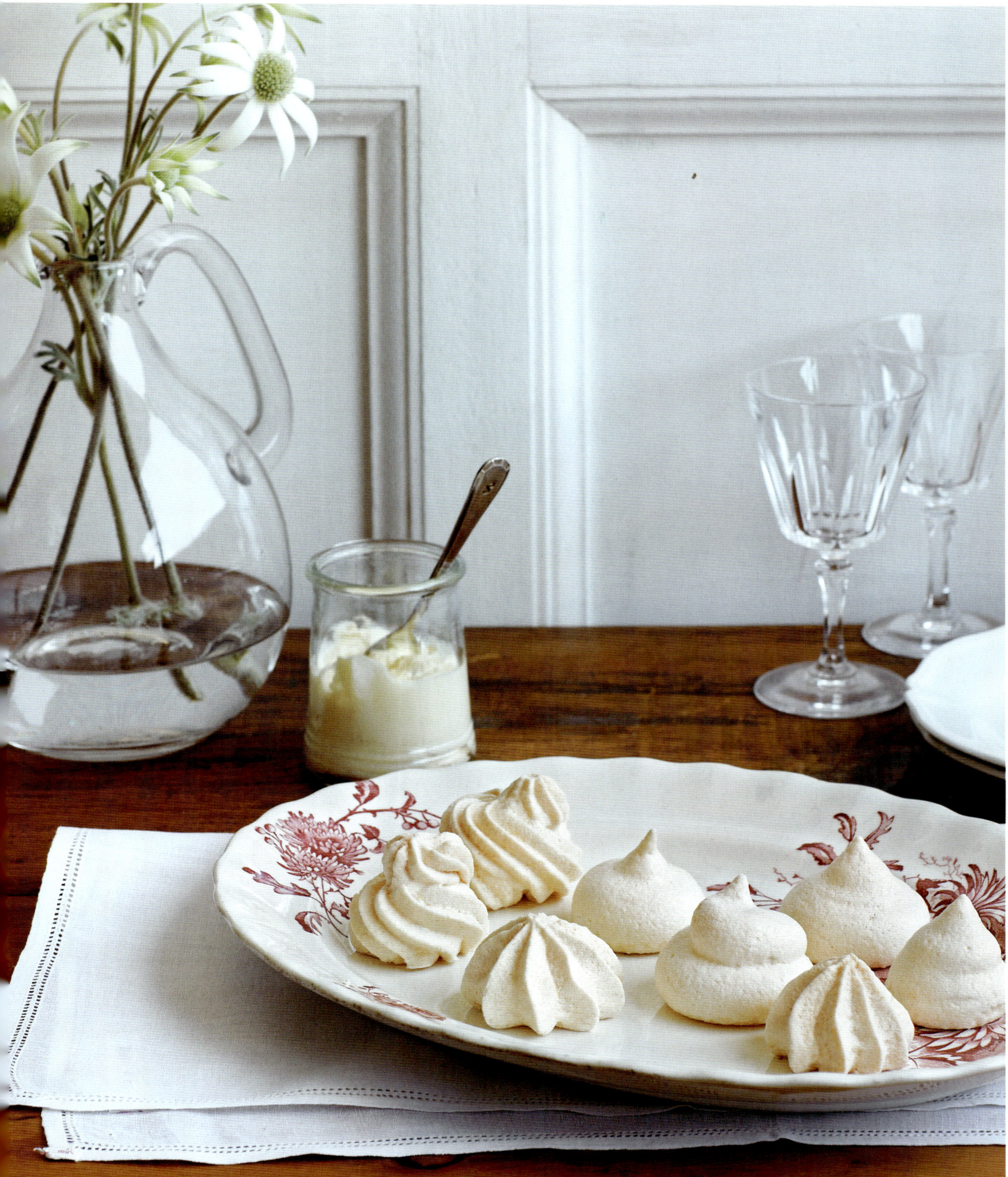

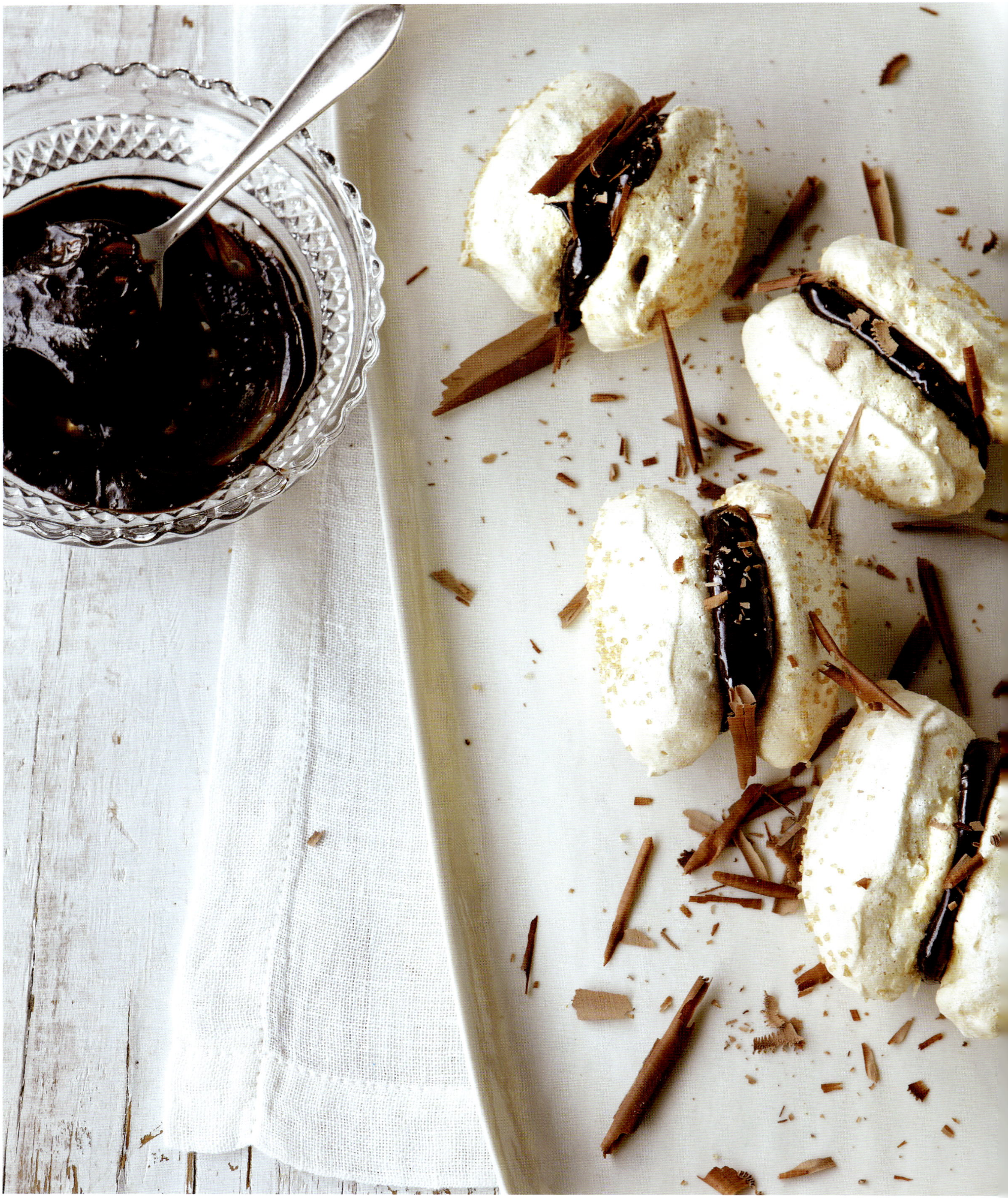

SMALL CAKES *macarons & meringues*

INGREDIENTS
½ cup (115 g) demerara sugar
2 large egg whites
⅓ cup canned unsweetened chestnut pureé
60 g chopped dark chocolate
½ cup cream
dark chocolate shavings to decorate

DEMERARA MERINGUES WITH CHESTNUT & CHOCOLATE CREAM

Demerara sugar is less refined than white sugar and still has much of the molasses left in the crystals, which gives it a distinctive, rich flavour. When used in making meringues, its flavour and texture make for a light meringue, pale bisque in colour. Dredging the tops of the unbaked meringue with a little extra demerara sugar adds a pretty, golden crystal finish. Demerara meringues make a decadent dessert when sandwiched with chestnut and chocolate cream. They also go well with whipped cream and a chocolate or caramel sauce on the side.

MAKES 6

METHOD

Spread the sugar out on a baking tray and place in the oven at 100°C for an hour or so to dry out. Leave to cool then place in a blender or food processor and grind the sugar fairly finely.

Beat the egg whites until they form soft peaks, then beat in half the sugar until the mixture is thick and shiny. Using a large metal spoon, gently fold in the remaining sugar. To do this, cut gently down through the mixture and lift some up and over onto the top, repeating until the whites and sugar are lightly mixed. It is not necessary to mix thoroughly; if the mixture is overworked the air cells in the meringue will break down.

To shape the meringues, use two wet dessertspoons. With one, scoop up a heaped spoonful of mixture. With the other spoon, scoop this mixture out onto a baking tray lined with baking paper, to form a half-egg shape. If necessary, neaten the shape with a knife dipped in cold water. Repeat until all the mixture is used. This should make 12 meringues.

Dredge the tops with a little extra demerara sugar and bake in a 120°C oven for 1 hour or longer until firm. Gently lift each meringue off the tray, press the base with your finger while still warm to make a hollow and return to the oven for a further 30 minutes until crisp and dry. Leave to cool in the turned-off oven. Store in an airtight container until needed.

To make the filling, heat the cream until bubbles are just beginning to form around the edge of the saucepan. Place the chopped chocolate in a heatproof bowl and pour the cream over it. Stir until the chocolate is melted and the mixture is smooth. Add the chestnut purée and stir until smooth. If lumpy, rub through a sieve. Leave to cool completely, then whip the cream and fold into the mixture. Chill until the filling is thick but spreadable.

Spread a good scoop of the filling onto the base of one meringue. Top with another meringue and place on a plate. Scatter with pieces of marrons glacés (poached chestnuts in syrup) and their syrup, or with shavings of dark chocolate, to decorate. Serve with a dollop of thick cream.

NOTE You could also scatter the meringues with pieces of marrons glacés (poached chestnuts in syrup) and drizzle their syrup over the meringues.

INGREDIENTS
2 large egg whites
½ cup (110 g) caster sugar

FILLING
½ cup cream
1 teaspoon caster sugar
a few drops of vanilla essence
chopped walnuts to decorate (optional)

MERINGUES CHANTILLY

These meringues have been given their pretty name because they are filled with crème Chantilly (sweetened, whipped vanilla-flavoured cream, in turn named after the town in France where it originated). Meringues should be made small if being served for afternoon teas – just one or two bites. When served as a dessert they may be larger.

MAKES 12

METHOD

Preheat the oven to 120°C. Grease a baking tray and lightly dust it with flour, or line it with baking paper.

Using a rotary beater or an electric mixer, beat the egg whites until they form soft peaks. Sift 2 tablespoons of the caster sugar over the whites and beat again until the mixture is stiff and shiny.

Sift half the remaining sugar over the whites and, using a large metal spoon, fold it in. Use two damp dessertspoons or tablespoons (depending on size you want the meringues to be) to shape the meringues. With one spoon, scoop up a heaped spoonful of the mixture. With the other spoon, scoop the meringue out onto the prepared baking tray to form a half-egg shape. Neaten with a knife dipped in cold water. If preferred, the meringue can be formed by piping, using a bag fitted with a large plain or rose tube.

Dredge with the remaining sugar and bake for about 1 hour or until a delicate beige colour. Peel the baking paper, if using, off the meringues or lift them carefully off the tray with a palette knife. Gently press the base of each meringue, while still warm, to make a hollow. Replace the meringues upside-down on the tray and return to the oven for a further 30 minutes or until crisp and dry. Cool on a wire rack.

Several hours before the meringues are required, whip the cream with the sugar and vanilla until stiff, and use to sandwich the meringues together in pairs. The cream may be piped or spread on. Place in the refrigerator until serving time. If you wish, sprinkle chopped walnuts on the cream just before serving.

SMALL CAKES *macarons & meringues*

INGREDIENTS
¼ cup ground almonds
¼ cup ground hazelnuts
¾ cup (120 g) icing sugar, sifted, plus extra to dust
1 egg white

BOULES DE NEIGE

Boules de neige, or 'snowballs', are little balls of almond and hazelnut meringue rolled in snowy white sugar and baked into the most delectable crisp sweet treat. Offer these as a petit four, after Christmas dinner, or package them into a pretty box or cellophane bag as a gift. You can buy pretty little paper cases designed for confectionery in a variety of colours, making the snowballs seem even more special.

MAKES ABOUT 18

METHOD
Preheat the oven to 160°C. Line a baking tray with baking paper.

Combine the ground nuts, sugar and egg white in a large bowl and mix to form a firm paste, which can be rolled in the hand.

Divide the mixture into pieces the size of large hazelnuts. Roll each ball in sifted icing sugar to coat thickly. Arrange on the prepared tray and bake for about 10 minutes, until well puffed.

Dust with icing sugar if liked. Cool and transfer to paper cases to serve. Store in an airtight container.

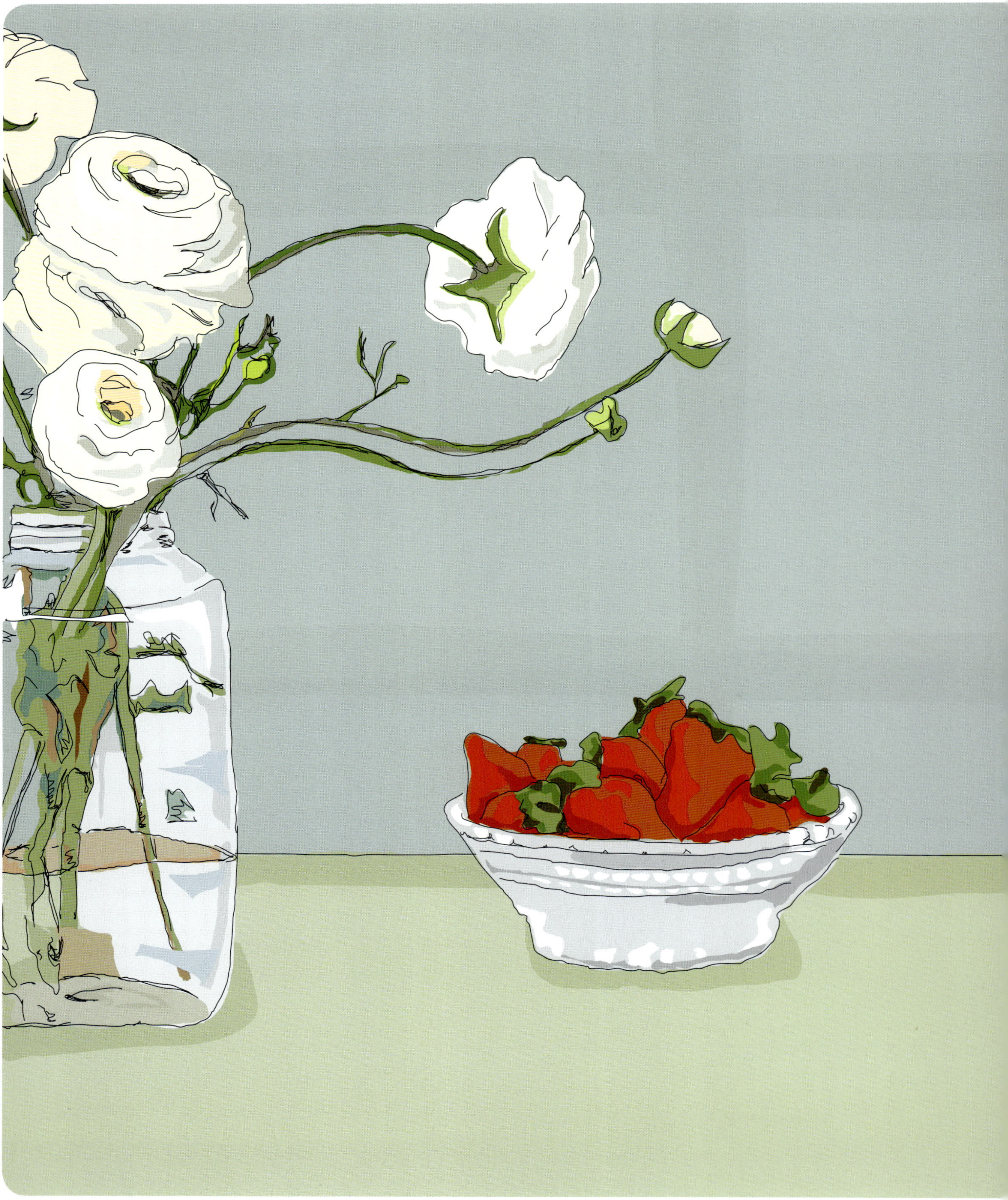

DESSERTS
CHAPTER 6

HINTS & TIPS

Many of us can always make room for dessert, and a delicious, well-presented dessert can be the most memorable and impressive course of a meal.

FRUIT DESSERTS

USE JUST-RIPE, GOOD-QUALITY FRUITS without bruising or soft patches. If the fruit is to be used raw, as in French-style tarts, it is particularly important that it be top-notch and flawless.

IF USING POACHED, CANNED OR THAWED FROZEN FRUITS, make sure the fruit is well drained, so that it will not make the dessert soggy.

FROZEN FRUITS CAN BE SUBSTITUTED FOR FRESH in many desserts where the fruit is to be cooked, or in cooked fruit sauces. Where it is to be served raw or as an accompaniment, use fresh fruit, as it has a better texture and appearance.

PUDDINGS

There are two types: steamed (which this book does not deal with) and baked. For baked puddings, you will need ovenproof baking dishes or moulds. Cake tins can also be used, thought they are less attractive for puddings that are to be served at the table.

MAKING PUDDINGS

BUTTER THE DISH, TIN OR MOULD WELL, so that the pudding is easily turned out or served. Wipe around the edges of the container before baking. The pudding is easier to handle if it is placed on a baking tray while cooking. Some puddings will need to be baked in a water bath; see opposite.

CHEESECAKES

There are two types: unbaked (not covered in this book) and baked. Cheesecakes may have a pastry crust or a crumb crust; the latter is made by combining finely ground biscuits with butter (and sometimes cream), pressing the mixture into the tin, then chilling before pouring in the filling. The filling may be made of cream cheese, ricotta or other soft cheeses, cream and/or condensed milk, plus other ingredients.

MAKING CHEESECAKES

A SPRINGFORM TIN IS ESSENTIAL for the traditional cheesecake, which can't be turned out. Generally the cost reflects the quality. To ensure even baking and help prevent warping it's worth investing in a quality brand with a good weight. Also, go for a reliable non-stick surface, which helps the crust release and makes cleaning easier.

FOR THE CRUMB CRUST, a plain, sweet biscuit is best – however use chocolate, ginger or cinnamon-flavoured biscuits for an alternative flavour.

WHEN PRESSING THE CRUMB CRUST INTO THE TIN, you may find it easier to achieve an even, firm crust by using a straight-sided glass, rather than your fingers, to press over the base and sides of the tin.

FOR THE FILLING, the creaminess of a well-known brand of cream cheese is hard to resist, but you can reduce the fat in your cheesecake by choosing a light cream cheese. Ricotta can be substituted; it is not as smooth, but is typical in Italian-style cheesecakes and similar desserts.

DESSERTS *hints & tips*

WHEN BEATING THE FILLING, use V-groove beaters or a paddle attachment rather than a whisk. The whisk will incorporate too much air, causing the cheesecake to puff up as it bakes before falling and cracking as it cools.

IF THE FILLING IS OVERCOOKED, it will dry out and lose creaminess. At the end of baking the filling should still have a little wobble in the centre. As it cools it will become firm. Overcooked cheesecakes usually crack.

SOUFFLÉS

The charm of a soufflé, apart from its delectable flavour and airy texture, is its spectacular appearance. Rising magnificently above the rim of the dish, its height is determined by the size of the dish. Sizes vary from individual serving dishes through to 5-and 6-cup dishes and larger.

MAKING SOUFFLÉS

TO PREPARE A DISH FOR A SWEET SOUFFLÉ, brush with melted butter and dust inside with a little caster sugar. Remove excess sugar by turning the dish upside down and tapping lightly on the work surface. For savoury soufflés, sometimes the dish is sprinkled with breadcrumbs.

FOR A HIGH SOUFFLÉ, tie a double band of baking paper around the dish to give it extra height. Cut a strip of baking paper 15 cm wide and wrap it around so that it stands like a collar above the edge of the dish. Tie with kitchen string.

SOUFFLÉS CAN BE PARTLY PREPARED AHEAD OF TIME. Prepare the soufflé base mixture (which may be custard or a fruit purée for a sweet soufflé, or a béchamel sauce for a savoury soufflé), cover and refrigerate until just before it is time to cook the soufflés. Then whisk the egg whites, combine with the base mixture, pour into the dishes and bake as directed in the recipe.

MERINGUES

A light meringue is often piled onto a baked, sweet pie or pudding and placed in a moderately hot oven just long enough to tint the meringue; it should be soft and marshmallow-like inside, while the crust may be crisp or soft, depending on the treatment. See Lemon Meringue Pie (page 362) and Lime Meringue Pie (page 361).

Another favourite meringue is the Pavlova (page 318), which, topped with whipped cream and tart-sweet passionfruit or strawberries, is a dessert sweet-tooths can never resist.

See page 259 for hints on working with meringue mixtures.

COOKING IN A WATER BATH

Some desserts (especially ones containing a custard mixture) are baked in a water bath (also known as a bain marie) to ensure that they cook evenly and don't curdle. Place the baking dish(es) in a baking tray, then pour boiling water into the baking tray to come to the specified level up the sides of the dishes (generally about halfway). Then carefully transfer the baking tray to the oven and bake as directed. When cooked, carefully remove the tray from the oven, then the dishes from the water.

INGREDIENTS

½ cup (110 g) caster sugar
juice and rind of 1 orange
1 bunch (450 g) rhubarb, trimmed and cut into 5 cm lengths
1 punnet (250 g) strawberries, washed, hulled and halved

CRUMBLE TOPPING

1 cup (150 g) plain flour
60 g butter, diced
¼ cup (55 g) caster sugar
½ teaspoon ground cinnamon
⅓ cup desiccated coconut

RHUBARB & STRAWBERRY CRUMBLE

Sweetened adequately, rhubarb is absolutely luscious, and surprisingly, it is also a great mixer. I love to combine it with apple, but it is also wonderful with oranges or strawberries. If you find rhubarb on its own too tart, it can be mellowed by adding an equal amount of apple.

SERVES 4

METHOD

Preheat the oven to 180°C. Grease a 5 cup (20 cm) ovenproof dish, or individual dishes.

Combine the sugar and orange juice in a saucepan. Stir over a medium heat until the sugar dissolves. Bring to the boil, then lower the heat and add the rhubarb and orange rind. Cover and simmer for 5 minutes, or until tender but not mushy. Stir in the strawberries.

To make the crumble topping, sift the flour into a bowl and rub the butter into it until the mixture resembles coarse breadcrumbs. Add the sugar, cinnamon and coconut and mix well.

Spoon the fruit into a the prepared dish. Sprinkle with the crumble topping and bake for about 30 minutes or until golden brown. If liked, serve with thick cream, natural yoghurt or vanilla ice cream.

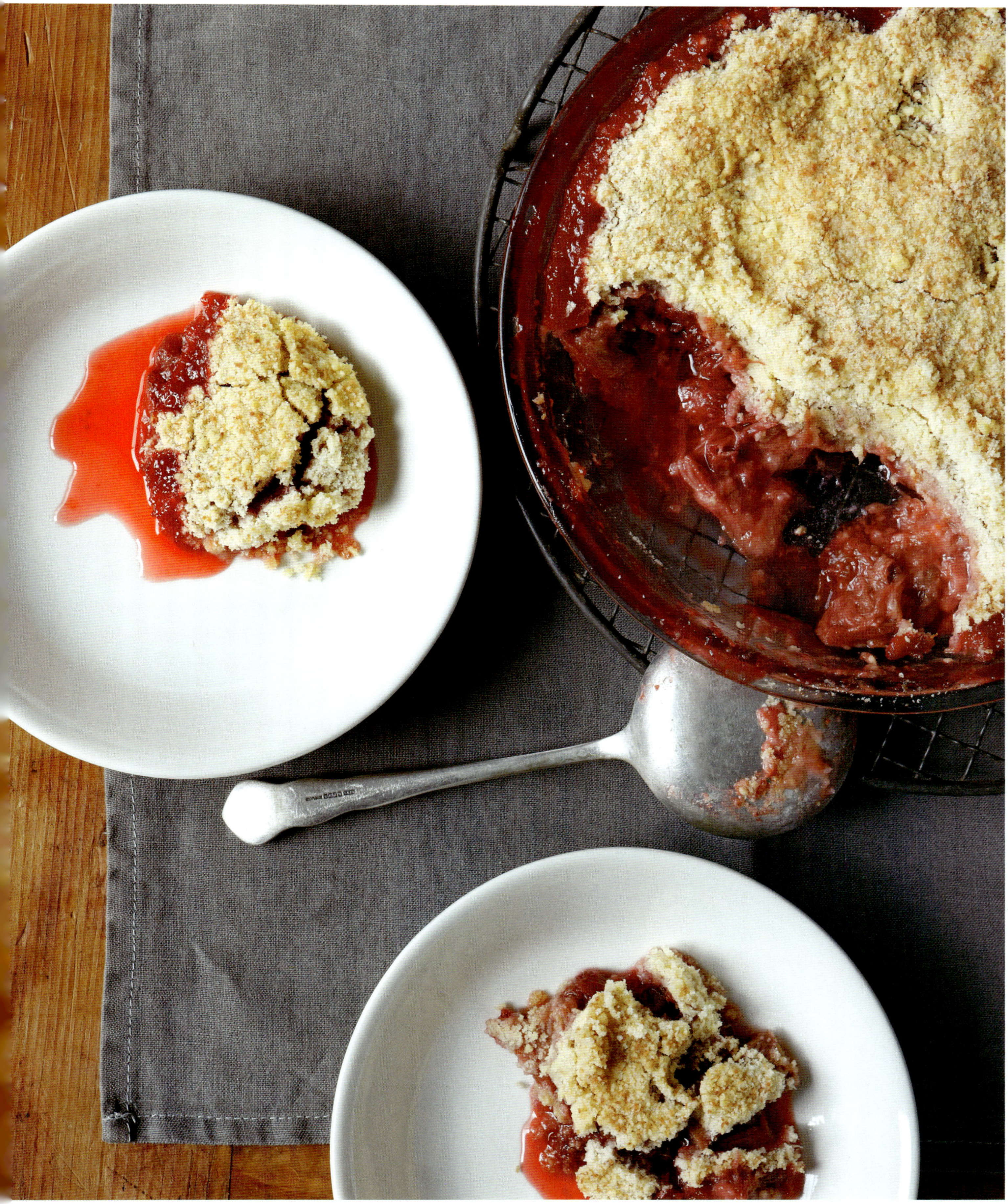

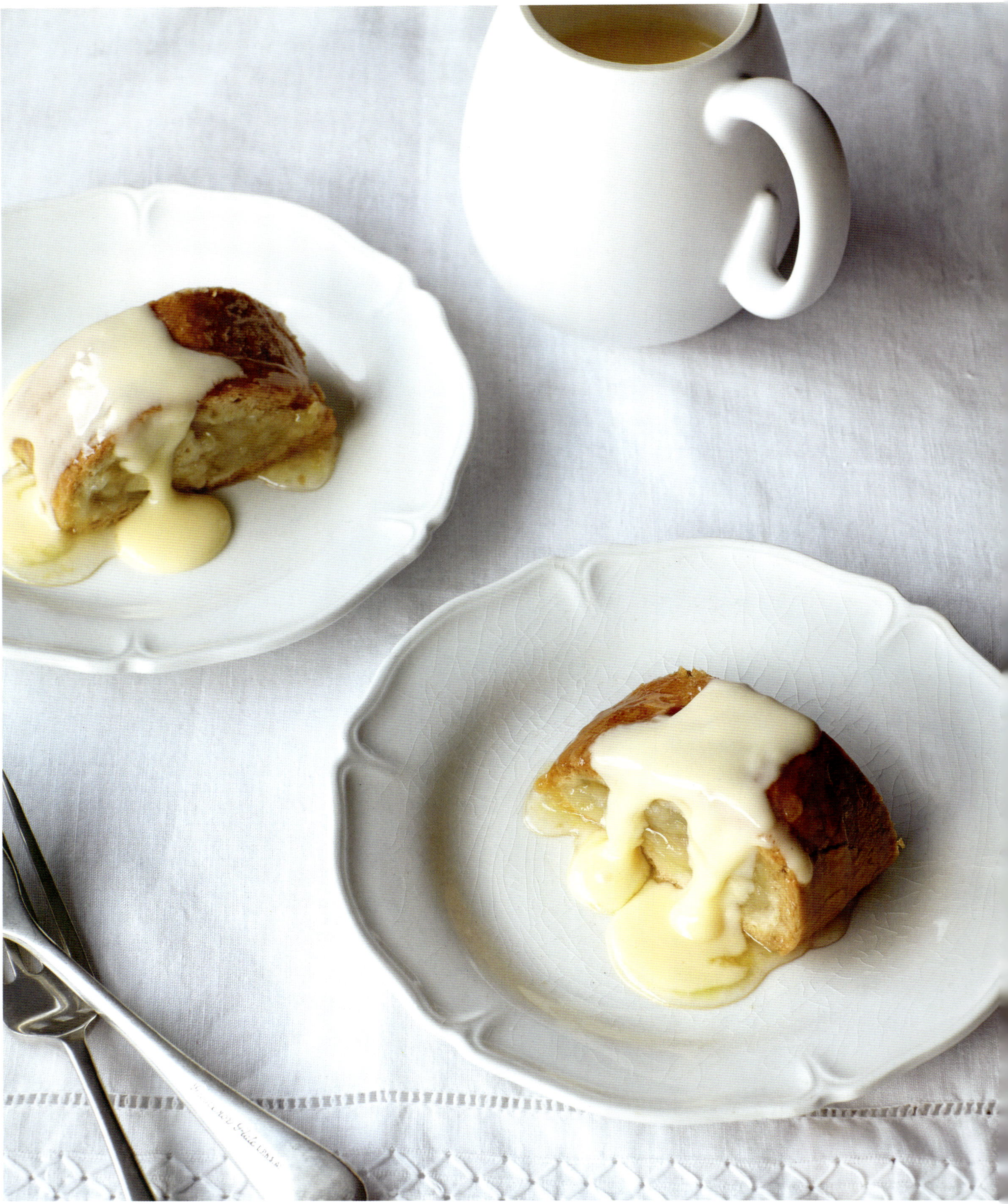

DESSERTS *fruit desserts*

INGREDIENTS

PASTRY
1½ cups (225 g) self-raising flour
½ teaspoon bicarbonate of soda
1 teaspoon cream of tartar
1 tablespoon butter
about 4 tablespoons iced water

FILLING
3 cooking apples, peeled, cored and thinly sliced

SYRUP
¾ cup (165 g) caster sugar
60 g butter
1 cup boiling water

BAKED APPLE ROLY-POLY

SERVES 6

METHOD

Preheat the oven to 180°C. Grease a large, shallow ovenproof dish about 30 cm x 20 cm.

To make the pastry, sift the dry igredients together, rub in the butter with your fingertips and mix in enough water to make a soft dough. Roll out the pastry to a rectangle about 30 cm x 18 cm.

Spread the apples over the pastry and shape the roly-poly by rolling it up from the long side like a Swiss roll. Lift into the prepared dish, seam side down.

Mix the syrup ingredients until the sugar is dissolved and pour over the roly-poly.

Bake for 1 hour, basting the roly-poly every 10 minutes with the syrup. Serve hot, cut into slices, with custard or cream.

VARIATIONS

JAM OR GOLDEN SYRUP ROLY-POLY Follow recipe for Apple Roly-Poly, but substitute about ½ cup jam or golden syrup for the apples. Roll out the pastry fairly thinly.

FRUIT ROLY-POLY Follow recipe for Apple Roly-Poly but substitute ¾ cup dried fruit for the apples.

INGREDIENTS

5 large cooking apples, peeled, cored and sliced
¼ cup water
½ cup (110 g) caster sugar
½ cup (110 g) firmly packed light brown sugar
½ teaspoon ground nutmeg
½ teaspoon ground cinnamon
¼ teaspoon salt
¾ cup (110 g) self-raising flour
125 g butter, diced

APPLE CRISP

Granny Smith apples, tart and firm, seem almost made for this delectable dessert. The sugary spices flavouring the topping give a lovely crisp crunch.

SERVES 6

METHOD

Preheat the oven to 180°C. Grease a shallow 4-cup ovenproof dish.

Put the apples in the prepared dish and add the water. Combine the sugars, nutmeg, cinnamon, salt and flour in a bowl. Cut in the butter until the mixture resembles coarse breadcrumbs. Spoon evenly over the apples.

Cover and bake for 30 minutes. Uncover and bake for a further 30 minutes or until the topping is golden and crisp. Serve hot or warm.

TIP When preparing fruits such as apples and pears that go brown due to oxidisation once peeled or cut, drop the pieces or slices as you prepare them into a bowl of water that has been acidulated with a squeeze of lemon juice. Drain and dry the fruit before using in the recipe.

INGREDIENTS
1 cup dried apricots
2 cups dried apples
2 cups fresh breadcrumbs
60 g butter, melted
1/3 cup chopped blanched almonds
grated rind of 1 orange
1/2 cup (110 g) firmly packed brown sugar
15 g butter

WINTER FRUIT BROWN BETTY

Brown betties are an old-time dessert often made with fresh fruit. This version calls for dried fruit, which is handy to have on hand. In place or apricots and apples, you could use 3 cups of a mixture of dried fruits, such as apples, apricots, pears, peaches and prunes – often sold as dried fruit salad, or ready chopped and labelled as fruit medley.

SERVES 6

METHOD

Preheat the oven to 200°C.

Roughly chop the apricots and apples and soak overnight in plenty of water to cover. Drain.

Toss the breadcrumbs in the melted butter. Spread a thin layer of crumbs in the bottom of a 4–5 cup baking or soufflé dish (about 20 cm round or square). Cover with a little of the chopped fruit. Sprinkle over a little of the almonds, orange rind and brown sugar. Repeat the layers until the dish is full, finishing with a layer of crumbs. Dot with the butter and sprinkle with any remaining sugar.

Bake for 30 minutes or until golden and crisp. Serve very hot with cream.

INGREDIENTS

1 punnet (125 g) blueberries
1 cup frozen raspberries
3 tablespoons blanched whole almonds
2 tablespoons plain flour
¾ cup milk
⅓ cup (75 g) caster sugar
2 large eggs
1 tablespoon port or sherry
¼ teaspoon salt
1 tablespoon cold unsalted butter, diced
icing sugar to dust (optional)
whipped cream to serve (optional)

BLUEBERRY & RASPBERRY CLAFOUTIS

This light dessert takes no time to put together, and it always impresses with its creamy silken texture and generous filling of berries. Plus it looks gorgeous brought to the table, dappled with bright colours and served with cream. Raspberries add a little tartness to the dish, while the blueberries are reliably sweet, together making the perfect pairing.

SERVES 4-6

METHOD

Preheat the oven to 200°C. Butter a 6-cup gratin dish or other ovenproof dish.

Tip the blueberries into the prepared dish and sprinkle the raspberries around.

In a blender or food processor, grind the almonds with the flour then add the milk, 4 tablespoons of the sugar, the eggs, the port or sherry and the salt, then blend the custard well. It will be necessary to stop the machine and scrape down the sides once or twice.

Pour the custard slowly over the fruit, dot with the butter and sprinkle with the remaining 2 tablespoons sugar.

Bake the clafoutis in the middle of the preheated oven for 30–40 minutes or until the top is golden and the custard is set. Transfer it to a wire rack and let it cool for 20 minutes. Dust with icing sugar if liked and serve the clafoutis warm with the whipped cream.

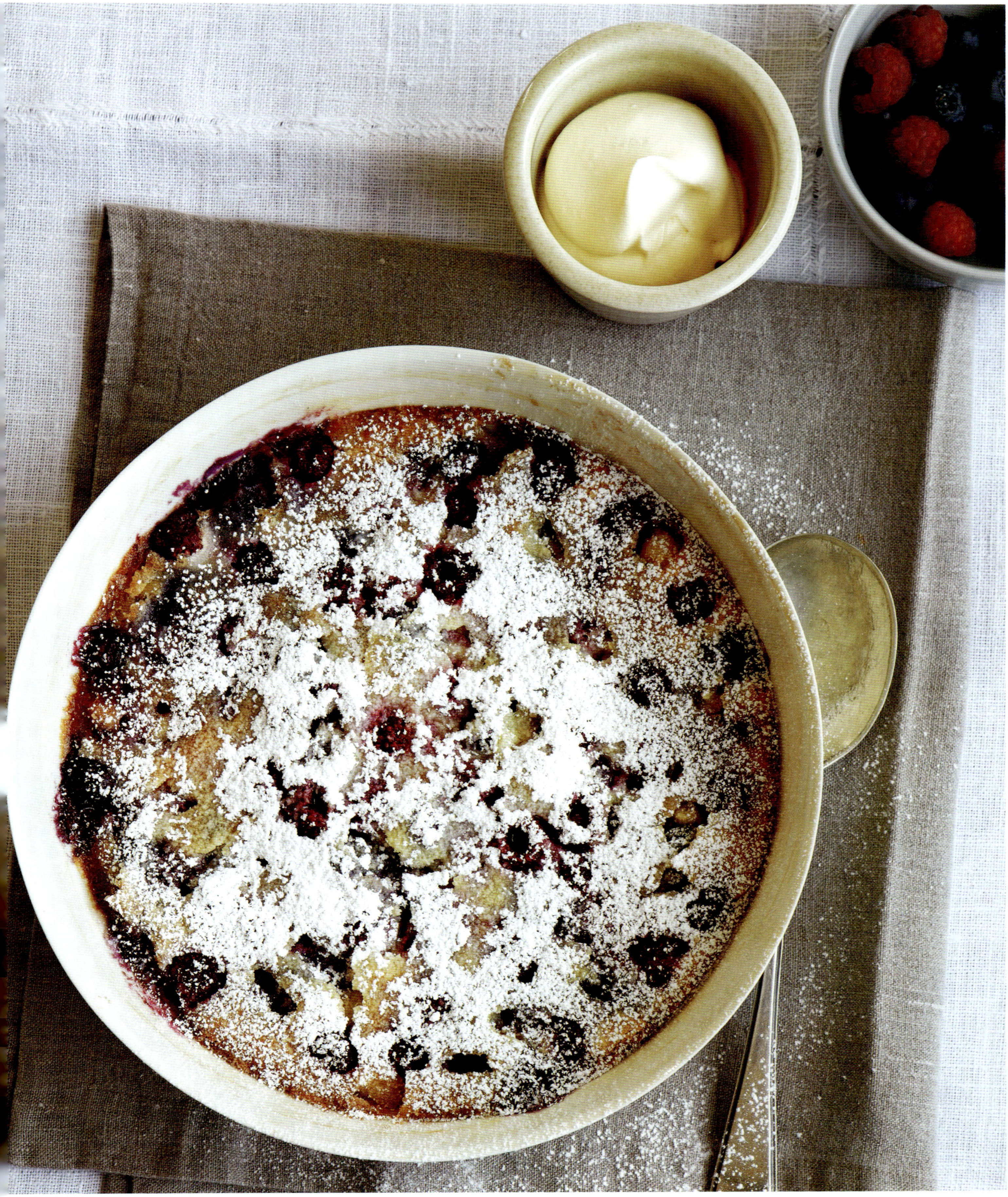

FRUIT SPONGE

INGREDIENTS
500 g fresh fruit (such as apricots, peaches, apples or pitted cherries)
½ cup (110 g) caster sugar, plus extra to sprinkle
100 g butter
2 eggs, beaten
1 cup (150 g) self-raising flour

SERVES 6

METHOD
Preheat the oven to 180°C. Grease a 4-cup pie dish.

Slice larger fruit; halve smaller fruit, or leave it whole. Arrange the fruit in the prepared dish. Sprinkle with sugar to taste and add a little water if required.

Cream together the butter and ½ cup sugar until light. Add the eggs gradually, beating well between each addition – if there is a sign of curdling, add some of the flour.

Sift the flour and stir lightly into the creamed mixture. Spread the mixture over the fruit.

Bake in the middle of the oven for 35–40 minutes. Serve hot or cold with cream or custard.

VARIATION
INDIVIDUAL FRUIT SPONGES Use six individual ovenproof dishes and bake as above for about 20 minutes.

NOTE The sponge may be made with canned fruit if liked. Drain juice from the fruit before arranging in the pie dish.

DESSERTS *puddings*

INGREDIENTS
90 g butter, softened
1/3 cup (75 g) caster sugar
3 eggs, separated
3 tablespoons cream or milk
1 tablespoon brandy (optional)
1 1/2 cups ground almonds
custard to serve

ALMOND CASTLES

SERVES 8

METHOD
Preheat the oven to 160°C. Grease eight dariole moulds (see Note).

Using an electric mixer, cream together the butter and sugar. Stir in the egg yolks, cream or milk, brandy, if using, and almonds. Whisk the egg whites to a stiff froth and fold lightly into the creamed mixture. Spoon into the prepared moulds, filling them three-quarters full.

Bake for 20–25 minutes or until the puddings are firm in the centre and golden brown. Turn out and serve with custard.

VARIATION
STEAMED ALMOND CASTLES If liked, the puddings may be steamed rather than baked – cover the moulds loosely with greased baking paper and steam for 40–50 minutes or until firm.

NOTE The almond mixture is cooked in dariole moulds – small, deep-sided moulds usually made of metal. They may be 1/2 or 1/3 cup in capacity and are perfect for small individual puddings. The moulds are also used for mousses and other individual desserts.

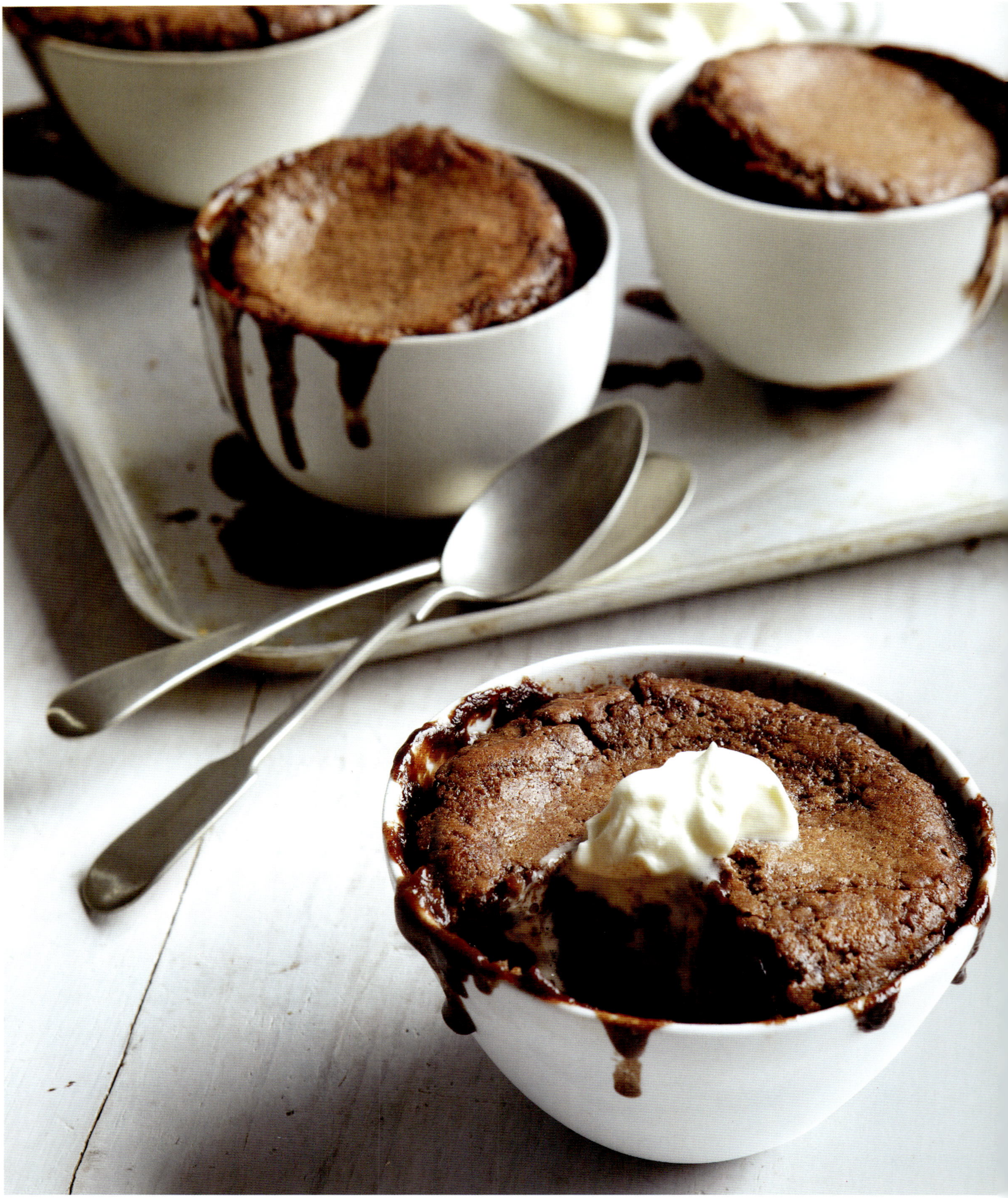

INGREDIENTS

1 cup (150 g) self-raising flour
2 tablespoons cocoa powder
125 g butter, softened
½ cup (110 g) caster sugar
2 eggs, lightly beaten
½ teaspoon vanilla essence
½ cup milk

SAUCE

½ cup (110 g) firmly packed brown sugar
1 tablespoon cocoa powder
2 cups hot water

SELF-SAUCING CHOCOLATE PUDDINGS

It seems such an extraordinary thing to do – pouring hot water over a chocolate pudding – but people love it, especially when it is baked in individual dishes. It makes a difference to use a good-quality Dutch cocoa. Years ago, I bought a pretty tin of Van Houten's Dutch Cocoa and have been extolling its virtues ever since. Look for Dutch (or 'dutched') cocoa in larger supermarkets, kitchen supply shops or good delis.

SERVES 4–5

METHOD

Preheat the oven to 200°C. Lightly butter a 4–5 cup soufflé dish or four or five 1-cup soufflé dishes or ovenproof bowls.

Sift the flour and cocoa together and set aside.

Using an electric mixer, cream the butter and sugar until light and fluffy, then add the eggs and vanilla, mixing well.

Lightly fold in the flour and cocoa mixture alternately with the milk. Spoon into the prepared soufflé dishes.

To make the sauce, combine the sugar and cocoa in a small bowl and sprinkle over the pudding mixture. Carefully pour the hot water over the pudding(s). Bake for 30–35 minutes for a large pudding and 20–25 minutes for individual puddings. Serve warm with whipped cream.

INGREDIENTS

3½ cups milk
1 piece vanilla bean, or 1 teaspoon vanilla essence
¼ cup butter, softened
8 slices French bread (centre portion, not the crusty end)
½ cup sultanas
3 eggs, or 5 egg yolks
⅓ cup (75 g) caster sugar
⅛ teaspoon salt
grated nutmeg to sprinkle

SULTANA BREAD PUDDING

Bread pudding was often made with a good loaf of white bread, sliced and the crusts removed. Often square loaves would be cut diagonally to produce triangles, for an attractive effect. I used to make this pudding for my father, who liked a 'wee dram', so I would add 2 tablespoons Scotch whisky to the milk. We all loved it.

SERVES 6–8

METHOD

Preheat the oven to 180°C. Grease a 6-cup ovenproof dish.

Scald the milk with the vanilla bean, if using. Simmer for 15 minutes. Cool, then discard the vanilla bean, if using, or add the vanilla essence.

Meanwhile, butter one side of each slice of bread. Arrange the slices in the prepared dish, buttered sides down, sprinkling the sultanas between the layers.

Beat the eggs or yolks with the sugar and salt and stir in the scalded milk. Pour over the bread. Let stand for 30 minutes.

Sprinkle with nutmeg. Stand the dish in a roasting tin, pour in hot water to come halfway up the sides of the dish and bake for about 1 hour or until a knife inserted in the centre comes out clean. Serve warm.

TIP Freshly grated nutmeg has the best flavour. Grate on the finest surface of the grater, or to save your knuckles, use a small rotary grater of the type often used for parmesan cheese.

DESSERTS *puddings*

INGREDIENTS

1¼ cups pitted dates
1¼ cups water
1½ teaspoons bicarbonate of soda
125 g unsalted butter, softened
¾ cup (165 g) caster sugar
3 large eggs
1 teaspoon vanilla essence
2 cups (300 g) self-raising flour
1 teaspoon ground ginger

CARAMEL SAUCE

1 cup cream
125 g unsalted butter
½ cup (110 g) firmly packed brown sugar
1 tablespoon golden syrup or maple syrup

STICKY DATE PUDDING

There's something homely about sticky date pudding. My preferred method of cooking this mixture is in individual pudding moulds. Alternatively, you can make one large pudding and bake it in a cake tin, then cut it into squares. Serve with caramel sauce or thick cream or, better still, with both!

SERVES 6-8

METHOD

Preheat the oven to 180°C. Grease a 22 cm square cake tin and line the base with baking paper, or grease six or eight 1-cup metal moulds.

Combine the dates and water in a small saucepan and bring slowly to the boil. Stir in the bicarbonate of soda and set aside.

Using an electric mixer, cream the butter and sugar until light and fluffy. Add the eggs one at a time, beating well after each addition, then add the vanilla.

Sift the flour with the ginger and fold into the butter mixture. Mash the date mixture with a fork (this can also be done in a food processor). Lightly fold into the batter. Spoon into the prepared tin and bake for 45 minutes to 1 hour for a large pudding or 20–25 minutes for individual puddings, or until a skewer inserted in the centre comes out clean.

Let the pudding cool in the tin for 10 minutes, then run a sharp knife around the edge. Invert the pudding onto a plate then re-invert it, top side up, onto a serving plate. Cut into squares. Invert individual moulds onto serving plates.

To make the caramel sauce, combine all the ingredients in a saucepan. Bring the mixture to the boil, stirring, and simmer for 8 minutes over a medium heat, until it thickens slightly. Pour the caramel sauce over the pudding to serve.

NOTE This luscious caramel sauce is wonderful served with ice cream or steamed puddings. Microwave on low, stirring occasionally, to reheat.

INGREDIENTS
100 g butter, softened
grated rind and juice of 1 large lemon
2/3 cup (150 g) caster sugar
3 eggs, separated
1/2 cup (75 g) self-raising flour, sifted
1 1/4 cups milk

LEMON DELICIOUS PUDDING

Generations of readers have written in praising this lemon delicious recipe, sometimes called lemon surprise pudding because underneath the sponge topping is a creamy lemon sauce. However, the surprise will only be there if the pudding is cooked the right amount. Too much and the sauce will be lost, too little and there won't be enough sponge topping. If there doesn't seem to be enough sponge, return the dish to the oven for a little longer.

SERVES 4

METHOD
Preheat the oven to 180°C. Butter four 1-cup individual ramekins.

Using an electric mixer, cream the butter with the lemon rind and sugar. When it is creamy and light, beat in the egg yolks. Stir in the sifted flour alternately with the milk.

Beat the egg whites until stiff and fold into the mixture with the lemon juice, lightly yet thoroughly.

Pour into the prepared ramekins and bake for about 40 minutes. Serve hot with thick cream.

VARIATION
LARGE LEMON DELICIOUS PUDDING Spoon the mixture into a greased 3–4 cup casserole or pie dish (about 20 cm in diameter) and bake in a preheated 180°C oven for 45–50 minutes.

TIP For a pretty effect on individual puddings, have ready metal skewers that have been heated to red-hot over a naked flame or on the stove element. As soon as the puddings come out of the oven, dust the tops with sifted icing sugar. Holding the skewers with an oven mitt, scorch the tops of the puddings quickly with the skewers. Do this one skewer at a time, leaving the other skewers on the heat as you work, to form a crosshatch pattern on the top of each pudding.

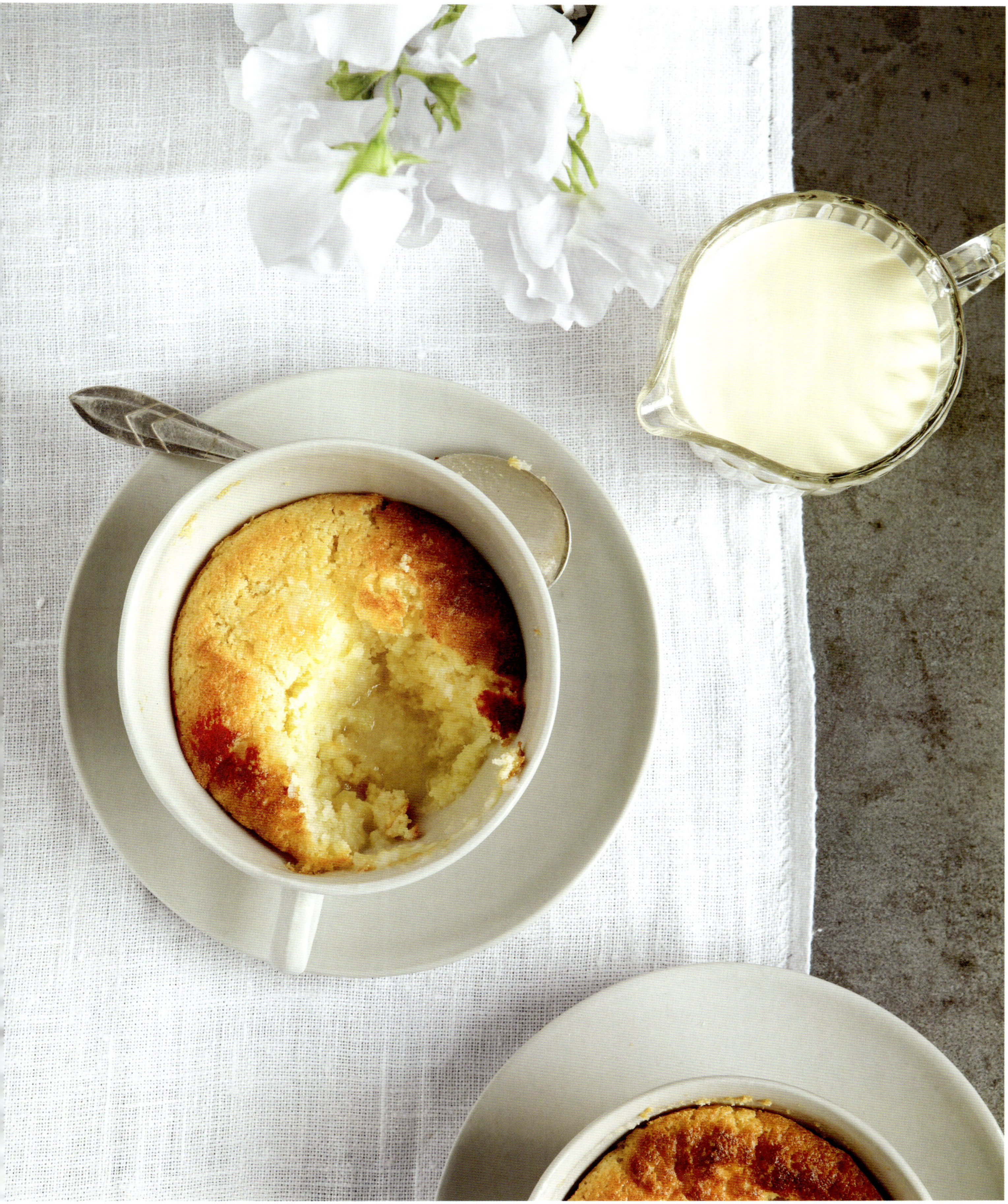

INGREDIENTS
1 cup (150 g) plain flour
2 tablespoons caster sugar
60 g butter, diced and chilled
2 egg yolks
½ teaspoon vanilla essence
thin slices of lemon to serve
icing sugar to dust
thick cream to serve

FILLING
2 cups ricotta
1 cup (220 g) caster sugar
grated rind and juice of 2 lemons
4 eggs
a pinch of salt
1 teaspoon vanilla essence

BAKED RICOTTA & LEMON TART

SERVES 10

METHOD

Put the flour, sugar and butter in a food processor and process with a pulse mode until crumbs are formed. Add the egg yolks and vanilla and continue to process on normal mode until a dough is formed. Turn out onto a floured board and knead lightly into a smooth ball. Wrap in plastic wrap and chill for 30 minutes before using.

Roll the pastry out to line a 23 cm loose-based flan tin. Trim the edges, prick the base lightly with a fork and chill again while making the filling.

Preheat the oven to 200°C. Using an electric mixer with paddle or V-groove beaters, beat the ricotta until softened, then gradually beat in the sugar until light and fluffy. Beat in the lemon rind and the eggs, one at a time, to prevent curdling. Beat in the salt, lemon juice and vanilla, until smooth and well blended.

Pour into the pastry shell and bake for 15 minutes. Reduce the heat to 190°C and bake for a further 35 minutes or until the pastry is cooked and the filling is pale golden.

Cool on a wire rack. Garnish with thinly sliced lemon and dust with icing sugar. Serve with thick cream.

DESSERTS *cheesecakes*

INGREDIENTS
1 quantity Plain Rich Shortcrust Pastry (page 329)
lightly beaten egg white to glaze
500 g ricotta
½ cup (110 g) caster sugar
⅔ cup honey
4 eggs
2 teaspoons cinnamon to sprinkle

HONEY CHEESECAKE SQUARES

There are many interesting honeys with different flavours depending on the flowers from which the bees collected the nectar – such as heather, or native Australian or New Zealand tree blossoms. These are known as 'flower honeys' and each has a distinctive taste. Experiment with various honeys then settle for the one you like best.

MAKES ABOUT 16 SQUARES

METHOD

Preheat the oven to 190°C. Grease a 20 cm square loose-based cake tin, or line a regular tin with baking paper, extending it a few centimetres over two opposite sides to aid with removal later.

Roll out the pastry to line the prepared tin. Brush the pastry with a little egg white, prick the bottom and sides well and bake blind for 10 minutes. Remove and allow to cool in the tin while preparing the filling.

To make the filling, beat together the ricotta, sugar and honey, add the eggs one at a time and beat until combined. Pour into the cooled pastry shell.

Reduce the oven temperature to 180°C and bake the cheesecake for 45–50 minutes or the until top is golden-brown. Turn off the heat and allow to cool in the oven.

Sprinkle with cinnamon and cut into squares or diamond shapes to serve.

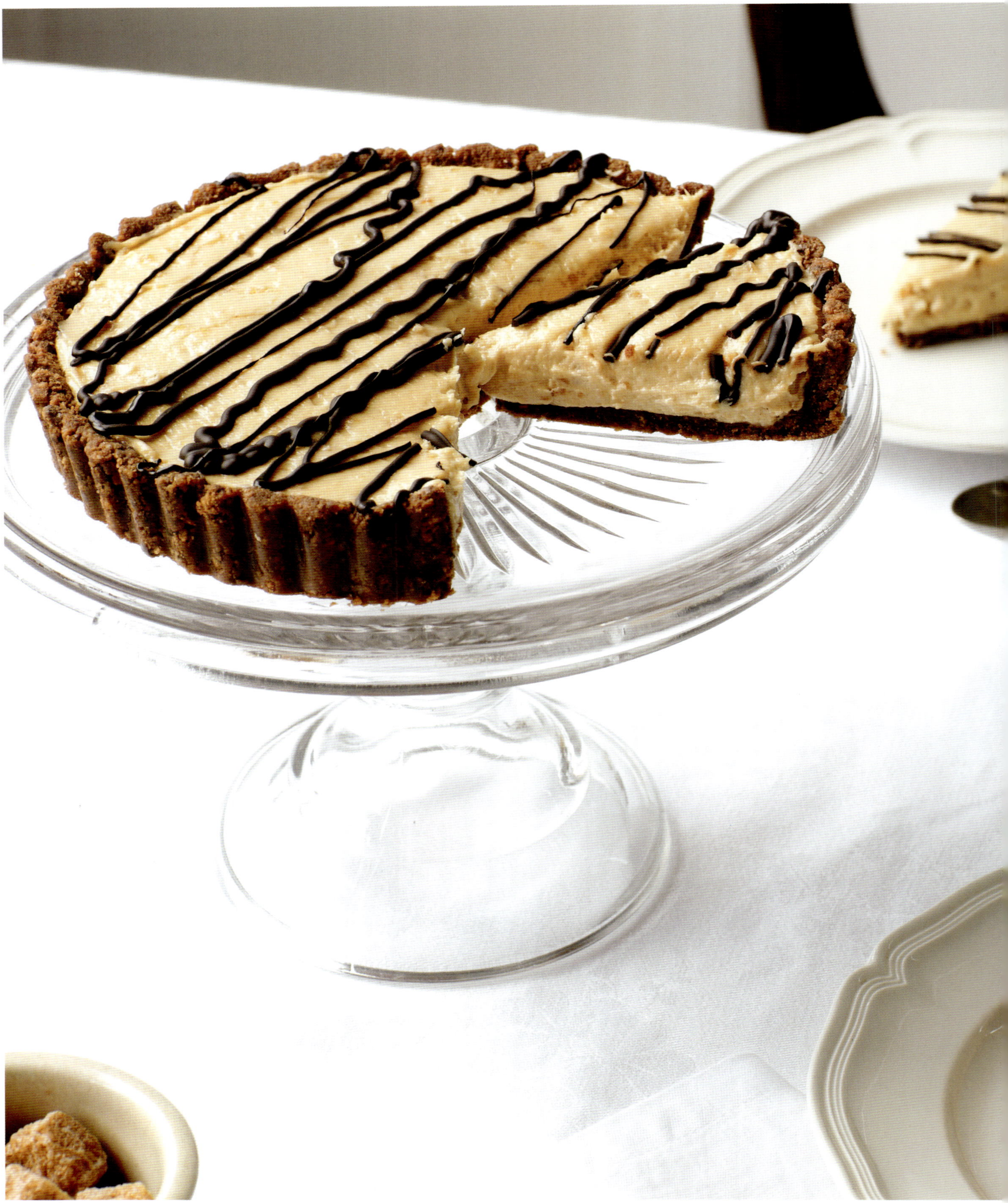

INGREDIENTS

200 g chocolate wheaten biscuits
60 g butter, melted
½ cup milk, plus 1 tablespoon extra
¾ cup crunchy peanut butter
250 g cream cheese
½ cup (110 g) caster sugar
30 g dark chocolate, melted

CHOCOLATE PEANUT BUTTER CHEESECAKE

Some people never get over their love of peanut butter. This recipe originated in America where peanut butter is very popular. I've adapted it to suit our tastes and it's a very pleasant way to enjoy good crunchy peanut butter.

SERVES 10

METHOD

Preheat the oven to 180°C. Line the base of a 20 cm loose-based flan tin with baking paper.

Crush or process the biscuits to fine crumbs. Add the melted butter and the extra tablespoon of milk and process until well combined. Press the mixture over the base and sides of the prepared tin. Bake for 15 minutes, then remove the tin to a wire rack and allow to cool completely.

To make the filling, combine the peanut butter and the ½ cup milk in a small saucepan on low heat and stir until smooth. Remove from the heat and cool.

Using an electric mixer with paddle or V-groove beaters, beat the cream cheese with sugar until smooth and stir in the peanut butter mixture. Spoon into the cooled chocolate crust, cover loosely with plastic wrap and chill for several hours until firm.

Put the melted chocolate in a small plastic bag and snip off a corner. Drizzle the melted chocolate finely back and forth over the cheesecake. Return to the refrigerator and leave to set for 15 minutes before cutting into wedges to serve.

INGREDIENTS

CRUMB CRUST
2 cups coarsely broken plain biscuits (such as Nice)
½ cup ground almonds
¼ cup thickened cream
75 g butter, melted

FILLING
750 g cream cheese, at room temperature
⅔ cup (150 g) caster sugar
2 eggs
grated rind of 1 lemon
1 tablespoon lemon juice

TOPPING
1½ cups sour cream
2 tablespoons caster sugar
½ teaspoon vanilla extract
½ teaspoon grated nutmeg to sprinkle

BISTRO CHEESECAKE

I've taken in lots of Broadway shows in New York over the years, and often called into the world-famous Lindy's afterwards for a piece of their sinfully rich but heavenly cheesecake. This is as good as it gets, and is a variation of the cheesecake that was so popular in my early days, when I used to demonstrate it.

SERVES 10

METHOD

Preheat the oven to 190°C.

Use a blender or food processor to process the broken biscuits into fine crumbs. Transfer to a bowl. Add the ground almonds, cream and melted butter and mix well. Using your fingers, press the crumb mixture into a 22 cm springform pan to come 4 cm up the sides. Chill while making the filling.

To make the filling, using an electric mixer, beat the cream cheese and sugar until smooth. Add the eggs one at a time, beating well after each addition. Beat in the lemon rind and juice. Pour the cream cheese mixture into the prepared crumb crust, spreading it evenly with a spatula. Bake for 25–30 minutes or until very lightly browned on top. Remove from the oven and cool to room temperature.

Increase the oven temperature to 220°C. Using an electric mixer, beat the sour cream, sugar and vanilla until smooth. Pour over the cheesecake and spread evenly. Bake for 5 minutes or until glazed and shiny. Remove from the oven and cool. Refrigerate overnight or for at least 6 hours. Sprinkle with grated nutmeg and serve.

VARIATIONS

CHERRY CHEESECAKE Drain canned cherries, pat dry and fold through the filling.

GINGER CHEESECAKE Use ginger biscuits in the base and stir chopped crystallised ginger through the filling. Sprinkle with ground ginger in place of nutmeg.

LEMON OR PASSIONFRUIT CHEESECAKE Replace the sour cream topping with Lemon or Passionfruit Butter (pages 254–255). There is no need to bake the filling in the oven for 5 minutes.

FRUIT-TOPPED CHEESECAKE Instead of nutmeg, decorate with passionfruit, strawberries, grated chocolate or sliced kiwi fruit.

TIP The cheesecake can be made a few days ahead and kept covered and chilled. If you don't have a food processor, place biscuits in a plastic bag and crush with a rolling pin or the base of a saucepan.

DESSERTS *cheesecakes*

This cheesecake became the signature dish at Johnnie Walker's bistro in Sydney. It was always a top seller and I used to make it at the cookery class I conducted there. Don't attempt to make it at the last moment – you need to prepare it a day ahead and then refrigerate it.

INGREDIENTS

3 teaspoons powdered gelatine
½ cup cold water
⅔ cup (150 g) caster sugar
⅛ teaspoon salt
3 eggs, separated
¼ cup brandy
¼ cup crème de cacao
2 cups cream, whipped
shaved or grated chocolate to decorate

CRUMB CRUST

1¼ cups sweet biscuit crumbs (Nice biscuits are ideal)
¼ cup (55 g) caster sugar
75 g butter, melted

BRANDY ALEXANDER PIE

SERVES 6-8

METHOD

Preheat the oven to 180°C.

Soften the gelatine in the cold water in a saucepan. Add half of the sugar, the salt and the egg yolks. Stir to blend. Heat over low heat, stirring, until the gelatine dissolves and the mixture thickens. Do not boil. Remove from the heat and stir in the brandy and crème de cacao. Chill until the mixture starts to thicken slightly.

To make the crumb crust, combine all the ingredients and press evenly over the bottom and sides of 23 cm pie plate or springform tin (see Note). Bake for 15 minutes, then remove the tin to a wire rack and allow to cool completely.

Using an electric mixer, beat the egg whites until stiff. Gradually beat in the remaining sugar and fold into the thickened mixture. Fold in half of the whipped cream. Tip into the cooled crust and chill for several hours or overnight.

Decorate with the remaining cream and the shaved or grated chocolate.

NOTE Look for a tart tin with sides about 2 cm deep. I use one with a removable base, as this makes it easy to remove and serve the finished pie.

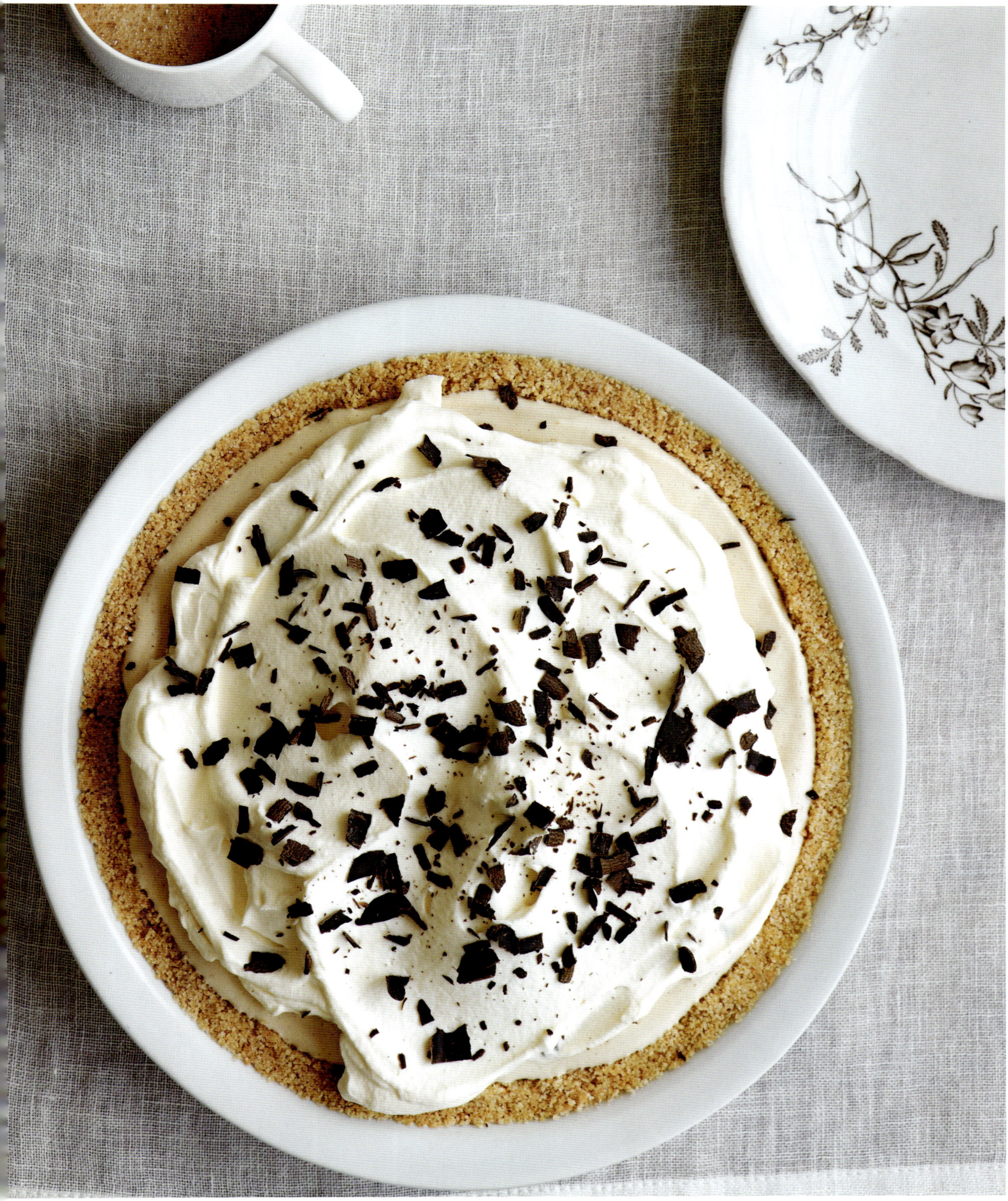

INGREDIENTS
45 g butter
1 tablespoon plain flour
1 cup milk
¼ teaspoon salt
½ cup (110 g) caster sugar plus extra to dust
a piece of vanilla bean
4 egg yolks
5 egg whites

BASIC SWEET SOUFFLÉ

The famous French soufflé is one of the lightest, most delectable, most useful dishes in a cook's repertoire. Any chef worth their salt can whip up a soufflé on demand and with today's excellent thermostatically controlled ovens it is easier to succeed than to fail in making soufflés. Don't be afraid. Making a soufflé is simply a matter of aerating custard with whipped egg whites, and baking it.

SERVES 6

METHOD
Preheat the oven to 180°C. Lightly butter a 6-cup soufflé dish and dust it with caster sugar.

Melt the butter in a saucepan, blend in the flour and cook for 1 minute. Remove from the heat and add the milk, stirring constantly. Add the salt, sugar and vanilla bean. Heat, stirring constantly, and when the sauce is thick and smooth, remove from the heat and allow to cool.

When the milk mixture is cool, remove the vanilla bean and stir in the egg yolks.

Whisk the egg whites until stiff and fold into the mixture. Spoon into the prepared soufflé dish. Bake for 35 minutes or until well risen and golden. Serve immediately.

VARIATIONS
PASSIONFRUIT SOUFFLÉ Add ½ cup sieved passionfruit pulp, retaining 1 teaspoon of seeds to add to the sauce with the egg yolks.

ORANGE LIQUEUR SOUFFLÉ Add 2 tablespoons Grand Marnier, Cointreau or other orange-flavoured liqueur to the sauce when adding the egg yolks.

CHOCOLATE SOUFFLÉ Finely chop 60 g dark chocolate and melt over hot water. Allow to cool slightly then add to the sauce.

DESSERTS *soufflés*

INGREDIENTS
100 g dark chocolate, chopped
⅓ cup (55 g) icing sugar, sifted
75 g unsalted butter
3 tablespoons plain flour, sifted
¼ cup cocoa powder, sifted
1 cup milk
a pinch of salt
2 tablespoons rum or brandy, or 1 teaspoon vanilla essence
4 egg yolks
5 egg whites
¼ teaspoon cream of tartar
thick cream and icing sugar to dust (optional)

CHOCOLATE SOUFFLÉS

For chocolate soufflés I like to use individual dishes and choose the best-quality dark chocolate. For an even richer chocolate flavour I also use a good Dutch cocoa.

SERVES 6

METHOD

Preheat the oven to 190°C. Melt the chocolate in a heatproof bowl set over a saucepan of hot (not boiling) water, or on low in the microwave.

Grease six 1-cup soufflé dishes or ramekins and dust the insides with a tablespoon of the measured icing sugar. Place on a baking tray and set aside.

Melt the butter in a saucepan over a low heat and stir in the flour and cocoa powder until blended. Add the milk and continue to stir, increasing the heat to medium, until a smooth, thick sauce forms. Add a pinch of salt, the melted chocolate and the rum or other flavouring, stirring until the mixture is smooth.

Cool for 5 minutes then whisk in the egg yolks, one at a time. The soufflé mixture can be made in advance to this point.

Whisk the egg whites and cream of tartar until soft peaks form, then gradually beat in the remaining icing sugar until stiff but not dry. Stir a large dollop of the egg-white mixture into the chocolate mixture and then gently fold in the remainder using a large metal spoon. Spoon the mixture into the prepared dishes and smooth the tops.

Bake for about 20 minutes or until risen and set, then transfer the dishes to warmed plates and serve immediately. You can, if you like, cut a slit in the tops of the soufflés on serving and add a dollop of thick cream, then sift a little icing sugar over the top.

NOTE Cream of tartar is is a fine white powder made from the crystals that form on the inside of wine barrels. It is used to stabilise beaten egg whites (as in meringue mixtures). It is also an ingredient in baking powder.

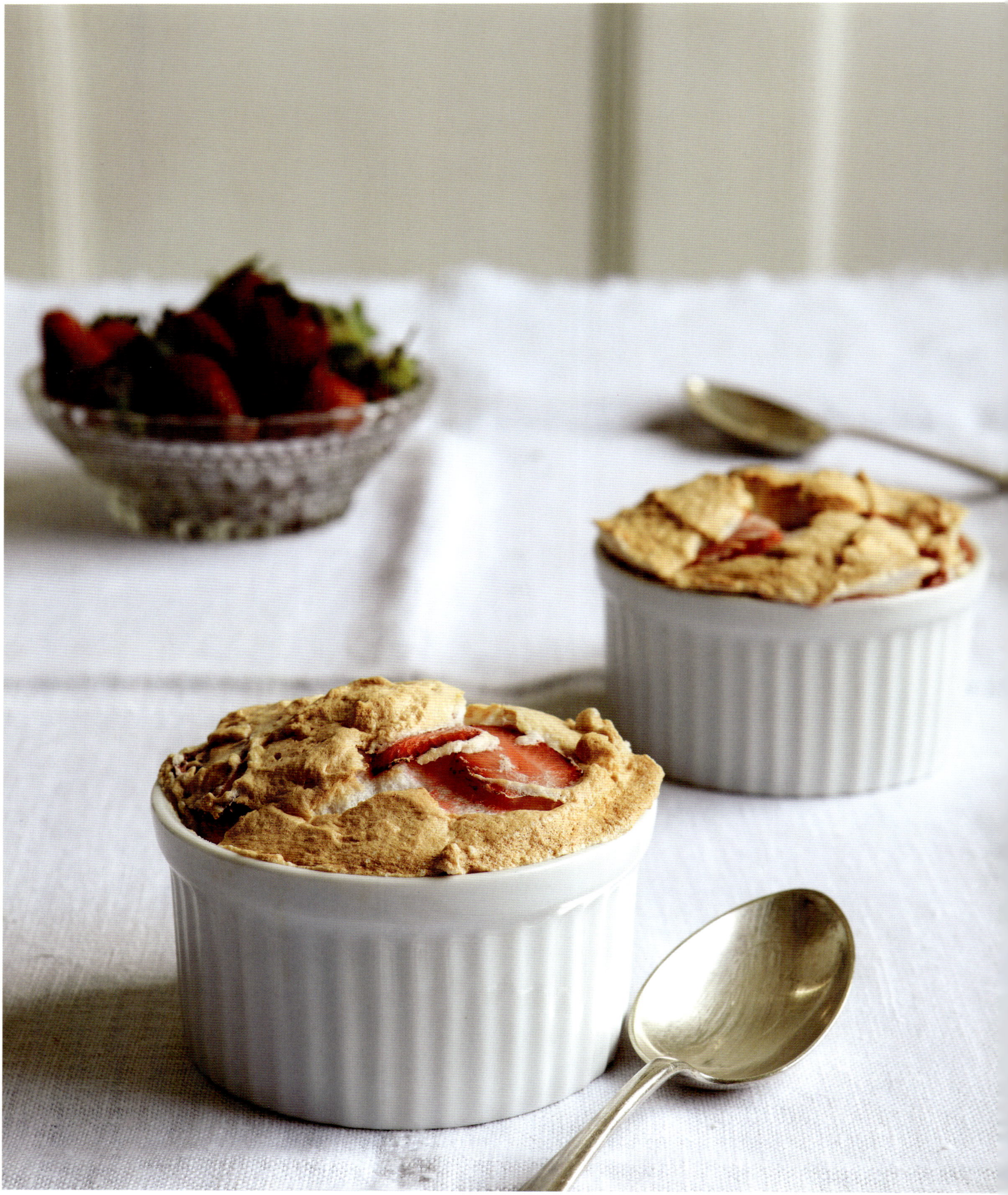

DESSERTS *soufflés*

INGREDIENTS
½ cup (110 g) caster sugar plus 2 tablespoons extra
1 punnet (250 g) strawberries, hulled and sliced
2 tablespoons Kirsch
5 egg whites
whipped cream to serve

BAKED STRAWBERRY SOUFFLÉS

This recipe differs from most soufflés in that it has no custard base, but instead uses a light meringue mixture. It is very simple to make. The sugared strawberries and Kirsch are a good combination.

SERVES 6

METHOD

Preheat the oven to 180°C. Grease 6 small (½–⅔ cup) soufflé dishes and use the 2 tablespoons of sugar to coat the sides and bottom.

Sprinkle the sliced strawberries with 2 tablespoons of the remaining sugar and the Kirsch, and macerate for 1 hour.

Beat the egg whites until stiff, then gradually beat in the remaining sugar to form a stiff meringue. Drain the strawberries and fold through the meringue, then spoon the mixture into the prepared dishes. Stand them in a baking tin and add enough hot water to come halfway up the sides of the dishes. Bake for 15–18 minutes or until puffed and lightly browned.

Serve immediately, with whipped cream.

INGREDIENTS

4 egg whites
1½ tablespoons plain flour
45 g ground hazelnuts
75 g ground almonds
½ cup (110 g) caster sugar
45 g butter, melted
1½ cups cream
½ teaspoon vanilla essence
1½ cups sliced peaches (fresh or drained canned)
sifted icing sugar to dust

ALMOND & HAZELNUT GALETTE

A galette is a round flat cake, either sweet or savoury, and very French. This version calls for peaches, but other fruits may be used.

SERVES 8

METHOD

Preheat the oven to 180°C. Cut out three rounds of baking paper 20 cm in diameter. Spray with non-stick cooking spray, and place on baking trays.

Whisk the egg whites until very stiff peaks form. Sift the flour, nuts and sugar into the egg whites, add the melted butter and fold together gently using a metal spoon. Divide the mixture into three and spread one portion out on each baking paper round.

Bake for 25–30 minutes or until pale gold. Place on wire racks, allow to cool then remove the baking paper rounds.

Whip the cream and add the vanilla. Place one meringue round on a serving platter, spoon one-third of the cream over and arrange half of the sliced peaches on the cream. Cover with the second meringue round. Repeat the layering with one-third of the cream and the remaining peaches and place the last meringue round on top. Dust with icing sugar and decorate with the remaining whipped cream.

VARIATIONS

APRICOT GALETTE You can use sliced apricots, either fresh or canned, instead of peaches.

STRAWBERRY GALETTE You can use fresh strawberries cut into thin slices instead of the peaches.

DESSERTS *meringue desserts*

INGREDIENTS
4 egg whites
a pinch of salt
$2/3$ cup (150 g) caster sugar plus extra to sprinkle
1 teaspoon cornflour
$1\frac{1}{2}$ teaspoons white vinegar
$\frac{1}{2}$ teaspoon vanilla essence
$1\frac{1}{4}$ cups cream
1 punnet (250 g) strawberries, hulled and sliced
pulp from 1–2 passionfruit
sifted icing sugar to dust

ROLLED PAVLOVA

SERVES 8

METHOD

Preheat the oven to 180°C. Line a 30 cm x 25 cm Swiss roll tin with baking paper.

Beat the egg whites with the salt until stiff peaks form. Beat in $1/2$ cup of the sugar, 2 tablespoons at a time. Gently fold in the remaining sugar, the cornflour, vinegar and vanilla and spoon into the prepared tin. Smooth the surface.

Bake for 12–15 minutes or until set on the top and springy to the touch. Turn out onto a clean tea towel sprinkled generously with caster sugar and leave for 5 minutes on a wire rack to cool. Roll up gently from the short end, using the tea towel to help with the rolling. Leave for 30 minutes or until cool.

Whip the cream to soft peaks, add half the sliced strawberries and fold through the cream. Unroll the pavlova, spread with the cream and scatter with the passionfruit pulp and remaining strawberries. Roll up again using the tea towel to assist and place, seam side down, on a serving plate. Refrigerate for at least 30 minutes.

Serve cut into thick slices and dusted with the sifted icing sugar.

INGREDIENTS
6 egg whites, at room temperature
a pinch of salt
2 cups (440 g) caster sugar
1½ teaspoons white vinegar
1½ teaspoons vanilla essence
1¼ cups cream
strawberries and raspberries, or other fruit of your choice

PAVLOVA

Pavlova, named after the Russian ballerina Anna Pavlova, is still just about the most popular party dessert in Australia. Everyone has their favourite texture, be it the crisp meringue shell or the delicate soft marshmallow. The following recipe was given to me by a churchgoer who won acclaim for her 'pavs' and made at least five a week for members of the congregation. The meringue puffs up as light as a feather, looking just like Pavlova's tutu, and the tart-sweet flavour of the strawberries adds a distinctive flavour to the dessert.

SERVES 6–8

METHOD

Preheat the oven to 200°C. Place a piece of baking paper on a baking tray and mark a 20 cm circle on it to use as a guide (the pavlova will spread a little).

In an electric mixer, beat the egg whites and salt at full speed until they stand in stiff peaks. Sift the sugar and gradually sprinkle it into the egg whites 1 tablespoon at a time, beating at high speed until all sugar has been added.

Lastly, fold in the vinegar and vanilla. Spoon large dollops of meringue inside the circle on the baking sheet to form a high mound and smooth over the top lightly. Place in the oven (immediately reducing the heat to 150°C) for 1 hour.

If using an electric oven, turn off the heat and leave the pavlova in the oven until cold. If using a gas oven, reduce heat to 120°C and cook for a further 30 minutes, then turn the heat off and leave the pavlova in the oven until completely cooled.

When the pavlova is cooled, slide onto a large, flat cake plate, removing the baking paper. Don't worry if it collapses slightly; you should also expect cracks on the surface. Whip the cream until stiff but still shiny and spoon over the top of the pavlova. Spoon berries over the cream and serve.

NOTE The meringue may also be sprinkled with blanched, slivered almonds before baking. They will toast to a golden brown.

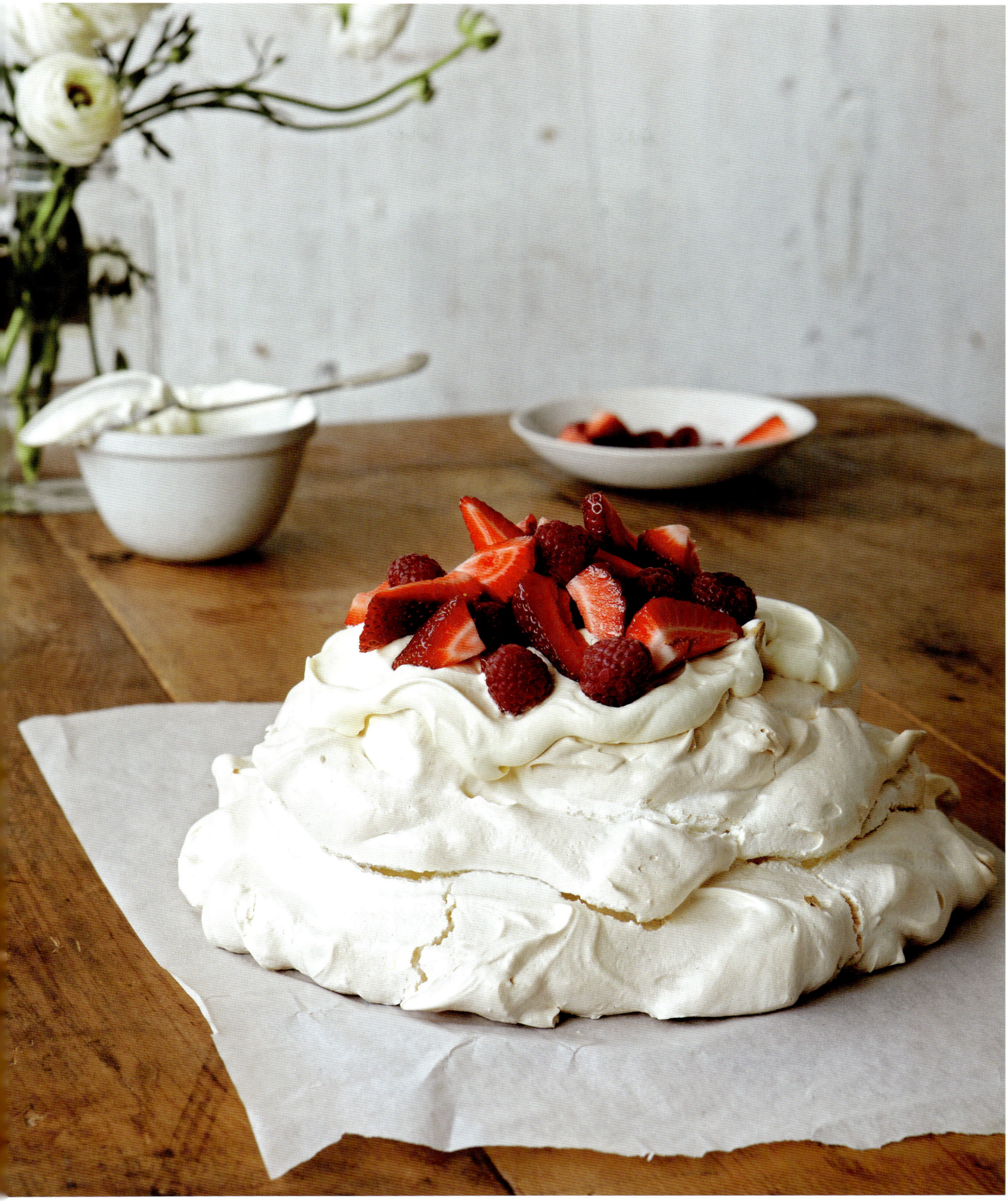

INGREDIENTS
6 eggs, separated
1 whole egg
¾ cup (165 g) caster sugar
1 cup ground hazelnuts
¾ cup fresh white breadcrumbs
1 teaspoon plain flour

FILLING
1½ cups cream
1 teaspoon caster sugar
1 teaspoon vanilla essence
½ cup ground hazelnuts

HAZELNUT TORTE

SERVES 10

METHOD

Preheat the oven to 150°C. Grease a 23 cm springform tin and dust with flour.

Beat the egg yolks and whole egg together until thick and pale yellow. Gradually beat in ½ cup of the sugar, then the nuts and breadcrumbs. Continue to beat until the mixture forms a dense, moist mass.

Whisk the egg whites in another bowl until they begin to foam, then gradually add the remaining sugar. Continue to whisk until the whites form stiff, glossy peaks.

Mix about half the egg whites into the hazelnut mixture, sprinkle the flour over and fold in the remaining egg whites. Turn into the prepared tin.

Bake for 35–45 minutes or until the cake shrinks away slightly from the sides of the tin. Remove from the oven, release the spring on the tin and remove the sides. Allow the cake to cool.

To make the filling, whip the cream and add the sugar and vanilla. Slice the cake into two layers and sandwich together with one-third of the cream. Using a spatula, cover the top and sides of the cake with the remaining cream, and scatter ground hazelnuts over the top and sides.

DESSERTS *meringue desserts*

INGREDIENTS

MERINGUE CASE
- 4 egg whites
- 1 cup (220 g) caster sugar
- ½ teaspoon cinnamon
- ¾ cup ground hazelnuts

COFFEE SAUCE
- ½ cup (110 g) caster sugar
- ¾ cup water
- 1 tablespoon instant coffee powder
- 2 tablespoons boiling water
- 1 tablespoon rum

FILLING
- ½ teaspoon instant coffee powder
- 2 tablespoons brown sugar
- 1 tablespoon hot water
- ¾ cup cream

DECORATION
- sifted icing sugar
- ½ cup whipped cream
- whole toasted hazelnuts

COFFEE VACHERIN

Vacherin is a luscious meringue dessert usually made into a case or basket to hold a filling of fruit, cream or ice cream. Sometimes the base is a disc of sweet pastry or almond paste with the meringue piped on in rings, one on top of the other, around the edge. The filling is then piled into the centre. Vacherins can also be assembled with discs of meringue layered with filling, as here, which is the easiest type to make.

SERVES 8

METHOD

Preheat the oven to 140°C. Mark two 20 cm circles on two sheets of baking paper and place each on a baking tray. Spray with non-stick cooking spray.

Whisk the egg whites until stiff. Add 2 tablespoons of the caster sugar and beat for 30 seconds longer. Sift the remaining sugar with the cinnamon and fold into the egg whites with the ground hazelnuts. Spread or pipe the meringue over the two baking paper circles.

Bake for 1–1¼ hours or until pale golden. Turn off the oven and allow the meringue to cool completely in the oven.

To make the coffee sauce, dissolve the sugar in ½ cup of the water over low heat. Increase the heat and boil without stirring until the syrup is a rich golden brown. Remove from the heat and carefully stir in the remaining cold water. Return to low heat and stir until the caramel dissolves. Pour into a heatproof bowl and allow to cool. As the syrup cools and begins to thicken, stir in the instant coffee, dissolved in the boiling water, and the rum. When cold, the sauce should be thick and syrupy.

To make the filling, mix the coffee and brown sugar with the hot water and allow to cool. Whip the cream and, as it begins to thicken, add the coffee and brown sugar mixture. Continue beating until the cream holds soft peaks.

Sandwich the two meringue rounds together with the filling. Dust the top of the gateau with sifted icing sugar and pipe rosettes of cream around the edge. Decorate the rosettes with whole hazelnuts. Serve with the coffee sauce.

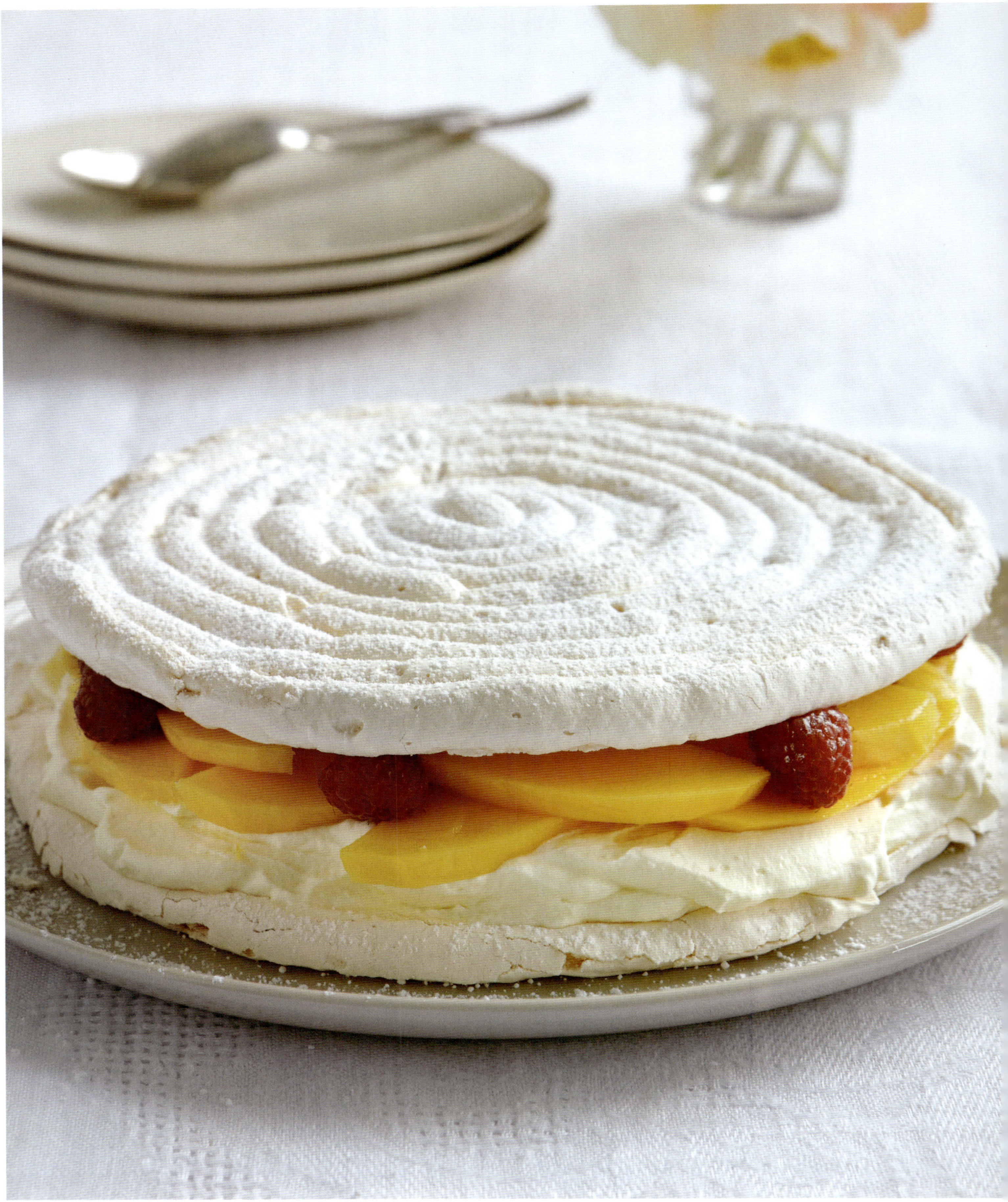

DESSERTS *meringue desserts*

INGREDIENTS

MERINGUE CASE
4 egg whites
1 cup (220 g) caster sugar
½ teaspoon vanilla essence

FILLING
1 cup cream, whipped (see Note)
1 cup sliced canned or fresh mangoes
½ cup fresh or frozen raspberries

MANGO VACHERIN

For this memorable dessert, two meringue cakes are filled with whipped cream (you could also use a good vanilla ice cream that has been softened) and fruit. We've used mangoes, but you could also use peaches in season.

SERVES 8

METHOD

Preheat the oven to 150°C. Cut two rounds of baking paper 20 cm in diameter, place each on a greased baking tray and spray with non-stick cooking spray.

To make the meringue case, whisk the egg whites and the sugar together until very thick and glossy. Fold in the vanilla. Spoon the mixture into a piping bag fitted with a plain 1 cm tube. Pipe a layer of meringue over each baking paper round. Alternatively, spread the mixture to cover the rounds.

Bake for 35–40 minutes or until crisp and pale golden. Turn off the oven and allow to cool completely in the oven with the door open.

Just before serving, spread one meringue round with whipped cream. Arrange the mango slices over, then the raspberries. Top with the other meringue round and serve immediately.

VARIATIONS

VACHERIN CHANTILLY WITH FRUITS Make the meringue case as above. Just before serving, whip 2 cups cream and fold in 2 tablespoons Grand Marnier and 1 tablespoon sifted icing sugar. Put a layer of fresh fruit, such as strawberries, or sliced peaches, bananas, apricots or grapes (or a mixture of fruits), in the meringue case. Pile whipped cream on top and decorate with a little more fruit. If using peaches or bananas, first sprinkle slices with lemon juice to prevent discolouration. Serve immediately.

VACHERIN MELBA Make the meringue case as above and fill with whipped cream (or softened ice cream; see below). Replace the mangoes with sliced peeled peaches.

NOTE The whipped cream can be replaced with 3 cups vanilla ice-cream, softened.

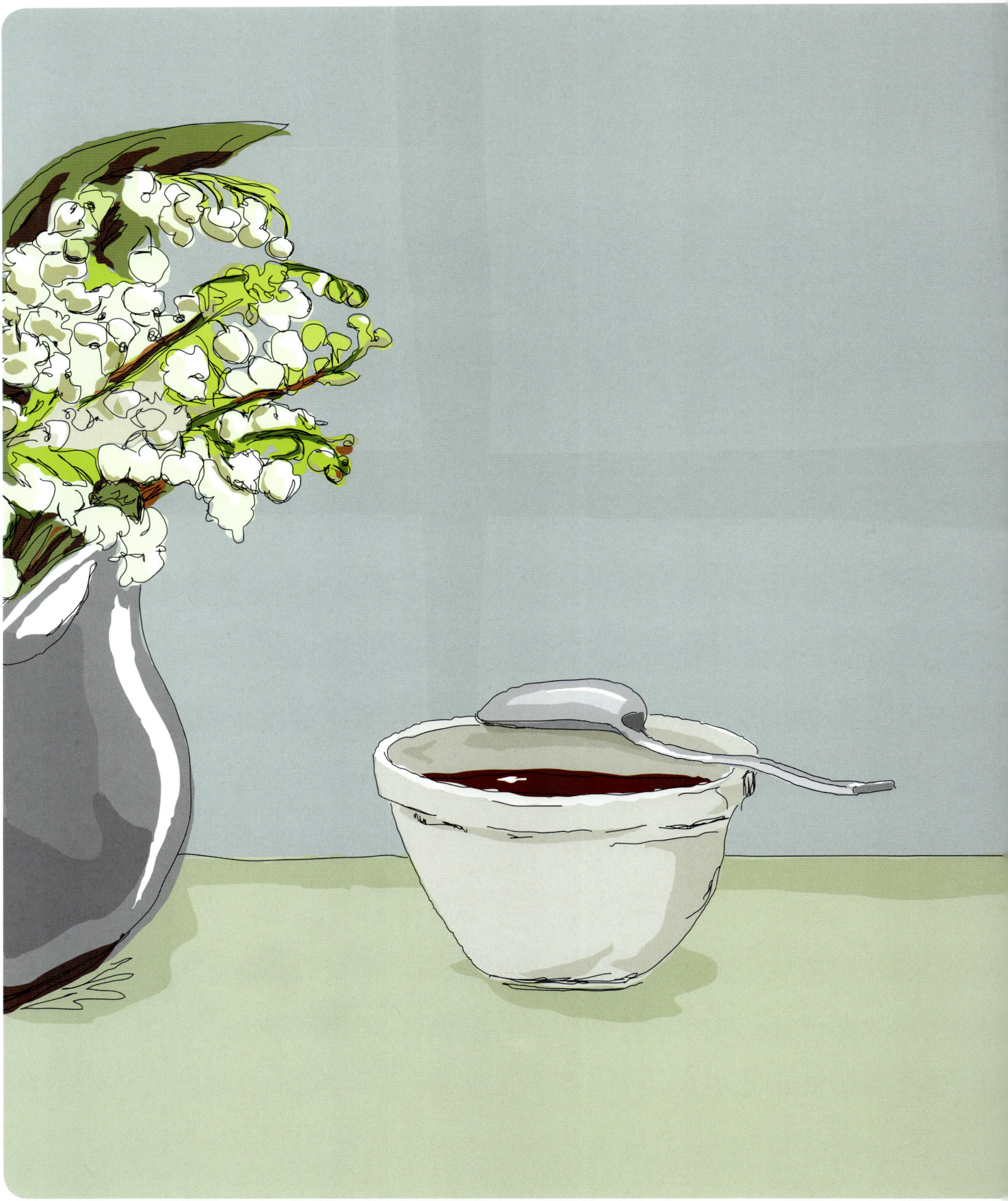

PASTRY
CHAPTER 7

HINTS & TIPS

Most pastries are a mixture of flour and fat bound with liquid, but variations in ingredients and in ways of mixing and cooking produce different results. A good pastry should be light, tender, crisp and somewhat flaky. Success in pastry-making is really a matter of practice. Certainly there are those whose delicate touch contributes to the lightness and tenderness of the pastry. But by following a few simple rules, anyone can make good pastry.

Start with simple pastries such as shortcrust, sweet flan or sour cream pastry, or use commercial brands that make it easy and foolproof to produce home-baked pastries. Supermarkets carry pastry mixes, packaged filo, ready-rolled frozen shortcrust or puff pastry, and ready to bake vol-au-vent cases.

SHORT PASTRIES

Most short pastries are made by mixing fat with flour and lightly stirring in just enough liquid to make the mixture hold together. There are several types of short pastry:

PLAIN SHORTCRUST Known in French as pâte brisée, this pastry does not contain sugar. It is used for savoury pies and pastries. It can also be made in the food processor.

RICH SHORTCRUST (pâte brisée à l'oeuf) is enriched with egg yolk. This pastry is crisper than plain shortcrust.

SWEET FLAN PASTRY (pâte sucrée) contains sugar and egg yolks. It is fine and crisp, and used for delicate sweet tarts.

MAKING SHORT PASTRY

HAVE INGREDIENTS AND EQUIPMENT COOL before starting, so that the fat will remain in tiny pieces without melting into the flour.

HANDLE THE PASTRY QUICKLY AND LIGHTLY once the liquid is added to avoid overdeveloping the gluten (elastic strands formed by the flour protein and moisture), which makes pastry tough and causes it to shrink when baked.

CHILL PASTRY FOR AT LEAST 30 MINUTES after mixing and before rolling out, and again when it has been shaped, before baking. This relaxes the gluten so that the pastry will be tender and won't shrink when baked. The longer the chilling time, the better – overnight is ideal – but be sure to remove it from the fridge at least 1 hour before shaping or you will be obliged to overhandle it.

LINING A FLAN TIN

USE A LOOSE-BOTTOMED FLAN TIN, or place a flan ring on a baking tray. If the pastry you are using contains sugar or egg, lightly grease the sides and base of the tin or ring – this is not necessary for plain pastry.

ROLL PASTRY OUT to a circle about 3 mm thick and about 4 cm bigger than the tin or ring. Lift the pastry over the rolling pin, then lift and lay the pastry over the tin or ring using the rolling pin. Ease the pastry carefully into the ring, without stretching it, then, with a floured forefinger or a small ball of pastry, press the pastry into the angle round the base. Use floured fingertips to press the pastry firmly against the sides of the tin or ring. If using a loose ring, steady it with the other hand while you do so.

ROLL ACROSS THE TOP of the tin or ring with the rolling pin to trim off surplus pastry. Press the pastry gently around the top edge to work it very slightly above the rim of the tin or ring, then work around the top, gently thumbing the pastry a fraction away from the tin or ring. Rest for 30 minutes before baking as recipe directs.

TO RELEASE THE BAKED SHELL OR TART from a loose-bottomed tin, place the tin on a jar and allow the sides to fall down. Slide the tart off the base onto a serving plate, or leave it on the base to serve. To release the shell from a flan ring, slide it off the tray onto a serving plate and lift the ring off.

BAKING BLIND

Flan cases and tart or tartlet shells are often baked 'blind', meaning without filling. A case or shell may be baked completely if the filling is not to be cooked with it, or partially baked to colour and crisp the pastry before adding the filling and finishing the cooking. Care must be taken to see that an empty case or shell doesn't puff up unevenly or buckle as it cooks. Oven temperatures used for baking blind vary with the type of pastry being used (see recipes). To bake tartlet shells blind, prick lightly all over the base with a fork, bake for 6 minutes then check. If any have puffed up, press down gently with a spoon then finish baking.

TO BAKE A LARGER PASTRY CASE BLIND, line it with crumpled baking paper and fill with rice, dried beans or baking beads (available from kitchenware stores). For partial pre-baking, bake the case for about 8 minutes or the until sides are just coloured. Lift out the paper with the rice, beans or beads, return the case to the oven and bake for about 5 minutes more to dry and colour the base. If the sides of the case are over-browning, protect them with foil. Remove from the oven, add the filling and finish cooking.

TO PRE-BAKE COMPLETELY, bake for 10–15 minutes after removing the paper and rice, beans or beads, or until shell is golden. Remove from oven and cool before filling.

TO MOISTURE-PROOF A PASTRY CASE that will have a juice or liquid filling, brush the inside of the cooked case or shell with lightly beaten egg or egg white or warm jam and place in a hot oven for 2–3 minutes to set.

FLAKY PASTRY

These pastries are made by folding together layers of pastry dough with butter or other fats in between. When baked, the pastry puffs up into separate thin, crisp 'leaves'. The basic dough for flaky pastries is damper and more elastic than for short pastries. This allows the pastry to stretch when it is folded, and also allows for taking up the extra flour needed for dusting.

MAKING FLAKY PASTRY

SO THAT THE FAT WILL REMAIN IN FIRM LAYERS, separating the pastry layers, have ingredients, equipment and your hands cool before starting. Chilling the pastry at intervals during preparation is also designed to keep fat layers firm.

TO ROLL FLAKY PASTRIES, first beat the pastry lightly and evenly with the rolling pin from front to back of the pastry, then bring the rolling pin down firmly on the pastry, give a short, sharp back-and-forth roll, lift the pin and repeat. The idea is to roll the pastry more thinly without pushing the fat about so that it breaks through the surface. Work your way from the front to the back of the pastry with these short, quick rolls, but stop just before you get to the back edge so that the pastry is not pushed out of shape. If fat does break through, sprinkle it with flour, refrigerate pastry for 10 minutes then continue. Keep corners square and edges straight. Correct the shape by pulling corners out gently rather than pushing the sides in.

FOLD THE PASTRY EXACTLY IN THREE with the edges level. Use a ruler as a guide and mark thirds with a fingertip on a long side before folding. Whatever shape you want to make from flaky pastries, always roll them straight along or straight across, keeping the rectangular shape.

IF MAKING ROUNDS, OVALS AND OTHER SHAPES, they must be cut from the pastry, not shaped by rolling. Cut cleanly with a sharp knife, and avoid the edges when glazing, so that the layers can separate as the pastry rises.

CHOUX PASTRY

Choux pastry is made by a different method than other pastries; flour is added to a mixture of water and melted butter and the resulting paste is cooked on the stovetop until it thickens, then eggs are beaten in.

MAKING CHOUX PASTRY

USE BAKING PAPER AS A FUNNEL to pour flour into the boiling liquid.

BEAT IN THE EGGS GRADUALLY, using a wooden spoon, until the paste is well combined, shiny and smooth.

TO FORM PUFFS, use a pastry bag and plain tube, or use two spoons to make well-shaped mounds of pastry on a tray.

TO FORM ÉCLAIRS, use a pastry bag and plain tube to pipe fingers of pastry on the tray.

CHOUX PASTRY STORES WELL in airtight containers. Do not fill until ready to serve. The pastries should be crispish; if necessary, recrisp them in a preheated 180°C oven for 5–10 minutes, cool on wire racks, fill and serve.

INGREDIENTS

1½ cups (225 g) plain flour
a pinch of salt
100 g chilled butter or firm cooking margarine, diced
about 3 tablespoons iced water
a squeeze of lemon juice

PLAIN SHORTCRUST PASTRY (PÂTE BRISÉE)

This pastry, which does not include sugar, is good for savoury pies and pastries, and is fairly easy to handle. Butter will give the best flavour, but firm cooking margarine can be used if preferred.

MAKES ENOUGH TO LINE A 20–23 CM PIE PLATE OR FLAN RING

METHOD

Sift the flour and salt into a large bowl. Add the diced fat and stir round with a knife until the pieces are coated with flour. Rub the fat into the flour between thumbs and fingertips, lifting your hands above the bowl to keep the mixture cool, until it resembles coarse breadcrumbs. Shake the bowl so that any large lumps come to the surface, then rub them in.

Mix the water and lemon juice. Add 2 tablespoons of the liquid to the flour mixture and stir in quickly with a round-ended knife. When the dough starts to cling together, use the fingers of one hand to gather it into a ball. Sprinkle in more liquid only if necessary to dampen any remaining dry mixture in the bowl, and use the ball of dough to gather it up. The dough should leave the bowl clean.

Place the pastry on a lightly floured surface and knead lightly by turning and pressing with the floured heel of your hand until smooth. Pat into a round, wrap in plastic wrap and chill for 30 minutes.

On a lightly floured surface, press the dough with your hand into a round or other shape as required. Lightly flour a rolling pin and roll out, lifting and turning the dough frequently and lightly flouring the work surface as needed to prevent sticking. Chill again after shaping and before baking.

Unless otherwise indicated, bake shortcrust pastry in a preheated 190°C oven.

VARIATION

LARGER PASTRY SHELLS For a 25 cm pastry shell or a two-crust 20–23 cm pie, follow recipe for Plain Shortcrust Pastry, using 2 cups (300 g) plain flour, 150 g butter or firm margarine and about 4 tablespoons iced water with a squeeze of lemon juice added. For a two-crust pie, use a little more than half of the dough for the bottom crust, and the the remainder for the lid. Scraps can be used to decorate the pie if liked.

INGREDIENTS
1½ cups (225 g) plain flour
a pinch of salt
¼ teaspoon baking powder
125 g chilled butter, diced
1 egg yolk
2 teaspoons iced water
a squeeze of lemon juice

PLAIN RICH SHORTCRUST PASTRY (PÂTE BRISÉE À L'OEUF)

This pastry is crisper and more moisture-proof than plain shortcrust. Use it for quiches and other pies and tarts with rich fillings. It is also ideal to use when making individual savoury or fruit tartlets or barquettes. Sweet rich shortcrust (see Variations) can be used for fruit tarts and tartlets.

MAKES ENOUGH TO LINE A 20–23 CM PIE PLATE OR FLAN RING

METHOD
Make pastry in same way as for Plain Shortcrust Pastry (opposite), using egg yolk mixed with water and lemon juice as the liquid. Unless otherwise indicated in the recipe, bake in a preheated 190°C oven.

VARIATIONS
LARGER PASTRY SHELLS For a 25 cm pastry shell or a two-crust 20–23 cm pie, follow the recipe for Plain Rich Shortcrust Pastry, using 2 cups (300 g) plain flour, a large pinch of salt, ½ teaspoon baking powder, 185 g butter, 1 egg yolk, about 1 tablespoon iced water and a squeeze of lemon juice. For a two-crust pie, use a little more than half the dough for the bottom crust, and the remainder for the lid. Scraps can be used to decorate the pie if liked.

SWEET RICH SHORTCRUST PASTRY Follow the recipe for Plain Rich Shortcrust Pastry, beating 2 teaspoons caster sugar with the egg and water before mixing with the dry ingredients.

SHORTCRUST PASTRY IN THE FOOD PROCESSOR
Place 2 cups (300 g) plain flour, 185 g diced frozen butter or firm cooking margarine (or a mixture of both) and ¼ teaspoon salt in a food processor fitted with a steel blade. Process, turning on and off rapidly, until the butter is cut into the flour and the mixture looks like coarse breadcrumbs. Mix 1 egg with about 2 tablespoons cold water and a squeeze of lemon juice. With the motor running, pour the liquid quickly through the feed tube. Do not use it all unless necessary – stop pouring as soon as a ball of dough forms around the blade. Wrap in plastic wrap and chill for 1 hour before using. Bake as for Plain Rich Shortcrust Pastry. For a sweet pastry, add ⅓ cup (75 g) caster sugar to the processor with the flour, butter and salt. Makes enough to line two 18–20 cm pie plates or flan tins.

INGREDIENTS
125 g cream cheese
125 g butter
1½ cups (225 g) plain flour

CREAM CHEESE PASTRY

This is a rich, tender pastry that is suitable for small turnovers and tartlets. It is rather fragile, so chill it well before using, to firm it up a little, and handle it carefully.

MAKES ENOUGH FOR ABOUT 24 SMALL PASTRIES

METHOD

Beat the cream cheese and butter in a large mixing bowl until soft. Sift in the flour and mix to a dough. Wrap in plastic wrap and chill for several hours or overnight. (If left overnight, allow to stand at room temperature for about 1 hour before rolling out.) Rolling it out between sheets of baking paper will make it easier to handle.

Unless otherwise indicated, bake in a preheated 190˚C oven.

INGREDIENTS
2¼ cups (335 g) plain flour
1 teaspoon salt
185 g chilled butter, diced
1 egg
½ cup sour cream

SOUR CREAM PASTRY

Use this rich, melting pastry for turnovers and individual tarts. It is very soft, so chill it well before rolling it out to make it easier to handle. It is good for both sweet and savoury tarts.

MAKES ENOUGH FOR TWELVE 8 CM TARTS OR TURNOVERS

METHOD

Sift the flour and salt into a large bowl. Add the butter and rub it into the flour until the mixture resembles coarse breadcrumbs. Make a well in the centre. Beat the egg and sour cream together and pour into the well. Stir from the centre, gradually incorporating the flour to make a soft, pliable dough. Wrap in plastic wrap and chill for 1 hour before using.

Unless otherwise indicated, bake sour cream pastry in a preheated 190˚C oven.

SWEET FLAN PASTRY (PÂTE SUCRÉE)

INGREDIENTS
1¼ cups (185 g) plain flour
a pinch of salt
80 g unsalted butter, diced
⅓ cup (75 g) caster sugar
1 teaspoon iced water
2 egg yolks
2 drops vanilla essence

MAKES ENOUGH FOR ONE 20–22 CM TART

METHOD
Sift the flour with the salt onto a pastry board and make a well in the centre. Place the remaining ingredients in the well and rub together with the fingertips of one hand. The movement of your fingertips working on these centre ingredients is rather like that of a chicken pecking corn.

Using a metal spatula, quickly draw in the flour to form a dough. Knead the pastry lightly until smooth. Wrap in plastic wrap and chill for 1 hour or more before using. Unless otherwise indicated, bake in a preheated 190°C oven.

VARIATIONS
FOOD PROCESSOR ALTERNATIVE Chill or freeze the butter. Fit the metal blade attachment. Sift the flour and salt into the food processor bowl. Add the butter and process for 15–20 seconds or until the mixture resembles fine breadcrumbs. Add the remaining ingredients and process for a further 20–30 seconds or until the mixture starts to cling together. Turn out onto a floured surface and shape into a ball. Knead lightly until smooth, then wrap in plastic wrap and chill before using.

BISCUIT PASTRY

INGREDIENTS
125 g butter, softened
½ cup (110 g) caster sugar
1 egg, beaten
1 cup (150 g) plain flour
⅔ cup (100 g) self-raising flour

This sweet, tender pastry is used for pies, tarts and tartlets and as the base for slices.

MAKES ENOUGH FOR A 2-CRUST 20–23 CM PIE OR 25–30 TARTLETS

METHOD
Using an electric mixer, cream the butter and gradually beat in the sugar until the mixture is white and fluffy. Beat in the egg, then stir in the sifted flours.

Knead lightly, wrap in plastic wrap and chill for about 20 minutes or until firm enough to roll. Bake as directed in the recipe.

INGREDIENTS

1 cup (150 g) plain flour
1 cup water
125 g butter, diced
½ teaspoon salt
1 teaspoon sugar (if making sweet puffs)
4 eggs, beaten

CHOUX PASTRY

Choux pastry is softer than other pastries and is shaped with a spoon or by squeezing from a piping bag. When it is cooked, it swells into crisp golden shells that are hollow inside. The secret of making shells that will hold their shape is to be sure that the pastry is cooked and dry right through. A well-cooked shell should be golden brown, firm to the touch and feel very light in the hand. Choux pastry is used to make profiteroles and éclairs.

MAKES ENOUGH FOR 12 MEDIUM ÉCLAIRS OR PUFFS

METHOD

Sift the flour onto a sheet of baking paper.

Put the water, butter, salt and sugar, if using, into a medium saucepan. Bring slowly to the boil (the butter must be melted before the water boils). Immediately remove from the heat, tip in the flour all at once and stir vigorously with a wooden spoon. Return to the heat and continue stirring until the mixture forms a mass, leaves the sides of the saucepan and begins to film the bottom – this will take only a short time. Remove from the heat and allow to cool.

Spoon the mixture into the bowl of an electric mixer or leave in the saucepan. Add the beaten egg to the dough, a little at a time, beating after each addition until thoroughly incorporated. Do not add all the egg unless necessary; the dough is ready when it is as shiny as satin and holds its shape on a spoon. Shape into puffs or éclairs while warm.

To form puffs or éclairs, use a pastry bag and plain tube to pipe even-sized quantities of pastry onto a baking tray lined with baking paper. Puffs may also be made using two spoons to make well-shaped mounds of pastry on the baking tray.

To cook, first place in a preheated 230°C oven so that the pastry puffs quickly, then reduce the heat to 180°C so that the pastry will cook without over-browning. To be failsafe, leave the cooked shells in the turned-off oven with the door slightly open for 20 minutes to ensure that they are thoroughly dried out.

PUFF PASTRY

INGREDIENTS
1 2/3 cups (250 g) plain flour
250 g butter, chilled
1/2–2/3 cup iced water
a squeeze of lemon juice

Use for fine pastries where maximum delicacy and high, even rising are required. Puff pastry is mostly eaten as a sweet little cake or puff, but when grated good cheese is added, as for gougères (page 414), you have a perfect savoury bite to accompany red wine.

MAKES ENOUGH FOR TWO 18 CM ROUNDS OR 12 SMALL PASTRIES OR TURNOVERS

METHOD

Sift the flour into a mixing bowl, add 30 g of the butter, and rub into the flour until the mixture resembles coarse breadcrumbs. Add the water mixed with the lemon juice and stir with a knife, then gather the dough together with your fingers. Place on a lightly floured surface, knead lightly and shape into a square pat. Wrap in plastic wrap and chill for 1 hour. At the same time, chill the remaining butter.

Remove the chilled dough and butter from the refrigerator. Put the butter into a loose plastic bag and beat it with a rolling pin to make it pliable, remove from the bag and then use a floured rolling pin roll it into a 15 cm square. The butter and dough should both be firm and of the same consistency.

Lightly flour a work surface and roll out the dough to a 25 cm square, pulling out the corners to make a neat shape. Place the butter diagonally on the centre of the dough and fold the four dough corners in, slightly overlapping, to make an envelope of dough completely enclosing the butter.

Flour the work surface and rolling pin and roll the dough and butter to a rectangle three times as long as it is wide, and 1 cm thick. Fold the bottom third up and the top third down and seal the edges by pressing lightly with the rolling pin. This is the first fold.

Turn the dough round at right angles so that the top flap is to your right, as if it were a book. Roll as before to a rectangle three times as long as it is wide and about 5 mm thick. Fold into three as before, place in a plastic bag and chill for about 30 minutes until firm but not hard. The dough has now had two folds.

Remove the dough from the refrigerator and roll and fold it twice more in the same manner. Chill again for about 30 minutes.

Roll and fold twice more (the dough has now had six folds). Chill again for 30 minutes, and the dough is ready to use. Roll out and cut as desired, then chill again for 30 minutes before baking. Unless otherwise indicated, bake puff pastry in a preheated 230°C oven.

INGREDIENTS

2 cups (300 g) plain flour
a pinch of salt
180 g butter, diced
about 2/3 cup iced water
a squeeze of lemon juice

ROUGH PUFF PASTRY

This is the simplest of the flaky pastries. Use it for sausage rolls, turnovers or other recipes for which you want crisp, tender layers, but where a very high, even rise is not required.

MAKES ENOUGH FOR TWO 20 CM ROUNDS OR 16–20 SMALL SAUSAGE ROLLS

METHOD

Sift the flour and salt into a large bowl. Have the butter cool and firm but not hard. Add the butter to the flour and stir around with a knife until the pieces are well coated. Mix the water and lemon juice and stir into the flour with a round-ended knife, without breaking up the butter. With floured fingers, gently gather the mixture into a ball, then place it on a floured work surface. Do not knead; use floured hands to shape it into a rectangular block.

Roll out to a rectangle three times as long as it is wide and 1 cm thick. Fold the bottom third up and the top third down and seal the edges by pressing lightly with the rolling pin. Turn the dough round at right angles so that the top flap is to your right, as if it were a book. Roll again to a rectangle about 5 mm thick and fold as before.

Repeat twice more, then place the folded dough in a plastic bag and chill for at least 30 minutes. The dough is now ready for use. Chill again after rolling out and cutting, before baking. Unless otherwise indicated, bake rough puff pastry in a preheated 230°C oven.

INGREDIENTS
2 cups (300 g) plain flour
a pinch of salt
90 g butter, diced
about ⅔ cup iced water
90 g lard

FLAKY PASTRY

Flaky pastry is easier to make and only a little less delicate and high-rise than puff pastry. Use for pie toppings, tarts, vol-au-vent cases, and the like. Lard is added as it makes a flakier crust that is excellent for meat pies.

MAKES ENOUGH FOR TWO 18 CM ROUNDS OR ABOUT 12 SMALL PASTRIES

METHOD

Sift the flour and salt into a mixing bowl, add half the butter and rub it in with your fingertips until the mixture resembles coarse breadcrumbs. Add the water, stir in with a knife and gather the dough into a ball with your fingers.

Knead the dough lightly on a floured work surface until smooth, then, with floured hands, shape it into a rectangular block. Flour the work surface and rolling pin and roll the dough to a rectangle three times as long as it is wide and about 5 mm thick.

Divide the lard in half and work each portion and the remaining butter separately with a wooden spoon until they are of the same consistency as the dough. Cut one half of the lard into small pieces and place in rows of about four, keeping well within the edges, on top of two-thirds of dough. Fold the bottom third of the dough up and the top third down and seal the edges by pressing lightly with the rolling pin.

Turn the dough round at right angles so that the edge of the top flap is to your right, as if it were a book. Roll as before to a rectangle three times as long as it is wide and 5 mm thick. Place the remaining butter on the top two-thirds, as you did with the lard, then fold, turn and roll out again. Repeat, using the remaining lard.

Place the folded dough in a plastic bag and chill for at least 30 minutes before using. Chill again after rolling out and cutting, before baking.

Unless otherwise indicated, bake flaky pastry in a preheated 230°C oven.

INGREDIENTS
1½ cups (225 g) baker's flour
¼ teaspoon salt
1 egg
½ cup lukewarm water
2 tablespoons white vinegar
2 tablespoons vegetable oil
melted butter

STRUDEL PASTRY

Strudel pastry should be made with high-gluten baker's flour so that it will be strong enough to be stretched without tearing. The process of gently pulling and stretching the dough to paper thinness is easier if two people work from opposite sides. Be sure to take off any rings, which may tear the dough, before you begin. Have the strudel filling ready before stretching the dough – once stretched, it should be used within 5 minutes or it will become brittle.

MAKES ENOUGH FOR ONE LARGE STRUDEL TO SERVE 10–12

METHOD

Sift the flour and salt into a bowl. Beat the egg until frothy, stir in the water, vinegar and oil and add to the flour. Mix with a wooden spoon until smooth, then turn the dough out onto a lightly floured work surface.

Knead thoroughly, scraping the dough off the surface as necessary with a knife. As you knead, keep lifting the dough and slapping it down hard on the surface. It will be sticky at first but as you continue it will become elastic, smooth and shiny, leaving the hands clean. Kneading will take about 15 minutes and dough should be beaten 100–150 times. Shape it into a ball and cover with a warm bowl. Leave for 20 minutes.

Meanwhile, cover a table with a cloth that hangs over the edges. Flour the cloth well. Brush the top of the dough with melted butter and lift it onto the floured cloth. Roll out until 3 mm thick. Now slip your closed fists, thumbs tucked in and palms downwards, under the dough. Working from the centre, lift and pull it out gently by pulling your hands apart. Work towards the edges and move around the table so that the dough is evenly stretched on all sides to a large square. If dry patches appear in the dough, brush with melted butter to keep them supple. If the dough tears, pinch it together. When the dough is as thin as paper, brush generously all over with melted butter and trim off thick edges with scissors.

Fill and bake as directed in the recipe.

PASTRY *pastry doughs*

INGREDIENTS
3 1/2 cups (525 g) plain flour
3/4 teaspoon salt
250 g lard
1/2 cup plus 2 tablespoons water

HOT WATER PASTRY

This pastry sets firm enough to stand by itself even before baking. It is the traditional pastry for English cold pies such as pork or veal and ham pie, even when these are made in a mould. It must be used while it is still warm since it becomes brittle when cold.

MAKES ENOUGH FOR A 20 CM COVERED PIE

METHOD
Warm the flour, then sift with the salt into a warm mixing bowl and make a well in the centre. Heat the lard with the water and, when boiling, tip into the well and mix with a wooden spoon until smooth. Use at once, keeping any dough not being worked in a covered bowl over hot water.

INGREDIENTS
1 2/3 cups (250 g) self-raising flour
a pinch of salt
125 g fresh suet or packaged shredded suet
about 1/3 cup cold water

SUET PASTRY

Suet pastry can be baked, but is usually boiled or steamed to make a soft crust for puddings or dumplings – unlike other pastries, it is not supposed to be crisp.

MAKES ENOUGH TO LINE A 4 CUP PUDDING BASIN

METHOD
Sift the flour and salt into a mixing bowl. If using fresh suet, remove any skin and chop the suet finely with a little of the measured flour to prevent it from sticking. Add to the flour and stir around with a knife, then add most of the water, and stir with a knife until the dough begins to cling together. Gather into a ball with your fingers. Sprinkle in more water only if necessary to dampen any remaining dry mixture in the bowl, and use the ball of dough to gather it up. Place on a lightly floured work surface and knead lightly by turning and pressing with the floured heel of your hand until smooth. Roll out and use at once.

VARIATION
SPONGE CRUST OR SWEET PUDDING For an extra light and spongy crust, 1/2 cup of the flour may be replaced by 1 cup loosely packed fresh white breadcrumbs. For a sweet pudding, 1 tablespoon white or brown sugar may be added to the flour.

INGREDIENTS
2 cups milk
4 egg yolks
¼ cup (30 g) cornflour
2 tablespoons plain flour
¼ cup (55 g) caster sugar

CRÈME PÂTISSIÈRE (PASTRY CREAM)

This classic French custard filling is often used in fruit tarts. If you like a fluffier pastry cream, you can fold ½ cup of whipped cream into the cooled pastry cream just before using.

MAKES 2¼ CUPS

METHOD

Heat the milk in a saucepan over medium heat, until bubbles start to appear.

Using an electric mixer, beat the egg yolks, cornflour and plain flour until combined. Add the sugar and beat until pale and thick.

Pour the hot milk onto the egg yolks, whisking continuously. Return to a clean saucepan. Cook on low heat for 8 minutes, stirring, until the mixture is thick and beginning to bubble.

Transfer to a bowl and cover the surface with a piece of baking paper. Cool before using.

VARIATIONS

RICH CRÈME PÂTISSIÈRE After cooling, fold in ¾ cup whipped cream.

TUTTI-FRUTTI CRÈME PÂTISSIÈRE Omit the vanilla bean. After cooling, fold in 2 tablespoons rum, brandy or fruit liqueur, and ¼ cup chopped glacé fruits.

FRANGIPANE CREAM After removing the crème pâtissière from the heat, beat in 60 g butter and ¼ cup crushed almond macaroons or chopped blanched almonds.

CHOCOLATE CRÈME PÂTISSIÈRE Combine 2 cups milk and 90 dark chocolate in a saucepan on medium heat, stirring, until the chocolate has melted and the mixture is smooth. Using an electric mixer, beat 4 egg yolks, ¼ cup (30 g) cornflour and 2 tablespoons plain flour until combined. Add ¼ cup (55 g) sugar and beat until pale and thick. Pour hot chocolate milk onto egg yolks, whisking continuously. Return the mixture to a clean saucepan. Cook on low heat for 8 minutes, stirring, until the mixture is thick and beginning to bubble. Transfer to a bowl and cover the surface with a piece of baking paper. Cool before using. If you like a fluffier pastry cream fold in ½ cup whipped cream.

PASTRY *fruit pies & tarts*

INGREDIENTS

- 1 quantity Plain Sweet Rich Shortcrust Pastry (page 329)
- 6 large cooking apples, peeled, cored and thinly sliced
- ¾ cup (165 g) caster sugar
- 1 tablespoon plain flour
- 1 teaspoon cinnamon
- ¼ teaspoon nutmeg
- a pinch of salt
- 30 g butter
- 1 egg white, lightly beaten
- extra sugar for sprinkling

APPLE PIE

Granny Smith apples, Australia's own apple, are now grown and enjoyed worldwide. Their crisp flesh is good raw and also stands up well to cooking. Golden delicious apples are not far behind, excellent for both eating and cooking. This two-crust apple pie is in the American style.

SERVES 6–8

METHOD

Preheat the oven to 200°C. Grease a 23 cm pie plate.

Reserve one-third of the pastry for the lid of the pie. Roll out the remainder to line the prepared pie plate.

Toss the apples with the sugar, flour, spices and salt. Spread evenly in the pastry case and dot with butter. Roll out the remaining pastry to cover the top of the pie, moisten the edges with milk and press firmly together. Press the edges with the tines of a fork to decorate. Make a few slits in the top crust for steam to escape, brush with egg white and sprinkle with extra sugar.

Bake for 10 minutes. Lower the oven temperature to 160°C and bake for a further 45 minutes or until the pastry is golden and the apples are tender. Serve warm.

INGREDIENTS

1 quantity Sweet Flan Pastry (page 331)
6–8 medium cooking apples
1 tablespoon water
½ cup (110 g) caster sugar
¼ cup brandy or 2 teaspoons vanilla essence
30 g butter
1 teaspoon lemon juice
1 extra tablespoon sugar

APRICOT GLAZE

½ cup apricot jam
1 tablespoon water

FRENCH APPLE TART

The French like their apple pies with one crust of pastry baked blind and then filled with a thick apple purée which is topped with thinly sliced apples and finished with apricot jam glaze. The result is both pretty and delicious.

SERVES 6

METHOD

Preheat the oven to 190°C. Line a 20 cm flan tin with pastry, then prick well and chill until firm. Line with baking paper, half-fill with pie weights or dried beans and bake blind (see page 326) for 10 minutes. Remove the paper and beans. Reduce the oven temperature to 180°C and bake for a further 5–10 minutes or until the crust is pale golden. Allow to cool.

Reserve two or three apples for the top of the tart. Peel, core and quarter the others. Slice roughly and put into a saucepan with the water, sugar, brandy or vanilla and half the butter. Cover and cook over a gentle heat for about 20 minutes, stirring occasionally, until tender.

Increase the heat and boil, stirring, until thick enough to hold in a mass in the spoon. Push through a sieve if necessary. Taste and add more sugar if the apple is not sweet enough. Spread in the cooled pastry shell.

Peel and core the reserved apples and slice very thinly. Sprinkle with the lemon juice and extra sugar. Arrange the slices in a pattern on top of the cooked apple. Melt the remaining butter and brush over the apple. Bake for about 30 minutes or until the apples are tender and browned lightly.

For the apricot glaze, heat the jam and water in a saucepan over low heat and stir until dissolved. Pass through a sieve, then return to the pan and bring to the boil. Cook gently until the glaze is clear and a thick but spreadable consistency is obtained.

Slide the cooked tart onto a wire rack or serving dish and brush the top and pastry with the apricot glaze. Serve the tart warm or cold with a bowl of whipped cream.

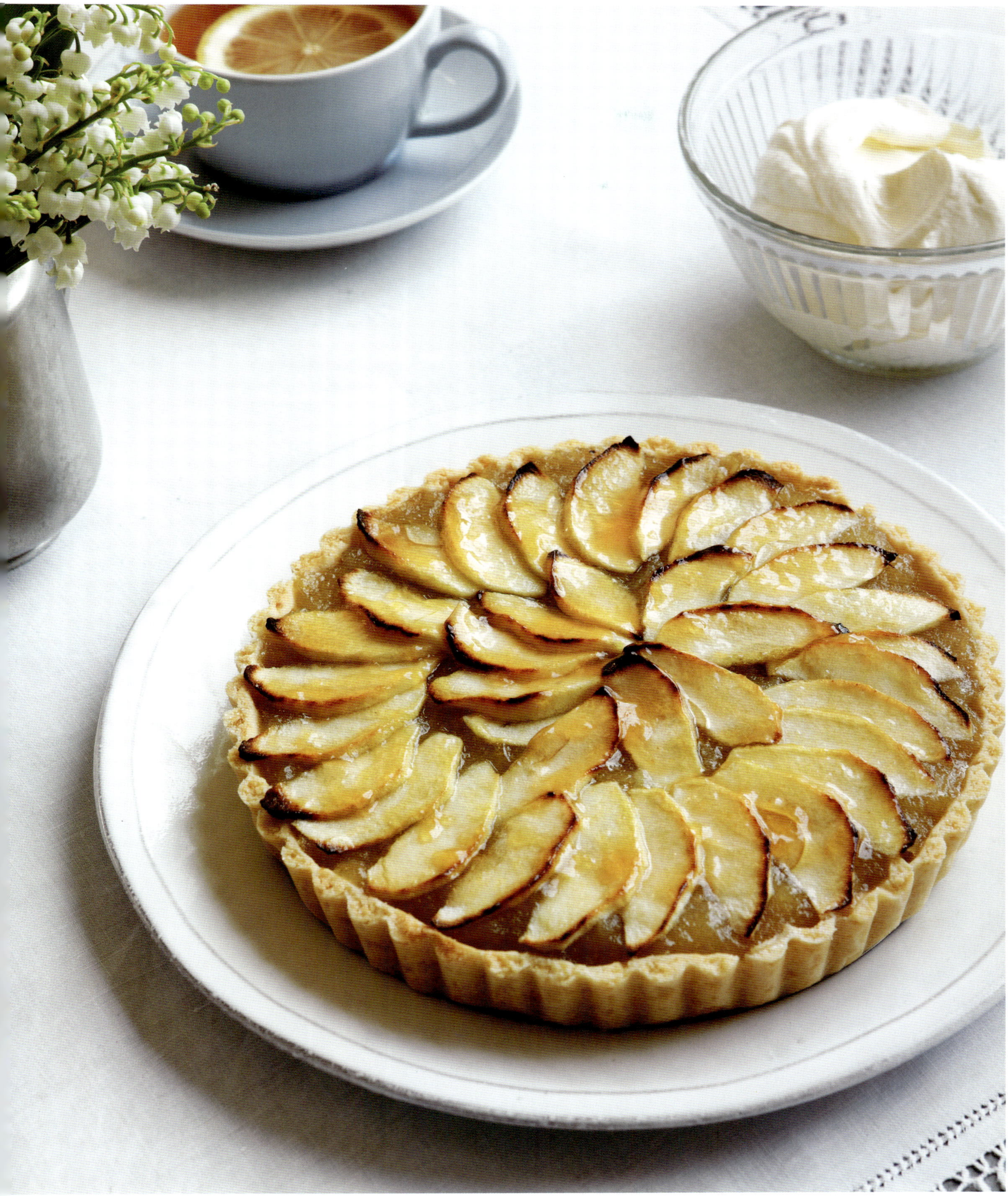

INGREDIENTS

6 large cooking apples, peeled, cored and thinly sliced
½ cup (110 g) caster sugar
1½ teaspoons ground cinnamon
½ cup sultanas
2 teaspoons grated lemon rind
1 quantity Strudel Pastry (page 336)
melted butter to brush
1 cup fresh breadcrumbs fried in 15 g butter

APPLE STRUDEL

A delicate filled pastry which is usually associated with Austrian cooking. Strudel is one of the best and most famous of desserts – a wonderfully crisp, tender and flaky construction of paper-thin pastry layers rolled round a filling.

SERVES 10–12

METHOD

Preheat the oven to 230°C. Grease a baking tray.

Mix the apples, sugar, cinnamon, sultanas and lemon rind together and set aside.

Brush the stretched-out strudel dough with the melted butter and sprinkle with the fried breadcrumbs.

Spoon the apple mixture in an 8–10 cm wide line along one side of the pastry, to within 5 cm of the edges. Fold the near edges of the pastry over the filling and roll up, starting from the filling end, by lifting the cloth to make the dough roll over and over on itself.

Lift the strudel onto the prepared baking tray, seam side down, curving it into a horseshoe if it is too long for the tray. Brush with more melted butter.

Bake for 10 minutes, then reduce the oven temperature to 200°C and bake for a further 20 minutes or until the strudel is crisp and brown. Brush several more times with melted butter while cooking, and again after removing from the oven. Serve warm, cut into wide diagonal slices.

NOTE Strudel should be served freshly baked, as the pastry toughens when cold. However, it can be frozen unbaked and then baked straight from the freezer. Remove from the freezer wrapping and place on a greased baking tray. Bake as directed in the recipe, but allow an extra 15–20 minutes baking time after reducing the oven temperature to 200°C. Test by inserting a fine skewer into the centre; the tip should be hot when withdrawn. Cover the strudel loosely with foil if the pastry is over-browning before the filling is cooked through.

PASTRY *fruit pies & tarts*

INGREDIENTS
4 large cooking apples, peeled, cored and thinly sliced
2 tablespoons brown sugar
1 teaspoon vanilla essence
250 g Puff Pastry (page 333)
125 g unsalted butter
½ cup fresh breadcrumbs
2 tablespoons redcurrant jelly
½ cup chopped blanched almonds
sifted icing sugar to dust
whipped cream to serve

QUICK APPLE STRUDEL

This version is simplified by using commercial puff pastry, rolled as thinly as possible. Use butter puff pastry if you can find it. The same method is used when making this recipe with classic Strudel Pastry (page 336).

SERVES 6–8

Sprinkle the apples with brown sugar and vanilla, toss well to coat the apples and stand for 1 hour.

Preheat the oven to 190°C. Grease a baking tray.

Roll out the pastry on a floured tea towel to an oblong shape about 50 cm x 35 cm.

Melt half the butter and sauté the breadcrumbs until golden.

Melt the remaining butter and brush half over the pastry, leaving a 5 cm margin along each side. Spread half the apples over the crumbs, dot with 1 tablespoon redcurrant jelly and sprinkle with half the almonds. Top with the remaining apples, jelly, almonds and breadcrumbs.

Fold in the edges of the pastry and brush with the remaining melted butter. Roll up like a Swiss roll and place the strudel, seam side down, on the prepared baking tray, curving it if necessary to fit. Brush the top with melted butter and bake for 45 minutes, brushing again with butter every 10 minutes. Remove from the oven and dust generously with icing sugar. Serve warm, with whipped cream.

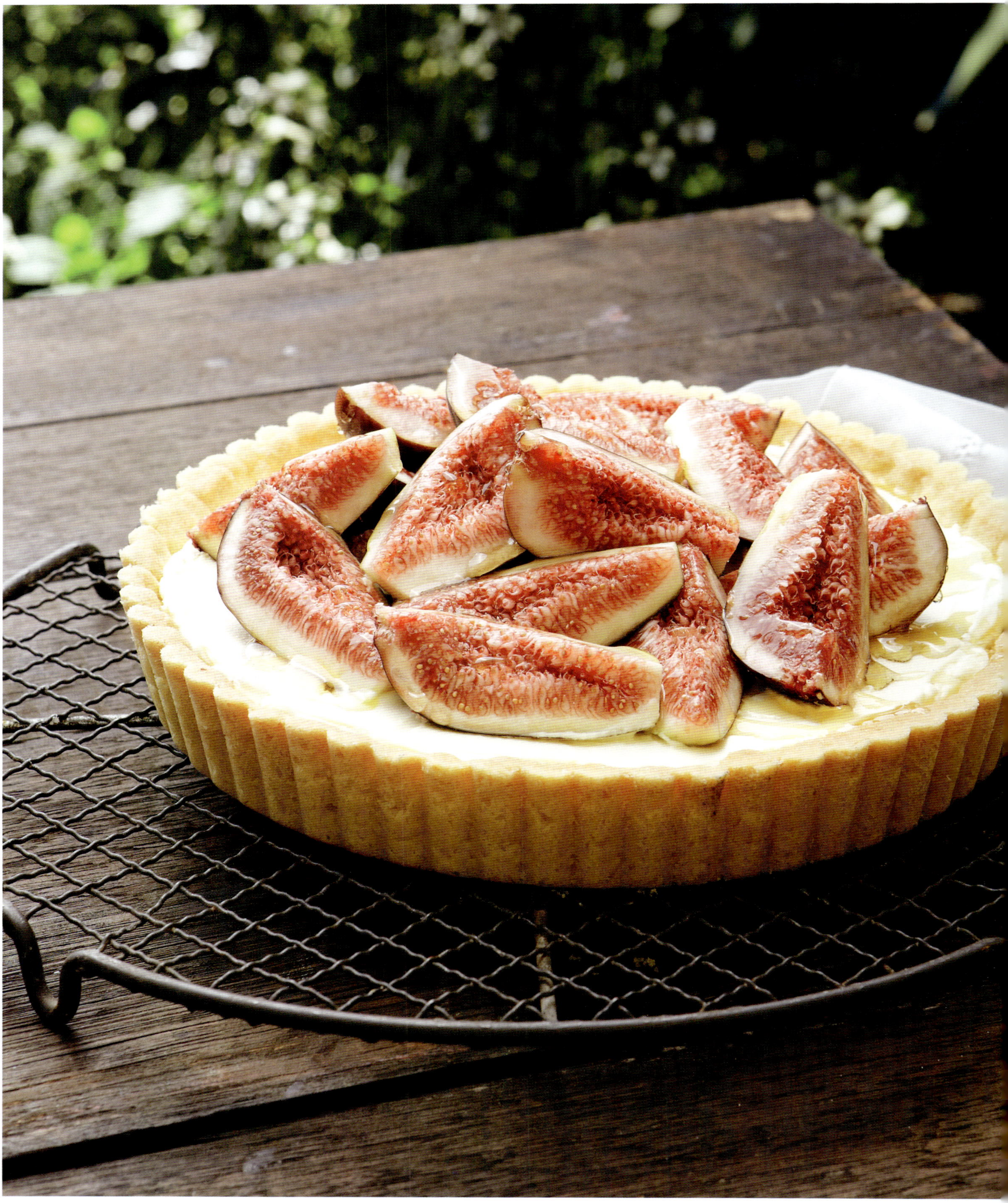

INGREDIENTS

2 cups (300 g) plain flour
½ cup (110 g) caster sugar
185 g unsalted butter, melted and cooled
a few drops of vanilla essence
1⅔ cups (600 g) mascarpone, chilled, sweetened and flavoured with honey and vanilla essence or orange-blossom water
6–8 fresh figs
extra sugar to caramelise (optional)

FRESH FIG & MASCARPONE TART

This fig and mascarpone dessert is hard to beat. I also like to make it with muscat grapes or blueberries, in the same way as set out in this recipe. The pastry is unusual, but it works well with soft fruit tarts such as this one. Small battery-run blowtorches, or gas torches, are available at good kitchen shops or some hardware stores. They are used to caramelise the sugar topping on foods, making a delicious crisp brown crust without heating the food underneath. This can also be done under a hot griller, but care has to be taken not to let the food beneath cook or warm.

SERVES 8-10

METHOD

Preheat the oven to 200°C. Lightly grease a 23 cm loose-based flan tin.

Sift the flour into a bowl and stir in the sugar. Make a well in the centre and add the melted butter and vanilla. Mix together to make a stiff dough.

Press the dough into a 23 cm loose-based flan tin, working up the edges evenly. Prick the base well, line with baking paper and fill with baking beads or dried beans. Bake for 20 minutes or until golden, removing the paper and beads or beans after 15 minutes. Remove from the oven and leave to cool completely.

Whip the chilled mascarpone until it holds its shape. Spread the mascarpone in the cooled tart case as evenly as possible.

Quarter the fresh figs and arrange them, cut side up, in the tin, as tightly as possible. Serve as is or sprinkle with extra sugar and place under a very hot grill for a minute or so. Alternatively, use a gas torch to caramelise the figs. Serve cut into wedges.

APRICOT TART

SERVES 10–12

INGREDIENTS
1 quantity Rough Puff Pastry (page 334)
1 tablespoon ground almonds
2 tablespoons caster sugar
850 g can apricot halves, drained (see Note)
¼ cup apricot jam
1 tablespoon water

METHOD

Preheat the oven to 220°C. Line a large baking tray with baking paper.

Halve the pastry and roll out each piece to a 32 cm x 22 cm rectangle. Place on the prepared tray. Lightly score a 1 cm border along the long edges. Use a fork to prick the pastry inside the borders and along the short edges.

Sprinkle the ground almonds and half of the sugar over the pastry, leaving the border free. Top with the apricots and sprinkle with the remaining sugar.

Combine the apricot jam and water in a small saucepan over low heat. Stir until smooth. Brush the apricots with half of the jam.

Bake for 30 minutes or until the pastry is puffed and golden and the apricots are beginning to brown.

Glaze the apricots and the pastry edges with the remaining apricot jam. Place under a preheated grill for 1–2 minutes or until caramelised. Serve warm.

NOTE This tart can also be made with fresh ripe apricots, halved and stoned. Six or seven should be sufficient, just enough to cover the ground almonds in a single layer. Bake as directed; if the apricots are still too firm after this time, bake for a further 5 minutes.

PASTRY *fruit pies & tarts*

INGREDIENTS

1 cup orange juice
½ cup water
1 cup seeded raisins
1½ cups (330 g) caster sugar
¼ cup (35 g) plain flour, sifted
3 tablespoons lemon juice
a large pinch of salt
1 quantity unsweetened Plain Rich Shortcrust Pastry made with 2 cups (300 g) plain flour (see Variation, page 329)
lightly beaten egg white and caster sugar to glaze

LATTICED RAISIN PIE

SERVES 6-8

METHOD

Bring the orange juice and water to the boil in a saucepan, remove from the heat and stir in the raisins. Stand for 2 hours, then stir in the sugar, flour, lemon juice and salt. Return to low heat and stir constantly until the mixture is boiling and well thickened. Cool completely.

Preheat the oven to 220°C.

Divide the pastry dough into two portions, one a little larger than the other. Roll out the larger portion and use it to line a 23 cm pie plate. Spoon in the raisin mixture, mounding it slightly. Roll out the remaining dough and cover the pie with a lattice top (see Note). Brush with egg white and sprinkle with caster sugar. Bake for 10 minutes, then reduce the heat to 180°C and bake for 25–30 minutes longer or until the top is browned.

NOTE A lattice top is a decorative finish to a pie with an attractive filling such as fruit. Roll out the dough and cut into strips 1-2 cm wide. The simplest method is to arrange the strips on the filling in crisscross rows. Or the strips can be woven as follows: lay half the strips on a piece of baking paper, about 2 cm apart. Fold back every second strip halfway. Place a strip at right angles across the unfolded strips. Unfold the doubled strips and fold back the alternate ones. Lay another cross strip about 2 cm from the first. Continue, working towards the edge, then repeat the process, starting from the other side of the centre line. Strips should be loosely arranged, without stretching. When the whole piece of paper is latticed, chill the lattice for 30 minutes. Moisten the edge of the bottom crust of the pie. After chilling, shake the lattice top carefully onto the pie. Press the edges well together and trim. Bake as directed in the recipe.

INGREDIENTS

Plain Rich Shortcrust Pastry for a two-crust, 23 cm pie (page 329)
4 cups fresh or frozen blackberries, or 3 cups drained, canned blackberries
¾ cup (165 g) caster sugar
1½ tablespoons cornflour
2 tablespoons lemon juice

BLACKBERRY PIE

The days of going to country fields or roadsides to pick blackberries are past, as blackberry bushes became a nuisance and were eradicated. Now we depend on store-bought fresh or frozen blackberries for this magical pie.

SERVES 6

METHOD

Preheat the oven to 200°C. Grease a 23 cm pie plate.

Divide the pastry into two pieces, one slightly larger than the other. Roll out the larger potion of pastry and use to line the prepared pie dish.

If using fresh blackberries, toss gently with the sugar, cornflour and lemon juice. If using sweetened, frozen or canned blackberries, add less sugar. Spoon into the pie crust. Dampen the edges of the pastry.

Roll out the remaining pastry and make a lattice for the top (see page 347).

Bake for 10 minutes, then reduce the oven temperature to 180°C and bake for a further 25 minutes or until the pastry is cooked and golden brown. Serve warm with cream, ice cream or custard.

NOTE If you don't want to make a lattice, roll out the second piece of pastry to slightly larger than the pie. Place on top of the pie, press into place, trim and crimp the edges. Make a few slashes in the top for steam to escape. Bake as directed.

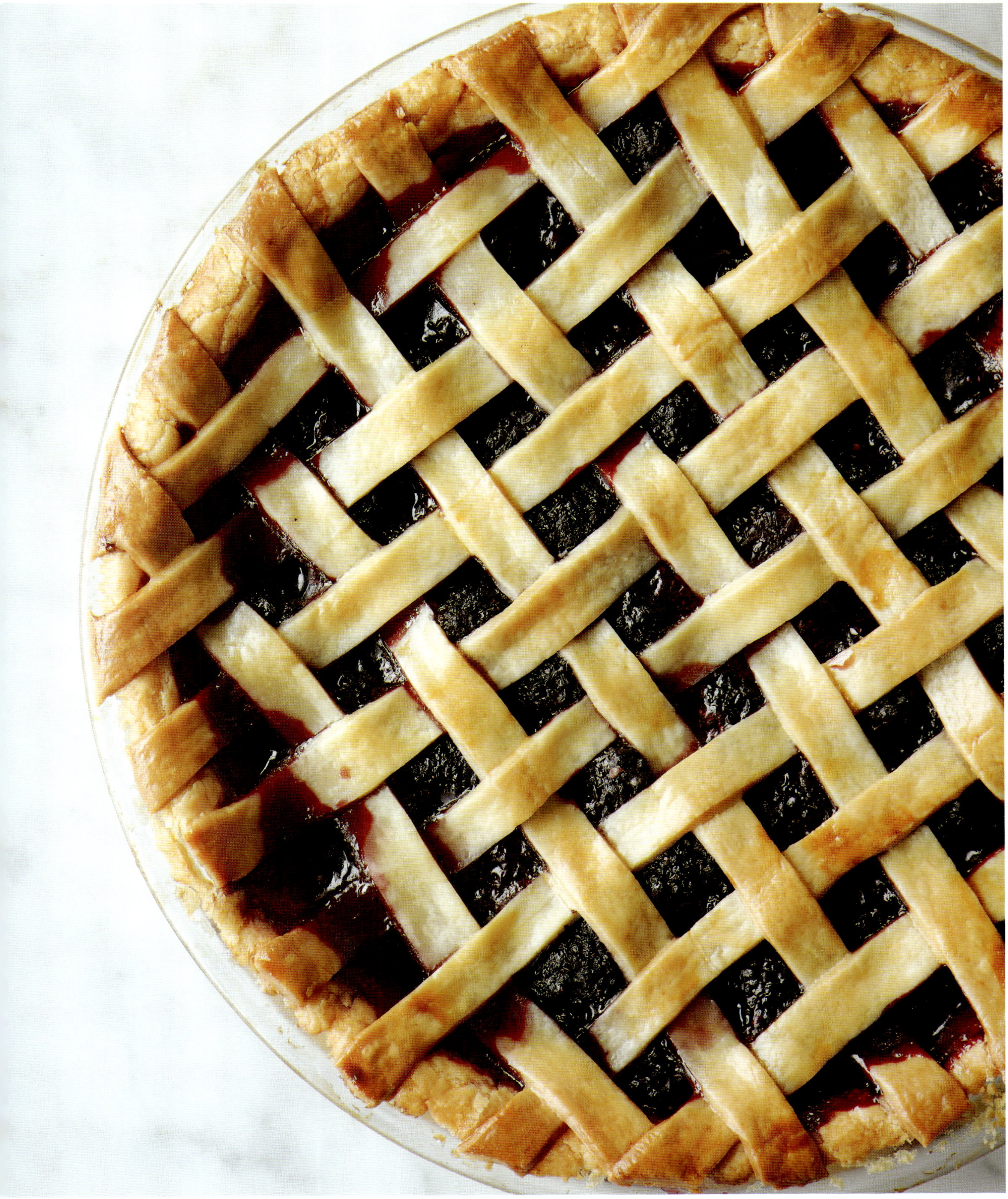

INGREDIENTS

20 cm tart shell made from Sweet Flan Pastry (page 331), baked blind (see page 326)
½ quantity Crème Pâtissière (page 338)
mixed fruits (strawberries, grapes, cherries, mandarin or orange segments, apricots or pears)
¼ cup sieved apricot jam
1 tablespoon water
a squeeze of lemon juice

FRENCH FRUIT TART (TARTE AUX FRUITS)

This tart has the tempting, glamorous look of the tarts seen in those superb French patisseries. The trick is to work in a tidy area, with nothing else on the go at the same time. The French fruit tart needs your undivided attention!

SERVES 6

METHOD

Prepare the fruit according to type.

Fill the cooled tart shell with crème pâtissière. Arrange the prepared fruit over the cream in a decorative fashion, in concentric circles, in any order. The cream should be completely covered with fruit.

To make the glaze, heat the apricot jam, water and lemon juice together in a saucepan, stirring, until the mixture hangs in heavy drops from the spoon. Brush over the fruit while the glaze is still warm.

Put the tart in the refrigerator to set the glaze until ready to serve.

NOTE For the best result this tart should be put together 1–2 hours before serving. Have the tart shell baked, the crème pâtissière and the glaze at the ready (it will have to be reheated) and then settle down to create a beautiful work of art.

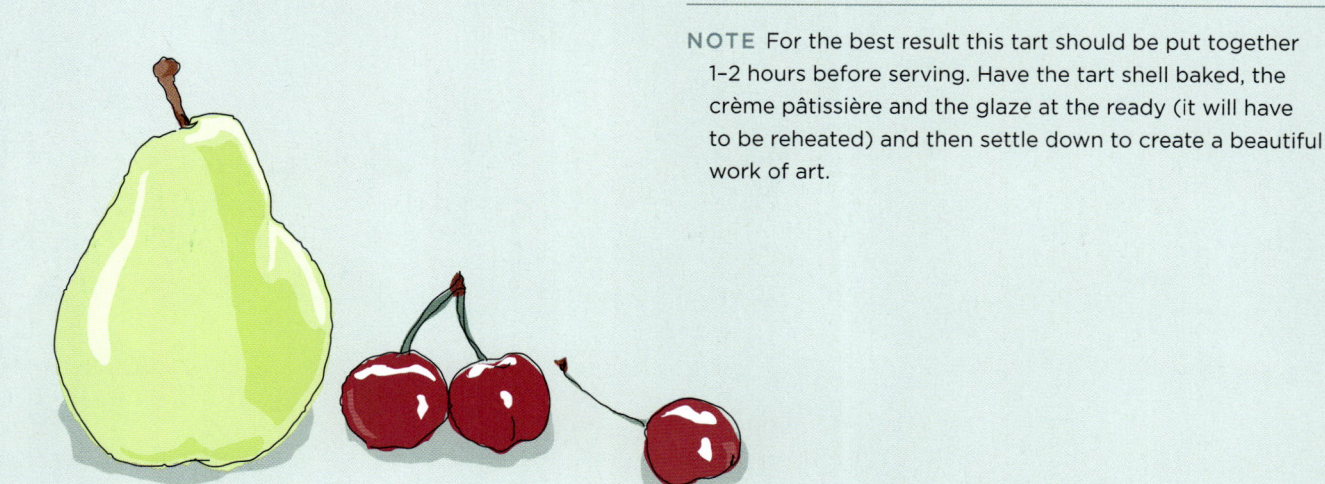

PASTRY *fruit pies & tarts*

INGREDIENTS
1 quantity Sweet Flan Pastry (page 331)

FILLING
2 eggs, separated
⅓ cup (75 g) caster sugar
2 tablespoons plain flour
¾ cup milk
1 teaspoon vanilla essence
6 ripe nectarines, halved and stoned
  (or use other fruit in season)
sifted icing sugar to dust (optional)

FRUIT SOUFFLÉ TART

When making tarts, the French always use whatever fruit is in season, when it is at its peak and cheapest, and are proud of their respect for time, quality ingredients and money. Use whatever variety of stone fruit is in season: nectarines, peaches, plums, cherries or apricots.

SERVES 6–8

METHOD

Make the pastry, chill for 1 hour or more, and use to line a 23 cm loose-based flan tin. Prick the base lightly and chill for about 15 minutes.

Meanwhile, preheat the oven to 190°C. Bake the pastry blind (see page 326) for about 15 minutes, until it is set. Remove the paper and pastry weights. Return the pastry case to the oven for a further 5 minutes to dry out the base. Cool slightly before filling and baking further.

Increase the oven temperature to 200°C.

To make the filling, beat the egg yolks with the sugar until the mixture forms a ribbon falling into the bowl when the beater is lifted. Stir in the flour.

Bring the milk to the boil and pour over the egg-yolk mixture, stirring well until mixed. Add the vanilla and transfer the egg-yolk mixture to the saucepan. Cook gently, stirring constantly until thickened, without letting it boil. Remove from the heat and cool to lukewarm, stirring occasionally.

Whisk the egg whites until stiff but not dry and fold them gently into the egg custard. Pour into the prepared flan tin. Arrange the nectarines or other fruit on the egg filling, rounded side down.

Bake for 20 minutes. Reduce the oven temperature to 180°C and bake for a further 20 minutes or until golden brown. Remove the tart from the oven and dust, if you like, with sifted icing sugar. Serve warm or at room temperature.

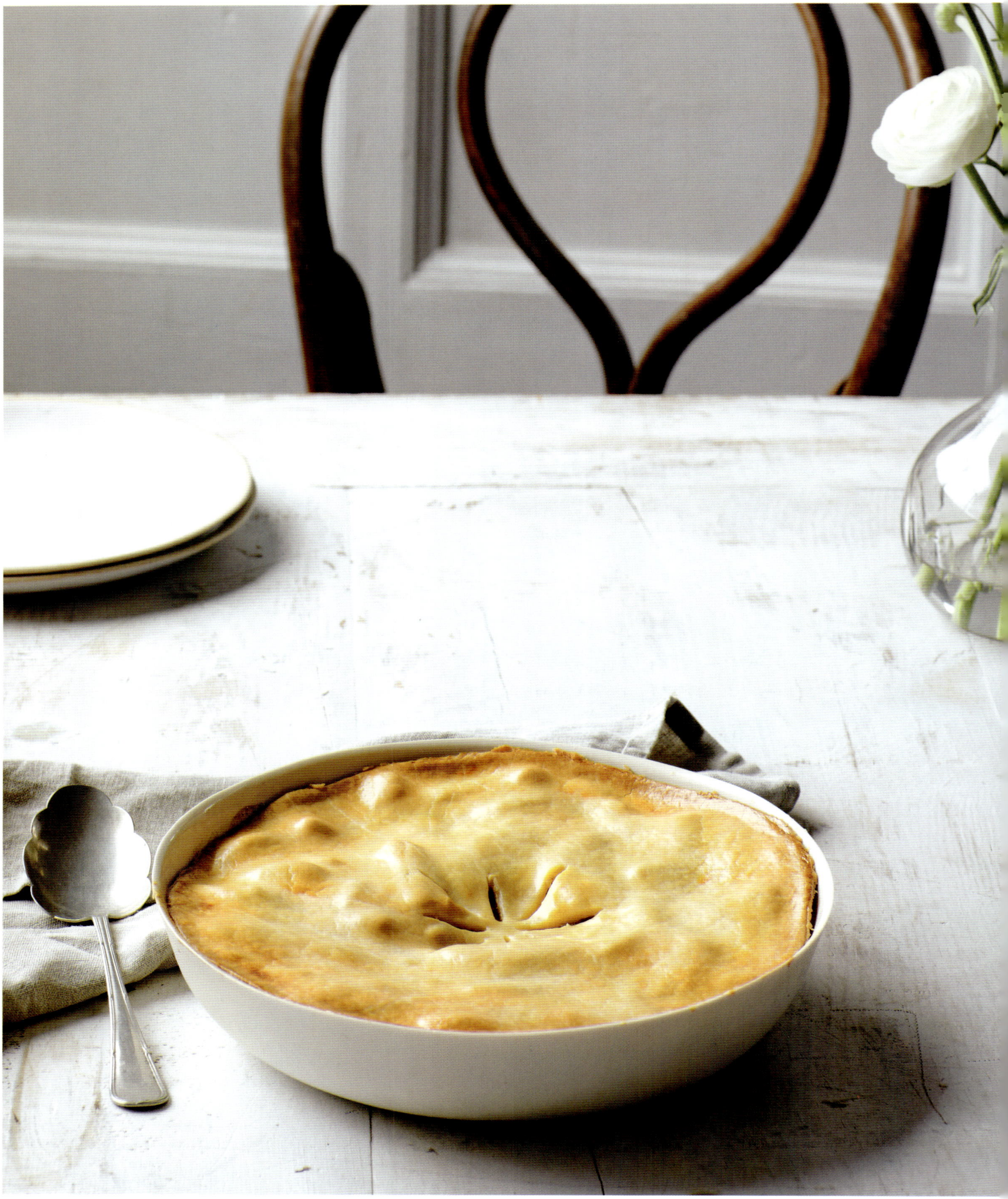

PASTRY *fruit pies & tarts*

INGREDIENTS

3 tablespoons quick-cooking tapioca (see Note)
¾ cup (165 g) caster sugar
⅓ cup (75 g) firmly packed dark brown sugar
¼ teaspoon salt
1 teaspoon ground cinnamon
½ teaspoon nutmeg
6 tart apples, peeled, cored and sliced
half of a 375 g packet frozen shortcrust, puff or flaky pastry, thawed
whipped cream flavoured with a little sugar and nutmeg to serve (optional)

DEEP DISH APPLE PIE

SERVES 6

METHOD

Preheat the oven to 220°C. Grease a deep 20 cm round or square dish.

Mix together the tapioca, sugars, salt, cinnamon, nutmeg and sliced apples. Pour into the prepared dish.

Roll out the pastry to fit the top of the dish. Cut several slits near the centre and lay the pastry over the apple mixture.

Bake for about 35 minutes, then reduce the oven temperature to 180°C and bake for a further 30 minutes. Serve with cream whipped with sugar and nutmeg if desired.

NOTE The quick-cooking tapioca helps to absorb the juices from the apples and to thicken them so that the filling is not runny.

INGREDIENTS

1 cup (150 g) flour
¼ cup (55 g) caster sugar
2 teaspoons cocoa powder
½ teaspoon cinnamon
a pinch of ground cloves
½ teaspoon baking powder
a pinch of salt
125 g ground almonds
125 g butter, chilled and diced
milk or Kirsch as needed
1½ cups raspberry or plum jam
beaten egg to glaze
sifted icing sugar to dust (optional)
whipped cream to serve

LINZER TORTE

Linzer torte, named after the town of Linz on the River Danube, is made in many parts of Austria. It is distinguished by its unique pastry made with ground nuts, either almonds or hazelnuts, and spices. This pastry is arranged in lattice strips over a jam filling, either plum or raspberry. Serve Linzer torte plain or dusted with icing sugar.

SERVES 8–10

METHOD

Preheat the oven to 190°C. Grease an 18 cm springform tin.

Sift the flour, sugar, cocoa, cinnamon, cloves, baking powder and salt into a mixing bowl. Add the ground almonds.

Rub in the butter and mix lightly with your fingertips to a dry dough, adding a little milk or Kirsch if necessary. Wrap the dough in foil and chill for at least 30 minutes.

Roll out two-thirds of the dough and press into the base of the prepared tin. Spread with the jam. Roll out the remaining dough, cut into 1 cm wide strips and arrange in lattice fashion (see page 347) on top, using the last strip as an edging around the tart. Press down lightly to seal and refrigerate for 30 minutes.

Remove the tart from the refrigerator, brush with beaten egg and bake for 35–40 minutes. Allow to cool in the tin.

Once cool, dust with icing sugar if desired. Serve with whipped cream.

PASTRY *fruit pies & tarts*

INGREDIENTS
1 kg apricots, halved and stoned
¾ cup (165 g) caster sugar
a pinch of salt
1 tablespoon grated lemon rind
2 tablespoons lemon juice
1 tablespoon cornflour
23 cm unbaked Plain Rich Shortcrust Pastry pie shell (page 329)

TOPPING
⅓ cup (75 g) firmly packed brown sugar
½ cup (150 g) plain flour, sifted
1 teaspoon cinnamon
90 g butter

APRICOT CRUMBLE PIE

When summer's stone fruits come on the market, apricots are a top purchase. They are good gently poached in a light sugar syrup, baked in the oven, or used in many desserts and cakes. A crumble is easy to make and loved by children and adults alike.

SERVES 6–8

METHOD
Preheat the oven to 200°C.

Mix together the apricots, sugar, salt, lemon rind and juice and cornflour. Pack into the pie shell.

For the topping, combine the sugar, flour and cinnamon and rub in the butter until the mixture resembles coarse breadcrumbs. Sprinkle over the apricots.

Bake for 15 minutes. Reduce the oven temperature to 180°C and bake for a further 30 minutes longer or until the apricots are tender. Serve warm with cream or custard.

INGREDIENTS

PASTRY
2 cups (300 g) plain flour
125 g butter, diced
2 tablespoons caster sugar
½ cup ground almonds
1 egg, beaten
a little grated lemon rind
1 tablespoon rum

FILLING
½ cup ground almonds
½ cup (110 g) caster sugar
600 g mixed berries
3 tablespoons icing sugar
whipped cream to serve (optional)

FREEFORM BERRY TART

SERVES 8

METHOD

Have all the ingredients at room temperature and place them in a bowl in the order listed. Handling the pastry quickly, mix all the ingredients together. This can be done by hand or in a food processor. Form into a round, wrap in plastic wrap and refrigerate for 1 hour before using.

When chilled, roll out on a piece of baking paper to a rough 30 cm circle. Transfer to a large baking tray and chill for 30 minutes.

Preheat the oven to 180°C.

To make the filling, sprinkle the tart shell with the ground almonds and 1 tablespoon of the sugar. Spread the fruit over the chilled pastry, leaving a border about 5 cm wide.

Fold the border over the filling, leaving a gap in the centre, and sprinkle the pastry with the remaining sugar.

Bake on the lowest rack of the oven for 45 minutes or until the pastry is golden. Cool on the tray, allowing it to stand until just warm. Dust with icing sugar before serving with whipped cream, if liked.

NOTE This is a rustic Italian way of making a fruit tart, which they call crostata. Other fruit can be used, such as plums; arrange them, cut side up, in circles, packing them tightly and reversing the direction of the fruit with each circle. Bake as directed.

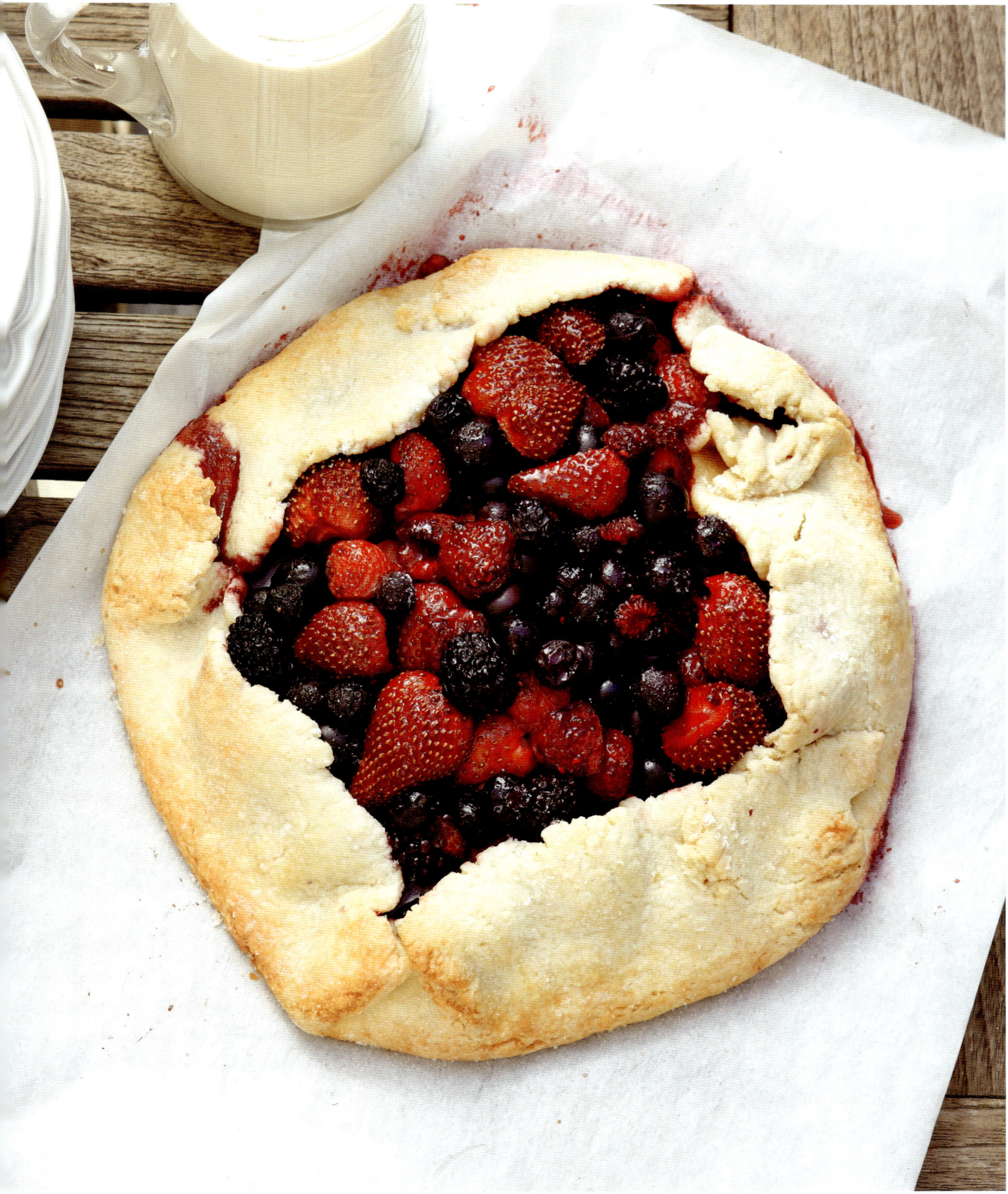

INGREDIENTS

1 teaspoon tea leaves
500 g large pitted dessert prunes
1 quantity Plain Rich Shortcrust Pastry (page 329)
1 egg
½ cup cream
1 teaspoon cornflour
¼ cup (55 g) caster sugar
2 tablespoons Cointreau or Grand Marnier
30 g butter
cream to serve

FLAN AUX PRUNEAUX (PRUNE TART)

A simple French tart. A good cook will have the pastry made ahead and rolled into the tart case, ready to be filled with the prepared prunes half an hour or so before required.

SERVES 6–8

METHOD

Make a weak tea (see Note), strain it and pour over the prunes. Allow to soak for 4 hours.

Preheat the oven to 200°C. Grease a 20 cm loose-based flan tin.

Roll out the pastry and use it to line the prepared flan tin. Drain and stone the prunes, then spread out in the pastry case. Bake for about 20 minutes.

Meanwhile, beat the egg with the cream, cornflour, sugar and liqueur. Remove the tart from the oven, pour the custard mixture over and dot with butter. Return to the oven and bake for further 10–15 minutes to set the custard. Cool on a wire rack and serve with either pouring cream, or softly whipped cream.

NOTE Use regular black tea, or Earl Grey if you like it.

PASTRY *fruit pies & tarts*

INGREDIENTS
PASTRY
2 cups (300 g) plain flour
150 g butter, softened
5 tablespoons icing sugar, sifted
2 egg yolks
¼ teaspoon vanilla essence

FILLING
30 g butter
1 kg cooking apples, peeled, cored and quartered
grated rind and juice of ½ lemon
½ cup (110 g) caster sugar
Glacé Icing (page 252) and 1 tablespoon redcurrant jelly (optional) to decorate

GALETTE NORMANDIE

A galette is a flat cake traditionally made with flaky pastry or yeast dough. It is the symbolic cake eaten on Twelfth Night in France. A more elaborate version can consist of meringue, fruit and nuts.

SERVES 8

METHOD

To the make pastry, sift the flour onto a work surface, make a well in the centre and add the butter, sugar, egg yolks and vanilla to the well. Work together into a smooth paste. Divide into three portions, wrap in plastic wrap and chill for 30 minutes.

To make the filling, melt the butter in a heavy saucepan, add the apples, lemon rind and juice, cover and cook gently until soft and pulpy. Mix in the sugar. Purée in a food processor or blender or push through a sieve.

Preheat the oven to 180°C. Line three baking trays with baking paper.

Roll out the pastry into three equal-sizes rounds about 20 cm in diameter. Bake on the prepared trays for about 15 minutes or until a pale golden colour. Allow to cool.

When the pastry is cold, sandwich together in layers with the apple mixture. Cover the top with a thin layer of glacé icing and marble with redcurrant jelly, if using.

NOTE Normandy, in northern France, is noted for its fine apples, apple brandy (Calvados) and cream. Any recipe with 'Normandy' or 'Normandie' in its name is likely to feature one or more of these ingredients.

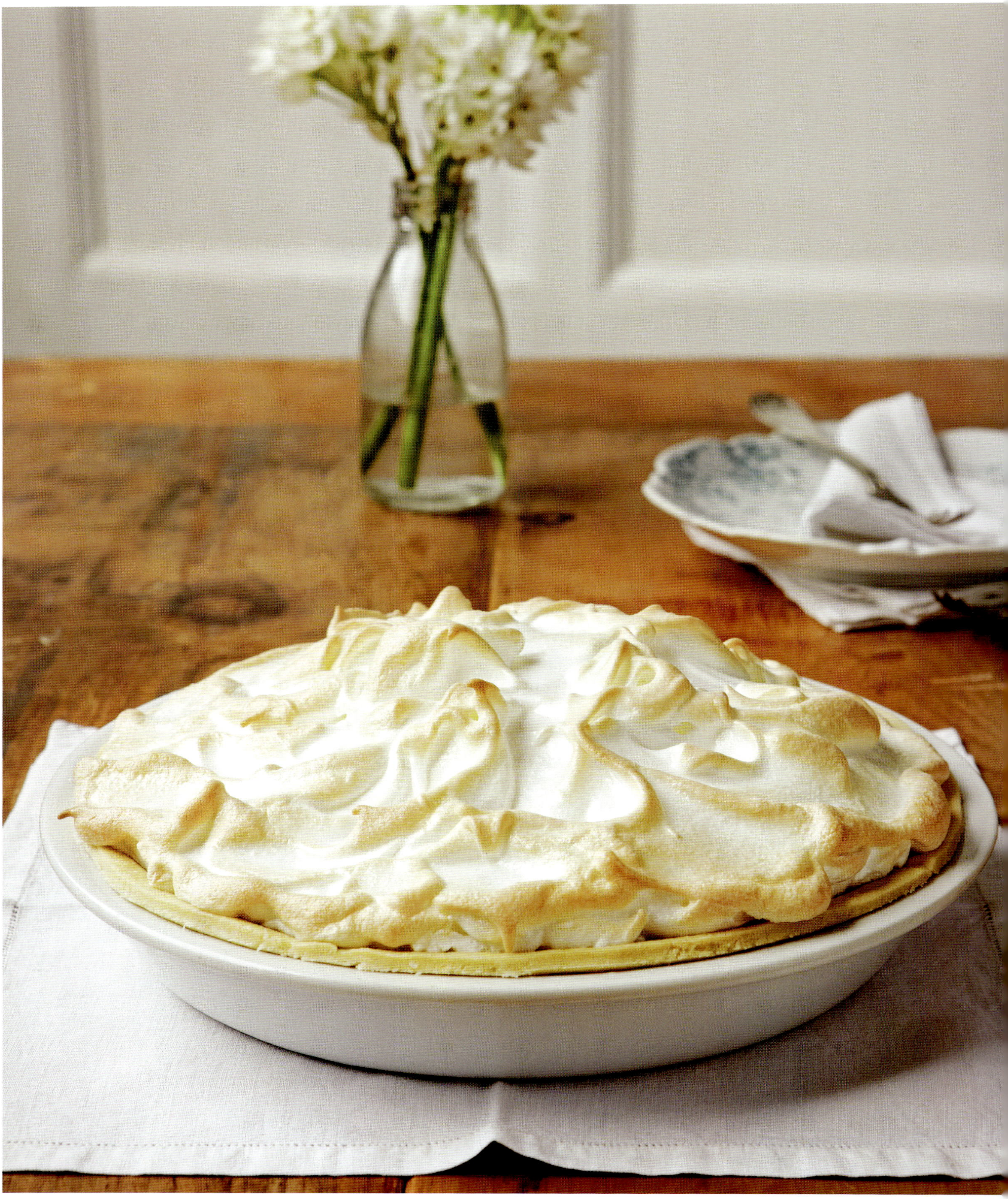

PASTRY *fruit pies & tarts*

INGREDIENTS
3 tablespoons cornflour
1¾ cups (385 g) sugar
½ cup lime juice
1 tablespoon grated lime rind
3 eggs, separated
1½ cups boiling water
23 cm Plain Shortcrust Pastry tart shell (page 328), baked blind (see page 326)
whipped cream to serve

LIME MERINGUE PIE

Don't be tempted to pile on the meringue with this recipe. There should be just a little more meringue than the filling. It's all about good proportions. A thin crust, a nice amount of lime filling and then a little more meringue – and the meringue shouldn't be too sweet.

SERVES 8

METHOD
Preheat the oven to 200°C.

Combine the cornflour, 1¼ cups (275 g) of the sugar, the lime juice and rind in a saucepan. Beat the egg yolks until thick and fluffy and add to the lime juice mixture. Gradually add the boiling water. Bring to a simmer over very gentle heat, stirring constantly until thickened. Simmer for a further 2–3 minutes. Pour into the pastry shell and leave to cool.

Beat the egg whites until stiff but not dry and gradually beat in the remaining sugar. Spread the meringue over the top of the pie, carefully sealing in all the filling and being sure it touches the edge of the pastry shell all around.

Bake for about 5 minutes or until very pale brown. Cool and serve with whipped cream.

INGREDIENTS

PASTRY
90 g butter, softened
1/3 cup (75 g) caster sugar
1 teaspoon vanilla essence
1 egg
3/4 cup (110 g) self-raising flour
3/4 cup (110 g) plain flour

FILLING
3 egg yolks
1/2 cup (110 g) caster sugar
2 tablespoons plain flour
grated rind and juice of 2 lemons
4 tablespoons water

MERINGUE
3 egg whites
pinch cream of tartar
1/4 cup (55 g) caster sugar

LEMON MERINGUE PIE

SERVES 8

METHOD

To make the pastry, cream the butter with the sugar and vanilla. Add the egg and beat well. Stir in the sifted flours, turn out onto a floured board and knead lightly. Wrap in plastic wrap and chill for 1 hour.

Preheat the oven to 200°C. Grease a 20–23 cm pie dish.

Roll out the pastry on a floured surface and use to line the prepared pie dish. Pinch the edges decoratively and prick the base well with a fork.

Bake for 15 minutes, then reduce the oven temperature to 180°C and bake for a further 5–10 minutes or until the crust is golden. Cool.

To make the filling, mix the egg yolks, sugar, flour and lemon rind in the top of a double saucepan and gradually stir in the lemon juice and water. Cook, stirring constantly, over boiling water until the mixture is smooth and thick. Cool, then pour into the cooled pie shell.

To make the meringue, beat the egg whites with the cream of tartar until thick. Gradually add the sugar, 2 tablespoons at a time, beating until the mixture is thick and glossy and the sugar is dissolved. Spread over the filling in the pie shell, sealing it completely with the meringue. Bake in a 180°C oven for 8–10 minutes or until meringue is golden. Serve cold.

PASTRY *fruit pies & tarts*

INGREDIENTS

CRUMB CRUST
1½ cups fine sweet biscuit crumbs, such as Nice
⅓ cup (75 g) caster sugar
75 g butter, melted

FILLING
3 teaspoons powdered gelatine
¼ cup cold water
1 cup (220 g) caster sugar
a pinch of salt
1 teaspoon grated lemon rind
½ cup lemon juice
4 eggs, separated
whipped cream to decorate

LEMON CHIFFON TART

SERVES 6–8

METHOD

Preheat the oven to 180°C. Lightly grease a 23 cm pie dish.

To make the crumb crust, mix the crumbs, sugar and butter in a bowl. Put the mixture into the prepared pie dish and press and pat it out evenly over the bottom and sides. Bake for 8–10 minutes, then allow to cool.

To make the filling, soften the gelatine in the cold water, then stir over simmering water until dissolved. Combine ½ cup of the sugar, the salt, lemon rind and lemon juice in the top of a double saucepan or a heatproof bowl that will fit over a saucepan. Add the egg yolks and gelatine mixture, stirring until well blended. Place over simmering water and stir until the mixture thickens a little. Pour into a bowl and chill until the mixture mounds when dropped from a spoon. Beat the egg whites until foamy, then gradually beat in the remaining sugar, beating until smooth and shiny. Fold the egg whites into the lemon mixture. Spread into the pie shell and chill until serving time. Decorate with whipped cream.

VARIATIONS

LIME CHIFFON TART Follow the recipe for Lemon Chiffon Tart, using gingersnap biscuit crumbs in the crust, and substituting grated lime rind and lime juice for the lemon rind and juice.

ORANGE CHIFFON TART Follow the recipe for Lemon Chiffon Tart, substituting 1 teaspoon grated orange rind and ½ cup orange juice mixed with 2 tablespoons lemon juice for the lemon rind and juice.

This luscious dessert of caramelised apples on a pastry crust appears on the menu of nearly every French restaurant. **Golden delicious apples should be used for best results.**

PASTRY *fruit pies & tarts*

INGREDIENTS

PASTRY
1 cup (150 g) plain flour
2 teaspoons caster sugar
90 g butter, cut into small dice
1 egg yolk
1 tablespoon cold water

FILLING
125 g butter
1⅓ cups (295 g) caster sugar
10 large, ripe golden delicious apples, peeled, cored and thinly sliced
whipped cream to serve (optional)

TART TATIN

SERVES 8

METHOD

To make the pastry, sift the flour and sugar into a bowl, make a well in the centre and place the butter, egg yolk and water in the well. Mix quickly with a fork to form a dough.

Alternatively, to make this pastry with an electric mixer, cream the sugar with the butter then incorporate the egg and water. Mix for a few seconds, then add the flour all at once. Do not beat any more once a dough is formed. Roll in plastic wrap and chill for 1 hour.

To make the filling, put the butter and sugar in a 23 cm round flameproof dish. Allow the butter to melt on a gentle heat. Remove from the heat and arrange the apples, flat, in circles in the dish, packing them very tightly together. Return to the heat and cook gently until the butter and sugar form a pale caramel. This will take about 15 minutes. Do not allow the caramel to become dark.

Preheat the oven to 190°C.

While the apples are cooking, carefully roll out the pastry dough to a 28 cm round. Remove the dish from the heat and cover the apples with the dough round, pushing the edges inside the dish.

Place the dish on a baking tray and bake for 45 minutes. If it begins to brown too much, cover it loosely with foil. Stand for 10 minutes before inverting the tart onto a heated dish. Serve warm, with lightly whipped cream if desired.

NOTE To make this tart you need a heavy, round flameproof dish – a cast-iron frying pan with a screw-on handle is one idea, a small paella pan another. These are available at specialty kitchen shops. It is worth looking for a special pan for this famous dish.

INGREDIENTS
1½ quantities Sweet Flan Pastry (page 331)

FILLING
250 g cream cheese, softened
½ cup (110 g) caster sugar
1 teaspoon grated lemon rind
1 tablespoon orange juice
1 tablespoon cream
1 punnet (250 g) strawberries, hulled and sliced if large

GLAZE
½ cup redcurrant jelly
1 tablespoon water
2 teaspoons Cointreau or Grand Marnier, or 2 tablespoons orange juice

GLAZED STRAWBERRY FLAN

The strawberries we take for granted these days result from careful crossbreeding of a small wild American strawberry with a juicy specimen from Chile. Wild strawberries are now cultivated, too, and they are valued for their fragrance. When chosing strawberries, an intense perfume is the best indicator of quality.

SERVES 6

METHOD

Roll out the pastry thinly and use it to line a lightly greased 20 cm loose-based round or square flan tin. Chill for at least 30 minutes.

Preheat the oven to 190°C.

Prick the base of the pastry all over with a fork, then bake blind (see page 326) for about 20 minutes or until the pastry is a pale biscuit colour. Allow to cool.

To make the filling, cream together all the ingredients except the strawberries and chill.

To make the glaze, heat the redcurrant jelly and water in a small saucepan, stirring until smooth. Cool slightly. Stir in the liqueur or orange juice.

To assemble, spoon the cream cheese filling into the flan case and smooth the surface with a spatula. Carefully decorate with the strawberries. Spoon or brush the glaze over them and chill until set.

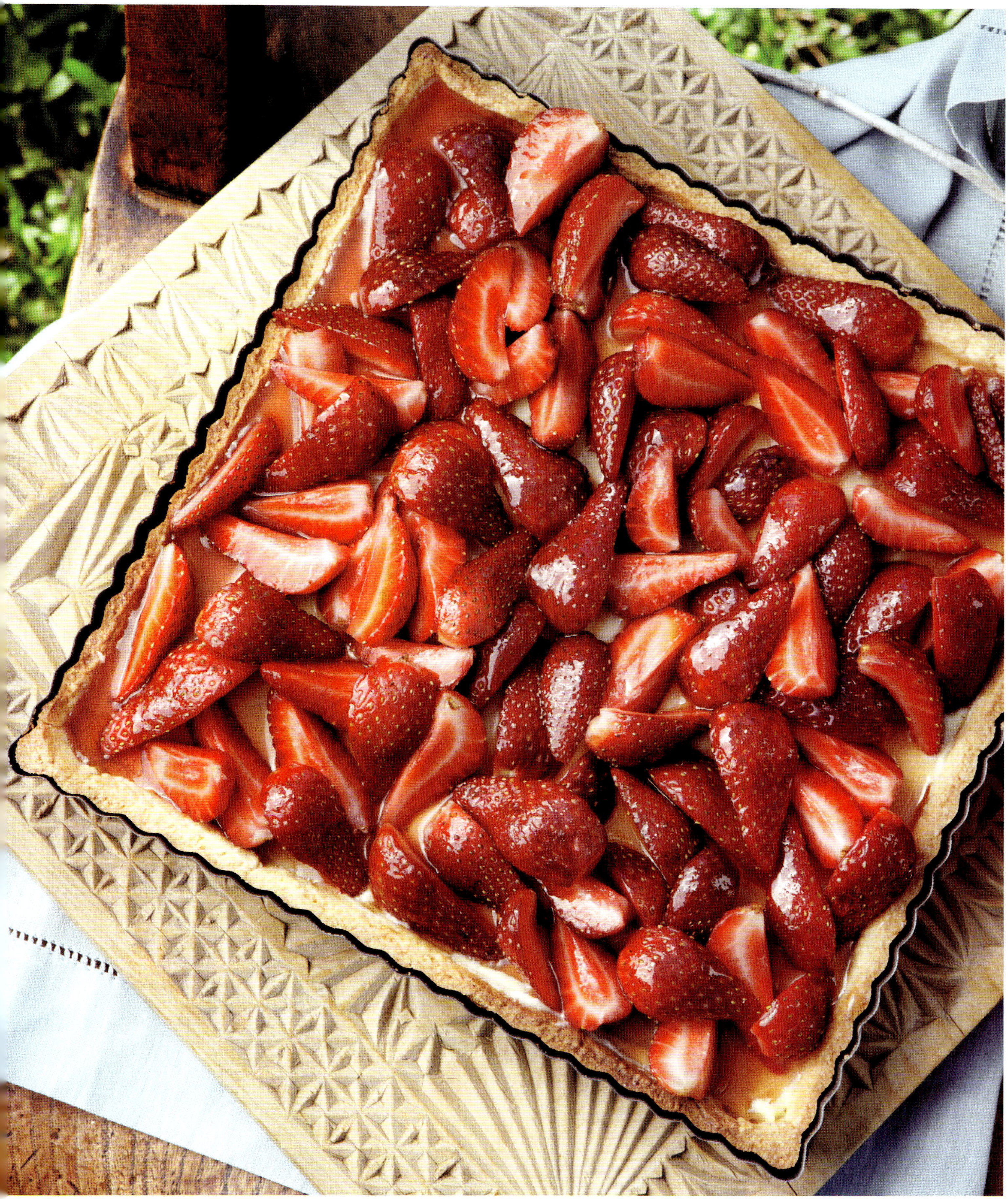

INGREDIENTS
1 cup (150 g) plain flour
3 tablespoons ground almonds
75 g butter, diced
¼ cup (40 g) icing sugar, sifted
1 egg yolk
a few drops of vanilla essence
a pinch of salt
icing sugar to dust

FILLING
4 eggs
¾ cup (165 g) caster sugar
grated rind and juice of 2 lemons
½ cup cream

LEMON TART

SERVES 8–10

METHOD

For the pastry, sift the flour with the ground almonds onto a work surface and make a large well in the centre. Put the butter in the well with the icing sugar, egg yolk, vanilla essence and salt, and work these centre ingredients with the fingertips of one hand into a soft paste. Gradually draw in the surrounding flour with a metal spatula and knead lightly to form a dough. Wrap and chill for 1 hour.

Roll out the dough to line a 23 cm loose-based flan tin, pressing the sides in well and trimming the excess. Lightly prick the base and chill for 15 minutes.

Preheat the oven to 200°C.

Once the pastry shell is chilled, bake blind (see page 326) for 15 minutes, then remove from the oven, lift away the paper and beans, and return to the oven for a further 5 minutes. Reduce the oven temperature to 180°C.

For the filling, beat the eggs in a bowl with the sugar until smooth. Stir in the lemon rind and juice. Lightly whip the cream and stir into the lemon mixture.

Pour the filling into the prepared pastry case and bake for about 45 minutes. Leave to cool for several hours before serving. Dust with icing sugar if liked.

INGREDIENTS

1 quantity Plain Rich Shortcrust Pastry (page 329)
2 egg whites
1 cup (220 g) caster sugar
2 cups flaked or slivered blanched almonds
¼ teaspoon ground cinnamon
1 teaspoon vanilla essence
icing sugar to dust

PARISIAN ALMOND TART

SERVES 8-10

METHOD

Preheat the oven to 190°C. Wrap the pastry in plastic wrap and chill for a least 1 hour.

Roll out the pastry on a floured board to fit a loose-based round flan tin at least 25 cm in diameter (or a 25 cm x 10 cm rectangular tin). Trim away any excess pastry and prick the base lightly with a fork. Line the shell with baking paper and half fill the paper with rice or dried beans. Chill for a further 15 minutes.

Bake for 15 minutes. Remove the paper and rice and bake the shell for a further 5 minutes or until pale golden. To make the filling, combine the egg whites, sugar, almonds, cinnamon and vanilla in a saucepan and heat, stirring constantly, until the mixture is hot without boiling.

Pour the filling into the shell and bake for 20–25 minutes or until the filling is golden and firm.

Dust with icing sugar if liked and cut the tart into wedges or squares while still warm. The tart will keep for several days.

NOTE Buy flaked or slivered almonds, or better still buy whole fresh shelled almonds, store in the freezer and use as required. To hull and blanch almonds, cover with hot water, and when the skins loosen, slip them off. To flake almonds, using a small sharp knife, slice off thin flakes of each almond; to sliver almonds, cut thicker lengthwise slices then cut into fatter needle shapes. When the almonds are dry, store in a glass jar.

INGREDIENTS

1 cup (220 g) caster sugar
¼ cup golden syrup or molasses
¼ cup water
¼ cup melted butter
3 eggs, well beaten
1 cup pecan halves
23 cm unbaked Plain Rich Shortcrust Pastry shell (page 329)

PECAN PIE

Pecans are an American nut of the hickory family, rather like a walnut in flavour and appearance. In many recipes walnuts and pecans are interchangeable. The name comes from the Native American word for these nuts, which were quickly adopted by the new settlers in North America. Of all the pecan dishes, perhaps the best known is pecan pie.

SERVES 8

METHOD

Preheat the oven to 200°C.

Mix together the sugar, golden syrup, water and melted butter. Add the eggs and pecans and stir well. Pour into the pastry shell.

Bake for 10 minutes, then reduce the oven temperature to 180°C and continue baking for about 30 minutes longer. Serve warm or cold.

USING A FLAN RING

Rather than using a flan tin, professional bakers and patissiers often use a flan ring. This resembles the outer ring of a springform tin (minus the clip). Its advantage is that it can be put on a baking sheet then the baked tart can simply be slid off the baking sheet and the flan ring lifted off, leaving the tart ready to serve.

PASTRY *nut tarts*

INGREDIENTS
1 cup maple syrup
½ cup water plus 3 tablespoons extra
3 tablespoons cornflour
60 g butter
1 quantity Plain Sweet Rich Shortcrust Pastry, made with 2 cups flour (see Variation, page 329)
1 cup coarsely chopped walnuts
whipped cream to serve (optional)

MAPLE WALNUT PIE

SERVES 6–8

METHOD

Bring the maple syrup and ½ cup water to the boil in a small saucepan and boil for 2 minutes.

Mix the cornflour and the remaining water together in a small bowl, then add to the boiling syrup, stirring constantly. Cook for about 2 minutes or until the mixture thickens. Remove from the heat, stir in the butter, and cool quickly by placing the pan in the refrigerator.

Preheat the oven to 200°C.

Divide the pastry into two portions, one slightly larger than the other. Roll out the larger portion and use it to line a 20 cm pie plate. Pour in the cooled syrup mixture and sprinkle the walnuts on top. Roll out the remaining pastry and cover the pie, crimping the edges to seal. Cut a few slashes in the centre of the pastry lid to allow steam to escape. Bake in the centre of the oven for 30 minutes.

Serve warm or at room temperature with a bowl of whipped cream if liked.

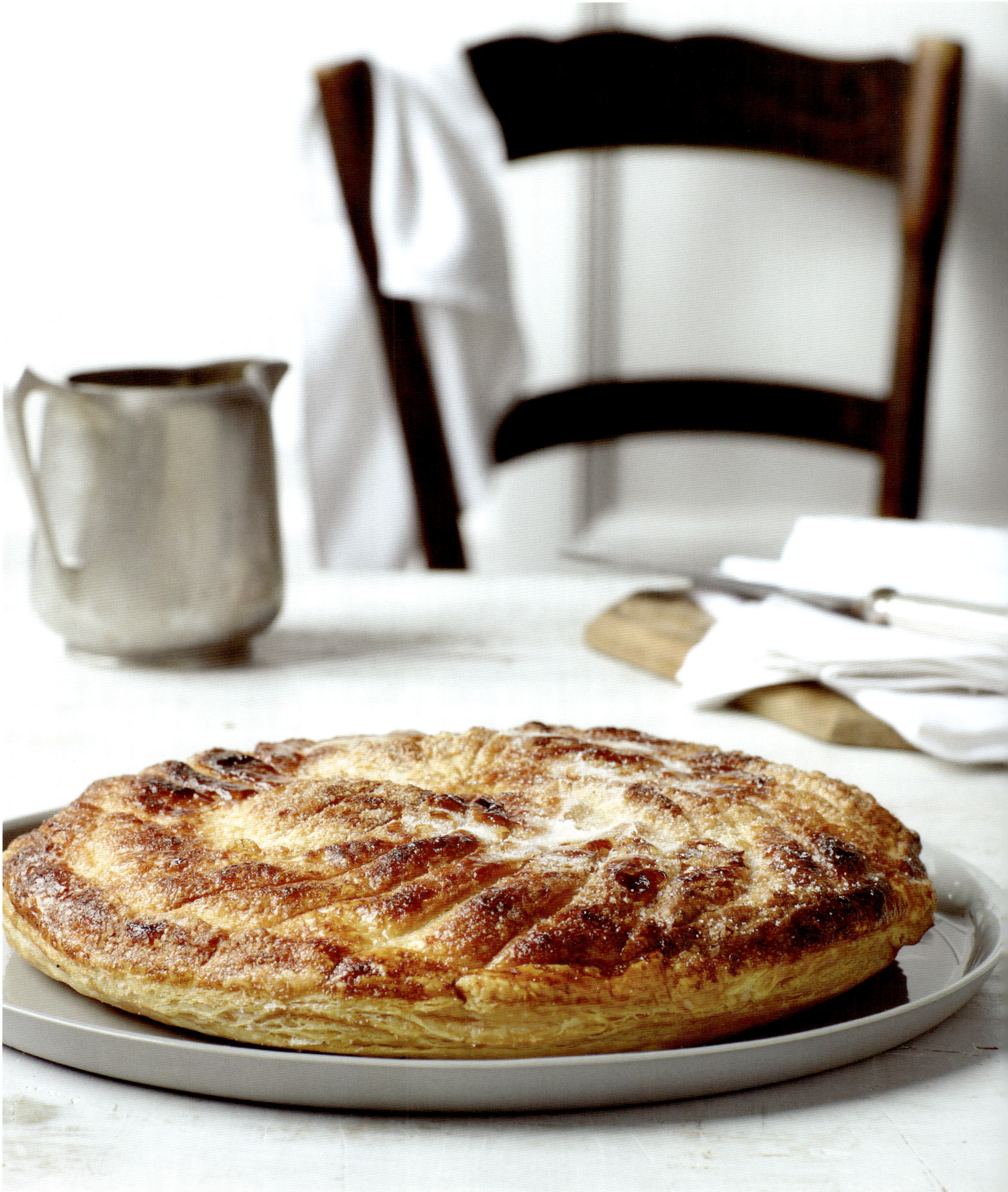

INGREDIENTS

2 sheets frozen puff pastry made with butter, just thawed
1 egg, beaten with ¼ teaspoon salt, to glaze
caster sugar to dust

ALMOND FILLING

125 g unsalted butter, softened
½ cup (110 g) sugar
1 egg
1 egg yolk
125 g whole blanched almonds, freshly ground (see Tip)
1 tablespoon plain flour
2 tablespoons rum

GATEAU DE PITHIVIERS

In France, a version of this cake is made flatter and known as galette des rois (cake of kings). This is a traditional Epiphany cake served on Twelfth Night (6 January), but it's usually available in pâtisseries from Christmas until the end of January. Traditionally a dried bean or silver trinket would be hidden in the almond paste, and the cake accompanied by a cardboard crown. The lucky person who found the bean in their piece of cake would wear the crown for the day.

SERVES 8–10

METHOD

To prepare the filling, cream the butter in a bowl. Add the sugar and beat until soft and light. Beat in the egg and egg yolk. Stir in the almonds, flour and rum; don't beat the mixture at this point or the oil will be drawn out of the almonds.

Using a cake tin as a guide, use a sharp knife to cut out a 23 cm round from each pastry sheet. Place one round on a baking sheet and mound the filling in the centre, leaving a 2.5 cm border. Brush the border with the egg glaze. Roll out the other round slightly so it is slightly larger than the first, lay it on top and press the edges together firmly.

Brush the gâteau with the egg glaze and, working from the centre, score the top in curves like the petals of a flower without cutting through to the filling.

Chill for 15–20 minutes.

Preheat the oven to 220°C. Pierce a few holes in the centre of the gâteau to allow steam to escape. Sprinkle it with sugar or icing sugar and bake for 20–25 minutes, or until puffed and brown on top. Lower the oven temperature to 200°C and continue baking for 15–20 minutes or until firm, lightly browned on the sides and glazed with melted sugar on top. If the sugar has not melted by the time the pastry is cooked, grill it quickly (watching it carefully) until shiny.

Cool the gateau on a wire rack. Serve warm or at room temperature.

TIP To freshly grind the almonds I use a small nut mill that I have had for years. The next best thing is a coffee grinder, kept especially for grinding nuts, or a food processor. Roughly chop the nuts first by hand, then grind using the pulse button, though not too finely. Little bits of almond give the filling a pleasing texture.

INGREDIENTS
1 quantity Plain Rich Shortcrust Pastry (page 329)
60 g butter, softened
3 tablespoons caster sugar
1 egg
4 tablespoons ground almonds
a few drops of vanilla or almond essence
raspberry jam or 500 g stewed fresh apple, pear or plum
extra caster sugar to sprinkle

BAKEWELL TART

This very old English recipe – originally called Bakewell pudding, after the town in Derbyshire – has many variations. The mixture can be baked in one large tart shell, as here, or in small tart cases.

SERVES 6–8

METHOD

Roll out the pastry and use it to line a 20 cm flan tin. Chill for about 20 minutes.

Bake blind (see page 326) for 15 minutes in a preheated 190°C oven. Remove the pastry from the oven and increase the oven temperature to 220°C.

Meanwhile, using an elelctric mixer, cream the butter and gradually beat in the sugar until the mixture is light and fluffy. Beat in the egg, then add the almonds and essence. Beat well.

Spread the partially baked pastry case with the fruit, straining off as much of the juice as possible, or with enough raspberry jam to cover the base. Spread the almond mixture on top.

Bake for about 30 minutes until golden brown. Sprinkle with the extra caster sugar. Serve cool.

INGREDIENTS
1 quantity Plain Rich Shortcrust Pastry (page 329)
1½ cups fresh breadcrumbs or plain cake crumbs
1 cup golden syrup
1 teaspoon ground ginger
1 egg, beaten
grated rind and juice of ½ lemon

RICH TREACLE TART

SERVES 6

METHOD
Preheat the oven to 200°C.

Roll out the pastry dough and use it to line a 22–23 cm pie plate. Chill for 20 minutes, then bake blind (see page 326) for 15 minutes.

Combine the remaining ingredients and pour into the pastry case. Use any remaining pastry to decorate the tart with a lattice design (see page 347).

Reduce the oven temperature to 180°C and bake for a further 35–40 minutes. Allow to cool, during which time the filling will set.

VARIATION
TREACLE AND COCONUT TART Make as above, then spread about ⅓ cup dessicated coconut over the filling before adding the lattice crust.

INGREDIENTS

1 cup milk
1 tablespoon powdered gelatine
100 g dark chocolate, chopped
¾ cup (165 g) caster sugar
¼ teaspoon salt
4 eggs, separated
1 teaspoon vanilla essence
2 tablespoons instant coffee powder
one 23 cm Sweet Rich Shortcrust Pastry shell (page 329), baked
sweetened whipped cream to serve (optional)
shaved chocolate, freshly grated nutmeg, chopped candied ginger, flaked coconut or chopped nuts to decorate (optional)

MOCHA CHIFFON PIE

An American tart of lightly set creamy mousse piled into a baked pastry shell and chilled until firm. I like it served with cream, then topped with shaved chocolate, candied ginger or chopped nuts.

SERVES 6–8

METHOD

Put the milk in a small heavy saucepan. Sprinkle the gelatine on the milk and allow to soften for 5 minutes.

Add the chocolate and stir over medium heat until it has melted and the gelatine has dissolved.

Beat ¼ cup (55 g) of the sugar and the salt with the egg yolks. Beat in the chocolate milk and pour back into the double saucepan. Put over simmering water and cook, stirring constantly, until the mixture is thickened and coats a metal spoon. Remove from the heat and add the vanilla and coffee. Chill until thickened but not firm.

Beat the egg whites until foamy. Gradually add the remaining sugar, beating until stiff but not dry. Fold into the gelatine mixture. Pile the filling lightly into the pastry shell and chill until firm.

Serve plain, or spread with sweetened whipped cream. If desired, sprinkle with shaved chocolate, freshly grated nutmeg, chopped candied ginger, flaked coconut or chopped nuts.

PASTRY *cream & cheese tarts*

INGREDIENTS
double quantity Sweet Flan Pastry (page 331)
2 cups (440 g) firmly packed brown sugar
1 cup cream
30 g butter
¼ teaspoon vanilla essence
a pinch of salt
2 eggs, beaten

BROWN SUGAR TART

SERVES 6–8

METHOD
Preheat the oven to 200°C.

Use two thirds of the pastry dough to line a 23 cm loose-based flan tin.

Combine the brown sugar and cream in a medium saucepan and bring to the boil, stirring. Simmer gently for about 15 minutes. Remove the pan from the heat and stir in the butter, vanilla and salt. Let the mixture cool to lukewarm.

Add the eggs and beat until well blended. Pour into the tart shell. Roll out the remaining one-third of the dough, then cut into strips. Arrange strips lattice-fashion over tart (see page 347), pressing lightly at the ends to join them to the sides of the base pastry.

Bake for 20–25 minutes or until the pastry is cooked and the filling is barely set. Cool on a wire rack.

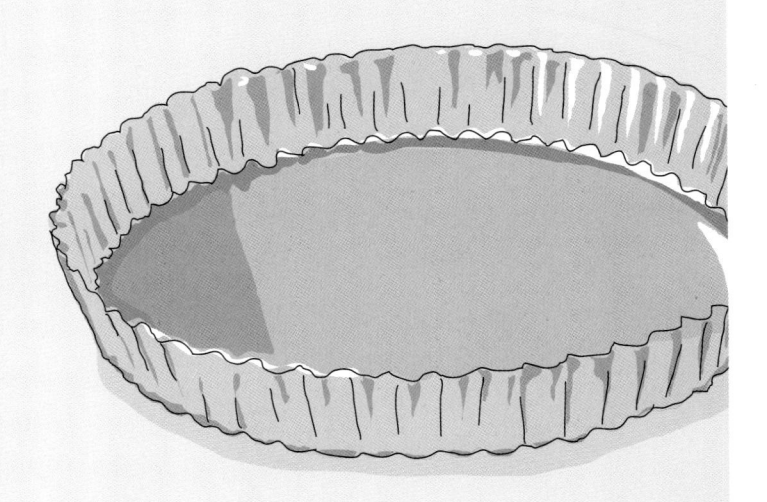

INGREDIENTS

1 quantity Sweet Flan Pastry (page 331)
125 g unsalted butter, softened
½ cup (110 g) caster sugar
250 g cream cheese, softened
2 eggs, beaten
a pinch of ground nutmeg
sifted icing sugar to dust

CREAM CHEESE TART

A very simple tart using cream cheese for a smooth texture. The only seasoning is nutmeg, so for the most aromatic and flavourful result, grate whole nutmeg yourself using a small tin grater or a rotary grater of the type used for parmesan cheese.

SERVES 6

METHOD

Preheat the oven to 190°C.

Roll out the pastry dough and use to line a 20 cm loose-based flan tin. Chill for 20 minutes.

Cream the butter with the sugar until light and fluffy. Add the cream cheese, beating until it is light and fluffy. Beat in the eggs little by little. Spread the mixture in the tart shell and sprinkle with nutmeg.

Bake for 30 minutes or until the filling is puffed and golden and the pastry is a pale gold. Protect the sides with crumpled foil if the pastry is browning too much.

Serve warm or cold, with icing sugar sifted over the top.

PASTRY *cream & cheese tarts*

INGREDIENTS

125 g butter, softened
1/3 cup (75 g) caster sugar
1 egg yolk
1 cup (150 g) plain flour
1/2 cup (75 g) self-raising flour
1 tablespoon cornflour

FILLING

3 eggs, sseparated
1/3 cup (75 g) caster sugar
3 teaspoons powdered gelatine
1/4 cup cold water
1 cup hot milk
300 ml cream, whipped
2 tablespoons rum
whipped cream to decorate
ground nutmeg to sprinkle

EGGNOG TART

SERVES 8

METHOD

Cream the butter and sugar well, add the egg yolk and beat in. Sift in the flours and cornflour and mix lightly. Knead, cover in plastic wrap and chill for 1 hour.

Roll out the pastry and use it to line a 23 cm tart plate or loose-based flan tin. Prick the base all over with a fork to prevent rising. Chill again for about 30 minutes.

Preheat the oven to 190°C. Line the tart shell with baking paper and half-fill with pie weights or dried beans. Bake blind (see page 326) for 15 minutes. Remove the paper and beans, reduce the oven temperature to 180°C and bake for a further 5–10 minutes or until the crust is golden. Remove to a wire rack and allow to cool.

To make the filling, beat the egg yolks and sugar in a double boiler over gentle heat until thick and pale. Soak the gelatine for 5 minutes in the water and milk and stir it into the mixture. Continue to cook, stirring constantly, until smooth. Stir the mixture over ice until it is cool and begins to set. Fold in the whipped cream.

Beat the egg whites until soft peaks form and fold in the custard with the rum. Spoon into the tart shell. Chill until set. Decorate with whipped cream and sprinkle with nutmeg to serve.

INGREDIENTS

4 cups milk
¾ cup (165 g) caster sugar
¾ cup fine semolina
1 cinnamon stick
1 teaspoon grated lemon rind
a pinch of salt
5 eggs, lightly beaten
1 teaspoon vanilla essence
250 g filo pastry
185 g unsalted butter, melted

SYRUP

1 cup water
1 cup (220 g) caster sugar
1 cinnamon stick
1 tablespoon lemon juice
1 strip lemon rind

GREEK CUSTARD PIE

SERVES 10–12

METHOD

Combine the milk, sugar, semolina, cinnamon, lemon rind and salt in a heavy saucepan and stir over low heat until thickened. Simmer for 5 minutes, then remove from the heat. Discard the cinnamon stick. Cover the surface of the mixture with plastic wrap to prevent a skin from forming, and allow to cool.

Preheat the oven to 180°C.

Lightly whisk the eggs and vanilla in a bowl and stir in the cooled milk mixture. Stack the sheets of filo between two dry tea towels with a dampened towel on top. Place one sheet of filo in a greased 33 cm x 23 cm ovenproof dish and brush it with melted butter. Repeat until you have used half the filo.

Pour in the custard mixture and top with the remaining filo, brushing each sheet with butter before it is placed in position. Trim the edges of the filo to fit the dish and brush the top with the remaining butter.

With a sharp knife, cut through the top three sheets of filo in a diamond pattern. Bake for 45 minutes or until the pastry is golden brown and a thin knife inserted into the custard comes out clean. Remove from the oven and cool in the dish.

To make the syrup, place all the ingredients in a saucepan and bring to the boil, stirring until all the sugar has dissolved. Boil over moderate heat for 10 minutes without letting it colour, then strain and cool to lukewarm. When the pie is cold, pour over the lukewarm syrup and leave to cool completely before serving.

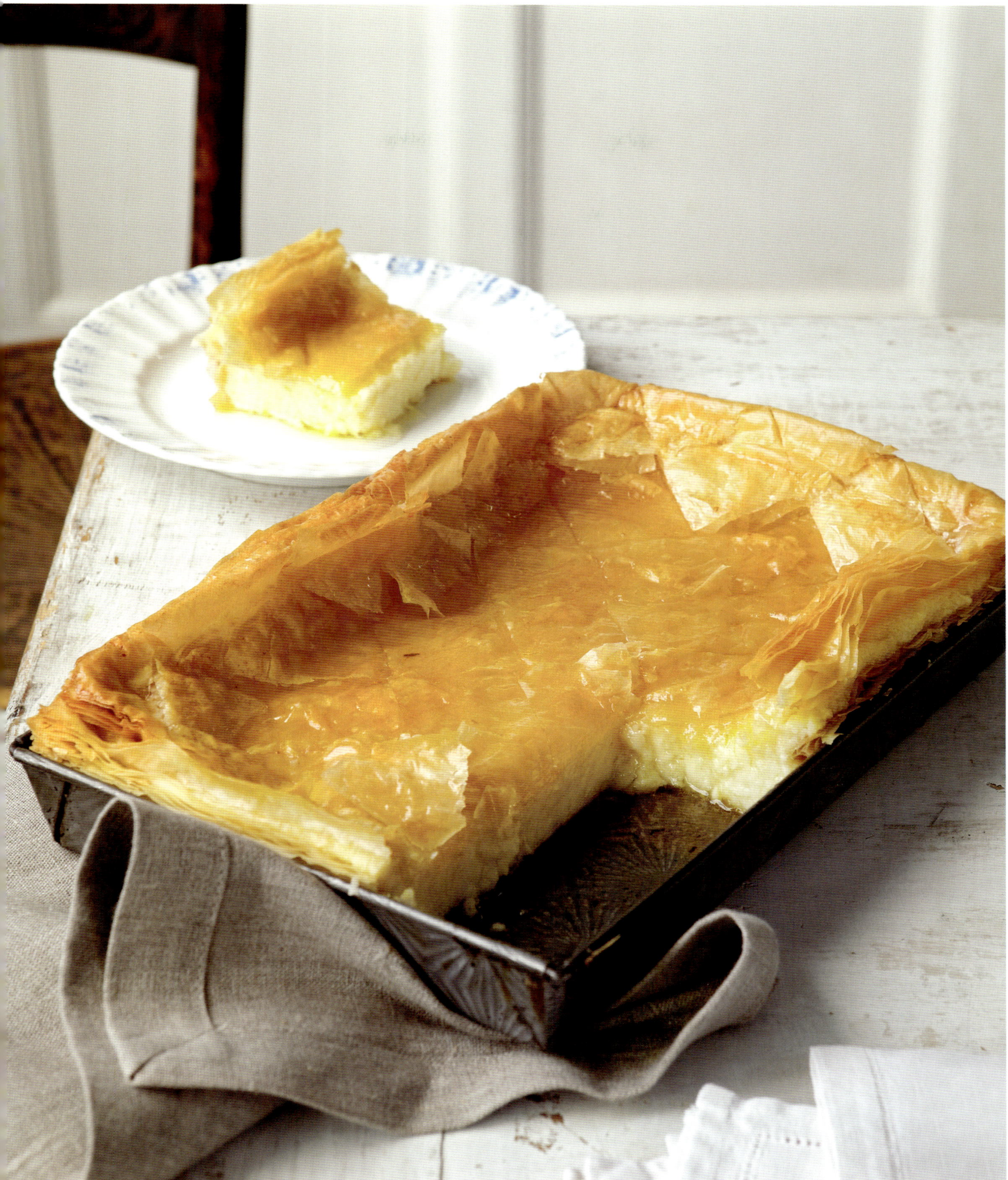

BASIC PROFITEROLES

MAKES ABOUT SIXTEEN 5 CM PROFITEROLES

INGREDIENTS

1 quantity sweetened or unsweetened Choux Pastry (page 332)
1 egg
a pinch of salt
2 cups Crème Pâtissière (page 338) or flavoured whipped cream to fill the profiteroles

METHOD

Preheat the oven to 230°C. Lightly grease a baking tray.

Using a piping bag fitted with a 1 cm plain tube, pipe choux pastry into small, high mounds, well apart, on the prepared tray. Pipe each mound with one steady pressure, and release the pressure before lifting the bag away, to avoid a long tail. For 5 cm profiteroles, make mounds about 3 cm in diameter.

Alternatively, take spoonfuls of the pastry and, with another spoon, push them off onto the baking tray. Do not try to change the shape of the choux pastry when putting it out, or it will rise in bumpy shapes instead of round ones.

Beat the egg with the salt and brush over the pastry mounds, pushing down the tails (the egg glaze may be omitted if the puffs are to be iced; just push down the tails with a damp finger).

Bake for 10 minutes. Reduce the oven temperature to 180°C and bake for a further 15–20 minutes or until the profiteroles are golden brown, firm and light in the hand. If the pastry is becoming too brown before it is cooked through, cover loosely with a sheet of foil.

Make a slit or hole with the point of a knife in the side of each profiterole. Return to the turned-off oven and leave with the door ajar for 20 minutes to ensure that the puffs are thoroughly dried out (this is the secret of puffs that will hold their shape without collapsing). Cool on a wire rack.

Fill by piping the desired filling through the holes in the sides, or by carefully cutting off the tops with a serrated knife, spooning in the filling and replacing the lids. Unfilled profiteroles will keep in an airtight container for 1–2 weeks.

VARIATIONS

CHOCOLATE PROFITEROLES Fill Basic Profiteroles with either 2 cups Crème Pâtissiere (page 338) or 1 cup cream that has been whipped with 2 teaspoons icing sugar and a few drops of vanilla essence. Pile into a serving dish and sift a little more icing sugar over the top. To make the hot chocolate sauce, break 185 g dark chocolate into pieces and place in a heatproof bowl with ½ cup water and 1 tablespoon rum or brandy (optional). Set the bowl over a saucepan of simmering water and stir until the chocolate melts. Cook for 1 minute longer, then pour the sauce into a heated jug and serve with the profiteroles (see page 384). Serves 6–8.

COFFEE PROFITEROLES Dissolve 1 teaspoon instant coffee powder in 2 teaspoons hot water and allow to cool. Whip 1 cup cream with 2 teaspoons sifted icing sugar, the coffee and 2 teaspoons brandy or whisky (optional). Fill Basic Profiteroles with this mixture and ice tops with 1 quantity Coffee Glacé Icing (page 252). Serves 6–8.

PRALINE PROFITEROLES Whip 1 cup cream and mix with ½ cup Crème Pâtissière (page 338) and 2 tablespoons Praline (right). Fill Basic Profiteroles with this mixture and sift a little icing sugar over the tops. Serves 6–8.

ORANGE PROFITEROLES Rub 3 sugar cubes over the rind of 1 orange until the sugar is saturated with orange oils. Squeeze the juice from half the orange, and pound the sugar cubes with 2 teaspoons of the juice until dissolved. Whip 1 cup cream with this orange syrup and 2 teaspoons brandy (optional). Use to fill Basic Profiteroles. To make the toffee topping, slowly cook 90 g caster sugar in a small, heavy saucepan, tilting the pan frequently from side to side so that the sugar heats evenly, until it melts and caramelises to a golden brown. Dip the base of the saucepan in cold water to stop further cooking. Dip the top of each profiterole in the toffee and place on a wire rack to set. Serves 6–8.

CREAM PUFFS Whip 1 cup cream with 1 tablespoon icing sugar and a few drops of vanilla essence. Fill Basic Profiteroles with this mixture and sift more icing sugar over the tops. Serves 6–8.

PRALINE

Praline is a confection of caramelised sugar and almonds, crushed or ground to a fine powder. Equal quantities of sugar and almonds are used. Sometimes about half the almonds are replaced by hazelnuts, but the method remains the same, as do the uses for the final product. Praline may be sprinkled on ice cream, a cold or hot soufflé or custard; added to a butter cream or crème pâtissière, to fill cakes and cream puffs; or used to decorate the top and sides of large cakes. Praline keeps well in an airtight container; it may also be stored in the freezer.

To make praline, cook 250 g caster sugar and 250 g whole unblanched almonds in a heavy-based saucepan over low heat until the sugar melts, turning the nuts over to brown evenly. Continue cooking until the sugar has become nut brown in colour. Pour into an oiled tin or plate. Allow to become quite cold and hard, then break into small pieces and crush with a rolling pin, or grind in a blender or nut mill. Store in an airtight container, or in the freezer. Makes about 1 cup.

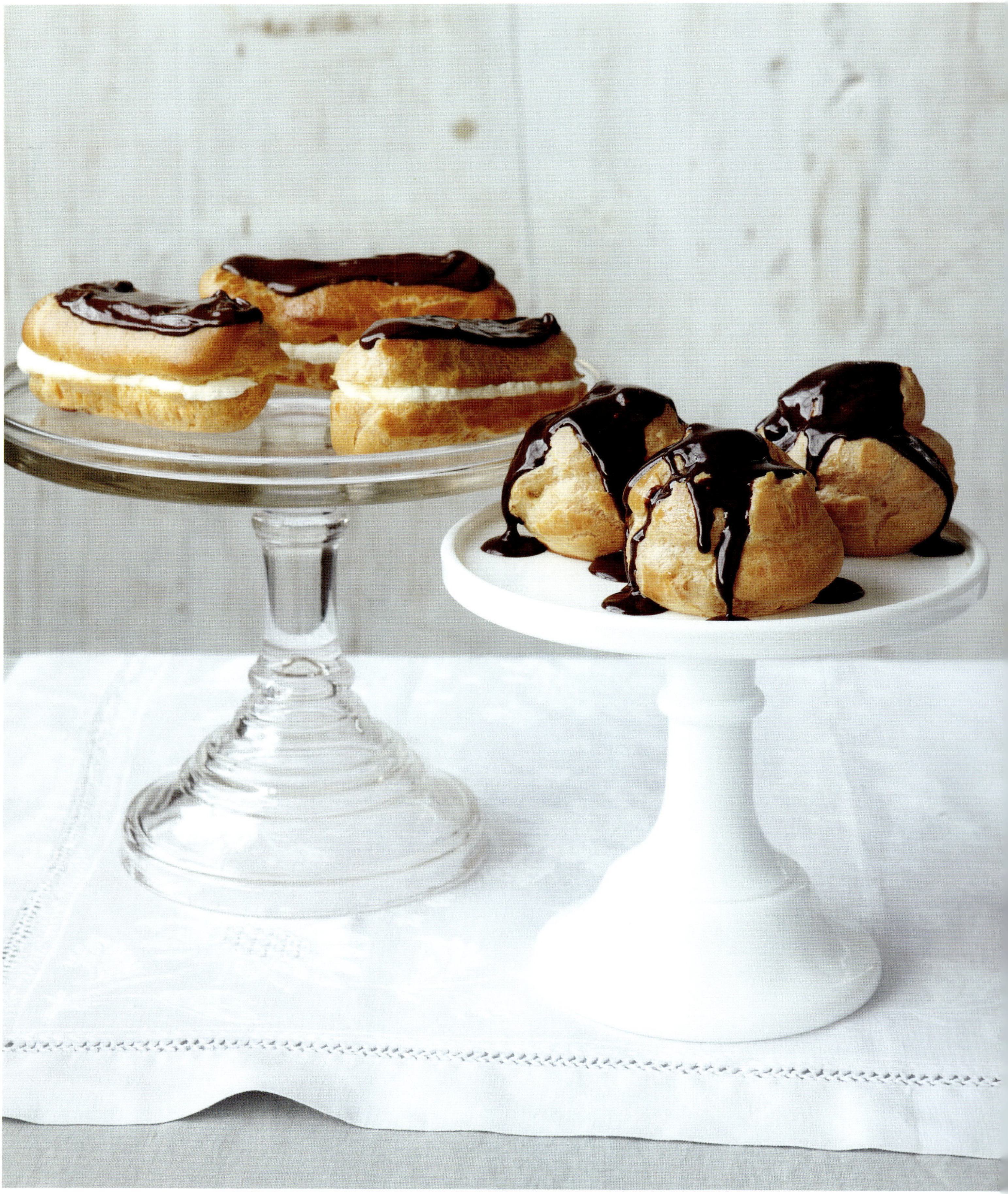

PASTRY *sweet tartlets & pastries*

INGREDIENTS
1 quantity sweetened Choux Pastry (page 332)
1 cup cream
1 teaspoon caster sugar

GLOSSY CHOCOLATE ICING
200 g dark chocolate, chopped
50 ml cream
1 tablespoon vegetable oil

CHOCOLATE ÉCLAIRS

Éclairs – finger-shaped puffs of choux pastry filled with whipped cream or sometimes flavoured Crème Pâtissière (page 338) – make one of the most delicate confections for afternoon tea or dessert. Served with profiteroles, they can make for a very pretty and decadent afternoon tea.

MAKES ABOUT 12

METHOD

Preheat the oven to 230°C. Grease two baking trays.

Spoon the choux pastry into a large piping bag fitted with a 1 cm plain tube. Pipe the mixture into 8 cm lengths about 5 cm apart on the prepared baking trays. Bake for 12 minutes, then reduce the oven temperature to 180°C and bake for a further 15–20 minutes or until golden brown, firm and light in the hand.

Slit each éclair along the side, turn off the oven and leave the éclairs in the oven to cool for 20 minutes with the door half open. Remove and cool completely on a wire rack.

When cold, whip the cream with the sugar and use to fill the éclairs.

To make the icing, put the chocolate and cream in a small heavy pan over low heat and stir until melted and smooth, Remove from the heat and stir in the oil. Spread over the tops of the éclairs and leave to set.

VARIATIONS

RASPBERRY OR STRAWBERRY ÉCLAIRS Make as for Chocolate Éclairs but fill with whole raspberries or sliced strawberries and whipped cream. Ice with Lemon Glacé Icing (page 252) tinted pink.

COFFEE ÉCLAIRS Make as for Chocolate Éclairs but fill with whipped cream flavoured with 1 tablespoon coffee liqueur, and ice with Coffee Glacé Icing (page 252).

GÂTEAU ST HONORÉ

INGREDIENTS
½ quantity Sweet Flan Pastry (page 331)
1 egg, beaten, to glaze
1 quantity Choux Pastry (page 332)

CHOUX PUFF FILLING
½ cup cream
vanilla essence

CARAMEL
1 cup (220 g) caster sugar
½ cup water

CRÈME ST HONORÉ
1 egg, separated
1 egg yolk
¼ cup (55 g) caster sugar
2 tablespoons plain flour
1 tablespoon cornflour
1½ cups milk
1 vanilla bean, scraped
½ cup cream

SERVES 10–12

METHOD

Preheat the oven to 200°C. Grease a baking tray. Roll out the sweet flan pastry to a 20 cm round and place on the prepared tray. Prick well with a fork and brush the edge with beaten egg.

Fill a piping bag fitted with a 1 cm plain tube with choux pastry. Pipe a border around the edge of the sweet flan pastry round, 5 mm in from outside to allow for spreading. Brush with beaten egg.

Pipe the remaining choux onto a greased baking tray in 14 small rounds the size of a walnut. Brush with beaten egg. Bake all the pastry for about 25 minutes for the choux puffs and about 30 minutes for the pastry base or until crisp and golden. Remove from the oven. Prick the base of each choux puff two or three times to allow steam to escape and cool on a wire rack.

Meanwhile, make the crème St Honoré. Beat the egg yolks with the sugar until creamy and very light in colour. Mix the flour and cornflour with a little cold milk to make a smooth paste and add to the egg yolk mixture. Scald the remaining milk with the vanilla bean, strain onto the egg yolk mixture, blend and return to the saucepan. Stir over a gentle heat until the the mixture boils.

Whisk the egg white until peaks form, add a little of the hot custard, mix thoroughly and pour back into the pan. Stir gently over low heat for 2–3 minutes. Chill. Whip the cream and fold through just before serving.

For the choux puff filling, whip the cream, flavour with vanilla essence and put in a piping bag. Cut a tiny hole in the side of each puff with the point of a knife and force in the cream through the hole.

For the caramel syrup, in a small heavy-based saucepan heat the sugar with the water until dissolved. Bring to the boil and boil, without stirring, until golden. Spoon a little caramel syrup onto the choux pastry rim and secure choux puffs on top. Fill the centre of the gâteau with crème St Honoré.

Return the caramel to the heat and cook until it is a rich amber colour. Immediately transfer the saucepan into cold water to prevent further cooking. Spoon over the puffs.

For a spectacular effect, dip two spoons into caramel, then pull and spin caramel strands around the gâteau. Serve immediately.

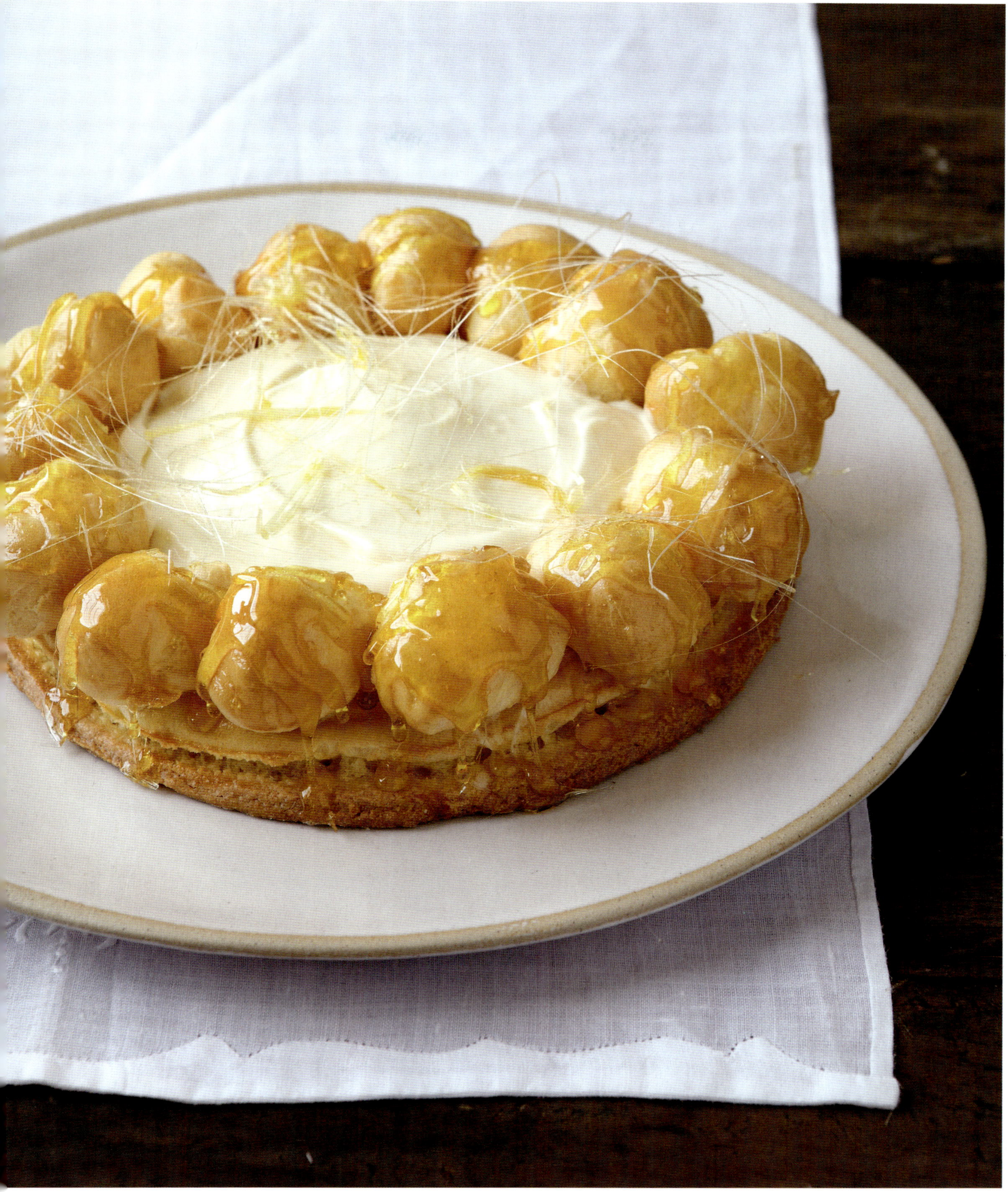

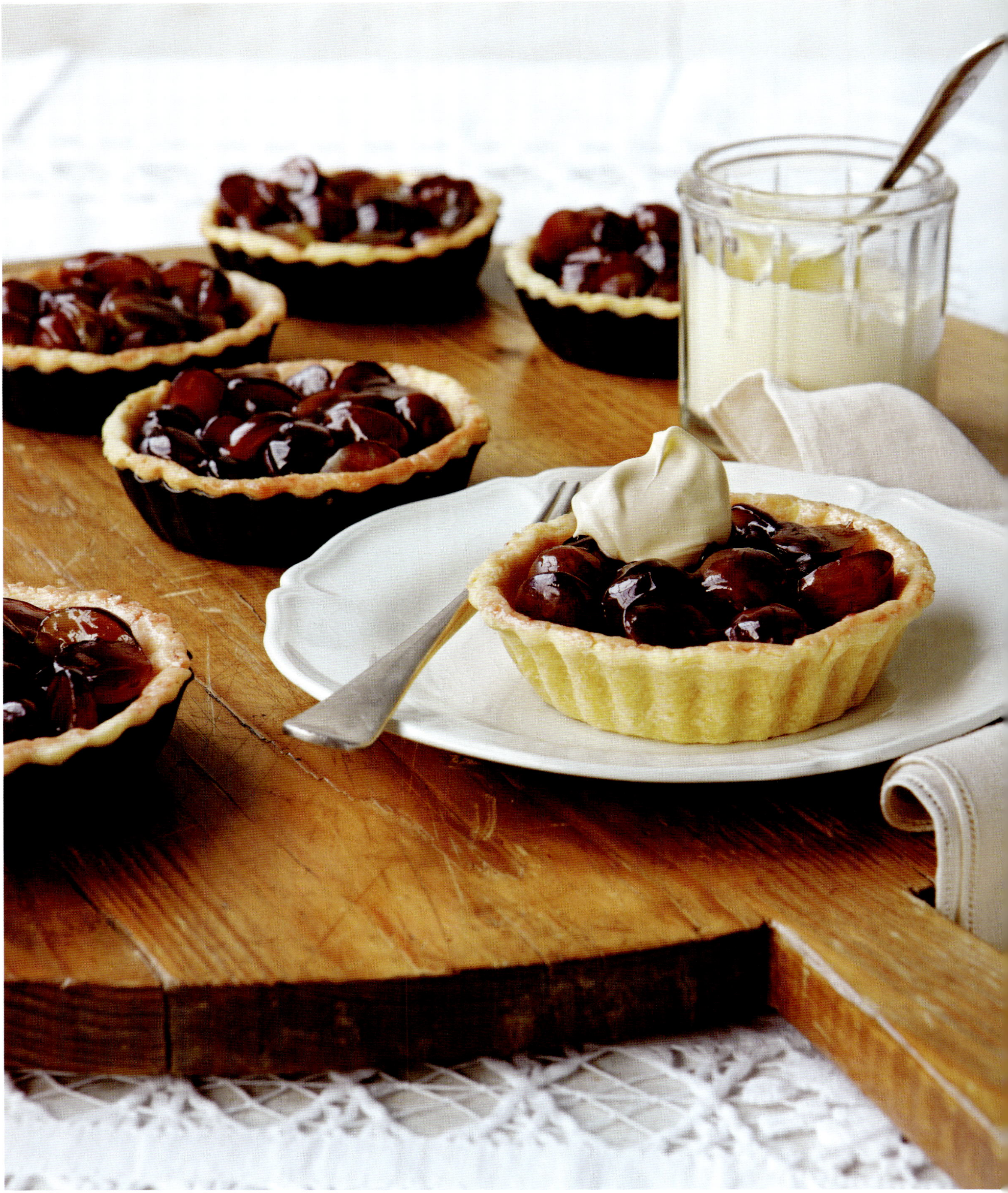

PASTRY *sweet tartlets & pastries*

INGREDIENTS

1½ quantities Sweet Flan Pastry (page 331)
500 g fresh fruit in season (see Variations)

GLAZE

1 cup sieved jam (use apricot for pale fruits and redcurrant for red fruits)
3 tablespoons water
1 tablespoon lemon juice

FRUIT TARTLETS

MAKES 6 LARGE OR 12 SMALL TARTLETS

METHOD

Roll out the pastry dough thinly and use to line six 8 cm tartlet tins. Chill for about 20 minutes. Prick the bottom of each tartlet with a fork and chill for a further 20 minutes.

Preheat the oven to 190°C. Blind bake the tartlet cases (see page 326) for 8–10 minutes or until the pastry is a pale biscuit colour. Do not allow to brown. Cool. To prepare the fruits for the tarts, see Variations.

To make the glaze, heat all the ingredients over gentle heat, stirring until the glaze hangs in heavy drops from the spoon. Brush the tartlet shells with the hot glaze. Pile the fruit into the tartlet shells and brush the fruit carefully with glaze until it glistens. Allow to set.

VARIATIONS

STRAWBERRIES Wash, dry carefully and hull. They can be left whole if small, or sliced or halved.

APRICOTS, PEACHES AND PLUMS Poach in a light syrup (½ cup/110 g caster sugar dissolved in 1 cup water) until just tender. Drain. Slit and remove stones. Small fruits may be used whole, larger fruits should be sliced or halved. Good-quality canned fruit may also be used.

GRAPES Wash, halve if desired and seed if necessary.

PEARS If using ripe pears, peel, slice finely and arrange in the tartlet shells. Brush with a little lemon juice to prevent discolouring. If the pears are not quite ripe, peel and poach in a light syrup until tender. Drain before slicing.

RHUBARB Use young rhubarb; wash well and cut into 4 cm lengths. Poach in a light syrup (½ cup/110 g caster sugar dissolved in 1 cup water) until tender but still holding its shape, and drain well.

MANDARINS Peel, remove outside skins with a sharp knife and cut between membranes to separate skinless segments. Dry segments on paper towels before using.

CHERRIES Wash, then remove stones with a cherry stoner, or halve cherries and lift stones out with a small sharp knife. Dry before placing in tartlet shells.

HOT APPLE TARTS

INGREDIENTS
375 g packet frozen puff pastry, thawed (see Tip)
4-6 eating apples such as red or golden delicious, peeled and cored
½ cup (110 g) caster sugar
125 g butter
a little warmed honey
whipped cream or crème fraîche to serve

SERVES 6

METHOD
Preheat the oven to 220°C. Dampen a baking tray.

Roll out the pastry dough thinly on a floured work surface. With a 15 cm round cutter or saucer, cut out six rounds. Turn the rounds over onto the prepared baking tray and chill for 30 minutes.

Slice the apples downwards very thinly. Arrange on the pastry rounds in overlapping rows. Sprinkle with the sugar and dot with butter. Bake for 20–25 minutes or until the apples and pastry are golden. Brush the tops with honey, and serve warm with chilled crème fraîche.

TIP If you can't find a block of puff pastry, use ready-rolled puff pastry sheets.

INGREDIENTS
1 cup (220 g) caster sugar
½ cup water
2 sheets ready-rolled puff pastry
3 medium mangoes
whipped or thick (double) cream to serve

CARAMELISED MANGO TARTLETS

These tartlets are simple to make and always a great success. They can be made with any soft fruit in season; peaches and nectarines are particularly good.

SERVES 6

METHOD

To make the caramel, put the sugar and water in a saucepan and heat gently until dissolved, stirring occasionally. Bring to the boil, without stirring, until the mixture starts to turn golden around the edge. (Do not stir the sugar while boiling as it may crystallise). Lower the heat and continue cooking until the caramel is golden.

Remove the saucepan from the heat and place the base of the saucepan into a bowl of cold water until the cooking stops. Pour the caramel into six individual pie tins, swirling quickly so the bottom is coated with a thin, even layer. Allow to cool.

Peel the mangoes with a small sharp knife. Cut each mango lengthwise on both sides of the stone. Cut each mango cheek into three slices. Arrange three slices per pie dish, cut side up, on top of the caramel.

Lay the pastry on a floured surface and cut it into six circles with a 12 cm biscuit cutter. Drape the rounds over the pie dishes and tuck the edge down around the mango slices. Chill for 15 minutes.

Preheat the oven to 200˚C.

Bake the tartlets on a baking tray for 20–25 minutes or until the pastry is golden brown. Allow to cool in the dishes for 2–3 minutes. Invert each tartlet onto a serving plate and serve with a dollop of cream.

INGREDIENTS

1 quantity Biscuit Pastry (page 331)
2–3 firm ripe pears
lemon juice
¾ cup (165 g) caster sugar
½–1 cup water
1 strip lemon rind
½ quantity Crème Pâtissiere (page 338)

INDIVIDUAL PEAR TARTS

An example of the simple yet impressive French way with fruit tarts. The fruit is arranged in a way that shows its lovely shape, over a layer of delicious crème pâtissière.

SERVES 6–8

METHOD

Roll out the pastry dough and use to line six or eight 10 cm loose-based individual flan tins. Chill for 30 minutes.

Preheat the oven to 180°C.

Bake the chilled tart cases blind (page 326) for 8 minutes. Remove the lining paper and rice or beans, return to the oven and bake for a further 5–10 minutes or until the shells are golden. Remove from the oven and allow to cool.

Peel, halve and core the pears. Brush each pear half with lemon juice as it is prepared, to prevent discolouration. Put the sugar, water and lemon rind into a heavy-based saucepan and bring to the boil. Add the pears, cover tightly and poach gently (just below a simmer) for 8–10 minutes or until the pears are just tender. Remove the saucepan from the heat and cool the pears in the syrup for 20 minutes. Remove them and drain on a cloth.

Spread a layer of crème pâtissière in each tart shell. On a board, place each pear half, cut side down, and cut lengthways into slices. Spread over the pastry cream in a tart shell, fanning the slices out.

Boil down the remaining poaching syrup until it is sticky, and brush over the pears. Warm the tarts slightly in a 120°C oven before serving.

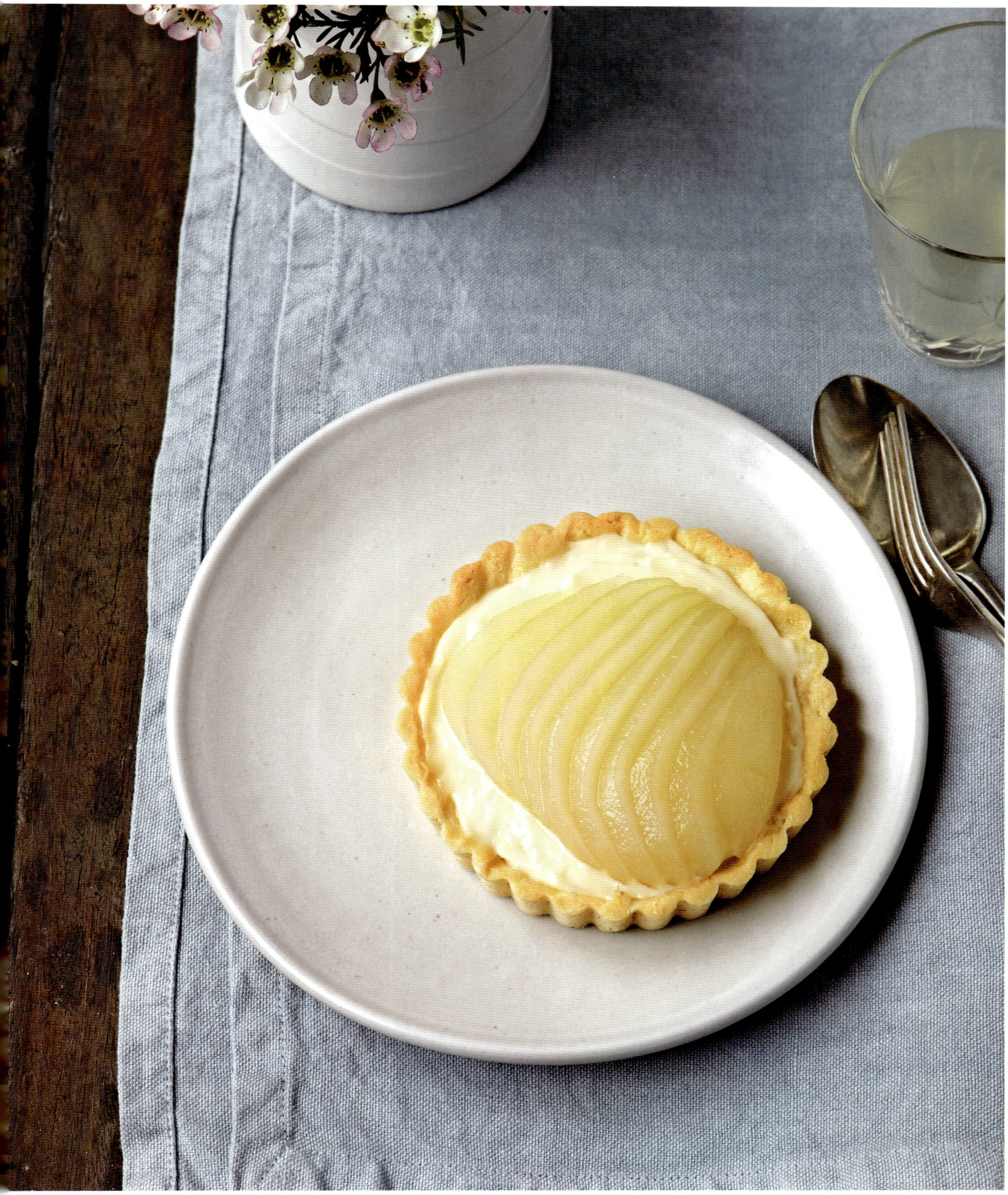

CHRISTMAS MINCE PIES

INGREDIENTS
PASTRY
2 cups (300 g) plain flour
¼ teaspoon baking powder
185 g unsalted butter, diced
¼ cup (55 g) caster sugar
2 egg yolks
1–2 tablespoons lemon juice or iced water

1 cup Fruit Mincemeat (opposite)
1 egg white, lightly beaten
sifted icing sugar to dust (optional)

Little mince pies are a universal favourite at Christmas time. I make them by the dozen to offer when friends drop in over the festive season. They store and keep well and can be gently heated in the oven before serving. Dust with icing sugar just before serving, for a pretty finish.

MAKES 24

METHOD

Preheat the oven to 200°C. Grease two 12-hole small, rounded or shallow patty tins, or mini muffin tins.

Make the pastry by sifting the flour and baking powder into a bowl. Rub in the butter using your fingertips until the mixture resembles breadcrumbs. Stir in the sugar. Add the egg yolks and enough lemon juice or water to bring the ingredients together to form a dough.

Knead the dough gently on a lightly floured surface until smooth. Halve, wrap in plastic wrap and chill for at least 30 minutes.

Roll out one of the pastry portions between two sheets of baking paper until 3–5 mm thick. Using a 6.5 cm round cutter, cut out 12 rounds. Place the rounds into the prepared patty tins. Spoon 2 teaspoons of the fruit mince into each. Re-knead the scraps and chill before rolling out again and using to line more patty tins.

Repeat with the remaining dough, reserving some pastry for decorating the tops.

Re-roll scraps of pastry and cut into small stars. Top each pie with a star. Brush with egg white. Bake for 20 minutes, until golden. Leave to cool completely in the pans. Serve warm or at room temperature, dusted with a little icing sugar, if you like.

NOTE Mince pies can be made ahead, frozen and reheated for about 10 minutes in a 180°C oven as required.

FRUIT MINCEMEAT

INGREDIENTS

3 cups raisins
3 cups currants
3 cups sultanas
¾ cup blanched almonds, chopped
2 large cooking apples, grated
1½ cups (330 g) firmly packed brown sugar
150 g butter, melted
¾ cup brandy or rum
½ teaspoon grated nutmeg
½ teaspoon ground cloves
1 teaspoon ground cinnamon
grated rind and juice of 2 oranges

MAKES ABOUT 9 CUPS

METHOD

Working in batches, pulse the dried fruit and almonds in a food processor to coarsely chop.

Spoon into a bowl and combine with the grated apple, sugar, butter, brandy or rum, spices, rind and juice.

Cover and chill, stirring daily, for at least 2 days before use.

NOTE This fruit mince stores for months, kept airtight, in the refrigerator. Make it well ahead of time – at least a few days, and up to several months, before needed.

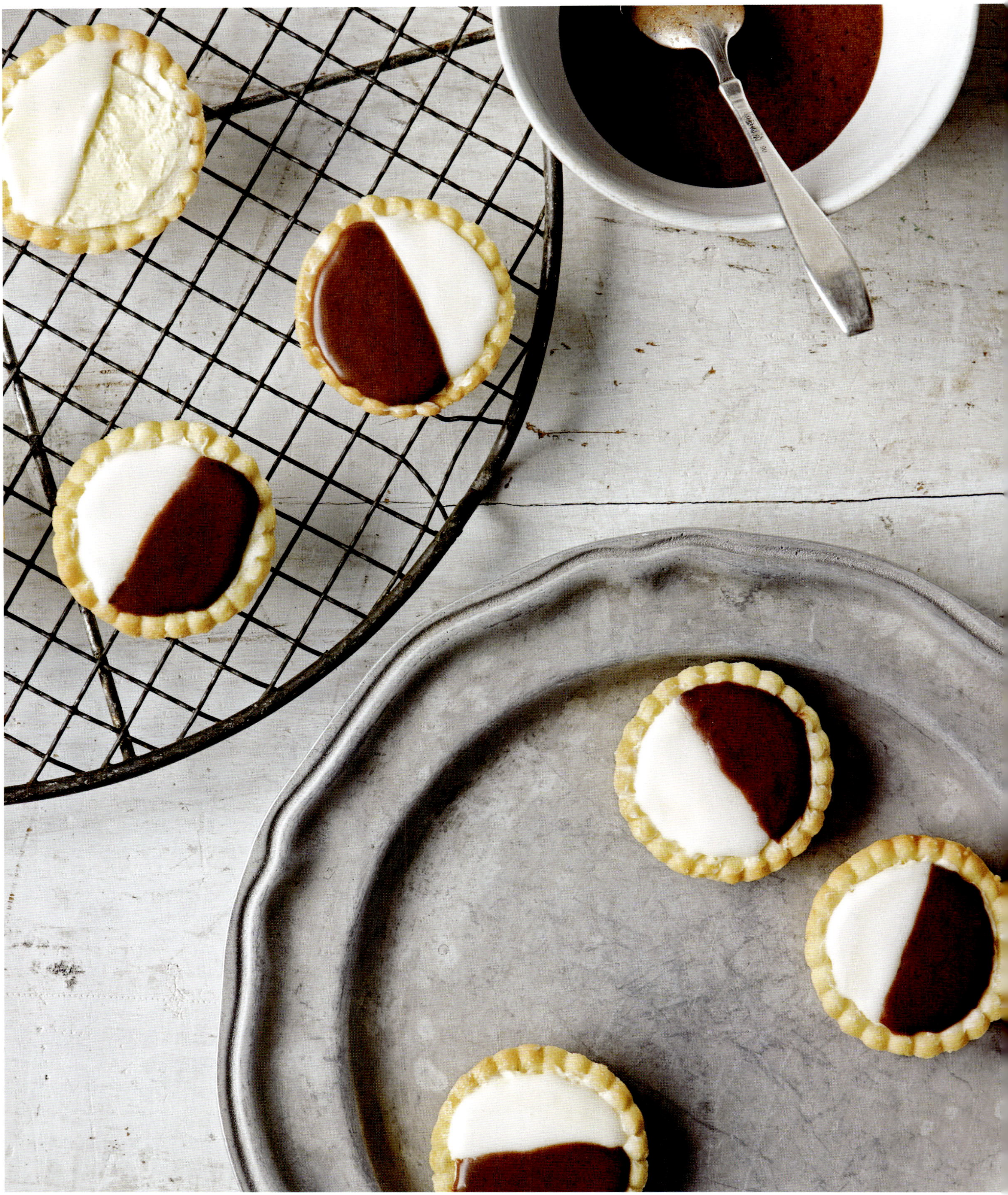

PASTRY *sweet tartlets & pastries*

INGREDIENTS

PASTRY
125 g butter, softened
½ cup (110 g) sugar
½ teaspoon almond essence
1 egg
1⅔ cups (250 g) plain flour, sifted
1 teaspoon baking powder
a pinch of salt

FILLING
90 g butter, softened
½ cup (80 g) icing sugar, sifted
3 tablespoons sweetened condensed milk
1 tablespoon lemon juice

ICING
1 cup (160 g) icing sugar
1 drop vanilla essence
1 tablespoon cocoa powder
1 teaspoon butter

NEENISH TARTS

MAKES 24

METHOD

To make the pastry, using an electric mixer, cream the butter with the sugar and almond essence until light and fluffy. Add the egg and beat well. Stir in the flour, baking powder and salt. Knead lightly, then form into a ball, wrap in plastic wrap and chill for 30 minutes.

Preheat the oven to 180°C. Grease two 12-hole shallow patty tins.

Roll out the pastry and cut into twenty-four 6 cm rounds. Fit into the prepared patty tins, prick lightly with a fork and chill for 20 minutes. Bake for 10–15 minutes or until a pale biscuit colour. Cool on wire racks.

To make the filling, beat the butter until fluffy, then beat in the icing sugar, condensed milk and lemon juice. Spoon into the cooled tarts, smooth flat with a palette knife and leave to set.

To make the icing, sift the icing sugar into a small heatproof bowl, add 1 tablespoon of hot water and heat over gently simmering water. Stir in the vanilla and when the icing will coat the back of a spoon, use it immediately to ice one half of each tart (see Tip).

Add the cocoa and butter to the remaining white icing in the bowl. Stand over simmering water and stir until the butter melts and the icing is smooth and glossy (you may have to beat in a little more hot water). Use at once to ice the other halves.

TIP To help make a clean line between the two icings, place a square of baking paper on top of one half so that the straight edge forms a guide for the white icing. Remove immediately. Repeat with all the white halves and leave to set completely. When adding the chocolate icing, tilt each tart as you ice so that the icing comes cleanly against the white edge.

INGREDIENTS

1 quantity Plain or Rich Shortcrust Pastry (page 328–329), Cream Cheese Pastry or Sour Cream Pastry (page 330), Rough Puff Pastry (page 334), or one 375 g (12 oz) packet frozen puff pastry, thawed
filling of your choice (see below)
lightly beaten egg or egg white
caster sugar (for sweet turnovers only)

TURNOVERS

A square or circle of pastry folded over a filling, a turnover is quicker and easier to make than a pie, is portable and is a treat for many occasions. Serve turnovers, large or small, sweet or savoury, as a main course or dessert, for picnics, packed lunches or as nibbles with drinks. Use plain or sweet shortcrust pastry, cream cheese or sour cream pastry, commercial or homemade flaky pastry or, speediest of all, frozen ready-rolled sheets of puff pastry. Turnovers can be baked or deep-fried. The filling must be completely cold when the pastry is folded around it.

MAKES ABOUT 12

METHOD

Roll out dough 5 mm thick and cut it into squares or circles of desired size. Mound your chosen cold filling (right) in the centre of one-half of each piece of pastry (if using squares of pastry, mound the filling in a corner so you end up with a triangular turnover.) Do not overfill; use about 1½ tablespoons filling for 10 cm turnovers, 1 tablespoon filling for 8 cm turnovers.

Brush the edges with beaten egg or egg white, fold the other half over and press edges to seal.

If using rough puff pastry, lightly tap the cut edges. If using shortcrust, cream cheese or sour cream pastry, press around the sealed edges with the tines of a fork or the point of a teaspoon for a decorative effect.

Place the turnovers on greased baking trays and chill for 20 minutes. Brush with beaten egg white, then sprinkle over caster sugar for sweet turnovers. Cut 2 or 3 slits in the top of each turnover to allow steam to escape then bake in a preheated oven until the pastry is golden brown. Bake shortcrust, rough puff or puff pastry turnovers at 200°C and cream cheese or sour cream pastry turnovers at 190°C.

SWEET FILLINGS FOR BASIC TURNOVERS

FRUIT Use apples or pears, stewed or thinly sliced and sprinkled with sugar and lemon juice; or use berries or other fresh or canned fruits. Drain canned fruits well.

DRIED FRUIT Use Fruit Mincemeat (page 395) or raisins, sultanas or mixed dried fruit, sprinkled with brown sugar and lemon juice.

CREAM CHEESE OR RICOTTA Use cream cheese, or ricotta cheese mixed with a little cream. Sweeten to taste with brown or white sugar, then add your choice of flavourings: ground cinnamon, cardamom or mixed spice, brandy or rum, chopped dried or glacé fruits, grated orange or lemon rind.

JAM OR LEMON CURD Use a good berry jam, apricot jam (which may be mixed with slivered almonds), marmalade sprinkled with cinnamon or a few drops of orange liqueur, or Lemon Butter (pages 254–255).

PASTRY *sweet tartlets & pastries*

INGREDIENTS
1 quantity Biscuit Pastry (page 331)
about ¼ cup jam
1 cup desiccated coconut
½ cup (110 g) caster sugar
1 egg, beaten

COCONUT TARTS

MAKES 12

METHOD

Preheat the oven to 180°C.

Roll out the dough and use it to line twelve small tart tins, about 8 cm in diameter. Place 1 teaspoon of the jam in the bottom of each pastry case.

Combine the coconut and sugar and beat in the egg. Place spoonfuls in the pastry cases on top of the jam.

Bake the tarts for about 20 minutes or until golden brown. Leave in the tins for a few minutes, then transfer to a wire rack to cool.

INGREDIENTS

½ of a 375 g packet frozen puff pastry, thawed, or 1 quantity Puff Pastry (page 333)
1 cup cream
3 tablespoons strawberry or raspberry jam

ICING

1 cup (160 g) icing sugar, sifted
1½ tablespoons water
2–3 drops vanilla essence

MILLE-FEUILLES

The name literally means 'a thousand leaves', and refers to the many flaky layers of crisp puff pastry used to make this beautiful French pastry. Puff pastry is layered alternately, usually with whipped cream and raspberry or strawberry jam. The top is glazed with icing or dusted with icing sugar. Crème Pâtissiere (page 338) is sometimes used instead of cream, with a thick fruit purée instead of jam and occasionally a Chocolate Glaze (page 252). Make your own puff pastry, or, if you prefer, use commercial frozen puff pastry.

MAKES ABOUT 8

METHOD

Roll out the pastry as thinly as possible to a rectangle about the size of a large baking tray. Lay this over a dampened baking tray, allowing the pastry to come right up to the edges. Prick well all over and chill for 15 minutes.

Preheat the oven to 200°C.

Bake the pastry for 5–10 minutes or until pale golden brown. Using a palette knife, carefully turn the pastry over and bake for a further 5 minutes. Remove from the oven and cool on a wire rack.

When cold, trim the edges and cut into three strips about 8 cm wide.

Whip the cream until it stands in soft peaks. Spread the flat side of one strip of pastry with half the jam and half the cream. Lay a second pastry strip on top and press down lightly. Spread with the remaining jam and cream. Top with the last pastry strip, flat side up. Press down lightly.

To make the icing, mix the icing sugar with enough water to make a creamy consistency. Add the vanilla. Stir over hot water until the icing is warm and glossy.

Spread the top pastry layer with warm icing. Cut across into slices 4 cm wide.

NOTE If desired, the cooked pastry trimmings can be crushed lightly and used to sprinkle over the top and sides of the finished pastries just before serving.

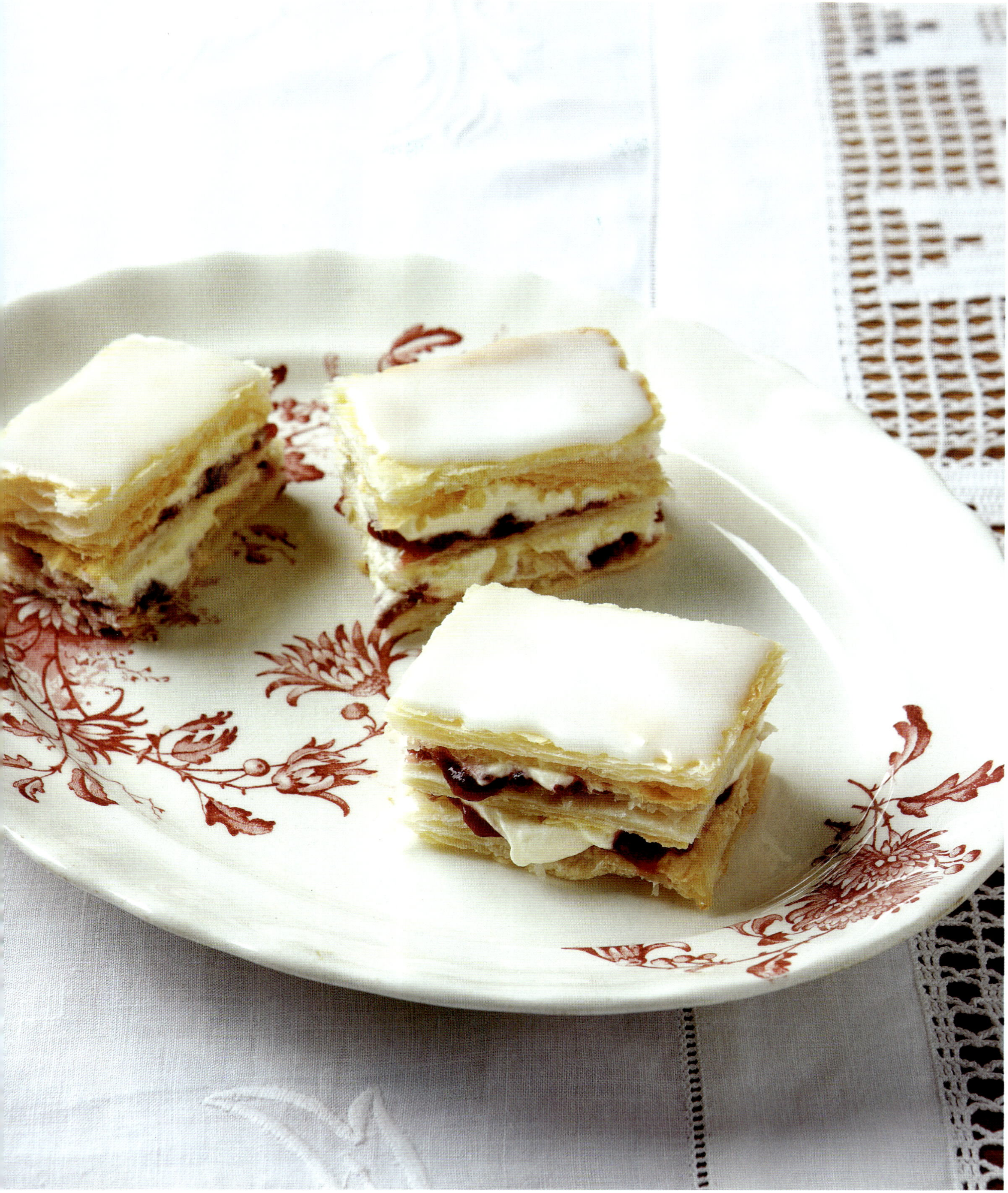

INGREDIENTS
¾ cup finely chopped walnuts
½ cup finely chopped almonds
1 teaspoon caster sugar
¼ teaspoon ground cinnamon
⅛ teaspoon grated nutmeg
10 sheets filo pastry
250 g butter, melted

CINNAMON HONEY SYRUP
1 cup (220 g) caster sugar
⅔ cup water
¼ cup honey
1 small cinnamon stick
1 teaspoon fresh lemon juice

NUT ROLLS

A Middle-Eastern delicacy made from crisp filo pastry rolled around spiced nuts, baked until golden, then finished off by being dipped in a sugar syrup until they glisten and gleam. A delicious confection.

MAKES 30

METHOD

Preheat the oven to 180°C. Grease a baking tray.

Mix together the nuts, sugar and spices.

Stack the filo between two dry tea towels with a dampened towel on top. Brush half of a sheet of filo with melted butter, fold the other half over and brush with butter so that you have a piece of filo 30 cm x 18 cm. Sprinkle with 1 tablespoon of the nut mixture.

Beginning at one end, roll the filo as you would a jam roll. Cut into three. Place on the prepared tray with the smooth side of the pastry rolls up and brush with melted butter.

Repeat with the remaining filo and nut filling. Bake for 20 minutes or until golden brown.

To make the syrup, mix all the ingredients together and simmer gently for 30 minutes. Cook only until light brown. While they are still hot from the oven, dip the nut rolls into the warm syrup. Allow to drain then transfer to a wire rack set over a baking sheet to catch the drips. Serve cold.

PASTRY *sweet tartlets & pastries*

INGREDIENTS
20 sheets filo pastry (about one 375 g packet)
185 g butter, melted
1½ cups finely chopped walnuts
¾ cup finely chopped almonds
¼ cup (55 g) caster sugar
2 teaspoons ground cinnamon
⅛ teaspoon ground cloves

SYRUP
2 cups (440 g) caster sugar
2 cups water
2 whole cloves
8 cm cinnamon stick
1 tablespoon lemon juice
a thin strip of lemon rind
2 tablespoons honey

BAKLAVA

MAKES 30

METHOD

Preheat the oven to 160°C. Grease a 33 cm x 23 cm x 5 cm baking dish.

Stack the filo between two dry tea towels with a dampened towel on top. Place one sheet of filo in the prepared baking dish, brush all over with melted butter and place another sheet on top. Continue adding sheets of filo, buttering in between, until nine sheets are used.

Mix the nuts with the sugar and spices and sprinkle half over the filo.

Add two more sheets of filo, brushing each with butter. Top with the remaining nuts and then nine more sheets of buttered filo. Trim the edges and brush the top layer with butter.

With a sharp knife, cut through the top few sheets of filo to make a diamond pattern. Sprinkle a little water over the surface to keep the pastry flat while baking, and bake in the centre of the oven for 30 minutes.

Move the baklava to a shelf placed above the centre and bake for a further 30 minutes. If the pastry is browning too much, cover with foil, but do not reduce the cooking time.

To make the syrup, place all the ingredients in a saucepan and stir over high heat until the sugar dissolves. Bring to the boil and boil over moderate heat for 10 minutes. Strain and cool before using.

Spoon the cooled syrup over the hot baklava as soon as it comes from the oven. Allow to cool, then cut into diamonds to serve.

INGREDIENTS

3–4 rashers bacon
One 20 cm Plain Shortcrust Pastry flan case (page 328), baked blind (see page 326)
2 eggs
1 teaspoon plain flour
a pinch of grated nutmeg
½ teaspoon salt
a pinch of cayenne pepper
½ cup cream
½ cup milk

QUICHE LORRAINE

A quiche is an open-faced tart with a savoury custard filling. Most widely known is quiche lorraine, which traditionally contains only eggs, cream or milk, and bacon or ham. The classic quiche lorraine contains no cheese, but a few tablespoons of grated cheese can be added to the egg mixture, if desired. Other quiche fillings may include cheese, tomatoes, onions, crabmeat, smoked salmon, mushrooms or other vegetables. There should be a lot of creamy filling encased in thin pastry shell.

SERVES 4–6

METHOD

Trim the rind off the bacon and grill or fry until crisp. Cut into dice. Place in the pastry case.

Preheat the oven to 190°C.

Beat together the eggs, flour, nutmeg, salt, cayenne, cream and milk, only until just combined (over-beating causes bubbles on top). Strain the mixture over the bacon.

Bake for 10 minutes. Reduce the oven temperature to 180°C and bake a further 20 minutes, or until a knife inserted in the custard comes out clean. Cool for 5 minutes in the tin before transferring to a serving place. Serve warm or cool, but not chilled.

VARIATIONS

CRAB QUICHE Substitute the bacon for 1 cup of flaked crabmeat and add a tablespoon of dry sherry to the egg and cream mixture.

SPINACH QUICHE Add ½ cup chopped, well-drained cooked English spinach, omitting the bacon and adding a little grated nutmeg.

NOTES Use a metal flan ring with fluted edges which can stand on a baking sheet. The tart will then easily slide onto a plate for serving. Quiches lend themselves to advance preparation. The flan ring lined with pastry may be made well ahead of time and chilled, while the filling can also be prepared in advance and stored in the refrigerator.

PASTRY *savoury pies & tarts*

INGREDIENTS

30 g butter
¼ cup water
½ teaspoon salt
1½ cups sliced leeks, white part only
2 eggs
¼–½ cup cream
½ cup milk
a pinch of grated nutmeg
a pinch of freshly ground pepper
½ cup grated gruyère cheese
one 20–22 cm Plain Shortcrust Pastry flan case (page 328), baked blind (see page 326)
2 teaspoons extra butter

LEEK QUICHE

SERVES 6

METHOD

Preheat the oven to 190°C.

In a heavy-based saucepan, heat the butter and water with the salt. Add the leeks, cover and cook for 6–8 minutes, or until the liquid in the pan has almost evaporated. Lower the heat and cook gently until the leeks are very soft. Cool.

Beat the eggs, cream and milk, nutmeg and pepper until just combined. Add the leeks and grated cheese. Pour into the prepared flan case and dot with small pieces of the extra butter.

Bake for 10 minutes, then lower the oven temperature to 180°C and bake a further 20 minutes or until the custard is set. Cool in the tin. Serve warm.

VARIATION

MUSHROOM QUICHE Cook 1 tablespoon chopped green onions in 30 g butter, but do not allow them to brown. Stir in 250 g finely sliced button mushrooms, ½ teaspoon salt and a squeeze of lemon juice. Cover and cook over a gentle heat for about 8 minutes. Uncover, raise the heat and boil until the liquid evaporates. Cool. Beat 2 eggs, a pinch of cayenne pepper, ½ cup cream, ¼–½ cup milk and 1 teaspoon plain flour until mixed. Gently stir in the mushroom mixture. Pour into a Plain Shortcrust Pastry flan case that has been baked blind (see page 326). Sprinkle with 2 tablespoons grated gruyère cheese. Bake in a preheated 190°C oven for 10 minutes. Reduce the oven temperature to 180°C and bake for a further 20 minutes or until set. Serve warm.

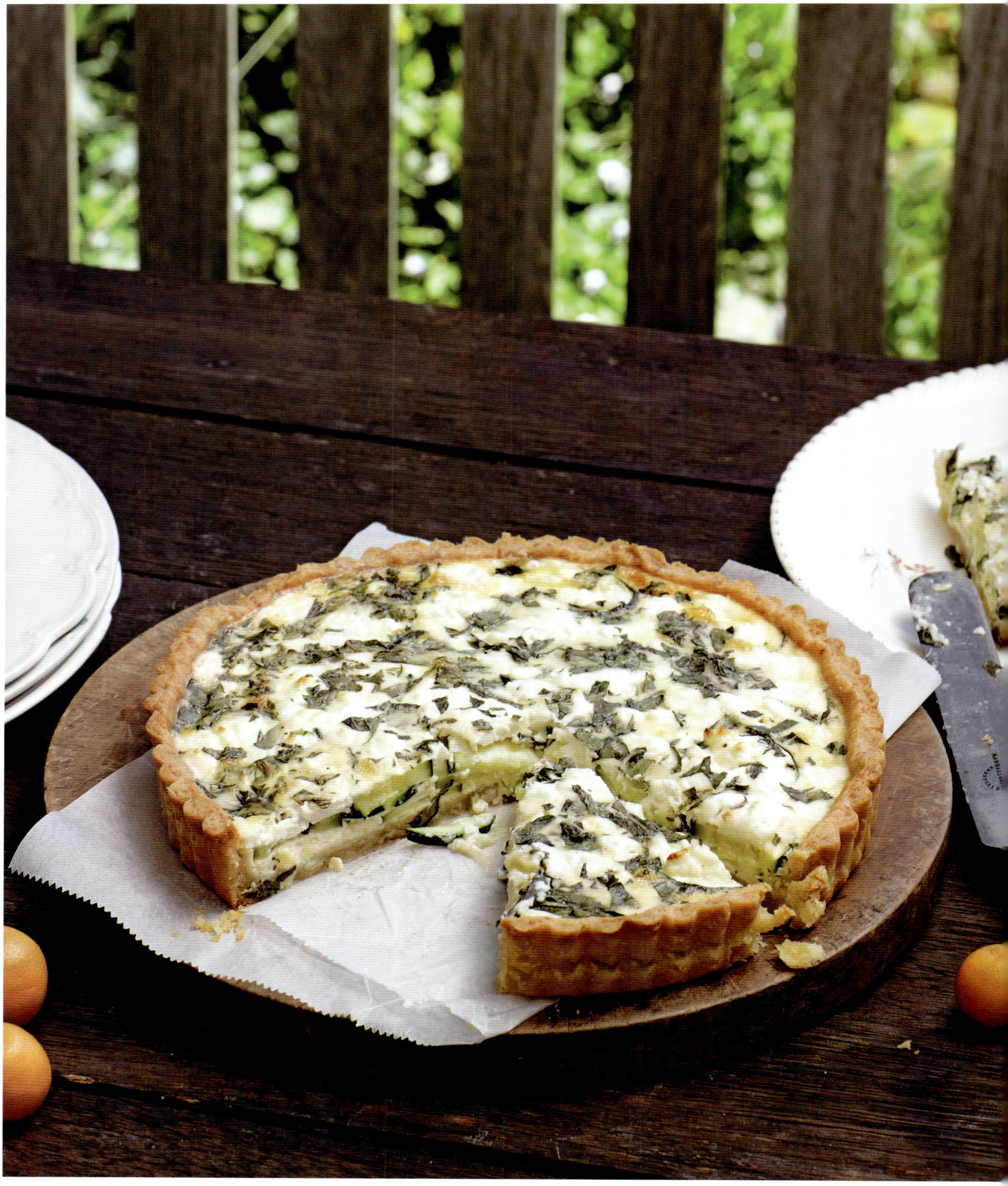

ZUCCHINI, MINT & GOAT'S CHEESE QUICHE

INGREDIENTS

PASTRY
2 cups (300 g) plain flour, sifted
170 g cold butter, diced
1½ cups grated tasty cheese
½ cup iced water

2 zucchini, sliced
120 g goat's cheese or feta
4 eggs, lightly beaten
¾ cup milk
½ cup roughly chopped mint

SERVES 8

METHOD

For the pastry, place the flour in the bowl of a food processor. Add the butter and process with a pulse mode until the mixture resembles breadcrumbs. Add the grated cheese. Add the water and process in a continuing mode until a dough has formed. Wrap in plastic wrap and chill for at least 10 minutes.

Lightly grease a 23 cm loose-based flan tin 4 cm deep.

Roll the dough out on a lightly floured surface to a 27 cm circle. Lift with the rolling pin and ease into the tin, pressing into the fluted edge. Trim the edges, prick the base with a fork and chill for 25 minutes.

Preheat the oven to 180°C.

Line the pastry shell with baking paper and pastry weights or rice and blind bake (see page 326) for 15 minutes. Remove the paper and rice and bake for a further 10 minutes.

Scatter the zucchini over the pastry base and crumble over the goat's cheese or feta and the mint.

Whisk together the eggs and milk and season well. Pour into the pastry shell and bake for 30–35 minutes, until set and golden. Serve warm.

VARIATIONS

ZUCCHINI AND BACON QUICHE Scatter a little cooked chopped bacon or pancetta over the zucchini.

MIXED VEGETABLE QUICHE For a fast evening meal, use frozen shortcrust pastry sheets for the base and scatter over left-over mixed vegetables (peas, corn, asparagus etc) before filling with the egg and cheese mixture.

BLUE CHEESE QUICHE Pan-fry sliced onions until very soft. Add a little brown sugar and balsamic vinegar to caramelise. Spread over the pastry shell and crumble over 150 g of your favourite blue cheese before filling with the egg mixture.

INGREDIENTS

1½ cups cream
2 eggs
2 egg yolks
2 tablespoons tomato paste
salt and freshly ground black pepper
4 tablespoons grated Swiss or gruyère cheese
25 cm Plain Shortcrust Pastry flan case (page 328), baked blind (see page 326)
2 tomatoes, cut into 1 cm slices
2 tablespoons chopped parsley
1 tablespoon chopped fresh mixed herbs (such as lemon thyme, oregano, basil, chives)
3 tablespoons grated parmesan cheese
2 teaspoons butter

HERBED TOMATO QUICHE

SERVES 6–8

METHOD

Preheat the oven to 190°C.

Combine the cream, eggs and yolks, tomato paste and salt and pepper to taste and beat lightly. Add 2 tablespoons of the Swiss or gruyère cheese. Spoon the custard into the flan case. Arrange the tomato slices on top and sprinkle with a litle more salt and pepper and the herbs. Top with the remaining Swiss and parmesan cheeses and dot with small pieces of butter.

Bake on the top shelf of the oven for 20–25 minutes or until the filling is set and the top is golden. Remove the quiche from the tin and cool on a wire rack.

INGREDIENTS

olive oil
3 French shallots (eschallots), chopped
500 g ricotta cheese
1 cup grated gruyère cheese
¾ cup grated parmesan cheese
½ cup sour cream
4 eggs, beaten
½ teaspoon dried tarragon
400 g can artichoke hearts, drained and quartered
salt and freshly ground black pepper
24 sheets filo pastry

RICOTTA & ARTICHOKE PIE

SERVES 8–10

METHOD

Preheat the oven to 200°C.

Heat 1 tablespoon of the oil in a small frying pan, add the shallots and cook until softened. Set aside.

Combine the ricotta, gruyère and parmesan cheeses in a large bowl and add the sour cream, eggs and tarragon. Mix until thoroughly combined. Stir in the shallots, artichoke hearts, and salt and pepper.

Stack the sheets of filo between two dry tea towels with a dampened towel on top.

Brush a 25 cm springform cake tin with oil. Line the tin with five sheets of filo pastry, each brushed lightly with oil, overlapping them and allowing the ends to hang over the sides of the tin.

Spread half of the cheese mixture over the filo. Top with five more sheets of filo, each brushed with oil. Add the remaining cheese mixture, spreading evenly, fold in the overhanging pastry and then top with the remaining filo sheets, each lightly brushed with oil. Tuck the overhanging ends down inside the tin, enclosing the filling completely.

Bake for 40–45 minutes or until the top is golden. Let the pie cool completely in the tin.

INGREDIENTS

PASTRY
3 cups (450 g) plain flour
a pinch of salt
150 g butter, diced
½ cup water

FILLING
1 kg onions, sliced
⅓ cup olive oil
4 medium tomatoes, sliced
12 anchovy fillets
20 pitted black olives

ONION & OLIVE TART

The French call this pissaladière, an onion and olive tart with a base of pastry (as we give here) or yeast dough. If you want a yeast base, refer to the pizza crust recipe (page 436).

SERVES 6–8

METHOD

Sift the flour and salt into a bowl. Rub in the butter until the mixture resembles breadcrumbs, then stir in the water and mix to form a dough. Wrap in plastic wrap and chill for 30 minutes.

Meanwhile, cook the onions in the oil over a very low heat for at least 30 minutes. When the onions are cooked, but not brown, remove from heat and drain, reserving the oil. Allow to cool.

Preheat the oven to 200°C.

Roll out the pastry and use it to line a 30 cm x 20 cm rectangular flan ring. Spread the cooled onions over the pastry and garnish with tomatoes, anchovy fillets and olives. Drizzle the reserved oil over the tart.

Bake for 40–45 minutes. Serve warm or cool, but not chilled.

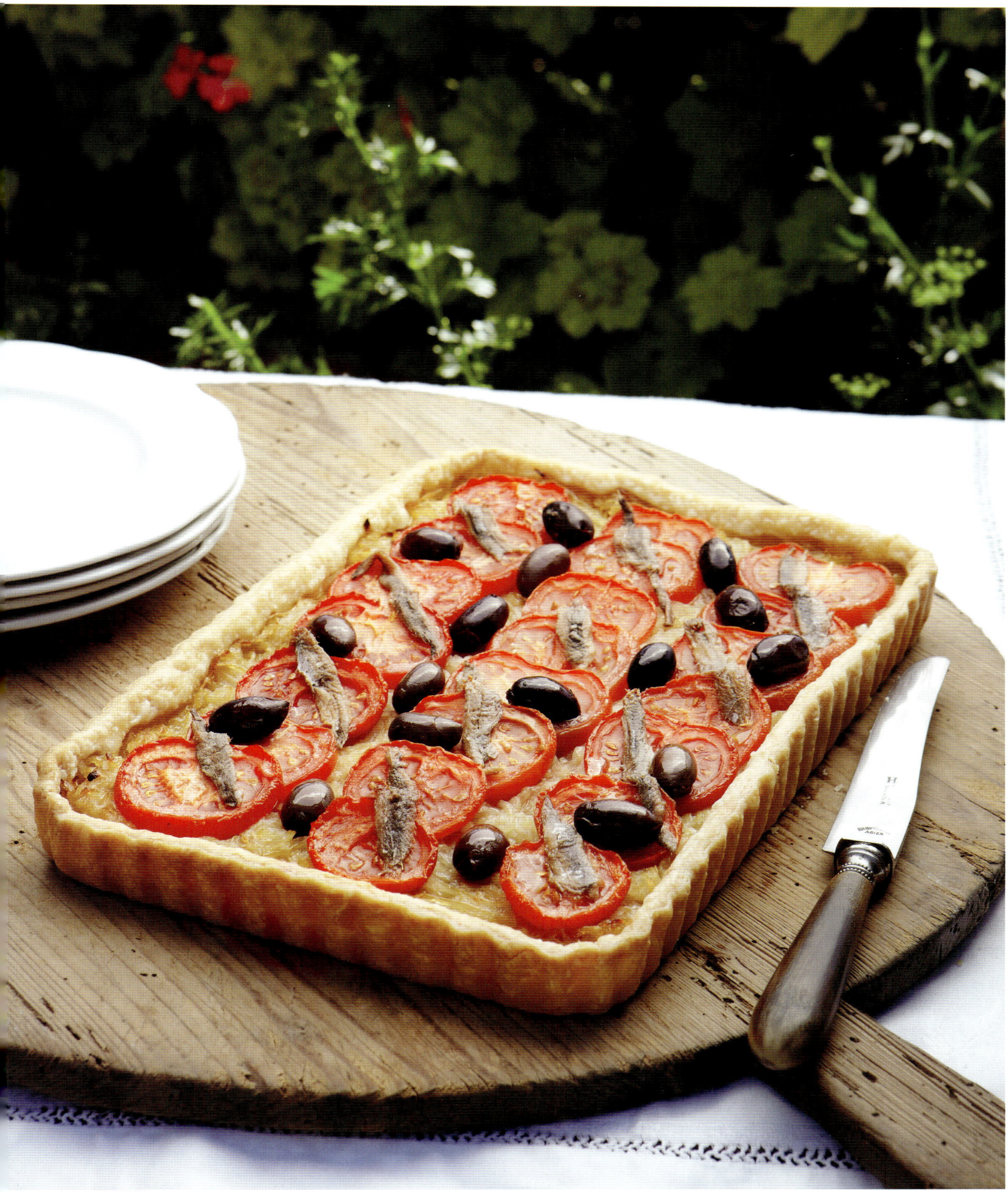

GREEK CHEESE PASTRIES (TIROPITAKIA)

INGREDIENTS
2 onions, finely chopped
30 g butter
300 g feta cheese, crumbled
300 g ricotta cheese
2 eggs
½ cup finely chopped parsley
salt and freshly ground black pepper
1 teaspoon nutmeg
24 sheets filo pastry
200 g butter, melted, extra

MAKES 72–96 (DEPENDING ON SIZE)

METHOD

Cook the onions gently in the 30 g butter until soft. Transfer to a plate to cool a little.

Preheat the oven to 190°C. Lightly grease baking trays.

Mix the feta and ricotta cheeses. Add the eggs, beat thoroughly and fold in the onions and parsley. Season with salt and pepper to taste and the nutmeg.

Unfold the filo pastry and, leaving it stacked, cut it lengthways in three or four strips, depending on the size you want your triangles to be. Stack the strips between two dry tea towels with a dampened towel on top.

Lay one strip on a work surface. Brush lightly with melted butter, fold lengthways in half and brush again with butter. Place 2 teaspoons of cheese filling on one end of the pastry strip. Fold the corner of pastry over the filling until it meets the folded edge of the pastry to form a triangle.

Continue to fold the pastry over in triangles until you come to the end of the strip. Brush the top with melted butter and place, seam side down, on a a prepared baking tray. Repeat with the remaining filling and pastry.

Bake the pastries for 15–20 minutes or until puffed and golden brown. Serve hot.

VARIATION

SPINACH PASTRIES Follow the recipe for Greek Cheese Pastries, but use the filling for Greek Spinach Pie (opposite) instead of cheese filling.

NOTES The pastries can be prepared and frozen unbaked until required. Bake straight from the freezer, allowing 10 minutes extra cooking time.

The recipe can also be halved.

PASTRY *savoury pies & tarts*

INGREDIENTS

1 kg spinach leaves, finely chopped
12 green onions, chopped
½ cup vegetable oil
1 onion, chopped
4 eggs, beaten
250 g feta cheese, crumbled
250 g cheddar cheese, grated
¼ teaspoon ground cinnamon
¼ teaspoon grated nutmeg
¼ teaspoon salt
freshly ground black pepper
20 sheets filo pastry

GREEK SPINACH PIE (SPANAKOPITA)

SERVES 6–8

METHOD

Preheat the oven to 180°C. Grease a 33 cm x 23 cm baking dish.

Combine the spinach, green onions and parsley in a large bowl.

Heat 2 tablespoons of the oil and gently fry the onion until soft. Add to the spinach mixture with the eggs, feta and cheddar cheeses, cinnamon, nutmeg and salt. Add pepper to taste and mix well.

Stack the filo sheets between two dry tea towels with a dampened towel on top. Lightly brush one sheet of filo pastry with oil and place in the prepared baking dish.

Repeat until ten sheets of filo have been used, brushing each with oil.

Spread the spinach mixture over the filo. Cover with the remaining sheets of filo, brushing each with oil. Sprinkle water over the top sheet of filo. Bake for 45 minutes or until golden brown.

Using a sharp knife, cut into diamond shapes for serving.

INGREDIENTS

1 cup (150 g) plain flour
1 cup water or milk, or a mixture of both
100 g unsalted butter
1 teaspoon sugar
½ teaspoon salt
4 eggs
100 g gruyère or other Swiss-style cheese, grated
1 egg, beaten

GOUGÈRES

Gougères – delectable little puffs of feather-light choux pastry flavoured with gruyere cheese – hail from Burgundy in France and are one of my favourite things to serve with a glass of red wine. To ensure they puff up properly, the dough should be cooled before beating in the eggs. At first the egg makes the dough separate into slippery clumps that don't want to mix, but keep going and the dough will eventually become smooth and shiny.

MAKES 30–40

METHOD

Preheat the oven to 200°C. Grease two baking trays.

Sift the flour onto a piece of baking paper.

Put the water and/or milk, butter, sugar and salt into a medium saucepan. Bring to a rapid boil and, using the baking paper as a funnel, pour the flour all at once into the boiling mixture. Over a gentle heat, incorporate the flour quickly and thoroughly with a wooden spoon and beat until the mixture balls around the spoon and leaves the sides of the pan (a bit of muscle is needed here). This process dries the paste and cooks the flour.

Remove from the heat, transfer the mixture to a bowl and allow to cool.

Beat in the eggs, one at a time, using an electric mixer with a paddle beater if you have one. If using a wooden spoon, beat each egg lightly first before adding. If the paste is very stiff, beat an extra egg and add it gradually until a pliable consistency is obtained. Beat until the mixture is well combined, shiny and smooth.

Add the cheese and mix lightly. Use two spoons to drop small balls of the mixture onto baking trays. Brush with a little beaten egg and bake for 20 minutes, until puffed and golden. Serve piping hot.

NOTE You can make the gougères ahead of time – shape them on a tray lined with baking paper and then freeze. When they are frozen they can be transferred into freezer bags ready for baking any time. Thaw for 10 minutes on the trays, then bake for 20–30 minutes.

PASTRY *savoury pastries & tartlets*

INGREDIENTS
1 quantity unsweetened Choux Pastry (page 332)

SAVOURY PROFITEROLES

Profiteroles are small choux pastry puffs with a sweet or savoury filling. They make superb party savouries or glamorous desserts or can star at morning or afternoon tea. Tiny profiteroles, filled or unfilled, are an elegant accompaniment to clear soup.

MAKES 30-40

METHOD

For cocktail-sized profiteroles (to serve with drinks or to accompany soup), make mounds of pastry about 2 cm in diameter and bake for 10 minutes in a 230°C oven, then reduce the oven temperature to 180°C and bake for a further 10 minutes. Leave the profiteroles in the turned-off oven with the door ajar for 20 minutes to dry them out.

For tiny unfilled puffs to accompany soup, make dots of pastry by squeezing it from a piping bag fitted with a plain 5 mm tube and cutting off in 5 mm lengths. Bake in a preheated 180°C oven for about 10 minutes or until crisp and brown. Leave the puffs in the turned-off oven with the door ajar for 20 minutes to dry them out.

NOTES Cold fillings that do not contain cream may be added 1-2 hours ahead of time; those with cream should not be added more than 30 minutes ahead, or the profiteroles may go soft. Hot fillings should be added at the last minute and the filled profiteroles placed in the oven for a few minutes if necessary to ensure they are very hot. If you are making cocktail-size profiteroles, the filling may be put in cold and heated in the shells. Place them in one layer on a baking tray, in a preheated 180°C oven for 20-25 minutes.

FILLINGS

COLD Fill with one of the following to serve cold with drinks or soup:
- Softened pâté.
- Finely chopped cooked ham, chicken or prawns, mixed with enough mayonnaise to bind.
- Softened blue cheese mashed with a little cream.
- Avocado mashed with a little cream cheese, lemon juice and seasonings.
- Finely chopped smoked salmon or other flaked, smoked fish mixed with cream cheese and seasoned with pepper and lemon juice.

HOT Fill with one of the following to serve hot with drinks:
- Chopped cooked spinach, flaked crab, chopped prawns or asparagus, mixed with mornay sauce.
- Chopped cooked chicken, ham or seafood, or fried mushrooms mixed with béchamel sauce.

ONION TARTLETS

INGREDIENTS
1 quantity Plain Rich Shortcrust Pastry (page 329)
8 onions, sliced
125 g butter
salt and freshly ground white pepper
2 tablespoons plain flour, sifted
1½ cups beef stock
2 tablespoons grated cheddar cheese
2–3 tablespoons grated parmesan cheese

SERVES 6

METHOD

Preheat the oven to 230°C.

Line six 10 cm tartlet tins with the pastry, prick well and bake blind (see page 326).

Cook the onions gently in half the butter until soft. Increase the heat a little and cook until they are a rich, even brown, stirring occasionally. Season with salt and pepper to taste and remove from the heat.

Melt the remaining butter in a saucepan, stir in the flour and cook over medium heat for 5–6 minutes or until the flour turns nut brown.

Gradually add the stock and simmer, stirring, for 5 minutes. Mix in the onions and spoon the mixture into the pastry cases. Mix the cheeses together and sprinkle over the top.

Bake for 5–10 minutes or until the cheese melts and colours slightly. Serve warm or cold.

PASTRY *savoury pastries & tartlets*

INGREDIENTS

PASTRY
3 ⅓ cups (450 g) flour
2 teaspoons paprika
½ teaspoon salt
250 g butter or lard, diced
cold water

FILLING
½ cup oil
1 onion, finely chopped
1 tomato, peeled, seeded and chopped
1 teaspoon paprika
1 kg lean stewing beef, trimmed and cut into 5 mm dice
2 teaspoons plain flour
½ cup beef stock
½ teaspoon ground cumin
salt
½ teaspoon chilli powder
1 hard-boiled egg, chopped
¼ cup pitted, chopped green olives
⅓ cup sultanas

EMPANADAS

These spicy meat turnovers are popular in several Latin American countries. Fillings vary from region to region, and the empanadas may be baked or deep-fried.

MAKES 18

METHOD

To make the pastry, sift the flour, paprika and salt together, and rub in the fat. Using a knife, stir in enough water to make a fairly stiff dough. Knead lightly, wrap in plastic wrap and chill for 30 minutes.

To prepare the filling, heat the oil in a large frying pan, add the onion and fry gently until golden brown. Add the tomato and paprika and cook slowly until soft.

Add the meat, flour, stock, cumin, salt to taste and chilli. Stir until the mixture comes to the boil. Cover and simmer for 15 minutes, then remove the lid and cook rapidly for 5–10 minutes to reduce the liquid by half. Allow to cool.

Divide the pastry into pieces about the size of an egg. Roll each piece thinly to form an 18 cm circle. Put 2 tablespoons of the meat filling, 1 teaspoon chopped egg, ½ teaspoon chopped olives and a few sultanas in the centre of each pastry circle.

Spread the filling over half the circle, leaving a 2 cm border. Moisten the edges of the pastry and fold over to make turnovers, pressing the edges firmly together.

Pinch the edge between thumb and finger and fold the pinched part over onto the unpinched part. Alternatively, fold the pastry circle to within 1 cm of the opposite edge, fold the lower half over the upper and crimp. Chill the empanadas for 20 minutes.

Preheat the oven to 200°C. Bake the empanadas for 15 minutes. Serve hot or warm.

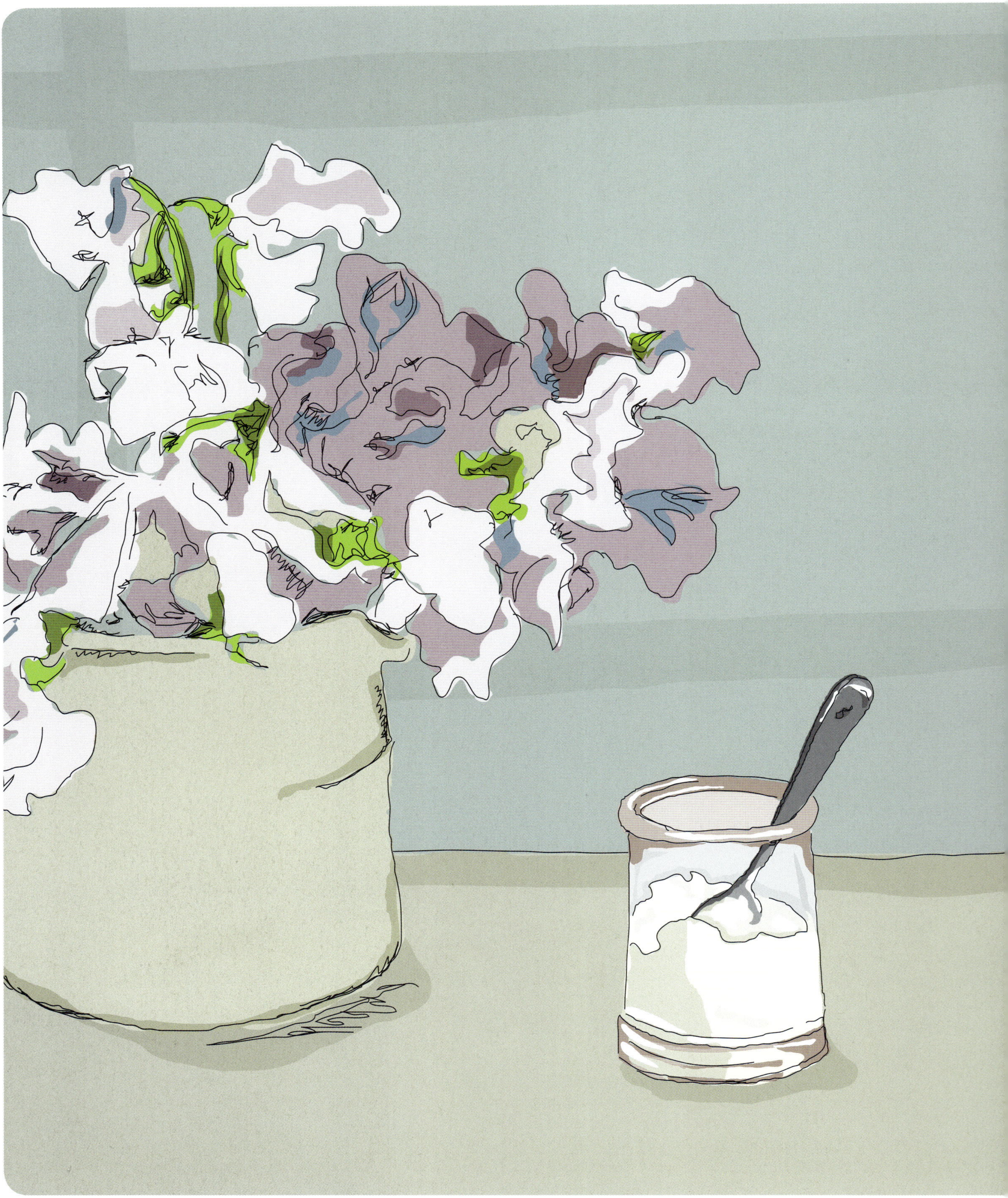

YEAST COOKERY
CHAPTER 8

HINTS & TIPS

Any cook using yeast for the first time comes under its fascinating spell once the warm, spicy fragrance of freshly baked breads and buns scents the kitchen.

There are few foods as wonderful as chewy-crusted homemade bread. Wholesome, traditionally made breads offer a burst of subtle and complex flavours that are so satisfying and bear little resemblance to their refined, additive-laden counterparts. You might think, 'Why bother? A loaf of bread is easy to buy and not that expensive', but take another look. Really good breads are getting more and more expensive as we develop a taste for them. Many are made by artisans who are justified to charge the higher prices over the factories that make pap.

These better breads don't contain the additives which, though they help keep bread fresh, and give a good colour and elasticity, also cause unpleasant allergic reactions in some people. So why don't more people bake their own bread? Mostly because the kneading is time-consuming and to some, a little tricky. Yet, on the whole, baking with yeast is easier and more foolproof than many think. We even include a recipe for a no-knead bread (page 430).

Cakes, too, can be baked with yeast. Before the introduction of mechanical raising agents such as baking powder and bicarbonate of soda in the mid-nineteenth century, all cakes used either yeast or beaten eggs to leaven them. Stollen, Savarin and Gugelhopf are all types of yeasted cake.

TYPES OF YEAST

Fresh yeast, obtainable in compressed form, and sold by the weight, will keep in the refrigerator for 2–3 days. Dehydrated (dry) yeast, sold in packets, and readily available at most supermarkets, will keep for several months if stored in a cool, dry place. For most cooks, dry yeast is the easy option.

When the yeast becomes active it creates the gas that gives bread and buns their light, characteristic texture. The temperature of the liquid used is most important; it must be lukewarm.

Dry yeast is added to the dry ingredients in a bowl and then the liquid ingredients are added. Compressed yeast is dissolved with a little sugar or liquid before the remaining liquid is added; this is known as 'creaming' the yeast. When yeast is added to liquid and left to activate, it will foam, double in size and smell yeasty; the resulting mixture is known as the yeast 'sponge'. If a sponge fails to form, the water may have been too hot, or the yeast too old.

FLOUR

Much bread is made with a special baker's flour, although plain flour may be used. Cracked wheat, rye or finely processed oats can be added. Whatever the flour used, it should be fresh. For yeasted cakes, brioche, savarins and stollens, plain white flour is recommended. Australian plain flour is a hard wheat flour ideal for bread making.

BASIC METHOD FOR WORKING WITH YEAST DOUGHS

Sift the dry ingredients into a warm bowl, make a well in centre, and pour in the liquids. Mix into a soft dough. Turn the dough out on a lightly floured work surface and knead to a smooth, elastic ball, which will take 5–10 minutes or the time specified in the recipe. Knead in as little extra flour as possible. Kneading is important as it distributes the yeast throughout the mixture, develops the gluten in the flour and influences the texture of the finished loaf. When kneading, use the heels of your hands to smear the dough across the work surface, then pick it up, give it a quarter turn and repeat until it is smooth and elastic.

Put the ball of dough in a clean, greased bowl and turn the dough over, so that the top is lightly greased. This keeps the top soft, allowing it to stretch easily as the dough rises. Cover with a clean tea towel.

The dough now needs to rise. 'Rising' is the word used to describe the standing time necessary for the dough to double in bulk before it is shaped. The bowl of dough must stand in a warm place free from draughts while it is rising. A warm place can be:
- In a barely warm oven.
- In a saucepan containing warm water that comes halfway up the sides of the bowl holding the dough.
- On top of an internal hot water cylinder.

Rising the dough will take 1–2 hours, or until it has doubled in bulk. If you are not in a hurry, you can cover the bowl of dough with baking paper, then foil, place in a fridge, and leave overnight. Remember it is heat that kills yeast, not cold. To test, press two fingers lightly and quickly in the top of the dough.

If the dent stays, the dough is ready. If it fills up, leave for 15 minutes longer and test again.

Once the dough has risen, knock it back (this process is also known as 'punching down'). This means to gently knead it until all the gas has been expelled. Next, knead the dough into its required shape, put into greased tins (or onto greased trays for buns freeform loaves), and leave to rise again in a warm place for 30 minutes to 1 hour (this rising is called 'proving'). For buns, allow 15–30 minutes, depending on size. The shaped 'proved' dough should be close to the final size, as it won't rise a great deal more once it is put in the oven.

Bake in a hot oven (200°C) for the first 15 minutes so that the heat kills the yeast and the dough won't over prove. Don't open the oven during this time.

To test whether it is cooked, tap the base of the bread (turning it out of the tin first) or the buns. If cooked, there will be a hollow sound. Otherwise, return the buns to the tray or the loaf to the tin and cook for a little longer. Home-baked bread is best eaten the same day. It does not keep as long as commercial bread, but it can be wrapped and frozen for up to 2 months. Thaw at room temperature then refresh in a preheated moderate oven for about 10 minutes. Alternatively slice the loaf before freezing then remove the required number of slices when needed.

YEAST TROUBLESHOOTING

If you find your efforts with yeast are not successful, the following may explain some of the common failures.

IF THE YEAST MIXTURE DOES NOT RISE OR FOAM, the yeast was stale; the liquid used for dissolving the yeast was too hot; the dough had too much flour, sugar, fat, salt or eggs; the dough was under- or over-kneaded or mixed; and/or the oven temperature was too low.

IF THE LOAF DIDN'T RISE OR ROSE POORLY, the dough had too much liquid or dough rose too much during first rising; the dough did not rise enough before the second rising; and/or the dough was too cold.

IF THE LOAF IS OVER-RISEN AND PUFFY, and the bread is heavy, dark and misshapen, the dough had too much yeast; it rose at too high a temperature, or rose too much during the second rising; and/or the heat was too low.

IF THE LOAF HAS UNEVEN COLOUR, the crust is pale and the crumb loose, with open holes, and the loaf is soft and puffy, the dough had too much yeast and rose too much during the second rising; and/or the heat was too low.

WORKING WITH SWEET YEAST MIXTURES

For savarins, babas and other sweet yeasted mixtures, the dough is often mixed with dried fruits and nuts. These mixtures are delicate, so maintaining the right technique at each stage of work is important, as is the right temperature.

BASIC BREAD

INGREDIENTS

625 g baker's flour or plain flour, or for wholemeal bread a mixture of half baker's flour and half wholemeal plain strong wheat flour
1½ teaspoons salt
30 g compressed yeast, or 14 g (2 sachets) dry yeast
1½–2 cups lukewarm water (or warm for dry yeast)
60 g butter, melted and cooled slightly

MAKES 2 LOAVES

METHOD

Sift the flour and salt into a large warmed bowl, then take out ½ cup and sift it onto a work surface.

Mix the yeast with ¼ cup water in a small bowl, stirring to dissolve.

Run your fingers through the flour in the bowl and make a well in the centre. Pour the yeast mixture into the well and add the butter (which should be warm, not hot) and 1½ cups of the water. Mix the flour and liquid ingredients with your fingers, then beat with your hand, adding a little more water if necessary to make a firm dough. With your hand, fold and slap the dough against the sides of the bowl until it begins to feel elastic and leaves the sides.

Scrape the dough out of the bowl onto the floured work surface and knead by folding the far edge towards you, then pushing it firmly away with the heel of the hand. Turn the dough a little and repeat. Continue kneading until the dough is smooth and elastic and springs back when you make a dent with your finger.

Place the dough in a clean, warm, oiled bowl, turn it so that it is lightly oiled all over, and cover with oiled plastic wrap and a cloth. Leave to rise in a warm place for 30 minutes to 1 hour (or in a cool place for longer – see Rising Times for Bread, opposite). Test by pushing a finger into the dough. If the indentation remains, it is ready.

Knock back the dough by punching it lightly with your fist several times, squeezing out any large bubbles. Turn it out onto a lightly floured surface and knead three or four times.

The loaves may be baked in two lightly oiled 23 cm x 12 cm bread tins, or the dough may be formed into any shape such as plaits, twists, cottage rounds or crescents and baked on a greased baking tray.

For loaves baked in tins, divide the dough equally into two and pat each piece into a round, then fold the sides under to form a neat oblong. Press together to seal and place in the prepared tins. Alternatively, shape as desired and place on a prepared baking tray. Cover loosely with oiled plastic wrap and a cloth and leave in a warm place until risen to the tops of the tins, or doubled in bulk if you are baking shapes on trays.

During the second rising, preheat the oven to 230°C.

Bake for 15 minutes, then turn the tins or trays around, reduce the oven temperature to 180°C and bake for a further 20–25 minutes for bread in tins and 18–20 minutes for shapes on trays, or until it is cooked; it should sound hollow when the underside is knocked with the knuckles. If not, return to the oven for more baking. If you want a crisp crust all over, take the bread out of the tins and bake directly on the oven bars for last 10 minutes. Remove the bread from the tins or trays as soon as it comes from the oven, and cool on a wire rack.

VARIATIONS

VIENNA TWIST Break off about one-fifth of the dough and set aside. Pat the remaining dough into a rectangle and roll it up towards you from a long side, tapering the dough toward the ends with your hands to make a long shape with pointed ends. Squeeze the edges together to seal and place, seam side down, on a greased baking tray. Divide the reserved dough in half, roll each piece into a long rope between your hands, twist the ropes together and lay on top of the loaf, pressing the ends to seal. Cover loosely with oiled plastic wrap. Allow to rise in a warm place until doubled in bulk. Bake as for loaves in tins.

BREAD ROLLS Pat the dough out into a rectangle, cut into 24 equal portions and shape each into a thick round. Turn under all around to make balls, pressing the edges together underneath to seal. Place on a greased baking trays, cover loosely with oiled plastic wrap and leave in a warm place until almost doubled in bulk. Bake in a preheated 200°C oven for about 25 minutes, turning the trays round halfway through the baking time.

TOPPINGS These may be varied. For a crisp crust, brush the dough with cold water and repeat several times during baking. For a golden shiny crust, brush with a little beaten egg; for a cottage loaf, dust the bread lightly with flour; for a rich crust, brush with melted butter. Coarse salt, poppy, sesame or caraway seeds, or coarse wheat can be sprinkled over the bread before baking for an attractive loaf with good flavour.

RISING TIMES FOR BREAD

Recipes usually say that yeast dough should be allowed to rise in a warm place, but if it suits you better, you can allow it to rise more slowly in a cool place or even in the refrigerator. A dough will take 30–60 minutes to double in bulk in a warm place, about 2 hours at normal room temperature, or up to 12 hours in a cool room or refrigerator. Keep the bowl covered with oiled plastic wrap and a cloth, or place the dough in a plastic bag large enough to allow for expansion; loosely tie the mouth. A slow rise is considered by many experts to give bread a better texture and flavour than a quickly risen loaf.

INGREDIENTS

5 cups (750 g) wholemeal flour, sifted
2 teaspoons salt
1 tablespoon caster sugar
30 g compressed yeast, or 15 g (2 sachets) dry yeast
1¾ cups lukewarm water
1 tablespoon oil
beaten egg to glaze

FARMHOUSE BREAD

MAKES TWO 500 G LOAVES

METHOD

Mix the flour, salt and sugar in a warmed bowl.

Blend the yeast with a little of the water, stirring to dissolve, then stir into the remaining water and add to the dry ingredients with the oil. Mix to a soft dough. Turn out onto a lightly floured surface and knead for 10 minutes, until the dough is smooth and does not stick to the fingers.

Place the dough in a lightly oiled plastic bag, and leave in a warm place for 1 hour or until doubled in size. Knock back firmly with your knuckles to remove air bubbles, then turn out onto a floured surface and knead again for 5 minutes.

Divide the dough into two pieces. Pat each one out to a rectangle, then fold into three and place in two greased 500 g (21 cm x 14 cm) loaf tins. Cover with a damp cloth and leave in a warm place for 30–40 minutes, until the dough has risen to the tops of the tins.

Preheat the oven to 230˚C.

Brush the tops with beaten egg and bake for 40 minutes, or until the loaves are well risen, brown and sound hollow when tapped on the bottom with your knuckles. Cool on a wire rack.

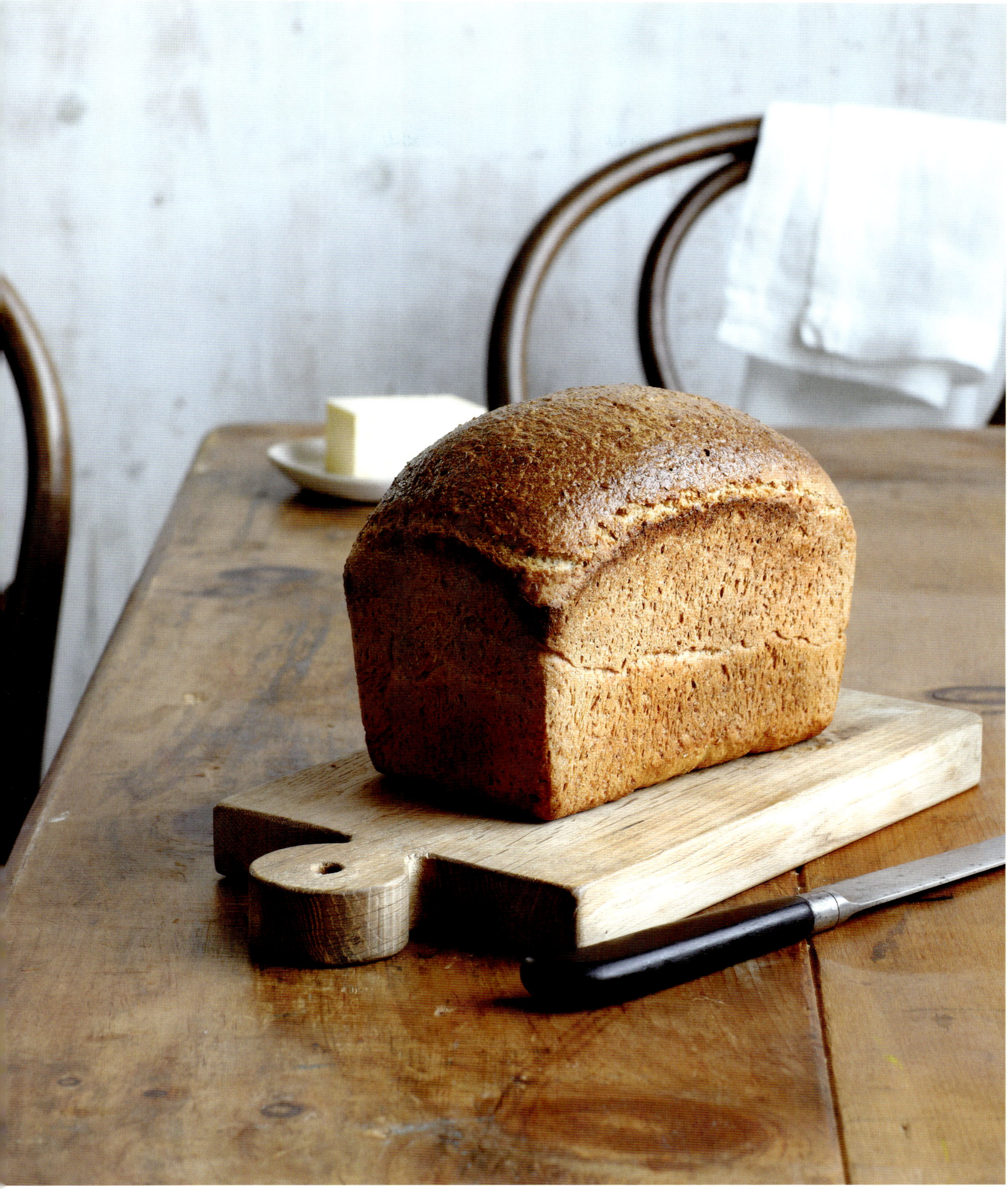

INGREDIENTS

4 cups (600 g) baker's flour or plain flour
1 teaspoon salt
15 g compressed yeast or 7 g (1 sachet) dry yeast
3 teaspoons sugar
1¼ cups milk
60 g butter

COTTAGE LOAF (BASIC MILK DOUGH)

MAKES 2

METHOD

Sift the flour and salt into a large mixing bowl. Make a well in the centre of the flour.

If using compressed yeast, cream the yeast with the sugar in a small bowl. If using dry yeast, stir it into the flour.

If using compressed yeast, heat ½ cup of the milk to lukewarm and add to the yeast and sugar mixture. Mix until dissolved, then pour into the well in the flour. Stir in a little of the surrounding flour, then cover with a cloth and leave in a warm place for 30 minutes. If using dry yeast, stir all the liquid into the flour to form a dough. Cover with a cloth and leave in a warm place for 30 minutes.

Melt the butter, add the remaining milk and warm slightly. Pour into the yeast batter in the bowl and gradually mix in the flour (if you are using compressed yeast and haven't already done so). The dough for a cottage loaf should be quite stiff, so add more flour if necessary. Knead the dough, then allow it to rise until it is doubled in bulk. Knock the dough back and knead lightly for 10 minutes.

Shape two thirds of the dough into a ball and place on a greased baking tray. Shape the remaining dough into a ball, place on top of the other dough, then press a floured finger right down the centre of both. Leave to rise for about 35 minutes or until doubled in bulk.

Preheat the oven to 230°C.

Brush the risen dough with milk, sprinkle with a little flour and bake in the centre of the oven for 20 minutes. Reduce the oven temperature to 180°C and bake for a further 20–25 minutes. To test whether the bread is cooked, knock firmly on the base: the bread should sound hollow. If it does not, bake for a little longer.

VARIATION

FRUIT LOAF Prepare dough as for Cottage Loaf, using a little more liquid. When the dough has doubled in bulk, knock it back and knead in 125 g mixed dried fruit. Cut the dough in half, shape each portion and place in two well-greased 21 cm x 11 cm loaf tins. Cover and leave to rise for 35–40 minutes. Bake in a preheated 230°C oven for 20 minutes, then reduce the oven temperature to 180°C and bake for a further 20–25 minutes. Paint the loaves with honey or thick milk and sugar syrup as soon as they come out of the oven. Cool on a wire rack.

MALT BREAD

MAKES 2 LOAVES

INGREDIENTS
3 cups (450 g) wholemeal plain flour
2 cups (300 g) plain flour
a pinch of salt
30 g compressed yeast or 14 g (2 sachets) dry yeast
1¾ cups lukewarm water
2 tablespoons molasses
2 tablespoons syrup-type malt extract
60 g sultanas (optional)
60 g butter, melted

SYRUP
2 tablespoons milk
2 tablespoons caster sugar

METHOD

Sift the flours and salt into large warmed mixing bowl.

If using compressed yeast, cream the yeast with the sugar in a small bowl. If using dry yeast, stir it into the flour.

Make a well in the centre of the flour mixture and pour in the yeast mixture (if using compressed yeast), treacle and malt extract. Add the sultanas, if using, and beat vigorously with your hand, mixing in the butter and the remaining water little by little, to form a soft dough. Turn out onto a floured board and knead for 5–10 minutes until the dough is even textured and well blended.

Place in a greased bowl and turn the greased side of the dough up. Cover with greased plastic wrap and a damp cloth and leave in a warm place to rise for about 2 hours or until the dough has doubled in bulk.

Knock down the dough, divide in half and put each half into a greased 500 g loaf tin, pressing down well. Cover and allow to rise again for about 45 minutes, or until the dough has doubled in bulk.

Preheat the oven to 180°C.

Bake the loaves for about 40 minutes, turning the tins around after first 25 minutes of cooking time.

To make the syrup, heat the milk and sugar, stirring until the sugar has dissolved. Brush the tops of the loaves with syrup and bake for a further 5 minutes. When cooked, the loaves will sound hollow when the undersides are knocked with the knuckles. Remove from the tins and cool on a wire rack.

VARIATIONS
BUNS If preferred, the dough can be shaped into 24 buns and baked on a greased baking tray for 15–20 minutes.

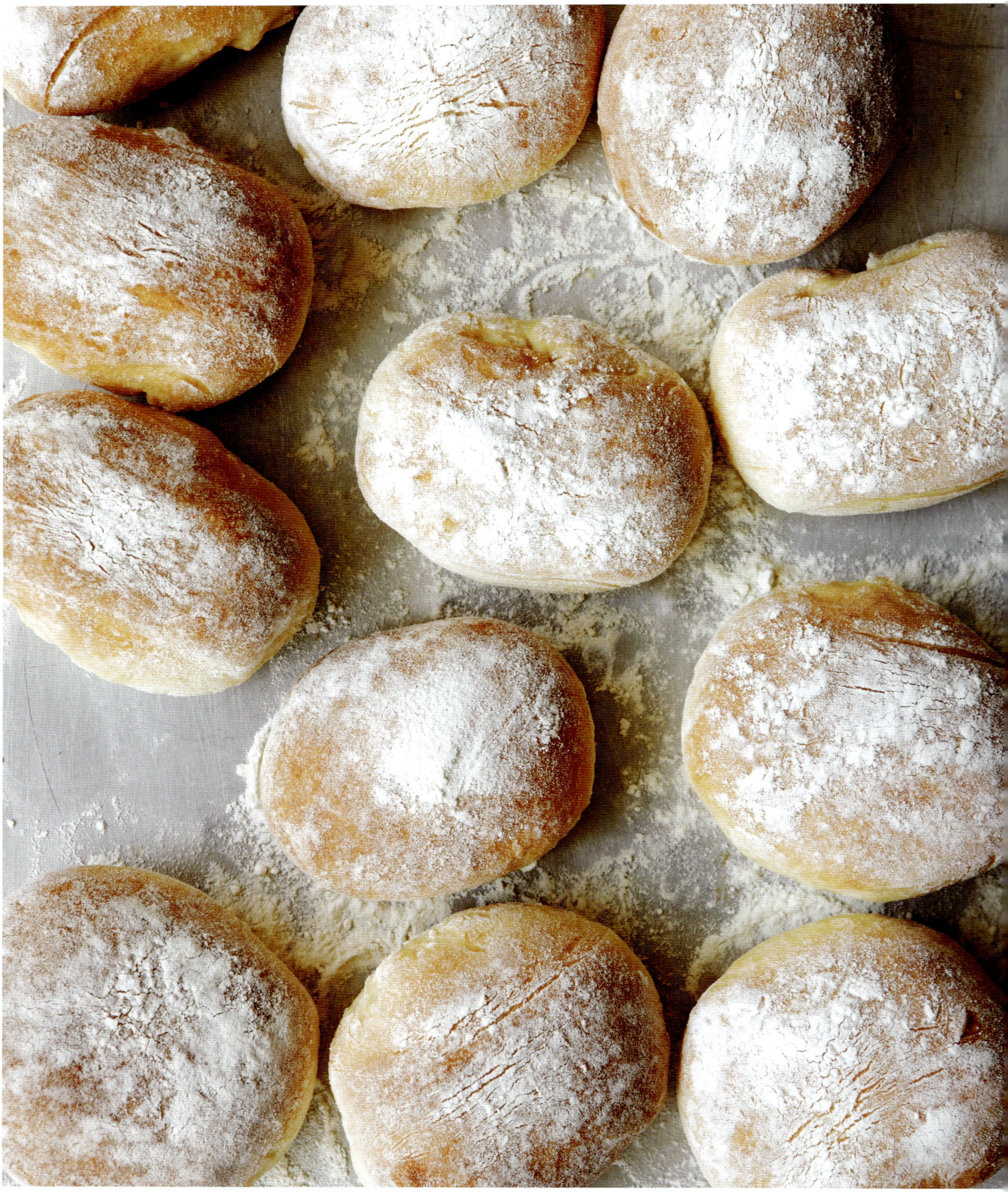

YEAST COOKERY *basic & savoury breads & rolls*

INGREDIENTS
4 cups (600 g) flour
1 teaspoon salt
¾ cup milk
½ cup water
60 g butter
15 g compressed yeast or 7 g (1 sachet) dry yeast
1 teaspoon sugar
a little extra milk and flour

FLOURY BAPS

These soft floury baps are Scottish, and a great breakfast bun. Early deliveries were made through villages, with the baker's carter calling out 'Baps!', and the children were often sent out to buy them.

MAKES 12

METHOD

Sift the flour with the salt into a bowl.

Heat the milk and water together to blood heat; add the butter and remove from the heat when the butter has melted.

If using compressed yeast, cream the yeast with the sugar in a small bowl and stir into the warm liquid. If you are using dry yeast, mix it with the flour.

Make a well in the centre of the flour and pour in the yeast mixture. If you are using dry yeast, add the milk at this stage. Stir in a little flour from the sides until the yeast mixture is the consistency of a thick batter. Cover with a folded cloth and place in a warm spot.

When the yeast mixture has doubled, and bubbles have formed, mix in the remaining flour. Turn the dough onto a floured work surface and knead for about 5 minutes or until smooth. Place in a clean, greased bowl and turn over so the top surface is also lightly greased. Cover with greased plastic wrap and leave in a warm place for 2 hours or until doubled in bulk.

Knock down and turn out onto a floured board. Knead lightly, divide into 12 pieces and shape each into a ball. Place the balls of dough on a greased baking tray. Cover and allow to rise in a warm place for 20 minutes.

Preheat the oven to 200°C.

Brush the risen baps with a little milk and sprinkle lightly with flour. Bake for 15–20 minutes or until very pale golden.

NO-KNEAD BREAD

MAKES A 1 KG LOAF

INGREDIENTS

- 4 cups (600 g) baker's flour or plain flour (you can use a mixture of white and wholemeal flour; see Variations)
- 1 teaspoon bread improver
- ¼ teaspoon dry yeast
- 1½ teaspoons salt
- 2¼ cups warm water
- plain flour (with burghul or cracked wheat if you like), cornmeal or wheat bran to dust and top

METHOD

In a large bowl, combine the flour, bread improver, yeast and salt. Add the water and stir, with a plastic or silicon spatula, until mixed. Cover the bowl with plastic wrap, then a tea towel. Set aside at room temperature for 10–12 hours, until the surface has many bubbles. In cold weather the dough will take longer to rise than in warm weather. Be sure to keep it out of draughts, and in the winter, put it in a sunny spot, well-covered with perhaps two tea towels.

Use a spatula to release the dough from the sides and fold the dough over on itself three or four times. Cover again with the same plastic wrap and tea towel and leave for another 6–8 hours, until the dough has doubled in volume.

Meanwhile, 15 minutes before baking, place a heavy-based covered pan (cast iron, enamel or ceramic) in the oven and set it to 240°C. When the dough is ready, carefully remove the pan from the oven and place it on a heatproof trivet. Sprinkle the base with a thick dusting of flour. With your hand under the bowl, turn the dough over into the pan. Shake the pan very lightly to distribute the dough evenly. Quickly sprinkle on the topping, if desired. If you like, use a sharp knife or scissors to cut a few slashes into the top of the dough, making a decorative pattern. Cover with the lid and bake for 40 minutes, then remove the lid and bake for another for 20 minutes, until the loaf is browned and crusty. The bread is cooked if it sounds hollow when the underside is knocked with the knuckles. Turn out and leave to cool on a wire rack.

VARIATIONS

CRISP CRUST For a crisper crust, you can reduce the length of time the pot is covered to 20 minutes and then increase the time the loaf bakes uncovered. For a crisp crust all over, take the bread out of the pan and bake it directly on the oven bars for the last 10 minutes. If not, return to the oven for more baking. Turn the bread out of the pan as soon as it comes from the oven, and cool on a wire rack.

WHOLEMEAL BREAD You can add up to half wholemeal to half plain flour if you like a denser loaf of bread. Baker's flour (from health food stores) is best because of its high gluten content, but you will still get good results with ordinary plain flour. Wholemeal soaks up more water than white flour so you may need to add more or less water, depending on the proportions you use.

NOTES Bread improver is available in many supermarkets and health food stores. It contains enzymes that help to strengthen the gluten in the flour. It also aids in earlier fermentation (replacing the need for a 'mother' starter), which gives a sourness much liked in sourdough and artisan breads. Yeast alone is missing this enzyme.

It is best not to double the quantities to make two loaves because it can be too unwieldy to manage.

YEAST COOKERY *basic & savoury breads & rolls*

This no-knead bread is adapted and very much simplified from a recipe by Jim Lahey, of New York's Sullivan Street Bakery. It is based on the principle that kneading can be omitted when making bread by using very little yeast, a soft, slack dough, a long rising time and by baking it in a preheated pan with a lid.

Once you master this simple method you'll want to make it regularly. It needs time but not labour; it's just a matter of mixing the flour, salt, yeast and a little bread improver and water in a bowl 20–24 hours before you want to bake it.

INGREDIENTS

4 cups (600 g) plain flour
1 teaspoon sea salt
2 teaspoons caster sugar
7 g (1 sachet) 1 sachet dry yeast
freshly ground black pepper
1/3 cup olive oil
1½ cups warm water
¾ cup black olives, pitted and roughly chopped

OLIVE BREAD

I picked up this recipe on a visit to Venice many years ago, when the sight of black olives in bread was a really new idea to me. Now we often make it when we go to my granddaughter's farm; the smell of baking bread welcomes everyone and puts us in that country holiday mood.

The best way to serve it is cut into chunks for dunking into a good extra-virgin olive oil, or topped with soft goat's cheese or a curled slice of prosciutto. Olive bread also makes a lovely base for savoury sandwiches and is good just sliced with ice-cold butter or your favourite dip.

SERVES 6–8

METHOD

Sift the flour into a large bowl with the salt and sugar. Stir in the yeast. Make a well in the centre and add the pepper, olive oil and warm water.

Gradually incorporate the wet ingredients into the flour mixture. Mix to a soft manageable dough, adding more water if necessary. Turn onto a floured surface and knead for 5–10 minutes or until the dough is smooth and elastic. Incorporate the olives until mixed through evenly.

Place the dough in a greased bowl and sprinkle with a few drops of water. Cover the bowl with plastic wrap, then a tea towel. Leave in a warm place for 1 hour.

Preheat the oven to 200°C. Grease and flour a baking tray.

Lightly knead the dough again, and shape into two loaves, each 25 cm long. Place on the tray, sprinkle with a little flour and cover with a cloth. Leave for 30 minutes, until doubled in size, then make slashes on the tops of the loaves with a sharp knife.

Bake the loaves for 20 minutes then reduce the oven temperature to 180°C and bake for a further 20–25 minutes, until the bread sounds hollow when tapped on the uunderside and is well risen and golden.

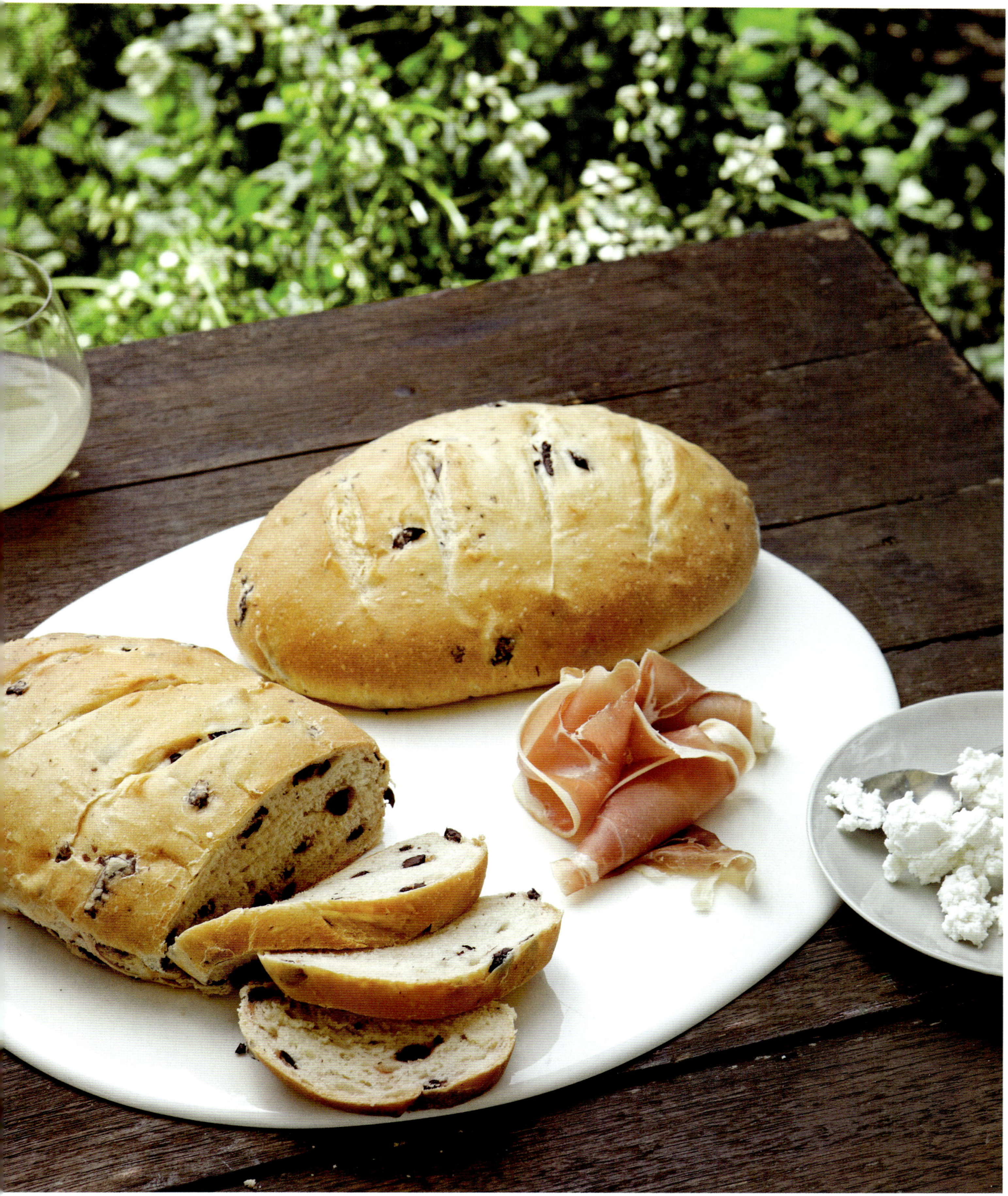

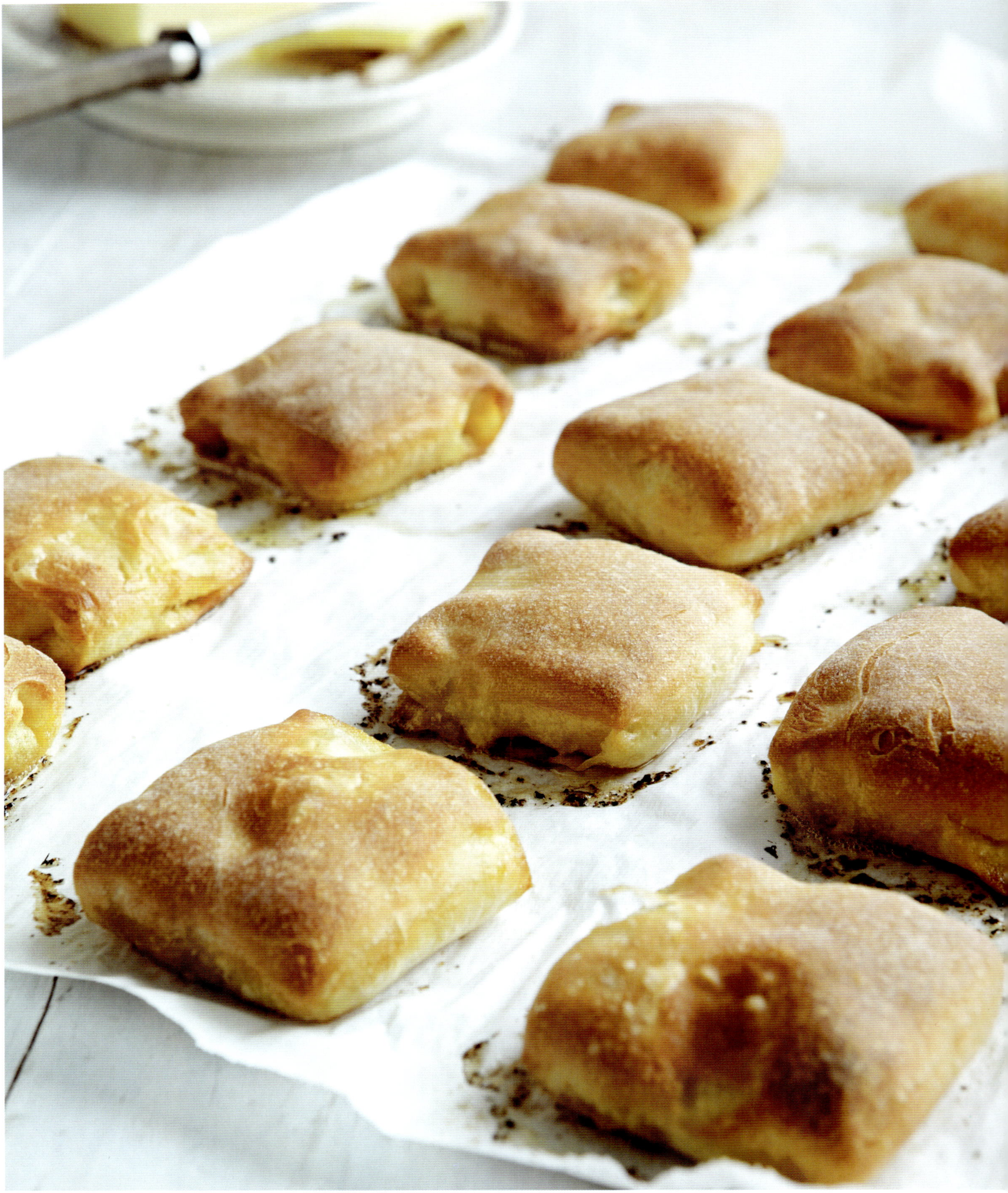

INGREDIENTS

15 g compressed or 7 g (1 sachet) dry yeast
1½ cups lukewarm water
3 cups (450 g) baker's flour or plain flour
½ teaspoon salt
125 g butter

NAIRN BUTTERIES

I was born in Nairn, Scotland, the home of these wonderful breakfast rolls. Elizabeth David, the famous English food writer, once said they are the best in the world, better than the French croissant.

MAKES 16–24

METHOD

In a small bowl, mix the compressed yeast, if using, and ¼ cup of the lukewarm water, stirring to dissolve.

Sift the flour and salt into a large bowl. Make a well in the centre and beat in the compressed yeast mixture or the dry yeast, if using, and enough warm water to make a medium-soft dough. You may need a little more or less according to the flour.

Turn the dough out onto a floured board and knead until smooth and elastic, then form into a ball. Put the dough into a buttered bowl, turn the ball round to lightly coat it with butter, cover with a damp cloth or plastic wrap and leave to rise in a warm place for 45 minutes or until doubled in bulk.

Meanwhile, divide the butter into two portions, each cut into little cubes. The butter should be cold but not too hard. Turn dough onto a lightly floured board and pat out to a 42 cm x 20 cm rectangle. Dot two thirds of the dough with half the cubes of butter and, from the short end, fold over like an envelope, with the unbuttered dough folded over one third of the buttered dough then the remaining buttered dough folded over. Press down with a rolling pin.

Wrap in plastic wrap and chill for 15–30 minutes. Roll out the dough into a rectangle, dot with the remaining butter and fold over in the same manner. Wrap and leave to rest in the refrigerator for 30 minutes or until you are ready to use the dough.

Finally, roll out or press the dough into a rectangle about 1 cm thick. With a sharp knife, cut into 16 or 24 squares, depending on whether you want small or larger rolls.

Transfer the pieces to the prepared baking tray and cover loosely with plastic wrap; leave for 30 minutes.

Preheat the oven to 220°C.

Bake the rolls for 10–15 minutes or until light golden. Serve warm with cold butter.

NOTE The dough can be made the night before needed, cut into squares and put on a greased tray. Cover with plastic wrap and refrigerate overnight, then remove from refrigerator and allow to rise before baking.

INGREDIENTS

15 g compressed yeast or 7 g (1 sachet) dry yeast
1 cup lukewarm water
½ teaspoon sugar
3 tablespoons olive oil
3 cups (450 g) plain flour, sifted
1½ teaspoons salt
freshly ground white pepper

PIZZA DOUGH

If you like a high, fluffy, bread-like crust, use this dough to make one 30 cm pizza. For a thinner, crisper crust, divide dough then roll and pat it out into three or four 30 cm rounds. For parties, bake pizza in a rectangular or square tin, which makes it easier to cut into serving-size portions.

MAKES 2 PIZZA CRUSTS

METHOD

If using compressed yeast, combine the yeast, water and sugar in a large bowl. Set aside for about 15 minutes or until the surface is foamy. Stir in the oil.

If using compressed yeast, sift the flour and salt over the yeast mixture. If using dry yeast, add it to the flour, then mix in the water.

Season with pepper and blend with a wooden spoon. Turn the dough onto a lightly floured work surface and knead gently until smooth and elastic. Place the dough in a large, greased bowl and turn the dough to grease it all over. Cover with a tea towel and leave in a warm place for 2 hours, or until doubled in bulk, light and spongy.

Turn out onto a lightly floured work surface, knock down and knead four or five times. Divide dough in half and roll out into two rounds 5 mm thick. Place on greased baking trays or pizza trays, cover and leave to rise in a warm place for about 15 minutes before adding toppings.

NOTE After the first rising, pizza dough can be wrapped in plastic wrap and refrigerated overnight. The next day, simply knock down, knead lightly, roll out, and allow to rise for 15 minutes before filling and baking.

FOUR SEASONS PIZZA

SERVES 6–8

INGREDIENTS

½ quantity Pizza Dough (opposite), patted out to a 30 cm round
½ quantity Pizza Sauce (below)

TOPPING 1
2 slices cooked ham, cut into strips
4 mushrooms, thinly sliced
salt and freshly ground black pepper

TOPPING 2
4 anchovy fillets, halved
2 tablespoons diced mozzarella cheese
2 teaspoons drained capers

TOPPING 3
4–5 slices salami, cut into strips
8 black olives, stoned

TOPPING 4
6 prawns, shelled and de-veined, or ¼ cup flaked tuna, or one 125 g can mussels, drained
4 thin slices mozzarella cheese
2 tablespoons olive oil and ¼ cup grated parmesan cheese to finish

METHOD

Preheat the oven to 200°C. Spread the cooled sauce over the dough and add the toppings, a different one for each quarter.

Sprinkle the olive oil and cheese over the whole pizza and bake for 18–20 minutes or until the crust is golden and crisp around the edges.

PIZZA SAUCE

This rich, flavourful tomato sauce is used as a base for many pizzas. It is spread over the bread dough before other toppings are added. Instead of fresh tomatoes, drained canned whole tomatoes may be used.

Place 750 g ripe tomatoes, peeled and chopped; 2 garlic cloves, crushed; 1 teaspoon dried oregano, 1 tablespoon chopped fresh basil or 1 teaspoon dried basil, 1 bay leaf, 1 tablespoon brown sugar, salt and freshly ground black pepper in a saucepan and simmer gently for 30–40 minutes, stirring often. Taste for seasoning, remove the bay leaf and cool before using. Makes enough for two 30 cm rounds, or two 35 x 30 cm rectangles.

PIZZA MARGHERITA

SERVES 12

INGREDIENTS
1 quantity Pizza Dough (page 436), patted out to two 35 cm x 30 cm rectangles or two 30 cm rounds
4 tablespoons olive oil
½ cup grated parmesan cheese

1 quantity Pizza Sauce (page 437)
2 cups diced mozzarella cheese
12 leaves fresh basil, torn
salt and freshly ground black pepper

METHOD
Preheat the oven to 200°C.

Brush the pizza dough with half of the olive oil and sprinkle with half of the parmesan cheese. Spoon the sauce over the top and then add the mozzarella and basil, seasoning with salt and pepper.

Sprinkle the remaining oil and parmesan cheese over and bake for for 18–20 minutes or until the crust is golden and cooked.

VARIATIONS

HAM & MUSHROOM PIZZA Make as for Pizza Margherita, replacing the mozzarella and basil with 250 g cooked ham, cut into strips, and 6–8 finely sliced mushrooms.

SALAMI PIZZA Make as for Pizza Margherita, replacing the mozzarella and basil with a 50 g can flat anchovy fillets, drained, 125 g Italian salami cut into strips, and 12 stoned and quartered black olives.

NEAPOLITAN PIZZA Make as for Pizza Margherita, omitting the basil and parmesan and adding a 50 g can flat anchovy fillets, drained, and 125 g Italian salami cut into strips. Olives are optional.

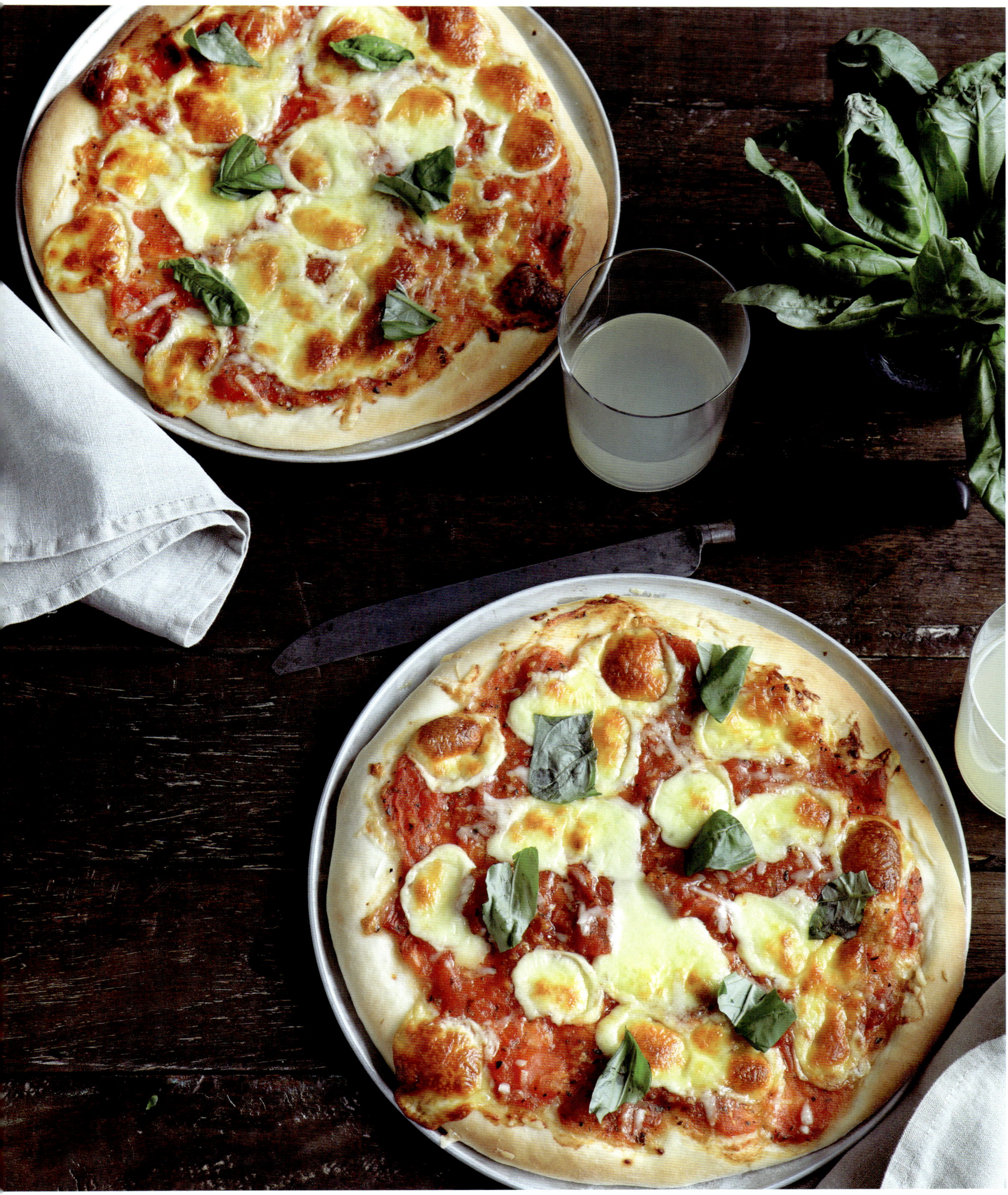

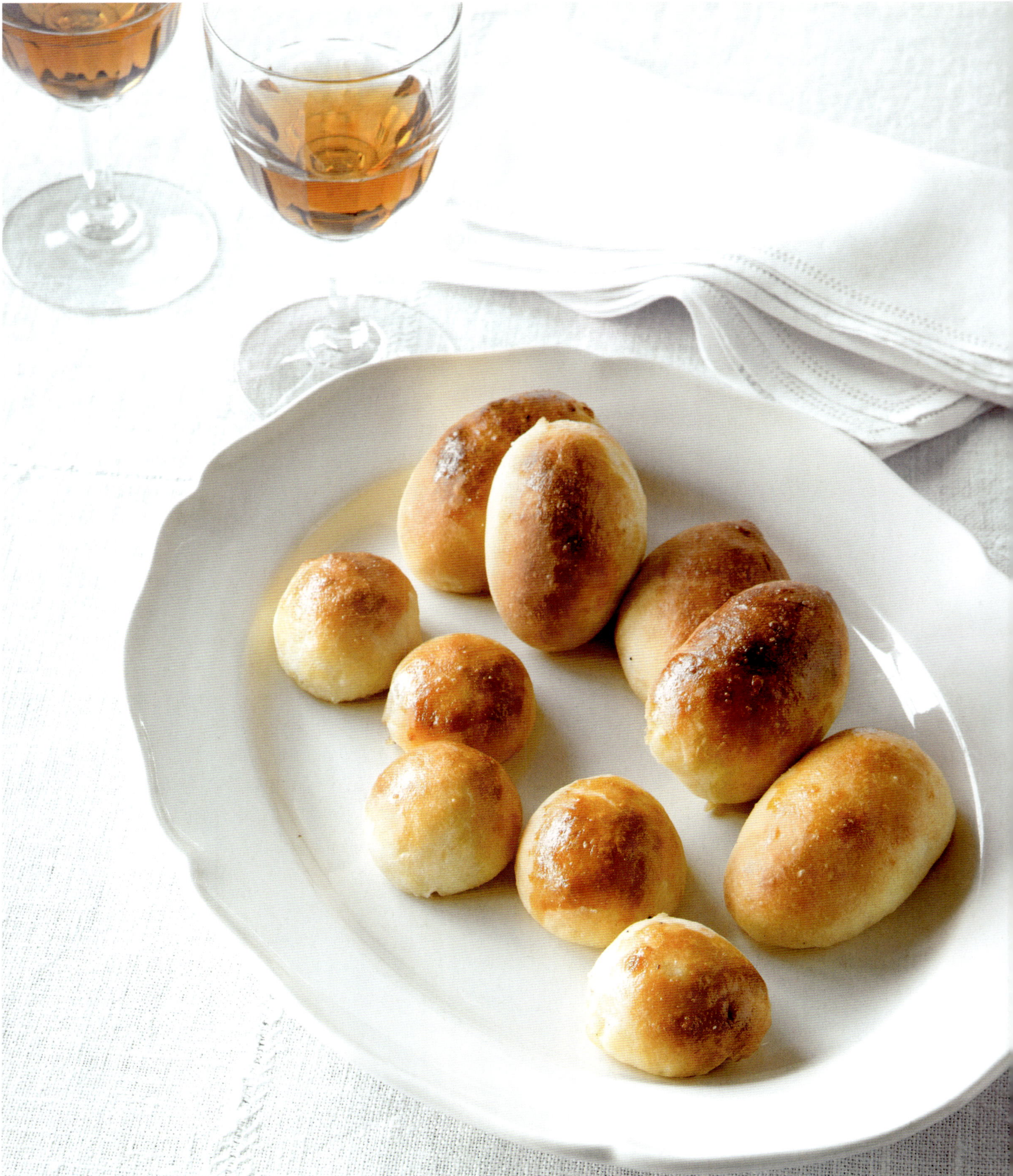

YEAST COOKERY *piroshki*

INGREDIENTS

1¼ cups milk
125 g butter
2 tablespoons sugar
3 cups (450 g) plain flour
2 teaspoons salt
7 g (1 sachet) dry yeast
1 egg yolk
beaten egg, to glaze

FILLING

3 large onions, finely chopped
60 g butter
250 g speck, or smoked streaky bacon, finely and neatly diced
freshly ground pepper

PIROSHKI

This recipe for soft buns filled with onion and smoked bacon or speck came into my life in the 1970s via a reader of *Woman's Day* when we were running a national bake-off. In those days the recipe seemed so exotic and different. I thought I'd never tasted anything so good and have been making them ever since. We, the judges, were so impressed they won a major prize. I have since learned that there are many variations to these Russian meat pies; many contain mince or cabbage, and often they are fried instead of baked. But this is still the recipe I like best.

MAKES 45–50 SMALL OR 30 LARGE

METHOD

Heat the milk, butter and sugar in a saucepan on low until lukewarm and the butter has melted, stirring occasionally.

Sift the flour with the salt into a large mixing bowl. Stir in the yeast. Make a well in centre and pour in the milk mixture and egg yolk. Stir with a wooden spoon, gradually incorporating flour. Beat dough for 3 minutes, until smooth and elastic. You can use your hand or the dough hook of an electric mixer to make the dough. Sprinkle a little flour on top, cover with plastic wrap then a folded tea towel, and leave in a warm place until doubled, about 1 hour.

Meanwhile, make the filling. Fry the onion in the butter on low heat, stirring, until golden, cool. Add the speck or bacon with a good grinding of pepper.

Preheat the oven to 230°C. Turn the dough out on to a floured board, knead lightly, and take a tablespoon-sized piece of dough. Top with a teaspoon of filling and fold edges of dough over to enclose filling. Mould into a ball. Place on lightly greased baking trays. Repeat with the remaining dough and filling, cover loosely with plastic wrap and leave in a warm place for 15 minutes.

Brush with beaten egg and bake for 10–15 minutes or until golden and cooked.

NOTE To freeze, pack in oven bags in serving-sized batches. It is a simple matter to lift them out of the freezer and pop them straight into a 180°C oven for about 10 minutes to reheat.

INGREDIENTS

15 g compressed yeast or 7 g (1 sachet) dry yeast
¼ cup lukewarm water
3 ⅓ cups (500 g) plain flour
a pinch of salt
2 tablespoons caster sugar
3 eggs, lightly beaten
¾ cup lukewarm milk
125 g butter, softened
beaten egg to glaze

BRIOCHE

This is a little topknot-shaped yeast bread which, along with croissants, spells breakfast to millions in France. Eat brioche warm with chilled butter, preferably unsalted, and fruit jam. Brioche are also delicious toasted, or may be hollowed out and used as a case for cooked savoury food such as seafood, pâté or mushrooms.

MAKES 12

METHOD

If using compressed yeast, dissolve the yeast in the water.

Sift the flour and salt into a large bowl. Take out ½ cup of the flour and work it gradually into the dissolved compressed yeast, or mix it with the dry yeast, if using, and the lukewarm water, to form a soft dough.

Form this dough into a ball and cut a cross in the top. Place the ball in a bowl of warm water and leave for about 5 minutes or until it doubles in bulk (it will rise to the surface when ready).

Meanwhile, make a well in the centre of the remaining flour, put in the sugar, eggs and milk and stir them together. Drain the yeast sponge, place it in the well and combine with the egg mixture. Stir in the surrounding flour gradually to form a soft dough. Beat the dough vigorously with your hand until well mixed, then beat in the butter.

Place the dough in a greased bowl, sprinkle lightly with flour, cover the bowl with plastic wrap and allow to rise in the refrigerator overnight or for at least 6 hours.

Remove from the refrigerator, punch the dough down and turn it onto a floured board. Knead lightly, then divide into pieces the size of an egg.

Cut off one third of each piece; roll the remainder of each piece into a ball and put into greased brioche moulds (deep fluted moulds). Roll small pieces of dough into little tadpole-shaped tops with tails. Cut a cross in the top of each brioche, open it a little and push the tops in, tail down. Leave to rise for 10–15 minutes in a warm place.

Preheat the oven to 220°C.

Brush the brioche with beaten egg and bake for about 15 minutes or until golden brown. Serve warm.

BASIC SWEET RICH DOUGH

INGREDIENTS

- 4 cups (600 g) plain flour
- a large pinch of salt
- ¾–1 cup milk
- 125 g butter
- 30 g compressed yeast or 14 g (2 sachets) dry yeast
- ½ cup (110 g) caster sugar
- 2 eggs, beaten

This basic dough makes many different loaves, rolls and twists of any size or shape you wish. Add spices, fruits, cherries or nuts; brush with melted butter and sprinkle with cinnamon and sugar before baking, or bake, cool and drizzle over some Glacé Icing (page 252).

SERVES 16

METHOD

Sift the flour with the salt into a large bowl. Stir in the dry yeast, if using.

Heat ¾ cup of the milk to lukewarm, add the butter and allow to melt, then add the compressed yeast, if using, and stir until dissolved. Mix in the sugar and beaten eggs.

Make a well in the flour, pour in the milk mixture and stir until smooth, first with a wooden spoon and then with your hand. Add more warm milk if necessary to make a soft dough. When the dough comes away cleanly from the sides of the bowl, turn it onto a floured work surface and knead until smooth and elastic. Only add a little more flour if the dough is too soft to knead.

Place the dough in a greased bowl and turn the dough over in the bowl so it is lightly greased. Cover with a damp cloth and leave it to rise in a warm place for 45–50 minutes or until doubled in bulk. Knock back the dough, pull the sides to the centre, turn over, then cover and allow to rise again for 30 minutes before shaping and baking.

WAYS TO USE BASIC SWEET RICH DOUGH

SUGARPLUM RING Use ½ quantity Basic Sweet Rich Dough. Leave to rise in a warm place until doubled in bulk. Pinch off bits of dough and form into 2.5 cm balls. Knead the balls lightly on a floured work surface. Roll balls of dough in melted butter, then in a mixture of brown sugar and cinnamon and place in a greased 20 cm ring tin. Leave a little space between each to allow for rising. Cover with a floured damp cloth and allow to rise in a warm place until almost doubled in bulk. Sprinkle over chopped walnuts or almonds. Bake in a preheated 180°C oven for 30–35 minutes. Serves 8.

CLOVERLEAF ROLLS Use ½ quantity Basic Sweet Rich Dough. Leave to rise in a warm place until doubled in bulk. Shape risen dough into walnut-sized balls. Grease muffin tins and put three balls of dough in each. Cover and let rise in a warm place for 30–45 minutes or until doubled in bulk. Brush rolls with milk or beaten egg and bake in a 200°C oven for about 15 minutes. Makes 12–18.

CRESCENTS Use ½ quantity Basic Sweet Rich Dough. Leave to rise in a warm place until doubled in bulk. Roll out the dough to the size of a dinner plate. Spread with softened butter and sprinkle with poppy seeds or sesame seeds. Cut into eight wedges and roll up each from the widest edge towards the point. Stretch dough gently and shape into a crescent. Place crescents well apart on a greased baking tray. Cover with a cloth and allow to rise in a warm place until doubled in size. Brush with beaten egg or milk and sprinkle over a few poppy seeds or sesame seeds. Bake in a preheated 230°C oven for 10–15 minutes or until the rolls are golden. Makes 8.

HOT CROSS BUNS

INGREDIENTS
- 4 cups (600 g) plain flour
- 1 teaspoon mixed spice
- ½ teaspoon ground cinnamon
- 1 teaspoon salt
- 30 g compressed yeast or 14 g (2 sachets) dry yeast
- 60 g butter, diced
- ¼ cup currants or sultanas
- ¼ cup chopped mixed candied peel
- ½ cup (110 g) caster sugar
- ½ cup lukewarm water
- ½ cup lukewarm milk
- 1 egg, lightly beaten

PASTE FOR CROSS
- ¼ cup (35 g) self-raising flour
- 2 tablespoons cold water

GLAZE
- ¼ teaspoon powdered gelatine
- 2 tablespoons water
- 1 tablespoon sugar to glaze

MAKES 12–14

METHOD

Sift the flour, mixed spice, cinnamon and salt into a bowl. Rub in the butter, then mix in currants or sultanas and peel. If using dry yeast, stir it in now, with the sugar. Make a well in the centre.

If using compressed yeast, cream the yeast with the sugar and add a little of the warm water to dissolve the yeast completely. Blend the remaining water and milk with the yeast and add with the beaten egg to the flour. Mix to form a soft dough. Turn onto a lightly floured work surface and knead until smooth and elastic.

Shape into a ball, place in a clean, greased bowl and turn the ball over so that the top of the dough is greased. Cover with a damp tea towel and leave to rise in a warm place for 1¼–1½ hours or until doubled in bulk.

Turn the risen dough onto a lightly floured work surface and gently press out to 1 cm thick. Divide the dough into 12–14 pieces and shape each into a small ball. Place balls on a greased baking tray, at least 2.5 cm apart, or arrange in greased round cake tins. Cover and leave to rise in a warm place for 20–30 minutes. Preheat the oven to 200°C.

To make the paste for the cross, combine the self-raising flour and water and beat to a smooth paste. Put into a baking paper funnel or a small piping bag fitted with a plain nozzle. Using a sharp knife, make a slight indentation in shape of a cross on top of each bun just before baking and pipe the prepared paste into cross.

Bake the buns for about 15 minutes.

Meanwhile, to make the glaze, sprinkle the gelatine over the water in a small saucepan. When softened, dissolve over a low heat. Add the sugar and stir until dissolved. Remove from the heat. Remove the buns from the oven and brush with the glaze while still hot. Stand the buns in a warm place, such as near the opened door of the turned-off oven. This helps to set the glaze.

VARIATION
ICING CROSS If liked, omit the paste cross and decorate with a sweet icing cross. Mix 1 cup sifted icing sugar with enough hot milk (about 2 teaspoons) to make a firm consistency. Spoon into a piping bag fitted with a plain tube and pipe crosses on the baked warm buns.

GREEK EASTER BREAD

INGREDIENTS
1 quantity Basic Sweet Rich Dough (page 443)
½ cup finely chopped mixed candied peel
¼ cup chopped almonds
½ teaspoon aniseeds (optional)
5 eggs
Glacé Icing (page 252)
pink or red food colouring
chopped nuts or fruit jellies to decorate

It's an old Greek custom to bake eggs in a nest of sweet dough. Use raw eggs, either natural white or brown, or colour them with Easter egg dye which you can find in many delicatessens.

SERVES 12–15

METHOD
Make the Basic Sweet Rich Dough as directed. After the second rising, turn the dough onto a floured work surface. Combine the peel, almonds and aniseeds, if using, and knead into the dough.

Divide the dough in half and roll each half into a rope about 60 cm long. Twist the ropes loosely together and shape into a ring on a large greased baking tray. Arrange the unshelled eggs in hollows evenly around the ring. Cover and leave to rise in a warm place for 30–40 minutes.

Preheat the oven to 190°C.

Bake the ring for 30–35 minutes, or until golden. Transfer to a wire rack to cool.

When cool, spread with glacé icing, tinted pale pink, leaving the eggs uncovered. Decorate with chopped nuts or brightly coloured fruit jellies.

INGREDIENTS

60 g butter
4 cups (600 g) plain flour, sifted
⅓ cup (75 g) caster sugar
a pinch of salt
30 g compressed yeast or 15 g (2 sachets) dry yeast
1 cup lukewarm milk

TO FINISH

1 beaten egg
2 tablespoons sugar, plus extra as needed
½ cup chopped nuts
2 tablespoons melted butter
1 tablespoon cinnamon
¼ cup currants
¼ cup sultanas

SWEDISH COFFEE BREADS

This recipe is perfect for entertaining as it serves a large number of people. There are three different variations so you can either make all three or you can choose one variation and make a larger quantity.

MAKES 3

METHOD

Melt the butter and allow to cool.

Put the flour in a bowl. Add the sugar and salt, mix and make a well in the centre.

In a small bowl, mix the yeast in a little of the milk and add to the flour with the butter and the remaining milk. Mix with a spoon until all the milk and butter have been absorbed, then put in a greased bowl, cover with a damp cloth and leave to rise in a warm place for 2 hours or until dough has doubled in size.

Knock back the dough and knead until it is soft and smooth. Divide into three portions and shape as follows.

VARIATIONS

COFFEE TWIST Take one portion of dough and divide it into three equal pieces. Roll each piece of dough between floured hands into a long strand. Plait strands together lightly, then cover and allow the twist to rise on a baking tray for 45 minutes. Brush with beaten egg, and sprinkle with sugar and chopped nuts. Bake in a preheated 180°C oven for 20–25 minutes. Serves 12.

CINNAMON RING Roll out the second portion of dough as thinly as possible on a floured work surface. Brush with melted butter and sprinkle heavily with sugar and cinnamon. Roll up like a Swiss roll and join the ends together to make a ring. Make sure the ends are well sealed. Place the ring on a baking tray to rise. Cut almost through the dough at 2.5 cm intervals with scissors. Turn the leaves of dough thus formed to alternate sides to expose the filling. Allow to rise again for 45 minutes. Brush with beaten egg and bake in a preheated 180°C oven for 15–20 minutes. Serves 12.

FRUIT AND NUT BUNS Roll out the remaining portion of dough as thinly as possible on a floured work surface. Brush with melted butter and sprinkle heavily with sugar, currants, sultanas and chopped nuts. Roll up like a Swiss roll and cut into 2.5 cm slices to form small buns. Decorate each bun by cutting with scissors in different patterns according to your imagination. Allow to rise on a baking tray for 45 minutes. Brush with beaten egg and bake in a preheated 180°C oven for 5–10 minutes. Makes about 12.

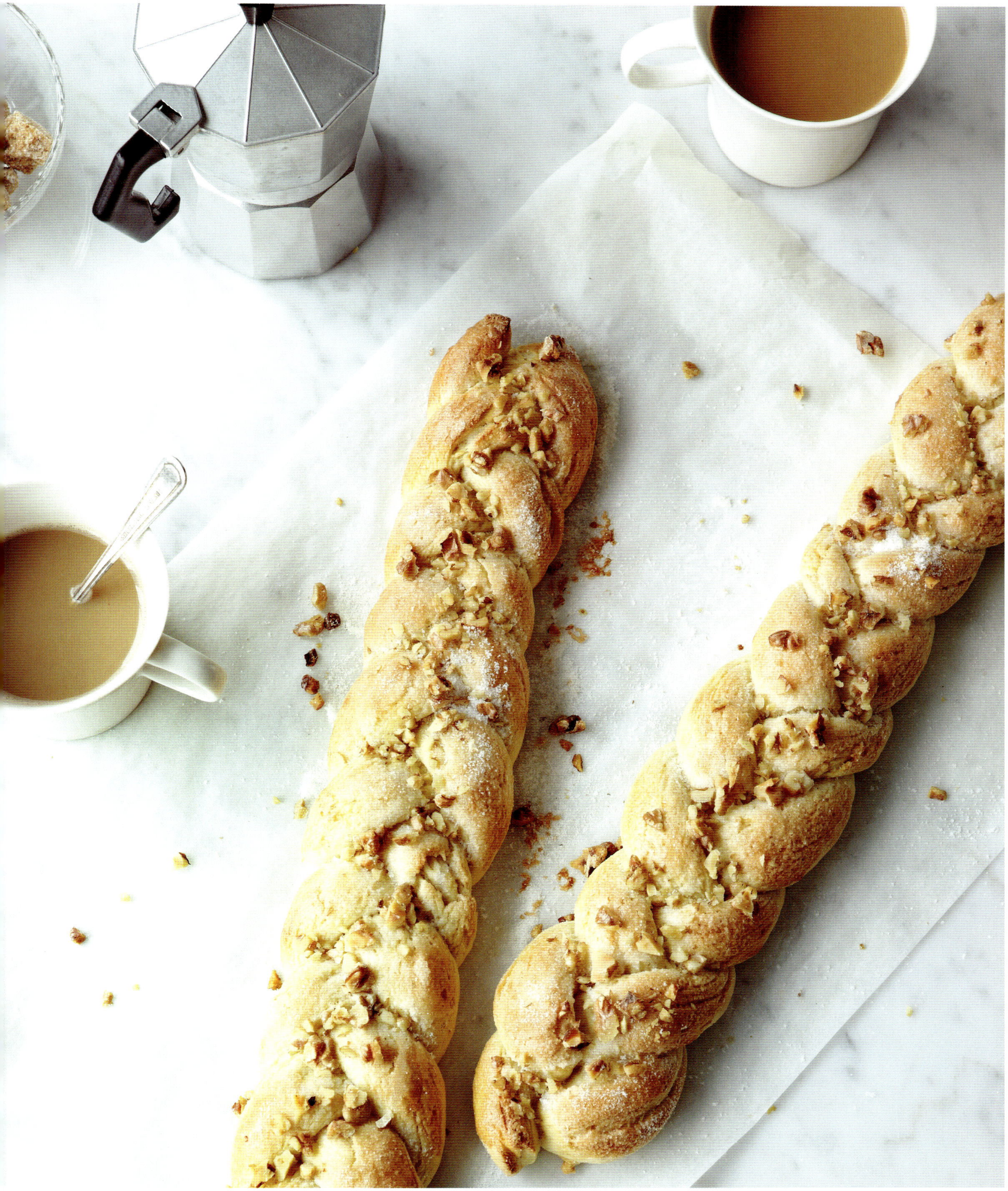

INGREDIENTS

30 g compressed yeast or 14 g (2 sachets) dry yeast
1¼ cups lukewarm milk
6 cups (900 g) plain flour, sifted
½ cup (110 g) caster sugar
3 teaspoons salt
½ teaspoon ground cloves
½ teaspoon freshly ground black pepper
1½ cups light beer
½ cup golden syrup
2 cups (300 g) rye flour
1 cup raisins

NORWEGIAN SWEET BREAD

In many parts of the world, beer is added to bread to give extra flavour and richness. This good-tasting Norwegian bread has a full flavour and delicious chewy texture. Rye flour is commonly used in Northern European breads.

MAKES 3

METHOD

If using compressed yeast, soften the yeast in the warm milk in a large bowl and let stand for 5 minutes. Beat in 1 cup of the plain flour, the sugar, salt, cloves and pepper.

If using dry yeast, add it to 1 cup of the plain flour then beat in the sugar, salt, cloves and pepper.

Cover the bowl with a tea towel and stand in a warm place for 40 minutes or until the dough is light and bubbly.

Add the beer and golden syrup. Beat in the rye flour and raisins, and enough of the remaining plain flour to make a moderately stiff dough. Turn the dough out onto a lightly floured work surface and knead for 8–10 minutes or until smooth and elastic.

Place in a greased bowl, turning the dough to grease the surface. Cover and allow to rise in a warm place for about 1 hour or until doubled in bulk.

Knock the dough back and rest for 10 minutes.

Divide the dough into thirds and shape into three round loaves. Place on greased baking trays, cover and let rise for 35–40 minutes or until doubled in bulk.

Preheat the oven to 190°C.

Bake the loaves for about 40 minutes or until golden.

YEAST COOKERY *sweet breads & rolls*

INGREDIENTS
4 cups (600 g) plain flour, sifted
1 teaspoon salt
30 g compressed yeast or 14 g (2 sachets) dry yeast
1 teaspoon caster sugar
2 eggs
1 egg yolk
1 cup cream
¼ cup lukewarm water
¼ cup milk and 3 teaspoons caster sugar to glaze

SALLY LUNN

An English soft sweet bun, popular for breakfast or tea-time. The recipe is said to have arrived with a French refugee in the seventeenth century.

MAKES 2

METHOD

If using dry yeast, place the flour, salt and yeast in a large bowl. Beat the whole eggs with the egg yolks and strain into the flour. Stir in the cream and the lukewarm water.

If using compressed yeast, mix the yeast with the sugar in a large bowl. Beat the whole eggs with the egg yolks and strain into the creamed yeast mixture. Stir in the cream and whisk until frothy. Add the lukewarm water. Pour the yeast mixture into the flour.

Mix to a soft dough, adding a little more water if necessary. Beat well, then put in a greased bowl and cover with lightly greased plastic wrap and a clean tea towel. Put in a warm place to rise for about 1½ hours or until doubled in bulk.

Preheat the oven to 200°C. Grease two 20 cm cake tins.

Turn the dough onto a lightly floured work surface and knead lightly. Halve the dough and shape into two rounds about 20 cm in diameter. Put the rounds into the prepared cake tins and bake for 20–25 minutes or until golden.

Combine the milk and sugar and heat gently to dissolve the sugar. Remove the cakes from the oven, brush with the milk and sugar glaze and return to the oven for 30 seconds to dry the glaze.

Serve warm with butter, or sliced, toasted and buttered.

ORANGE ROLLS

INGREDIENTS
1 quantity Basic Rich Sweet Dough (page 443)
1 cup (220 g) caster sugar
grated rind of 1 orange
½ cup sultanas (optional)
60 g melted butter

ORANGE ICING
2 cups (250 g) icing sugar, sifted
2 tablespoons orange juice

MAKES 2; SERVES 16

METHOD

Prepare the dough and chill.

When ready to shape, combine the sugar, orange rind and sultanas. Divide the dough in half and roll each half out on a well-floured surface to a rectangle 46 cm x 23 cm. Brush with the melted butter and sprinkle with the sugar and sultana mixture. Roll up from one long side, like a Swiss roll.

Cut into 12 thick slices and place, cut sides up, in two lightly greased 20 cm sandwich tins. Cover and let rise in a warm place for about 1 hour or until doubled in bulk.

Meanwhile, preheat the oven to 190°C.

Bake the rolls for about 25 minutes.

For the orange icing, combine the icing sugar and orange juice to make a thin icing.

Remove the rolls from the tins and drizzle with the orange icing while warm.

VARIATION

CINNAMON PINWHEELS Follow the recipe for orange rolls above, omitting the orange rind and using instead 2 teaspoons cinnamon and a little extra butter.

YEAST COOKERY *sweet breads & rolls*

INGREDIENTS
½ quantity Basic Sweet Rich Dough (page 443)
1–2 teaspoons ground cardamom
1 egg
2 teaspoons milk
caster sugar to sprinkle

CARDAMOM BRAID

MAKES 1 LARGE BRAID

METHOD

Make up the basic sweet dough as directed, adding the ground cardamom to the flour before sifting. Leave in a warm place until doubled in bulk.

Turn onto a floured surface and knead lightly. Divide the dough into three equal portions. Shape each piece into a rope about 2.5 cm across. Line the ropes up on a greased baking tray and, starting from the middle, plait loosely towards the ends, taking care not to stretch the dough. Seal the ends by pinching them well together. Cover and leave in a warm place to rise until doubled in bulk.

Preheat the oven to 180°C.

Beat the egg and milk then brush over the braid. Sprinkle the braid generously with caster sugar and bake for about 30–35 minutes or until brown.

Transfer to a wire rack and loosely cover with a clean tea towel. Leave to cool before slicing.

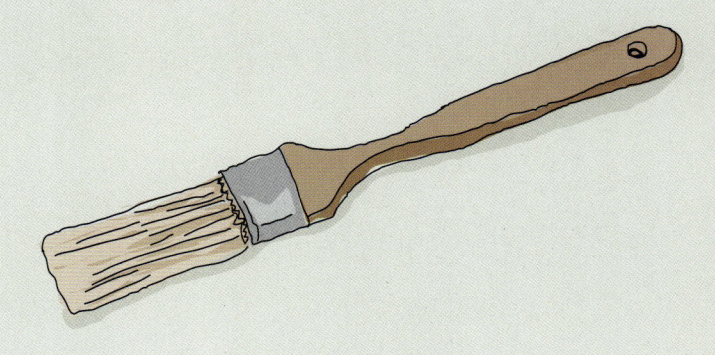

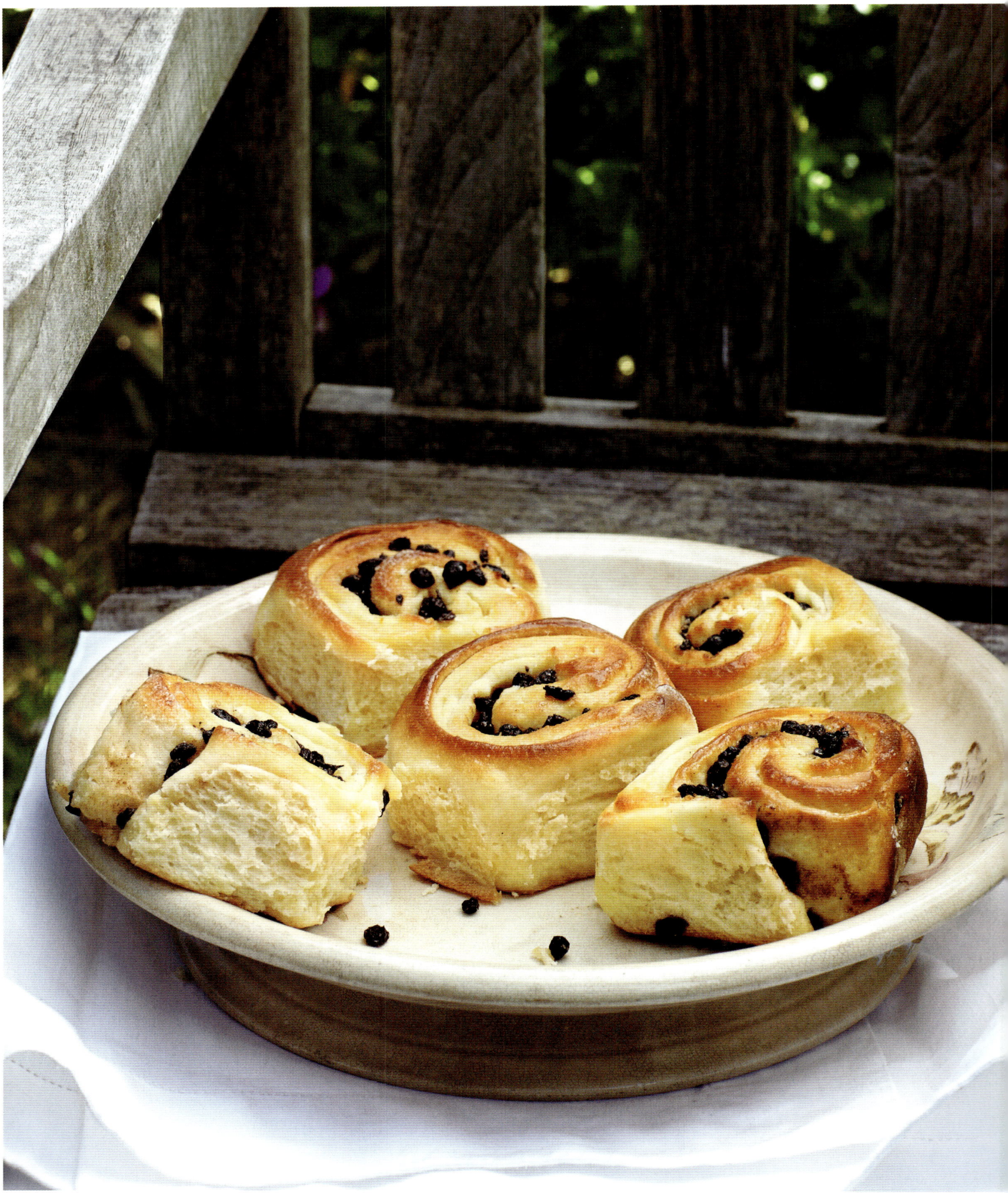

CHELSEA BUNS

INGREDIENTS
1 quantity Basic Sweet Rich Dough (page 443)
60 g butter, softened
¼ cup (55 g) caster sugar
1 cup currants
1 teaspoon mixed spice
extra caster sugar

GLAZE
¼ cup (55 g) caster sugar
⅓ cup water

This sweet yeast bun, an English creation, is now enjoyed wherever there are good commercial or home bakers. The buns look impressive but are not difficult to make.

MAKES 12

METHOD
Make the sweet rich dough as directed. After the first rising, turn the dough onto a floured work surface, knead lightly and roll out to a rectangle about 30 cm x 20 cm. Spread with softened butter and sprinkle with 1 tablespoon sugar. Fold each end over to meet in the centre, then fold the dough in half and roll out again.

Sprinkle with the rest of sugar, the currants and spice. Roll up from one long side like a Swiss roll. Cut into 12 equal slices. Arrange the slices, cut side up and almost touching, in a well-greased 20 cm sandwich tin. Cover loosely with a clean tea towel and leave to rise in a warm place for about 20 minutes, after which time the buns should now be touching.

Preheat the oven to 200°C.

Sprinkle the risen buns with extra caster sugar. Bake for about 20 minutes or until golden.

Meanwhile, to make the glaze, combine the sugar and water in a saucepan and stir over gentle heat until the sugar has dissolved. Increase the heat and boil, without stirring, for 3 minutes.

Remove the buns from the oven, brush with the glaze and return to the oven for 30 seconds to dry the glaze. Leave to cool before separating the buns. Serve warm or cool with plenty of butter.

INGREDIENTS

5 cups (750 g) plain flour, sifted
½ teaspoon salt
15 g compressed yeast or 7 g (1 sachet) dry yeast
¼ cup plus ½ teaspoon sugar
2¼ cups lukewarm milk
90 g butter
1 egg, beaten
½ cup currants

GLAZE

¼ cup (55 g) sugar
½ cup water

OLD-FASHIONED PENNY BUNS

MAKES ABOUT 15

METHOD

If using dry yeast, place 2½ cups of the flour, the salt and the yeast in a large bowl. Stir in about ½ cup of the milk until dissolved. Mix to a soft dough, using a little more milk if necessary, and beat well. Put in a greased bowl, cover with a damp tea towel and set aside to rise for 30–40 minutes.

If using compressed yeast, cream the yeast with the ½ teaspoon sugar in a small bowl. Stir in about ½ cup of the milk until dissolved. Make a well in the flour and pour in the yeast mixture. Mix to a soft dough, using a little more milk if necessary, and beat well. Put in a greased bowl, cover with damp tea towel and set aside to rise for 30–40 minutes.

Warm the remaining milk and melt the butter in it. Allow to cool to lukewarm, then add the egg. Stir into the risen flour mixture together with the currants, the remaining flour and sugar. Beat well, then cover the bowl with lightly oiled plastic wrap and a clean tea towel. Set aside to rise in a warm place for about 1½ hours or until doubled in bulk. Turn onto a floured work surface, punch your fist into the dough and knead lightly. Shape pieces of dough into small buns and place on a greased baking tray so the buns are just touching each other. Cover loosely with a cloth and allow to rise for 15 minutes.

Preheat the oven to 200°C.

Bake the buns for 15–20 minutes, or until golden.

Meanwhile, to make the glaze, put the sugar and water in a small saucepan and heat gently, stirring until the sugar dissolves. Increase the heat and boil for 3 minutes, without stirring. Remove the buns from the oven, brush with glaze and replace in the hot oven for about 30 seconds to dry the glaze. Serve warm from the oven, with or without butter; or cold, sliced and spread with butter, or toasted with butter.

INGREDIENTS

15 g compressed yeast or 7 g (1 sachet) dry yeast
1¼ cups warm milk
4 cups (600 g) plain flour
1 teaspoon salt
45 g lard or butter
1½ tablespoons caster sugar
¾ cup currants
2 tablespoons chopped mixed candied peel
milk to glaze

YORKSHIRE TEA CAKES

MAKES 6–8

METHOD

If using compressed yeast, dissolve the yeast in the warm milk and leave in a warm place for about 10 minutes or until the mixture becomes frothy.

Sift the flour and salt into a large bowl, add the dry yeast, if using, and rub in the lard or butter. Stir in the sugar, currants and peel. Add the milk and yeast mixture (if using compressed yeast) and mix to a firm dough (you may need to add a little more flour).

Turn the dough onto a lightly floured work surface and knead for about 10 minutes or until smooth and elastic. Form into a ball, return to the clean, very lightly oiled bowl and turn the dough round to coat it lightly with oil. Cover with a tea towel and leave to rise in a warm place for about 1 hour or until the dough has doubled in bulk.

Turn onto a lightly floured surface, knock the dough down and knead until smooth. Divide into six or eight pieces. Shape each into a ball and roll out to rounds 15–18 cm in diameter. Then place the tea cakes on two or three greased baking trays, brush the tops with milk and cover with oiled plastic wrap. Allow to rise in a warm place for about 40 minutes or until almost doubled in size.

Preheat the oven to 200°C.

Bake for about 20 minutes or until well risen and golden brown. Cool on a wire rack. Serve warm or toasted, split open and spread with plenty of butter.

NOTE If you would like the buns to have a sticky top, brush with clear honey or syrup as soon as you remove them from the oven.

INGREDIENTS

½ quantity Basic Sweet Rich Dough (page 443)
30 g butter, softened
¼ cup (55 g) caster sugar
⅓ cup raisins
2 teaspoons ground cinnamon
Glacé Icing (page 252)
walnut halves, glacé cherries and candied angelica to decorate

TEA RING

MAKES 1

METHOD

Prepare the basic sweet rich dough as instructed. After the second rising, turn the dough onto a floured work surface and roll out to a rectangle about 1 cm thick. Dot the surface with softened butter and sprinkle with sugar, raisins and cinnamon. Roll up the dough tightly, beginning at the longer side, and seal by pinching the edges well together.

Curl the dough into a ring, joining the ends together well, and place on a greased baking tray. Using scissors or a sharp knife, snip the ring at 2.5 cm intervals around the outside edge, making each cut or snip two-thirds through the dough. Cover with a cloth and leave to rise for 15–20 minutes.

Preheat the oven to 190°C.

Bake the tea ring for about 25 minutes or until golden brown and a skewer inserted in the centre comes out clean.

Make a thin glacé icing and brush over the ring while still warm, then decorate with nuts, cherries and angelica.

YEAST COOKERY *yeasted cakes*

INGREDIENTS

- 2 strips candied angelica, cut into 1 cm dice
- 1/3 cup raisins
- 1/2 cup currants
- 1/2 cup glacé cherries, halved
- 2/3 cup chopped mixed candied peel
- 1/3 cup rum
- 5 cups (750 g) plain flour
- a large pinch of salt
- 1/3 cup warm milk
- 45 g compressed yeast
- 185 g butter, softened
- 1/2 cup (110 g) caster sugar
- 2 eggs, lightly beaten
- 1/2 cup blanched slivered almonds
- melted butter, caster sugar and sifted icing sugar to decorate

STOLLEN

MAKES 2

METHOD

Put the angelica, raisins, currants, cherries and peel in a bowl and pour the rum over. Toss well, cover and allow to stand for 2 hours or preferably overnight.

Sift the flour and salt into a bowl.

Put the warm milk in another bowl, add the yeast and butter and stir until the yeast is dissolved. Mix in the sugar and eggs. Make a well in the centre of the flour, pour in the yeast mixture and mix until smooth, commencing with a wooden spoon and then finishing off with your hand. When the dough leaves the sides of the bowl, turn onto a lightly floured board and knead until smooth and elastic – this may take 10–15 minutes. Place the dough into a clean greased bowl, cover with a damp cloth and leave to rise in a warm place for 50–60 minutes or until doubled in bulk.

When risen, knock the dough down and shape into a square. Drain the rum-soaked fruits, dry well on paper towels and toss in a little flour. Spoon into the middle of the dough square with the almonds. Fold the dough over the fruits, and knead the fruits lightly into the dough. Return to the greased bowl, cover and leave in a warm place to rise for 30–45 minutes.

Knock the dough down and turn onto a floured board. Halve the dough. Roll out each portion into an oval about 2 cm thick. Brush with melted butter and sprinkle with a little caster sugar. Fold each portion's long edges inwards, overlapping the centre with each edge by about 2.5 cm. Press the edges gently to keep them in place and leave the roll this side up.

With lightly floured hands, taper the ends slightly and pat the sides to mound the stollen in the centre. The finished loaves should be about 8 cm wide. Place on a greased baking tray. Brush with a little butter and let rise in a warm place for about 1 hour or until doubled in bulk.

Preheat the oven to 190°C. Bake the loaves for about 45 minutes or until golden brown and crusty. Cool on a wire rack. Dust heavily with sifted icing sugar before slicing and buttering.

VARIATION

POPPY SEED STOLLEN (MOHNSTOLLEN) Omit all fruit; use almonds only. When each portion of dough is rolled into a flat oval, brush with melted butter and fill each with half of following mixture: 250 g poppy seeds, ground and simmered in 1 cup milk with 2/3 cup raisins for 5 minutes; 2/3 cup chopped mixed candied peel; 1/2 cup (110 g) sugar; 1/2 teaspoon cinnamon; 1 tablespoon rum; and a few drops of rosewater. Fold and bake as for Stollen.

SAVARIN

INGREDIENTS

- 2 cups (300 g) plain flour
- ¼ teaspoon salt
- 15 g compressed yeast or 7 g (1 sachet) dry yeast
- 3 teaspoons caster sugar
- ½ cup warm milk
- 2 eggs (60 g size)
- 125 g butter, softened
- ½ cup Apricot Glaze (page 389)
- 1 cup fruit (strawberries, raspberries, cherries, blackberries, etc), sprinkled with 2 tablespoons Kirsch and 1 tablespoon sugar

SYRUP

- 1 cup water
- 1 cup (220 g) caster sugar
- 2.5 cm piece vanilla bean
- ⅓ cup Kirsch

A wonderful liqueur-soaked yeast cake, said to have been invented by the great French chef Jean Brillat-Savarin. A savarin is usually baked in a special savarin ring mould. The syrup is flavoured with Kirsch, and the centre can be filled with whipped cream, custard or a fruit filling. A savarin is usually glazed, and can be decorated with almonds, glacé fruits or fresh berries, if desired.

SERVES 6–8

METHOD

Sift the flour and salt into a large warmed bowl. Add the dry yeast, if using.

If using compressed yeast, cream the yeast with the sugar in a small bowl, then add the warm milk.

Make a well in the centre of the flour and add the compressed yeast mixture, if using, or the sugar and warm milk, if using dry yeast. Sprinkle a little flour from the side over the top, cover with a cloth and leave in a warm place for 15 minutes for the yeast to sponge.

Beat the eggs into the butter and add to the yeast mixture. Beat vigorously using the hand until all the flour is incorporated and the dough is smooth and elastic. Cover with a cloth and leave the dough to rise in a warm place until doubled in bulk. This will take 30–40 minutes.

Spoon the dough into a well-greased 23 cm savarin mould or ring tin. Allow to rise in a warm place until the dough reaches the top of the tin. Preheat the oven to 200°C. Bake for about 20 minutes or until golden brown and beginning to shrink a little from the sides of the tin.

To make the syrup, combine the water, sugar and vanilla bean in a saucepan. Stir over medium heat until the sugar dissolves. Bring to the boil and boil for 10 minutes. Discard the vanilla bean. Stir in the Kirsch.

Remove the savarin from the oven and cool in the tin for 5 minutes. Turn out onto a wire rack and place a dish under the rack to catch any syrup that runs off the cake. Prick the savarin with a fine skewer all over and while still hot, spoon the warm syrup over, a little at a time, until all the syrup has been absorbed. Allow the savarin to cool. Carefully slide onto a serving dish, brush lightly with apricot glaze and fill the centre with fruit sprinkled with sugar and Kirsch.

NOTE The centre of the savarin may be filled with 2 cups of whipped cream flavoured with Kirsch, 2 cups Crème Pâtissière (page 338) flavoured with vanilla and Kirsch, or a mixture of fresh fruits such as cherries, pears, apricots and pineapple sprinkled with sugar and Kirsch. A bowl of whipped cream may accompany the savarin if you like.

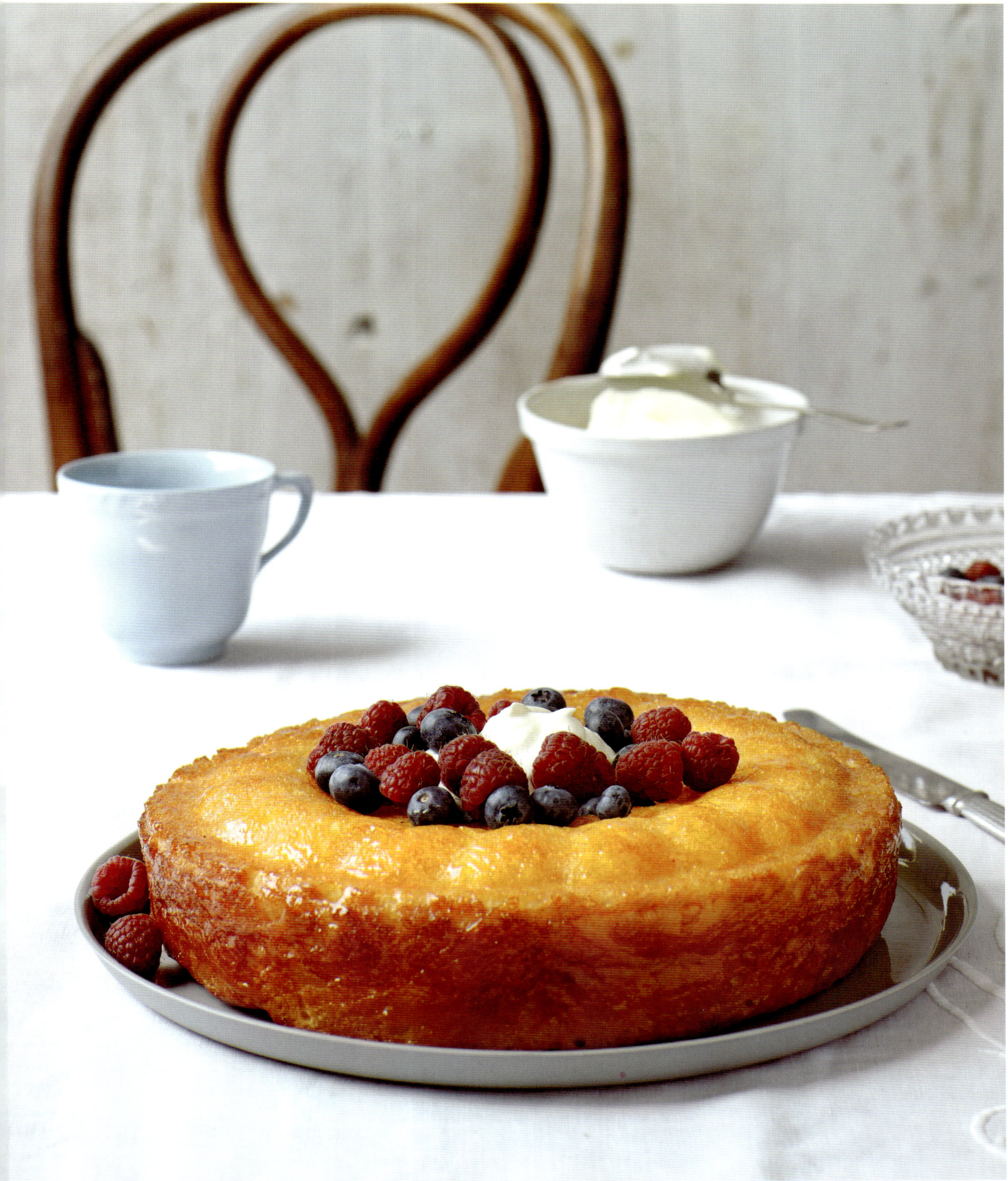

APPLE KUCHEN

INGREDIENTS
2 cups (300 g) plain flour
½ teaspoon salt
15 g compressed yeast or 7 g (1 sachet) dry yeast
2 tablespoons caster sugar
1 egg, beaten
½ cup warm milk
60 g butter, melted
¼ cup raisins
1 apple, peeled, cored and sliced
caster sugar to sprinkle
1 teaspoon ground cinnamon

SERVES 6-8

METHOD

Grease a 20–22 cm cake tin or deep sandwich tin.

Sift the flour and salt into a large bowl. Add the dry yeast if using, and the sugar. Mix in the egg, milk and butter. Beat thoroughly, then leave to rise in a warm place until doubled in bulk.

If using compressed yeast, cream the yeast with the sugar. Mix into the flour with the egg, milk and butter. Beat thoroughly, then leave to rise in a warm place until doubled in bulk.

Turn out onto a floured board and knead lightly. Work the raisins into the dough. Shape into a large bun with floured hands and put into the prepared tin. Flatten the top with your fist and cover with sliced apple, pressing the sharp edge of the slices into the dough.

Brush lightly with a thin syrup (3 tablespoons water and 1 tablespoon sugar boiled for 1 minute) or with water alone, then sprinkle thickly with caster sugar mixed with the cinnamon, and leave to prove for 20 minutes.

Preheat the oven to 190°C.

Bake for 40–45 minutes or until well risen and golden.

GUGELHOPF (KUGELHUPF)

INGREDIENTS
- ⅓ cup slivered almonds
- ½ cup currants
- ½ cup raisins
- 3 tablespoons rum
- ¾ cup lukewarm milk
- 30 g compressed yeast or 14 g (2 sachets) dry yeast
- 3 cups (450 g) plain flour
- a pinch of salt
- 1½ tablespoons caster sugar
- 3 eggs, lightly beaten
- 125 g butter, melted and slightly cooled
- sifted icing sugar to dust

This is the yeast cake of Alsace from which babas and savarins were developed. Gugelhopf is studded with rum-soaked currants and is cooked in a distinctive fluted ring mould.

SERVES 10–12

METHOD

Generously butter a 20 cm gugelhopf tin or fluted ring tin and press the slivered almonds into the butter. Refrigerate until needed.

Soak the currants and raisins in the rum.

If using compressed yeast, pour the lukewarm milk onto the yeast and stir until dissolved.

Sift the flour and salt into a warm bowl. Add the dry yeast, if using. Make a well in the centre and add the yeast mixture (if using compressed yeast) or the lukewarm milk (if using dry yeast), the sugar, eggs and melted butter. Beat well and add the soaked fruits and their liquid. Turn the batter into the prepared tin (which should be three-quarters full).

Cover with a oiled plastic wrap and stand in a warm place for 20–30 minutes or until the mixture has risen to 2.5 cm below the top of the tin.

Preheat the oven to 190°C.

Bake for 50–60 minutes or until a skewer inserted in the centre comes out clean. Stand for a few minutes, then turn out onto a wire rack to cool.

Dust with icing sugar and serve in slices with coffee or white wine.

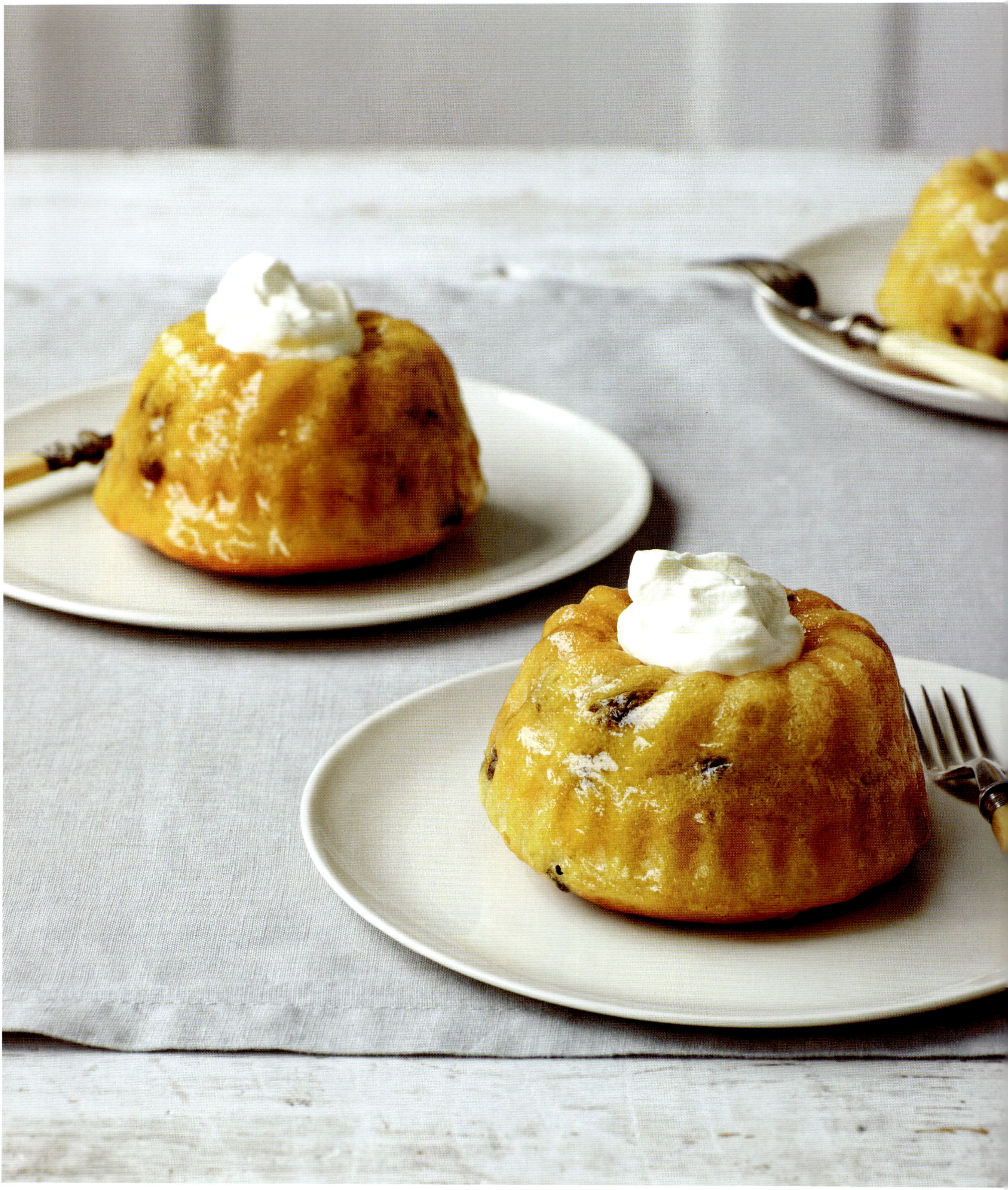

INGREDIENTS

- ¼ cup currants
- ½ cup sultanas
- ¼ cup dark rum
- 15 g compressed yeast or 7 g (1 sachet) dry yeast
- ½ cup lukewarm milk
- 3 tablespoons caster sugar plus a pinch extra
- 2 cups (300 g) plain flour
- ½ teaspoon salt
- 4 eggs, lightly beaten
- 125 g butter, softened
- whipped cream to serve

SYRUP
- 1½ cups water
- 1½ cups (330 g) sugar
- 4 tablespoons dark rum

GLAZE (OPTIONAL)
- 1 cup apricot jam
- 2 tablespoons water
- 2 tablespoons dark rum

BABA AU RHUM

A delectable French dessert cake made of yeast dough containing currants and soaked in rum-flavoured syrup. Large babas are baked in a tall, cylindrical mould and small ones in individual baba, dariole or pudding moulds.

MAKES 6–8

METHOD

Soak the currants and sultanas in the rum, covered, overnight.

If using compressed yeast, cream the yeast with the milk and a pinch of sugar and stand for 10 minutes.

Sift the flour, the remaining sugar and the salt into a large warmed bowl, make a well in the centre and add the yeast mixture or the dry yeast, if using. Sprinkle a little flour from the sides over the liquid, cover with plastic wrap and leave in a warm place for 20 minutes.

Add the eggs and butter to the flour–yeast mixture and beat vigorously until the dough is smooth and elastic. Drain the fruit and mix into the dough.

Cover with oiled plastic wrap and a cloth and leave in a warm place to rise for about 1 hour until doubled in bulk.

Pipe or spoon the baba dough into 6–8 buttered individual baba moulds (about 10 cm across the top of the tin), filling them one-third full. Let the dough rise for 30–40 minutes or until it reaches the tops of the moulds.

Preheat the oven to 230°C.

Place the babas in the oven, then immediately reduce the oven temperature to 200°C. Bake for 15 minutes or until well browned.

Remove the babas from the moulds and cool on a wire rack until lukewarm.

To make the syrup, combine the water and sugar and cook, stirring, until the sugar dissolves. Boil for 10 minutes without stirring, then remove from the heat and add the rum. Cool until warm.

Place the rack of babas over a tray and slowly spoon the warm syrup over the babas so they absorb as much as possible. As the syrup collects in the tray, re-spoon it over the babas.

To make the glaze, heat the jam and water together, stirring until the jam melts. Stir in rum, then rub mixture through a sieve. Brush over the babas. Serve with whipped cream.

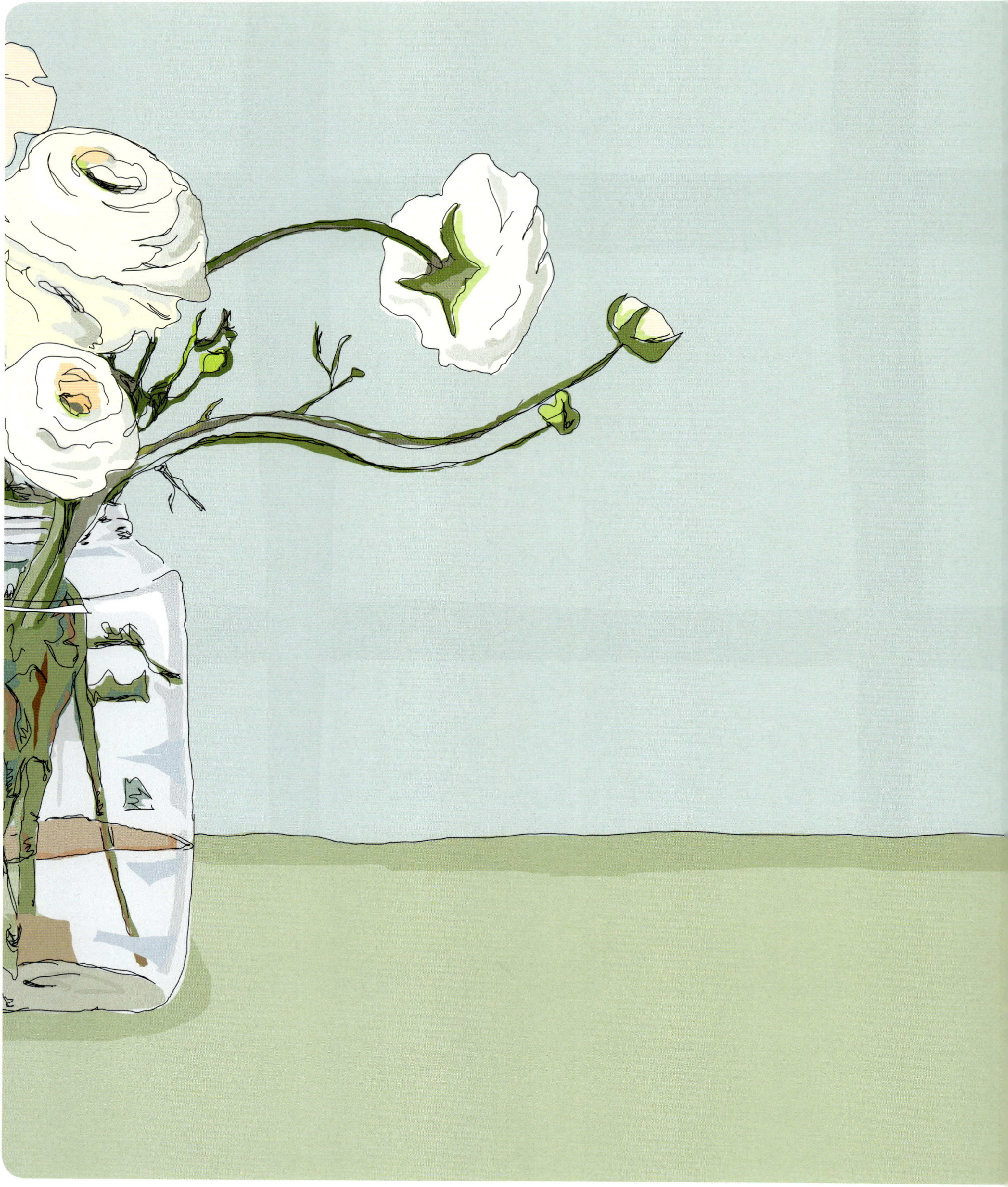

GLOSSARY & INDEX

GLOSSARY

Most ingredients used in baking are readily available supermarket staples. This glossary lists some ingredients commonly used in baking, with information on how to purchase, use and store them. As with any cooking, you will get the best results if you use the best-quality ingredients you can find or afford.

BUTTER Butter is made by churning cream until it forms a solid mass. Salted butter keeps longer than unsalted, as the salt acts as a preservative. Store butter well wrapped in the refrigerator, away from strong-smelling foods, as butter absorbs odours and flavours readily. Salted butter contains more milk solids than unsalted so burns more quickly. Be sure to use unsalted butter if a recipe specifies it as the flavour of some cakes and biscuits depends on it.

BUTTERMILK Formerly a by-product of buttermaking, this was the liquid left over after cream was churned to make butter. Now it is generally made by adding a bacterial culture to skim milk to thicken it and give it a tang. Buttermilk has less than 1 per cent fat. It is used in baking to add flavour and to act as a raising agent (its acidity reacts with bicarbonate of soda).

CARDAMOM One of the most exotic spices, the whole seed pods and small black seeds (whole or crushed) of cardamom are used in baking and sweet dishes as well as pilaus, curries and pickles. Like all spices, cardamom loses pungency once ground, so it is best to grind the seeds yourself as needed, using a spice mill or a coffee grinder kept especially for spices.

CHEESE Fresh and soft cheeses such as cream cheese, mascarpone and ricotta are often used in baking and desserts. Ricotta is made from whey, a by-product of cheesemaking. These cheeses have a fresh, mild taste and are best eaten soon after purchase, but can be stored in the fridge for a few days.

CHOCOLATE Chocolate is made by roasting and grinding cocoa beans with water until cocoa liquor (also known as cocoa mass) forms. Further processing produces cocoa butter and a paste that is dried to form cocoa powder. High-quality chocolate is made by conching (kneading) cocoa mass with other ingredients for up to 72 hours – the longer the kneading, the better the quality. Good-quality chocolate contains at least 50 per cent cocoa liquor and no vegetable fats. Check the label and the ingredients list, and always buy the best quality you can find or afford. DARK CHOCOLATE has the most intense flavour as it contains the greatest proportion of cocoa liquor, as well as sugar, cocoa butter, vanilla and other flavours. MILK CHOCOLATE has milk solids added to it; it is sweeter, creamier and less intensely flavoured than dark chocolate. WHITE CHOCOLATE is not strictly chocolate as it contains no cocoa liquor; it is made from cocoa butter, sugar, milk solids and flavourings. COMPOUND (BAKING) CHOCOLATE contains vegetable fat rather than cocoa butter and lacks the rich texture and depth of flavour of dark chocolate. It is more stable than other types of chocolate, so is good for making chocolate decorations, but is best avoided otherwise due to its inferior flavour and texture.

When melting chocolate, do so gently and without exposing it to any moisture, as this will cause it to 'seize' (stiffen and become grainy). Melt in the microwave on low, stirring frequently, or in a bowl over (not touching) barely simmering water in a saucepan.

COCOA POWDER A by-product of chocolate-making. Use Dutch or 'dutched' cocoa powder for preference, as it has a more pronounced yet less bitter flavour than regular cocoa powder. Cocoa powder adds a chocolate flavour to baked goods without adding the fat and sugar of solid chocolate. To dust tins or trays when making chocolate cakes or brownies, use cocoa powder, or a mixture of cocoa and flour; this helps preserve the dark colour of the finished product.

COCONUT The fruit of the coconut palm, one of the most important trees of the tropics. The hard, brown, hairy shell protects a layer of white, sweet, edible flesh which can be grated or shredded and eaten as is or used for cooking. Or it may be dried to make desiccated and shredded coconut, which may be moist or dried.

CORNFLOUR *See* Flour.

CORNMEAL *See* Polenta.

CREAM Cream varies in richness depending on how much butterfat it contains; the more butterfat, the thicker it is. Reduced-fat cream has between 18–25 per cent butterfat and cannot be whipped. Cream that is to be whipped must have at least 35 per cent butterfat. Pouring cream has 35–48 per cent butterfat. Thick (double/heavy) cream has at least 40 per cent butterfat; some types have gelatine added to give them more body. The thickest of cream of all is clotted, scalded or Devonshire cream, with 55 per cent butterfat. When whipping cream, first chill the bowl in the fridge. A balloon whisk will give the greatest volume. If using electric beaters, be careful not to overbeat the cream as you will produce butter.
See also Sour cream, Crème fraiche.

CRÈME FRAÎCHE Although the French name means 'fresh cream', crème fraîche is a cultured cream with a pleasantly sour tang. It can be boiled without curdling. It can be substituted for sour cream in baking or used as an accompaniment to fruit and desserts.

DATES Dates grow in huge, hanging bunches up to 10 kg on the date palm, and can be eaten either fresh or dried. Dried dates can be bought either pitted or unpitted; pitted dates have been processed by machine and some remnants of stones may remain, so check them carefully. Store fresh dates at room temperature or refrigerate in an airtight container. Store dried dates in an airtight container in a cool, dark, dry place.

EGGS Eggs are graded according to weight; the recipes in this book are based on 60 g eggs. There is no difference in nutritive value between brown and white eggs; the colour depends only on the breed of hen. Store eggs in their cardboard carton or a sealed container in the fridge, but allow them to come to room temperature before use; cold egg whites do not whisk as well as those at room temperature.

When whisking egg whites, the bowl and beaters must be scrupulously clean, as the merest trace of fat or grease (incuding egg yolk) will reduce the volume of the whites. Whisk gently at first, then more vigorously until the desired consistency is achieved. At 'soft peak' stage, the peaks on the whisked whites will flop when the beater or whisk is removed; at 'stiff peak' stage, only the very tips of the peaks will flop. Do not overbeat as this will dry out the whites and eventually make the mixture deflate and become watery; once this happens it cannot be saved. Beating egg whites with sugar stabilises them and prevents this from happening.

ESSENCES These concentrated liquid flavourings (which include vanilla, almond and peppermint essences) are made by distillation. They are also known as extracts. Be sure to use natural essences or extracts wherever possible as they have a superior flavour to artificial versions.
See also Vanilla.

FATS Fats tenderise and add flavour and richness to baked goods. BUTTER is the most commonly used fat in baking. MARGARINE is synthesised from various oils and other additives; it lacks the flavour and richness of butter. OIL is used instead of butter in some cakes and breads, but it cannot be sbstituted for it in other recipes. All-purpose oils such as polyunsaturated vegetable oil are suitable for baking; olive oil is usually too strong in flavour, though it is sometimes called for. LARD is pig fat; SUET is the firm white fat around the kidneys of beef, mutton or lamb. Formerly much used in baking, both are now much less popular due to concerns about their high levels of saturated fat.
See also Butter.

FLOUR Flour is produced by grinding grains such as wheat, rye or buckwheat; vegetables or legumes such as potatoes or chickpeas; or nuts such as chestnuts. Where no grain is specified, 'flour' means wheat flour. In baking, the most commonly used flours are white wheat flours that have been refined to remove the bran and wheatgerm. Wheat crops vary according to where they are grown, and may give 'soft' or 'hard' grains (and thus soft or hard flours). **PLAIN FLOUR** is a mixture of soft and hard flour, and is used for cakes, pastries and breads (although for breads it will not give as good a result as bread flour). To make plain flour rise, a raising agent (baking powder, bicarbonate of soda or yeast) must be added to it. **SELF-RAISING FLOUR** is plain flour with a raising agent added. **WHOLEMEAL FLOUR** is made from the whole wheat grain. As it contains the bran, it is more nutritious but heavier than white flour, and does not rise as well. **BAKER'S FLOUR** (also known as strong flour or bread flour) is made from hard wheat with a high gluten content. The gluten develops when the flour is mixed with liquid and the dough kneaded, producing the characteristic chewy texture of bread. **CAKE FLOUR** is made from soft wheat. Low in protein and high in starch, it produces light, tender cakes with a delicate crumb. **CORNFLOUR** is a fine white powder milled from corn. True cornflour contains no gluten. Some types are milled from wheat and labelled as wheaten cornflour; if cooking for people who cannot tolerate gluten, be sure to buy true cornflour.

GELATINE This colourless and almost flavourless protein is used as a setting agent, mostly for desserts. It may lose its setting power if boiled or used with acidic liquids. Certain fruits (such as papaya, pineapple and figs) contain an enzyme that eats the protein in gelatine and prevents it from setting. Gelatine must be soaked in cold water first to soften it, then added to the hot liquid that is to be set and stirred to dissolve. **POWDERED GELATINE** is the more widely available type and consists of granules. **LEAF (SHEET) GELATINE** comes in the form of rectangular sheets. Gelatine is made commercially from the bones and tendons of cows or pigs, so is unsuitable for vegetarians.

GINGER A bold perennial plant with a heavenly scented flower. The edible rhizome can be used fresh, chopped or grated, in both sweet and savoury dishes, or dried and ground to a powder as a spice.

GLACÉ (CANDIED) FRUITS AND GINGER These have been preserved by boiling them in a sugar syrup. They are used to flavour and decorate baked products and confectionery. Glacé cherries are often dyed bright red or green; undyed cherries are a darker, more natural red.

HAZELNUTS Hazelnuts are very popular in European cookery. Their mealy texture makes them perfect for puddings, cakes and Continental tortes. They are highly nutritious, being rich in protein, fat, iron and thiamine. To roast and skin hazelnuts, put them on a baking tray in a preheated 180º oven for about 10 minutes, shaking the tray occasionally, until the nuts are fragrant (watch carefully, as they burn easily). Tip them into a clean tea towel, gather the corners up into a bundle and rub them to remove the skins (not all the skins will come off; don't worry about those that don't). For storage, see Nuts.

HONEY Made by bees from flower nectar, honey varies in strength and flavour according to the type of blossom from which it was gathered. Regular honey is clear; creamed honey (which has been deliberately crystallised) is also available. If clear honey begins to crystallise and solidify, it can be returned to its liquid state by immersing the jar in hot water. Blended honey (often just labelled as 'honey') is a good all-purpose type suitable for cooking. Flower honey comes from one type of blossom. Good honey is best kept for eating, not cooking. Honey is sweeter than sugar and should not generally be substituted for it in recipes. To accurately measure honey, dip the measuring spoon or cup into hot water, then into the honey; the honey will then flow off easily.

LIQUEURS Used in baking as flavourings, liqueurs are alcoholic syrups distilled from wine or brandy and flavoured with such ingredients as herbs, spices or fruits. Where used in small amounts, in most cases they can be omitted if desired, or replaced by a liquid with a similar flavour (such as orange juice rather than orange liqueur).

GLOSSARY

MILK Unless otherwise indicated, assume that whole milk is called for in baking recipes. Using reduced-fat milk may give a different result. 'Soured milk', if specified in a recipe, does not mean spoilt milk; use buttermilk, or add a little lemon juice to regular milk to sour it. **EVAPORATED MILK** has been heated so that most of the water content evaporates. **SWEETENED CONDENSED MILK** is made in the same way as evaporated milk but with the addition of sugar. It is used in confectionery and for filling tarts, slices and cheesecakes. *See also* Buttermilk.

NUTS AND NUT MEALS Many nuts have high levels of oil which can become rancid and bitter if exposed to heat; for this reason nuts are best stored in the freezer. Whole nuts last longer than whole or chopped nuts, so it is best to chop or grind nuts only as needed. Nut meals may also be packaged as ground nuts.

OILS *See* Fats.

POLENTA Another name for cornmeal; it comes in fine, medium and coarse grades and is used in baking cornbread and some cakes.

RAISING AGENTS These react with the liquid in mixtures and with heat to help cakes and breads to rise. There are both natural raising agents (yeast and beaten egg whites) and chemical raising agents (bicarbonate of soda, baking powder and cream of tartar). Yeast and chemical raising agents lose their potency over time, so make sure they are fresh. *See also* Yeast.

SOUR CREAM Formerly made by allowing cream to sour naturally, but now made by adding a bacterial culture to pouring cream or thick cream. The bacteria produce lactic acid, thickening the cream and giving it a slightly sour taste. Stabilisers such as gelatine may also be added to increase the shelf life. In baking, sour cream is used in cakes, slices, cheesecakes and tarts.

SPICES Spices such as cardamom, cinnamon, pepper, nutmeg and ginger are produced from the roots, rhizomes, seeds or woody parts of various plants. Most are available in both whole and ground forms. All spices lose pungency once ground, so it is best to grind them yourself as needed, using a spice mill or coffee grinder (or, in the case of nutmeg, a small rotary grater – the type sometimes used for grating parmesan cheese). Store whole and ground spices in an airtight container in a cool, dark, dry place.

SUGAR A sweet substance extracted from many plants, chiefly sugar cane, sugar beet, sugar maple and various species of palm. **ORDINARY WHITE GRANULATED SUGAR** is the most common type, used as an everyday sweetener. **CASTER SUGAR** is a fine white sugar, best for creaming and beating cake and icing mixtures and where a less grainy result is wanted. **BROWN SUGAR** is sugar that has been refined further and then coated with a film of molasses. It can replace white sugar in any recipe where the flavour will not be harmed by a note of molasses. **ICING SUGAR** is powdered sugar with extremely fine grains. Pure icing sugar is used to make icing for fine 'piped' decoration of cakes as well as a firm covering. Soft icing mixture is pure icing sugar with cornflour, which helps keep the grains soft. It is used in icings and frostings where a soft finish is required. **DEMERARA SUGAR** is the least refined sugar; it still has much of the molasses left in the crystals, giving it a distinctive rich flavour which is excellent for baking, making chutneys and desserts.

VANILLA Vanilla comes from the dried, fermented bean of a species of Central American orchid. Vanilla essence, vanilla extract and vanilla paste all result from processing vanilla beans and vary in strength of flavour. Vanilla beans, extract or paste will give a unique vanilla flavour. Imitation vanilla is just that, a flavoured syrup; it lacks the complex flavour of the real thing.

YEAST Yeast is a living organism and needs food, warmth and moisture to grow. When mixed with liquid, the yeast starts to work and the carbon dioxide created makes bread doughs rise and gives breads, buns and other yeast mixtures their characteristic light texture. The liquid used with yeast must be only lukewarm; too much heat will kill the yeast. See also pages 420–421.

INDEX

NOTE References in *italics* indicate text in Tips or Notes sections; references in **bold** indicate photographs.

A

abbreviations 10
almonds
    almond biscuits 61
    almond butter balls **52**, 53
    almond castles 297
    almond cheese rounds 76
    almond and hazelnut galette 316
    almond paste 218
    almond roll **210**, 211
    almond tuiles 31
    almonds, toasting *222*
    amaretti 56, **57**
    caramel almond torte 235
    coffee & almond slice 93
    coffee almond layer cake 250
    friands **264**, 265
    gateau de pithiviers **372**, 373
    Linzer torte 354
    orange & almond cake 238
    Parisian almond tart 369
    praline 383
    raspberry & almond slab cake 182, **183**
amaretti 56, **57**
American strawberry shortcake 139
angel cake 201
anise drop biscuits 17
Anzac biscuits 19
apples
    apple cider & sultana muffins 117
    apple crisp 292
    apple crumble muffins 114, **115**
    apple kuchen 460
    apple pie 339
    apple strudel 342
    apple tea cake 188
    baked apple roly-poly **290**, 291
    deep-dish apple pie **352**, 353
    French apple tart 340, **341**
    galette Normandie 359
    German apple cake **236**, 237
    hot apple tarts 390
    quick apple strudel 343
    tart Tatin 364–5
apricots
    apricot crumble pie 355
    apricot fingers 92
    apricot shortcake 141
    apricot tart 346
    apricot tartlets 389
    apricot upside-down cake 240, **241**
    dried apricot & coconut slice 102, **103**

B

baba au rhum 463
bacon muffins 112
bain marie 287
Bakewell tart 374
baking cases, paper *208*
baking paper
    extending *245*
    lining tins with *161*
baking trays, cooling *51, 70*
baklava 403
banana cake 184
banana nut bread 157
barabrith (Welsh fruit bread) 154
bars *see* slices, bars and fingers
berries
    berry muffins 112
    blackberry pie 348, **349**
    freeform berry tart 356, **357**
    savarin 458, **459**
    see also blueberries; raspberries; strawberries
bienenstich 224, **225**
biscuit pastry 331
biscuits *14–15, 17, 51, 71*
    see also drop biscuits; refrigerator biscuits; rolled biscuits; shaped biscuits
bishop's cake 219
bistro cheesecake 308–9
Black Forest cherry torte 247
blackberry pie 348, **349**
blind baking 327
blue cheese quiche 407
blueberries
    blueberry bran muffins **118**, 119
    blueberry and raspberry clafoutis 294, **295**
    blueberry upside-down cupcakes 262
    orange & blueberry cake **198**, 199
boules de neige 283
brandy Alexander pie 310, **311**
brandy snap baskets 26
brandy snaps 26–7
bread *420–1*
    basic recipe 422–3
    bread improver 430
    bread rolls 423
    corn bread 144
    cottage loaf (basic milk dough) 426
    damper 146, **147**
    farmhouse bread 424, **425**
    floury baps **428**, 429
    malt bread 427
    no-knead bread 430–1
    olive bread 432, **433**
    rising times 423
    toppings 423
    Vienna twist 423
    wholemeal bread 430
    see also quickbreads; soda bread; sweet breads/rolls
brioche 442
brown sugar tart 377
brownies 82–3
    cranberry chocolate, with cream cheese topping 89
    easy blondies **90**, 91
    easy chocolate 84
    fudge 85
    marbled cheesecake 88
    two-tone 86, **87**
burnt butter biscuits 50
butter 468
    clarifying *270*
butter cakes 160, *163*
    banana cake 184
    basic recipe 164

INDEX

chocolate cake 172
chocolate sandwich cake 173
cinnamon layered cake **170**, 171
coconut cake 176
frosted lemon & buttermilk cake 180
glazed coffee cake **178**, 179
honey chocolate cake 174, **175**
Madeira cake 165
marble cake 169
nutmeg cake 177
orange cake 168
orange marmalade cake 166, **167**
raspberry & almond slab cake 182, **183**
seed cake 164
sultana cake 181
butter cream filling (crème au beurre) 255
butter cream icing (Vienna icing) 253
butter shortbread biscuits 63
butter wafers 23
butterfly cakes 260, *260*
buttermilk 468
buttermilk bread 148
buttermilk cornmeal muffins 127
buttermilk scones 132
frosted lemon & buttermilk cake 180

C

cake fillings 254
butter cream (crème au beurre) 255
butterscotch 255
firm lemon butter 254–5
lemon butter 255
passionfruit butter 255
ricotta rum 255
cake tins, lining 161
cakes *160–3*
see also butter cakes; Continental cakes; fruit cakes; quick-mix cakes; small cakes; sponge cakes; tea cakes; yeasted cakes
caramel
caramel almond torte 235
caramel nut cake 196, **197**
caramel sauce 301
caramelised mango tartlets 391
chocolate caramel slice **106**, 107
pecan caramel slice 99

cardamom 468
cardamom braid 451
cardamon cookies 51
carrot cake **194**, 195
cats' tongues 55
cheese *308*, 468
almond cheese rounds 76
blue cheese quiche 407
cheese, capsicum & shallot muffins 124, **125**
cheese biscuits **78**, 79
cheese scones 129
cheese and walnut shortbreads 75
cheese-topped scone loaf 129
gougères 414
Greek cheese pastries 412
rosemary & cheese biscuits **58**, 59
zucchini, mint & goat's cheese quiche **406**, 407
zucchini & cheese quickbread 145
see also cream cheese; ricotta
cheesecakes *286–7*
baked ricotta & lemon tart 304
bistro cheesecake 308–9
chocolate peanut butter cheesecake **306**, 307
honey cheesecake squares 305
marbled cheesecake brownies 88
passionfruit cheesecake 308–9
Chelsea buns **452**, 453
cherries
Black Forest cherry torte 247
cherry cheesecake 308–9
cherry currant drops 22
cherry drop biscuits 16
cherry raisin drops 22
cherry sultana drops 22
cherry tartlets **388**, 389
cherry wink cookies 20, **21**
chocolate 468
Black Forest cherry torte 247
chocolate seven-minute frosting 254
chocolate butter cake 164
chocolate butter cream filling 255
chocolate butter cream icing 253
chocolate butter wafers 23
chocolate cake 172
chocolate caramel slice **106**, 107
chocolate cream cheese frosting 254
chocolate crème pâtissière 328
chocolate drop biscuits 16

chocolate éclairs **384**, 385
chocolate glacé icing 252
chocolate glaze 252
chocolate liqueur soufflé 312
chocolate madeleines 270
chocolate peanut biscuits 18
chocolate peanut butter cheesecake **306**, 307
chocolate profiteroles 383
chocolate roll 208
chocolate sandwich cake 173
chocolate soufflés 313
chocolate toffee cake 223
cranberry chocolate brownies with cream cheese topping 89
double chocolate cake **228**, 229
easy chocolate brownies 84
economical chocolate icing 253
espresso chocolate & hazelnut cake 246
ganache-filled macarons **274**, 275
hazelnut & chocolate roulade 212
honey chocolate cake 174, **175**
lamingtons 266, *266*
melt & mix chocolate cake 193
melting chocolate 84
rich chocolate fudge cake 248, **249**
rich chocolate icing 252
rum chocolate frosting 253
self-saucing chocolate puddings **298**, 299
sour cream chocolate cake 243
choux pastry 327, 332
Christmas cake 218
Christmas mince pies 394
Christmas spice biscuits 70
cinnamon crinkles 48, **49**
cinnamon honey syrup 402
cinnamon layered cake **170**, 171
cinnamon pinwheels 450
cinnamon tea cake 185
citrus shortbread 37
cloverleaf rolls 443
cocoa powder *18*, 468–9
coconut 469
coconut cake 176
coconut drops 38
coconut raspberry slice 94, **95**
coconut tarts 399
dried apricot & coconut slice 102, **103**
treacle & coconut tart 375

coffee
- coffee almond layer cake 250
- coffee and almond slice 93
- coffee butter cream filling 255
- coffee butter wafers 23
- coffee éclairs 385
- coffee glacé icing 252
- coffee kisses 277
- coffee macarons 276
- coffee and nut doboztorte 226
- coffee profiteroles 383
- coffee syrup cake 222
- coffee vacherin 321
- glazed coffee cake **178**, 179
- iced coffee cakes 268

Continental cakes 161, *163*
- apricot upside-down cake 240, **241**
- bienenstich 224, **225**
- Black Forest cherry torte 247
- caramel almond torte 235
- chocolate toffee cake 223
- coffee almond layer cake 250
- coffee and nut doboztorte 226
- coffee syrup cake 222
- double chocolate cake **228**, 229
- espresso chocolate & hazelnut cake 246
- Finnish sour cream cake 227
- German apple cake **236**, 237
- gingerbread 231
- Greek walnut cake 234
- griestorte 232, **233**
- mocha nut cake 251
- orange & almond cake 238
- pineapple upside-down cake 239
- poppy seed cake 230
- rich chocolate fudge cake 248, **249**
- rich ginger cake 242
- sour cream chocolate cake 243
- sour cream streusel cake **244**, 245

Continental strawberry shortcake 138
corn muffins 126
cornmeal (polenta) 471
- buttermilk cornmeal muffins 127
- corn bread 144
- corn muffins 144

cottage loaf (basic milk dough) 426
crab quiche 404
cranberry chocolate brownies with cream cheese topping 89
cream 469

cream cheese
- chocolate cream cheese frosting 254
- cranberry chocolate brownies with cream cheese topping 89
- cream cheese pastry 330
- cream cheese slices 105
- cream cheese tart 378
- cream cheese turnovers 398
- *see also* cheesecakes

cream puffs 383
cream of tartar 313
crème au beurre 255
crème fraîche 469
crème pâtissière 338
crusted orange scones 129
cupcakes *258*, 260–1, *260*
- iced coffee cakes 268
- queen cakes 263
- quick upside-down fruit cupcakes 262

custard pie, Greek 380

D

damper 146, **147**
Danish raspberry shortcake **140**, 141
dates 47, 469
- date bars 96
- date slice 97
- date surprises 47
- frosted date bars 101
- orange & date quickbread 155
- sticky date pudding 301

demerara meringues with chestnut & chocolate cream **280**, 281
desserts *286–7*
- almond & hazelnut galette 316
- almond castles 297
- apple crisp 292
- apple strudel 342
- baba au rhum 463
- baked apple roly-poly **290**, 291
- bistro cheesecake 308–9
- blueberry & raspberry clafoutis 294, **295**
- chocolate peanut butter cheesecake **306**, 307
- fruit sponges 296
- galette Normandie 359
- gâteau St Honoré 386, **387**
- glazed strawberry flan 366, **367**
- hazelnut torte 320
- honey cheesecake squares 305
- Linzer torte 354
- pavlova 287, 318, **319**
- rhubarb & strawberry crumble 288, **289**
- rolled pavlova 317
- winter fruit brown betty 293
- *see also* flans; meringue; pies, sweet; puddings; soufflés; tarts, sweet; vacherins

dough *see* yeast
drop biscuits 14
- almond tuiles 31
- anise biscuits 17
- Anzac biscuits 19
- basic recipe 16
- brandy snaps 26–7
- butter wafers 23
- cherry biscuits 16
- cherry raisin drops 22
- cherry wink cookies 20, **21**
- chocolate biscuits 16
- chocolate peanut biscuits 18
- Florentines **28**, 29
- ginger biscuits 16
- Highland oatmeal cookies 30
- nut biscuits 16
- tollhouse cookies **24**, 25

Dundee cake 216, **217**

E

easy blondies **90**, 91
éclairs, chocolate **384**, 385
eggnog tart 379
empanadas 417
English madeleines 270
equipment 8–9
espresso chocolate & hazelnut cake 246

F

farmhouse bread 424, **425**
figs
- fig bars 96
- fresh fig & mascarpone tart **344**, 345

fillings *see* cake fillings
filo pastry 105
fingers *see* slices, bars and fingers
Finnish sour cream cake 227
flaky pastry 327, 335
flan rings 370, 404
flan tins, lining *326*

INDEX

flans
- flan aux pruneaux 358
- glazed strawberry flan 366, **367**

Florentines **28**, 29
flour 470
floury baps **428**, 429
four-seasons pizza 437
frangipane cream 338
freeform berry tart 356, **357**
French apple tart 340, **341**
French fruit tart 350
friand tins 265
friands *258*, **264**, 265
frostings *see* icings and frostings
fruit
- dried fruit muffins 112
- dried fruit turnovers 398
- French fruit tart 350
- fruit desserts *286*
- fruit loaf 426
- fruit mincemeat 395
- fruit and nut tea ring **152**, 153
- fruit roly-poly 291
- fruit scones 129
- fruit soufflé tart 351
- fruit tartlets **388**, 389
- fruit turnovers 398
- fruit-topped cheesecake 308–9
- glacé fruits 470
- preventing browning *292*
- quick upside-down fruit cupcakes 262
- Welsh fruit bread 154
- winter fruit brown betty 293

fruit cakes *161*, *163*, 192
- bishop's cake 219
- Christmas cake 218
- Dundee cake 216, **217**
- light 214
- rich 215
- Siena cake **220**, 221

fruit sponges 296
fudge
- fudge brownies 85
- rich chocolate fudge cake 248, **249**

G

galettes
- almond & hazelnut 316
- galette Normandie 359

ganache-filled macarons **274**, 275
gâteau de pithiviers **372**, 373

gâteau St Honoré 386, **387**
gelatine 470
gem scones 269
Génoise cake *160*, 202–3
German apple cake **236**, 237
ginger 470
- candied 470
- ginger cheesecake 308–9
- ginger crisp biscuits 71
- ginger daisies 64, **65**
- ginger drop biscuits 16
- ginger oatmeal scones 133
- ginger slice 97
- gingerbread 231
- gingerbread men 67
- gingernuts 43
- old-fashioned ginger cake 200
- rich ginger cake 242
- shortbread biscuits 63

glacé cherries 20
glacé or warm icing 252
- softening *268*

glazes *see* icings and frostings
golden syrup roly-poly 291
gougères 414
grape tartlets 389
Greek cheese pastries (tiropitakia) 412
Greek custard pie 380
Greek Easter bread 445
Greek spinach pie 413
Greek walnut cake 234
griestorte 232, **233**
gugelhopf 461

H

ham muffins 112
ham and mushroom pizza 438
hazelnuts 470
- almond & hazelnut galette 316
- espresso chocolate & hazelnut cake 246
- hazelnut & chocolate roulade 212
- hazelnut cookies 66
- hazelnut crescents 42
- hazelnut torte 320
- pistachio–hazelnut friands 265

herb scones 129
herbed tomato quiche 408
Highland oatmeal cookies 30
honey 470
- bienenstich 224, **225**
- cinnamon honey syrup 402

honey buns 40, **41**
honey cheesecake squares 305
honey chocolate cake 174, **175**
honey spice cookies 74
honey spiced sponge roll 213
honey tea cake **186**, 187
hot cross buns 444
hot water pastry 337

I

icings and frostings 252
- apricot glaze 340
- butter cream icing (Vienna icing) 253
- chocolate cream cheese frosting 254
- chocolate glaze 252
- economical chocolate icing 253
- glacé or warm icing 252
- marshmallow frostings 253, 254
- rich chocolate icing 252
- rum chocolate frosting 253
- seven-minute frosting 254

J

jam doughnut muffins 123
jam lamingtons 266
jam roly-poly 291
jam turnovers 398

K

kugelhupf 461

L

lamingtons 266, *266*
langues des chats (cats' tongues) 55
latticed raisin pie 347
lavash 149
leek quiche 405
lemons
- firm lemon butter 254–5
- frosted lemon & buttermilk cake 180
- lemon butter cake 164
- lemon butter cream icing 253
- lemon butter filling 255
- lemon cheesecake 308–9
- lemon chiffon tart 363
- lemon curd turnovers 398
- lemon delicious puddings 302, *302*, **303**
- lemon glacé icing 252

lemon melting moments **44**, 45
lemon meringue pie 362
lemon sponge fingers 104
lemon tart 368
lemon tea loaf 190, **191**
lemon yoghurt muffins 113
lime chiffon tart 363
lime meringue pie **360**, 361
Linzer biscuits **68**, 69
Linzer torte 354
liqueur butter cream icing 253

M
macarons *258–9, 276*
    coffee 276
    ganache-filled **274**, 275
    strawberry 273
    vanilla 273
Madeira cake 165
madeleine tins 270
madeleines 270, **271**
malt bread/buns 427
mandarin tartlets 389
mango tartlets, caramelised 391
mango vacherin **322**, 323
maple walnut pie 371
marble cake 169
marbled cheesecake brownies 88
marshmallow frostings 253, 254
mascarpone and fresh fig tart **344**, 345
measurements 8–9
melting moments, lemon **44**, 45
meringue *259, 287*
    almond & hazelnut galette 316
    baked strawberry soufflés **314**, 315
    boules de neige 283
    coffee kisses 277
    demerara meringues with chestnut & chocolate cream **280**, 281
    hazelnut torte 320
    lemon meringue pie 362
    lime meringue pie **360**, 361
    meringues Chantilly 282
    mini meringues 278, **279**
    pavlova 287, 318, **319**
    rolled pavlova 317
    shells 278
    see also vacherins
mille-feuilles 400, **401**
mince pies 394
mocha chiffon pie 376
mocha nut cake 251

muffins *110–11, 116*
    apple cider and sultana 117
    apple crumble 114, **115**
    basic recipe 112
    blueberry bran **118**, 119
    buttermilk cornmeal 127
    cheese, capsicum & shallot 124, **125**
    cornmeal 144
    fresh corn 126
    jam doughnut 123
    lemon yoghurt 113
    raisin and bran 116
    sour cream and prune 122
    spiced breakfast 120–1
mushroom quiche 405

N
Nairn butteries **434**, 435
neenish tarts **396**, 397
Neapolitan pizza 438
no-knead bread 430–1
Norwegian sweet bread 448
nutmeg, grating *300*
nutmeg cake 177
nuts 471
    banana nut bread 157
    caramel nut cake 196, **197**
    coffee & nut doboztorte 226
    fruit & nut tea ring **152**, 153
    mocha nut cake 251
    nut drop biscuits 16
    nut muffins 112
    nut rolls 402
    vanilla kippels 32, **33**
    see also almonds; coconut; hazelnuts; peanuts; pecans; walnuts

O
oats
    ginger oatmeal scones 133
    Highland oatmeal cookies 30
    oat and raisin bread 156
    oatcakes 77
    oatmeal 77
    oatmeal raisin cookies 39
    oatmeal soda bread 143
    rolled oat squares 100
    spicy oat biscuits 30
old-fashioned ginger cake 200
old-fashioned penny buns 454
olive bread 432, **433**

onion & olive tart 410, **411**
onion tartlets 416
oranges
    crusted orange scones 129
    orange and almond cake 238
    orange and blueberry cake **198**, 199
    orange butter cream icing 253
    orange cake 168
    orange chiffon tart 363
    orange and date quickbread 155
    orange liqueur soufflé 312
    orange madeleines 270
    orange marmalade cake 166, **167**
    orange profiteroles 383
    orange rolls 450
    orange and sultana loaf 189
    orange tuiles 31
    wholemeal orange muffins 112
oven temperatures 10

P
panforte **220**, 221
Parisian almond tart 369
passionfruit cheesecake 308–9
passionfruit soufflé 312
pastry *326–7*
    baking blind *327*
    biscuit pastry 331
    choux pastry 327, 332
    cream cheese pastry 330
    flaky pastry 327, 335
    in food processor *99*
    hot water pastry 337
    lining a flan tin *326*
    pastry cream 338
    puff pastry 333
    rough puff pastry 334
    short pastries 326–7
    sour cream pastry 330
    strudel pastry 336, *342*
    suet pastry 337
    see also shortcrust pastry; sweet flan pastry
pastry case, moisture-proofing *327*
pastry cream 338
pâte brisée 326, 328
pâte brisée à l'oeuf 326, 329
pâte sucrée 326, 331
pavlova 287, 317, 318, **319**
peanuts
    allergy to 18
    chocolate peanut biscuits 18

INDEX

chocolate peanut butter cheesecake **306**, 307
    peanut butter biscuits 60
pears
    individual pear tarts 392, **393**
    pear tartlets 389
pecans 99
    pecan caramel slice **98**, 99
    pecan pie 370
peppermint seven-minute frosting 254
petticoat tails 37
pfeffernusse (spice biscuits) 35
pies, savoury
    piroshki **440**, 441
    ricotta & artichoke pie 409
    spanakopita (Greek spinach pie) 413
    see also tarts, savoury
pies, sweet
    apple pie 339
    apricot crumble pie 355
    blackberry pie 348, **349**
    brandy Alexander pie 310, **311**
    Christmas mince pies 394
    deep-dish apple pie **352**, 353
    Greek custard pie 380
    latticed raisin pie 347
    lemon meringue pie 362
    lime meringue pie **360**, 361
    maple walnut pie 371
    mocha chiffon pie 376
    pecan pie 370
    see also tarts, sweet
pineapple upside-down cake 239
piroshki **440**, 441
pistachio–hazelnut friands 265
pizzas
    four-seasons 437
    ham and mushroom 438
    Neapolitan 438
    pizza dough 436
    pizza margherita 438, **439**
    pizza sauce 437
    salami 438
plain shortcrust pastry 326, 328
plum tartlets 389
plum upside-down cupcakes 262
polenta *see* cornmeal
poppy seed butter wafers 23
poppy seed cake 230
poppy seed stollen 457
praline 383

profiteroles
    basic 382
    chocolate 383
    coffee 383
    cream puffs 383
    orange 383
    praline 383
    savoury 415
prunes
    prune bars 96
    prune tart 358
    sour cream & prune muffins 122
puddings 286
    lemon delicious 302, **303**
    self-saucing chocolate **298**, 299
    steamed almond castles 297
    sticky date 301
    sultana bread pudding 300
puff pastry 333, 334
pumpkin scones **130**, 131

Q

queen cakes 263
quiches
    blue cheese 407
    crab 404
    herbed tomato 408
    leek 405
    mixed vegetable 407
    mushroom 405
    quiche Lorraine 404
    spinach 404
    zucchini, mint & goat's cheese **406**, 407
    zucchini and bacon 407
quick upside-down fruit cupcakes 262
quickbreads 110, *111*
    banana nut bread 157
    barabrith (Welsh fruit bread) 154
    buttermilk bread 148
    corn bread 144
    damper 146, **147**
    fruit & nut tea ring **152**, 153
    lavash 149
    oat & raisin bread 156
    orange & date 155
    raisin & walnut loaf 151
    simple walnut tea bread 150
    zucchini & cheese 145
    see also soda bread
quick-mix cakes 160
    caramel nut cake 196, **197**

carrot cake **194**, 195
melt & mix chocolate cake 193
old-fashioned ginger cake 200
orange & blueberry cake **198**, 199

R

raisin & bran muffins 116
raisin & walnut loaf 151
raising agents 420, 471
raspberries
    blueberry & raspberry clafoutis 294, **295**
    Danish raspberry shortcake **140**, 141
    raspberry & almond slab cake 182, **183**
    raspberry éclairs 385
    raspberry upside-down cupcakes 262
refrigerator biscuits 14, 54
rhubarb & strawberry crumble 288, **289**
rhubarb tartlets 389
rich shortcrust pastry 326, 329
    in food processor 329
ricotta
    baked ricotta & lemon tart 304
    honey cheesecake squares 305
    ricotta & artichoke pie 409
    ricotta rum filling 255
    ricotta turnovers 398
rock cakes 272
rolled biscuits 14
    almond biscuits 61
    almond cheese rounds 76
    cheese biscuits **78**, 79
    Christmas spice biscuits 70
    ginger crisp biscuits 71
    ginger daisies 64, **65**
    ginger shortbread biscuits 63
    gingerbread men 67
    hazelnut cookies 66
    honey spice cookies 74
    Linzer biscuits **68**, 69
    oatcakes 77
    peanut butter biscuits 60
    speculaas 72, **73**
    see also shortbread
rolled oat squares 100
rolled pavlova 317
rosemary & cheese biscuits **58**, 59
rough puff pastry 334
rum butter cream filling 255
rum chocolate frosting 253

S

sablés 62
salami pizza 438
Sally Lunn 449
savarin 458, **459**
savoury scone ring 136, **137**
scones 110, *111*
   basic recipe 128
   buttermilk 132
   cheese 129
   crusted orange 129
   fruit 129
   ginger oatmeal 133
   herb 129
   pumpkin **130**, 131
   treacle 134
   wholemeal 135
seed cake 164
seven-minute frostings 254
shaped biscuits 14
   almond butter balls **52**, 53
   amaretti 56, **57**
   burnt butter biscuits 50
   cardamon cookies 51
   cats' tongues 55
   cinnamon crinkles 48, **49**
   coconut drops 38
   date surprises 47
   gingernuts 43
   hazelnut crescents 42
   honey buns 40, **41**
   lemon melting moments **44**, 45
   oatmeal raisin cookies 39
   pfeffernusse (spice biscuits) 35
   rosemary & cheese biscuits **58**, 59
   vanilla biscuits 34
   vanilla kippels 32, **33**
   walnut butter biscuits 46
   see also shortbread
shortbread **36**, 37
   butter 63
   cheese & walnut 75
   citrus 37
   ginger 63
   sablés 62
shortcakes 110, *111*
   American strawberry 139
   apricot 141
   Continental strawberry 138
   Danish raspberry **140**, 141

shortcrust pastry
   in food processor 329
   plain 326, 328
   sweet flan pastry 326, 331
   see also rich shortcrust pastry
Siena cake **220**, 221
slices, bars and fingers *82*, *83*
   apricot fingers 92
   chocolate caramel slice **106**, 107
   coconut raspberry slice 94, **95**
   coffee and almond slice 93
   cream cheese slices 105
   date bars 96, 101
   dried apricot & coconut slice 102, **103**
   lemon sponge fingers 104
   pecan caramel slice **98**, 99
   rolled oat squares 100
   sultana slice 97
small cakes 258
   coffee kisses 277
   friands *258*, **264**, 265
   gem scones 269
   iced coffee cakes 268
   lamingtons 266
   queen cakes 263
   rock cakes 272
   Vienna cakes 267
   see also cupcakes; macarons; madeleines; meringues
soda bread 142
   brown 142
   oatmeal 143
   treacle 142
soufflés 287
   baked strawberry **314**, 315
   basic sweet 312
   chocolate 313
sour cream 471
sour cream chocolate cake 243
sour cream pastry 330
sour cream and prune muffins 122
sour cream streusel cake **244**, 245
spanakopita (Greek spinach pie) 413
speculaas 72, **73**
spices 471
   Christmas spice biscuits 70
   honey spice cookies 74
   honey spiced sponge roll 213
   pfeffernusse 35
   shortbread 63
   spice cake 164

spice glacé icing 252
spiced breakfast muffins 120
spiced fruit pinwheels 129
spicy oat biscuits 30
   see also cardamom; cinnamon
spinach
   spanakopita 413
   spinach pastries 412
   spinach quiche 404
sponge cakes 160–1, *163*
   almond roll **210**, 211
   angel cake 201
   chocolate roll 208
   Génoise cake *160*, 202–3
   hazelnut & chocolate roulade 212
   honey spiced sponge roll 213
   sponge sandwich 207
   Swiss roll 209
   turning out *206*
   Victoria sponge 204, **205**
   whisked sponge 206
springform tins 286
sticky date pudding 301
stollen 457
strawberries
   American strawberry shortcake 139
   baked strawberry soufflés **314**, 315
   Continental strawberry shortcake 138
   glazed strawberry flan 366, **367**
   rhubarb & strawberry crumble 288, **289**
   strawberry éclairs 385
   strawberry macarons 273
   strawberry tartlets 389
   strawberry upside-down cupcakes 262
strudel, apple 342, *342*, 343
strudel pastry 336, *342*
suet pastry 337
sugarplum ring 443
sultanas
   apple cider & sultana muffins 117
   orange & sultana loaf 189
   sultana bread pudding 300
   sultana cake 164, 181
   sultana slice 97
   sultana spice cake 164, 181
Swedish coffee breads 446, **447**
sweet breads/rolls
   basic sweet rich dough 443
   brioche 442

INDEX

cardamom braid 451
Chelsea buns **452**, 453
cloverleaf rolls 443
crescents 443
Greek Easter bread 445
hot cross buns 444
Norwegian sweet bread 448
old-fashioned penny buns 454
orange rolls 450
Sally Lunn 449
sugarplum ring 443
Swedish coffee breads 446, **447**
Yorkshire tea cakes 455
sweet flan pastry 326, 331
sweet rich dough, basic 443
sweet rich shortcrust pastry 329
Swiss roll 209

T
tarts, savoury
    onion & olive tart 410, **411**
    onion tartlets 416
    see also pies, savoury; quiches
tarts, sweet
    apricot tart 346
    baked ricotta & lemon 304
    Bakewell tart 374
    brown sugar tart 377
    caramelised mango tartlets 391
    coconut tarts 399
    cream cheese tart 378
    eggnog tart 379
    freeform berry tart 356, **357**
    French apple tart 340, **341**
    French fruit tart 350
    fresh fig & mascarpone **344**, 345
    fruit soufflé tart 351
    fruit tartlets **388**, 389
    galette Normandie 359
    gâteau St Honoré 386, **387**
    hot apple tarts 390
    individual pear tarts 392, **393**
    lemon chiffon tart 363
    lemon tart 368
    Linzer torte 354
    neenish tarts **396**, 397
    Parisian almond tart 369
    prune tart 358
    rich treacle tart 375
    tart Tatin 364–5
    treacle & coconut tart 375
    see also pies, sweet

tea bread, simple walnut 150
tea cakes 160, *163*
    apple 188
    cinnamon 185
    honey **186**, 187
    Yorkshire 455
tea loaf
    lemon 190, **191**
    orange & sultana 189
tea ring 456
    fruit & nut **152**, 153
tiropitakia 412
tollhouse cookies **24**, 25
tomato quiche, herbed 408
treacle & coconut tart 375
treacle scones 134
treacle soda bread 142
treacle tart, rich 375
tuiles 31
turnovers 398
tutti-frutti crème pâtissière 338
two-tone brownies 86, **87**

V
vacherins
    coffee vacherin 321
    mango vacherin **322**, 323
    vacherin Chantilly with fruits 323
    vacherin Melba 323
vanilla 34, 471
vanilla biscuits 34
vanilla kippels 32, **33**
vanilla macarons 273
vanilla sugar 32, 34
vanilla tuiles 31
vegetable quiche 407
Victoria sponge 204, **205**
Vienna cakes 267
Vienna icing 253
Vienna twist 423

W
walnuts
    cheese & walnut shortbreads 75
    Greek walnut cake 234
    maple walnut pie 371
    raisin & walnut loaf 151
    simple walnut tea bread 150
    storing walnuts *46*
    walnut butter biscuits 46
    walnut butter cream icing 253
water baths 287

Welsh fruit bread 154
whisked sponge cake 206
wholemeal muffins 112
wholemeal orange muffins 112
wholemeal scones 135

Y
yeast *420–1*, 471
yeasted cakes
    apple kuchen 460
    baba au rhum 463
    gugelhopf (kugelhupf) 461
    savarin 458, **459**
    stollen 457
    tea ring 456
Yorkshire tea cakes 455

Z
zucchini, mint & goat's cheese quiche **406**, 407
zucchini & bacon quiche 407
zucchini & cheese quickbread 145

ACKNOWLEDGEMENTS

My kitchen and table would have been very different without my daughter Suzanne and granddaughters Kate and Louise. Ever since Suzanne returned from London with a Cordon Bleu Diploma, our working lives have been closely knitted and our family meals have been immensely pleasurable, fascinating and satisfying. And I can't tell you how nice it is as a grandmother to have Kate and Louise pick up the baton and share our joy and love of all things good from the kitchen. It makes for an especially happy life.

I'm enormously grateful to Hardie Grant Books, in particular Paul McNally. He knew that there was a wealth of knowledge and a bank of recipes that needed to be put in one very special book for all to share.

I also want to thank Gordana Trifunovic for her unwavering dedication towards all aspects of the book from conception to photography right through to the final days of printing. She was so caring, constant and diligent, and kept a steady eye on the job.

The book seem to come together beautifully thanks in no small way to the superb editing talent of Janine Flew, who in the nicest way possible kept the book simmering along gently.

I'd like to thank Grace Campbell, Brett Sargent and Andrew de Sousa for assisting with the baking on the photoshoot and for doing such a wonderful job.

Thank you also Vanessa Levis and Leesa O'Reilly for the beautiful photographs and styling – you've both given a meaning to the food, and helped make the book welcoming and appealing.

Last but not least, because we can't live without good design, I would like to thank Sarah Odgers for her beautiful design for the book and for the wonderful illustrations which help make the book a joy to behold.

ACKNOWLEDGEMENTS

BOOKS BY MARGARET FULTON

Margaret has written more than 25 cookbooks over the course of her long career, some of which are still in print today. Her books have been treasured for generations, and Margaret hopes to continue to inspire and encourage a new generation of curious and interested cooks.

The Margaret Fulton Cookbook, 1968
Margaret Fulton's Ice Cream Wonderland, 1970
The Woman's Day Cookbook, 1970
Canned Fruit and Meat Recipe Book, 1971
Entertaining with Margaret Fulton, 1971
Margaret Fulton Cookery Course, 1973
Margaret Fulton's Favourite Recipes, 1973
Margaret Fulton's Italian Cookbook, 1973
The Complete Margaret Fulton Cookbook, 1974
Margaret Fulton's Crockpot Cookbook, 1976
Cooking for Good Health, 1978
Margaret Fulton Oven Magic, 1978
My Very Special Cookbook, 1980
The Margaret Fulton Creative Cooking Course, 1981
Superb Restaurant Dishes, 1982
Cooking for Family and Friends, 1983
The Everyday Cookery Book, 1983
Margaret Fulton's Encyclopedia of Food and Cookery, 1983
The New Idea Cookbook, 1986
Margaret Fulton's Book of Cooking for Two, 1989
Margaret Fulton's New Cookbook, 1993
Cooking for One and Two, 1995
A Passionate Cook, 1998
I Sang for My Supper: Memoirs of a Food Writer, 1999
Cooking for Dummies (co-author Barbara Beckett), 2001
Margaret Fulton's Kitchen, 2007
Margaret Fulton Christmas, 2008

NOTE The year indicates the first year of publication. Many of these books have since been fully revised and updated.

Published in 2012 by Hardie Grant Books

Hardie Grant Books (Australia)
Ground Floor, Building 1
658 Church Street
Richmond, Victoria 3121
www.hardiegrant.com.au

Hardie Grant Books (UK)
Dudley House, North Suite
34–35 Southampton Street
London WC2E 7HF
www.hardiegrant.co.uk

All rights reserved. No part of this publication may be reproduced, stored in a retrieval system or transmitted in any form by any means, electronic, mechanical, photocopying, recording or otherwise, without the prior written permission of the publishers and copyright holders.

The moral rights of the author have been asserted.

Copyright text © Margaret Fulton 2012
Copyright photography © Hardie Grant 2012

National Library of Australia Cataloguing-in-Publication data:

Author: Fulton, Margaret.
Title: Margaret Fulton : baking / Margaret Fulton.
ISBN: 978 1 74270 028 1 (hbk.)
Notes: Includes index.
Subjects: Baking. Cooking. 641.815

PUBLISHER Paul McNally
PROJECT EDITOR Gordana Trifunovic
EDITOR Janine Flew
DESIGN MANAGER Heather Menzies
DESIGNER & ILLUSTRATOR Sarah Odgers
PHOTOGRAPHER Vanessa Levis
STYLIST Leesa O'Reilly
FOOD PREPARATION Grace Campbell, Andrew De Sousa, Brett Sargent
PRODUCTION Penny Sanderson

Colour reproduction by Splitting Image Colour Studio
Printed and bound in China by 1010 Printing International Limited.

Australian metric cup and tablespoon measures have been used throughout. For explanations and imperial conversions, see pages 8–9.